HJT Training Immigration Manual

© 2014 HJT Training

Further information and copies of this manual can be obtained from:

HJT Training Ltd
28 Queen Street
London
EC4R 1BB

DX: 582 London/City

T: +44 (0) 20 3405 2942
E: enquiries@hjt-training.co.uk

HJT Training is a company limited by guarantee. Registered in England and Wales. Reg no. 4891943

Although great care has been taken in the compilation and preparation of this book to ensure accuracy, the publishers cannot in any circumstances accept responsibility for any errors or omissions.

ISBN: 978-0-9572058-4-0

Version 14

Contents

INTRODUCTION 16

THE HJT IMMIGRATION MANUAL 16

THE LAW SOCIETY'S IMMIGRATION AND ASYLUM ACCREDITATION SCHEME (IAAS) 17

THE OISC REGISTRATION SCHEME 18

SOURCES OF INFORMATION ON IMMIGRATION LAW 19

CHAPTER 1: IMMIGRATION CONTROL 21

KEY CONCEPTS 21

    Exclusionary principle 21

    Exemption from control 21

        Right of abode 22

        European Community law 22

FORMS OF CONTROL 23

PERMISSION TO TRAVEL, ENTER AND REMAIN 24

    Entry clearance 26

    Leave to enter or remain 28

    Immigration categories or purposes 29

SOURCES OF LAW 31

    Primary legislation 32

    Secondary legislation 36

    Immigration rules 37

    Operational Guidance 38

MAKING AN APPLICATION 39

    Timing 40

        Automatic extension of leave (also known as 'continuing leave' or '3C leave') .. 41

        Effect of an invalid application 42

    Application forms and fees 44

        Visa/entry clearance applications 44

        In-country extension and regularisation applications 45

    Fee exemption 49

    Decisions 50

CHAPTER 2: GENERAL REQUIREMENTS AND POLICIES 52

NAVIGATING THE IMMIGRATION RULES 52

    Transitional provisions 53

COMMON REQUIREMENTS OF THE IMMIGRATION RULES 54

    Specified documents 54

    Evidential flexibility 55

    Maintenance 55

        Meaning of public funds 56

        Required level of income 58

        Third party support 58

        Sponsors and undertakings 60

        Joint sponsors 60

Adequate accommodation 60
Reporting and other conditions 62
Knowledge of language and life in the UK 62
Tuberculosis tests 64
General grounds for refusal 64
    Mandatory or discretionary grounds? 65
Refusal of entry clearance or leave to enter 66
Refusal of leave to enter in relation to a person in possession of an entry clearance, and grounds on which leave to enter or remain which is in force is to be cancelled at port or while the holder is outside the United Kingdom (rules 321 and 321A) .. 72
Refusal of leave to remain (rule 322) 73
Refusal of indefinite leave to enter or remain (rule 322(1C)) ... 73
Curtailment (rule 323) 74
POLICIES, CONCESSIONS AND OPERATIONAL GUIDANCE 74
    Legacy cases 76
    Deliberately delayed consideration of asylum claim 77
    Seven-year children concession 78
    Duty to safeguard children 79
    Delay in asylum and human rights cases 80
    Age and enforcement action 81
    Carers policy 81
    Family court proceedings 82
    Children in the care of a Local Authority 82
    Policies, concessions and the law 83
        Legitimate expectation 83
        Judicial review 84
        The immigration tribunal 84
  RETURNING RESIDENTS 85

CHAPTER 3: VISITORS 88
  General visitor (paras 41- 46) 88
  Intention to leave 90
  Frequent and successive visits 91
  Switching and extensions for visitors 92
  Appeals for visitors 92
  Tactics 93
  OTHER TYPES OF VISIT VISA 93
    Child visitor (paras 46A-46F) 93
    Business visitor (paras 46G-46L) 93
    Sports visitor (paras 46M-46R) 94
    Entertainer visitor (paras 46S-46X) 94
    Visitor in transit (paras 47-50) 94
    Private medical treatment visitor (paras 51-56) 95
    Parent of a child at school (paras 56A to 56C) 95
    Visitors seeking to enter for the purposes of marriage or to enter a civil partnership (paras 56D-56F) 95

Visitors seeking leave to enter under the Approved Destinations Status (ADS) agreement with China (paras 56G-56J) 96

Student visitor (paras 56K-56M) 96

Prospective Entrepreneur (paras 56N-56Q) 96

Visitors undertaking permitted paid engagements (paras 56X to 56Z) 96

CHAPTER 4: EMPLOYMENT CATEGORIES OUTSIDE THE PBS **97**

UK ancestry visas (paragraphs 186-192) 97

CHAPTER 5: LONG RESIDENCE AND PRIVATE LIFE **99**

Ten year rule 99

Other considerations 101

Tactics 101

Private life 102

Suitability 103

Not be reasonable to expect the applicant to leave the UK 104

Very significant obstacles to integration 106

Rule 276ADE(1) and Article 8 (ECHR) 107

Private life outside the rules 108

Making a private life application 109

Decision 110

CHAPTER 6: FAMILY-BASED APPLICATIONS **112**

FAMILY LIFE UNDER APPENDIX FM 112

Navigating Appendix FM 114

Operational guidance 115

Transitional provisions 116

Section GEN 117

Suitability 117

Making a family life application 119

Family life as a Partner under Appendix FM 120

Relationship 120

English language requirement 124

Financial requirement 125

Appendix FM-SE 128

The income threshold and Article 8 129

Immigration status 130

Section EX: Exceptions to certain eligibility requirements for leave 131

to remain as a partner or parent 131

Reasonable to expect the child to leave the UK 132

Insurmountable obstacles 133

Decision 134

Indefinite leave to remain 135

Marriages that have ended during the probationary period 136

Bereaved spouses or partners 136

Victims of domestic violence 136

Destitution domestic violence (DDV) concession 139

Getting married in the UK 139

Parent of a child in the UK 142
    Relationship requirements 142
    Other requirements 144
    Grants of leave 144
Children of partners and parents 145
Adult dependent relatives 145
    Relationship requirements 146
    The 'threshold' requirement 146
    Financial requirement 148
    Decision 149
CHILDREN OF SETTLED PARENT(S) 149
    In-country applications 150
Sole responsibility 150
Serious and compelling circumstances making exclusion undesirable 152
Other definitions 152
Adopted children 153
Children born in the UK 154

CHAPTER 7: POINTS BASED SYSTEM 155

INTRODUCTION 155
THE BASICS 156
    Migration Advisory Committee 158
SPONSORSHIP UNDER THE POINTS-BASED SYSTEM 158
Applying for sponsorship 158
Sponsor duties 159
    Codes of practice 161
DOCUMENTARY EVIDENCE, POLICY GUIDANCE AND ALVI 162
Status of the policy guidance 162
Specified evidence and evidential flexibility 163
Other general considerations 1655
    Overstaying and extension applications 165
    Payment of application fees 166
    Continuity of residence 167
Maintenance.. 167
English language 169
Curtailment of leave 169
TIER 1: HIGHLY VALUED 170
Tier 1 (General) 170
Tier 1 (Post study work) 171
TIER 1 (ENTREPRENEUR) 171
Attributes 172
    Initial applications 172
    Subsequent applications 173
Genuine entrepreneurs 174
Language 176
Maintenance.. 176
Switching 177

Period and conditions of leave, curtailment and settlement 177
TIER 1 (INVESTOR) 178
  Attributes.. 179
    Initial applications... 179
    Subsequent applications 179
  For those who apply to enter the category on or after 6 November 2014, the full minimum sum of £2m must be invested to qualify the migrant for an extension. 180
  Genuineness 180
  Switching 180
  Period and conditions of leave, and curtailment 181
  Settlement 181
TIER 1 (EXCEPTIONAL TALENT) 181
TIER 1 (GRADUATE ENTREPRENEUR) 183
TIER 2: SKILLED WORKERS 184
TIER 2 (GENERAL) 186
  Quotas for the issue of Certificates of Sponsorship to employers 186
  Attributes.. 186
  Resident labour market test (RLMT) 187
  Maintenance.. 187
  English language skills 188
  Genuineness 188
  Switching 188
  Period and conditions of leave, and curtailment 188
  Settlement 189
TIER 2 (INTRA-COMPANY TRANSFER) 190
TIER 2 (SPORTSPERSON) 191
TIER 2 (MINISTERS OF RELIGION).. 191
TIER 4: STUDENTS 192
  Requirement to have a sponsor 193
    Licensing of sponsors... 193
TIER 4 (GENERAL)... 195
  Eligibility... 195
  Low risk countries.. 196
  Age restrictions.. 196
  Security clearance... 196
  Maximum length of stay as a student 197
  Genuine student provision 198
  The CAS... 199
  English language 201
  Funds and maintenance 202
    Length and conditions of leave 203
    Extensions... 204
TIER 4 (CHILD) 205
TIER 5: YOUTH MOBILITY AND TEMPORARY WORKERS................................ 206
  Tier 5 (Youth Mobility Scheme)... 207
  Tier 5 (Temporary worker) 208
    Creative and sporting category 209

Charity worker category 210

Religious worker category 210

Government authorised exchange category 211

International agreement category 212

FAMILY MEMBERS OF PBS MIGRANTS 212

CHALLENGING PBS DECISIONS 213

ADMINISTRATIVE REVIEW 214

CHAPTER 8: INTERNATIONAL PROTECTION 216

THE REFUGEE CONVENTION 216

Sources of refugee law 217

ASYLUM SEEKERS 218

WELL-FOUNDED FEAR 218

Fear 219

Well-foundedness 219

Standard of proof 220

Credibility 221

Qualification Directive 221

Asylum and Immigration (Treatment of Claimants etc) Act 2004 2233

Inconsistencies 224

Plausibility 226

Dishonesty 228

Demeanour 228

Future risk 228

Country information 229

Relevance of past experiences to future risk 232

Specific individual risk 232

Generic risk cases 233

Activities in the United Kingdom and claims made in bad faith 233

Future activities 236

BEING PERSECUTED 239

Actors of persecution 238

Acts of persecution 239

Human rights analysis 240

Subjective nature of being persecuted 241

Role of Convention reasons 242

Prosecution and persecution 243

Military service 244

Civil war 245

THE CONVENTION REASONS 246

Race 247

Religion 247

Nationality 247

Membership of a particular social group 247

Political opinion 249

Attributed Convention reasons 249

PROTECTION AND RELOCATION 250

Protection from non-state persecution 250
Internal relocation 252
Non Refoulement 255
Cessation Clauses 255
Exclusion clauses 257
Article 1(D) 257
Article 1(F) 257
Nexus to acts falling within Article 1F 258
Evidence 260
Relevance and definition of terrorist acts 260
Procedure 261
Article 33(2) 262
Humanitarian Protection 263
Serious harm 263
Article 15(c) 265
"Conflict" 265
Standard of Proof 265
"Indiscriminate violence" 266
"Life or Person" 266
The critical question 267
Victims of trafficking 267
The convention against trafficking 267
Definition of trafficking 268
Referral Process 268

CHAPTER 9: ASYLUM PROCESS AND PRACTICE 271

Claiming asylum 271
Screening interview 272
Routing 273
The role of the representative 273
Asylum interview 274
Decision 274
Further grounds: Section 120 statement 274
Lodging the appeal 275
Asylum Support 275
Age disputes 276
Relevance of age 276
Challenging an age assessment 277
Fast-track appeals 279
Safe Third Country Cases 281
Dublin 3 281
Safe third country certificates 284
Returns to EEA countries 284
Substance of safe third country challenges 285
'Clearly unfounded' certificates 286
Prohibition on further appeals or raising grounds late 287
Fresh claims 288

Legal test 288

Exceptional circumstances 290

    Fresh claims and clearly unfounded certificates 291

Case law on fresh claims 292

Evidence 293

    Previously available evidence 293

    Sur place style arguments 295

    Article 8 private and family life 297

BENEFITS OF RECOGNITION AS A REFUGEE 299

Refugees and immigration status 299

Settlement protection 299

Refugee family reunion 299

    Pre-existing family 300

    'Post flight' and other family members 300

Travel documents 301

Refugees and work, benefits and education 301

BENEFITS OF HUMANITARIAN PROTECTION 301

Immigration status 301

Exclusion 302

Family reunion and travel documents 302

CHAPTER 10: HUMAN RIGHTS LAW 304

HUMAN RIGHTS ACT 1998 304

Interpretation of statute 304

Effect on public authorities 305

Damages and compensation 305

Human rights as a ground of appeal 306

EUROPEAN CONVENTION ON HUMAN RIGHTS 306

Articles of the ECHR 306

Categories of rights 308

Standard of Proof 308

ECHR AND IMMIGRATION LAW 309

Applicability of ECHR in immigration cases 309

ARTICLE 2 309

ARTICLE 3 310

Absolute nature of Article 3 311

Torture 312

Inhuman treatment or punishment 312

Degrading treatment or punishment 313

Specific types of Article 3 case 315

    Absence of exclusion clauses 315

    Absence of Convention reasons 316

    Sufficiency of protection test 316

    Destitution in the UK 316

    Unavailability of medical treatment abroad 316

    Effect of the act of removal 320

    Successful Article 2, 3 and 8 claims and leave to remain 320

ARTICLE 4 320
ARTICLE 5 321
ARTICLE 6 322
ARTICLE 8 324
   Interference with Article 8 rights 325
      Family relationships 325
      Private life 327
      Threshold for interference in foreign cases 329
      Relocating the family 330
      Applying for entry clearance from abroad 332
   In accordance with the law 333
   For a legitimate aim 333
   Necessary in a democratic society 334
      Effect on children 335
      Home Office delay 336
      Failure to apply a policy 338
      Third party rights 338
      Part 5A, 2002 Act considerations 339
   Article 8 and the Immigration Rules 340
ARTICLE 14 342
DISCRETIONARY LEAVE 342
      Old DL 342
      New DL 342
TRAVEL DOCUMENTS 344

CHAPTER 11: EUROPEAN COMMUNITY LAW 345

UNDERLYING LEGAL PRINCIPLES 345
COUNTRIES TO WHICH EC LAW APPLIES 346
INTERACTION OF UK AND EC LAW 346
   Rights not privileges 346
   Implementation of EC law 347
   Choice of method of entry/residence 349
   EC law and the ECHR 349
WHO BENEFITS FROM FREE MOVEMENT? 350
   EEA nationals exercising Treaty rights 350
QUALIFIED PERSONS 351
      Jobseekers 351
      Workers 352
      Posted workers 353
      Self-employed persons 354
      Self-sufficient persons 354
      Students 355
      Comprehensive sickness insurance cover 355
   British citizens exercising Treaty rights 356
   Family members of qualified persons 358
      Ordinary family members 359
      Other family members 361

BENEFITS OF THE EXERCISE OF TREATY RIGHTS..363

    Admission 364

    Initial right of residence..365

    Extended right of residence 366

    Permanent residence 367

    Retained rights of residence...368

    Derivative right of residence 371

        Chen..372

        Teixeira and Ibrahim...372

        Ruiz Zambrano 373

        Ruiz Zambrano and Appendix FM 374

        General considerations...375

    Dual nationals and McCarthy 375

    Application forms 377

EXCLUDING AND REMOVING EEA NATIONALS FROM UK....................................378

    Ceasing to be qualified 378

    Public policy removals and exclusions 378

RIGHTS OF APPEAL 381

THE ANKARA AGREEMENT 382

    Workers 383

        A worker and legally employed 383

        Duly registered as belonging to the labour force........................384

        "Legal employment" for one of three possible time periods 385

        Rights of residence 386

        Expulsion..386

        Family members 387

    Self-employed..387

        Rights of Establishment 387

        Lawful entry 388

        Applications 389

        Appeals 389

    Additional agreements 390

CHAPTER 12: BRITISH NATIONALITY LAW **391**

A BRIEF HISTORY OF NATIONALITY LAW 391

    Pre 1948..391

    1948 to 1983...391

    1983 onwards 392

    2002 legislation...393

    2006 legislation...394

    2009 legislation...394

    2014 legislation...395

BIRTH OR ADOPTION IN THE UK 395

    Parent is British or settled 396

    Children born inside UK to members of the armed forces 398

    Abandoned minors 398

    Registration on parents becoming British or settled 398

Registration due to early years spent in UK 399

Minors adopted by British citizens 400

BIRTH OUTSIDE THE UK 400

Acquisition by descent 401

Acquisition by registration 401

ACQUISITION BY REGISTRATION AS AN ADULT 403

NATURALISATION 404

Period of residence 405

Non-spouse cases 405

Spouse cases 405

In breach of the immigration laws 405

The good character requirement 406

Sufficient knowledge of language and life in the UK 407

Intention to live in the UK 407

Citizenship ceremonies 407

CHALLENGING NATIONALITY DECISIONS 409

STOPPING BEING BRITISH 409

Loss of British nationality 409

Renunciation of British nationality 410

Deprivation of nationality 410

CHAPTER 13: ENFORCEMENT: DETENTION, REMOVAL AND DEPORTATION 412

DETENTION 412

Power to detain 412

Criteria for detention 415

Presumption of liberty 415

Reasons to detain 416

Factors militating against detention 417

Deportation cases 418

Families and children 419

Detained fast track 419

Detention reviews 420

RELEASE AND BAIL 421

Temporary admission and CIO bail 421

Tribunal bail 423

Power to grant bail 423

Factors relevant to bail 424

Sureties and recognisance 425

Bail conditions 427

Preparing bail applications 427

National security cases 429

Challenges to lawfulness of detention 429

ADMINISTRATIVE REMOVAL 430

Challenging removal decisions 431

Removal under the Immigration Act 2014 433

DEPORTATION 435

Power to deport 435

Procedure for deportation 436
    Discretionary deportation 437
    Security cases 437
    Automatic deportation 438
Appeal rights under the 2014 Act 439
Revocation of deportation order... 442
Substantive considerations 444

CHAPTER 14: THE LAW OF APPEALS... **451**

RIGHT OF APPEAL.. 452
  Decisions attracting a right of appeal.. 452
    Validity of the notice of decision 454
  Limitations on the right of appeal 456
    Students and deportees 457
  In-country and out-of-country appeals 458
GROUNDS OF APPEAL 459
  Statement of additional grounds 459
APPEALS STRUCTURE 462
  Sources of law, practice and procedure.. 463
FIRST-TIER TRIBUNAL 464
  Overriding Objective... 464
  Lodging appeals 465
    Deadline for appeal 465
    Extension of time for lodging notice of appeal 466
  Case management powers 466
  Documents to be sent to tribunal by the Home Office...................... 468
  Response... 468
  Variation of grounds of appeal 469
  Adjournments... 469
  Conduct of the appeal 470
    Concessions by the Home Office.. 471
    Natural justice 471
    Public hearing 472
    Hearing in the absence of a party 472
    Determination without a hearing.. 472
    Combined hearings.. 473
    Evidence.. 473
    Forgery and authenticity of documents 473
    Evaluating country reports 474
  Abandonment of appeals 474
  Decisions by the Home Office to withdraw the decision 475
  Authority to represent... 475
  Irregularities and corrections 476
  Second or subsequent appeals... 476
  Decisions 477
SEEKING PERMISSION TO APPEAL TO THE UT FROM THE FTT................................ 477
  Basis of application.. 478

Application to the First-tier Tribunal 478
Review process 479
FTT considers whether to review the decision... 479
Seeking permission to appeal from the UT 480
Status and race relations appeals.. 480
PURSUING AN UPPER TRIBUNAL APPEAL 480
Non-compliance in the UT... 480
Respondent's response to appeal 481
Further evidence 482
Initial hearing.. 483
APPEALS TO THE COURT OF APPEAL... 484
Seeking permission from the UT 484
UT self-review.. 485
TRIBUNAL DETERMINATIONS AS PRECEDENTS 486
Reported tribunal cases... 486
'Country Guideline' decisions.. 486
APPEALS UNDER THE IMMIGRATION ACT 2014.. 487
Rights of appeal 487
Grounds of appeal 488
From where may appeals be brought? 490
ADMINISTRATIVE REVIEW 490
Procedure 492

CHAPTER 15: CRIMINAL OFFENCES 495

INTRODUCTION... 495
IMMIGRATION OFFICERS AND POLICE POWERS... 495
ARTICLE 31 DEFENCE AGAINST PROSECUTION 496
TRAFFICKING.. 497
OFFENCES UNDER THE IMMIGRATION ACT 1971 498
Illegal entry and stay: s.24 to 24A 498
Assisting: s.25 to 25D.. 498
General offences: s.26 500
Registration cards and immigration stamps 501
Offences connected with ships or ports... 501
Powers of entry and search 501
OFFENCES UNDER THE 2004 ACT 502
Immigration document offence: s.2... 502
Duty to co-operate: s.35 503
OFFENCES IN NATIONALITY ACTS 503
EMPLOYER AND FINANCIAL INSTITUTION OFFENCES 503
Civil penalties.. 503
Sections 135 to 139 of the 2002 Act 504
GIVING IMMIGRATION ADVICE: THE OISC 504
Section 91 of the Immigration and Asylum Act 1999...................................... 504
Section 84 of the Immigration and Asylum Act 1999...................................... 505
OFFENCES CONNECTED WITH SUPPORT... 506
False and dishonest representations, delay or obstruction 506

Section 107 of the 1999 Act 506
Failure of a sponsor to maintain 507
Offences under Schedule 3 of the NIA 2002 507

CHAPTER 16: PROFESSIONAL ETHICS 508

GENERAL DUTIES 508
BASIC PRINCIPLES 509
FALSE REPRESENTATIONS 509
APPEALS 510
COSTS AND CLIENT CARE 511
    Addressing status of the fee earner in the client care letter 511
SUPERVISION 511
LIENS – RETENTION OF DOCUMENTS 512
STANDARD OF WORK 513
SUPERVISION OF STAFF 513
CONFLICT OF INTEREST 514
CONFIDENTIALITY 518
    Basic duty 518
    Exceptions to the rule on confidentiality 520
MONEY LAUNDERING 521
    Terrorism, Money Laundering and Confidentiality 521
DUTIES TO THE COURT 522
COMPLAINTS PROCEDURES 524
    Responsibility for complaints 525
    Practical solutions 525
    Third party instructions 525

CHAPTER 17: PRACTICAL SKILLS 528

ASYLUM APPLICATIONS 528
    Taking instructions 528
    Substance of instructions 529
    Substance of initial advice 530
    Dealing with interpreters 530
    Minors 531
    Unaccompanied Asylum Seeking Children 532
    Disputed minors 532
    Women 533
    Vulnerable clients 534
PROFESSIONAL CONDUCT REGARDING ASYLUM CLAIMS 535
EXPERT EVIDENCE PRACTICE DIRECTION 535
COMMISSIONING MEDICAL EVIDENCE 537
    Identifying the issues 537
    Corroboration 538
    Credibility 538
    Reviewing the medical report 539
    Checklist for medical evidence 540
    Submitting the medical report to the court 541

Referral onwards 541
Practicalities... 541
COMMISSIONING COUNTRY EXPERT EVIDENCE.. 542
When to commission country expert evidence 542
Examples of the assistance that expert evidence can give 542
Finding an expert witness... 543
Testing the expert witness 543
Duties of expert witnesses 544
Doctrine of ultimate issue 545
Letter of instructions 545
The report.. 546
Reusing expert reports 547

LIST OF CASES **548**

Introduction

The HJT immigration manual

This manual was originally devised and written with a view to training practitioners for the immigration and asylum accreditation scheme now run by the Law Society. It retains that function but is also now aimed at those advisers seeking registration or increasing their level of registration with the Office of the Immigration Services Commissioner.

Since the first edition, the manual has been extensively rewritten and revised to reflect changes in the law and to improve the delivery of the information the manual contains. This latest edition continues that tradition of continual improvement.

During its lifetime, the manual has evolved to become the leading introductory text for new immigration practitioners and for students of immigration law. Thousands of new immigration lawyers and advisers have been trained by HJT Training using this manual.

The original contributors included Gail Elliman, David Jones, David Robinson, Mark Symes and Colin Yeo. Recent editions have been extensively re-written and updated by Julian Bild and formatted by Jo Severs. Thanks go to Androulla Demetriou for her design flair and her patience and hard work in producing the printed edition.

Thanks must also go to Colin Yeo for his ever more popular and always engrossing Free Movement blog, the excellent and bang up to date Free Movement CPD Training courses and eBooks.

Both UK and EU immigration law and practice continue to evolve rapidly as the control of immigration in the UK becomes ever more politicised. This edition covers changes to the Immigration Rules and Immigration (EEA) Regulations as well as those parts of the Immigration Act 2014 that impact on immigration decision making, particularly where now in force.

This 14th edition has been fully updated in late October 2014, including changes brought into force on 20 October 2014; to appeal rights, the Tribunal procedure rules, and to the Immigration Rules as a result of Statement of Changes HC693

The Law Society's Immigration and Asylum Accreditation Scheme (IAAS)

The Legal Aid Agency (LAA), the government agency responsible for public legal funding, requires all advisers working under a legal aid contract in immigration law to be accredited under the IAAS. The IAAS is also open to solicitors and their staff who do not do publically funded work. There are three levels to this scheme. This manual is suitable for those sitting assessments at Level 1 (including Level 1 probationary) and Level 2.

It is beyond the scope of the manual to describe the requirements of the accreditation scheme and the nature of the examinations at levels 1 and 2. HJT Training runs revision courses which address these issues.

Information on the Law Society's immigration and asylum accreditation scheme is not easy to obtain. Responsibility for the scheme is divided between several organisations, as follows:

- **The LAA** requires those providing advice and representation under an immigration legal aid contract to be accredited under the Law Society scheme. The LAA website (now incorporated into the Ministry of Justice's website) is notoriously difficult to navigate but is the place to look for information about the requirement to be accredited (and reaccredited).

- **The Law Society**. The accreditation scheme is run by the Law Society. The Law Society website is the place to look for information about the requirements of the scheme.

  See www.lawsociety.org.uk > Member Services > Accreditation schemes > Immigration and Asylum

  Guidance on the standards you need to achieve at each level is extremely scant. The current 'Guidance' dated June 2013 simply lays out the broad areas of knowledge and understanding that are required. There are no longer any syllabuses for levels 1 and 2.

- **Central Law Training**. CLT administer the examinations and their website is the place to look for information about when the next round of examinations is scheduled. The website also contains a past paper in each category (i.e. written exam, drafting assessment and interview assessment) for practise purposes

Further past examination papers are not publicly available. Those attending HJT Training courses will be given access to training materials, including sample questions, not available on the CLT website.

The OISC registration scheme

The Office of the Immigration Services Commissioner (OISC) was created by the Immigration Act 1999 and regulates immigration advisers who are not solicitors and barristers or supervised by them. The OISC also regulates the provision of immigration advice in the not-for-profit sector.

Again, it is beyond the scope of the manual to describe the OISC scheme in detail. As with the LAA scheme, there are knowledge and skills examinations and assessments that must be completed in order to register with the OISC. The OISC scheme also requires an applicant to show knowledge of the OISC Code of Standards and Commissioner's Rules, the Guidance on Competence, and the existence of certain minimum best practice business practices. The assessments are administered and run directly by the OISC itself. See www.oisc.gov.uk for further details.

From July 2013, the OISC requires all those registering at each level (who are not accredited under the IAAS) to pass formal written assessments. HJT Training has a contract with the OISC to draft and mark the assessment papers. There are sample papers, a mark scheme and detailed syllabuses at:
http://oisc.homeoffice.gov.uk/how_to_become_a_regulated_immigration_adviser/ how_do_i_apply_for_exemption/competence_assessment/.

As with the IAAS, those attending HJT Training courses will be given access to further preparatory and practise materials including further sample papers and mark schemes, and tips and techniques for those intending to take the OISC assessments.

The OISC has the responsibility to ensure that its regulated advisers understand the law and procedures of UK and EEA immigration control and how to apply it properly to their clients' cases, and consequently the tests require examinees to clearly show their knowledge. The OISC assessments are not easy to pass. Many have underestimated their difficulty and the failure rate is consequently high.

Neither HJT Training nor any other training provider can provide OISC accreditation or registration as this lies with the OISC alone. However, HJT Training does offer training that will assist a person seeking registration with the OISC and is an approved OISC Continuing Professional Development (CPD) training provider.

The levels of the OISC and LSC schemes broadly correspond as follows:

Law Society	OISC
Probationer	Level 1
Level 1 (accredited caseworker)	Level 1/2
Level 2 (senior caseworker)	Level 2/3
Level 3 (advanced caseworker)	No equivalent

Sources of information on immigration law

Immigration law changes on a very frequent basis. As will be seen in the following chapter, new immigration Acts of Parliament are now passed on an annual basis, most recently the Immigration Act 2014, and immigration law is additionally cursed by a plethora of interlinked conventions, secondary legislation, rules (which are amended on a monthly basis), European directives, regulations and guidance material. It is an extremely complex subject area. Mastering it is difficult, and staying up to date is time consuming.

As well as this manual, HJT can recommend the following as sources of information on immigration law and practice:

ILPA. Membership of the Immigration Law Practitioners Association is essential for any serious immigration lawyer or caseworker. The monthly ILPA mailing to members, ILPA emails and sub-committee email lists are invaluable and unrivalled sources of information. The various ILPA best practice guides are essential reading for any new immigration adviser aspiring to become a good immigration adviser. The specialist training provided by ILPA is second to none.

JCWI. The Joint Council for the Welfare of Refugees publishes the famous JCWI Handbook every few years and this is one of the standard reference works for immigration lawyers. The last edition is very out of date now, but a new one is in preparation for 2015.

Macdonald's Immigration Law and Practice (8th edition). This is the gold standard immigration law reference book, still very useful but also quite out of date. A new edition is to be published shortly.

Immigration Law Handbook 2013 (Phelan and Gillespie). A useful compendium of the statutes, regulatory material, and rules governing UK and EEA immigration law, including international materials. Also out of date now, but new editions are published quite regularly.

Symes and Jorro, Asylum and Human Rights Law and Practice (2nd edition). This is the gold standard asylum, human rights and international protection reference book.

RLG. The Refugee Legal Group is a members-only internet forum of around 900 members administered by Asylum Aid. It is an invaluable source of information for immigration and asylum advisers. Go to http://www.asylumaid.org.uk/refugee-legal-group/ to join the RLG

Update websites. There are various websites that provide updates on immigration and asylum law, including:

- UK Visas and Immigration information on the GOV.UK website:

  Services and guidance page (including latest news)
  https://www.gov.uk/government/organisations/uk-visas-and-immigration

  A-Z
  https://www.gov.uk/browse/visas-immigration

  The Immigration Rules
  https://www.gov.uk/government/collections/immigration-rules

  Operational Guidance
  https://www.gov.uk/immigration-operational-guidance

  The old archived website for things you cannot find on the new one!
  http://webarchive.nationalarchives.gov.uk/*/http:/www.ukba.homeoffice.gov.uk/

- ILPA: www.ilpa.org.uk

- The Electronic Immigration Network (EIN): http://www.ein.org.uk/

- Free Movement blog: www.freemovement.org.uk

- Right to Remain: http://righttoremain.org.uk/resources/index.html

- The UN Refugee Agency: http://www.unhcr.org/

- BAILII (for case law): http://www.bailii.org/, with reported decisions of the Upper Tribunal (IAC) at: http://www.bailii.org/uk/cases/UKUT/IAC/

Chapter 1: Immigration control

Key concepts

Exclusionary principle

The fundamental rule of immigration control is that it is exclusive in nature. That is, everyone is excluded from lawful entry or residence unless they are either exempted from control or have permission, called 'leave'.

General rule

- Everyone is excluded

Unless

- Not subject to immigration control, or
- Permission ('leave') is granted

This basic rule, the founding principal of immigration law, is derived from s.1 Immigration Act 1971. The 1971 Act still provides the framework for the UK's system of immigration control despite heavy amendments over the intervening years:

> s.1(1) All those who are in this Act expressed to have the right of abode in the United Kingdom shall be free to live in and to come and go into and from, the United Kingdom without let or hindrance...
>
> (2) Those not having that right may live, work and settle in the United Kingdom by permission and subject to such regulation and control of their entry into, stay in and departure from the United Kingdom as is imposed by this Act...

Section 1(1) states that a person with 'the right of abode' will be free of immigration control, and section 1(2) that all others will need permission to come, stay, live, work, settle and depart.

Exemption from control

Sections 1(1) and 1(2) do not quite provide the full picture as to who is subject to or exempt from immigration control.

Those not subject to immigration control include those with the 'right of abode'. This group includes all British citizens, but a few others too, who may be British nationals (but not British citizens) or citizens of Commonwealth countries who were settled in the UK or married to men settled in the UK when the Immigration Act 1971 came into force.

EEA nationals and their family members are not subject to UK immigration control either, and will usually have a right to admission and to reside in the UK under European Community law. There are some restrictions on EEA nationals though, where they are economically inactive or criminals. So EEA nationals and their family members do not have the right of abode, and are subject to some restrictions on their freedom of movement, but do not usually need to seek the permission of UK immigration officers to come or stay in the UK.

Additionally, some foreign soldiers, members of international organisations and diplomats may also be exempt from immigration control.

Right of abode

The right of abode is an example of legacy terminology carried over from an earlier era of immigration control. As is discussed in the chapter on nationality law, before 1948 anyone born in the UK or in any of its many colonies was a British Subject. From 1948, most British Subjects became Citizens of the United Kingdom and Colonies ('CUKC'). That status persisted until the great reform of citizenship laws in the British Nationality Act 1981. For the two decades prior to the 1981 Act, however, politicians had sought to limit the right of residents of the colonies to live in the United Kingdom itself. The way in which this was achieved was to introduce the concept of the 'right of abode', which was independent from citizenship status. A person could therefore be a CUKC but not possess the right of abode, and therefore have no right to come to the UK itself unless they could meet certain requirements.

When the right of abode was initially introduced it was linked to another new concept, that of 'patriality'. Put simply, the right of abode was acquired through one's male ancestors having been born in the territory of the United Kingdom (rather than its colonies). The original version of section 2 of the Immigration Act 1971 must be consulted if a query arises about the original meaning of the right of abode. The law has moved on considerably since those dark days, but the concept of the right of abode still persists.

Today, British citizens hold the right of abode. Some individuals hold the right of abode but are not British citizens, but they are few in number and are addressed in the chapter on nationality.

European Community law

It can be seen that section 1 of the 1971 Act, enacted prior to the UK joining the European Union, makes no mention of any exception or carve out for European Union or European Economic Area ('EEA') citizens and their families. However, section 7 of the Immigration Act 1988 exempts them from the requirement to hold leave to enter or remain. In fact, it is prohibited under European Community law that an Immigration Officer even endorse any form of immigration status in a passport of an EEA citizen, and they do not require passports to travel within the

European Economic Area if they can otherwise prove that they are nationals of a member state.

This subject is addressed in detail in the chapter on European Community law. Suffice it to say that the principles that apply to domestic UK immigration law have little or no place when considering the rights of EEA citizens. The terminology is also very different. Do not get confused between the two.

Forms of control

In order to apply and enforce immigration laws, a number of forms of control have been introduced, operated by different officials. These officials work under the direction of the Secretary of State for the Home Department (SSHD). According to statute, it is the SSHD who makes immigration decisions, though she delegates the overwhelming majority of these to her civil servants.

As with everything that touches on UK immigration law and practice, understanding the organisations responsible for immigration control is difficult.

From April 2013, at least on paper, immigration officials operate within a number of separate departments of the Home Office, UK Visas and Immigration (UKVI), the Immigration Enforcement Directorate (also called 'Home Office Immigration Enforcement'), and the UK Border Force. The first two previously operated as the UK Border Agency (UKBA). The UK Border Force was split off from the UKBA in March 2012.

The UK Border Force is responsible for controls at the border such as passport checks, juxtaposed controls operating from various ports abroad, and customs.

In earlier times, the functions of these three new entities were performed mainly by the Immigration and Nationality Directorate ('IND') of the Home Office. This was then briefly re-constituted as the Border and Immigration Agency ('BIA') before morphing into the UKBA.

Entry clearance work abroad (see below) was in previous years carried out by an organisation called UK Visas, a joint operation between the Home Office and Foreign and Commonwealth Office. The separate identity for UK Visas has now been abandoned and the visa operation is carried out within the UKVI by Entry Clearance Officers (ECO).

References to these predecessor organisations, particularly the UKBA, will still be encountered regularly. As the control of immigration is a direct function of the Home Office, we will usually refer in this manual to the body of immigration officials who make decisions on applications and enforce controls as 'the Home Office'.

The main forms of immigration control (and the personnel responsible) are as follows:

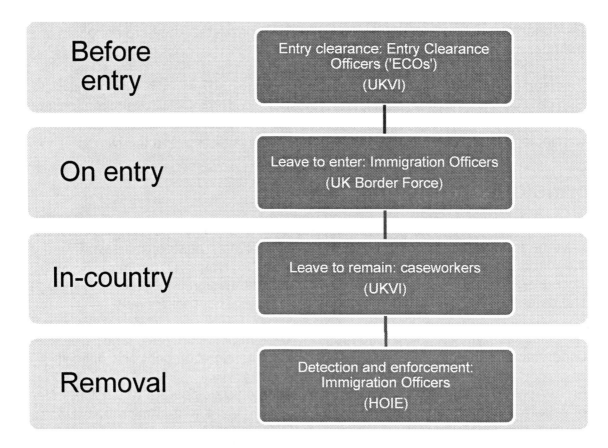

There are additional controls on employers and educational institutions. The UKVI must authorise them to recruit overseas workers and students through the system of sponsor licences, and can penalise them if those they recruit breach immigration laws. The Immigration Act 2014 introduces further controls, to be exercised by marriage registrars, private landlords, banks and the DVLA. Civil penalty schemes and criminal offences provide the incentive for these organisations to enforce immigration controls

Immigration officers are endowed by legislation with wide powers to enforce immigration laws. Most of these powers originate in the 1971 Act (as amended) and include the power to search, seize, detain, question, arrest and enforce departure. These powers are not restricted to use on foreign nationals without the right of abode: an Immigration Officer also has the power to detain and question a British citizen in order to establish that they are indeed a British citizen.

Permission to travel, enter and remain

For those with a right of abode, they will be able to travel to and enter the U.K. with a British citizen passport, or another passport if stamped with 'right of abode' or a certificate of entitlement to the right of abode, without let or hindrance. It can be also be seen from section 1 of the 1971 Act that for those not exempt from UK immigration control, their entry into, stay in and departure from the United Kingdom and their ability to live, work and settle in the UK is determined by the Act. In short, they must have permission to do any of these things.

The word for 'permission' used in immigration law throughout the Immigration Acts is usually that of 'leave', although we also need to mention permission grant by way of 'entry clearance' at this stage:

Entry clearance

- Pre-entry control, more commonly referred to as a 'visa'

Leave to enter

- Permission to enter into the UK, either incorporated into the visa, or granted at port (to non-visa nationalsvisiting the UK)

Leave to remain

- Leave to remain in the UK, usually granted in-country

Limited leave

- Time limited leave (to enter or remain), granted for a certain period with a specified expiry date

Indefinite leave to enter or remain

- Unlimited leave that has no expiry date (but which can be lost, see below)

Example

Elvis is Kosovar. He entered the UK illegally in the back of a lorry. He remained illegally for several years, never making any application to the Home Office. He decides to try to regularise his position by applying for leave.

Technically he is actually seeking leave to enter even though he has been here for many years. If his application were to succeed it might well be endorsed as leave to remain by the Home Office, simply because the decision will be made by officials of the UKVI working within the UK rather than at the border. There is no substantive difference between leave to enter and leave to remain once it is granted.

Entry clearance

Entry clearance is a form of pre-arrival control. Rather than allowing any person to arrive at a UK port and seek entry at that stage, requiring an Immigration Officer to make a snap decision on a potentially complex case, many migrants seeking to enter the UK are required to possess entry clearance, a visa, before they physically arrive at an entry point to the UK.

If a person is required to have entry clearance and does not they must be refused entry (immigration rule 320(5)).

The rules on who does and does not require entry clearance are as follows:

'Visa nationals'

- Always required: Nationals of countries listed in Appendix 1 to the Immigration Rules

Stay of more than 6 months

- Always required: immigration rule 24

If category-specific rule says so

- Always required: check individual rules (e.g. fiancé or marriage visitor)

Example

Alasdair is Canadian and wishes to enter the UK for a two week holiday. Canada is not listed in Appendix 1 of the Immigration Rules and Alasdair is not therefore a visa national. Entry as a visitor is granted for six months or less and the rule does not require that entry clearance is obtained.

Alasdair does not require entry clearance before he travels.

Maria is Colombian and wishes to enter the UK for a one year computing course. Colombia is listed at Appendix 1 and so Maria is a visa national. In addition, she is seeking entry for a period exceeding six months, and the Tier 4 (General) rule under which she needs to apply does specify that prior entry clearance is mandatory.

Maria very definitely requires entry clearance before she travels.

A non-visa national can, optionally, apply for entry clearance to travel to the UK for a visit, and (until Part 2 of the Immigration Act 2014 comes into force) if refused on arrival at port will then potentially have an in-country right of appeal. This would be very useful advice to give to a person who is at risk of refusal on arrival, for example because of a poor prior immigration history, or having less than concrete ties to their country of nationality (i.e. being young, footloose and fancy free).

Entry clearance is sought from an Entry Clearance Officer ('ECO') at a British embassy, High Commission or consulate in the country of origin. If granted, it takes the form of a sticker or vignette in the holder's passport, which is then presented to an Immigration Officer on arrival.

Top tip

British High Commissions exist in Commonwealth countries, British embassies in non-Commonwealth countries and consulates are just smaller posts away from the main High Commission or embassy in a given country. Much of the visa process though is now outsourced to the 'commercial partners' of the diplomatic post.

Usually, by virtue of the Immigration (Leave to Enter and Remain) Order 2000, an entry clearance will also include the grant of leave to enter, which becomes effective on entry to the UK. However, on arrival an Immigration Officer may examine the leave to enter and has the power to cancel the entry clearance which contains the leave to enter under certain limited circumstances including:

➢ False representations or material facts not disclosed, with or without knowledge, in writing or orally

➢ Change in circumstances since entry clearance issued

➢ Restricted returnability, medical grounds, criminal record, subject to a deportation order or exclusion conducive to public good

➢ Criminal offending

See 1971 Act, Schedule 2, paragraph 2A and immigration rule 321A.

Example

> Tasneem applied for entry clearance as a Tier 4 Migrant (a student). The application was granted. While Tasneem was making arrangements to travel to the UK, though, her mother fell ill. She felt unable to leave her and did not travel.
>
> Her mother recovers and 4 months later Tasneem seeks entry to the UK. In the meantime, her course has started and her college has informed the Home Office that she has not enrolled.
>
> When Tasneem arrives in the UK she is stopped by an Immigration Officer and refused entry, even though she has a valid entry clearance. The basis of the refusal is Immigration Rule 321A(1), because there has been a change of circumstances since the entry clearance was granted.

There are a number of other relevant provisions relating to entry clearance (see part 1 of the Immigration Rules), including:

> ➢ Entry clearance applications for any purpose other than a visit must be made in the overseas post where the applicant resides or the nearest designated post if there is none: immigration rule 28.
>
> ➢ An application for entry clearance is to be decided in the light of the circumstances existing at the time of the decision, except that an applicant will not be refused an entry clearance where entry is sought in one of the categories contained in paragraphs 296-316 or paragraph EC-C of Appendix FM (i.e. the rules relating to children coming to the UK with a view to settlement) solely on account of his attaining the age of 18 years between receipt of his application and the date of the decision on it: immigration rule 27.
>
> ➢ The entry clearance application will not be treated as having been made until the correct fee is paid: immigration rule 30

Most entry clearance posts now employ an agent or courier firm to accept and process applications before forwarding them to the entry clearance post for decision. The visa application is made, usually on-line, to a Visa Application Centre (VAC) operated by these 'commercial partners'. The applicant is then given an appointment to attend the VAC in person, where they will submit any necessary documentation, pay the fee, have their biometrics enrolled, and be interviewed if necessary.

Leave to enter or remain

There is no real difference between leave to enter and leave to remain other than where it is granted, either at port (e.g. Dover, Heathrow) or in-country.

Leave to enter will be granted on initial entry, and then if a further period of leave is sought and granted it will be called leave to remain. Where limited leave to enter or remain has been granted and remains current, the holder can depart from and re-enter the UK using that leave (unless it was granted for a single entry as a visitor).

Leave can either be granted for a specific period, in which case it is referred to as limited leave, or can be granted for an indefinite period. Indefinite leave is usually encountered as Indefinite Leave to Remain, or 'ILR'. This may also be referred to as 'settlement', as that is what it amounts to. There are a few immigration categories in which Indefinite Leave to Enter is granted right at the outset (for children of settled parents and Adult Dependent Relatives), though most migrants will need one or more periods of limited leave before being able to apply for settlement.

Top tip

When immigration lawyers refer to extensions of leave, they are often referring to an extension of leave in the same immigration category. For example, a Tier 4 student will be granted a limited period of leave to enter the UK to undertake the course for which they have been sponsored, and will then have to apply for further periods of leave to remain if undertaking further studies.

Immigration lawyers often refer to an application for an extension of leave in a different immigration category as a variation application or as 'switching'. For example, a Tier 4 student might meet the love of his or her life, get married and want to apply for leave to remain as a spouse. Whether in the same category, or a different one, both are extensions of leave (or 'extensions of stay' as they are referred to in the Immigration Rules).

Immigration categories or purposes

When entry clearance or a form of leave is sought, it must be sought for a specific purpose, such as to visit, study, work or live with a family member in the UK. The 'Immigration Rules', a document forming a key part of the UK's system of immigration control, sets out the different purposes for which entry to the UK can be sought.

The Immigration Rules are a unique form of legislation that the Secretary of State is authorised to amend by a relatively simple Parliamentary process called the negative resolution procedure. Essentially, any change to the rules is simply laid before Parliament and then automatically becomes law. These changes are published in documents called Statements of Changes. An objection to an amendment can be made by a Member of Parliament, but the objection only triggers a debate, and does not actually prevent the rule changes being implemented.

The current set of Immigration Rules ('the rules') is officially called HC 395 (the reference number of the document in the House of Commons library). They current rules were first introduced in 1994 and have been very heavily amended in subsequent years, growing from some 30 pages to well over 1000 as successive governments have sought to limit immigration into the UK. Amendments are made every month or two. The plethora of amendments and different drafting techniques used by different draughtsmen over the years make the rules difficult to navigate.

The following chapters examine the specific categories in more detail. Common examples include:

- Partners
- Parents of a child in the U.K.
- Visitors
- Students (Tier 4 of the Points Based System)
- Workers (Tiers 2 or 5 of the Points Based System)
- Investment and business (Tier 1 of the Points Based System)
- Asylum claims

However, there are many other categories under the rules, some of which only exist for a relatively small number of immigrants.

The following flowcharts provide examples of the different stages of immigration control a migrant will pass through in various categories of the rules. The examples all assume that everything goes according to plan for the potential migrant – refusals, appeals and removals are not dealt with here.

Visitors	Partners	Employment
(Apply for Entry Clearance)	Apply for Entry Clearance	Apply for Entry Clearance
(Entry Clearance and leave to enter granted for 6 months)	Entry Clearance and leave to enter granted for 33 months	Entry Clearance and leave to enter granted for 5 yrs and 1 month or 3 yrs and 1 month
Arrive at UK port	Arrive at UK port	Arrive at UK port
Leave to Enter granted for 6 months or date of entry endorsed on visa	Date fo entry endorsed on passport	Date of entry endorsed on passport
Usually must depart before expiry	Apply for an extension of stay 30 months after entry	Apply for an extension of stay to maximum of 6 years*
	Apply for ILR 60 months after entry	(or Apply for ILR 60 months after entry)*

Brackets have been used around some of the stages as they may not apply in all cases (i.e. to non-visa nationals arriving in the UK as visitors).

*The employment category above refers to Tier 2 (General), the Points–based System category for skilled workers. Some Tier 2 (General) migrants can settle after 5 years, others cannot and must leave after a maximum of 6 years.

Sources of law

It is essential as an adviser to be able to navigate around the various pieces of law that govern UK and EU immigration control. This takes a lot of practise, and will always remain a challenge. Immigration control is maintained through primary legislation, secondary legislation, the Immigration Rules, Home Office policy, obligations under international conventions, and the discretion of the Secretary of State to admit a person who does not satisfy any of the above.

All of these sources are amended from time to time and it will only be the most recently amended versions which will represent the current state of the law. The Immigration Rules are updated several times a year, the Immigration (EEA) Regulations which govern the free movement regime have been amended many times in the last couple of years, and statutes are regularly amended too. The Immigration Act 2014, currently being implemented section by section, will give rise to many further changes to the Immigration Rules, and to older statutes, and will no doubt give rise to new and amended regulations. Reliance on old materials can produce serious problems for your clients, yet it is not always easy to find up to date versions.

We list below some of the most important legal sources and provisions.

Primary legislation

Available at http://www.legislation.gov.uk/ - usually, but not always up to date!

Immigration Act 1971

- ➤ Continues to provide the framework of immigration control
- ➤ All persons without a right of abode are subject to immigration control (s.1)
- ➤ The Secretary of State must lay down the rules to be followed (s.1(4))
- ➤ Defines who has a right of abode (amended by other legislation) (s.2)
- ➤ Provides that entry/stay is regulated by the grant of leave to enter or remain for either a limited or indefinite period (s.3), and that leave continues whilst an application is awaiting decision (s.3C)
- ➤ Provides for regulation and control of entry into and stay in the UK by the Secretary of State through powers (delegated to entry clearance officers and immigration officers and under-secretaries at the Home Office) to grant (s.4):
  - Entry clearance
  - Leave to enter
  - Leave to remain/further leave to remain
  - Make a decision to remove
  - Make a decision to deport
  - Make a decision to revoke a deportation order
- ➤ Provides for when a person may become liable for deportation (s.3(5))
- ➤ Gives the power to remove only to certain countries or territories – specified in paragraph 8 of Schedule 2
- ➤ Defines various terms including illegal entrant (s.33)
- ➤ Provides for the power to examine passengers and detain passengers (Schedule 2)
- ➤ Provides for the grant of bail (Schedule 2)

British Nationality Act 1981

- ➤ Redefined nationality and citizenship and limited 'right of abode' to newly created 'British citizens' (replacing Citizens of the United Kingdom and Commonwealth with six new categories of nationality and citizenship). While the Act may at first glance appear indecipherable, patience will be rewarded:
  - s.1 defines acquisition by birth or adoption
  - s.2 defines acquisition by descent
  - s.3 sets out the provisions for the registration of minors born outside the UK
  - s.6 and Schedule 1 set out the criteria for acquisition by naturalisation
  - s.4 to s.4C sets out other registration provisions
  - s.11 defines who acquired citizenship on commencement of the Act

- s.14 defines a 'British citizen by descent' and, in effect, also 'otherwise than by descent'. The distinction is important, as will be seen in the nationality law chapter.
- s.40 deprivation of citizenship

Special Immigration Appeals Commission Act 1997

➤ Created SIAC for security-sensitive appeals

Human Rights Act 1998

➤ Incorporates the European Convention of Human Rights into UK law. Provides for a domestic remedy (rather than having to go to the court in Strasbourg) for those asserting that a public official has breached their human rights protected under the ECHR

Immigration and Asylum Act 1999

➤ Largely superseded, but still relevant in certain important respects:
- amends IA 1971 to provide for entry clearance to have effect as leave to enter (s.3)
- provides powers of administrative removal for persons (s.10)
- provides for the registration of immigration advisors through the Office of the Immigration Services Commissioner (OISC), including the introduction of related criminal offences and enforcement powers
- provides for the support and dispersal of asylum seekers
- provides for suspicious marriages to be reported by registrars
- creates new offences relating to facilitating/harbouring illegal entrants and increases powers of arrest and power to search premises and persons

Nationality, Immigration and Asylum Act 2002

- sets out rights of appeal to the immigration tribunal
- provides for certain asylum and human rights claims to be certified as clearly unfounded. The right to challenge such decisions is to be exercised from abroad only (commonly referred to as non-suspensive appeals because the removal process is not suspended to allow the appeal to take place) (s.94)
- provides for establishment of accommodation centres and removal centres (ss.16-42)
- allows for revocation of indefinite leave to remain (s.76)
- grounds of appeal (s.84)
- limitations on appeal rights (ss.88-99)
- gives domestic life to Article 33(2) of the Refugee Convention (s.72)
- provisions for juxtaposed controls with EEA countries
- a new Part 5, commencing on 28 July 2014, provides certain considerations as to the public interest that judges must have regard to when assessing an Article 8 claim

- The appeals provisions are to be heavily amended, leaving only those who have made asylum or human rights claims with a right of appeal, when Part 2 of the Immigration Act 2014 comes into force

Asylum and Immigration (Treatment of Claimants etc) Act 2004

➢ Current provisions include:
- immigration criminal offences aimed particularly at asylum seekers, including arriving without an immigration document (s.2), not co-operating with removal (s.35) and trafficking (s.4)
- statutory negative presumptions about the assessment of credibility in asylum cases (s.8)
- a regime for returning asylum seekers to safe third countries
- various regulation-making powers, including to partially designate countries or groups for 'non-suspensive' appeals
- powers for electronic monitoring, or 'tagging', as a form of reporting restriction for those on bail or temporary admission

Immigration, Asylum and Nationality Act 2006

➢ The major change introduced in this legislation was the abolition of appeal rights against entry clearance decisions for students and employment categories, which came into effect under the Points Based System (s.4). Most other changes were relatively minor:
- introduces a new regime of civil penalty notices and fines for employers who employ immigrants without permission to work as well as a new criminal offence to replace s.8 1996 Act (s.15 to 26)
- various provisions relating to information sharing and other enforcement powers (s.27 to 42)
- removes registration as a British citizen as of right by introducing a good character requirement (s.58)

UK Borders Act 2007

➢ The changes instituted under the Act generally have little impact on day to day casework:
- the exception to this are the provisions on automatic deportations, subject to a human rights exemption and other exemptions
- provision for biometric immigration documents
- provision for imposing conditions on reporting and residence on those granted limited leave
- enhanced powers of detention for immigration officers

Tribunals, Courts and Enforcement Act 2007

➢ Creates a unified tribunal structure consisting of the First-tier Tribunal and the Upper Tribunal. Each is divided into different speciality 'chambers'.
➢ Immigration appeals were belatedly merged into the unified tribunal structure as of 2010 by the 2009 Act (below). An Immigration and Asylum Chamber was created in both the First-tier and Upper Tribunals.

➢ The right of appeal to the Court of Appeal is restricted by a second appeals test

Criminal Justice and Immigration Act 2008

➢ Sections 130-137 of this Act provide for a special immigration status for individuals who cannot be removed to their country of origin because of human rights concerns, but who have committed crimes falling under s.72 NIAA 2002 or are excluded from refugee status by virtue of Article 1F of the Refugee Convention. Spouses, civil partners and children may also be subjected to the same status. The status can prohibit the person from working, subject them to heavy reporting and residence conditions and leaves them on a reduced welfare support package. It has not been introduced yet.

Borders, Citizenship and Immigration Act 2009

➢ New citizenship provisions were enacted, but the coalition government has stated that these provisions will never be commenced.
➢ Abolished Asylum and Immigration Tribunal and merged immigration adjudication into the unified tribunal structure.
➢ Power to transfer fresh claim judicial reviews to the Upper Tribunal (a process which will reach its culmination on 1 November 2013 from when almost all immigration JRs will be heard in the Upper Tribunal)
➢ Powers to restrict what studies a person can undertake in the UK
➢ Most importantly, a new duty to safeguard and promote the welfare of children: section 55

Legal Aid, Sentencing and Punishment of Offenders Act 2012

➢ Largely removes immigration matters from funding under legal aid
➢ Excludes migrants from the rehabilitation of offenders provisions

Crime and Courts Act 2013

➢ Allows for decisions to refuse an extension and to remove to be made at the same time
➢ Removes right of appeal for family visitors
➢ Restricts in-country appeal rights for those facing deportation on national security grounds

Immigration Act 2014

➢ Streamlines the decision-making process for removing migrants who do not have permission to be in the UK
➢ Restricts appeal rights to those who have made asylum or human rights claims
➢ Provisions to prevent private landlords, banks and the DVLA providing their services to irregular migrants

➢ Restrictions on bail applications
➢ New rules for registering marriages

Secondary legislation

Some of this material is available on http://www.legislation.gov.uk/, but never in the amended form, so itis usually necessary to look separately at the original regulations and then any amendments to those regulations. The Immigration Law Handbook is a useful source for the consolidated (i.e. amended) regulations.

Immigration (Notices) Regulations 2003

➢ Governs the content of notices of immigration decisions
➢ Governs the service of the notice
➢ Requires a Notice of Appeal to be served with a Notice of Decision in certain circumstances
➢ Requires notices to be re-served where an asylum or human rights claim is made post-decision

Tribunal Procedure (First-tier Tribunal) (Immigration and Asylum Chamber) Rules 2014

➢ Regulates appeal procedure in the Immigration and Asylum Chamber of the First-tier Tribunal, including time limits for lodging appeals. Now includes The Fast Track Rules. This is the place to start your search when look for anything relating to appeals procedure.

Tribunal Procedure (Upper Tribunal) Rules 2008

➢ Governs appeals procedure in the entire Upper Tribunal, including the Immigration and Asylum Chamber

Immigration (European Economic Area) Regulations 2006

➢ Transposes into domestic law EC freedom of movement law, and regulates appeal rights and residence rights for EEA nationals and their family members. For a consolidated (but unofficial) version go to: http://www.eearegulations.co.uk/versions/latest.php

Immigration Orders

➢ There are many Orders made under secondary legislation powers that can have an effect on immigration law. The most important is the Immigration (Leave to Enter and Remain) Order 2000, which simplified immigration control for persons with visas. Under this Order, entry clearance takes effect as leave to enter if it specifies the purpose for which the holder wishes to enter the country and if it is endorsed with the conditions to which it is subject. Multi-entry visit visas operate as leave to enter on an unlimited number of occasions for so long as they are valid (for six months if six months or more remain of the visa's period of validity; or for the visa's remaining period of validity, if less than six months). Leave given for more than six months, or which was conferred by entry clearance (other than single-entry visit visas), does not normally lapse when a person leaves the Common Travel Area.

➤ There are many other orders, the most useful of which are included in the secondary legislation section of Phelan and Gillespie's Immigration Law Handbook.

Commencement Orders

➤ Bring into force the specific provisions of primary and sometimes secondary legislation.

Immigration rules

Immigration Rules (HC395)

➤ Referred to in this manual as 'the rules'
➤ https://www.gov.uk/government/collections/immigration-rules
➤ Unique legal status different to secondary legislation
➤ Regulates who may and may not be granted entry clearance and/or leave to enter or remain.
➤ HC395 is not actually law or secondary legislation as such and the SSHD retains discretion to allow entry outside the rules. SSHD cannot act more restrictively than is set out in HC395 as, assuming there is a right of appeal, the decision will be overturned on appeal or failing that would be susceptible to judicial review. The Immigration Rules are made under section 3(5) of the 1971 Act.
➤ Where the Secretary of State stipulates that certain requirements must be met in order to succeed in an application made under the Immigration Rules, all those requirements, including the requirement to provide specified evidence in support of the application, must appear within the Immigration Rules themselves. This was held to be the case in the landmark Supreme Court judgment in Alvi [2012] UKSC 33. As a consequence, much of the Home Office's guidance as to how the Immigration Rules are to be applied, and the supporting documentation that must be provided, has been added to the Immigration Rules and to several appendices to the Immigration Rules.

Statements of Changes

➤ Statements of Changes amend the Immigration Rules (HC395). They are available at:
https://www.gov.uk/government/collections/immigration-rules-statement-of-changes

Operational Guidance

The Home Office publishes the guidance it provides to its immigration officials on how the Immigration Rules and other provisions should be interpreted and applied both generally and in specific circumstances. These important policy documents also contain concessions, outlining circumstances in which discretion might be exercised, exceptionally, to grant leave outside the Immigration Rules.

The Operational Guidance, previously referred to on the old UKBA website as 'Staff instructions', can be found at: https://www.gov.uk/immigration-operational-guidance and includes the;

➤ Immigration Directorate Instructions (IDIs)
➤ Entry Clearance Guidance (ECG)
➤ Modernised Guidance
➤ Business and commercial caseworker guidance
➤ Asylum Policy
➤ Nationality Instructions
➤ European casework instructions
➤ Enforcement Instructions and Guidance (EIG)

These documents, voluminous and regularly updated, are vital tools in the armoury of the immigration adviser. They allow the adviser to step into the shoes of the Home Office decision maker to see how an application will be assessed against the Immigration Rules. Where the guidance is helpful to a case, it should be quoted in the covering letter or representations, and on appeal or judicial review.

Top tip

HJT Training and the Immigration Law Practitioners Association jointly publish an invaluable compendium of historic Home Office policies and also regularly run a joint training session with materials to keep the publication up to date.

See the HJT Training website for further information.

For more on 'Operational guidance' see the section on 'Policies, concessions and Operation Guidance'.

Making an application

Applications for entry clearance must be made from abroad, usually now on-line. Leave to remain/extension applications are usually made from within the UK, though there is no bar on making them from outside the UK.

Applications for leave to remain can be made in person by appointment at the UKVI's premium service centre, by post or courier, and sometimes on-line.

It is particularly important that an in-country application is 'valid'. A 'valid application' is defined in paragraph 6 of the rules as an application made in accordance with the requirements of Part 1 of the rules. There are a number of elements to making a valid application:

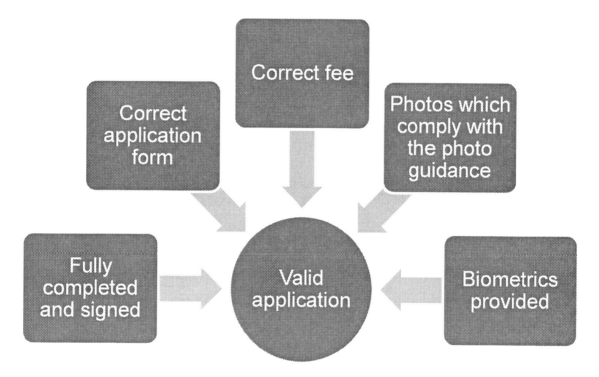

As discussed below, if an application does not comply with the required formalities, even down to wrongly sized photographs, there may be very serious consequences for the applicant.

The provisions as to validity for in-country applications can be found at Immigration Rules A34 to 34D. Advisers need to be particularly aware of the mandatory requirements of rule 34A for a postal application or application made in person.

The mandatory requirements are:

➢ Use of the specified form, and the most up to date version of it (see list of forms below). Always download the forms directly from the UKVI website, and check that they remain up to date before finalising the application. Note though that rule 34I allows for an old version of a form to be used for up to 21 days after a new version goes on-line.

➢ The payment of a specified fee. Ensure, if the payment page is used, that the account is in funds and remains in funds until the fee is collected. A full list of fees can be found at: https://www.gov.uk/government/publications/visa-regulations-revised-table

➢ Inclusion of specified biographical information

➢ Photographs as described in the photo guidance. Ensure you keep a photocopy of the photos, paperclipped to the form, so you will be able to prove they have been sent with the application if the Home Office alleges they have not.

➢ Completion of the 'confirmation box' (i.e. signing the form (which may also require a signature from others (e.g. partner or parent)) and other sections of the form stated to be mandatory

➢ Compliance with biometric requirements, i.e. attending the Home Office or a post office for face and fingerprint scans within a specified timeframe

➢ Attendance at a Home Office appointment if required

➢ Where the application is made on-line, mandatory documents must be submitted within 15 working days of submission of the online application, and biometric information must be enrolled within 45 days (rule A34)

Note that the guidance on validity, in the Modernised Guidance on Specified application forms and procedures, states;

> If the application was received more than three months ago and does not meet the specified form requirements, you must use discretion and accept it as valid. This is because the applicant may be unfairly disadvantaged if you reject their application after this length of time

Where stated an application form can include dependants within it, anfd that may now include, where applicable, children over 18 (rule 34D).

Timing

A postal application for an extension of stay is treated as having been made on the day it is posted (rule 34G(i)). It is vital therefore to send applications by recorded delivery and to keep evidence of the date of posting in case of later dispute.

Applications for an extension of stay should be made whilst the applicant has current leave to remain. The Home Office recommends the application is made no earlier than 28 days before the current leave expires.

That being said, the Immigration Rules do allow applications to be made where the applicant has overstayed by no more than 28 days. 'Overstaying' is defined in paragraph 6 of the Immigration Rules as staying beyond the latest of:

> (i) the time limit attached to the last period of leave granted, or
>
> (ii) beyond the period that his leave was extended under sections 3C or 3D of the Immigration Act 1971.

Whilst an application made within that 28 day period following expiry of leave will be considered under the Immigration Rules in the normal way, the applicant will still have become an overstayer. That may have serious consequences. They will have lost their continuity of residence, and their right to work. They will also have lost their right of appeal if the application is refused (until the introduction of the appeals provisions of the Immigration Act 2014). Every effort must therefore be made to make an in-time application. The 28 day disregard should be relied on only where there is no other option.

Automatic extension of leave (also known as 'continuing leave' or '3C leave')

The Home Office takes several weeks or months (or even years in some cases) to make a decision on an application for an extension of stay. This delay will usually result in the person's leave apparently expiring while the application is awaiting an initial decision.

Section 3C of the Immigration Act 1971 was enacted to deal with this problem. It automatically extends leave while an in-time application is pending, and then, if the application is refused, by a further 10 business days from the receipt of the decision to allow the applicant to lodge an appeal with the First-tier Tribunal (IAC) (or an application for Administrative Review when the Part 2 of the Immigration Act 2014 is commenced). Leave is further extended if an in-time appeal (or application for Administrative Review) is lodged and remains pending (i.e. not finally decided). S3C also extends the conditions attached to the previous grant of leave.

Where an out of time appeal is lodged, 3C leave is restored, retrospectively, if an extension of time is granted by the Tribunal.

A similar provision at Section 3D of the Immigration Act 1971 automatically extends the leave of those whose leave has been curtailed whilst they appeal against the curtailment. On the implementation of Part 2 of the Immigration Act 2014, there will no longer be a right of appeal against a decision to curtail leave, though it is likely such a decision will be Administrative Reviewable.

An adviser may have to confirm to an employer or other body that an in-time application or appeal or application for Administrative Review is pending and that the employee therefore has continuing leave to remain in the UK. It is unlawful to dismiss a person on the basis of their immigration status whilst they have continuing leave under these statutory provisions. Problems will particularly arise where the employer rings the Home Office's execrable 'hotline', which is meant to confirm a migrant's entitlement to work but often gets the answer wrong, often simply because the in-time application has not been logged in the Home Office's immigration database. In such cases, the employer should be reminded of the decision in _Klusova v London Borough of Hounslow [2007] EWCA Civ 1127_

Effect of an invalid application

The decision on whether an application is valid is made by the Initial Consideration Unit or, for those attending in person, the Public Enquiry Office. The forms and accompanying documents are checked for compliance, and the merits of the application disregarded at that stage.

Where a postal application is made, the Home Office should contact the applicant informing them that their application is invalid, before rejecting it as invalid, to give them an opportunity to correct it. This common sense practice now has support in the rules at paragraph 34C(b). An applicant should be given 10 business days to correct the application after such contact.

Invalid applications are returned to applicants or their advisers, endorsed with the defects which need remedying on a Notice of Invalidity. It will be returned undecided (i.e. neither refused nor granted). This can have very serious consequences. The applicant will be in much the same position as they would have been if the application had not been made at all, i.e. they will have become an overstayer on receiving the Notice of Invalidity if their leave expired after making the application.

If the invalid application was made in-time, the applicant will be able to make one further application in the 28 day period allowed for as above. By applying out of time however they will have lost any appeal rights they may have had. But if the invalid application was made by a person who had already overstayed, any further application is likely to be rejected as the applicant would have, by then, overstayed by more than 28 days. Clearly, it is always vitally important that the application is validly made to the satisfaction of the Initial Consideration Unit or Public Enquiry Office. Very careful regard must be had to rules A34 and 34A.

Note though that mistakes are regularly made by the Home Office and valid applications are wrongly rejected as being invalid, commonly where it is wrongly alleged that no photos have been provided or that the application has not been accompanied by the fee.

Example

Graeme has been studying in the UK for eight years. He has always complied with immigration requirements and the next course he wants to undertake will end after another two years, meaning that he would be then eligible to apply for settlement after 10 years of continuous lawful residence (see next chapter).

However, when he makes his latest immigration application he forgets to sign the cheque. He submits the application on 20 January. His leave expires on 31 January. The Home Office return the application to him on 28 February and notify him that it is invalid.

Graeme has unwittingly become an overstayer (as from the date the application is returned to him) and is committing a criminal offence by remaining in the UK. He has also lost any right he had to work in the UK. He can though make a further application and that must be made within 28 days of the invalid application being returned to him.

If that application is refused he will not have a right of appeal, nor will he be able to make a third attempt (as he will now have overstayed by more than 28 days).

If the application is successful though, his future long residence application may be saved by a concession in the rules which allows the Home Office to ignore up to 28 days of overstaying between the expiry of a grant of leave and a new application being made when considering his continuity of residence over the 10 year period.

As a further important point for those in the UK studying under Tier 4, Graeme, as an overstayer when making his second application, will not now be able to rely on the 'having an established presence' provision which requires that he has current leave at the date of application. This provision substantially reduces the maintenance requirement under Tier 4 so, having made an invalid application, he will have completely lost his chance of extending his stay unless he can meet the more onerous maintenance requirement.

The implications of making an application on the wrong form are slightly mitigated by the judgment in *JH (Zimbabwe) v SSHD* [2009] EWCA Civ 78. The Court of Appeal held that an application made on the wrong form (e.g. on a SET form rather than an FLR form) may in fact be a valid immigration application, even if it was ultimately doomed to fail as the applicant could not meet the requirements for settlement. The Court went on to find that it is possible to vary an application by applying for a different form of immigration status on a different application form, up until the time that a decision is made by the Secretary of State on the application. It had previously been thought that once leave was extended automatically by section 3C Immigration Act 1971, it was not possible to vary an application (see also rules 34E to 34G).

Note also that rule 34I allows an out of date form to be used for up to 21 days after the new version goes online.

See also the section in this manual on overstaying and extension applications in Chapter 3: Points Based System. This includes a discussion on the important cases of *Basnet* and *Kobir* where the courts have found the Home Office's system of processing payments with postal applications risks falling into procedural unfairness, and that the Home Office should sometimes use their discretion outside the Immigration Rules when incorrect fees have been paid.

Application forms and fees

Forms, and a list of current fees can be found on the GOV.UK website at: https://www.gov.uk/immigration-operational-guidance/fees-forms

Visa/entry clearance applications

Information on entry clearance applications, processing times and local administrative arrangements for submitting an application can be found on the GOV.UK website, which provides links as necessary to the visa application website (http://www.visa4uk.fco.gov.uk/), and to the websites of the commercial partners' and the local embassy and High Commission.

Visa processing times can be found at: https://www.gov.uk/visa-processing-times

Visa applications must usually be made on-line (though a few posts still require a paper application, and some give you the option of either).

An application for entry clearance should be made from the country in which the applicant is living (i.e. not merely passing through). Visit visas are an exception – they can be made at any post designated to accept such applications (rule 28), as are some Tier 5 and Tier 1 applications (rule 28A).

An application is not legally made unless and until it is accompanied by the appropriate fee in local currency: rule 30. If the fee can be paid online, the application date will be the date the online application is submitted. Otherwise, the fee will be paid when the applicant attends the VAC in person for the biometric appointment. In the latter case, even if made online some time before the appointment date, the application will still be treated as having been made when the fee is paid at the VAC on the date of the appointment.

The date of application may be important. Where the immigration rules that apply to the application have been amended between the date of the on-line application and the date the fee is paid, it will the amended rule that will be applied to the application (and the application is therefore likely to be refused as not meeting the amended requirements).

Additionally, under rule 27, a child applicant must apply before their 18th birthday, but having done so will continue to be treated as under 18 throughout the decision making process.

Visa fees in local currency can be found at: https://www.gov.uk/visa-fees. The fees for some of the main types of entry clearance application as of 6 April 2014 are as follows:

Visa	Fee
Short term visit	£83
Family member (partner/child)	£885
Adult Dependent relative	£1,982
Certificate of Entitlement	£289
Tier 1	£874
Tier 1 Graduate Entrepreneur	£310
Tier 2 (General, Sport, MOR & ICT long term)	£514
Tier 2 (ICT short term)	£428
Tier 4	£310
Tier 5	£208

The above list is not comprehensive and reduced fees sometimes apply for Council of Europe Social Charter (CESC) nationals. The Immigration Act 2014 gives the UKVI to amend fees more regularly than at present, and for a mandatory surcharge to be charged to cover access to NHS services. Always look at the GOV.UK website for details of the up to date fees.

EEA family permits, and applications under the family reunion rules from the pre-existing families of refugees remain free of charge.

In-country extension and regularisation applications

The main non-PBS, non-EEA application forms are as follows:

Form NTL (No Time Limit)

Use this form to apply for an indefinite leave stamp (No Time Limit) to be endorsed in a new passport or travel document of a person who already has indefinite leave to enter, or to remain in the United Kingdom

Form FLR (M)

Use this form to apply for an extension of stay as the partner (together with any dependent children) of a person present and settled in the UK, or of a person with limited leave in the UK with refugee leave or humanitarian protection.

Form FLR (O)

Use this form to apply for an extension of stay for applications in any of the following categories:

- Academic visitor
- Domestic worker in a private household
- Academic visitor
- UK ancestry
- Visitor for private medical treatment
- Dependant of a person who has limited leave to enter or remain in the UK other than under the points based system
- General visitor
- Other purposes/reasons not covered by other application forms

Form FLR (FP)

Use this form to apply for an extension of stay for applications in any of the following categories:

- Private life in the UK
- Family life as a partner (10 year route)
- Family life as a parent of a child in the UK (5 year & 10 year routes)

Form FLR (LR)

This form is to apply for an extension of stay in the UK under the 10 year long residence rule.

Form FLR (AF)

Use this form to apply for an extension of stay for applications in any of the following categories:

- Limited leave as a HM Forces member on discharge
- Limited leave as the partner and child of a British or foreign or Commonwealth HM Forces sponsor under Appendix Armed Forces
- Limited leave as the partner or child whose sponsor was discharged from HM Forces
- Limited leave as the partner and child of a British HM forces sponsor applying under transitional arrangements under Part 8 of the Immigration Rules
- Limited leave as the partner and child of a foreign or Commonwealth HM forces sponsor applying under transitional arrangements under Part 7 of the Immigration Rules

For settlement the form is SET(AF).

Form FLR (P)

Use this form to apply for an extension of stay in the UK as a child under the age of 18 of a relative with limited leave to enter or remain in the UK as a refugee or beneficiary of humanitarian protection. Or as parents, grandparents or other dependent relatives aged over 18 of persons with limited leave to enter or remain in the UK as a refugee or beneficiary of humanitarian protection and for a biometric immigration document

Form FLR (BUS)

Use this form to apply for an extension of stay as a Retired Person of Independent Means or as a Representative of an Overseas Business

Form DL

Form DL is for anyone who following refusal of asylum has been granted:

• Discretionary Leave or

• Less than four years Exceptional Leave

and is now applying for a further period of Discretionary Leave or settlement, in accordance with the published Home Office Asylum Instruction on Discretionary Leave. This form must not be used by applicants applying for further leave on Article 3 medical grounds who must use the FLR(O) form.

Form FLR (S)

This form is to apply for leave to remain in the UK, and a biometric residence permit, as a stateless person.

Form SET (M)

Use this form to apply for indefinite leave to remain in the United Kingdom as the spouse (husband or wife), civil partner or unmarried partner of a person who is present and settled in the U.K.

Form SET (DV)

This form is used specifically for applying for settlement under the Immigration Rules for victims of domestic violence whose relationships have broken down during the probationary period because of that domestic violence

Form SET (F)

Use this form to apply for indefinite leave to remain as the:

- Child under age of 18 of a parent, parents or a relative present and settled in the UK
- Adopted child under the age of 18 of a parent or parents present and settled in the UK
- Child aged over 18 of persons present and settled in the UK

Form SET (BUS)

Use this form to apply for indefinite leave to remain as a Retired Person of Independent Means or as a Representative of an Overseas Business

Form SET (O)

Use this form to apply for indefinite leave to remain in the United Kingdom when approaching five years of continuous leave to remain in the United Kingdom in one of the following categories:

- work permit holder or dependant
- employment not requiring a work permit
- businessperson, innovator or investor
- highly skilled migrant, highly skilled migrant under the terms of the HSMP indefinite leave to remain (ILR) judicial review policy document
- self-employed lawyer
- writer, composer or artist
- Tier 1 migrants
- Tier 2 migrants
- PBS dependants
- UK ancestry
- bereaved partner
- other purposes/reasons not covered by other application forms

Form SET (P)

Use this form to apply for indefinite leave to remain in the United Kingdom when approaching five years of continuous leave to remain in the United Kingdom as a refugee or person granted humanitarian protection

Form SET (LR))

Use this form to apply for indefinite leave to remain (settlement) in the UK under the 10 year long residence rules.

These forms must be accompanied by the correct fee, where applicable. Fees are reduced for applications from citizens of countries that are signatory to the European Social Charter. The most commonly encountered fees, as of 6 April 2014 are as follows:

Application	Principal fee	Dependant's fee
ILR postal	£1093	£1093
LTR postal	£601	£601
Tier 1 (Entrep/Inv/ET) postal	£1093	£1093
Tier 2 (G/ICTLTS/SP/MOR))*	£601	£601
Tier 4 postal	£422	£422
Tier 5 postal	£200	£208

*Different fees apply under Tier 2, dependent upon whether the job is in a shortage occupation, and the length of extension applied for.

The fees above are for postal applications. For applications made in person at the public enquiry office the fee is the postal fee plus £400 (which includes a £100 appointment booking fee which is returnable).

A Super Premium service, where a mobile Home Office unit comes to you, costs an additional £6000.

Some individuals are exempt from paying fees for applications:

➢ people applying for Indefinite Leave to Remain on the grounds of domestic violence where, at the time of making the application, the applicant appears to be destitute (or has been granted leave under the DDV concession);

➢ children under 18 and receiving local authority support;

➢ persons granted limited leave to remain whilst they were under 18 on the rejection of their claim for asylum and who are now applying for further leave to remain;

➢ nationals of Turkey and their dependants who are applying for leave to remain under the terms of the Turkish European Community Association Agreement; (the 'Ankara Agreement');

➢ rejected asylum seekers who are seeking extensions of discretionary leave to remain;

➢ those applying for leave to remain where the basis of their claim is asylum or Article 3 ECHR.

On 1 July 2013, the Home Office introduced a flat rate fee of £55.00 for EEA residence documents for EEA nationals and their family members. Family permit applications remain free.

Fee exemption

Those applying for leave on Article 8 grounds will have to pay a fee, but if they are destitute, they can apply for a fee exemption on form Appendix 1 FLR(FP) FLR(O) The form can be found at:
https://www.gov.uk/government/publications/application-to-extend-stay-in-the-uk-appendix-1-flrfp-flro
Guidance can be found in the IDIs at:
https://www.gov.uk/government/publications/chapter-1a-applications-for-fee-waiver-and-refunds
The Administrative Court found the guidance to be unlawful in *Carter, R* (On the Application Of) v SSHD [2014] EWHC 2603 (Admin), though that decision is currently being appeal by the Secretary of State to the Court of Appeal (see:

https://www.gov.uk/government/publications/application-to-extend-stay-in-the-uk-appendix-1-flrfp-flro/fee-waiver-applications-for-flro-and-flr-fp-information-for-applicants)

Decisions

A well prepared and properly evidenced application which meets the requirements of the Immigration Rules should be allowed by the Home Office. In practice though, many such applications are refused for very silly reasons. Home Office decision makers, both in the UK and abroad, routinely ignore documents that have been submitted, and often appear to have no proper understanding of the law. Advisers should always warn their clients that they may receive a perverse decision, and that appeals, where available, are routinely allowed by immigration judges in such cases. This is frustrating for advisers and their clients, but something that advisers need to get used to.

It will become even more frustrating when the right of appeal disappears for all but asylum and human rights claims with the commencement of Part 2 of the Immigration Act 2014. In some cases, where the right of appeal has been taken away, there will be a new system of Administrative Reviews where, for a fee, a specialised team of UKVI caseworkers will reconsider the decision. However, the administrative review process only allows for the correction of caseworking errors, so is much more limited in scope than an appeal to the Tribunal (which, for instance, can consider how the law should have been interpreted in a particular case). If there is no right to administrative review in a particular case, or the administrative review fails, or where the administrative review regime is not appropriate, the remedy will be an application for judicial review made to the Upper Tribunal (Immigration and Asylum Chamber).

It will always reduce the chance of a silly decision if the application is well prepared, in form as well as in content. The documentation should be easy to find and well ordered. Every application must be supported by a covering letter laying out the basic law relied upon, usually a category of the Immigration Rules or a provision of the Immigration (EEA) Regulations 2006, listing the enclosures, and explaining why the enclosures show that each of the requirements of the law is met.

On receipt of a negative decision advisers should look carefully at the validity of the Notice of Decision, and the reasons of refusal, and then consider the availability of an appropriate remedy, if any. Currently, it is rare that the Home Office will simply review a decision on polite request unless there is a specific policy to do so (see e.g. the *Alvi* policy and the Reconsiderations policy in the Modernised guidance/other cross-cutting information). So a request for a review outside the policy is likely to be a waste of time unless it is accompanied by a formal complaint, or comes from an MP, or is put in the form of a pre-action protocol letter (i.e. one informing the Home Office that you will a seek judicial review if the decision is not changed), or the Parliamentary and Health Service Ombudsman gets involved.

Acting in the best interests of your client, it will always be necessary to give them an honest assessment of the merits of their case. There no point embarking on lengthy and costly applications and remedies, and it might be a breach of your professional duties to do so, if they are likely to fail (unless your client has given fully informed consent for you to do so.

Chapter 2: General requirements and policies

Navigating the Immigration Rules

The Immigration Rules (HC 395) set out the rules for entry to and stay in the UK for people who are subject to immigration control, and is the single most important document in immigration law. They must be consulted and strictly adhered to for all type of immigration application for people subject to immigration control

The power to make the rules comes from section 3(2) of the Immigration Act 1971:

> The Secretary of State shall from time to time (and as soon as may be) lay before Parliament statements of the rules, or of any changes in the rules, laid down by him as to the practice to be followed in the administration of this Act for regulating the entry into and stay in the United Kingdom of persons required by this Act to have leave to enter, including any rules as to the period for which leave is to be given and the conditions to be attached in different circumstances...

The rules include a list of the purposes or categories under which people can enter and/or remain in the UK – e.g. for protection, to visit, to study, for employment, business and investment, and for family reasons. A few purposes though remain outside the rules (see e.g. the concessions relating to carers and those involved in family proceedings in the section on policies and concessions).

The landmark Supreme Court judgement in Alvi [2012] UKSC 33, held that all mandatory requirements, including evidential requirements, must be listed in the Immigration Rules. Before Alvi, many of these requirements could only be found in guidance documents. Together with the government's policy of increasingly micro-managing immigration, this means that the Immigration Rules have become extremely long and convoluted. This manual can only really provide an overview of the Immigration Rules, which now run to more than 1000 pages.

There is no alternative but for advisers to work directly from the Immigration Rules themselves. The only up to date and comprehensive version of the Immigration Rules is on the GOV.UK website at:
https://www.gov.uk/government/collections/immigration-rules.
An index to the rules is at:
https://www.gov.uk/government/publications/immigration-rules-index.

The Immigration Rules are difficult to navigate. Critical information has been placed into the Immigration Rules in arbitrary places, and into an increasing number of appendices. Even the paragraph numbering scheme often fails to follow any rational pattern; but nevertheless advisers must avoid the temptation to work solely from the guidance to applicants provided on the GOV.UK website as this is neither comprehensive nor always accurate, and can be misleading.

Each category of the Immigration Rules (e.g. visitors in Part 2, the Points-based system in Part 6A, family members in Appendix FM) has been drafted in different formats, but will generally contain;

- An outline of the purpose of the category
- A definition of criteria used in the category (though paragraph 6 of the Immigration Rules also contains important definitions of key words and phrases). It cannot be presumed that words in the Immigration Rules have their ordinary or common sense meaning, so it is important to see how they are defined for the purpose of a particular rule.
- The specific requirements that must be met for entry clearance or leave to enter, for an extension of stay, and for indefinite leave to remain where available. The requirements of the rules are different for each of these types of application
- Specified (i.e. mandatory) documents – detailing both their form and content – that must be submitted with the application
- The period of leave that will be granted
- The conditions that will be placed on the grant of leave (e.g. no recourse to public funds, prohibition on working – see more on conditions below)
- The circumstances in which the application will be refused

Top tip

No two categories follow the same pattern. It is important to read the Immigration Rules carefully and look for what is NOT in the Immigration Rules as much as what IS in them. For example, the student category (Tier 4 of the Points-based system) contains no provision relating to a grant of ILR, so a migrant who is in the U.K. as a student cannot apply for ILR under the student category. Similarly, the Tier 5 categories make no reference to English language requirements (unusually for the PBS), so there are none.

Transitional provisions

When changes are made to the Immigration Rules, transitional provisions are introduced which then disapply those changes to those who have already made applications or entered the UK before the changes were made. So, depending on the particular transitional provisions, the 'old' rules will continue to apply to some migrants, and the new rules to others. In effect, there will be two or more sets of rules running side by side, covering similar purposes, but applicable to different migrants.

As an example, those who applied under the partner provisions as they were before 9 July 2012 (which are in Part 8 of the Immigration Rules), will have different requirements to meet from those who first applied after that date (under the rules in Appendix FM). The rules incorporate the transitional provisions (see rules A277 to A280 (and weep!)), and it is necessary to carefully consider which particular rules and requirements apply to a particular case, depending on the migrant's date of first application in that category or date of entry.

Also, over the years, and particularly with the introduction of the points-based system (PBS) from 2008, many categories within the Immigration Rules have been closed to new applicants. These include, in recent times, Tier 1 (General) and Tier 1 (Post-study work). These categories are for most purposes obsolete, but they remain in the Immigration Rules (either in the main body of the rules or relocated to the appendices) for those who were granted leave in those categories before they were closed, and who may still be able to make extension or ILR applications, or sponsor dependants in those categories.

For those pursuing appeals or judicial reviews in categories that have been amended after they received their decision, the applicable rules will be those as they were at the date of decision. Usefully, there are archived versions of the Immigration Rules as they stood at various dates in the past on the GOV.UK website (see the 'Archive: Immigration Rules' link on the Immigration Rules page).

Common requirements of the Immigration Rules

Many different immigration categories include similar provisions, and rather than repeat the information it is more convenient to deal with them in one place.

Specified documents

Rule 39B lays out the general requirements as to 'specified' documents (i.e. specified in the Immigration Rules) that must be provided in support of an application. Where specified, supporting documentation must meet the requirements of the rules both in respect of form and content. A 'nearly' document just won't do!

There is no requirement that a specified document be named as such, so long as it is referred to in the Immigration Rules. It must be verifiable, and so must include the contact details of the person or organisation creating the document, and original (unless stated otherwise). Where not in English or Welsh, it must be accompanied by a full translation which includes the translator's credentials, the date and the translator's signature, and confirms that it is an accurate translation.

Evidential flexibility

Where a document or an original document is not available, a full explanation should be provided in a covering letter. The necessary document should be provided as soon as possible, and before a decision is made on the application.

In a points-based system (PBS) or Appendix FM case however, by reason of rule 245AA(a) and paragraph D(a) of Appendix FM-SE, a document provided after the date of application may simply be ignored by the Home Office decision-maker.

This annoyingly inflexible provision was upheld by the Court of Appeal in the case of Secretary of State for the Home Department v Raju & Ors [2013] EWCA Civ 754, overturning the more flexible approach taken by the Upper Tribunal in Khatel and others (s85A; effect of continuing application) [2013] UKUT 44 (IAC).

Nevertheless a document provided late, rather than never, but then ignored by the Home Office, does raise the question of fairness and may ground a legal challenge to the decision.

There has been much litigation around the scope of earlier versions of the Home Office's PBS evidential flexibility policy, but the current policy (in the Modernised Guidance/Other cross-cutting information) merely reflects the current rules.

There is no general requirement that the Home Office contact an applicant where documents are in the wrong form or missing, though they should do so in the specific circumstances outlined in rule 245AA(b) relating to the PBS applications, and paragraph D(b) of Appendix FM-SE for family life applications (see more on this in the sections on the PBS and Appendix FM categories).

Maintenance

Entry, leave to remain and settlement are usually contingent on a person being able to adequately maintain and accommodate themselves and any dependants without recourse to public funds. It is now enshrined in statute, at s117B(3) of the Nationality, Immigration and Asylum Act 2002 (as amended by the Immigration Act 2014) that;

> It is in the public interest, and in particular in the interests of the economic well-being of the United Kingdom, that persons who seek to enter or remain in the United Kingdom are financially independent, because such persons—
>
> (a)are not a burden on taxpayers, and
>
> (b)are better able to integrate into society.

This principle is operated by a maintenance requirement which appears in most categories, and by a condition placed on any grant of leave in those categories denying the migrant recourse to public funds (which they would in any case be unable to claim due to benefits legislation).

Maintenance Exception (handwritten margin note)

Exceptions to this principle include refugees and those with humanitarian protection, their pre-existing families, those applying under the long residence, private life, bereaved partners and victims of domestic violence categories, and where the EX1 exception applies under the family life categories in Appendix FM.

Where the principle applies, the rules differ as to precisely how the requirement is to be met. They will either;

- stipulate that a person must be able to maintain and accommodate themselves adequately without recourse to public funds;
- provide, as under the Points Based System, that an applicant has to demonstrate a fixed amount of savings in a prescribed form or,
- require, as under the family life categories of Appendix FM, a specified level of income and/or savings (unless the sponsor is in receipt of particular benefits).

This section looks at the requirements an applicant will need to meet in cases where the rule stipulates that they must be able *to maintain and accommodate themselves and any dependants adequately in the UK without recourse to public funds*.

Key principles on maintenance

- 'Public funds' are exhaustively defined
- There must be no additional recourse
- Income support provides an objective measure as to adequacy
- The adequacy requirement is not an excuse for inquiry into lifestyle
- Third party support is permitted in law, unless excluded by a specific rule (as it generally is now under the PBS and Appendix FM).

Meaning of public funds

The definition of 'public funds' is relevant both to the requirements of certain categories, and also to the condition on grants of leave prohibiting recourse.

Public funds are exhaustively listed in rule 6 of HC395. The list is exhaustive in the sense that any benefit not included in the rule is not considered to be a public fund for the purposes of the immigration rules. As can be seen, there are some public funds, such as legal aid, education, contributory benefits such as contributory job seekers' allowance, and NHS care that are not included in the definition and are not therefore treated as public funds:

"public funds" means

(a) housing under Part VI or VII of the Housing Act 1996 and under Part II of the Housing Act 1985, Part I or II of the Housing (Scotland) Act 1987, Part II of the

Housing (Northern Ireland) Order 1981 or Part II of the Housing (Northern Ireland) Order 1988;

(b) attendance allowance, severe disablement allowance, carer's allowance and disability living allowance under Part III of the Social Security Contribution and Benefits Act 1992; income support, council tax benefit and housing benefit under Part VII of that Act; a social fund payment under Part VIII of that Act; child benefit under Part IX of that Act; income based jobseeker's allowance under the Jobseekers Act 1995, income related allowance under Part 1 of the Welfare Reform Act 2007 (employment and support allowance) state pension credit under the State Pension Credit Act 2002; or child tax credit and working tax credit under Part 1 of the Tax Credits Act 2002;

(c) attendance allowance, severe disablement allowance, carer's allowance and disability living allowance under Part III of the Social Security Contribution and Benefits (Northern Ireland) Act 1992; income support, council tax benefit and, housing benefit under Part VII of that Act; a social fund payment under Part VIII of that Act; child benefit under Part IX of that Act; income based jobseeker's allowance under the Jobseekers (Northern Ireland) Order 1995 or income related allowance under Part 1 of the Welfare Reform Act (Northern Ireland) 2007;

(d) Universal Credit under Part 1 of the Welfare Reform Act 2012 or Personal Independence Payment under Part 4 of that Act;

(e) Universal Credit, Personal Independence Payment or any domestic rate relief under the Northern Ireland Welfare Reform Act 2013;

(f) a council tax reduction under a council tax reduction scheme made under section 13A of the Local Government Finance Act 1992 in relation to England or Wales or a council tax reduction pursuant to the Council Tax Reduction (Scotland) Regulations 2012 or the Council Tax Reduction (State Pension Credit) (Scotland) Regulations 2012.

Importantly, a person should not claim public funds or other services to which they are not legally entitled if they are to avoid problems with later immigration applications (see e.g. the section on General Grounds for Refusal), or removal for breaching conditions. The fact that a public fund or service is wrongly granted to them will not protect the applicant if they were not entitled to it.

The expression 'without recourse to public funds' is further defined in rules 6A to 6C of HC395. In short, this explicitly states that entry is not prohibited where the sponsor is already claiming public funds but will be prohibited where the migrant relies on their sponsor's entitlement to increased or additional public funds as a result of their arrival in the U.K. It also enables the sponsor to use their pre-existing public funds to support the applicant, as long as the level of support is still 'adequate' (see below). This means that, for example, a sponsor already in receipt of disability living allowance can use those funds to support an applicant. This reflects the judgment in *MK (Somalia) v Entry Clearance Officer* [2007] EWCA Civ 1521, which settled a long running legal dispute in this area. It is also explicitly provided for in Appendix FM where a partner or parent is in receipt of specified disability related benefits.

Rule 6C prevents reliance on future additional entitlement to child benefit or tax credit in an entry clearance application, but permits reliance on those sources of funds in extension or settlement applications.

Required level of income

Outside the Points Based System and the income/savings-based requirements in Appendix FM, the level of maintenance required is stated in the Immigration Rules as 'adequate', which is defined in paragraph 6 of the Immigration Rules as;

> "'adequate' and 'adequately' in relation to a maintenance and accommodation requirement shall mean that, after income tax, national insurance contributions and housing costs have been deducted, there must be available to the family the level of income that would be available to them if the family was in receipt of income support."

This definition was introduced on 9 July 2012, largely reflecting well established principles as to the meaning of 'adequate maintenance' outlined in judgements such as *KA and Others (Adequacy of maintenance) Pakistan* [2006] UKAIT 00065. Those judgments established that providing the level of maintenance is equivalent to that of a person or family receiving income support then that will be considered to be adequate for the purposes of the immigration rules. In *Yarce (adequate maintenance: benefits)* [2012] UKUT 00425(IAC), the Upper Tribunal did not understand the new paragraph 6 definition to require a departure from the approach taken in KA.

The current level of income support for a couple both aged 18 or over is £113.70 per week. The latest and historic benefit levels can be checked on Rightsnet's website (www.rightsnet.org.uk). Rightsnet provides a useful benefit rates poster at http://www.rightsnet.org.uk/toolkit/benefit-tax-credit-rates.

Ahmed (benefits: proof of receipt; evidence) [2013] UKUT 84(IAC) usefully sets out the information the Tribunal requires from an Appellant in an entry clearance appeal seeking to establish that the adequate maintenance requirement is met.

Where preparing an Appendix FM application, the specified evidence requirements for those relying on 'adequate maintenance' are set out in paragraphs 12 and 12A of Appendix FM-SE. The documentation must be in the format specified in paragraph 1.

Third party support

'Third party support' refers to support that is provided by an additional party, such as a parent, other relative or friend. This issue has been contentious, with the government long seeking to exclude such reliance.

In the case of *Mahad and Others [2009]* UKSC 16, the Supreme Court settled a long running legal dispute about whether the maintenance rules permitted support from third parties to be taken into account. The court held that such support is permissible, though the evidential requirements to establish its availability will be onerous. Subsequent rule changes however make Mahad largely irrelevant to applications made under Appendix FM and the PBS.

An applicant under Appendix FM cannot rely on third party support except as allowed for in paragraph 1(b) of Appendix FM-SE which states;

> Promises of third party support will not be accepted. Third party support will only be accepted in the form of:
>
> (i) payments from a former partner of the applicant for the maintenance of the applicant or any children of the applicant and the former partner, and payments from a former partner of the applicant's partner for the maintenance of that partner;
>
> (ii) income from a dependent child who has turned 18, remains in the same UK household as the applicant and continues to be counted towards the financial requirement under Appendix FM;
>
> (iii) gift of cash savings (whose source must be declared) evidenced at paragraph 1(a)(iii), provided that the cash savings have been held by the person or persons at paragraph 1(a)(iii) for at least 6 months prior to the date of application and are under their control; and
>
> (iv) a maintenance grant or stipend associated with undergraduate study or postgraduate study or research.

Example

Azim has been studying in the UK with the support of an uncle. He has now married a British citizen and wishes to remain as a partner. Neither he nor his spouse have jobs, but Azim's uncle is happy to support them until they can manage on their own.

In this case, where the uncle already has a history of providing support, there is good reason to think that the support will be adequate and that the offer is well considered and genuine. The uncle's support could have been relied upon for spouse applications made before 9 July 2012, but not now. Azim will have to ask his uncle to give him £62,500 as a lump sum. If his uncle obliges, and Azim then holds this amount for 6 months before the application is made, it will treated as his own savings rather than third party support.

Were Azim applying as a visitor, say, or under the ancestry category, he could still rely on his uncle's third party support.

Sponsors and undertakings

A maintenance undertaking is mandatory under the adult dependent relative category of Appendix FM, which states;

> E-ECDR.3.2. If the applicant's sponsor is a British Citizen or settled in the UK, the applicant must provide an undertaking signed by the sponsor confirming that the applicant will have no recourse to public funds, and that the sponsor will be responsible for their maintenance, accommodation and care, for a period of 5 years from the date the applicant enters the UK if they are granted indefinite leave to enter.

The undertaking will be legally enforceable (see Immigration Rule 35). In other categories though, an undertaking will be of no real value.

Joint sponsors

In *AM (Ethiopia) & Ors v Entry Clearance Officer [2008] EWCA Civ 1082*, the Court of Appeal found that under immigration rule 317, the old version of the adult dependent relative category, it was possible for joint sponsors (e.g. two siblings) to give undertakings. This principle was upheld by the Supreme Court in Mahad and Others [2009] UKSC 16.

The equivalent category under Appendix FM, for adult dependent relatives, though, does not appear to allow for joint sponsors.

Adequate accommodation

Most categories of the Immigration Rules (but not the PBS) require that the applicant(s) and any family members they are joining in the UK have adequate accommodation available to them.

Key principles on accommodation

- Third party provision is permitted
- Statutory overcrowding renders accommodation inadequate
- Adequacy can have a wider meaning

Unlike with maintenance, there has never been a problem with accommodation being provided by a third party: AB (Third-party provision of accommodation) [2008] UKAIT 00018 and Mahad and Others [2009] UKSC 16.

Accommodation must be adequate for the person coming to the UK and for those already occupying the accommodation. For people seeking entry on a long-term basis there are three considerations to the question of whether accommodation is adequate.

Firstly, in family cases, the sponsor/applicant must 'own or exclusively occupy' the proposed accommodation. This is not quite as onerous as it sounds as the guidance states that:

'Accommodation can be shared with other members of a family provided that at least part of the accommodation is for the exclusive use of the sponsor and his dependants. The unit of accommodation may be as small as a separate bedroom but must be owned or legally occupied by the sponsor and its occupation must not contravene public health regulations and must not cause overcrowding as defined in the Housing Act 1985'

The Immigration tribunal analysed this requirement in the case of KJ ("Own or occupy exclusively") Jamaica [2008] UKAIT 00006 and concluded that the approach in the IDIs is the correct one.

Secondly, the proposed accommodation must not be overcrowded once the applicant arrives. Overcrowding is defined in paragraph 6 of the Immigration Rules by reference to the Housing Act 1985, the Housing (Scotland) Act 1987 or the Housing (Northern Ireland) Order 1988 (as appropriate). The test for whether a property will be overcrowded is based on the permitted number of persons in a room, and in the property as a whole.

The guidance states;

A house is considered to be overcrowded if 2 persons aged 10 years or more of opposite sexes, who are not living together as husband and wife, must sleep in the same room. The Act also details the maximum number of people allowed for a given number of rooms or a given room floor area.

Account is taken only of rooms with a floor area larger than 50 square feet and rooms of a type used either as a living room or bedroom.

Rooms such as kitchens or bathrooms are excluded.

Under the Housing Act, the number of people sleeping in accommodation must not exceed the following:

Rooms	Persons permitted
1	2
2	3
3	5
4	7.5
5	10
*	with an additional 2 persons for each room in excess of 5

For the purpose of the Act:

- a child under 1 does not count as a person.
- a child aged 1-10 years counts as only half a person.

Reporting and other conditions

Under rules 325-326, any foreign national aged 16 or over from countries or territories listed in Appendix 2 to the Immigration Rules needs to register with the police (or, if in London, at the Overseas Visitors Registration Office), as do the stateless and those holding non-national travel documents (e.g. a Refugee Convention travel document), where they are given limited leave to enter the United Kingdom for longer than six months or given limited leave which takes them over 6 months from arrival.

Exempt from this requirement are seasonal agricultural workers, Tier 5 private servants in diplomatic households and overseas government employee, Tier 2 ministers of religion, persons granted leave as partners of a person settled in the United Kingdom, parents of children at school, and those given leave following the grant of asylum. Exceptionally, the requirement can be imposed on any other foreign national where the Immigration Officer considers it necessary to ensure that he complies with the terms of the leave.

Where the immigration rules provide for them, conditions will be applied to a grant of limited leave which prevent or restrict the right to take employment, which require a Tier 4 student to study at a particular college, and which prohibit recourse to public funds. These conditions will be specified on the document granting leave (i.e. the visa or Biometric Residence Permit). If the grant of leave is silent in respect of a particular issue (i.e. the right to take employment), there will be no prohibition in that regard. The Home Office can also impose reporting, residence and other conditions on foreign nationals who are granted limited leave to enter or remain in the UK but this is not common.

Breach of condition

A breach of conditions may and often does lead to removal from the UK under s10(1)(a) of the Immigration Act 1999. S10 of the 1999 Act is to be amended by s1 of the Immigration Act 2014 to simply allow for the removal of those in the UK without permission. Where a condition of leave has been breached the UKVI can curtail that leave under provisions in immigration rule 323, leading to removal under the amended s10. A breach of conditions can also be the ground upon which a subsequent application for an extension (rule 322(3)) or entry clearance (rules 320(7B) and 320(11)) is refused.

Knowledge of language and life in the UK

In order to obtain settlement (ILR) most applicants must demonstrate knowledge of language and life in the UK (KOLL), or that they meet the narrow criteria for exemption.

Those applying for ILR in the refugee, humanitarian protection, bereaved spouses and domestic violence categories, and those with discretionary leave, do not have to meet this requirement.

On October 2013, major changes were introduced to the KOLL requirement. All applicants needing to meet these requirements, now provided for in Appendix KOLL to the Immigration Rules, have to pass the Life in the UK test and separately evidence that they can speak and understand English language at minimum B1 level of the Common European Framework of Reference for Languages (equivalent to an ESOL qualification at entry level 3).

The Life in the UK Test requirement is met by sitting and passing an examination with multiple choice questions based on the book 'Life in the United Kingdom: A Guide for New Residents'. The ESOL route (i.e. passing an ESOL qualification taught with citizenship materials) is no longer available.

The official website for those booking and preparing to take the test is:
https://www.gov.uk/life-in-the-uk-test.

The language requirement can be met in a number of different ways;

➢ By being a national of a country listed in paragraph 2.2(a)(i) of Appendix KOLL
➢ By passing an English language test in speaking and listening at the minimum level with a provider approved by the Secretary of State (as specified in Appendix O to the Immigration Rules)
➢ Having an academic qualification at Bachelor's degree or higher level (excluding professional and vocational qualifications) from a college in a country listed in paragraph 2.2(a)(iii) of Appendix KOLL
➢ Having an academic qualification at Bachelor's degree or higher level (excluding professional and vocational qualifications) taught in English
➢ Acquiring a regulated ESOL qualification at minimum Entry level 3
➢ Having already met the B1 requirement in a previous grant of leave, and having had unbroken leave since that grant

Part 3 of Appendix KOLL lays out the exemptions; for those aged under 18 or over 65 at the date of their applications, and where the UKVI considers that, because of the applicant's mental or physical condition, it would be unreasonable to expect them to fulfil that requirement.

Those who just cannot pass either or both of the KOLL tests, and provide specified evidence of their efforts to learn English, may be able to rely on a reduced requirement after having spent 15 years on one of the routes to settlement specified in paragraph 3.2 of Appendix KOLL. They will need only an English language qualification at Level A2 of the CEFR (or ESOL equivalent). This option is not available to nationals of the list of countries at 3.2(d), who must therefore take and pass the Life in the UK test, however long that takes.

The specified documents that must be submitted with the ILR application are in Part 4 of Appendix KOLL.

Guidance on the KOLL requirements is at:
https://www.gov.uk/government/publications/knowledge-of-life-and-language-in-the-uk

A new rule 39C allows the UKVI, as from 6 November 2014, to interview applicants for settlement to satisfy the Secretary of State that the KOLL requirements are met. If the decision-maker has reasonable cause to doubt (on examination or interview or on any other basis) that any document submitted by an applicant for the purposes of satisfying the requirements of Appendix KoLL was genuinely obtained, that document may be discounted for the purposes of the application.

Tuberculosis tests

Under rule A39, any person applying to enter the UK for more than six months or as a fiance(e) or proposed civil partner from a country listed in Appendix T Part 1 must present, at the time of application, a valid medical certificate issued by a medical practitioner listed in Appendix T Part 2, confirming that they have undergone screening for active pulmonary tuberculosis and that this tuberculosis is not present in the applicant.

General grounds for refusal

The Immigration Rules at Part 9 specify that an applicant can or sometimes must be refused leave if one of the general grounds for refusal applies. An application may meet all the category specific requirements of the rules, but still fall to be refused under the General Grounds.

General grounds of refusal can be applied to any application, from entry clearance to settlement, and to existing leave which can be cancelled or curtailed. They are applied as follows;

Rule 320:	Refusal of entry clearance or leave to enter the United Kingdom
Rule 321:	Refusal of leave to enter in relation to a person in possession of an entry clearance
Rule 321A:	Grounds on which leave to enter or remain which is in force is to be cancelled at port or while the holder is outside the United Kingdom
Rule 322:	Refusal of leave to remain, variation of leave to enter or remain or curtailment of leave
Rule 323:	Grounds on which leave to enter or remain may be curtailed
Rule 323A:	Curtailment of leave in relation to a Tier 2 Migrant, a Tier 5 Migrant or a Tier 4 Migrant
Rule 323AA:	Prohibited changes to employment for Tier 2 Migrants and Tier 5 Migrants
Rule 323B:	Curtailment of leave in relation to a Tier 1 (Exceptional Talent) Migrant
Rule 323C:	Curtailment of leave in relation to a Tier 1 (Graduate Entrepreneur) Migrant
Rule 324:	Crew members

These provisions have become an important part of the Home Office's armoury for reducing migration into the UK, and are amended regularly. It will always be necessary to consider Part 9 when taking a client's instructions, if necessary by asking direct questions to your client, in respect of criminal convictions (in the U.K. or abroad), their UK immigration history, and money owed to the NHS.

The burden to prove one of the general grounds for refusal always rests with the Home Office: he who asserts must prove. The standard of proof for allegations is the normal civil standard. Any allegation (e.g. of forgery) must be backed by evidence.

The Home Office provides detailed guidance to its caseworkers on the use of the general grounds. It can be found on the GOV.UK website;

> in the Modernised Guidance at:
> https://www.gov.uk/government/collections/general-grounds-for-refusal-modernised-guidance,
> and in the Entry Clearance Guidance at RFL03-RFL10
> https://www.gov.uk/government/collections/refusals-entry-clearance-guidance).
> Guidance on curtailment is available at:
> https://www.gov.uk/government/publications/curtailment-of-leave

The Part 9 provisions have been subject to much litigation over the years. In addition to the guidance, it will be a good idea to consider the case law (which is too voluminous for this manual) if they have been or may be applied in a particular case.

Mandatory or discretionary grounds?

The general grounds are divided into those that are mandatory, i.e. that must be applied by the decision maker, and those that are discretionary, where the decision maker can decide to apply them or not. Where there is discretion, the exercise of discretion should be considered in accordance with Home Office policy as outlined in their Operational Guidance.

You can see from the wording of the section heading that contains the particular rule whether the application 'is to be refused' on the basis of the general ground (i.e. a mandatory ground), or 'should normally be refused' (a discretionary ground).

Where a discretionary ground of refusal has been applied against the migrant, an adviser should consider whether there actually has been an exercise of discretion, or whether the ground may been applied without consideration of the exercise of discretion. In the latter circumstance, the decision may be unlawful.

Example

Fatima wants to come to the UK as an entrepreneur. Some years ago she spent time in the UK as a student, and had a baby here. The NHS hospital charged her £7000.00 for the cost of maternity services, but she left the UK without fully paying the debt. She came to an agreement with the NHS to pay off the debt at £100.00 per month and the debt is nearly cleared. She explains this in her covering letter when making her visa application. The ECO ignores her agreement with the NHS, and without giving any additional reasons refuses her application under rule 320(22). By failing to consider the agreement between Fatima and the NHS, the ECO has failed to exercise their discretion (i.e. has failed to consider all the relevant circumstances before deciding to refuse the application on a discretionary ground). She can rely on this breach of rules by the ECO in her Administrative Review application or subsequent judicial review of the decision.

Where a discretionary ground has been applied against the applicant, and there is a right of appeal, the Tribunal judge will be able to exercise their discretion differently under s84(1)(f) of the Nationality, Immigration and Asylum Act 2002 and allow the appeal. A Tribunal judge will not though be able to disapply a mandatory ground where the ground is properly made out on the facts of the case.

On Administrative Review, a failure to exercise discretion may amount to a caseworking error, but a decision to exercise discretion against the applicant may not be challengeable other than by judicial review.

Refusal of entry clearance or leave to enter

At rule 320 there are a number of grounds on which entry clearance or leave to enter can or will be refused. Note though that rule A320 exempts family applications under Appendix FM and private life applications under rule 276ADE(1) from most of the provisions of rule 320 (and rule 322). Rule A320 states:

> Paragraphs 320 (except subparagraph (3), (10) and (11)) and 322 do not apply to an application for entry clearance, leave to enter or leave to remain as a Family Member under Appendix FM, and Part 9 (except for paragraph 322(1)) does not apply to an application for leave to remain on the grounds of private life under paragraphs 276ADE-276DH.

Note though, that Appendix FM applicants may be refused under the discretionary ground at 320(11), where they have a particularly bad immigration history (see below). They must also not fall for refusal under the 'suitability' requirements of Appendix FM (which in large part reflect the general grounds in Part 9). Importantly though, they will not be subject to the mandatory re-entry ban provided for in rule 320(7B) (see below).

The grounds in rules 320(1) to 320(7D) are mandatory (i.e. the application "must be refused"), and they are as follows:

Grounds on which entry clearance or leave to enter the United Kingdom is to be refused

(1) the fact that entry is being sought for a purpose not covered by these Rules;

(2) 320(2) the fact that the person seeking entry to the United Kingdom:

(a) is currently the subject of a deportation order; or

(b) has been convicted of an offence for which they have been sentenced to a period of imprisonment of at least 4 years; or

(c) has been convicted of an offence for which they have been sentenced to a period of imprisonment of at least 12 months but less than 4 years, unless a period of 10 years has passed since the end of the sentence; or

(d) has been convicted of an offence for which they have been sentenced to a period of imprisonment of less than 12 months, unless a period of 5 years has passed since the end of the sentence.

Where this paragraph applies, unless refusal would be contrary to the Human Rights Convention or the Convention and Protocol Relating to the Status of Refugees, it will only be in exceptional circumstances that the public interest in maintaining refusal will be outweighed by compelling factors.

(3) failure by the person seeking entry to the United Kingdom to produce to the Immigration Officer a valid national passport or other document satisfactorily establishing his identity and nationality;

(4) failure to satisfy the Immigration Officer, in the case of a person arriving in the United Kingdom or seeking entry through the Channel Tunnel with the intention of entering any other part of the common travel area, that he is acceptable to the immigration authorities there;

(5) failure, in the case of a visa national, to produce to the Immigration Officer a passport or other identity document endorsed with a valid and current United Kingdom entry clearance issued for the purpose for which entry is sought;

(6) where the Secretary of State has personally directed that the exclusion of a person from the United Kingdom is conducive to the public good;

(7) save in relation to a person settled in the United Kingdom or where the Immigration Officer is satisfied that there are strong compassionate reasons justifying admission, confirmation from the Medical Inspector that, for medical reasons, it is undesirable to admit a person seeking leave to enter the United Kingdom.

(7A) where false representations have been made or false documents or information have been submitted (whether or not material to the application, and whether or not to the applicant's knowledge), or material facts have not been disclosed, in relation to the application *or* in order to obtain documents from the Secretary of State or a third party required in support of the application.

(7B) where the applicant has previously breached the UK's immigration laws (and was 18 or over at the time of his most recent breach)by:

(a) Overstaying;

(b) breaching a condition attached to his leave;

(c) being an Illegal Entrant;

(d) using Deception in an application for entry clearance, leave to enter or remain, or in order to obtain documents from the Secretary of State or a third party required in support of the application (whether successful or not);

unless the applicant:

(i) Overstayed for 90 days or less and left the UK voluntarily, not at the expense (directly or indirectly) of the Secretary of State;

(ii) used Deception in an application for entry clearance more than 10 years ago;

(iii) left the UK voluntarily, not at the expense (directly or indirectly) of the Secretary of State, more than 12 months ago;

(iv) left the UK voluntarily, at the expense (directly or indirectly) of the Secretary of State, more than 2 years ago; and the date the person left the UK was no more than 6 months after the date on which the person was given notice of the removal decision, or no more than 6 months after the date on which the person no longer had a pending appeal; whichever is the later;

(v) left the UK voluntarily, at the expense (directly or indirectly) of the Secretary of State, more than 5 years ago;

(vi) was removed or deported from the UK more than 10 years ago or;

(vii) left or was removed from the UK as a condition of a caution issued in accordance with section 22 of the Criminal Justice Act 2003 more than 5 years ago.

Where more than one breach of the UK's immigration laws has occurred, only the breach which leads to the longest period of absence from the UK will be relevant under this paragraph.

(7D) failure, without providing a reasonable explanation, to comply with a request made on behalf of the Entry Clearance Officer to attend for interview.

The mandatory entry ban at rule 320(2), for those sentenced to a period of imprisonment, was added in January 2013. Criminality had previously been only a discretionary ground of refusal. The rule does however acknowledge that decisions cannot be made in breach of the Conventions (i.e. the Refugee Convention and the European Convention of Human Rights) and that there may therefore be exceptions to the rule.

Immigration Rule 320(7A) mandates automatic refusal of any entry clearance application where deception is used or there is material non-disclosure, whether knowingly or unknowingly. It operates as an absolute bar to the use of deception in an application for entry clearance. However, in *AA (Nigeria) v SSHD* [2010] EWCA Civ 773 the Court of Appeal held that false representations must be deliberately false rather than accidentally incorrect in order to engage these general grounds. The Entry Clearance Guidance (ECG) reflects this principle (see ECG RFL05).

Rule 320(7A) operates in respect of the current application, but a migrant who has used deception in an application for entry clearance is likely to face a 10 year re-entry ban under r.320(7B) unless exempt from that provision.

Immigration Rule 320(7B) is intended to prevent breaches of immigration law by immigrants currently in the UK, by creating a serious immigration sanction against those who do breach immigration laws. It is also intended to punish past breaches of immigration law and is retrospective in operation.

Rule 320(7B) is broken into two parts. The first part lists the proscribed activities that might then engage the second part. The second part consists of the various periods of exclusion, which are expressed as being conditional on factors such as voluntary removal at one's own expense. It is not an easy provision to apply. As well as for those applying under Appendix FM, exemptions apply to those under 18 at the time of the most recent breach, those whose only offence is to overstay by up to 90 days, and those who have been accepted by the Home Office to be victims of trafficking (see RFL3.5 in the ECG).

The grounds in rules 320(8) to 320(22) are discretionary (i.e. the application "should normally be refused"), and they are as follows:

> **Grounds on which entry clearance or leave to enter the United Kingdom should normally be refused**
>
> (8) failure by a person arriving in the United Kingdom to furnish the Immigration Officer with such information as may be required for the purpose of deciding whether he requires leave to enter and, if so, whether and on what terms leave should be given;
>
> (8A) where the person seeking leave is outside the United Kingdom, failure by him to supply any information, documents, copy documents or medical report requested by an Immigration Officer;
>
> (9) failure by a person seeking leave to enter as a returning resident to satisfy the Immigration Officer that he meets the requirements of paragraph 18 of these Rules, or that he seeks leave to enter for the same purpose as that for which his earlier leave was granted;
>
> (10) production by the person seeking leave to enter the United Kingdom of a national passport or travel document issued by a territorial entity or authority which is not recognised by Her Majesty's Government as a state or is not dealt with as a government by them, or which does not accept valid United Kingdom passports for

the purpose of its own immigration control; or a passport or travel document which does not comply with international passport practice;

(11) where the applicant has previously contrived in a significant way to frustrate the intentions of the Rules by:

(i) overstaying; or

(ii) breaching a condition attached to his leave; or

(iii) being an illegal entrant; or

(iv) using deception in an application for entry clearance, leave to enter or remain or in order to obtain documents from the Secretary of State or a third party required in support of the application (whether successful or not); and

there are other aggravating circumstances, such as absconding, not meeting temporary admission/reporting restrictions or bail conditions, using an assumed identity or multiple identities, switching nationality, making frivolous applications or not complying with the re-documentation process.

(12) DELETED

(13) failure, except by a person eligible for admission to the United Kingdom for settlement, to satisfy the Immigration Officer that he will be admitted to another country after a stay in the United Kingdom;

(14) refusal by a sponsor of a person seeking leave to enter the United Kingdom to give, if requested to do so, an undertaking in writing to be responsible for that person's maintenance and accommodation for the period of any leave granted;

(16) failure, in the case of a child under the age of 18 years seeking leave to enter the United Kingdom otherwise than in conjunction with an application made by his parent(s) or legal guardian to provide the Immigration Officer, if required to do so, with written consent to the application from his parent(s) or legal guardian; save that the requirement as to written consent does not apply in the case of a child seeking admission to the United Kingdom as an asylum seeker;

(17) save in relation to a person settled in the United Kingdom, refusal to undergo a medical examination when required to do so by the Immigration Officer;

(18) DELETED

(18A) within the 12 months preceding the date of the application, the person has been convicted of or admitted an offence for which they received a non-custodial sentence or other out of court disposal that is recorded on their criminal record;

(18B) in the view of the Secretary of State:

(a) the person's offending has caused serious harm; or

(b) the person is a persistent offender who shows a particular disregard for the law.

(19) The immigration officer deems the exclusion of the person from the United Kingdom to be conducive to the public good. For example, because the person's conduct (including convictions which do not fall within paragraph 320(2)), character, associations, or other reasons, make it undesirable to grant them leave to enter.

(20) failure by a person seeking entry into the United Kingdom to comply with a requirement relating to the provision of physical data to which he is subject by regulations made under section 126 of the Nationality, Immigration and Asylum Act 2002.

(21) DELETED

(22) where one or more relevant NHS body has notified the Secretary of State that the person seeking entry or leave to enter has failed to pay a charge or charges with a total value of at least £1000 in accordance with the relevant NHS regulations on charges to overseas visitors.

The phrase, 'previously contrived in a significant way to frustrate the intentions of the Rules' (rule 320(11), is given further definition in the Entry Clearance Guidance (at RFL07).

The guidance lists, in addition to the offences referred to in r.320(11)(i)-(iv), the obtaining of services or support to which the person is not entitled, including non-exhaustively;

- obtaining asylum benefits
- state benefits
- housing and housing benefits
- tax credits
- employment
- goods or services
- NHS care using an assumed identity or multiple identities or to which not entitled.

As the obtaining of services is not referred to in 320(11), it cannot in itself be a ground for refusal, but will often also amount to a breach of conditions.

The breach of immigration laws must include 'aggravating features', which are listed non-exhaustively as the following:

- absconding;
- not complying with temporary admission / temporary reporting conditions / bail conditions;
- not complying with reporting restrictions;
- failing to comply with removal directions (RDs) after port refusal of leave to enter (RLE);
- failing to comply with RDs after illegal entry;
- previous working in breach on visitor conditions within short time of arrive in the UK (ie pre-meditated intention to work);
- previous recourse to NHS treatment when not entitled;
- previous receipt of benefits (income, housing, child, incapacity or otherwise) or NASS benefits when not entitled;
- using an assumed identity or multiple identities;

- previous use of a different identity or multiple identities for deceptive reasons;
- vexatious attempts to prevent removal from the UK, eg feigning illness;
- active attempt to frustrate arrest or detention by UK Border Agency or police;
- a sham marriage / marriage of convenience / polygamous marriage in the UK;
- harbouring an immigration offender;
- facilitation / people smuggling;
- escaping from UK Border Agency detention;
- switching of nationality;
- vexatious or frivolous applications;
- not complying with re-documentation process.

It must be arguable that this provision cannot be applied where both the offence and the aggravating feature are one in the same.

Refusal of leave to enter in relation to a person in possession of an entry clearance, and grounds on which leave to enter or remain which is in force is to be cancelled at port or while the holder is outside the United Kingdom (rules 321 and 321A)

A person who holds prior entry clearance can also be refused leave to enter under rule 321 on the basis that:

➤ whether or not to the holder's knowledge, false representations were employed or material facts not disclosed for the purpose of obtaining the entry clearance, or in order to obtain documents to support the application

➤ circumstances have changed since issue of the entry clearance which has removed the basis of the person's claim to admission

➤ and on grounds of criminality, or where it is deemed conducive to the public good

However, following the interpretation provided in *Khaliq (entry clearance; para 321) Pakistan* [2011] UKUT 350 (IAC), it is difficult to see in what circumstances this provision might be used as a grant of entry clearance itself has effect as a grant of leave to enter (i.e. they are granted at one and the same time by the ECO), and what has already been granted cannot be refused.

Similar powers apply though under r.321A. These allow for the cancellation leave to enter of both a person entering on a visa for the first time, and of a person who has entered the U.K. but has then travelled outside the U.K. (i.e. to prevent re-entry on the existing leave).

The power in rule 321A to cancel leave overlaps with that of curtailment, for example under r.323(ii) where circumstances have changed such that the person no longer meets the requirements of the rules under which his leave to enter was granted. Curtailment however is a discretionary power, and from the migrant's perspective, although both curtailment and cancellation give rise to an in-country right of appeal, it is much to be preferred. A person whose leave is curtailed will have continuing leave (under s3D of the 1971 Act) pending the conclusion of their appeal and, additionally, the Tribunal will be able exercise their own discretion if they disagree with the decision. In *Fiaz (cancellation of leave to remain-fairness)* [2012] UKUT 00057(IAC), the Upper Tribunal found that in some circumstances the duty of fairness requires that leave be curtailed rather than cancelled.

Refusal of leave to remain (rule 322)

An application for leave to remain must be refused where it is for a purpose not covered by the Immigration Rules, or where false representations or false documents have been submitted, and should normally be refused on the grounds of;

➢ false representations made in respect of an earlier grant of leave

➢ failure to comply with any conditions attached to a stay

➢ failure to maintain and accommodate without recourse to public funds

➢ undesirability on the grounds of a person's character, conduct or for national security reasons, including offending causing serious harm, or persistent offending by a person who shows a particular disregard for the law

➢ refusal by a sponsor to give an undertaking

➢ failure to honour a declaration or undertaking as to the intended duration and/or purpose of stay

➢ non-returnability

➢ failure to produce documents, and failure to attend an interview

➢ failure of a child to have written consent from a parent where required

➢ owing the NHS £1000 or more

Refusal of indefinite leave to enter or remain (rule 322(1C))

Under provisions introduced in December 2012, ILE/R will be refused to a person where;

➢ they have been convicted of an offence for which they have been sentenced to imprisonment for at least 4 years; or

➢ they have been convicted of an offence for which they have been sentenced to imprisonment for at least 12 months but less than 4 years, unless a period of 15 years has passed since the end of the sentence; or

> ➤ they have been convicted of an offence for which they have been sentenced to imprisonment for less than 12 months, unless a period of 7 years has passed since the end of the sentence; or

> ➤ they have, within the 24 months preceding the date of the application, been convicted of or admitted an offence for which they have received a non-custodial sentence or other out of court disposal that is recorded on their criminal record.

Curtailment (rule 323)

Rule 323 provides for the discretionary curtailment of leave under the same discretionary grounds available under r.322 and, in addition, where a person;

> ➤ ceases to meet the requirements of the rules under which his leave to enter or remain was granted

> ➤ has had their refugee status or humanitarian protection revoked (or is a dependant of such a person)

> ➤ where a person has, within the first 6 months of being granted leave to enter, committed an offence for which they are subsequently sentenced to a period of imprisonment

> ➤ has leave as a dependant of a person whose leave is curtailed

For those granted leave under the PBS, there are discretionary and mandatory grounds to curtail or alter the duration of a person's leave;

> ➤ who fails to commence or ceases their studies or employment

> ➤ where sponsorship is withdrawn, or the migrant is dismissed from their course or job

> ➤ where the sponsor ceases to hold a sponsor licence

or where;

> ➤ there is a prohibited change to employment as defined in r.323AA

> ➤ a Tier 1 (Exceptional Talent) endorsement is withdrawn

> ➤ a Tier 1 (Graduate Entrepreneur) sponsor loses its status, has their licence withdrawn or downgraded, or withdraws its endorsement

Policies, concessions and Operational Guidance

Knowledge of policies and concessions is an important part of an immigration caseworker's arsenal. There used to be many important concessions entirely outside the rules, but most of these have now been withdrawn or incorporated into the rules. There are still policies though that an adviser must be aware of. Some of these – e.g. the carers policy – represent categories that do not exist in the Immigration Rules, others clarify how the rules are to be applied in certain circumstances and mitigate the apparent inflexibility of some of them. Several of these have been touched upon above – for example, the provision that applications on family and private life grounds might be granted outside the rules where there are exceptional circumstances.

The majority of policies and concessions can be located in one or more of several collections of documents – the various instructions to Home Office caseworkers, Immigration Officers and Entry Clearance Officers - now found on the GOV.UK website under the title, <u>Operational Guidance</u>. These collections are broken down as follows:

➢ **Asylum policy**: previously called the 'Asylum Policy Instructions' and the 'Asylum Process Guidance': guidance to Home Office staff dealing with asylum cases. Covers screening and routing, asylum support, children, detention and reporting, decision making, country information, appeals, and voluntary departures.

➢ **Immigration Directorate Instructions (IDIs)**: guidance, mainly for Home Office caseworkers making decisions on non-asylum in-country applications, though often an overlap with the ECG and Modernised Guidance (see below). Includes many current policies and concessions, sometimes in the annexes, on a wide range of issues connected with immigration applications.

➢ **Entry Clearance Guidance (ECG)**: these comprise instructions to ECOs on how to interpret the Immigration Rules and assess applications

➢ **Enforcement Guidance and Instructions (EIG)**: formerly known as the Operation Enforcement Manual (EIG), these are instructions to Immigration Officers carrying out removals and other enforcement action. The sections on bail and detention are useful. The chapters of the manual were re-numbered, rendering references to specific chapters in case law obsolete.

➢ **European Casework Instructions (ECI)**: guidance on assessing EC law applications

➢ **Nationality Instructions (NIs)**: for nationality applications

➢ **Modernised Guidance**: Various policies from the sections referred to above are being rewritten, put into a new format and can now be found here

These are very large documents and are frequently altered, so there is little point in keeping a hard copy. It will be useful to though save (as PDFs) copies of polices you are relying on as they may alter or sometimes disappear before your client's application is finally decided.

We outline some of the important policies here. Many have passed their sell-by date, but they may still apply to a few individuals whose cases have been in the system for a very long time but are not yet concluded.

Legacy cases

On 25 July 2006, the then Home Secretary John Reid announced that his officials had found around 400,000 to 450,000 unclosed asylum files. These 'unresolved cases' soon came to be known as 'legacy' cases to most in the sector, and the Home Office committed itself to 'resolving' these cases by 2011. Some non-asylum files found themselves becoming legacy cases too. The exercise was officially referred to as the 'case resolution exercise' and a large team of Home Office caseworkers, the Casework Resolution Directorate (CRD) was established to deal with the backlog.

The Home Office announced in the summer of 2011 that the casework resolution exercise had been completed and that the CRD was to be wound up. The announcement said that all those who had not been granted leave under the exercise were either awaiting removal or were those with whom the Home Office had lost contact. However, there remains many thousands within the legacy who do not fit into either of those categories, and the announcement that the exercise was complete was clearly made many years prematurely! The remaining files, some 35,000 at the end of 2013, are being dealt with by the UKVI's Older Live Cases Unit in Liverpool.

Those granted leave under the case resolution exercise were granted ILR, until an unannounced change of policy on 20 July 2011, following which those granted leave were given only 3 years of discretionary leave. The many legal challenges to this change of policy have been unsuccessful (see e.g. _Geraldo & Ors, R (on the application of) v SSHD_ [2013] EWHC 2763 (Admin)).

One issue which did come to light in the litigation was an apparent practice of the Home Office to grant leave under the legacy to those whose removal had been delayed by more than six years through no fault of the applicant. This practice conformed to the policy laid out in the Enforcement Instructions and Guidance at Chapter 53. It was most recently considered in _Okonkwo (legacy/Hakemi; health claim) Nigeria_ [2013] UKUT 401 (IAC), but was found not to be applicable in that case. The Upper Tribunal did though find that, _'It may be unfair for the Secretary of State to fail to apply the terms of a policy to a case that fell within the terms of the policy when it was in existence'_ (i.e. in this case, a failure to consider the case under the legacy process at all). See more on this policy below (under Delay in asylum and human rights cases).

This policy may be even more valuable now that the Older Live Cases Unit is refusing leave altogether in many of the old legacy cases, even where removal is impracticable. The position of the Upper Tribunal in _R (on the application of Shou Lin Xu) v SSHD (Legacy cases - "conclusion" issue) IJR_ [2014] UKUT 375(IAC) is that the policy of resolving cases under the legacy did not require a grant of leave or removal. It is acceptable for the Home Office to resolve a legacy case by deciding that it should not be resolved.

Deliberately delayed consideration of asylum claim

In the case of *R (on the application of S) v SSHD* [2007] EWCA Civ 546 the Court of Appeal held that it was unlawful for the Home Office to have delayed consideration of a person's case in order to meet new targets they had been set for consideration of new cases, thereby depriving that person of a benefit to which he would otherwise have been entitled.

The case was brought be an Afghan who had entered the UK at the same time as his cousin in 1999. His cousin had been granted four years of Exceptional Leave to Remain (ELR), in line with the policy then in existence not to return anyone to Afghanistan. The cousin was then, as was normal, granted ILR after four years.

S himself was not so fortunate. His claim was deliberately delayed by the Home Office as a matter of policy in order to meet the new targets. By the time a decision was reached on S's case, it was 2004 and there was no longer a policy to grant ELR to Afghans. His application was turned down and he then lost his appeal.

The Court of Appeal decided this was a 'textbook' example of unlawful fettering of discretion. The Home Office had delayed S's case purely to meet Treasury-imposed targets and thereby deprived him of the benefit of a policy to which he would otherwise have been entitled.

In September 2008 the Home Office responded to the judgment by publishing a new policy applying to those who should have qualified for ELR at the time they applied for asylum. This was then withdrawn on 20 December 2010 and replaced with a 'case by case consideration' approach.

Any person who was later granted ELR of less than four years and was therefore not eligible for ILR could also apply under the policy. There is no need for the person to have remained in the UK continuously, or even to be in the UK at the time of belatedly seeking ILR from the Home Office: see *R (on the application of K) v SSHD* [2010] EWHC 3102 (Admin).

Example

Justin from Sierra Leone entered the UK in July 2001 and claimed asylum on arrival. At that time there was a policy to grant ELR to people from Sierra Leone. However, the Home Office did not make a decision on Justin's case until 2002, by which time the policy had been withdrawn. He was refused asylum at this time.

On appeal, the adjudicator dismissed Justin's asylum appeal. Justin became 'appeal rights exhausted', in Home Office speak, but remained in the UK.

Justin qualifies for ILR under the approach taken to cases following R (S).

The list of old ELR policies (in force at 1 January 2001) to which the Home Office policy applied is as follows:

Country	Date ELR policy ended
Angola (non-Luandan claimants only)	31 October 2002
Afghanistan	18 April 2002
Burundi	7 October 2002
Iraq (Government Controlled Iraq (GCI) claimants only)	20 February 2003
Liberia	7 October 2002
Rwanda	27 August 2002
Sierra Leone	6 September 2001
Somalia	10 September 2001

There will be few, if any, migrants who still fall to be considered under this policy in 2014.

Seven-year children concession

This concession used to apply to children with continuous residence in the UK of 7 years or more. It was abolished as of 9 December 2008.

Cases involving children seeking to regularise their stay on the basis of long residence will now be considered under rule 276ADE(1) or Section EX of Appendix FM. These rules represent the government's current view on how private life and best interests considerations should apply to children. They incorporate into the Immigration Rules, to a limited extent, the 7-year concession, but now require the child to also show that it is not reasonable to expect them to leave the UK.

Cases already under consideration at the time the old policy was scrapped should still be considered under its terms. There will be very few.

For this reason it is useful to set out the terms of the policy, which were follows when announced by Under-Secretary of State for the Home Department Mr O'Brien on 24 February 1999:

> Whilst it is important that each individual case must be considered on its merits, there are specific factors which are likely to be of particular relevance when considering whether enforcement action should proceed or be initiated against parents who have children who have lengthy residence in the United Kingdom. For the purposes of proceeding with enforcement action in a case involving a child, the general presumption is that we would not usually proceed with enforcement action in cases where a child was born here and has lived here continuously to the age of seven or over, or where, having come to the United Kingdom at an early age, they have accumulated seven years or more continuous residence. However, there may be circumstances in which it is considered that enforcement action is still appropriate despite the lengthy residence of the child, for example in cases where the parents have a particularly poor immigration history and have deliberately seriously delayed consideration of their case. In all cases the following factors are relevant in reaching a judgement on whether enforcement action should proceed:
>
> - the length of the parents' residence without leave; whether removal has been delayed through protracted (and often repetitive) representations or by the parents going to ground;
>
> - the age of the children;
>
> - whether the children were conceived at a time when either of the parents had leave to remain;
>
> - whether return to the parents' country of origin would cause extreme hardship for the children or put their health seriously at risk;
>
> - whether either of the parents has a history of criminal behaviour or deception.
>
> It is important that full reasons are given making clear that each case is considered on its individual merits.

One real benefit under the concession was that children would be granted settlement, rather than have to embark on the perilous 10 year route to settlement as now.

For more on children who have been in the UK for 7 years, see the section on 'unreasonable to expect the child to leave the UK' in the section on 'private life' applications (above).

Duty to safeguard children

Section 55 of the Borders, Citizenship and Immigration Act 2009 introduced an obligation to make arrangements to ensure that immigration functions are discharged having regard to the need to safeguard and promote the welfare of children who are in the United Kingdom. In so doing the Act aligns the duty imposed with that imposed on public authorities under the Children Act 2004, s.11(2).

The duty applies to the Home Office and also to those performing immigration functions, broadly defined. It only applies to children present in the UK, although the guidance (see below) encourages officials abroad to act compatibly.

By section 55(3), a person exercising any of the specified functions must, in so exercising them, have regard to any guidance given to the person by the Secretary of State for the purpose specified in BCIA 2009, s 55(1). The statutory guidance Every Child Matters: Change for Children was issued in November 2009.

Section 55 is a binding legal obligation rather than a policy, but it is convenient to remind readers of the existence of this duty in this section of the manual, particularly as the duty is enforced primarily by means of making the huge number of Home Office policies compliant with it.

Where children are affected by enforcement action (e.g. detention and removal), either directly or indirectly, the Office of the Children's Champion offers advice to UKVI decision-makers on the implications for the children's welfare, to enable an informed decision to be made giving due weight to their best interests. As far as the Home Office is concerned, neither the advice nor the best interests of the children need be determinative of the outcome of the case.

Delay in asylum and human rights cases

In the summer of 2009 the Home Office amended Chapter 53 of the Enforcement Guidance and Instructions in order to attach more weight to length of residence in the UK and delay by the Home Office when considering whether to enforce removal of failed asylum seekers.

The relevant passages are at 53.1.1 in the section dealing with exceptional circumstances. The most pertinent parts suggest caseworkers place weight on significant delay in cases including:

- "Family" cases where delay by the Home Office, or factors preventing departure, have contributed to a significant period of residence (for the purposes of this guidance,"family" cases means parent as defined in the Immigration Rules and children who are emotionally and financially dependent on the parent, and under the age of 18 at the date of the decision). Following an individual assessment of the prospect of enforcing removal, and where the factors outlined in "Character" and "Compliance" do not weight against the individual, family cases may also be considered exceptionally on grounds of delay where the dependent child has lived in the UK for more than 3 years or more whilst under the age of 18.

- Any other case where the length of delay by the Home Office in deciding the application, or where there were factors preventing departure, the case worker following an individual assessment of the prospect of enforcing removal, and where the factors outlined in "Character" and "Compliance" do not weight against the individual, concludes that the person will have been in the UK for more than 6 years.

Age and enforcement action

It was previously the case that enforcement action (i.e. removal or deportation) would not be pursued against the over-65s. That policy was withdrawn in late 2004. The current policy is at chapter 53.7 of the EIG, and states:

> Ministers have agreed that a person's age is not by itself, a realistic or reliable indicator of a person's health, mobility or ability to care for themselves. Many older people are able to enjoy active and independent lives. Cases must be assessed on their individual merits.
>
> The onus is on the applicant to show that there are extenuating circumstances, such as particularly poor health, close dependency on family members in the UK coupled with a lack of family and care facilities in the country of origin, which might warrant a grant of leave.

Carers policy

There is no provision in the Immigration Rules for those seeking to enter the UK to care for a sick family member or friend. A person who wishes to enter the UK to provide short-term care or make alternative arrangements for the long term care of a friend/relative may do so under the Rules relating to general visitors.

Where an extension of stay is sought purely for the purpose of caring, the policy published at Chapter 17, section 2 of the IDIs will be applied. It states, that:

> Whilst each case must be looked at on its individual merits, when considering whether a period of leave to remain should be granted, the following points are amongst those that should be borne in mind by caseworkers:
> • the type of illness/condition (this should be supported by a Consultant's letter); and
> • the type of care required; and
> • care which is available (e.g. from the Social Services or other relatives/friends); and
> • the long-term prognosis.

The policy on carers suggests that 3 months leave to remain will be granted initially, with further periods of up to 12 months at a time to follow in exceptional cases subject to favourable medical and welfare reports. The grant of 3 months leave is granted 'on the strict understanding that during this period arrangements will be made for the future care of the patient by a person who is not subject to the Immigration Rules' (IDIs at 17.3.1). There is also a duty on the Home Office to make enquiries as to the provision of satisfactory care for the person receiving care in the event of removal of the carer.

Family court proceedings

In the case of *MS (Ivory Coast) v SSHD* [2007] EWCA Civ 133 it emerged that the Home Office had a policy whereby removal or deportation action will not pursued where family proceedings are pending. The facts of that case were somewhat unsympathetic: a mother had commenced family proceedings and it was very far from clear that she would succeed in her application for contact given her conviction for abuse of her own children, her mental health difficulties and the time that had elapsed since her last contact.

The reported Upper Tribunal decision in *RS (immigration and family court proceedings) India* [2012] UKUT 00218(IAC) lays out the proper approach to cases involving deport proceedings where they begin before the completion of Family Court proceedings concerning an affected child. Following the conclusion of the proceedings in RS, the case was considered again in a further reported decision of the Upper Tribunal in *RS (immigration/family court liaison: outcome)* [2013] UKUT 82(IAC). Communications between the Family Court and the immigration tribunals in such cases are governed by the Protocol on communications between judges of the Family Court and Immigration and Asylum Chambers of the First-tier Tribunal and Upper Tribunal.

There appears to be no published guidance on granting leave where family proceedings are pending, but in practise it seems that leave outside the rules will be granted for 3 or 6 months at a time until the proceedings are concluded.

A person who has been granted leave pending the outcome of family court proceedings may be able to apply to extend that leave under the parent category of Appendix FM at the conclusion of the proceedings (see paragraph E-LTRPT.3.1.(b) of Appendix FM).

Children in the care of a Local Authority

Section 8 of Annex 3.2 FM (see Chapter 8 - Appendix FM of the IDIs) states:

Children in care

Decisions about the future of children in the care of the local authority should be left primarily in the hands of their social services department as they will be best placed to act in the child's best interests.

While the local authority may look into the possibility of arranging the repatriation of a child in their care, such action will only be taken if it is in the child's best interests. Where they consider it may be in the child's best interests to be repatriated, they will normally make full enquiries to ensure that suitable arrangements are made for the child's care and to satisfy themselves that repatriation is indeed in the child's best interests. We should ask to be kept informed of developments.

If the social services advise that it would be appropriate for the child to remain in the United Kingdom, consideration should be given to granting the child leave to remain.

If there is a realistic possibility of the child returning to his parent(s) and/or country of origin in the future, the child may be granted limited leave for periods of 12 months on Code 1. Where there is no prospect of the child leaving, the child may be granted leave to remain for 4 years on Code 1. In both cases, after 4 years of limited leave to remain, if there is no prospect of removal, indefinite leave to remain may be granted.

Policies, concessions and the law

The Home Office cannot operate a policy that is stricter than the Immigration Rules. They can however operate policies that are more generous than the rules or to cover situations not dealt with under the Rules. Where an ECO or the Home Office fails to act on a policy *outside the rules*, there may be remedies available, even though the policy or concession is not the law as such (being neither primary nor secondary legislation).

The Supreme Court found in *Munir & Anor, R (on the application of) v SSHD* [2012] UKSC 32 that the Home Office was not required, subject to any transitional provisions, to consider a case under a policy which had been withdrawn, even where the migrant would have qualified under the policy as at the date it was withdrawn. Nor was the Secretary of State required to put such a change of policy before parliament.

Legitimate expectation

There have been a number of cases involving a claim of legitimate expectation by a migrant, typically where the rule or policy has changed between making the application and it being decided, or where a policy outside the rules has been ignored.

However, it is important to understand that there is, generally speaking, no legitimate expectation in immigration law that the rules or policies will remain the same over time. The facts of the case of Odelola v SSHD [2009] 3 All ER 1061, which went as far as the House of Lords, illustrate how unfair this can be. Ms Odelola applied for leave and at the time she applied she met all of the requirements of the Immigration Rules. However, there was a delay in considering her case and by the time the decision was made the rules had been changed in such a way that she did not qualify. She challenged the refusal under the new rules but lost her case, the House of Lords holding that there was no legitimate expectation.

To succeed on the grounds of legitimate expectation a clear promise has to be made that the rules will remain the same. The case of R (on the application of Bapio Action Ltd) v SSHD [2008] UKHL 27 provides a rare example of a case that succeeded on this basis. The action was brought by Bapio Action Ltd, a company formed by the British Association of Physicians of Indian Origin to represent the interests of junior overseas doctors who had been lured to the UK by promises of a career here but after arrival were being deprived of an opportunity to apply for jobs.

The judgments differ considerably in their reasoning. Lord Bingham held that the email that effectively made the change sent out by a Home Office official was an unlawful exercise of the power to regulate immigration status that can only be exercised by the Secretary of State (and is rather critical of the attempt to affect so many lives by such informal, ill-considered means). Lord Carswell agreed with him, more or less. Lord Mance disagrees and decides that the email did not directly affect immigration status, but that the email was a breach of legitimate expectation. Lord Rodger agrees with Lord Mance. Lord Scott disagrees with all of them and allows the Home Office appeal. The result is therefore clear in that the application was allowed, but there is no majority reasoning as such.

Similarly, in R (on the application of HSMP Forum Ltd) v SSHD [2008] EWHC 664 (Admin) Mr Justice Bean held that a promise was made to those that were enticed to enter the UK under the HSMP scheme and leave behind them their jobs in order to make new lives for themselves and their families in the UK. The promise was that the rules under which they entered the UK would be the rules under which their settlement applications would be decided in four years' time. In fact, the Home Office tightened up the rules considerably, preventing many from qualifying for settlement. The court held that there was a legitimate expectation on the part of the migrants.

Judicial review

Where it can be established that the Home Office has acted contrary to a policy, or ignored a policy, the decision may be amenable to judicial review on the basis of breach of legitimate expectation or even abuse of process by the Home Office. Such judicial review applications are currently made to a High Court judge in the Administrative Court, and the judge has the power to quash a decision of the Home Office. From 1 November 2013, judicial review applications in regard to immigration matters will, but for a few exceptions, be heard in the Upper Tribunal (IAC)

Usually, this remedy will only be able to achieve proper consideration by the Secretary of State under a policy – the nature of policies and concessions are that they are discretionary, and unless they are expressed in absolute terms the courts will not force the Secretary of State to make a particular discretionary choice.

Judicial review cannot be pursued where there is an alternative remedy, such as an appeal to the immigration tribunal. However, appeal rights are limited, particularly by s.82 of the 2002 Act and the restricted definition of an 'immigration decision', so it may be the case that JR is the only available remedy.

The immigration tribunal

There are two ways in which enforcement of a policy or concession might be pursued within an immigration tribunal appeal. The tribunal case of AG and others (Policies; executive discretions; Tribunal's powers) Kosovo [2007] UKAIT 00082 examines both of these options.

Not in accordance with the law

Where a client has a right to an appeal to the immigration tribunal, it can be argued that a decision is "not in accordance with the law" where it can be shown that an appellant has been wrongly denied the benefit of a Home Office policy due to, for example, a misapprehension of the facts of the case (e.g. *Abdi v SSHD* [1996] Imm AR 148) or abuse of process (e.g. in *Rashid [2005] EWCA Civ 744 and A, H and AH* [2006] EWHC 526 (Admin)). It was thought that the immigration tribunal could not force the Secretary of State to make a particular choice but could intervene to force him to consider the case within the terms of the policy in question – and also make factual finding that would in effect bind the hands of the Secretary of State and force him to act in a certain way. However, the case of Fouzia Baig v SSHD [2005] EWCA Civ 1246 suggests that the immigration tribunal can go beyond this constraint and actually allow an appeal outright on the basis of failure to follow a policy. AG (above) agrees that this is the case, but only where the policy in question does not involve the exercise of discretion on the part of the SSHD; where the claimant clearly falls under a policy and that policy is quite clear in demanding that leave be granted, the immigration tribunal may follow this course.

That might be the case now, for example, in appeals relying on the ten-year long residence concession (which ignores gaps in continuity of residence of up to 28 days). In *OS (ten years' lawful residence) Hong Kong* [2006] UKAIT 00031, the Tribunal found that the terms of the ten year concession were not to be used as an aid to interpretation of the rules. On that basis, they found that the judge lower down had erred in conflating the rule and the concession and allowing the appeal substantively on that basis. However the Tribunal did find that a person who does not meet the requirements of the rules may have the benefit of the Secretary of State's exercise of discretion under the concession. When OS, was heard, though, the concession was in quite vague terms. The Tribunal allowed the appeal only to the extent that the decision had to be remade by the Secretary of State as she had ignored the policy when refusing the application. The concession is now clear in that gaps of up to 28 days will be ignored, and a Tribunal may well be able to allow an appeal which falls foul of the rule, but where the application falls clearly within the terms of the current concession.

Article 8 ECHR

As discussed in the chapter on human rights, where an immigrant falls within the scope of an existing policy, usually because they have been here a long time, or have immediate family here, and that policy has not been applied to them, a decision to expel them from (or refuse to admit them again to) the United Kingdom, is likely to be disproportionate and therefore a breach of their Article 8 right to respect for their family or private life.

Returning residents

If a person has ILR leaves the UK, they should usually be re-admitted for settlement if they:

- had indefinite leave to enter/remain when they last left the UK

- have not been away for more than 2 years

- did not receive assistance towards the cost of leaving

- now seek admission to continue their settled life in the UK

A person who has been away for more than two years may be admitted to the UK as a returning resident if, for example, he has lived here all his life and the only other bar to admission is that he has been away for more than two years (rule19). In fact, the IDIs, at Chapter 1, Section 3, Annexe K, are quite generous in their interpretation of this rule:

> **2. FACTORS TO BE CONSIDERED IN CASES WHERE PARAGRAPH 19 OF HC 395 MAY APPLY**
>
> The factors that should be considered in assessing whether a person comes within Paragraph 19 are set out below:
> - the length of his original residence here;
> - the time the applicant has been outside the United Kingdom;
> - the reason for the delay beyond the 2 years - was it through his own wish or no fault of his own? Could he reasonably have been expected to return within 2 years?
> - why did he go abroad when he did and what were his intentions?
> - the nature of his family ties here - how close are they, and to what extent has he maintained them in his absence?
> - whether he has a home in the United Kingdom and, if admitted, would resume his residency.
>
> The longer a person has remained outside the United Kingdom over 2 years, the more difficult it will be for him to qualify for admission under the discretion contained in Paragraph 19.
>
> **2.1 Other circumstances to be considered**
>
> Other more specific circumstances which might apply in favour of an individual are:
> - travel and service abroad with a particular employer prior to returning with him;
> - service abroad for the United Kingdom Government, as an employee of a quasi/government body, a British company or a United Nations organisation;
> - employment abroad in the public service of a friendly country by a person who could not reasonably be expected to settle in that country permanently;
> - a prolonged period of study abroad by a person who wished to rejoin his family here at the end of his studies;
> - prolonged medical treatment abroad of a kind not available here;
> - whether the person contacted a post abroad within 2 years to express his future intention to return to the United Kingdom.

Nevertheless, the person's leave automatically lapses by operation of law if he or she has remained outside the UK for more than two years, and he or she will be required to seek leave to enter, which will not be automatically granted. The application should be made to an entry clearance officer before the person returns to the U.K. Where a person who has not applied for a visa to return is refused leave to enter as a returning resident at the port, the Immigration Officer will usually grant a period of six months leave to enter as a visitor. There is no provision to appeal against that decision, and an application will have to be made outside the rules for the reinstatement of ILR. That being said though, a decision to grant leave to enter for 6 months may be unlawful if the immigration officer has failed to consider whether or not it is appropriate to grant entry as a returning resident (see _Anderson FE (AP), Re Judicial Review_ [2013] ScotCS CSOH_52).

Chapter 3: Visitors

There are a number of different types of visit visa for those coming to the U.K. for various short-term purposes. These can be found in Part 2 of the Immigration Rules, beginning at rule 40. Each category of visit visa has its own extensive guidance document in the Modernised Guidance:
https://www.gov.uk/government/collections/visiting-modernised-guidance).

Different types of visitor

- e.g. general, business, sports, entertainer

Intention to leave normally required

- Though extensions are available in some categories

Main conditions

- 6 months leave normal maximum stay
- Switching not normally possible
- No working

Limited right to appeal

We start this section with a look at the general visit visa. Some information about other the types of visit visas is provided at the end of the chapter.

General visitor (paras 41- 46)

As most of the requirements of the general visitor category must also be met by other types of visitor, we provide them in full;

> 41. The requirements to be met by a person seeking leave to enter the United Kingdom as a general visitor are that he:
>
> (i) is genuinely seeking entry as a general visitor for a limited period as stated by him, not exceeding 6 months or not exceeding 12 months in the case of a person seeking entry to accompany an academic visitor as their child, spouse or partner, provided in the latter case the visitor accompanying the academic visitor has entry clearance; and
>
> (ii) intends to leave the United Kingdom at the end of the period of the visit as stated by him; and does not intend to live for extended periods in the United Kingdom through frequent or successive visits; and
>
> (iii) does not intend to take employment in the United Kingdom; and

(iv) does not intend to produce goods or provide services within the United Kingdom, including the selling of goods or services direct to members of the public; and

(v) Save to the extent provided by paragraph 43A, does not intend to undertake a course of study; and

(vi) will maintain and accommodate himself and any dependants adequately out of resources available to him without recourse to public funds or taking employment; or will, with any dependants, be maintained and/or accommodated adequately by relatives or friends who can demonstrate they are able and intend to do so, and are legally present in the United Kingdom, or will be at the time of their visit; and

(vii) can meet the cost of the return or onward journey.; and

(viii) is not a child under the age of 18.

(ix) does not intend to do any of the activities provided for in paragraphs 46G (iii), 46M (iii) or 46S (iii); and

(x) does not, during his visit, intend to marry or form a civil partnership, or to give notice of marriage or civil partnership; and

(xi) does not intend to receive private medical treatment during his visit; and

(xii) is not in transit to a country outside the common travel area.

(xiii) where he is seeking leave to enter as a general visitor to take part in archaeological excavations, provides a letter from the director or organiser of the excavation stating the length of their visit and, where appropriate, what arrangements have been made for their accommodation and maintenance.".

'General' visitors are usually tourists or those intending to visit family or friends. However, as long as a visit to the UK does not breach the specific rules for general visitors, and there are a lot of them (i.e. intention to return, no employment, study, marriage, business and so forth), then the visit can be for any purpose at all.

Specific provision is made for those visiting the UK to act as an organ donor in rule 41A.

There is no separate provision for family visitors (and from 25 June 2013 no full right of appeal for those refused a visit visa applied for with the intention of visiting family members in the UK).

Although a grant of leave to enter as a visitor will usually be for 6 months, it is important to note that the intention of the visitor must be to visit *for a limited period as stated by him*. A visitor who spends substantially more time in the UK than that stated in the visa application form or to the Border Force officer on entry may well find that that rebounds on them when making a subsequent application, even where they have left the UK within the period of their leave.

Rule 41(v) now allows business and general visitors to undertake a short period of study. Rule 43A sets out the limits to that study, providing two categories of study, each restricted to a maximum of 30 days. Study must be either;

➢ recreational (e.g. pottery and horse riding, but not English language), or
➢ study in a regulated institution (which can be English Language or anything else)
➢ provided that is not the main purpose of their visit.

Intention to leave

Key principles on intention to leave

- Should not be based purely on suspicion but once raised, realistically, it is hard to dislodge suspicion
- Being poor is not a proper reason to refuse
- People are willing to spend a lot on family visits
- Objective factors provide the best guide

Proving an Intention to leave the UK was widely required throughout the Immigration Rules until the advent of the Points Based System. The principle categories to which it applies now are visitors under Part 2 of the Immigration Rules (including prospective entrepreneurs), domestic workers in private households (Part 5), and dependants of PBS migrants (Part 8). It is most often applied to visitors and will often be the issue on which an application for a visit visa or leave to enter as a visitor stands or falls.

In considering an intention to leave the United Kingdom the decision maker can look at all the circumstances of the applicant but must not make decisions based purely on suspicion. Case law has consistently stated that although an incentive to return can be evidence of an intention to return, financial incentives (or lack of financial incentives) cannot legitimately be used to raise a presumption that an applicant will remain in the UK.

Relevant factors for the ECO will include:

➢ Immigration history (previous compliance with immigration laws is an excellent indicator of intention to leave)

➢ Family links with own country, such as wife and children or elderly parents

➢ Other links, such as a job to return to or studies to complete

➢ Levels of income (not decisive taken alone, but it is not possible to argue this is not a relevant consideration)

➢ Absence or otherwise of links in the UK – this could cut both ways, as having a sponsor is helpful, especially if he or she can give evidence at an appeal hearing, and having someone to visit provides a visit-like purpose. On the other hand, if the family here has shown a 'pattern of immigration', some ECOs would suspect that like their family members already here, the applicant will never leave.

Examples

Saleem is from Bangladesh. He is applying for a student visit visa. He is 19 years old and has never left Bangladesh before, and he wants to study English. He has a strong academic background and wants to go into business when he returns.

Yolande is from Uganda. She is also applying for a student visit visa. She is 22 and also wants to study English. She has a sister in the UK who is a nurse under Tier 2 and Yolande previously visited her sister and returned to Uganda in accordance with the rules.

Their situations differ little, but Yolande is in a stronger position to argue that she possesses the requisite intention to return as she has already proven that she abides by the rules. There is no real reason to suspect that Saleem will break the rules, but sadly this is the assumption that may well be made by many ECOs examining his case.

Frequent and successive visits

A person granted a 2, 5, or 10 year multi-entry visit visa, will be able to make repeat visits to the U.K. within the period of the visa, but no single visit can last for more than 6 months.

The Immigration Rules do not stipulate any period of time that must elapse between visits to the UK. In *Sawmynaden (Family visitors – considerations)* [2012] UKUT 00161(IAC), the Upper Tribunal allowed the appeal of an Appellant who, following her retirement, had spent and wanted to continue spending a significant amount of time in the UK visiting her children who are settled here.

Not long after Sawmynaden was reported, however, the Secretary of State added a new requirement to the visit rules that the applicant must *not intend to live for extended periods in the United Kingdom through frequent or successive visits* (rule 41(ii). It is a moot point as to whether Ms Sawmynaden's appeal would have succeeded under the current rule.

The Modernised Guidance gives examples of those who would be in breach of the new provision;

- where an individual spends five or six months in the UK during a visit and returns after a short break in their home country for a further five or six months, or
- if they are living in the UK for successive short periods and breaking this by leaving for a couple of days, for example, someone living in the UK during the week and breaking this by leaving the UK at the weekends.

The guidance also provides a useful list of factors that will be relevant to the assessment as to whether the visitor is residing in the UK through frequent, successive visits.

Switching and extensions for visitors

As six months is generally the maximum period a person can stay on any single visit (there are exceptions in some of the categories above, as for private medical treatment) an extension will not be granted if the period sought will result in a stay of longer than six months. Applications are sometimes exceptionally granted outside the Immigration Rules, however – see the discussion of the policy on carers.

A person with leave as a visitor, other than in the prospective entrepreneur category, will not be able to switch to another category of the Immigration Rules. They will need to go home to apply for a visa to return.

Appeals for visitors

There is no right to appeal the refusal of a visit visa other than on human rights or race discrimination grounds. The full right of appeal for family visitors was removed (by Section 52 of the Crime and Courts Act 2013) for those making a visa application on or after 25 June 2013.

It is the view of the government that for a person refused a visit visa, the cheaper and quicker option is to apply again, and to address in the new application the reasons for refusal by providing better supporting evidence to show that they do in fact meet the requirements of the Immigration Rules. However, where a person has been refused on the grounds of genuineness or intention, they might find it difficult to produce better evidence to support a further application.

Now that we have lost the family visit appeal, it will be interesting to see how the Tribunal will deal with family visit appeals made solely on Article 8 and/or race discrimination grounds as there are no reported cases dealing with the extent to which a family visit might engage a person's right to respect for their family life.

A person with entry clearance, who is refused entry at port, will have a right of appeal (until the commencement of Part 2 of the Immigration Act 2014).

For detailed advice as to how to challenge visit visa refusals, Colin Yeo has produced a very handy eBook, 'Visit visa refusals: how to challenge decisions' available from the Free Movement blog (http://www.freemovement.org.uk/shop/)

Tactics

There are many applicants who will find it difficult to succeed in an application for a general visit visa, particularly those who are from developing countries and who are not high net-worth individuals. The quality of the application will be fundamental to the prospects of success. Applicants should consider providing a detailed itinerary and costing for the trip, evidence of accommodation, and of how they will spend their time here (e.g. invitations from family members, or research into the sights they intend to visit), evidence of funds, their provenance and their accessibility. More evidence rather than less. If the applicant is working, payslips and bank statements, and letters from the employer (on headed notepaper) should be provided. If not, and in any case, other evidence of income from property or land, business accounts, tax returns etc should be provided. If the applicant is studying, then plenty of evidence of that, and their progress in their studies, and an explanation as to how they can afford the time and funds for the trip.

Those who are non-visa nationals may want to consider applying for a visa in any case if they fear they may not be granted leave to enter without one. It is not uncommon for non-visa nationals to be refused entry, particularly where they are from countries where the Home Office considers their nationals do not have the requisite respect for the UK's immigration laws. The Home Office has a secret list of some 44 such countries, though is (not surprisingly) unwilling to disclose it.

Other types of visit visa

Child visitor (paras 46A-46F)

This category is for those below the age of 18 travelling without a parent and includes some additional requirements to those of the general visitor. Under this category, a child may visit the U.K. for a holiday, or for study. The applicant must demonstrate that suitable arrangements have been made for his travel to, and reception and care in the United Kingdom and that he has a parent or guardian in his home country or country of habitual residence who is responsible for his care. There is considerable additional detail in the Modernised Guidance about the mechanisms for ensuring these requirements are met and recorded. The principle behind these changes is to recognize the duty upon the Home Office to protect the interests of children who cross international borders. This manual cannot address this issue in detail but the reader may want to source "Safeguarding children", a Government policy document designed to address the growing problem of child trafficking.

Business visitor (paras 46G-46L)

This category exists for those who are visiting the UK for a period of six months or less to carry out specified business activities. Reference needs to be made to the rules for the exhaustive list of activities the business visitor can carry out under this provision. The business visitor cannot receive payment from a source within the UK for any business they transact here. Any such business is supposed to be incidental to their main business or employment back home.

Some of the specific activities provided for include visiting professors accompanying students undertaking study abroad programmes, short term secondees from overseas companies and board level directors attending board meetings in the UK, where not employed by the UK company, (who may be paid a fee for attending the particular meeting).

As an exception to the 6-month rule, an Academic visitor (defined in rule 46G(d)) can be granted a maximum period of 12 months leave.

Sports visitor (paras 46M-46R)

This category is for sports visitors who are not going to be employed in the UK. The permitted activities are as follows:

> To take part in a particular sporting event, tournament or series of events (as further defined in the rule)

> To take part in a specific one off charity sporting event, provided no payment is received other than for travelling and other expenses

> To join, as an amateur, a wholly or predominantly amateur team provided no payment is received other than for board and lodging and reasonable expenses

> To serve as a member of the technical or personal staff, or as an official, attending the same event as a visiting sportsperson coming for one or more of the purposes listed above.

Entertainer visitor (paras 46S-46X)

This route is for entertainers, both amateur and professional, and their crew, to visit the UK to fulfil a particular engagement, or perform in a particular competition or event. Employment is prohibited. The Points Based System must be used for an entertainer seeking to work in the UK for even a relatively short time if it is beyond a single short event. Amateur entertainers will find entry as a visitor slightly more straightforward than professionals, and 'amateur' is defined at rule 6 of the immigration rules as a person who engages in a sport or creative activity solely for personal enjoyment and who is not seeking to derive a living from the activity.

Visitor in transit (paras 47-50)

A visitor in transit can apply for leave to enter for up to 48 hours. They must be in transit to a country outside the common travel area, have both the means and the intention of proceeding at once to another country, and be assured of entry there, and must intend and be able to leave the United Kingdom within 48 hours. They can be given leave to enter for a maximum of 48 hours.

Visa nationals will need a transit visa unless they meet the requirements of the 'Transit Without Visa Scheme', currently a concession outside the rules, but to be incorporated into the rules (at rule 50A) from 1 December 2014.

Private medical treatment visitor (paras 51-56)

This category enables those who can afford it to travel to the UK for the specific purpose of receiving medical treatment in the UK. They must meet most of the requirements of the general visit visa and also show that the cost of the medical treatment can be met and that the medical treatment is of 'finite duration'. They will be required to produce evidence of their medical condition and treatment, the estimated cost and likely duration of the treatment, and sufficient funds. The Home Office may also require evidence that arrangements have been made for the necessary consultation and treatment, though this is at the discretion of the decision maker.

A person will be granted 6 months leave to enter (or up to 11 months in certain circumstances), and can then apply for extensions of stay of up to 6 months. There is no bar on the length of time a person may remain in the UK as a private medical treatment visitor. Evidence from an appropriately qualified NHS consultant or doctor on the Specialist Register of the General Medical Council is needed for an extension application.

In the Modernised Guidance and in the case of LB (Medical treatment of "finite" duration) Bangladesh [2005] UKAIT 00175 it states that 'finite' might well be a substantial period of time, even years, for example for fertility treatment, but the proposed treatment must have a proposed end point and a prospect of success.

The guidance says that there is no provision or concession for a person to enter or remain as a surrogate mother, and that any such application will be refused. A person applying to come to the U.K. to be a live organ donor may be granted leave outside the rules.

Unusually for a visit category, a person can apply in-country to switch into this provision.

Parent of a child at school (paras 56A to 56C)

This category, set out at rules 56A to 56C, allows a parent of a child studying in the U.K. to stay in the U.K. until the child reaches 12 years of age.

Visitors seeking to enter for the purposes of marriage or to enter a civil partnership (paras 56D-56F)

The category is for those who wish to travel to the UK to get married or register a civil partnership and then return home afterwards. It is not suitable for those wanting to remain in the UK after marriage. Entry clearance is mandatory.

The couple will need to produce satisfactory evidence, if required to do so, of the arrangements for giving notice of the marriage or civil partnership, or for the wedding or civil partnership ceremony to take place. The marriage needs to be planned for the period of the visit.

From 6 November 2014, the applicant will need to show that their intention is not to enter into a sham marriage or civil partnership.

Visitors seeking leave to enter under the Approved Destinations Status (ADS) agreement with China (paras 56G-56J)

This provision allows nationals of China to visit the U.K. in tour groups of 5 or more people for a maximum period of 30 days. An application for a visa must be submitted through an accredited Chinese travel agency.

Student visitor (paras 56K-56M)

For those seeking entry for a short course of study, this is probably the appropriate visa. The maximum length of stay is 6 months, though by way of a concession (see the Modernised Guidance/Visiting) students studying English can be granted up to 11 months. Extensions and variations are not otherwise possible so this route is solely for those planning to study a short course, at a college with a sponsor licence or one that is accredited or subject to appropriate educational oversight, and then leave the UK afterwards.

Prospective Entrepreneur (paras 56N-56Q)

A Prospective Entrepreneur can come to the U.K. to have discussions with potential funders and, if successful in raising the necessary funds, then switch into the Tier 1 (Entrepreneur) route. The application must be supported by specified evidence from the potential funder(s). Entry clearance is mandatory.

Given the recently added requirement under the Tier 1(Entrepreneur) category that *the applicant genuinely intends and is able to establish, take over or become a director of one or more businesses in the UK within the next six months*, it is likely that an entry clearance application as a prospective entrepreneur is going to be subject to very careful scrutiny.

Visitors undertaking permitted paid engagements (paras 56X to 56Z)

This route is for those coming to the U.K. for pre-arranged engagements to which they have been formally invited and which relate to their area of expertise or qualifications or occupation. Permitted engagements include the examination and selection of students for U.K. institutions, giving lectures, assessing pilots, to participate as a lawyer in court or tribunal proceedings, or undertaking by invitation an activity relating to the arts, entertainment or sporting professions.

Chapter 4: Employment categories outside the PBS

Most of the employment categories are now to be found within the Points Based System. Those outside the PBS (which are also largely outside the scope of this manual) include:

> Representatives of overseas businesses (paragraphs 144-149)

  A route for senior employers of overseas companies wanting to establish a base in the U.K, or for journalists of overseas news organisations on long term assignments in the U.K.

> Domestic workers in private households (paragraphs 159A–159H)

  Changes introduced from 6 April 2012 limit this category to those accompanying their employer on a visit to the UK, with a maximum stay of 6 months.

  Those who entered under the rules in place before that date will continue to be able to apply for extensions for periods of 12 months at a time, and for settlement after 5 years residence as a domestic worker.

> Professional and Linguistic Assessments Board (PLAB tests), Objective Structured Clinical Examination (OSCE), clinical attachment and dental observer posts (75A-M)

> Provisions relating to HM Forces and their family members are in Appendix Armed Forces and Appendix FM.

> UK Ancestry (paragraphs 186-192) see below

UK ancestry visas (paragraphs 186-192)

This provision is for the grandchildren of British citizens who emigrated from the UK in times past. The children, born outside the UK, of such a British citizen (or British Subject or Citizen of the UK and Colonies as they may have been at the time) will usually have been born British, and will be free of immigration control, but their children born outside the UK will not have been born British. In some circumstances those second generation children born outside the UK may have been able to register as British citizens, but if they could not or did not, they may be able to come to the UK and settle under the relatively benign requirements of the UK ancestry route.

A visa allowing free employment or self-employment and leading to settlement is available to a person who can show adequate maintenance and accommodation and:

➢ is a Commonwealth citizen; and

➢ is aged 17 or over; and

➢ can prove a relationship by blood or recognised adoption with a grandparent born in the United Kingdom and Islands; and

➢ is able to work and intends to take or seek employment in the United Kingdom.

It is not possible to switch to an ancestry visa from within the UK (rule 189(ii)). Entry clearance must be obtained from the British Embassy or High Commission in the home country of the applicant.

One of the main attractions of the ancestry visa is that it leads to settlement after five years. In addition, there are no restrictions on employment and the Modernised Guidance on UK ancestry suggests that examination of the applicant's ability to maintain him or herself is relatively limited, providing they can do so by some means that include some sort of employment. It is not strictly necessary to show employment when applying for extensions, although it would certainly be helpful to be able to be able to do so.

An up to date list of Commonwealth countries is at:
http://www.royal.gov.uk/monarchandcommonwealth/commonwealthmembers/membersofthecommonwealth.aspx

As there is no specified evidence under this category (except under rule 192(vi) for settlement), evidence of ancestry must be provided that is compelling. That should include, when relying on blood relationships, the full birth certificates of the applicant, the relevant parent, and the grand-parent, as well as marriage certificates where the applicant or direct ascendant relative has changed their names on marriage. An ability and intention to work can be proven by way of evidence of qualifications, current and previous work experience, CVs, job applications or offers in the UK, and, where there is a disability or illness, additional medical information confirming an ability to work.

Chapter 5: Long residence and private life

The long residence and private life provisions begin at rule 276A. They should be read alongside the Modernised Guidance (see Modernised Guidance: Other immigration categories: Long residence. The drafting of this provision, and its numerous amendments over time, make it somewhat difficult to navigate.

Until 9 July 2012, there were two routes to settlement on the grounds of long residence:

- 10 years continuous and lawful residence, or

- 14 years of continuous residence (whether lawful, unlawful or a combination of the two).

The 14 year category is now closed but for a person granted an extension of stay on this basis following an application made prior to 9 July 2012 (who will be able to apply for ILR once the requirements of the old rule are fully met). The 14 year rule has been replaced by the provisions of the new 'private life' category at rule 276ADE(1) (see below).

Ten year rule

Under the ten year rule (276A to 276D), the leave must be continuous and lawful. The terms "continuous residence" and "lawful residence" are defined in rule 276A as follows:

> (a) "continuous residence" means residence in the United Kingdom for an unbroken period, and for these purposes a period shall not be considered to have been broken where an applicant is absent from the United Kingdom for a period of 6 months or less at any one time, provided that the applicant in question has existing limited leave to enter or remain upon their departure and return, but shall be considered to have been broken if the applicant:
>
> (i) has been removed under Schedule 2 of the 1971 Act, section 10 of the 1999 Act, has been deported or has left the United Kingdom having been refused leave to enter or remain here; or
>
> (ii) has left the United Kingdom and, on doing so, evidenced a clear intention not to return; or
>
> (iii) left the United Kingdom in circumstances in which he could have had no reasonable expectation at the time of leaving that he would lawfully be able to return; or
>
> (iv) has been convicted of an offence and was sentenced to a period of imprisonment or was directed to be detained in an institution other than a prison

(including, in particular, a hospital or an institution for young offenders), provided that the sentence in question was not a suspended sentence; or

(v) has spent a total of more than 18 months absent from the United Kingdom during the period in question.

(b) "lawful residence" means residence which is continuous residence pursuant to:

(i) existing leave to enter or remain; or

(ii) temporary admission within section 11 of the 1971 Act where leave to enter or remain is subsequently granted; or

(iii) an exemption from immigration control, including where an exemption ceases to apply if it is immediately followed by a grant of leave to enter or remain.

Where it says in 276A that absence from the U.K. for a period of 6 months or less does not break a person's continuous residence, *provided that the applicant in question has existing limited leave to enter or remain upon their departure and return*, the grant of leave with which they return to the U.K. does not have to be the same grant of leave that they had when they left. A person therefore could leave the U.K. with existing leave, which then expires, and return on a new grant of leave (subject to the other provisions in 276A(a)).

In a significant concession in the guidance, the Home Office states that breaks of up to 28 days between the expiry of a grant of leave and the making of the next application for an extension during the qualifying period will also be disregarded when considering continuity of residence, as will longer periods in exceptional circumstances (e.g. hospitalisation). An application made more than 28 days before the qualifying period is completed will be refused.

The Modernised Guidance (Other categories) also states (or stated, given that it now appears to have disappeared);

➢ Once an applicant has built up a period of 10 years continuous lawful residence, there is no limit on the length of time afterwards when they can apply. This means they could leave the UK, re-enter and apply for settlement based on a 10 year period of continuous lawful residence they built up in the past. This is subject to the provision that the applicant must not be in the UK in breach of immigration laws at the date of application, except for any period of overstaying of 28 days or less.

➢ Time spent in the Republic of Ireland, Channel Islands or the Isle of Man does not count as residence in the UK for the purposes of long residence even though they form part of the common travel area.

➢ Time spent in the U.K. with a right to reside under the EEA regulations will be treated as lawful residence (by way of an exercise of discretion).

➢ Where the 10 years of residence has accrued during a period of continuing leave under s3C or 3D of the 1971 Act, an application can be submitted to the Home Office to vary the existing application, or to the Tribunal under the s120 as applicable.

Other considerations

Having met the 10 year requirement, the Home Office will then consider whether:

> (ii) having regard to the public interest there are no reasons why it would be undesirable for him to be given indefinite leave to remain on the ground of long residence, taking into account his:
>
> (a) age; and
>
> (b) strength of connections in the United Kingdom; and
>
> (c) personal history, including character, conduct, associations and employment record; and
>
> (d) domestic circumstances; and
>
> (e) compassionate circumstances; and
>
> (f) any representations received on the person's behalf;

These factors enable the Home Office to exercise discretion not to grant leave, though it is not common for an application to be refused on these bases. Where, due to criminality, the application falls foul of rule 322(1C)(ii)(iv), limited leave can be granted until the relevant time period has elapsed.

The Court of Appeal has in at least two cases been critical of the Home Office and immigration tribunal tendency to undermine the purpose of the long residence rule by taking too restrictive an approach to the latter set of considerations. In *ZH (Bangladesh) v SSHD [2009] EWCA Civ 8* the Court of Appeal held that illegal working is not sufficient to exclude a person from the benefits of the long residence rule.

For a grant of indefinite leave, the applicant will also have to meet the knowledge of English language and life in the U.K. requirement. If they do not, and they have spent less than 20 years in the U.K, they will be granted a further 2 years leave on the same conditions as their previous grant of leave. Otherwise they will be granted ILR with no conditions.

Applications under the 10 year long residence category are made on forms FLR(LR) and SET(LR).

Tactics

What can you suggest to a client who is nearly but not quite at the 10 year point of continuous lawful residence in the UK? An application under the 10-year rule cannot be made more than 28 days before the qualifying period is met. However, the client may be able to make an application to extend their stay in a different category, and if they reach the 10 year point before that application is decided, can then apply to vary that application (i.e. submit a new application under the 10-year rule which will replace the earlier undecided application). They will have reached the 10-year point whilst their leave is extended under s3C of the 1971 Act, but that is no problem. Their leave has been lawful and continuous.

If they reach the 10-year point after the extension application is refused, their leave may be extended under 3C whilst an appeal or Administrative Review (predicting the coming into force of Part 2 of the Immigration Act 2014) can be brought, or is pending. They may then be able to rely on the Statement of Additional Grounds procedure under s120 of the 2002 Act to raise the 10-year rule as part of their appeal. Alternatively, they can withdraw the appeal or Administrative Review application, become an overstayer, and make the application within the 28 day period of overstaying. The latter option, although it might sound more straightforward, may not be the better option as the applicant will become an overstayer and lose their right to work in the UK whilst they wait a decision.

Following the commencement of Part 2of the 2014 Act, an applicant may be able to put their 10 year application to the UKVI as a human rights application in reliance on Article 8 of the ECHR to give them a right of appeal (unless certified as clearly unfounded).

Private life

The concept of 'private life' comes from Article 8 of the European Convention on Human Rights, the "right to respect for one's private and family life, his home and his correspondence".

The private life category of the Immigration Rules, at rule 276ADE(1), allows an applicant to apply to regularise their stay in the UK on private life grounds, essentially long residence where some or all of that residence has not been lawful.

For applications made on or after 09 July 2012, rule 276ADE(1) defines, subject to 'suitability' requirements (which appear in Appendix FM at Section S-LTR of the partner category), a person who will be entitled to a grant of leave to remain on private life grounds as one who;

> (iii) has lived continuously in the UK for at least 20 years (discounting any period of imprisonment); or
>
> (iv) is under the age of 18 years and has lived continuously in the UK for at least 7 years (discounting any period of imprisonment) and it would not be reasonable to expect the applicant to leave the UK; or
>
> (v) is aged 18 years or above and under 25 years and has spent at least half of his life living continuously in the UK (discounting any period of imprisonment); or
>
> (vi) subject to sub-paragraph (2), is aged 18 years or above, has lived continuously in the UK for less than 20 years (discounting any period of imprisonment) but there

would be very significant obstacles to the applicant's integration into the country to which he would have to go if required to leave the UK.

The reference at 276ADE(1)(vi) to sub-paragraph 2, relates to third country removals under the Dublin Regulations.

Periods of imprisonment will be deducted from the total period of residence, (i.e. rather than requiring the applicant to start from scratch following release). For those familiar with the now closed 14-year unlawful residence category, note the absence of a clock-stopping provision under 276ADE(1).

As with the 14 year rule, the evidential requirements are set high. It is expected that applicants will be able to provide independent evidence of each 12 month period they have lived in the U.K, plus travel documents covering the whole period, unless a very good explanation has been provided as to why they cannot. A large envelope will be required.

The new rules will not be applied to applications relying on Article 8 private life made prior to 09 July 2012 (see *Edgehill & Anor v SSHD* [2014] EWCA Civ 402).

Suitability

Rule A320 exempts a private life application from most of the general grounds of refusal in Part 9 of the Immigration Rules. Instead, the first consideration will be whether it falls to be refused under the 'suitability' requirements in paragraphs S-LTR 1.2 to S-LTR 2.3 and S-LTR3.1 of Appendix FM (under the 'partner' category). Under these provisions, the applicant will be refused leave on mandatory grounds if;

➢ they are the subject of a deportation order,

➢ they have been sentenced to a period of imprisonment of 12 months or more,

➢ in the view of the Secretary of State, their offending has caused serious harm or they are a persistent offender who shows a particular disregard for the law,

➢ their conduct (including convictions which do not fall within the above criteria), character, associations, or other reasons, make it undesirable to allow them to remain in the UK, or

➢ they have failed without reasonable excuse to attend an interview; provide requested information; provide requested physical data; or undergo a medical examination or provide a medical report, when required to do so.

The applicant may be refused on discretionary grounds if;

➢ whether or not to their knowledge, false information, representations or documents have been submitted in relation to the application (including false information submitted to any person to obtain a document used in support of the application); or there has been a failure to disclose material facts in relation to the application, or

➢ one or more relevant NHS body has notified the Secretary of State that they have failed to pay charges in accordance with the relevant NHS regulations on charges to overseas visitors and the outstanding charges have a total value of at least £1000, or

➢ Failure to provide a maintenance undertaking.

Not be reasonable to expect the applicant to leave the UK

This requirement appears both in the private life rules for children (276ADE(1)(iv)), and in the Exception (paragraph EX1) which applies to partners and parents under Appendix FM who have children who are British citizens or have lived in the UK for seven years or more.

Whether it is reasonable to expect the child to leave the UK has become a core issue in UK immigration control. The Home Office are refusing nearly all the many applicants seeking to rely on this requirement. It is the Home Office's view that children here irregularly should leave the UK with their families however long they have lived here.

It is therefore worth looking at the history of this provision and the arguments in support of such applications in some detail. It will be central to the many tens of thousands of families who have children who have lived in the UK more than 7 years and who are attempting to regularise their stay on that basis[1].

Until 2008 children who resided in the UK for seven years would be permitted to remain under a Home Office policy called DP5/96, as would their parents. There were certain public interest 'escape' clauses for the Home Office – if the parents had deliberately gone to ground, committed offences or similar – but most applications under this policy would succeed. Seven years was recognised as an important if arbitrary period of residence for children by the previous President of the Upper Tribunal in *EM (Zimbabwe) CG* [2011] UKUT 98 (IAC) and continued to be recognised in other cases including *Azimi-Moayed and others (decisions affecting children; onward appeals)* [2013] UKUT 197 (IAC). When the Immigration Rules were changed in July 2012 (Statement of Changes HC 194), seven years of residence by a child was formally incorporated into the rules as a sufficient period to justify continued residence by the child and parents. The explanatory notes accompanying that particular change (paragraph 7.6) stated that:

---

[1] For more detail, read the Free Movement article at http://www.freemovement.org.uk/can-children-and-parents-apply-to-remain-after-seven-years-residence/#more-16941

> The key test for a non-British citizen child remaining on a permanent basis is the length of residence in the UK of the child – which the rules set at least the last seven years, subject to countervailing factors.

The Grounds of compatibility with Article 8 of the European Convention on Human Rights: Statement by the Home Office (13 June 2012) that accompanied the new rules went even further at paragraph 27:

> The Rules deal clearly with how to treat British citizen and other children in cases where we would otherwise intend to remove their parent(s) and how countervailing factors should weigh in the decision. There are some circumstances where children may be allowed to stay on a permanent or temporary basis on best interests grounds. The key test for remaining on a permanent basis is around the length of continuous residence of a child in the UK – which we have set at 7 years, subject to countervailing factors. We consider that a period of 7 continuous years spent in the UK as a child will generally establish a sufficient level of integration for family and private life to exist such that removal would normally not be in the best interests of the child. A period of 7 years also echoes a previous policy (known as DP5/96) under which children who had accumulated 7 years' continuous residence in the UK were not deported, which is still referenced by the Courts on occasion. In policy terms, we would not propose a period of less than 7 years as this would enable migrants who entered the UK on a temporary route (for example a route limited to 5 years in the UK) to qualify for settlement if they had brought children with them. The changes are designed to bring consistency and transparency to decision-making.

In December 2012, though, a new criterion of whether it would be reasonable for the child to leave the UK was added by Statement of Changes HC 760. Since then, the new statutory human rights presumptions at Part 5A of the 2002 Act also incorporate this new two stage test of seven years residence *and* that it would not be reasonable for the child to leave the UK.

In this context the reasonableness test need not be interpreted as a particularly high threshold and that in many cases where seven years residence is achieved, an application should succeed under the Immigration Rules without any need to refer to or import human rights considerations.

From a child's perspective seven years of residence can be literally a lifetime. It is the sum of all the child's experience and is all they know, rather than merely a given seven year period in the life of an adult. In *Azimi-Moayed and others (decisions affecting children; onward appeals)* [2013] UKUT 197 (IAC), it is suggested that residence from birth for a child is less significant than residence later on, on the basis that a young child's private life will be almost wholly within the family at the age of seven and will not have much to lose if they are forced to live elsewhere with their family. This though arguably treats children as mere parcels or as appendages of their parents rather than autonomous bearers of rights, as required by the UN Convention on the Rights of the Child. A young child in particular does not exercise choice about country of residence in the way that an adult does: an adult might make an informed choice to move to another country in the knowledge that he or she may have a precarious status and should not put down roots. That is not true of a child.

The word "reasonable" in paragraph 276ADE(1) and EX.1. is subject to the normal rules of statutory interpretation and is to be given its normal meaning. It is a term or test like many others in the Immigration Rules, such as 'adequate', 'sole responsibility', 'genuine and subsisting' and so on. Importantly, it does not import any sort of 'exceptionalness' threshold or similar because it is a normal application that is made under the Immigration Rules. There is no justification for the Home Office's preferred ultra-stringent approach.

Where a person with leave applies for an extension of leave on the basis of paragraph 276ADE(1) and/or EX.1., that application should normally be granted if the period of residence is satisfied and there is no bad behaviour by the applicants, they are well settled and integrated and therefore it would not be reasonable for the child to have to start over with their life again in another country. Indeed, even where the family is in the UK irregularly, there should be no need for a proportionality assessment, and no consideration of Part 5A of the 2002 Act, when considering the question within the rules, as the rules do not provide for such an assessment. It is only when the reasonableness test is clearly not met that such considerations come into play.

Very significant obstacles to integration

Rule 276ADE(1)(vi) requires that (as from 28 July 2014) 'there would be very significant obstacles to the applicant's integration into the country to which he would have to go if required to leave the UK'. This formulation replaced an earlier version which required the claimant to have 'no ties' to the other country.

The guidance indicated that the threshold for the 'no ties' category (276ADE(iv)) had been set extremely high. Factors such as language, cultural background, the length of time spent in the country of origin, family friends and social network, would be considered. A connection under any heading including, for example, an ability to communicate competently in a language spoken in the country of nationality 'with sympathetic interlocutors', or 'has spent their time in the UK living mainly amongst a diaspora community from their country of origin' will have sufficed to demonstrate that ties exist.

In Ogundimu (Article 8 - new rules) Nigeria [2013] UKUT 60 (IAC), looking specifically at the 'no ties' requirement under that earlier version of 276ADE(1)(vi), and the Home Office's guidance as to its meaning, the tribunal decided;

> The natural and ordinary meaning of the word 'ties' imports, we think, a concept involving something more than merely remote and abstract links to the country of proposed deportation or removal. It involves there being a continued connection to life in that country; something that ties a claimant to his or her country of origin... We recognise that the text under the rules is an exacting one. Consideration of whether a person has 'no ties' to such country must involve a rounded assessment of all the relevant circumstances and is not to be limited to 'social, cultural and family' circumstances. Nevertheless, we are satisfied that the appellant has no ties with Nigeria. He is a stranger to the country, the people, and the way of life. His father may have ties but they are not ties of the appellant or any ties that could result in support to the appellant in the event of his return there.

Whilst the wording of the rule has changed, the guidance in Ogundimu may be found relevant to an assessment of whether the 'very significant obstacles to the applicant's integration' threshold is met in a particular case. No doubt the Modernised Guidance on the long residence and private life provisions, when it appears back on the website, will indicate the Home Office's understanding of the new phrase which has not yet been subject to judicial consideration.

The significant obstacles test is future looking. Preparing a case on this basis will require a consideration of the applicant's ties to the UK, but more importantly the problems they will face in returning to their country of origin. Relevant to that assessment will be (non-exhaustively);

> The age they came to the UK. The more experience they have had of living in that country, particularly as an adult, the weaker their case will be
> The extent to which they will be able to find work and accommodation in that country. In some countries, it is hard find work without the practical support of others in the country, even to the extent of setting oneself up as a roadside trader. Expert evidence may be useful here. Relevant though will be the extent of any funds that might be expected for their support from family and friends in the UK, or available to them under the Home Office's voluntary return arrangements (see e.g. the Choices Service run by Refugee Action at: http://www.choices-avr.org.uk/)
> Their health
> Their sex or sexuality, which might lead them to being exploited or oppressed, particularly where young or psychologically vulnerable
> The extent to which their country is in a state of upheaval (e.g. by reason of war or environmental disaster)

Rule 276ADE(1) and Article 8 (ECHR)

In the Statement of Intent: Family Migration, published shortly before the 09 July 2012 rule changes were introduced, the government explained the changes thus;

> The new [private and family life] rules will reflect fully the factors which can weigh for or against an Article 8 claim. They will set proportionate requirements that reflect, as a matter of public policy, the Government's and Parliament's view of how individual rights to respect for private or family life should be qualified in the public interest to safeguard the economic well-being of the UK by controlling immigration and to protect the public from foreign criminals. This will mean that failure to meet the requirements of the rules will normally mean failure to establish an Article 8 claim to enter or remain in the UK, and no grant of leave on that basis...The [private life category] will provide a basis on which a person without family life can remain in the UK through long residence and social integration in the UK, consistent with the approach of Strasbourg and UK case law in this area... on the basis of the Article 8 right to respect for private life.

The rule changes, including rule 276ADE(1), the private life provision, thus represent an attempt by the government to bring Article 8 human rights considerations fully into the Immigration Rules.

Private life outside the rules

The UKVI's guidance[2] though acknowledges that where the requirements are not met, a decision to refuse a private life application and to require the person to leave the U.K. may nevertheless be a breach of Article 8 where there are 'exceptional circumstances'. The factors to be considered by UKVI caseworkers when deciding whether there are such circumstances are laid out in the guidance. The guidance states;

> 'Exceptional' does not mean 'unusual' or 'unique'. Although all cases are to some extent unique, those unique factors do not generally render them exceptional. A case is not exceptional just because the criteria set out in the private life Immigration Rules have been missed by a small margin.

Exceptional factors include;

> - the extent to which roots were put down whilst the applicant was in the UK legally,
> - exceptional legal or cultural factors which prevent or severely limit the applicant
>   from enjoying private life in their country of origin,
> - specific barriers to communication (such as a disability that would prevent the applicant from learning the language of the country of origin)
> - cumulative factors, such as family relationships where they cannot be counted as giving rise to family life

In almost all cases though applications outside the rules will be refused. Where there are particularly strong elements though, the UKVI may decide not to certify the application as clearly unfounded, allowing the applicant an in-country right of appeal. 'Near misses' in respect of the number of years the applicant has lived in the UK will not in themselves amount to exceptional circumstances, but where a substantial period has been spent in the UK legally, with a substantial private life developed during that period, that will certainly go to the applicants side of the balance when proportionality is to be assessed.

The current case law concerning the new private life and other Article 8 provisions in the rules accepts that a judge who finds the rules are not met, must go on and make a full proportionality assessment on established Article 8 principles when deciding the appeal.

The Immigration Act 2014 inserts (as from 28 July 2014[3]) a requirement that judges 'in considering the public interest question', have regard to the fact that;

---

[2] Which has disappeared from GOV.UK website pending amendment

[3] By adding a new Part 5A to the Nationality, Immigration and Asylum Act 2002, specifically here section 117B(4) of that Act.

> (4) Little weight should be given to—
>
> (a) a private life, or
> (b)...
>
> that is established by a person at a time when the person is in the United Kingdom
> unlawfully.
>
> (5) Little weight should be given to a private life established by a person at a time when the person's immigration status is precarious.

By putting this consideration into statutory form, the government hope to skew most Article 8 proportionality assessments made by the Tribunals and courts in their favour. It is the Government's view that now Parliament has set out its stall in the Immigration Rules on exactly how an Article 8 assessment should be carried out, the judiciary should defer to that view. The government has stated that only in exceptional circumstances should an appeal succeed on private and family life grounds if the refused application did not meet the requirements of the new rules.

That being said, the other statutory considerations in Part 5A may assist an appellant where, for instance, they have been supporting themselves without recourse to public funds (even if by working illegally) and speak English.

Making a private life application

A migrant in the UK irregularly can make an application under rule 276ADE(1). The application will be treated as an application under the rules made on Article 8 private life grounds.

The application is made on form FLR(FP), and currently costs £601.

An application for a fee exemption can be made where they do not have accommodation or the means of obtaining it or they cannot meet their essential living needs (on form Appendix 1 FLR(FP) FLR(O)).
https://www.gov.uk/government/publications/application-to-extend-stay-in-the-uk-appendix-1-flrfp-flro

As acknowledged though, by the provisions in rule 276A0, an Article 8 claim can be made in other ways. Rule 276A0 (as slightly amended from 6 November 2014) states;

> For the purposes of paragraph 276ADE(1) the requirement to make a valid application will not apply when the Article 8 claim is raised:
>
> (i) as part of an asylum claim, or as part of a further submission in person after an asylum claim has been refused;

> (ii) where a migrant is in immigration detention. A migrant in immigration detention or their representative must submit any application or claim raising Article 8 to a prison officer, a prisoner custody officer, a detainee custody officer or a member of Home Office staff at the migrant's place of detention; or
>
> (iii) in an appeal (subject to the consent of the Secretary of State where applicable).

So the Article 8 private life claim can be made by way of a fresh claim (i.e. further submissions made under rule 353), on appeal, or by representations made against removal. In each case it will be the criteria under 276ADE(1) that is applied.

Importantly, if a person receives a Notice of Decision to Remove (IS151B), the human rights claim can then be made by way of representations to the UKVI, usually by fax to the local enforcement team, and must be considered before removal.

Decision

Regardless of the form in which the claim is made, or whether the decision is made within or outside the rules, a successful claimant will be granted 30 months leave to remain on a 10 year route to settlement. They will need to make 3 further applications under 276ADE(1) to extend their stay. When they have completed at least 120 months of continuous leave on private life grounds, do not fall for refusal under the general grounds of refusal, and have met the Appendix KOLL requirements they can then apply for ILR.

The grants of limited leave will be subject to a condition of no recourse to public funds unless the UKVI considers that the person should not be subject to such a condition. Where the client is likely to be left destitute as a result of a condition being placed on their leave denying them recourse to public funds, they can make representations with the application, or post-decision if necessary, requesting that the condition is not applied or removed.

Post-decision, an application can be made for a change to condition on a form available at: https://www.gov.uk/government/publications/application-for-change-of-conditions-of-leave-to-allow-access-to-public-funds-if-your-circumstances-change

Where applications or claims made under the private life rules are refused, there may be no right of appeal under the current appeal provisions (as no further appealable decision need be made). That situation should change when Part 2 of the Immigration Act 2014 comes into force, making a decision to refuse a human rights claim (e.g. an application made under rule 276ADE(1)) an appealable decision.

Example

Maria is from Ecuador. She has been in the UK for just over 20 years. She entered as a visitor and overstayed, working for various individuals over the years as a cleaner. However, with moving around she lost her original passport.

Her first problem is proving when she entered the UK. But even if she can do that, she also has to prove she remained for the relevant period. A passport with an entry stamp and no evidence of departure will not prove her length of residence as she may have travelled abroad and returned on a different passport. Sometimes employers past or present are willing to give evidence, which would be very helpful. Support from well-respected members of the community who are willing to vouch for the applicant's length of residence from their own experience may help too. Friends and family will usually be willing to give evidence, though their evidence will not always be given a great deal of weight.

Sometimes it is possible to obtain official or semi-official records. An attempt to contact the Home Office to obtain evidence of Maria's application for entry clearance (if she made one) or leave to enter could be made, although the chances of success are limited. Doctor or hospital or library records or school records would be of considerable assistance, as would bank or utility bills. An unlawful immigrant may well not have generated such records, however, in which case they may not be able to establish their case.

If Maria has been in the UK less than 20 years, the case would be very different. In order to meet the rules, she would need to show very significant obstacles to re-integration into Ecuador, which may be difficult if she left the country as an adult. Outside the rules, she would need to show very substantial and compelling ties to the UK above and beyond the normal friendships one would make over time, usually requiring, at least, cumulative factors which might include a large extended family here and very substantial activities in her community.

Chapter 6: Family-based applications

Family life under Appendix FM

Subject to the transitional provisions (see below), applications made to join or remain with settled family members in the UK are, from 9 July 2012, made under Appendix FM to the Immigration Rules. When brought into force, these rules represented a huge shake up to the system of family migration into the UK and, as with the private life provisions, remain legally controversial.

We will outline here the new rules under Appendix FM and, where necessary, the 'old' rules (in brief) for those applying under the transitional provisions.

Appendix FM deals with four categories of family migration, providing a route to enter and remain in the UK for those with family life as;

a partner

- including those whose relationships have ended due to domestic violence or bereavement

A parent

- of a child in the UK

A child

- of a partner or parent

An adult dependent relative

In all categories, applicants will always need to meet 'suitability' and some 'eligibility' requirements.

The suitability requirements largely mirror the general grounds of refusal in Part 9 of the Immigration rules i.e. grounds for refusal relating to criminality, deception and owing money to the NHS.

The eligibility requirements relate to one or more of the following criteria;

Relationship

- always mandatory
- the sponsor must be a British citizen, settled, or have leave as a refugee or on the basis of humanitarian protection
- other relationship requirements are category specific

Financial

- minimum income requirements for parent and child categories
- adequate maintenance for others
- adequate accommodation
- no financial requirements where EX1 applies

English language

- basic English
- for partners and parents
- no English requirements where EX1 applies

Immigration status

- switching in-country
- except for fiancés and adult dependent relatives
- few immigration status requirements where EX1 applies

As laid out in paragraph section GEN 1.1 of Appendix FM (below), Appendix FM was drafted with a view to incorporating Article 8 considerations into the rules; here the right to respect for family life. The rules were also designed to incorporate the government's duty to give safeguard and promote the welfare of children in the UK (i.e. the 'best interests of the child' principle).

Purpose

GEN.1.1. This route is for those seeking to enter or remain in the UK on the basis of their family life with a person who is a British Citizen, is settled in the UK, or is in the UK with limited leave as a refugee or person granted humanitarian protection (and the applicant cannot seek leave to enter or remain in the UK as their family member under Part 11 of these rules). It sets out the requirements to be met and, in considering applications under this route, it reflects how, under Article 8 of the Human Rights Convention, the balance will be struck between the right to respect for private and family life and the legitimate aims of protecting national security, public safety and the economic well-being of the UK; the prevention of disorder and crime; the protection of health or morals; and the protection of the rights and freedoms of others s (and in doing so also reflects the relevant public interest considerations as set out in Part 5A of the Nationality, Immigration and Asylum Act 2002). It also takes into account the need to safeguard and promote the welfare of children in the UK, in line with the Secretary of State's duty under section 55 of the Borders, Citizenship and Immigration Act 2009..

As with the private life category, where the Appendix FM requirements are not met, the government's intention is that family life applications should be allowed only in exceptional circumstances.

Navigating Appendix FM

Navigating Appendix FM is never easy. Rather than providing a numbering system for the paragraphs of Appendix FM, as with the rest of the Immigration Rules, the individual paragraphs of Appendix FM are referenced by a complex lettering scheme, and one that is not in alphabetic order.

Top tip

To help you navigate Appendix FM, print out the useful contents page which is in the Statement of Changes (HC194) at page 19. Unhelpfully, the content page did not make it to the consolidated Immigration Rules as they appear on the GOV.UK website. We provide it here;

The sections of this Appendix are set out in the following order –

General
Section GEN: General

Family life as a partner
Section EC-P: Entry clearance as a partner
Section S-EC: Suitability-entry clearance
Section E-ECP: Eligibility for entry clearance as a partner
Section D-ECP: Decision on application for entry clearance as a partner
Section R-LTRP: Requirements for limited leave to remain as a partner
Section S-LTR: Suitability-leave to remain
Section E-LTRP: Eligibility for limited leave to remain as a partner
Section D-LTRP: Decision on application for limited leave to remain as a partner
Section R-ILRP: Requirements for indefinite leave to remain (settlement) as a partner
Section S-ILR; Suitability-indefinite leave to remain
Section E-ILRP: Eligibility for indefinite leave to remain as a partner
Section D-ILRP: Decision on application for indefinite leave to remain as a partner

Exception
Section EX: Exception

Bereaved partner
Section BPILR: Indefinite leave to remain (settlement) as a bereaved partner
Section E-BPILR: Eligibility for indefinite leave to remain as a bereaved partner
Section D-BPILR: Decision on application for indefinite leave to remain as a bereaved partner

Victim of domestic violence
Section DVILR: Indefinite leave to remain (settlement) as a victim of domestic violence
Section E-DVILR: Eligibility for indefinite leave to remain as a victim of domestic violence
Section D-DVILR: Decision on application for indefinite leave to remain as a victim of domestic violence

Family life as a child of a parent with limited leave as a partner or parent
Section EC-C: Entry clearance as a child
Section E-ECC: Eligibility for entry clearance as a child
Section D-ECC: Decision on application for entry clearance as a child
Section R-LTR-C: Requirements for leave to remain as a child
Section E-LTRC: Eligibility for leave to remain as a child
Section D-LTRC: Decision on application for leave to remain as a child 20

Family life as a parent
Section EC-PT: Entry clearance as a parent
Section E-ECPT: Eligibility for entry clearance as a parent
Section D-ECPT: Decision on application for entry clearance as a parent
Section R-LTRPT: Requirements for limited leave to remain as a parent
Section E-LTRPT: Eligibility for limited leave to remain as a parent
Section D-LTRPT: Decision on application for limited leave to remain as a parent
Section R-ILRPT: Requirements for indefinite leave to remain (settlement) as a parent
Section E-ILRPT: Eligibility for indefinite leave to remain as a parent
Section D-ILRPT: Decision on application for indefinite leave to remain as a parent

Adult dependent relatives
Section EC-DR: Entry clearance as an adult dependent relative
Section E-ECDR: Eligibility for entry clearance as an adult dependent relative
Section D-ECDR: Decision on application for entry clearance as an adult dependent relative
Section R-ILRDR: Requirements for indefinite leave to remain as an adult dependent relative
Section E-ILRDR: Eligibility for indefinite leave to remain as an adult dependent relative
Section D-ILRDR: Decision on application for indefinite leave to remain as an adult dependent relative

Operational guidance

Guidance on Appendix FM is unhelpfully spread across two Chapter 8s of the IDIs - Chapter 08: appendix FM family members, and Chapter 08: family members – as well as in the Modernised Guidance. It is best to search in all these locations as documents within often overlap.

Broadly, guidance on Appendix FM can be found in;

> the Immigration Directorate Instructions (IDIs) for most categories (including the children of settled parents under Part 8) (https://www.gov.uk/government/publications/chapter-8-appendix-fm-family-members)

> the Modernised Guidance for applications made under the domestic violence provisions (https://www.gov.uk/government/publications/victims-of-domestic-violence).

For guidance on the transitional provisions;

> i.e. those still entitled to apply under the old rules, see the IDIs at: https://www.gov.uk/government/collections/chapter-8-family-members-transitional-arrangements-immigration-directorate-instructions

> adopted children – see the Modernised Guidance at: https://www.gov.uk/government/publications/adopted-children

Transitional provisions

The transitional provisions are at rules A277 to A280 of Part 8 of the Immigration Rules. Part 8 is where you will find the 'old' family categories and, as stated by rule A277;

> A277 From 9 July 2012 Appendix FM will apply to all applications to which Part 8 of these rules applied on or before 8 July 2012 except where the provisions of Part 8 are preserved and continue to apply, as set out in paragraph A280.

Essentially, the following transitional provisions will be applied;

> Applications in Part 8 categories made prior to 9 July 2012 and undecided at that date will be decided in accordance with the provisions in Part 8 and the new 'suitability' requirements of Appendix FM.

> Those who had been granted entry clearance, or leave to enter or remain under a Part 8 category before that date will continue their route to settlement as provided for under Part 8, but also subject to the new 'suitability' requirements of Appendix FM. So, for instance, a person granted leave as a fiancé prior to that date, would be able to apply for an extension and then settlement as a spouse under the old rules.

> Applications under the children of settled parents provisions (rules 297-300), and those relating to children born in the U.K. (rules 304-309) will continue to be considered under Part 8 regardless of when the application is or was made.

> The Part 8 rules concerning adopted children will continue to apply for applications made after 9 July 2012, subject to the new financial requirements under Appendix FM in some circumstances.

Section GEN

Appendix FM begins with Section GEN: General. This section provides definitions of terms used elsewhere in Appendix FM, and includes an important procedural provision at GEN.1.9. as to the circumstances in which the family life rules will be applied.

GEN.1.2. defines the relationships considered under the 'family life as a partner' category.

GEN.1.3. allows applicants living outside the UK with their British citizen or settled partner or child to seek entry clearance to accompany them to the UK.

> GEN.1.3. For the purposes of this Appendix
>
> (a) "application for leave to remain" also includes an application for variation of leave to enter or remain by a person in the UK;
> (b) references to a person being present and settled in the UK also include a person who is being admitted for settlement on the same occasion as the applicant; and
> (c) references to a British Citizen in the UK also include a British Citizen who is coming to the UK with the applicant as their partner or parent.
>
> GEN.1.4. In this Appendix "specified" means specified in Appendix FM-SE, unless otherwise stated.

GEN.1.4. links Appendix FM to the specified evidence requirements in Appendix FM-SE.

GEN.1.6. lists the majority-English speaking countries whose nationals will automatically meet the English language requirement in the partner and parent categories.

GEN.1.8. incorporates into Appendix FM the provisions in Part 8 of the rules relating to polygamous marriages and the children thereof.

GEN.1.9. outlines the circumstances in which there will be no need to make a valid application in order to access the family life provisions in Appendix FM (see below).

Suitability

Those applying under either Part 8 or Appendix FM categories must not fall to be refused under the 'suitability' provisions. These largely reflect the Part 9 general grounds of refusal that apply in other categories. They apply regardless of the date the application was made, and are located in sections S-EC, S-LTR and S-ILR under the partner category (though applicable to all the family categories).

Appendix FM applications are largely exempted, by rule A320, from the general grounds of refusal relating to entry clearance and leave to remain. They are not exempt however from paragraphs 320(3), (10) and (11). It is particularly important to remember that although there is no mandatory re-entry ban for those who have previously breached the immigration laws, those with a very poor immigration history can be refused on discretionary grounds under rule 320(11) (i.e. "where the applicant has previously contrived in a significant way to frustrate the intentions of the Rules").

As with the general grounds, the suitability provisions can be mandatory (e.g. S-EC.1.1 to 1.8) or discretionary (e.g. S-EC.2.1 to 2.5).

The suitability requirements for entry clearance are;

Section S-EC: Suitability-entry clearance
S-EC.1.1. The applicant will be refused entry clearance on grounds of suitability if any of paragraphs S-EC.1.2. to 1.8. apply.

S-EC.1.2. The Secretary of State has personally directed that the exclusion of the applicant from the UK is conducive to the public good.

S-EC.1.3. The applicant is at the date of application the subject of a deportation order.

S-EC.1.4. The exclusion of the applicant from the UK is conducive to the public good because they have:

(a) been convicted of an offence for which they have been sentenced to a period of imprisonment of at least 4 years; or

(b) been convicted of an offence for which they have been sentenced to a period of imprisonment of at least 12 months but less than 4 years, unless a period of 10 years has passed since the end of the sentence; or

(c) been convicted of an offence for which they have been sentenced to a period of imprisonment of less than 12 months, unless a period of 5 years has passed since the end of the sentence.

Where this paragraph applies, unless refusal would be contrary to the Human Rights Convention or the Convention and Protocol Relating to the Status of Refugees, it will only be in exceptional circumstances that the public interest in maintaining refusal will be outweighed by compelling factors.

S-EC.1.5. The exclusion of the applicant from the UK is conducive to the public good because, for example, the applicant's conduct (including convictions which do not fall within paragraph S-EC.1.4.), character, associations, or other reasons, make it undesirable to grant them entry clearance.

S-EC.1.6. The applicant has failed without reasonable excuse to comply with a requirement to-

(a) attend an interview;

(b) provide information;

(c) provide physical data; or

(d) undergo a medical examination or provide a medical report.

S-EC.1.7. It is undesirable to grant entry clearance to the applicant for medical reasons.

S-EC.1.8. The applicant left or was removed from the UK as a condition of a caution issued in accordance with section 134 of the Legal Aid, Sentencing and Punishment of Offenders Act 2012 less than 5 years prior to the date on which the application is decided.

S-EC.2.1. The applicant will normally be refused on grounds of suitability if any of paragraphs S-EC.2.2. to 2.5. apply.

S-EC.2.2. Whether or not to the applicant's knowledge-

(a) false information, representations or documents have been submitted in relation to the application (including false information submitted to any person to obtain a document used in support of the application); or

(b) there has been a failure to disclose material facts in relation to the application.

S-EC.2.3. One or more relevant NHS body has notified the Secretary of State that the applicant has failed to pay charges in accordance with the relevant NHS regulations on charges to overseas visitors and the outstanding charges have a total value of at least £1000.

S-EC.2.4. A maintenance and accommodation undertaking has been requested or required under paragraph 35 of these Rules or otherwise and has not been provided.

S-EC.2.5. The exclusion of the applicant from the UK is conducive to the public good because:
(a) within the 12 months preceding the date of the application, the person has been convicted of or admitted an offence for which they received a non-custodial sentence or other out of court disposal that is recorded on their criminal record; or

(b) in the view of the Secretary of State:

(i) the person's offending has caused serious harm; or

(ii) the person is a persistent offender who shows a particular disregard for the law.

Making a family life application

Fiancés/proposed civil partners and adult dependent relatives can only apply from overseas. Other applications can be made from overseas, or from within the UK in certain circumstances.

As with private life applications, an application made under Appendix FM will be treated as a human rights claim. A valid application will not be required when the human rights claim is made (see GEN.1.9.);

(i) as part of an asylum claim, or as part of a further submission in person after an asylum claim has been refused;

(ii) where a migrant is in immigration detention. A migrant in immigration detention or their representative must submit any application or claim raising Article 8 to a prison officer, a prisoner custody officer, a detainee custody officer or a member of Home Office staff at the migrant's place of detention; or

(iii) in an appeal (subject to the consent of the Secretary of State where applicable);

In the appropriate circumstances, therefore, a human rights claim can be made as further submissions under the fresh claims procedure (rule 353), as representations, or on a Statement of Additional Grounds (a s120 Notice).

Applications for leave to remain should be made on form FLR(M), for partners who meet all the requirements of the rules, or otherwise on form FLR(FP) for those relying on the Exception.

Family life as a Partner under Appendix FM

This category provides for entry clearance, leave to remain and indefinite leave to remain for partners, defined at GEN.1.2. as;

(i) the applicant's spouse;
(ii) the applicant's civil partner;
(iii) the applicant's fiancé(e) or proposed civil partner; or
(iv) a person who has been living together with the applicant in a relationship akin to a marriage or civil partnership for at least two years prior to the date of application,

unless a different meaning of partner applies elsewhere in this Appendix.

Note here that the definition of unmarried partner in GEN.1.2. (iv) differs to that elsewhere in the Immigration Rules (e.g. 352AA relating to refugee family reunion for unmarried partners), where the requirement is that "parties have been living together in a relationship akin to either a marriage or a civil partnership which has subsisted for two years or more". That does not require two years cohabitation, but two years subsistence of the relationship (see: *Fetle (Partners: two year requirement)* [2014] UKUT 00267).

In addition to the suitability criteria, there are relationship, financial, English language and immigration status requirements. Where 'Section EX: Exceptions to certain eligibility requirements for leave to remain as a partner or parent' applies, the applicant will not need to meet the financial, English language or most of the immigration status requirements.

Relationship

The relationship requirements for partners are largely as they were prior to 9 July 2012.

The applicant's partner must be;

    (a) a British Citizen in the UK, subject to paragraph GEN.1.3.(c); or
    (b) present and settled in the UK, subject to paragraph GEN.1.3.(b); or
    (c) in the UK with refugee leave or with humanitarian protection.

The reference to GEN.1.3. (see Section GEN above) concerns British citizen and settled partners living outside the UK and returning to the UK with the applicant. The partners will be treated as being in the UK for the purposes of the application.

Additionally;

> The applicant and partner must be aged 18 or over at the date of application.
> The applicant and their partner must not be within the prohibited degree of relationship.
> The applicant and their partner must have met in person.
> The relationship between the applicant and their partner must be genuine and subsisting.
> If the applicant and partner are married or in a civil partnership it must be a valid marriage or civil partnership, as specified.
> If the applicant is a fiancé(e) or proposed civil partner they must be seeking entry to the UK to enable their marriage or civil partnership to take place.
> Any previous relationship of the applicant or their partner must have broken down permanently, unless it is a relationship which falls within paragraph 278(i) of these Rules.
> The applicant and partner must intend to live together permanently in the UK.

'Pre-flight' partners of refugees and those with humanitarian protection continue to be dealt with under the family reunion provisions in Part 11 of the rules. Sub-paragraph (c) above relates only to whose relationship (as defined in GEN.1.2.) was formed after the partner left their country of nationality.

Fiancés and proposed civil partners must apply for entry clearance. They must be seeking entry to the UK to enable their marriage or civil partnership to take place within 6 months of arriving here. They cannot apply from within the U.K.

The meaning of 'present and settled' and 'settled in the United Kingdom' is set out in rule 6 of the Immigration Rules and in essence means possession of ILR or the right of abode combined with physical presence in the UK. An EEA national or non-EEA family member with a permanent right of residence in the UK must be considered as present and settled.

The parties to a marriage or civil partnership will need to show that they are legally married according to the laws of the country in which the marriage took place (although see below for polygamous marriages), or that they have contracted a legal civil partnership in a country in which such partnerships are recognised. These countries are listed at Schedule 20 of the Civil Partnership Act 2004. At the time of writing this numbered some 75 jurisdictions (see: the IDIs at Chapter 8, section 2, Annex H for the list as it was in January 2013).

The rule that marriages will be recognised if legally contracted in the country in which they take place is a long standing rule of international private law. For authority see Berthiaume v. Dastous [1930] AC 79 and Rule 67 of Dicey 14th edition. This means that even quite unusual marriage arrangements, such as marriages by proxy, must be recognised (CB (Validity of marriage: proxy marriage) Brazil [2008] UKAIT 00080). More recently, the Upper Tribunal (IAC) may have misunderstood this principle in its judgment in *TA and Others (Kareem explained) Ghana* [2014] UKUT 316 (IAC)[4].

The requirement that the marriage is legal will in some cases mean that relevant formal divorce papers or other evidence of a divorce that was effective in the country in which it took place will need to be produced. The complex issue of domicile may also arise in some spouse cases.

In addition, the applicant must demonstrate that he or she has an intention to live permanently with the other (defined as below) and, if married or in a civil partnership, that the marriage is genuine and subsisting.

> "intention to live permanently with the other" or "intend to live together permanently" means an intention to live together, evidenced by a clear commitment from both parties that they will live together permanently in the UK immediately following the outcome of the application in question or as soon as circumstances permit thereafter. However, where an application is made under Appendix Armed Forces the words "in the UK" in this definition do not apply."[5]

The words 'subsisting marriage' have no precise definition. In the starred determination of GA ("Subsisting" marriage) Ghana [2006] UKAIT 00046 the tribunal held that this sub-rule requires the relationship to have more than formal legal validity, but did not explore any further what it does mean, other than to say that it is an examination of the present state of the relationship rather than looking backwards or looking forwards in time, and that the past conduct of the parties can provide an indication of future intention.

If an ECO believes that the marriage is a sham marriage entered into for the sole purpose of gaining entry to the UK and that the spouses actually have no intention of living permanently with each other, then these two sub-rules will form the basis of refusal. However, they are not equivalent to the old 'primary purpose' rule, which used to require applicants to demonstrate that the application was not being made for the primary purpose of gaining entry to the UK, irrespective of whether the couple actually did intend to live together afterwards.

---

[4] See article on Free Movement blog http://www.freemovement.org.uk/
[5] Rule 6 of the Immigration Rules

The guidance (<u>in the IDIs</u>) on assessing whether a relationship is genuine and subsisting or not sets out factors which may be associated with each possibility. Where factors in a case might indicate a relationship may not be, it will be a good idea for the applicant's and partner's statements to show how, despite the adverse factor(s), the relationship is indeed genuine and subsisting.

The couple must have met at the time of the application. This allows for arranged marriages, where the couple do not meet until the day of the wedding, but it may exclude some marriages that would be legal in the country in which they take place, such as marriages in absentia, by telephone or by proxy, unless the couple have met by the time of the application.

Under the immigration rules the spouse in a polygamous marriage is not permitted to enter or remain in the UK on the basis of the marriage if there is another person living who is the spouse of the sponsor and who at any time since their marriage has been in the UK or has been granted a certificate of entitlement (see rule 278). This does not mean that polygamous marriages are not recognised or lawful in the UK, but rather that only one wife (or husband?) from such a marriage may enter the UK.

Prohibited degree of relationship is defined in rule 6 as having the same meaning as in the Marriage Act 1949, the Marriage (Prohibited Degrees of Relationship) Act 1986 and the Civil Partnership Act 2004.

The minimum age for both the person seeking a visa and the UK-based sponsor is now 18 (at the date of application). An earlier rule change raising the age to 21 was found to be unlawful by the Supreme Court in Quila & Anor, R (on the application of) v Secretary of State for the Home Department [2011] UKSC 45.

The justification put forward by the Home Office at the time of the change was that it would help to prevent forced marriages. The Supreme Court found that the rule change was not a lawful way of deterring or preventing forced marriages. The actual effect, at least in some cases, was to force the young British spouse to live abroad until aged 21, away from home, friends and family.

There are no specified evidence requirements in the partner rules for proving that the relationship requirements are met. So it is a matter of collecting the best available evidence that the relationship is legally valid, genuine and subsisting. Interviews and home visits by the UKVI are not unusual, and nor indeed are immigration officials turning up as unwanted guests at marriages in the UK and whisking one party into detention. Investigating potentially sham marriages is a priority for the UKVI.

The reported decisions of the Upper Tribunal in *Goudey (subsisting marriage – evidence) Sudan* [2012] UKUT 00041(IAC) and *Naz (subsisting marriage – standard of proof) Pakistan* [2012] UKUT 00040(IAC) are useful when considering how best to prove a relationship is genuine and subsisting.

Applicants and their partners should submit original;

- evidence of registered relationships (e.g. birth, divorce and marriage certificates), with translations where necessary
- statements from both parties giving some history to the relationship and intentions for the future
- evidence of cohabitation
- photos and other evidence of any ceremony, and time spent together (but not DVDs or video cassettes)
- phone records – with itemised billing where possible, but phone cards if that is all there is (see *Goudey* above)
- other evidence of contact (e.g. emails, social media, cards, plane tickets)

Whilst there is no longer a requirement to seek permission from the Home Office to get married in the UK, registrars already have powers to notify the Home Office of suspicious marriages. The provisions of the Immigration Act 2014, operational in April 2015, will extend the length of time needed to give notice of marriage from 15 to 28 days, and will require registrars to notify the Home Office of all marriages involving a non-EEA party who is not settled in the UK. The immigration authorities will then have the power to delay marriages for up to 70 days whilst they investigate the immigration status of the parties, the genuineness of the marriage, and to take enforcement action where appropriate[6].

English language requirement

As under the old rules, applicants in the partner category have to submit with their application proof that they meet the English language requirement. The precise evidence that must be submitted is specified in Appendix FM-SE (at paragraphs 27 to 32).

The English language requirement can be met in four ways;

- by being a national of a specified majority English speaking country listed in GEN.1.6.
- by having passed an approved English language speaking and listening test at minimum level A1 of the Common European Framework of Reference for Languages (CEFR) with a provider approved by the Secretary of State (as specified in Appendix O)
- by having obtained an academic (not vocational or professional) qualification at degree level or above taught in English
- by exemption

  Exempt from the requirement are:
- those aged 65 or over at the date of application; and

---

[6] Read more on the new provisions relating to marriages in Immigration Bill Factsheet 12

> those who have a physical or mental condition that would prevent them from meeting the requirement; and
> where there are exceptional compassionate circumstances that would prevent the applicant from meeting the requirement.

The concession relating to long term residents of countries where there is no approved test centre in that country was withdrawn on 24 July 2014 for applications made on or after that date (or for some countries on or after 14 August 2014). Where an applicant is unable to travel to another country to take the test, they will now have to provide reasons why it is not practicable or reasonable, which will normally require more than inconvenience or reluctance (see Guidance at Annex FM 1.21 in the IDIs).

Lots of applicants find it hard to meet the English language requirement. They may be poorly educated or very unconfident at their ability to learn a new language, but finding it difficult or even very difficult to learn some basic English is not grounds for an exemption.

From 6 November 2014, new provisions at paragraphs 32A-32D of Appendix FM-SE deal with the aftermath of the recent scandal, when some approved test providers were found to be selling test certificates to thousands of migrants who, it is alleged, did not actually sit the test. Applicants previously relying on dodgy certificates can be required to provide new test certificates.

Financial requirement

For applications made under the transitional provisions (i.e. under the old rules), the applicant will need to show adequate maintenance and accommodation without recourse to public funds (as defined in rule 6). Applicants under Appendix FM will need to meet the very onerous income threshold (in addition to having adequate accommodation) unless the partner is in receipt of specified disability- related benefits.

For applications for entry clearance under the Partner category;

E-ECP.3.1. The applicant must provide specified evidence, from the sources listed in paragraph E-ECP.3.2., of-

(a) a specified gross annual income of at least-

(i) £18,600;
(ii) an additional £3,800 for the first child; and
(iii) an additional £2,400 for each additional child; alone or in combination with

(b) specified savings of-

(i) £16,000; and
(ii) additional savings of an amount equivalent to 2.5 times the amount which is the difference between the gross annual income from the sources listed in paragraph E-ECP.3.2.(a)-(d) and the total amount required under paragraph E-ECP.3.1.(a); or

(c) the requirements in paragraph E-ECP.3.3.being met.

In this paragraph "child" means a dependent child of the applicant who is-

(a) under the age of 18 years, or who was under the age of 18 years when they were first granted entry under this route;

(b) applying for entry clearance as a dependant of the applicant, or has limited leave to enter or remain in the UK;

(c) not a British Citizen or settled in the UK; and

(d) not an EEA national with a right to be admitted under the Immigration (EEA) Regulations 2006.

E-ECP.3.2. When determining whether the financial requirement in paragraph EECP.
3.1. is met only the following sources will be taken into account-

(a) income of the partner from specified employment or self-employment, which, in respect of a partner returning to the UK with the applicant, can include specified employment or self-employment overseas and in the UK;

(b) specified pension income of the applicant and partner;

(c) any specified maternity allowance or bereavement benefit received by the partner in the UK or any specified payment relating to service in HM Forces received by the
applicant or partner;

(d) other specified income of the applicant and partner; and

(e) specified savings of the applicant and partner.

E-ECP.3.3. The requirements to be met under this paragraph are-

(a) the applicant's partner must be receiving one or more of the following -

(i) disability living allowance;
(ii) severe disablement allowance;
(iii) industrial injury disablement benefit;
(iv) attendance allowance;
(v) carer's allowance;
(vi) personal independence payment;
(ii) Armed Forces Independence Payment or Guaranteed Income Payment under the Armed Forces Compensation Scheme; or
(viii) Constant Attendance Allowance, Mobility Supplement or War Disablement Pension under the War Pensions Scheme; and

(b) the applicant must provide evidence that their partner is able to maintain and accommodate themselves, the applicant and any dependants adequately in the UK without recourse to public funds.

E-ECP.3.4. The applicant must provide evidence that there will be adequate accommodation, without recourse to public funds, for the family, including other

> family members who are not included in the application but who live in the same household, which the family own or occupy exclusively: accommodation will not be regarded as adequate if-
>
> (a) it is, or will be, overcrowded; or
> (b) it contravenes public health regulations.

References to 'specified' refer to the mandatory provisions and requirements laid out in Appendix FM-SE. It is essential to consider the financial requirements in Appendix FM alongside the very complex additional requirements in Appendix FM-SE.

Detailed guidance on the financial requirements is in the IDIs at Annex FM 1.7. Where the partner is in receipt of one of the benefits listed in E-ECP.3.3, the guidance is in Annex FM 1.7a.

Points to note:

➢ a specified gross annual income of £18,600 is required (unless relying on E-ECP.3.3.)

➢ plus an additional amount for each child

The definition of 'child' excludes children who are settled, British citizens, or who have a right to admission under the EEA Regulations, but includes those already in the U.K. with limited leave. Note that where a British partner has children living abroad, they will often be British citizens, and there will therefore be no increased income threshold in such cases.

➢ For entry clearance applications, it is only the sponsor's income from employment which is relevant (i.e. the applicant's current income or income from future employment is ignored). Where application is made in-country, the applicant's income from lawful employment and self-employment can count toward meeting the income threshold.

➢ Where the income of the partner, or where relevant the partner and applicant, is below the minimum threshold, savings may make up the shortfall. A complicated formula must be applied to savings. The first £16000 of savings are disregarded. The balance must then be divided by 2.5, and the resulting figure can then be treated as income.

An easier approach will be to take the shortfall (i.e. the minimum income level that applies less the actual income), multiply that figure by 2.5 and add £16,000 to give the level of savings that will make up the shortfall.

➢ Where the sponsor is on benefits as listed in E-ECP.3.3, the income threshold does not apply. The financial requirement will be met by 'adequate maintenance and accommodation' as defined in paragraph 6 of the rules.

Appendix FM-SE

Appendix FM-SE contains many substantive and complex requirements in addition to those in Appendix FM. These apply largely, but not wholly, in respect of the financial requirements. These include (but are not limited to):

➢ As with the PBS, the decision-maker will only consider documents that have been submitted with the application unless they have contacted the applicant under the evidential flexibility rule at paragraph D(b).

➢ Where a specified document is missing or in the wrong format or does not contain all the specified information, the decision maker should contact the applicant and give them a few days to provide the correct document unless the application also falls to be refused on other grounds.

➢ For those relying on income from salaried employment, they will be able to use their gross annual salary at its current level from their current employment only where they have been employed with the same employer for a minimum of 6 months, and only where they have been paid at that level for that 6 month period (i.e. the level of gross annual salary will be taken as being the lowest income of that 6 month period). If this provision is not met, the sponsor will need to rely on their actual earnings over the previous 12 months.

➢ Where the British citizen is living outside the UK with their partner, they will both need to meet the financial requirement in respect of income earned abroad, and have a source of income available to them when they return to the UK (see e.g. paragraph 4).

➢ Under Appendix FM-SE, an application cannot rely on third party support, other than for maintenance payments, income from a dependent child of age 18 or over who remains part of the household, gifts of cash savings held for at least 6 months, and a maintenance grant for studies (paragraph 1(b)).

➢ Appendix FM-SE requires a great deal of specified evidence to be provided of the partners and applicants income, in its various forms, and savings. As an example, for those relying on income from salaried employment, they must provide wage-slips, bank statements and a letter from the employer (answering 5 specified questions) for the 6 month or 12 month period. Additionally, the Home Office reserves the right to request P60s and a contract of employment. For those relying wholly or partly on self-employed or other forms of income, completely different but even more onerous requirements apply.

➢ Detailed provisions as to the form that documents must take are laid out in paragraph 1. An application can be refused, for example, if the employer's letter is not on company-headed paper and signed by a senior manager.

> The specified documents evidencing income and savings are provided for in paragraphs 2 to 11. Where the sponsor is relying on certain benefits under E-ECP3.3, only paragraphs 12 and 12A apply.

> On the basis of the specified evidence provided under paragraphs 2 to 11, the income will then be calculated in accordance with paragraphs 13-20A. Paragraph 21 removes benefit and tax credit payments and any other source of income not specified elsewhere from the gross annual income calculation.

Even where the applicant meet the financial requirements, many will find it very difficult to provide all the specified evidence. Unless, paragraph D(e) applies, their application stands to be refused if they do not.

In addition to the financial requirements, Appendix FM-SE specifies the evidence required to prove the marriage or civil partnership, that the English Language requirement is met, and for all the key requirements of the adult dependent relative category.

The income threshold and Article 8

Almost exactly a year after the new rules were introduced, Mr Justice Blake, sitting in the High Court in the case of MM & Ors v Secretary of State for the Home Department [2013] EWHC 1900 (Admin), found that in cases where the partner of the applicant is a refugee or a British citizen (i.e. where it would be unreasonable to expect them to live elsewhere), the £18,600 minimum income requirement was 'unjustified and disproportionate'.

The absence of any flexibility in the scheme, and several aggravating features, contributed heavily to the court's conclusion that the requirement may breach the partners' right to respect for family life under Article 8. The aggravating features included:

> The setting of the minimum income level at above £13,400, i.e. that which would be earned by those on a minimum wage and working a 40 hour week. The claimants in the case had shown that of the 422 occupations listed in the 2011 UK Earnings Index, only 301 were above the £18,600 threshold. The government themselves accepted that some 45% of the UK working population earn less than the minimum income requirement.

> The disregard of the first £16,000 of savings.

> The disregard of even credible and reliable evidence of undertakings of third party support (e.g. where effected by deed and supported by evidence of ability to fund).

> The disregard of the migrant partner's own earning capacity during the thirty month period of initial entry.

On 26 July 2013, the Home Office lodged an appeal to the Court of Appeal against the High Court's decision in MM. At the same time, they put on hold decisions in respect of applications which would have been refused for failing to meet minimum income threshold, including the specified evidence requirements in Appendix FM-SE.

The Court of Appeal's judgement in MM & Ors, R (On the Application Of) v SSHD [2014] EWCA Civ 985 was issued on 11 July 2014. It was disappointing for all those couples (some 4000 or more) whose applications had been put on hold, overturning the High Court's decision, and finding that the rule itself was not incompatible with Article 8 or irrational. The Court did not though rule out the possibility of an Article 8 claim succeeding outside the rules, merely finding that the rule itself did not amount to a disproportionate interference with family life.

At paragraph 161 the court stated;

> If, as is suggested in the evidence of the respondents, decision makers have not been applying their minds to whether a "proportionality" test has to be used when considering "Exceptional circumstances" [i.e. applications outside the rules] in individual cases, then that is not a basis on which to challenge the lawfulness of the [minimum income rules] themselves. Such an approach may be a ground for challenging an individual decision; but that is not the object of the present litigation.

Those refused a visa for failing to meet the financial requirements in appendices FM and FM-SE will have a right of appeal to the First-tier Tribunal (Immigration and Asylum Chamber). The right of appeal will remain when Part 2 of the Immigration Act 2014 comes into force as a partner application should automatically be treated as a human rights claim. If the judge decides that the rules are not met, they will then need to consider whether the application of the financial requirement in the particular circumstances of the case amounts to a breach of Article 8.

For extension applications, applicants can rely on EX.1 (see below) where the financial requirements are not met. Any appeal will focus then on whether it is reasonable for the couple to live elsewhere. Whilst EX.1 is not available to applicants for entry clearance, it is likely the appeal against refusal of entry clearance will have the same focus.

Immigration status

The immigration status requirements for applying for leave to remain (i.e. from within the UK) as a partner are at:

> E-LTRP.2.1. The applicant must not be in the UK-
>
> (a) as a visitor;
>
> (b) with valid leave granted for a period of 6 months or less, unless that leave is as a fiancé(e) or proposed civil partner, or was granted pending the outcome of family court or divorce proceedings
>
> E-LTRP.2.2. The applicant must not be in the UK-

(a) on temporary admission or temporary release, unless paragraph EX.1. applies; or

(b) in breach of immigration laws (disregarding any period of overstaying for a period of 28 days or less), unless paragraph EX.1. applies.

This is more generous than the old Part 8 provision which required current leave within the rules in order to switch from another category. It allows switching for those who have overstayed up to 28 days, and for those who are in the U.K. outside the Immigration Rules, e.g. with a right to reside under EEA law, or with discretionary leave.

It is odd indeed that a visitor or person granted leave for 6 months or less cannot apply within the rules by relying on EX.1, but an illegal entrant or overstayer can. Advisers will have to use their judgement as to whether a visitor or other person with leave should overstay before making the application, but such a suggestion would be equally odd (and possibly unlawful given that it would require an adviser to advise a person to breach the law - both a professional conduct issue and a criminal offence).

Section EX: Exceptions to certain eligibility requirements for leave to remain as a partner or parent

EX.1. This paragraph applies if

(a) (i) the applicant has a genuine and subsisting parental relationship with a child who-

(aa) is under the age of 18 years, or was under the age of 18 years when the applicant was first granted leave on the basis that this paragraph applied;

(bb) is in the UK;

(cc) is a British Citizen or has lived in the UK continuously for at least the 7 years immediately preceding the date of application; and

(ii) it would not be reasonable to expect the child to leave the UK; or

the applicant has a genuine and subsisting relationship with a partner who is in the UK and is a British Citizen, settled in the UK or in the UK with refugee leave or humanitarian protection, and there are insurmountable obstacles to family life with that partner continuing outside the UK.

EX.2. For the purposes of paragraph EX.1.(b) "insurmountable obstacles" means the very significant difficulties which would be faced by the applicant or their partner in continuing their family life together outside the UK and which could not be overcome or would entail very serious hardship for the applicant or their partner.

Where paragraph EX1 applies, an application for leave to remain under the Appendix FM 'partner' or 'parent' categories will only have to meet the 'suitability', 'relationship' and part of the 'immigration status' requirements. (see e.g. paragraph R-LTRP.1.(d)). The financial, English language and immigration status requirements will not apply.

Note that EX1 does not apply to entry clearance applications.

The criteria outlined in EX1 were particularly designed to reflect the government's view as to the proper application of their duties under Article 8 and s55. Migrants can rely on EX1 where they are in the UK irregularly as illegal entrants or overstayers, or cannot meet the financial or English language requirements. Before the coming into force of Appendix FM, applications made in these circumstances would have been made outside the rules, and a successful applicant would have been granted 3 years discretionary leave on a six-year route to settlement. Now they will be granted 30 months within the rules, but on a ten-year route to settlement.

EX1 applies to two situations;

➢ where the couple cannot reasonably be expected to live in another country, and/or

➢ where the couple (or under the 'parent' category, a separated parent) has responsibility for a child who is entitled to remain in the UK.

In the latter case, there is also an overlap between EX1 and the circumstances that would give rise to an EEA derived right of residence under the principles in Ruiz Zambrano (see Regulation 15A(4A) of the Immigration (EEA) Regulations 2006 (as amended)), and a parent could potentially succeed in both an application under the rules, and for a derivative residence card. Both options have their pros and cons.

Reasonable to expect the child to leave the UK

We looked at this issue in the section on private life in regard to the provision in rule 276ADE(1)(iv). The same principles apply here, albeit the subject matter of the application will be a partner's right to stay rather than the child's. In paragraph 117B(6) of the 2002 Act, it helpfully states that in respect of parents that;

> (6) In the case of a person who is not liable to deportation, the public interest does not require the person's removal where—
> (a)   the person has a genuine and subsisting parental relationship with a qualifying child, and
> (b)   it would not be reasonable to expect the child to leave the United Kingdom.

A qualifying child under the Act is defined in exactly the same way as under EX.1. If it can be established that the child cannot reasonably be expected to leave the UK, as under paragraph 276ADE(1)(iv), the parent who is also a partner will succeed in his or her application.

Where the child is a British citizen, there will be a strong case both under the principles in ZH (Tanzania) and Ruiz Zambrano that it is unreasonable to expect the child to leave the UK. The case will be more difficult where the child is not British, but has lived in the UK for seven or more years.

For more on this, see the sections on rule 276ADE(1) and on 'relocating the family' in the section on Article 8.

Insurmountable obstacles

The 'insurmountable obstacles' test that appears in the rules at EX.1. (and appeared in the Part 13 of the rules relating to deportation and Article 8 until recently) originates in some very early domestic case law on Article 8 (see e.g. *Mahmood, R(On Application of)* v SSHD [2000] EWCA Civ 315. It was decisively laid to rest as an appropriate legal test in the authoritative judgement in *VW (Uganda)* v *SSHD* [2009] EWCA Civ 5. In paragraph 24 of VW(Uganda), Sedley LJ stated;

> EB (Kosovo) now confirms that the material question in gauging the proportionality of a removal or deportation which will or may break up a family unless the family itself decamps is not whether there is an insuperable obstacle to this happening but whether it is reasonable to expect the family to leave with the appellant. It is to be hoped that reliance on what was a misreading of Mahmood, as this court had already explained in LM (DRC) [2008] EWCA Civ 325 (and as Collins J had previously done in Bakir [2002] UKIAT 01176, § 9), will now cease.

The 'reasonable test' sets a much lower threshold than 'insurmountable obstacles'. As Lord Justice Sedley pointed out in *LM (DRC) v Home Secretary* there are very few obstacles that one literally cannot surmount, which would be far too high a test in this context.

The insertion of the 'insurmountable obstacles' into the rules, many years after it had been laid to rest by the higher courts, was driven by the Secretary of State's policy of narrowing the circumstances in which Article 8 could be used to thwart removal.

The 'insurmountable test' now exists in the rules and its application is not dependent upon an Article 8 proportionality assessment being carried out. However, if the rules are not met, the proportionality test will have to be undertaken and, as confirmed by the Court of Appeal in *MF (Nigeria) v Secretary of State for the Home Department* [2013] EWCA Civ 1192 [49],

> We would observe that, if "insurmountable" obstacles are literally obstacles which it is impossible to surmount, their scope is very limited indeed. We shall confine ourselves to saying that we incline to the view that, for the reasons stated in detail by the UT in Izuazu at paras 53 to 59, such a stringent approach would be contrary to article 8.

Perhaps with this in mind, EX.1 was amended from 28 July 2014. Insurmountable obstacles is now defined in the rules as meaning;

'very significant difficulties which would be faced by the applicant or their partner in continuing their family life together outside the UK and which could not be overcome or would entail very serious hardship for the applicant or their partner'.

This exact formulation of the test has not been considered in the courts yet. It is an attempt to blur the differences between the rules and the principles that must be applied to a proportionality assessment made outside the rules.

Examples

Duncan is a failed asylum seeker from Colombia, but has been living in the U.K. with a Colombian man with refugee status for two years in a genuine and subsisting relationship akin to marriage. His partner has a current well-founded fear of persecution in Colombia so there are insurmountable obstacles to the couple returning there to live, and Duncan can therefore rely on EX.1. He can apply for leave to remain as a partner, with no other requirements to meet but for the suitability requirements. He will be granted 30 months leave as a partner on a ten-year route to settlement.

Mabel came to the U.K. as a visitor from Kazakhstan. Whilst here, she has a relationship with a British guy and falls pregnant. The couple marry. She overstays and has her baby. She can rely on EX1 to overcome the fact that she has overstayed. She can argue that it is both unreasonable to expect her British citizen baby to leave the UK, and that there are therefore insurmountable obstacles to the family living in Kazakhstan. If she is no longer in a relationship with the baby's father, she can do the same by making her arguments under the parent category.

Decision

Spouses, civil partners and unmarried partners will be granted (see Section D-LTRP);

➢ 33 months leave to enter or
➢ 30 months leave remain
   o on a 60 month route to settlement or
   o on a 120 month route if relying on EX1

Fiancés and proposed civil partners will be granted 6 months leave to enter.

In all cases, including those of a fiancé or proposed civil partner granted 6 months leave to enter who has now registered their relationship, further leave to remain will usually be granted for 30 months at a time until the migrant becomes entitled to ILR.

Where the applicant has extant leave at the date of decision, the remaining period of that extant leave up to a maximum of 28 days will be added to the period of limited leave to remain granted under that paragraph (which may therefore exceed 30 months).

A person granted 30 months leave on the 120 month route will, if they meet all the requirements of the rules for their next extension application (i.e. they no longer have to rely on EX1), be able to switch into the 60 month route at that point, but any time spent on the 120 month route will not count towards the 60 month requirement. This will reduce their route to settlement from 120 months to 90 months.

There is a prohibition on employment, and no recourse to public funds for fiancés and proposed civil partners. For those granted 33 or 30 months leave there will be no recourse to public funds on the 60 month route, and on the 120 month route unless the Secretary of State considers that the person should not be subject to such a condition' (see D-LTRP.1.2.). The exceptional circumstances in which the UKVI will not prohibit recourse to public funds, or remove the prohibition on request, are in section 12 of Appendix FM1.0b of Chapter 8 of the IDIs. (For more on seeking removal of the prohibition, see the section Private life: Decision above)

Under the old rules, a spouse, civil partner or unmarried partner would have been granted 27 months leave to enter, or 24 months leave to remain, with no recourse to public funds. Those still in the UK with limited leave under the old rules, can apply for ILR after 24 months in the U.K.

Indefinite leave to remain

Whether applying for ILR under the partner category in Appendix FM or under the old rules, substantially the same relationship and financial requirements apply as for leave to enter and remain.

The couple will need to show their relationship is subsisting and that they continue to intend to live together permanently in the UK. The financial requirement under Appendix FM is slightly different though in that it does not require the applicant to divide their saving by 2.5. All savings over £16000 can be used to meet the income threshold where it partners cannot meet it form their income alone.

Under the 24 month route, the partner must not fall foul of the general grounds of refusal (particularly 322(1C) relating to criminality). For those applying under Appendix FM, essentially the same grounds apply but are instead found in the 'suitability' provisions (S-ILR).

Applicants for settlement under the age of 65 must meet the knowledge of English language and life in the U.K. (KOLL) requirements under Appendix KOLL unless exceptions apply: see section on Settlement (above).

Where the KOLL requirements are not yet met, or the application for ILR must be delayed due to the criminality provisions, the applicant will be able to apply for further limited leave.

Marriages that have ended during the probationary period

Normally, if a marriage or partnership has ended during the probationary period, the foreign national is expected to leave the UK unless they can qualify under another category (e.g. as the parent of a child in the U.K). However, in the following two circumstances partners will be able to apply for ILR notwithstanding the end of the relationship. These provisions are essentially the same under the old and new rules.

They apply only to partners of British citizens and those with ILR (see T, R (on the application of) v SSHD [2014] EWHC 2453 (Admin).

Bereaved spouses or partners

Bereaved partners will be entitled to apply for indefinite leave to remain if the partner they joined in the U.K. died during the 24, 60 or 120 month probationary period if the relationship was extant at the time of the bereavement. Applications will subject to the suitability provisions, but not the KOLL requirement.

Victims of domestic violence

Victims of domestic violence may be granted indefinite leave to remain where the marriage or relationship breaks down permanently during the probationary period as a result of domestic violence (under paragraph 289A and section DVILR1.1).

This provision applies only to those granted limited leave as a spouse, civil partner or unmarried partner of a British citizen or a person settled in the U.K. It does not apply where the migrant's partner is a refugee or has humanitarian protection.

There is no requirement to have current leave. No fee is payable where the applicant can show they are destitute. The suitability provisions apply, but not the KOLL requirements.

Domestic violence can be physical, emotional, sexual or financial abuse. It can come from a person other than the partner (e.g. from their family members). As stated in the Modernised Guidance;

> From 31 March 2013 a new cross government definition of domestic violence was implemented.

136

The definition of domestic violence and abuse is any incident or pattern of incidents controlling, coercive or threatening behaviour, violence or abuse between those aged 16 or over who are or have been intimate partners or family members regardless of gender or sexuality. This can include, but is not limited to, the following types of abuse:

o psychological
o physical
o sexual
o financial
o emotional.

Controlling behaviour is a range of acts designed to make a person subordinate and/or dependent by:

o isolating them from sources of support
o exploiting their resources and capacities for personal gain
o depriving them of the means needed for independence
o resistance and escape, and
o regulating their everyday behaviour.

Coercive behaviour is:

o an act or a pattern of acts of assault, threats, humiliation and intimidation, or
o other abuse that is used to harm, punish, or frighten their victim.

It will always be necessary to show that the relationship has broken down as a result of the domestic violence. Domestic violence is widely defined and an adviser needs to be sensitive to certain behaviour even if the client does not recognise it to be domestic violence. Signs of domestic violence include (see: http://www.southallblacksisters.org.uk/domestic-violence/);

Forced marriage: family members, including extended family members, who use physical violence or emotional pressure to make you to marry someone, without your free and full consent;

Threats regarding 'honour': immediate and extended family members, partners and ex-partners justifying a range of abusive and violent behaviour (listed below) in the name of 'honour'. For example, using violence to prevent you from bringing dishonour or shame upon yourself or them.

Destructive criticism and verbal abuse:
shouting/mocking/humiliating/accusing/name calling/verbally threatening;

Pressure tactics: sulking; threatening to withhold money, disconnect the telephone, take the car away, commit suicide, take the children away, report you to welfare agencies unless you comply with his demands regarding bringing up the children; lying to your friends and family about you; telling you that you have no choice in any decisions, demanding more dowry;

Disrespect and humiliation: persistently putting you down in front of other people; not listening or responding when you talk; interrupting your telephone calls; taking money from your purse without asking; refusing to help with childcare or housework;

Breaking trust: lying to you; withholding information from you; being jealous; having other relationships; breaking promises and shared agreements;

Isolation: monitoring or blocking your telephone calls; telling you where you can and cannot go; preventing you from contacting friends and relatives; accompanying you wherever you go.

Harassment: following you; checking up on you; opening your mail; repeatedly checking to see who has telephoned you; embarrassing you in public;

Threats: making angry gestures; using physical size to intimidate; shouting you down; destroying your possessions; breaking things; punching walls; wielding a knife or a gun;

Sexual violence: using force, threats or intimidation to make you perform sexual acts; having sex with you when you don't want to have sex; any degrading treatment based on your sexual orientation;

Physical violence: punching; slapping; hitting; biting; pinching; kicking; pulling hair out; pushing; shoving; burning; strangling; raping;

Denial: saying the abuse doesn't happen; saying you caused the abusive behaviour; being publicly gentle and patient; crying and begging for forgiveness; saying it will never happen again;

Suicide: acting in ways which make you feel suicidal or encouraging you to contemplate or commit suicide.

The Home Office specifies in the Modernised Guidance certain types of evidence that they expect to be submitted. This list is less prescriptive than it used to be and does tell caseworkers that other evidence may be considered, but in practice anything that is not considered to be 'impartial and objective' risks rejection. It might be thought that an expectation of evidence that is 'impartial and objective' in relation to violence that is by its nature private and experienced only by the victim is unreasonable and impossible. On appeal the immigration tribunal can consider any relevant evidence including personal testimony (see Ishtiaq v SSHD [2007] EWCA Civ 386).

The Home Office evidence preferences are for one of the following forms of evidence:

➢ an injunction, non-molestation order or other protection order made against the sponsor (other than an ex-parte or interim order); or

➢ a relevant court conviction against the sponsor; or

➢ full details of a relevant police caution issued against the sponsor.

As an alternative, the guidance state that more than one of the following forms of evidence will usually be accepted as proving the case adequately:

➢ a medical report from a hospital doctor confirming that the applicant has injuries consistent with being a victim of domestic violence; OR, a letter from a GMC registered family practitioner who has examined the applicant and is satisfied that the applicant has injuries consistent with being a victim of domestic violence;

➢ an undertaking given to a court that the perpetrator of the violence will not approach the applicant who is the victim of the violence;

➤ a police report confirming attendance at the home of the applicant as a result of a domestic violence incident;

➤ a letter from a social services department confirming its involvement in connection with domestic violence;

➤ a letter of support or a report from a domestic violence support organisation.

Where such evidence is not available the more relaxed approach to evidence laid down in Ishtiaq is very helpful. Nevertheless, every attempt should be made to obtain evidence as outlined in the Home Office guidance.

Top tip

The domestic violence rule does not require the applicant to possess leave at the time of application. However, the relationship must have been caused permanently to break down during the two year probationary period, which can be a problem where there has not been a clean separation between the couple. Helpfully, **LA (para 289A: causes of breakdown) Pakistan** [2009] UKAIT 00019 reminds judges that they *'must be careful to assess the evidence in the round, looking at the totality of the evidence and remembering that a broken marriage may have ended before the parties separate and the marriage may have broken down as a result of domestic violence even if other grounds are given in matrimonial proceedings or raised before the Tribunal'.*

Destitution domestic violence (DDV) concession

A concession was introduced on 1 April 2012, allowing prospective applicants under the domestic violence rule, who are destitute, to apply for three months of discretionary leave to allow them to claim benefits and secure temporary accommodation whilst they make and await a decision on the domestic violence application. Details of the concession and an application form are at: https://www.gov.uk/government/publications/application-for-benefits-for-visa-holder-domestic-violence. A person granted DDV leave will not have to pay a fee when applying for ILR under the rules.

Getting married in the UK

There is no requirement for migrants planning to marry in the UK to seek the permission of the Home Office to do so. The Certificate of Approval scheme, introduced under the Asylum and Immigration (Treatment of Claimants etc) Act 2004, and designed to introduce such a requirement, was abolished on 9 May 2011. The scheme was held to be unlawful by the House of Lords in 2008 in the case of Baiai [2009] 1 AC 287. After several modifications it was finally abandoned.

One part of the original scheme does remain, which is the requirement to give notice to marry or register the civil partnership at a 'designated office'. All registration offices in Scotland and Northern Ireland are designated offices, as are 76 offices in England and Wales. Both parties will need proof of their name, age and nationality, but there is no prescribed way of evidencing these.

Registrars have a duty under s24 of the Immigration and Asylum Act 1999 to report to the Home Office any marriage that they have reasonable grounds for suspecting to be a sham marriage. Under s24(5);

> "Sham marriage" means a marriage (whether or not void) –
>
> (a) entered into between a person ("A") who is neither a British national nor a national of an EEA State other than the United Kingdom and another person (whether or not such a person or such a national): and
>
> (b) entered into by A for the purpose of avoiding the effect of one or more provisions of United Kingdom immigration law or the immigration rules.

Part 4 of the Immigration Act 2014 amends the definition of "sham marriage", and amends the procedure for marriage and civil partnership. It also creates new powers for duties to report sham marriages and for the investigation and preventing of them. Some of these provisions commence 14 July 2014.

The new definition of "sham marriage" will read;

> (5) A marriage (whether or not it is void) is a "sham marriage" if—
>
> (a) either, or both, of the parties to the marriage is not a relevant national,
> (b) there is no genuine relationship between the parties to the marriage, and
> (c) either, or both, of the parties to the marriage enter into the marriage for one or more of these purposes—
>
> (i) avoiding the effect of one or more provisions of United Kingdom immigration law or the immigration rules;
> (ii) enabling a party to the marriage to obtain a right conferred by that law or those rules to reside in the United Kingdom.
>
> (6) In subsection (5)—
>
> "relevant national" means—
>
> (a) a British citizen,
> (b) a national of an EEA State other than the United Kingdom, or
> (c) a national of Switzerland
>
> "United Kingdom immigration law" includes any subordinate legislation concerning the right of relevant nationals to move between and reside in member States."

The Home Office estimates that under the new provisions, 35,000 marriages per year will need to be referred to the Home Office for potential investigation and that 6,000 marriages will be investigated.

In future notice of all marriages in England and Wales must be given 28 days in advance of the marriage taking place, replacing the current notice period of 15 days.

Where one of the parties to the marriage is a non-EEA national marrying in the Church of England (or Church in Wales), the parties will need to undertake civil preliminaries and will no longer be able to use Banns instead.

The 28 day notice period can be reduced on application where there are compelling reasons to do so because of exceptional circumstances. The Registrar General can still authorise marriage in death bed cases without the notice period being complied with.

Where one of the parties is a non EEA national, both parties to a marriage will need to attend in person to give notice at a designated Registry Office and for notice to be taken specified evidence, including specified evidence of nationality, must be provided.

In addition to the s24 duties, where one of the parties is a non EEA national and might gain immigration advantage the notice of marriage will be referred to the Home Office.

If the Home Office decides not to investigate then the Home Office should inform the registrar and the marriage can proceed after the conclusion of the normal 28 day notice period. If the Home Office does decide to investigate further, then the notice period is extended to 70 days to allow time for investigation and for enforcement action to be taken.

The Home Office may prevent the marriage taking place where the parties fail to co-operate with the investigation.

Examples of risk factors which may identify the marriage as being at high risk of being a sham include[7]:

➢ Is of a nationality at high risk of involvement in a sham, on the basis of objective information and intelligence about sham cases.
➢ Holds a visa in a category linked by objective information and intelligence to sham cases.
➢ Has no immigration status or holds leave which is due to expire shortly.

---

[7] SHAM MARRIAGES AND CIVIL PARTNERSHIPS BACKGROUND INFORMATION AND PROPOSED REFERRAL AND INVESTIGATION SCHEME, Home Office November 2013

> ➤ Has had an application to remain in the UK refused.
> ➤ Has previously sponsored another spouse or partner to enter or remain in the UK.
> ➤ Is or has been the subject of a credible section 24/24A report, which explains for example how the couple could not communicate in a common language and did not know basic information about each other.

Parent of a child in the UK

The Appendix FM category, 'family life as a parent of a child in the UK' is, according to the guidance (section 5 of Annex FM 1.0a to chapter 8 of the IDIs),

> a route intended for a parent who has responsibility for or access to their child following the breakdown of their relationship with the child's other parent. The route is for single parent applicants who:
>
> ▪ have sole parental responsibility for their child; or
>
> ▪ do not live with the child (who lives with a British or settled parent or carer), but they have access rights to the child; or
>
> ▪ (for a leave to remain application) are the parent with whom the child normally lives, rather than the child's other parent who is British or settled.

This category replaced the 'exercising rights of access to a child resident in the United Kingdom' category (paragraphs 248-248F of the Immigration Rules) which was closed to new applicants from 9 July 2012. It is not easy to understand either conceptually or practically.

Relationship requirements

'A parent' is defined under paragraph 6 of the Immigration Rules;

> **"a parent"** includes
> (a) the stepfather of a child whose father is dead and the reference to stepfather includes a relationship arising through civil partnership;
> (b) the stepmother of a child whose mother is dead and the reference to stepmother includes a relationship arising through civil partnership and;
> (c) the father as well as the mother of an illegitimate child where he is proved to be the father;
> (d) an adoptive parent, where a child was adopted in accordance with a decision taken by the competent administrative authority or court in a country whose adoption orders are recognised by the United Kingdom or where a child is the subject of a de facto adoption in accordance with the requirements of paragraph 309A of these Rules (except that an adopted child or a child who is the subject of a de facto adoption may not make an application for leave to enter or remain in order to accompany, join or remain with an adoptive parent under paragraphs 297-303);
> (e) in the case of a child born in the United Kingdom who is not a British citizen, a person to whom there has been a genuine transfer of parental responsibility on the ground of the original parent(s)' inability to care for the child.

For applications for entry clearance as a parent, the relevant child must be under 18 at the date of application, a British citizen or settled in the U.K, and living in the U.K. (or if the child is British Citizen, one who is coming to the UK to live or have contact with the applicant).

For applications for leave to remain, where paragraph EX1 applies, the relevant child may be one who has lived in the UK continuously for at least the 7 years immediately preceding the date of application, and for whom it is not reasonable to expect them to leave the UK.

The parent must have sole parental responsibility, or access rights to the child and provide evidence that they are taking and intend to continue to take an active role in the child's upbringing.

Where the application is for access rights, the parent or carer with whom the child normally lives must be-

> (i) a British Citizen in the UK or settled in the UK;
> (ii) not the partner of the applicant; and
> (iii) the applicant must not be eligible to apply for entry clearance as a partner under this Appendix.

So an application from a parent who is the partner of the child's other parent will fall to be refused under this category as they will be expected to apply under the partner category. That will be the case even if they cannot meet the requirements of the partner category.

A parent applying for leave for access rights the child must be 'taking [in the present tense] an active role in the child's upbringing'. This requirement is designed to prevent a parent who has not previously taken an active role from applying under the rule in order to begin doing so. A parent who has yet to take an active role for whatever reason, even if it is because they are outside the U.K, but now genuinely wants to do so, will have to make an application outside the rules.

The concept of 'sole parental responsibility' is not defined in the rules. In the guidance it is used interchangeably with the term 'sole responsibility'. The guidance defines 'sole responsibility' thus;

> Sole responsibility means that one parent has abdicated or abandoned parental responsibility and the remaining parent is instead exercising sole control in setting and providing the day to day direction for the child's welfare.

'Parental responsibility' is a legal concept and a central part of the regime for parents as set out in the Children Act 1989. In normal circumstances both parents will have parental responsibility from the child's birth if both appear on the birth certificate. There is no suggestion though that that Act is a reference point for assessing the parental roles under the Immigration Rules.

To add to the confusion as to the various parental relationships referred to in the rules, we have the concept of 'a genuine and subsisting parental relationship with a child' which appears in EX1. It is not clear how this concept contrasts with 'sole responsibility', 'sole parental responsibility', 'parental responsibility' and 'taking an active role'.

It is also important to note that a parent who succeeds in establishing a right to reside under the CJEU judgement in Ruiz Zambrano (implemented at regulation 15A(4A) of the Immigration (EEA) Regulations 2006) will also usually be entitled to a grant of leave under the parent category. The guidance at Appendix FM Section 1.0b of the IDIs states that a parent application that falls to be refused under the criminality provisions in Appendix FM should then be passed to the European Casework section if the circumstances give rise to a right to reside for the parent.

Other requirements

The 'suitability' requirements always need to be met. Unless Section EX: Exception applies, the same immigration status and English language requirements apply as for the Partner category. The financial requirement is for the applicant to adequately maintain and accommodate themselves and any dependants in the UK without recourse to public funds (and not the far higher minimum income requirement in the Partner and Child categories of Appendix FM.

Grants of leave

As with the Partner category, successful applicants will be granted 33 months on entry clearance or 30 months leave to remain, to begin a 60 month route to settlement, or 120 months where EX1 has been applied at any stage. There will be a condition prohibiting recourse to public funds unless they can show they are destitute.

A parent may though fail to complete the route if the relevant child ages out before settlement has been granted. The Statement of Intent states in this regard that:

> On the 10 year family route, the limited leave period of 30 months will not be shortened if a child in whose best interests the migrant is to remain in the UK will turn 18 before that leave period expires. But, to continue on or complete the route, the migrant parent or carer will have to satisfy the UK Border Agency at the next application stage that, where the child has turned 18, there continues to be a reason why it would breach Article 8 for the migrant parent/carer to be removed from the UK.

For extensions beyond their youngest child's 18th birthday, they will need to show the child remains dependent on them. This presents a daunting prospect for any parent who is first granted leave under this rule when their child is over 8 years old.

144

Children of partners and parents

This Appendix FM category is for a child whose parent has or is being granted limited leave as a partner or parent under Appendix FM. Children applying together with their parent can be added to the parent's application.

Children whose parent or parents are settled or applying for settlement in the U.K. will apply under the rules in Part 8.

As with other provisions for children in the Immigration Rules, the child must be under 18 at the date of their first application in this category, but not when making subsequent applications. This means that a child who ages out before they are entitled to a further extension of leave or settlement will still be treated as if they are under 18 when the subsequent application is considered. For all children though, regardless of age, whether on initial application or at any stage before they are settled, they must not be married or in a civil partnership, must not have formed an independent family unit and must not be leading an independent life (as defined in paragraph 6).

For entry clearance, the child must be coming to the UK with or to join a parent, who has limited leave as a partner or parent. Where that parent is not the partner of the child's other parent, the parent must have sole responsibility for the child, or there must be serious and compelling family or other considerations which make exclusion of the child undesirable. We consider the definitions of 'sole responsibility' and 'exclusion undesirable' below in the section on the children of settled parents.

For applications for leave to remain, there is no immigration status requirement, so the child can be here irregularly. The financial requirement is as for the Partner category, though it will be the parent's income and savings that is relevant. There will be no financial requirement to meet where the parent is on the 120 month route to settlement. Leave will be granted in line with the non-settled parent.

The child's application for ILR at the end of the parent's 5- or 10-year route will be made under rule 298 at the same time as the parent's application (see: Children of settled parents (below)).

Adult dependent relatives

This Appendix FM category, 'Adult dependent relative' (ADR), replaced the Part 8 (Rule 317) provisions for 'Other family members' for applications made on or after 9 July 2012. In very narrow circumstances, it provides the opportunity for an adult British citizen, settled person, refugee or person with humanitarian protection to sponsor a parent, grandparent, sibling or child over 18 to settle in the UK.

JCWI's report on the ADR category, 'Harsh, Unjust, Unnecessary', published in July 2014, states that;

It is almost impossible to succeed in this visa category. Fit and healthy parents and grandparents cannot even apply. The All-Party Parliamentary Group on Migration (APPG) has stated that this visa category has "in effect been closed".

The report also records that for the first year of its operation, only 34 settlement visas were issued under this route, many following appeal hearings.

Applications under this category can only be made from outside the U.K.

Guidance on this category is in the IDIs at chapter 8, Annex FM 6.0.

Relationship requirements

E-ECDR.2.1. The applicant must be the-

(a) parent aged 18 years or over;
(b) grandparent;
(c) brother or sister aged 18 years or over; or
(d) son or daughter aged 18 years or over

of a person ("the sponsor") who is in the UK.

E-ECDR.2.2. If the applicant is the sponsor's parent or grandparent they must not be in a subsisting relationship with a partner unless that partner is also the sponsor's parent or grandparent and is applying for entry clearance at the same time as the applicant.

E-ECDR.2.3. The sponsor must at the date of application be-

(a) aged 18 years or over; and
(b) (i) a British Citizen in the UK; or
    (ii) present and settled in the UK; or
    (iii) in the UK with refugee leave or humanitarian protection.

This is a considerably narrower set of relatives than was provided for in rule 317. Although there is no longer a requirement that the applicant is living alone, if they are not, it will be all the more difficult for them to meet the threshold requirement at E-ECDR.2.5.

Additionally, E-ECDR2.2 excludes parents and grandparents who are in a subsisting relationship with a person who is not also the sponsor's parent or grandparent, though it should be remembered that a parent can include a step-parent where the biological parent is dead (see paragraph 6 definition).

The 'threshold' requirement

E-ECDR.2.4. The applicant or, if the applicant and their partner are the sponsor's parents or grandparents, the applicant's partner, must as a result of age, illness or disability require long-term personal care to perform everyday tasks.

E-ECDR.2.5. The applicant or, if the applicant and their partner are the sponsor's parents or grandparents, the applicant's partner, must be unable, even with the practical and financial help of the sponsor, to obtain the required level of care in the country where they are living, because-

(a) it is not available and there is no person in that country who can reasonably provide it; or
(b) it is not affordable.

An indication of the difficulty of meeting this requirement is given in the examples provided in the guidance;

Example (e)

A person (aged 85) lives alone in Afghanistan. With the onset of age he has developed very poor eyesight, which means that he has had a series of falls, one of which resulted in a hip replacement. His only son lives in the UK and sends money to enable his father to pay for a carer to visit each day to help him wash and dress, and to cook meals for him. **This would not meet the criteria because the sponsor is able to arrange the required level of care in Afghanistan.**

Evidential requirements are specified in Appendix FM-SE as below;

Adult dependent relatives

33. Evidence of the family relationship between the applicant(s) and the sponsor should take the form of birth or adoption certificates, or other documentary evidence.

34. Evidence that, as a result of age, illness or disability, the applicant requires long-term personal care should take the form of:

(a) Independent medical evidence that the applicant's physical or mental condition means that they cannot perform everyday tasks; and
(b) This must be from a doctor or other health professional.

35. Independent evidence that the applicant is unable, even with the practical and financial help of the sponsor in the UK, to obtain the required level of care in the country where they are living should be from:

(a) a central or local health authority;
(b) a local authority; or
(c) a doctor or other health professional.

36. If the applicant's required care has previously been provided through a private arrangement, the applicant must provide details of that arrangement and why it is no longer available.

37. If the applicant's required level of care is not, or is no longer, affordable because payment previously made for arranging this care is no longer being made, the applicant must provide records of that payment and an explanation of why that payment cannot continue. If financial support has been provided by the sponsor or other close family in the UK, the applicant must provide an explanation of why this cannot continue or is no longer sufficient to enable the required level of care to be provided.

Additionally, the guidance states that;

> Under paragraphs 36-39 of the Immigration Rules, the ECO has the power to refer the applicant for medical examination and to require that this be undertaken by a doctor or other health professional on a list approved by the British Embassy or High Commission.

As to the care not being or no longer being affordable in the applicant's own country the guidance states;

> If payment was made for arranging this care, the ECO should ask to see records and an explanation of why this payment cannot continue. If financial support has been provided by the sponsor or other close family in the UK, the ECO should ask for an explanation of why this cannot continue or is no longer sufficient to enable the required level of care to be provided.

Financial requirement

> E-ECDR.3.1. The applicant must provide evidence that they can be adequately maintained, accommodated and cared for in the UK by the sponsor without recourse to public funds.
>
> E-ECDR.3.2. If the applicant's sponsor is a British Citizen or settled in the UK, the applicant must provide an undertaking signed by the sponsor confirming that the applicant will have no recourse to public funds, and that the sponsor will be responsible for their maintenance, accommodation and care, for a period of 5 years from the date the applicant enters the UK if they are granted indefinite leave to enter.

The sponsor's undertaking will be legally binding (see rule 35 of the Immigration Rules).

The guidance states that;

> In addition, in all cases the applicant must provide evidence from the sponsor that the sponsor can provide the maintenance, accommodation and care required, in the form of any or all of the following:
>
> (a) Original bank statements covering the last six months;
> (b) Other evidence of income – such as pay slips, income from savings, shares, bonds – covering the last six months;
> (c) Relevant information on outgoings, e.g. Council Tax, utilities, etc, and on support for anyone else who is dependent on the sponsor;
> (d) A copy of a mortgage or tenancy agreement showing ownership or occupancy of a property; and
> (e) Planned care arrangements for the applicant in the UK (which can involve other family members in the UK) and the cost of these (which must be met by the sponsor, without undertakings of third party support).

The requirement that the sponsor can provide the required care, in addition to maintenance and accommodation, is a new one. 'Care' is not defined in the Immigration Rules. It remains open to question therefore whether a successful applicant will be entitled to free NHS treatment. They are unlikely to be excluded under NHS regulations, or under the no recourse to public funds provision, but the government could decide that the NHS is nevertheless entitled to be reimbursed for the cost of any such treatment by the person signing the undertaking.

Decision

Successful applicants sponsored by a British citizen or settled person will be given indefinite leave to enter. They will have no recourse to public funds for the length of the sponsor's undertaking (i.e. five years from the date of entry).

Those sponsored by a relative with limited leave as a refugee or person with humanitarian protection will be granted leave in line, and can apply for ILR at the same time as the sponsor. The sponsor will not need to provide an undertaking on entry, but the applicant will have no recourse to public funds as a condition of entry. The 5-year sponsorship undertaking will have to be signed by the sponsor at the ILR stage.

Children of settled parent(s)

This category remains under Part 8 of the Immigration Rules, paragraphs 296 to 300, and is unaffected by the new provisions of Appendix FM.

Position of the parents

- All remaining parents in or coming to UK
- OR sole responsibility
- OR exclusion undesirable

Position of the child

- Under 18
- Not living independent life

Maintenance and accommodation

Under paragraph 296, where a parent is party to a polygamous marriage, and that parent would be refused under paragraphs 278 or 278A, their children may be refused too (even where they would otherwise meet the requirements of paragraph 297). This provision has been considered by the Tribunal in the case of SG (child of polygamous marriage) Nepal [2012] UKUT 00265(IAC)

For entry clearance, the child must be seeking to join or accompany a parent who is present and settled in the UK in the following circumstances:

1. both parents are present and settled or being admitted for settlement or

2. one parent present and settled and the other being admitted for settlement or

3. one parent present and settled or being admitted for settlement who can show that they have had sole responsibility for the child's upbringing or

4. one parent is present and settled in the United Kingdom or being admitted on the same occasion for settlement and the other parent is dead or

5. a parent or another relative present and settled or being admitted for settlement where there are serious and compelling family or other considerations which made the exclusion of the child undesirable and where there are suitable arrangements made for the child's care

Under options 1, 2, and 4, the application will be relatively straightforward. In addition to proving that both parents are settled in the UK, or that one parent is dead, the applicant will need to show they are not leading an independent life (as defined in paragraph 6 of the Immigration Rules), and that they can be maintained and accommodated adequately without recourse to public funds.

It is in respect of options 3 and 5 that complications can arise. It can be seen that there are additional requirements that apply where one of the parents resides outside the UK with no intention of joining the child in the UK, or where the child is seeking to join a relative who is not a parent. In such cases, the UK-based parent or relative will have to show a very good reason why the child should be allowed to settle in the UK rather than continue their life in the country in which they are living. These reasons, (i.e. 'sole responsibility' and 'exclusion undesirable') are examined in more detail below.

Prior entry clearance is required where the child is seeking indefinite leave to enter. A child may also apply for ILR from within the UK.

In-country applications

Under rule 298, a child who is under 18 at the date of application can apply for indefinite leave to remain if they have or have had limited leave in any category. A child who is here as a visitor, for example, can apply from within the UK to settle in the UK if both parents are settled, or one is settled and the other is dead, or the parent here has sole responsibility, or a parent or relative is settled and exclusion of the child is undesirable.

If the child is over 18 at the date of application, they must have previously been granted limited leave as a child in a category leading to settlement.

Sole responsibility

In order to show that the sponsoring parent in the UK has sole responsibility for the child, notwithstanding that they live in different countries, he or she will need to show that they have been, so far as is possible at arm's length, exercising the normal role played by a caring parent. It is acceptable that the child's day to day care is delegated to another person in the child's own country but evidence that ultimate control rests with the sponsoring parent is required.

The IDIs (chapter 8, Section 5A <u>Annex M</u>) elaborate on the meaning of sole responsibility and state that the following factors are to be used as guidance on how to assess it:

➢ the period for which the parent in the United Kingdom has been separated from the child;

➢ what the arrangements were for the care of the child before that parent migrated to this country;

➢ who has been entrusted with day to day care and control of the child since the sponsoring parent migrated here;

➢ who provides, and in what proportion, the financial support for the child's care and upbringing;

➢ who takes the important decisions about the child's upbringing, such as where and with whom the child lives, the choice of school, religious practice etc;

➢ the degree of contact that has been maintained between the child and the parent claiming "sole responsibility";

➢ what part in the child's care and upbringing is played by the parent not in the United Kingdom and his relatives.

The IDIs also say that sole responsibility should have been exercised for a substantial period of time. The Court of Appeal case of Nmaju v ECO [2000] EWCA Civ 505 (C/2000/6263) 31 July 2000, however, states that this is not the case, sole responsibility could be exercised for a short period of time and that the two key factors are:

1. What quality of control is involved?

2. For what period of time must this quality of control be exercised?

The tribunal case of TD (Paragraph 297(i)(e): "sole responsibility") Yemen [2006] UKAIT 00049 includes a useful summary of the relevant case law on this issue and holds that the test is whether the parent has continuing control and direction over the child's upbringing, including making all the important decisions in the child's life.

Example

Fatima, from Egypt, entered the UK as a work permit holder and has worked as a nurse for over 5 years. She now has ILR. She is sponsoring her husband and child to come to the UK. This will be a straightforward application on both counts.

However, if Fatima was applying for only the child to come to the UK to join her, it would be a far more problematic application if the father remains involved in the child's life. She would have to demonstrate sole responsibility (i.e. that the father did not financially support or take any important decisions in the child's life) or that the exclusion of the child would be undesirable.

If there is no father involved, and the child has been looked after by Fatima's family in Egypt whilst she has been in the UK, Fatima will still need to show that she meets the sole responsibility requirement, that is that she has directed the child's upbringing and has not fully delegated that direction to her family.

Serious and compelling circumstances making exclusion undesirable

There is no particular definition of what may constitute serious and compelling circumstances but the phrase 'family or other circumstances' suggests that real benefit to the child *or* to the sponsoring parent/s or other relative could be a valid consideration in interpreting this part of the rule.

However, in Hardward v SSHD (00/TH/01522) 12 July 2000, the Tribunal suggested, after reviewing the case law that the key factors are:

➢ willingness and ability of the overseas adult to care for the child

➢ poor living conditions – but not necessarily intolerable

➢ greater vulnerability of small children.

Article 8 and best interest principles will usually now play an important role in showing the test is met. In Mundeba (s.55 and para 297(i)(f)) Democratic Republic of Congo [2013] UKUT 88 (IAC), the Upper Tribunal adopts a more inclusive approach to the 'exclusion undesirable' test than has traditionally been the case, reading into it at least some of the more child-centred modern considerations one would expect in this day and age. Still, though, the test seems to require something more than best interests.

Other definitions

Under rule 6 of HC395 the definition of a 'parent' is deemed to include:

➢ stepfather of a child whose father is dead

➤ stepmother of a child whose mother is dead

➤ father or mother of an illegitimate child (providing he can prove paternity)

➤ an adoptive parent where the child was adopted in accordance with a decision taken by the competent court or administrative authority in a country whose adoption orders are recognised in the UK

Adopted children

The admission of adopted children and those being brought to the UK for adoption is provided for in rules 309A to 316F of HC395.

The rules for adopted children apply to some *de facto* adopted children as well as those adopted through an appropriate and acceptable court process. *De facto* adoption - not a formal one - or one that is formal but not recognised in the UK is defined in r.309A. It must be shown that:

➤ immediately preceding the application the adoptive parent/parents have been living abroad (if two parents, living together) for at least eighteen months of which the twelve months preceding the application must have been spent living with the child

➤ the adoptive parents must have assumed the role of the child's parents since the beginning of the eighteen month period so that there has been a genuine transfer of parental responsibility

Otherwise, the child must have been adopted in accordance with a decision taken by the competent administrative authority or court in his country of origin or the country in which he is resident, being a country whose adoption orders are recognised by the United Kingdom.

If the above requirements are met then the child must also show that they meet a further set of requirements in addition to those for natural children. These require that the child:

➤ has the same rights and obligations as any other child of the adoptive parent's or parents' family; and

➤ was adopted due to the inability of the original parent(s) or current carer(s) to care for him and there has been a genuine transfer of parental responsibility to the adoptive parents; and

➤ has lost or broken his ties with his family of origin; and

➤ was adopted, but the adoption is not one of convenience arranged to facilitate his admission to or remaining in the United Kingdom.

If successful, the child will be granted indefinite leave to enter the UK.

Given that the provisions for adopted children are so narrowly drawn, adoption cases are often argued under Article 8 ECHR. See e.g. the case of Singh v Entry Clearance Officer New Delhi [2004] EWCA Civ 1075. Home Office guidance on adopted children is in the Modernised Guidance (in the Family of people settled or coming to settle in the UK section).

Children born in the UK

A child born in the UK cannot be born in breach of immigration control.

However, rules 304 to 309 allow for a child born in the U.K. to be given leave in line with their parents, which will be particularly important if the family want to travel and return to the U.K. Children of settled parents, or those in respect of whom the parental rights and duties are vested solely in a local authority, can apply for indefinite leave. Where parents are here without leave, a child may be granted leave for a period not exceeding 3 months if both of his parents are in the United Kingdom and it appears unlikely that they will be removed in the immediate future, and there is no other person outside the United Kingdom who could reasonably be expected to care for him.

Guidance on these provisions is in the IDIs at Chapter 8 <u>Section 4A</u>

Chapter 7: Points Based System

Introduction

The Points-based System (PBS) is the part of the immigration rules which provides for leave to be granted to entrepreneurs, investors, the exceptionally talented, skilled workers, students, temporary workers, and under the youth mobility scheme.

The PBS was introduced in 2008 to simplify and consolidate the key 'managed migration' routes into the UK, to introduce objective criteria for granting visas and leave under these routes, and to reduce opportunities for abuse of immigration control.

Some 6 years into the PBS, few would argue that it has met these key intentions. In practice, the PBS turned out to be far from simple or objective.

To share responsibility for reducing abuse with those benefitting from managed migration, i.e. employers and education providers, the PBS introduced the concept of licensed sponsors who must take responsibility for ensuring only those migrants who meet the requirements of the rules, and who thereafter abide by the requirements of immigration control, will be granted leave.

The immigration rules for the PBS are in Part 6A of the Immigration Rules and in some 20 appendices. The rules run to hundreds of pages and are extremely detailed. The paragraph numbering scheme of Part 6A, which begins at paragraph 245AAA and finishes at paragraph 245ZZE is difficult to navigate. Over time, the rules have become fragmented and disjointed and the mandatory requirements of the scheme are spread large and wide across the Immigration Rules.

As a result of perceived abuses, the documentation that must be provided in support of applications has been prescribed as to form and content to such an extent that it has become extremely difficult to succeed in an application without expert advice. Advisers working with PBS applicants have to navigate through an extensive minefield of regulation, with apparently trivial mistakes having fatal consequences. Patience and an attention to detail are absolutely essential.

In a major about-face, the government decided in 2012 that the objective criteria of the PBS, the very essence of the new system, provided it with insufficient control over decision making. Basically, too many applicants were succeeding under the points-based requirements, and that was not good for the government's policy of reducing migration into the UK. Recent amendments have now substantially re-introduced the subjective criteria of the old, pre-PBS routes. In addition to proving that they have accrued the necessary points, students, entrepreneurs and some workers must now establish that their intentions are genuine. This has had a profound effect in some areas with, for example, the approval rate of entrepreneur applications dropping from 80% to a little over 30%.

The basics

The PBS groups the various routes within it under 5 'tiers'. They are as follows:

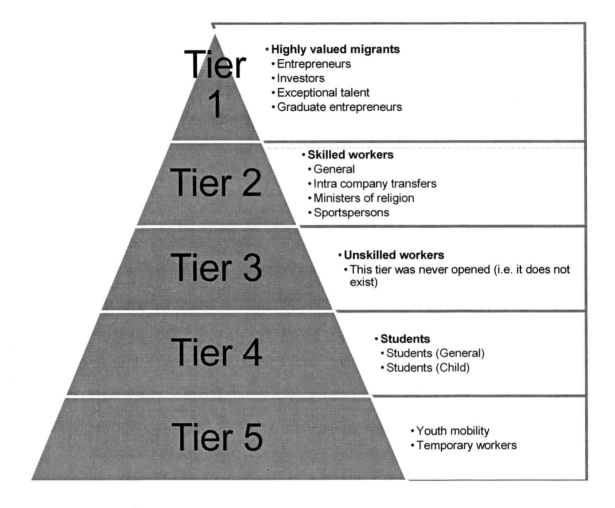

Under the PBS, an applicant has to show they are entitled to the requisite number of points under some or all of 3 sets of criteria (see below). Additionally, there are 'genuineness' requirements for entrepreneurs, Ministers of Religion, students and temporary workers

Attributes

- Appendix A
- Investment funds, valid sponsorship, minimum income
- English language for students

English language

- Appendix B
- for those routes leading to settlement

Maintenance (funds)

- Appendix C
- Savings (that must be held for a minimum period of 28 or 90 days prior to the application being made)

Genuineness

- Intentions, and sources of investment funds

There is no separate accommodation requirement as the funds requirement is set at a level that includes accommodation costs.

The number of points required under each of these 3 criteria, and the genuineness provisions, are laid out in Part 6A of the Immigration Rules. The basis upon which the requisite points are acquired, and the associated specified evidence, is provided for in Appendices A, B and C respectively (i.e. for Attributes, English language skills, and funds respectively).

And just to make things even more complicated, there are lots of 'transitional provisions'. Due to the very many amendments made to the PBS over the years, different rules can apply to applications made under the same route, dependent upon the date of application or the date the applicant was previously granted leave under that route. As an example, under Tier 2 (General), the question as to whether an employee will be able to settle in the UK will be, in part, dependent upon the rules at the time they were first granted leave under Tier 2.

There is a myriad of guidance to sponsors and applicants for the various PBS routes on the GOV.UK website, but it is not always easy to find. There is formal Policy Guidance for each route, and Operational Guidance for UKVI decision makers.

Remember though that the guidance is not the law. That was made clear in the Supreme Court's important decision in the case of Alvi [2012] UKSC 33 (see more on Alvi below). The Immigration Rules is the complete legal code that applies to the PBS, and for advisers it is the rules that need to be considered first and foremost. The guidance, though useful sometimes to help explain what the rules mean, is not always accurate, up to date and comprehensive. In attempting to simplify the Immigration Rules, it can sometimes be misleading. To the extent that the guidance provides the Home Office's interpretation of the rules, and particularly where that interpretation serves to limit their application, it carries little weight. A different interpretation may be just as valid.

Given the level of detail within the PBS, and it's frequent amendment, this section of the manual can provide only an overview of the various routes.

Migration Advisory Committee

To assist with the design of the Points Based System, the Home Office created the Migration Advisory Committee (MAC), an independent body of experts able to carry out research into the migration needs of the UK economy. This provides advice to government on the UK labour market generally, including skills shortages, and on the efficacy of the investment routes. The MAC has also advised the coalition government on the large scale changes to the PBS over time, as the economy's needs and government policy changes, and has been more recently involved in establishing the controversial minimum income threshold in the Appendix FM partner category.

Sponsorship under the points-based system

United Kingdom employers and education providers must apply to the Home Office for a sponsor licence in order to employ non-EEA migrants and to recruit non-EEA students. Sponsorship is required for applicants under the Tier 1 (Graduate Entrepreneur) route, and under tiers 2, 4 and 5. A successful sponsor must comply with their duties under their sponsorship scheme.

Comprehensive guidance is available to sponsors on the GOV.UK website (https://www.gov.uk/government/collections/sponsorship-information-for-employers-and-educators). This section of the manual aims to provide only the outline of the scheme.

The sponsor licensing scheme was considered by the Supreme Court in R (on the application of New London College Ltd) v SSHD [2013] UKSC 51. The scheme was held to be lawful, notwithstanding that it remains outside the immigration rules and any other known form of law. For a more detailed analysis of the judgement see:
http://www.freemovement.org.uk/2013/07/23/supreme-court-upholds-points-based-system-sponsor-licensing-scheme/.

Applying for sponsorship

Sponsors must apply, online, for a licence. If awarded a licence, they are then added to the register of sponsors, and will be able to issue a limited number of;

> 'certificates of sponsorship' (a 'CoS', essentially, for prospective employees, the offer of a job), or

> 'confirmations of acceptance for studies' (a 'CAS', for students, an offer of a place on a course).

The granting of sponsorship (in the form of a CoS or CAS), will be the core requirement for a student or employee who wants to enter or remain in the UK under the PBS. Presuming the sponsorship is valid – correctly granted by the sponsor under the terms of their sponsor licence and the immigration rules – it will provide the applicant with the points they need for 'Attributes'. When a migrant is issued with a CAS or CoS, presuming they meet the other requirements of the PBS rules, they will then be able to make their application for a visa or extension of stay.

A sponsor licence is valid for four years, starting from the day it is issued.

There are three principal questions investigated on a licence application:

> Firstly, is this a genuine organisation operating legally in the United Kingdom?

> Secondly, it is trustworthy? The history and background of the organisation, its key personnel and those in ownership and control of it will be investigated. Any history of dishonesty or immigration crime will be viewed particularly seriously and can lead to refusal of the application.

> Thirdly, is the organisation capable of carrying out its sponsorship duties? This will involve an investigation of its internal processes, including human resources practices.

Sponsor duties

Sponsors must comply with certain duties, including a duty to inform the Home Office if those they recruit do not turn up for their job or course, or if they are absent without permission for a significant period. Sponsors must also keep records of the migrants they have sponsored, including contact details and changes of circumstances. Initial information and updates on each CoS and CAS that is issued by a sponsor is provided to the Home Office by way of the Sponsor Management System, an online system that allows the Home Office to maintain a constant check on the sponsor's performance.

The Home Office closely monitors sponsors' behaviour and compliance with their duties. In particular the Home Office will:

> set a limit on the number of CoSs and CASs a sponsor can assign, and review its performance after it has assigned a certain number;

> make visits, pre-arranged or not, to check compliance; and

> ➤ issue civil penalties where evidence is found that the sponsor has been breaching the illegal working regulations, or refer the sponsor for prosecution where appropriate.

All Tier 2 and 5 sponsors will be rated A or B according to the Home Office's assessment of their ability to fulfil their sponsor duties. Any sponsor that is B-rated must comply with a time-limited action plan, which will set out the steps it needs to take in order to gain or regain an A-rating. If the sponsor does not comply with this action plan, it is likely to lose its licence altogether.

Where the Home Office considers that a sponsor has not been complying with its duties, has been dishonest in its dealings with the Home Office or otherwise poses a threat to immigration control, its licence may be withdrawn or it may be downgraded to a B-rating.

A B-rating is transitional, and holders will be given a Sponsorship Action Plan. This might include, for example, making specific improvements to record keeping, improving control over the staff employed to issue certificates of sponsorship or improving communication between different branches of the business so it knows when a migrant has not turned up for work. The sponsor will be expected, within a relatively short period (around three months), to have improved performance sufficiently to be upgraded to an A-rating, or risk having their licence withdrawn.

If the plan has not been met by the end of the three months the Home Office will normally withdraw the licence, though where significant progress has been made, they may instead decide to keep the organisation on a B-rating and have a new action plan drawn up. In deciding whether to draw up a new sponsorship action plan in these circumstances, they will take all the circumstances into account, including the following:

> ➤ whether genuine attempts have been made to meet the requirements of the action plan; and

> ➤ whether circumstances outside the control of the organisation prevented it from meeting the requirements.

The absolute maximum period on an action plan is 12 months. A B-rated organisation will automatically lose its licence after that time.

B-rated sponsors may be subject to additional duties. For example, a B-rated sponsor may be required to report to the Home Office when a migrant arrives for work, rather than simply reporting when they do not turn up. Such duties will be notified. B-rated sponsors are likely to be subject to more frequent and exacting inspections by the Home Office.

For an application under Tiers 2 and 5, where the applicant must show that they have sufficient funds to support themselves (the maintenance requirement), they may rely instead (i.e. where the applicant's savings are inadequate) on an undertaking from an A-rated (but not B-rated) sponsor to financially support them for the initial period of their leave.

Education providers must be A-rated before they can gain a licence, and must achieve Highly Trusted Sponsor status within 12 months of being issued with a licence. If they do not, their licence will be revoked. These provisions and failures by sponsors generally have resulted in many hundreds of education providers losing their licence, leaving thousands of students high and dry.

If a sponsor licence is suspended, that will have no immediate effect on the workers and students being sponsored, but the sponsor will not be allowed to issue new CoSs or CASs. If the sponsor licence is revoked, those who have been sponsored, who are not implicated in the reasons for revocation, will be given 60 days to find a new sponsor, failing which their leave will be curtailed. Where workers or students are implicated, their leave will be immediately curtailed.

Problems have arisen for many thousands of students who have made an application for an extension, relying on a valid CAS, but before a decision is made on the application the Home Office revokes their sponsor's licence, rendering the CAS invalid. The Home Office then refuses the application. The Upper Tribunal in Patel (revocation of sponsor licence – fairness) India [2011] UKUT 00211 (IAC) found that process to be unlawful due to the inherent unfairness of giving the students no opportunity in those circumstances to find a new sponsor before being refused. Patel was the first of a number of reported decisions of the Upper Tribunal which have focussed on the inherently unfair practices of the Home Office under the PBS. The UKVI generally does amend its practises following such decisions, and now writes to students before refusing them, to give them an opportunity to find a new sponsor.

Codes of practice

Codes of practice have been created for Tiers 2 and 5 of the Points Based System. These are aimed at sponsoring employers and exist for all sectors. They list, in Appendix J to the Immigration Rules:

➢ all the skilled jobs in the UK for which sponsors can issue a certificate of sponsorship;

➢ the minimum appropriate salary for the job (so as not to undermine domestic labour rates); and

➢ the acceptable media and methods for passing the resident labour market test (to ensure that the skilled post cannot be filled from the domestic labour market).

Documentary evidence, policy guidance and Alvi

One of the features of the Points Based System as initially designed was that the Immigration Rules set out only some of the mandatory criteria governing the various routes. The documentary evidence that had to be submitted was specified in very lengthy 'policy guidance' documents outside the rules.

This caused considerable controversy, largely because the policy guidance was so extremely prescriptive and inflexible. Many immigrants who could meet the substantive requirements of the PBS scheme failed in their applications because they misunderstood the guidance or were unable to obtain the requisite paperwork.

Status of the policy guidance

In the case of Pankina [2010] EWCA Civ 719, the Court of Appeal held that the policy guidance is just guidance. It does not have the status of law and must therefore be interpreted sensibly and flexibly.

The specific provision of the guidance under challenge in Pankina was the requirement for the applicant to have held the necessary level of funds for at least three months prior to making an application. This requirement featured only in the policy guidance, the rules themselves stating only that an applicant must hold a certain level of funds. The immediate effect of the decision in Pankina was that the funds must be held only at the date of application, but need not (as the guidance required) be held for the three preceding months.

A very similar judgment swiftly followed Pankina, in R (on the application of English UK) v SSHD [2010] EWHC 1726 (Admin). In English UK, Mr Justice Foskett held to be unlawful the requirement set out in the policy guidance, but not in the Immigration Rules, for a mandatory minimum level of English for those wanting to study English language in the UK.

Rather than accepting a degree of flexibility in the scheme, the Home Office responded to these judgments by incorporating most of the requirements of the policy guidance directly into the Immigration Rules. Almost immediately following the judgements in Pankina and UK English, for example, the three month rule on holding funds and the requirement for a minimum level of English for English language students were put into the Immigration Rules and became mandatory again.

The process of migrating the guidance into the Immigration Rules turned from a trickle into a flood following the Supreme Court's judgment in Alvi, R (on the application of) v Secretary of State for the Home Department [2012] UKSC 33. In Alvi, the Supreme Court decided that all substantive requirements that must be satisfied for an application to succeed must be laid before Parliament in the form of proper Immigration Rules under s.3(2) of the Immigration Act 1971. Attempting to import or incorporate requirements into the Immigration Rules by documents such as 'policy guidance' outside the rules was found to be unlawful.

With extraordinary haste, the day after Alvi was reported, a massive new Statement of Changes, Cm 8423, was published and brought into effect a day later on 20 July 2012. In addition to substantial amendments to Part 6A and to the existing appendices (A,B, & C), eight new appendices were added to the Immigration Rules as below;

➢ Appendix J: Codes of practice for Tier 2 sponsors, Tier 5 sponsors and employers of work permit holders
➢ Appendix K: Shortage occupation list
➢ Appendix L: Designated competent body criteria for Tier 1 (Exceptional talent) applications
➢ Appendix M: Sports governing bodies for Tier 2 (Sportsperson) and Tier 5 (Temporary worker - creative and sporting) applications
➢ Appendix N: Approved Tier 5 Government authorised exchange schemes
➢ Appendix O: List of English Language tests that have been assessed as meeting the Home Office's requirements
➢ Appendix P: Lists of financial institutions that do not satisfactorily verify financial statements, or whose financial statements are accepted
➢ Appendix Q: Statement of written terms and conditions of employment required in paragraph 245ZO(f)(ii) and paragraph 245 ZQ (e)(ii)

Further appendices have been added over time. This incorporation into the rules of what was previously guidance makes it all the more important that the rules are read and followed with extreme care, notwithstanding their length and complexity. The rules contain detailed provisions as to the precise format of documents that must be provided, in addition to their content. Particular care must be taken in this regard as the requirements as to format are usually in a different part of the rules to the requirements as to content.

Specified evidence and evidential flexibility

As per paragraph 39B of HC395, specified documents must be submitted in support of an application. They must be original documents, which are verifiable, and must be accompanied by a certified translation if not in English or Welsh.

Rule 245AA in its current form requires all specified documents to be submitted with the application itself. Documents submitted later may not be considered unless submitted in line with rule 245AA(b);

(b) If the applicant has submitted specified documents in which:

(i) Some of the documents in a sequence have been omitted (for example, if one bank statement from a series is missing);

(ii) A document is in the wrong format (for example, if a letter is not on letterhead paper as specified); or

(iii) A document is a copy and not an original document; or

(iv)A document does not contain all of the specified information;

the Entry Clearance Officer, Immigration Officer or the Secretary of State may contact the applicant or his representative in writing, and request the correct documents. The requested documents must be received at the address specified in the request within 7 working days of the date of the request.

Nor can additional documents be provided on appeal, due to the restrictions on the jurisdiction of the Tribunal in section 85A of the Nationality, Immigration and Asylum Act. The effect of s85A is that in appeals against Points-based System decisions an appellant cannot rely on evidence that was not submitted to the Home Office with the application except in very limited circumstances.

The exceptions are:

➢ to support grounds not referred to in s85A(3)(c) e.g. human rights grounds

➢ to prove a document is genuine or valid

➢ to show the refusal was wrong on grounds other than the acquisition of points under the Points Based System e.g. the general grounds of refusal, or 'genuineness' under the Tier 4 (General) and Tier 1 (Entrepreneur) routes.

The point of this provision is to encourage applicants, where there is a shortfall in the supporting documents, to apply again to the Home Office, and to pay a new fee, rather than try to make good the application on appeal to the Tribunal.

S85A, along with the right of appeal for refusals of extension applications is to be deleted by the Immigration Act 2014 when Part 2 is brought into force.

Various attempts have been made to challenge the lack of flexibility in the PBS in respect of specified documents. Once such is currently on appeal to the Supreme Court. Largely, the challenges have been in respect of the evidential flexibility *policy* which, at one time, was arguably broader than rule 245AA. The current policy simply guides UKVI decision makers as to the process that must be followed when applying the rule. For more on these challenges, see the Free Movement post at: http://www.freemovement.org.uk/another-evidential-flexibility-case/ .

See also the section on evidential flexibility at page 49.

The UKVI has gone some way to meet these challenges, positively, by amending and expanding rule 245AA. As of 1 October 2013 rule 245AA includes a provision whereby a caseworker should contact an applicant before refusing an application where a document has been provided that does not contain all the specified information. This will not assist an applicant who fails to submit a specified document at all, but will do so where a document that has been submitted falls short in regard to content.

Other general considerations

Overstaying and extension applications

The PBS rules explicitly allow for out of time extension applications. Up to 28 days of overstaying is disregarded when considering an extension application, but it is not disregarded for other purposes. Overstaying, even by one day, is always unwise. It is a criminal offence (see chapter on criminal offences), albeit rarely one that is prosecuted, and also leads to loss of appeal rights. More importantly for PBS migrants, an overstayer cannot lawfully work in the U.K, and may also have to leave any course of study. There will be little point applying for leave as an overstayer where the sponsor has withdrawn their sponsorship as a result.

The 28 day disregard allows for an extension application to be made;

➢ up to 28 days after the applicant's leave has expired, or
➢ up to 28 days after an applicant has received a Notice of Invalidity following an in-time application for an extension, or
➢ up to 28 days after continuing leave under 3C has expired (see definition of overstaying in rule 6).

A Notice of Invalidity will be sent when the application does not meet the requirements of rule 34.

Note that overstaying in excess of 90 days risks engaging immigration rule 320(7B) if the person departs from the UK and seeks re-entry (i.e. the 12-month re-entry ban).

It is important to be aware however that there are serious pitfalls for those applying as overstayers. Particularly, in addition to the problems mentioned above;

➢ Students, who overstay their leave, even by 1 day, cannot rely on the *'having an established presence'* provision (paragraphs 11 and 14 of Appendix C) which substantially reduces the amount of money they will need to show in their bank account when applying for an extension. Students who carefully plan their finances so that they have the requisite amount of money in their bank accounts for an extension application will not then be able to meet the very much higher maintenance requirement that will apply if they make a late application.

➢ Students cannot rely on money they have earned whilst overstaying to meet the funds requirement (paragraph 1A(d) of Appendix C).

It is important therefore to make sure that the initial in-time application exactly conforms to the requirements of the Immigration Rules, including the provisions on specified evidence. In many cases, applicants will not be able to repair the damage caused to them by refused or invalid applications by either applying again or appealing. They may instead need to go home to apply for a visa to return, presuming the sponsor allows them to do so.

Payment of application fees

Many applicants find their applications returned as invalid because the Home Office alleges that they have not been able to collect the fee, or the correct fee was not paid.

In Basnet (validity of application - respondent) Nepal [2012] UKUT 113 (IAC) (04 April 2012), the Home Office alleged that the applicant's bank had refused payment of the fee. The Tribunal identified that the proper question before them was whether the application was accompanied by the fee (i.e. whether the correct information had been provided to enable the Home Office to collect the fee), rather than whether the Home Office did actually collect it. The Tribunal found the burden was on the Home Office to prove non-payment (i.e. how the fee fell not to be paid), which they were unable to do in this case as they had destroyed the payment information provided by the applicant. The Tribunal also found the Home Office's system for processing payments to be unfair. The Tribunal decided that in cases where the Home Office fail to collect the fee, there should be prompt communication with the applicant to afford an opportunity to check or correct the billing data, as there is with applications made in person.

In *R (on the application of Kobir)* [2011] EWHC 2515 (Admin), where an applicant had failed to pay the correct fee, the court found it was:

> manifestly unfair and unreasonable for the Defendant not to have looked very carefully indeed at the full history with a view to exercising her discretion outside the rules rather than simply refusing it within the rules

Top tip

Some immigrants and advisers have found that it is possible to mitigate the effects of some of the stringent requirements of the PBS by lodging what may prove to be a hopeless appeal against a decision to refuse an in-time application and, in the meantime, preparing a fresh application ensuring that the PBS requirements are fully complied with.

If the appeal fails, or is withdrawn, an out of time application can then be made within 28 days with all the documents in order. Note that new applications cannot be submitted to the Home Office whilst there is an outstanding appeal by reason of section 3C 1971 Act.

Where a person is not able to make a further application for any reason (i.e. because they have overstayed more than 28 days or no longer meet the funds requirements) it is always a good idea to check that any previous applications that were returned as invalid or refused were lawfully rejected (e.g. on Alvi grounds).

Continuity of residence

Paragraph 245AAA defines, for the purposes of an ILR application, the term "continuous period of 5 years lawfully in the UK". This requires an unbroken period of leave, but the following circumstances will not amount to such a break;

> (i) the applicant has been absent from the UK for a period of 180 days or less in any of the five consecutive 12 month periods preceding the date of the application for leave to remain;
> (ii) the applicant has existing limited leave to enter or remain upon their departure and return except that where that leave expired no more than 28 days prior to a further application for entry clearance, that period and any period pending the determination of an application made within that 28 day period shall be disregarded; and
> (iii) the applicant has any period of overstaying between periods of entry clearance, leave to enter or leave to remain of up to 28 days and any period of overstaying pending the determination of an application made within that 28 day period disregarded.

Paragraph 245(a)(i) (above) allows a PBS migrant to spend up to 180 days per year outside the U.K, but paragraph 245(C) qualifies this for PBS migrants other than those with leave as a Tier 1(Investor) Migrant, a Tier 1(Entrepreneur) Migrant, a Tier 1(Exceptional Talent) Migrant or a highly skilled migrant, by requiring that;

> any absences from the UK during the five years must have been for a purpose that is consistent with the applicant's basis of stay here, including paid annual leave, or for serious or compelling reasons.

Paragraph 245(b) requires sponsored employees to have worked in accordance with their sponsorship throughout the relevant period, disregarding breaks of up to 60 days when changing employer.

Paragraphs 245(a)(ii) & (iii) disregard from the definition of 'unbroken period with valid leave' gaps of up to 28 days between the expiry of a previous grant of leave expired and the date of the next application, whether that is made in-country or from abroad.

Maintenance

Appendix C sets out the maintenance requirements. The general requirements are in paragraphs 1A, and requirements as to specified evidence in paragraph

1B. Subsequent paragraphs lay out the maintenance requirements for each of the PBS routes (except for Tier 1 (Investor) and Tier 1 (Exceptional Talent) where there is no maintenance requirement). They are, in outline;

➢ The applicant must have the requisite funds at the date of application, and for a consecutive 90 day period beforehand (except under Tier 4 where they must be held for a consecutive 28 day period).

In regard to this requirement, the Tribunal found in NA & Others (Tier 1 Post-Study Work-funds) [2009] UKAIT 00025, that the sums in question must be shown on each and every day of the period;

➢ The date of the closing balance of the relevant account must be no earlier than 31 days before the date of application. Where two or more accounts are submitted, the relevant date will be the closing balance of the most favourable account.

➢ Where the funds are in one or more foreign currencies, the applicant must have the specified level of funds when converted to pound sterling (£) using the spot exchange rate which appears on www.oanda.com for the date of the application;

➢ Where the funds were obtained when the applicant was in the UK, the funds must have been obtained while the applicant had valid leave and was not acting in breach of any conditions attached to that leave;

Where the PBS migrant is applying together with their partner or children, each applicant must have the requisite funds. If any applicant does not meet their funds requirement, all the applications will be refused;

➢ No points will be awarded where the specified documents show that the funds are held in a financial institution listed in Appendix P as being an institution with which the Home Office is unable to make satisfactory verification checks;

➢ Maintenance must be in the form of cash funds. Other accounts or financial instruments such as shares, bonds, pension funds etc, regardless of notice period are not acceptable;

➢ If the applicant wishes to rely on a joint account as evidence of available funds, the applicant (or for children under 18 years of age, the applicant's parent or legal guardian who is legally present in the United Kingdom) must be named on the account as one of the account holders;

➢ Overdraft facilities will not be considered towards funds that are available or under an applicant's own control;

➢ The specified documents required to evidence funds must be in the form laid out in paragraph 1B of Appendix C.

English language

Appendix B sets out the English language requirements of each route. Those seeking leave as a Tier 1 (Investor), and for the first time as a Tier 1 (Exceptional talent) migrant are exempt from English language requirements, as are those under Tier 2 (ICT) and Tier 5.

The levels of English language required are shown in Table 1. Available points for English language are shown in Table 2. Points are available for;

➢ nationals of a majority English speaking country listed in paragraph 6, or

➢ for a degree taught in English (paragraphs 7-9), or

➢ for passing an approved English language test (listed in Appendix O) at the appropriate level (paragraph10), or

➢ having met the requirement in a previous grant of leave (paragraphs 11-15), or

➢ for exemption under transitional arrangements (which are set out in paragraphs 16-18)

Curtailment of leave

In addition to the general grounds of refusal that are relevant to all applicants, there are specific grounds for the mandatory or discretionary curtailment (or variation of the duration of) leave granted under the PBS. These are at paragraphs 323A to 323C of the Immigration Rules and include curtailment;

➢ for failing to commence work or study, or for ceasing work or study

➢ where the sponsor ceases to hold a sponsor licence, or transfers the business to someone who does not have a licence and who fails to apply for one within 28 days of the date or is refused an appropriate licence

➢ where the migrant's undergoes a prohibited change of employment as defined in r.323AA

➢ where a Tier 1 Exceptional Talent or Graduate Entrepreneur migrant loses their endorsement

Tier 1: highly valued

The different routes currently open within Tier 1 are as follows:

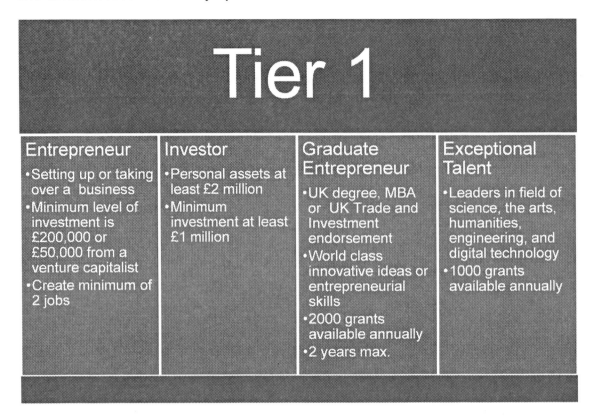

Two routes, Tier 1 (General) and Tier 1 (Post-study work) were closed by the current government for new entrants. They will still be relevant for those in the UK granted leave before they were closed.

Tier 1 (General)

The category of Tier 1 (General), which in pre-PBS days was called the Highly Skilled Migrant Programme, was designed to allow highly skilled people to come to the United Kingdom to look for work or self-employment opportunities. Points for Attributes were awarded on the basis of education, previous earnings, United Kingdom experience, and age. There was no requirement to have a job offer or for sponsorship.

Tier 1 (General) was closed to new applicants from overseas from 23 December 2010, and for new in-country applicants from 6 April 2011 (other than for those switching from a few pre-PBS categories).

Existing Tier 1 (General) migrants can still apply for extensions and settlement under rules 245C to 245CD, but this route closes for further applications for leave to remain from 6 April 2015, and for ILR from 6 April 2018.

Because the scheme is closed to new applicants, we are not addressing the criteria here. Guidance is on the GOV.UK website. The IDIs at:

https://www.gov.uk/government/uploads/system/uploads/attachment_data/file/26 3097/section1.pdf deal with settlement applications under Tier 1, including Tier 1 (General). Policy guidance on Tier 1 (General) is at: https://www.gov.uk/government/uploads/system/uploads/attachment_data/file/33 9377/T1_G_Guidance_08-14.pdf

Tier 1 (Post study work)

This route was closed to new entrants from 06 April 2012. It replaced the International Graduates and Scottish Fresh Talent schemes, enabling graduates of UK universities to apply to remain in the UK to work for up to two years following the successful completion of their studies. Those still in the UK with leave under this route may be able to switch into other PBS categories at the end of the 2 year period (or earlier if they choose).

As some compensation for the closure of the PSW route, the Home Office opened a new Graduate Entrepreneur route and also made it easier for graduates to switch directly into the Tier 1 (Entrepreneur) and Tier 2 (General) routes.

Tier 1 (Entrepreneur)

Starting at paragraph 245D, this route allows a migrant to come to or stay in the UK to invest in or set up a business with a substantial investment of his or her own money.

A business is defined as an enterprise as a sole trader, a partnership or a company registered in the UK.

A prospective entrepreneur visit visa is available (at rule 56N) for those who need to come to the UK to secure funding from venture capitalist firms, a UK entrepreneurial seed funding competition or from a UK government department. Having secured the necessary funding as a visitor, the migrant can then extend their stay under the Tier 1 (entrepreneur) category.

The Modernised Guidance for this route is at: https://www.gov.uk/government/uploads/system/uploads/attachment_data/file/34 2868/Tier_1_Entrepreneur_6.0_EXT.pdf
The Policy Guidance is at: https://www.gov.uk/government/uploads/system/uploads/attachment_data/file/33 9364/T1_E_Guidance_08-14_.pdf

Attributes

Initial applications

The migrant(s) applying for the first time for leave as a Tier 1 (Entrepreneur) must score all of the following points:

Investment and business activity	Points

(a) The applicant has access to not less than £200,000, or
 	
(b) The applicant has access to not less than £50,000 from:
 	
    (i) one or more registered venture capitalist firms regulated by the Financial Services Authority,
 	
    (ii) one or more UK Entrepreneurial seed funding competitions which is listed as endorsed on the UK Trade & Investment website, or
 	
    (iii) one or more UK Government Departments, and made available by the Department(s) for the specific purpose of establishing or expanding a UK business, or
 	
(c) The applicant:
 	
    (i) is applying for leave to remain,
 	
    (ii) has, or was last granted, leave as a Tier 1 (Graduate Entrepreneur) Migrant, and
 	
    (iii) has access to not less than £50,000, or
 	
(d) The applicant:
 	
    (i) is applying for leave to remain,
 	
    (ii) has, or was lasted granted, leave as a Tier 1 (Post-Study Work) Migrant,
 	
    (iii) since before 11 July 2014 and up to the date of his application, has been continuously engaged in business activity which was not, or did not amount to, activity pursuant to a contract of service with a business other than his own and, during such period, has been continuously:
 	
    (1) registered with HM Revenue & Customs as self-employed, or
    (2) registered with Companies House as a director of a new or an existing business. Directors who are on the list of disqualified directors provided by Companies House will not be awarded points,
 	
    (iv) since before 11 July 2014 and up to the date of his application, has continuously been working in an occupation which appears on the list of occupations skilled to National Qualifications Framework level 4 or above, as stated in the Codes of Practice in Appendix J, and provides the specified evidence in paragraph 41-SD. "Working" in this context means that the core service his business provides to its customers or clients involves the business delivering a service in an occupation at this level. It excludes any work involved in administration, marketing or website functions for the business, and
	25

(v) has access to not less than £50,000.	
The money is held in one or more regulated financial institutions	25
The money is disposable in the UK

If the applicant is applying for leave to remain, the money must be held in the UK. | 25 |

An entrepreneurial team (i.e. two applicants) can apply together relying on the same funds and business activity (see paragraph 52 of Appendix A).

Specified documents must be provided (under paragraph 41-SD of Appendix A) to show access to funding to the amount required, and that the applicant has permission to use the money to invest in a business in the UK. Further provisions in Appendix A go to the source and disposability of the funds, and in regard to funds invested in the business prior to an application having been made.

Particularly problematic in this regard has been the requirement (now at paragraph 41-SD(c)(10) of Appendix A) to provide a letter from the bank of a third party funder confirming the money in the third party's account is available for the use of the applicant. This requirement was considered by the Upper Tribunal in the reported case of Durrani (Entrepreneurs: bank letters; evidential flexibility) (Rev 1) [2014] UKUT 295 (IAC) in which it was held that the requirement for such a letter was not an absurdity. Changes introduced from 30 June 2014 have in any case made this provision easier to meet.

A regulated financial institution is one which is regulated by the appropriate regulatory body for the country in which the financial institution operates. Where a financial institution does business in the UK, the appropriate regulators are the Financial Conduct Authority and the Prudential Regulation Authority.

Money is disposable in the UK if all of the money is held in a UK based financial institution or if the money is freely transferable to the UK and convertible to sterling. Funds in a foreign currency will be converted to pounds sterling (£) using the spot exchange rate which appeared on www.oanda.com on the date on which the application was made.

Subsequent applications

Migrants who possess or were last granted leave as a Tier 1 (Entrepreneur), businessperson or innovator must score all of the points from the following table:

Investment and business activity	Points
The applicant has invested, or had invested on his behalf, not less than £200,000 (or £50,000 if, in his last grant of leave, he was awarded points for funds of £50,000 from one of the sources listed above) in cash directly into one or more businesses in the UK.	20
The applicant has:
    (a) registered with HM Revenue and Customs as self-employed, or
    (b) registered a new business in which he is a director, or
    (c) registered as a director of an existing business.

Where the applicant's last grant of entry clearance, leave to enter or leave to remain was | 20 |

as a Tier 1 (Entrepreneur) Migrant, the above condition must have been met within 6 months of his entry to the UK (if he was granted entry clearance as a Tier 1 (Entrepreneur) Migrant and there is evidence to establish his date of arrival to the UK), or, in any other case, the date of the grant of leave to remain.	

On a date no earlier than three months prior to the date of application, the applicant was:
    (a) registered with HM revenue and Customs as self-employed, or
    (b) registered a new business in which he is a director, or
    (c) registered as a director of an existing business.
	15

The applicant has: (a) established a new business or businesses that has or have created the equivalent of at least two new full time jobs for persons settled in the UK, or (b) taken over or invested in an existing business or businesses and his services or investment have resulted in a net increase in the employment provided by the business or businesses for persons settled in the UK by creating the equivalent of at least two new full time jobs. Where the applicant's last grant of entry clearance or leave to enter or remain was as a Tier 1 (Entrepreneur) Migrant, the jobs must have existed for at least 12 months of the period for which the previous leave was granted.	20

Specified documents must be provided as evidence of any investment and business activity that took place when the applicant last had leave as a Tier 1 (Entrepreneur) Migrant.

The investment must not include the value of any residential accommodation, property development or property management. The investment must not be in the form of a director's loan, unless it is unsecured and in favour of the business.

For the requirement that the applicant's activities have resulted in the creation of 2 full time jobs, a full time job is one involving at least 30 hours' work a week. Two or more part time jobs that add up to 30 hours a week will count as one full time job. Where the applicant's last grant of entry clearance or leave was as a Tier 1 (Entrepreneur) Migrant, the jobs must have existed for a total of at least 12 months during the period during which the migrant had leave in that category. This need not consist of 12 consecutive months and the jobs need not exist at the date of application, provided they existed for at least 12 months during the period of leave that the migrant is seeking to extend.

Genuine entrepreneurs

In addition to meeting the points-based requirements for Attributes, English language and Funds, an applicant making an initial application for entry or stay under this category must satisfy the decision maker that;

➢ they genuinely intend and are able to establish, take over or become a director of (if they have not already done so) one or more businesses in the UK within the next six months

➢ they genuinely intend to invest the money required under Appendix A in the relevant business or businesses

> the money referred to in Appendix A is genuinely available to the applicant, and will remain available to him until such time as it is spent by his business or businesses.

> that the applicant does not intend to take employment in the United Kingdom other than under the terms of paragraph 245DC (see below).

In making the assessment, the decision maker may take into account;

> the evidence the applicant has submitted;
> the viability and credibility of the source of the money referred to in Table 4 of Appendix A;
> the viability and credibility of the applicant's business plans and market research into their chosen business sector;
> the applicant's previous educational and business experience (or lack thereof);
> the applicant's immigration history and previous activity in the UK; and
> any other relevant information.

The requirements as to genuineness, introduced in 2013, are by their nature subjective. An applicant will not only have to evidence that they have the necessary funds, but also now impress the Home Office as to the provenance of those funds, and the viability of the intended entrepreneurial project. An applicant is now unlikely to succeed unless they have prepared an impressive business plan, and one they can talk to eloquently at a telephone or face to face interview. An applicant will effectively have to show that they can hit the ground running with their business as soon as the leave is granted, or that it is already up and running and successful.

Around two thirds of applications are now refused under the genuineness provisions.

Little guidance is given to applicants in respect of the genuineness requirements, but for a brief mention in the Policy Guidance. At paragraph 103 it states;

> 103. Where we have concerns about whether you are genuinely intending to pursue a business in the UK, we reserve the right to ask for more information and may ask you to attend an interview. We may ask for information about your business intentions, your previous educational and business experience and your immigration history and previous activity in the UK. If you have already registered in the UK as self-employed or as the director of a business, we may check any compliance with requirements for your sector, and we may request additional information and evidence to support the assessment. Any requested documents must be received by the Home Office at the address specified in the request within 28 working days of the date of the request. We will not carry out the assessment if your application already falls for refusal on other grounds, but we reserve the right to carry out this assessment in any reconsideration of our decision.

More guidance though is provided to decision makers in the Modernised Guidance. It is more helpful to applicants than the policy guidance. It states, for example, that where an interview is to be held, the UKVI can request, where applicable;

- ➤ A curriculum vitae (CV) to assess the applicant's previous experience in the field and in business.
- ➤ A business plan and any market research (if the business is in its infancy) to assess how much consideration the applicant has put into starting up, these can be purchased as a package, so plans that appear general may not be useful.
- ➤ Evidence of appropriate accreditation, registration or insurance for the relevant business section (if the business is established).
- ➤ Financial information overseen by a bank, for example a small business loan.
- ➤ Hierarchy charts of larger businesses.
- ➤ Evidence of advertising.
- ➤ Contracts showing trading, if the business is established.
- ➤ Tax documentation (for example, returns or evidence of registration with HMRC) but only if the business is actually trading. Non-trading businesses may still be registered (but you must note applicants switching from Tier 1(Post-study work) will not score points for working in a skilled occupation if their business is not trading).
- ➤ Affidavit from any mentors – for example if the applicant is being mentored by a member of the British Business Angels Association.
- ➤ Evidence of previous businesses owned by the applicant.
- ➤ Details of trading premises, and permissions if the business is trading in the applicant's home.

Applicants may sensibly provide this information with their application, which may forestall the need for an interview.

Language

The applicant will need to show competence in the English language by:

- ➤ passing a specified test in English equivalent to level B1 of the CEFR;

- ➤ coming from a majority English speaking country; or

- ➤ having taken a degree taught in English (verified using national academic recognition information centre (NARIC) data).

Further details on each of these routes are available in Appendix B.

Maintenance

If applying for entry clearance, the applicant must show £3,310 of personal savings which has to have been held for at least three months prior to the date of application. This level of funds must be proven using specified documents, and the level of funds must not dip below £3,310 during the three month period.

If applying for leave to remain, the applicant must show £945 in personal savings held for at least three months prior to making the application. As with entry clearance applications, the funds must not drop below the specified level and specified documents must be submitted as proof of funds.

Switching

To apply for an extension of leave as a Tier 1 (Entrepreneur) the applicant must possess or last have been granted leave in one of the following categories (taken from paragraph 245DD(e)):

(i) as a Highly Skilled Migrant,
(ii) as a Tier 1 (General) Migrant,
(iii) as a Tier 1 (Entrepreneur) Migrant,
(iv) as a Tier 1 (Investor) Migrant,
(v) as a Tier 1 (Graduate Entrepreneur) Migrant,
(vi) as a Tier 1 (Post-Study Work) Migrant,
(vii) as a Businessperson,
(viii) as an Innovator,
(ix) as an Investor,
(x) as a Participant in the Fresh Talent: Working in Scotland Scheme,
(xi) as a Participant in the International Graduates Scheme (or its predecessor, the Science and Engineering Graduates Scheme),
(xii) as a Postgraduate Doctor or Dentist,
(xiii) as a Self-employed Lawyer,
(xiv) as a Student,
(xv) as a Student Nurse,
(xvi) as a Student Re-sitting an Examination,
(xvii) as a Student Writing Up a Thesis,
(xviii) as a Work Permit Holder,
(xix) as a Writer, Composer or Artist,
(xx) as a Tier 2 Migrant,
(xxi) as a Tier 4 Migrant, or
(xxii) as a Prospective Entrepreneur

Rule changes introduced on 11 July 2014 'in response to evidence of widespread abuse' largely suspended the provisions allowing those from study categories, including Tier 4 and Tier 1 (Post-Study Work), to switch into the Tier 1 (Entrepreneur) route.

Period and conditions of leave, curtailment and settlement

Initial applicants will be granted leave for 3 years and 4 months (or 3 years if already in the U.K), with a prohibition on recourse to public funds, a requirement to register with the police (where required by paragraph 326), and no employment other than working for the business(es) the applicant has established, joined or taken over.

As far as employment is concerned, rule 245DC (and its equivalent for leave to remain applications) states;

> no employment other than working for the business(es) the applicant has established, joined or taken over, but working for such business(es) does not include anything undertaken by the applicant pursuant to a contract of service or apprenticeship, whether express or implied and whether oral or written, with another business

This provisions has been designed to prevent entrepreneurs working in a de facto employment relationship with another employer whilst claiming to be self-employed.

Extensions will be granted for 2 years with the same conditions.

Leave can be curtailed, in addition to the reasons under paragraph 323, if the migrant has not registered themselves as self-employed, or their new business, or as a director of an existing business within 6 months of being entry clearance, entering the U.K. or being granted leave to remain.

ILR will be granted after 3 years where the migrant has created at least 10 jobs, or where their activities have produced £5 million or more income during that period, or after 5 years in all other cases.

Tier 1 (Investor)

Starting at rule 245E, this category is for high net worth individuals making a substantial financial investment in the UK.

Two recent reports into the Investor route, by the Migration Advisory Committee and the Home Affairs Select Committee, gave rise to substantial changes brought into force for applications made on or after 6 November 2014. The changes include an increase in the minimum investment threshold, and an end to sourcing the investment sum as a loan.

Modernised guidance on this route is at:
https://www.gov.uk/government/publications/points-based-system-tier-1-investor
Policy guidance is at:
https://www.gov.uk/government/publications/guidance-on-application-for-uk-visa-as-tier-1-investor

This is a very complex route, particularly in respect of the evidence required to prove the applicant holds and has under their control the necessary investment sum. Those preparing applications will have to have very close regard to the copious requirements of Part 6A and Appendix A.

There are no English language or maintenance requirements under this route.

Attributes

Initial applications

Those applying for the first time on or after 6 November 2014 as a Tier 1 (Investor) must the following requirement (under Appendix A):

Assets	Points
The applicant has money of his own under his control held in a regulated financial institution and disposable in the UK amounting to not less than £2 million	75

Money is disposable in the UK if all of the money is held in a UK based financial institution or if the money is freely transferable to the UK and convertible to sterling. Funds in a foreign currency will be converted to pounds sterling (£) using the spot exchange rate which appeared on www.oanda.com on the date on which the application was made.

'Money of his own', and 'personal assets' include money or assets belonging to the applicant's spouse, civil partner or unmarried or same-sex partner, provided that specified documents are provided to show that the money or assets are under the applicant's control and that they are free to invest them.

Investment excludes investment by the applicant by way of deposits with a bank, building society or other enterprise whose normal course of business includes the acceptance of deposits.

Subsequent applications

Where an extension application is made by an existing Tier 1 (Investor), all of the following points must be obtained:

Assets and investment	Points
The applicant: (a) has money of his own under his control in the UK amounting to not less than £1 million, or (b) (i) owns personal assets which, taking into account any liabilities to which they are subject, have a value of not less than £2 million, and (ii) has money under his control and disposable in the UK amounting to not less than £1 million which has been loaned to him by a financial institution regulated by the Financial Services Authority.	30
The applicant has invested not less than £750,000 of his capital in the UK by way of UK Government bonds, share capital or loan capital in active and trading UK registered companies and has invested the remaining balance of £1,000,000 in the UK by the purchase of assets or by maintaining the money on deposit in a UK regulated financial institution.	30
(i) The investment referred to above was made:	15

179

> (1) within 3 months of the applicant's entry to the UK, if he was granted entry clearance as a Tier 1 (Investor) Migrant and there is evidence to establish his date of entry to the UK, unless there are exceptionally compelling reasons for the delay in investing, or
>
> (2) within 3 months of the date of the grant of entry clearance or leave to remain as a Tier 1 (Investor) Migrant, unless there are exceptionally compelling reasons for the delay in investing, or
>
> (3) no earlier than 12 months before the date of the application which led to the first grant of leave as a Tier 1 (Investor) Migrant, and in each case the investment has been maintained for the whole of the remaining period of that leave; or
>
> (ii) The migrant has, or was last granted, entry clearance, leave to enter or leave to remain as an Investor.
>
> Reasons for delay in investing must be unforeseeable and outside of the applicant's control. Delays caused by the applicant failing to take timely action will not be accepted.

For those who apply to enter the category on or after 6 November 2014, the full minimum sum of £2m must be invested to qualify the migrant for an extension.

Genuineness

As from 6 November 2014, the UKVI will be able to refuse an investor's application where they have concerns as to the applicant's control of and liberty to freely invest the money specified in their application, as to the legality of the conduct in acquiring the investment funds, and as to the character, conduct or associations of a third party funder.

Switching

Migrants who have or were last granted leave in the following categories can apply for an extension as a Tier 1 (Investor) (taken from paragraph 245ED(c):

(i)   as a Highly Skilled Migrant,
(ii)   as a Tier 1 (General) Migrant,
(iii)   as a Tier 1 (Entrepreneur) Migrant,
(iv)   as a Tier 1 (Investor) Migrant,
(v)   as a Tier 1 (Post-Study Work) Migrant,
(vi)   as a Businessperson,
(vii)   as an Innovator,
(viii) as an Investor,
(ix)   as a Student,
(x)   as a Student Nurse,
(xi)   as a Student Re-Sitting an Examination,
(xii)   as a Student Writing Up a Thesis,
(xiii) as a Work Permit Holder,
(xiv)   as a Writer, Composer or Artist,
(xv)   as a Tier 2 Migrant, or
(xvi)   as a Tier 4 Migrant.

Period and conditions of leave, and curtailment

Initial applicants will be granted leave for 3 years and 4 months (or 3 years if already in the U.K), with a prohibition on recourse to public funds, a requirement to register with the police (where required by paragraph 326). There is no prohibition on the investor taking employment, other than as a doctor or dentist in training or as a professional sportsperson. Extensions will be granted for 2 years with the same conditions.

Leave to enter or remain as a Tier 1 (Investor) Migrant may be curtailed if within 3 months of the entry, the grant of entry clearance or the grant of leave to remain, the applicant has not invested, or had invested on his behalf, at least £750,000 of his capital in the UK by way of UK Government bonds, share capital or loan capital in active and trading UK registered companies other than those principally engaged in property investment, or fails to maintain the investment at that level throughout the remaining period of his leave. That figure rises to £2 million for those granted leave under the rules in place from 6 November 2014.

Settlement

The period of time the investor must spend in the UK, taking account of the continuous residence provisions in rule 245AAA, before applying for settlement, is dependent on the level of the migrant's assets, and the extent of their investments in the UK economy.

Essentially, those with £10 million or more can settle after 2 years, those with £5 million or more after 3 years, and those with £1million or more after 5 years. A minimum of 75% of the total must be invested in UK Government bonds, share capital or loan capital in active and trading UK registered companies, and the rest in the purchase of assets or maintained on deposit in a UK regulated financial institution.

For those applying to enter this route from 6 November 2014, the level of investment of the relevant sum will be need to be 100% of the total, and the minimum sum will be £2 million.

Tier 1 (Exceptional Talent)

Starting at rule 245B, Tier 1 (Exceptional Talent) is for exceptionally talented individuals in particular field, who wish to work in the UK. These individuals are those who are already internationally recognised at the highest level as world leaders in their particular field, or who have already demonstrated exceptional promise and are likely to become world leaders in their particular area.

Essentially, there are a maximum of 1000 grants of leave per year under this route for applicants whose exceptional talent must be endorsed by one of the five 'Designated Competent Bodies':

> ➤ The Arts Council – for arts and culture applications (including those with exceptional promise of becoming exceptionally talented: see HC628)

> ➤ The British Academy – for humanities and social science applications

> ➤ The Royal Society – for natural sciences and medical science research applications

> ➤ The Royal Academy of Engineering – for engineering applications

> ➤ Tech City UK – for digital technology applications

Modernised guidance on this route can be found at: https://www.gov.uk/government/uploads/system/uploads/attachment_data/file/31 4019/Tier_1_Exceptional_talent_v5_0_EXT.pdf.

An applicant under this route must first apply to the UKVI for the Designated Competent Body's endorsement. The five bodies determine who may enter under this scheme and set their own criteria to decide who has sufficient talent. An endorsed potential applicant must then apply for leave.

Application forms and guidance for the application for endorsement are at: https://www.gov.uk/government/publications/application-for-endorsement-for-tier-1-exceptional-talent-visa.

The application for endorsement is made on form Tier 1 (ET) REG. 75 points are required for Attributes, and will be awarded for the obtaining the appropriate endorsement.

An applicant refused endorsement can request a review of the decision (see paragraph 19 and Annex A to the Policy Guidance.

An endorsed applicant can apply for entry clearance, or switch into this route from Tier 1, Tier 2 and Tier 5 (Temporary Worker) (in the latter case where sponsored in the Government Authorised Exchange sub-category in an exchange scheme for sponsored researchers).

There are no English language or maintenance requirements.

Initial applicants will be granted leave for 3 years and 4 months (or 3 years if already in the U.K), with a prohibition on recourse to public funds, and a requirement to register with the police (where required by paragraph 326). There is no prohibition on taking employment other than as a Doctor or Dentist in Training, or professional sportsperson.

For applications made on or after 6 November, initial applications for entry clearance will be granted for 5 years and 4 months, and for leave to remain for 5 years.

For extensions, the exceptionally talented person will need to show, with specified evidence, that they have earned money in the UK (defined at paragraph 6A of Appendix A) as a result of employment or self-employment in their expert field; and that the Designated Competent Body has not withdrawn its endorsement of the applicant. They will also now need to evidence a knowledge of English at minimum level B1 of the Council of Europe's Common European Framework for Language Learning (CEFR). Extensions will be granted for 2 years with the same conditions.

Settlement applications can be made after five years.

Tier 1 (Graduate Entrepreneur)

This route, beginning at rule 245F, opened on 06 April 2012 as a part-replacement for the Tier (1) Post-study Work route. It is for:

➢ UK graduates who have been identified by Higher Education Institutions as having developed genuine and credible business ideas and entrepreneurial skills to extend their stay in the UK after graduation to establish one or more businesses in the UK; and

➢ Graduates who have been identified by UK Trade and Investment as elite global graduate entrepreneurs to establish one or more businesses in the UK.

Modernised guidance on this route can be found at:
https://www.gov.uk/government/uploads/system/uploads/attachment_data/file/34 2863/Tier_1__Graduate_entrepreneur__v8.0_EXT.pdf

Policy guidance for this route is at:
https://www.gov.uk/government/publications/guidance-on-applications-under-tier-1-graduate-entrepreneur

Essentially, those who have graduated in the UK under Tier 4 may apply for leave for up to two further years to establish a business in the UK. In addition to utilising the fruits of their academic success, they will require the endorsement of a licenced UK Higher Education Institution (usually the one they graduate from) for the period of their leave. Some places in the scheme are also open to individuals endorsed by UK Trade and Investment.

There is a limit of 2000 Tier 1 (Graduate Entrepreneur) new approvals per year to be divided between participating institutions and UK Trade and Investment. Up to a maximum of 20 endorsements will be granted per institution. Qualifying institutions must be able to show that they have established processes and competence for identifying, nurturing and developing entrepreneurs among their undergraduate and postgraduate population.

Applicants can apply for entry clearance, or can switch into this route from Tier 4 and Tier 2 (General).

For Attributes, 75 points are required. 25 points will be awarded for each of the following:

➤ The applicant has been endorsed by UK Trade and Investment, or by a UK Higher Education Institution which has Highly Trusted Sponsor status under Tier 4 of the Points based system (and is an A-rated Sponsor if a Tier 2 or Tier 5 licence is also held), has degree awarding powers and has established processes and competence for identifying, nurturing and developing entrepreneurs amongst its undergraduate and postgraduate population.

➤ The applicant has been awarded a degree qualification (not a qualification of equivalent level which is not a degree) which meets or exceeds the recognised standard of a Bachelor's degree in the UK. For overseas qualifications, the standard must be confirmed by UK NARIC.

➤ The endorsement must confirm that the institution has assessed the applicant and considers that they have a genuine, credible and innovative business idea, and the applicant will be spending the majority of their working time on developing business ventures, and if the applicant's previous grant was under this route, they have made satisfactory progress in developing their business since that leave was granted.

An applicant will also need 10 points for English language (at level B1) and 10 points for maintenance (£1890 for entry clearance, £945 for leave to remain).

Leave to remain will be granted for one year at a time, up to a maximum of two years. There is no prohibition on employment other than as a Doctor or Dentist in Training, or professional sportsperson. After the end of the maximum period, successful Graduate entrepreneurs can apply to switch into Tier 1 (Entrepreneur) or Tier 2.

Tier 2: skilled workers

Tier 2 allows employers to recruit skilled employees from outside the United Kingdom and European Economic Area (EEA) to fill a particular post that cannot be filled by a British or EEA worker.

Tier 2 is broken down into the following four categories:

Tier 2

General	Intra Company Transfer	Sportsperson	Minister of religion
• Skilled workers • Quota applies • Must pass resident labour test • Or fill shortage occupation	• Employees of multinational firms • Long-term staff • Short-term staff • Graduate trainee • Skills transfer	• Internationally established at highest level • Must make significant contribution	• Preaching and pastoral work, missionaries or members of religious orders

This manual looks firstly at the provisions which apply across the four categories, and then at those specific to each.

Common provisionsModernised guidance for Tier 2 is at:
https://www.gov.uk/government/publications/points-based-system-tier-2
Policy guidance for applicants is at:
https://www.gov.uk/government/publications/guidance-on-application-for-uk-visa-as-tier-2-worker

All those wishing to apply under any of the Tier 2 categories will need a job offer in the UK from an employer who has a sponsor licence granted to them by the Home Office.

The detail of the processes through which an employer must go in order to become a registered sponsor are beyond the scope of this section. The policy guidance for sponsors is at:
https://www.gov.uk/government/publications/sponsor-a-tier-2-or-5-worker-guidance-for-employers

The sponsoring employer will provide their prospective employee with a Certificate of Sponsorship (CoS) reference number generated by the sponsor management system.

Applicants require a total of 70 points as below:

➢ Attributes (50 points)

➢ English language (10 points)

➢ Maintenance (10 points)

Tier 2 (General)

Tier 2 (General), beginning at rule 245H, enables UK employers to recruit workers from outside the EEA to fill a particular vacancy that cannot be filled by a British or EEA worker.

The relevant vacancy must be for an occupation skilled to National Qualifications Framework (NQF) 6 or above (subject to some exceptions, see para. 77E of Appendix A). A full list of posts at the appropriate skills level is in the codes of practice at Appendix J of the Immigration Rules.

The minimum age for applicants is 16.

Except where the applicant is to be paid a salary of £153,500 or more, an applicant for entry clearance must not have had leave as a Tier 2 migrant in the 12 months preceding their application, and where the sponsor is a limited company must not own more than 10% of its shares. Additionally;

➢ the certificate of sponsorship reference number must be used within 3 months of issue, and the application for entry clearance must be made no more than 3 months before the commencement of employment

➢ the applicant must not previously applied for leave using the same certificate of sponsorship reference number

➢ the sponsor must be A-rated, unless exceptions apply

Quotas for the issue of Certificates of Sponsorship to employers

After being granted a licence, a Sponsor must apply to the Secretary of State for a Certificate of Sponsorship (CoS) for issue to each prospective employee. A quota applies to certificates for new entrants: limited to 20,700 per year. The quota does not apply for those coming to the UK with a salary of £153,500 or over, or for those already sponsored under Tier 2 (General) who are seeking an extension or settlement.

The quota is divided into monthly allocations of 1725 certificates (see Appendix A). If the quota is unused for a particular month then the unused quota rolls over to the following month. If the number of applications in any month exceeds the monthly quota by no more than 100, all the applications will be granted. If there are more, then applications are granted on the basis of how many points they attract. Points are awarded on a sliding scale starting with shortage occupations (see Appendix K to the Immigration Rules), followed by PhD level jobs and lastly for those passing the resident labour market test. Additional points are then awarded for salary levels, starting at £20,300.

Attributes

An applicant requires 50 points for Attributes. So long as the employer has issued the CoS in accordance with the Tier 2 (General) rules, and the appropriate salary (as provided in Appendix J) is paid, the applicant will have the necessary points.

Certificate of Sponsorship	Points	Appropriate salary	Points
Job offer passes Resident Labour Market Test	30	Appropriate salary	20
Resident Labour Market Test exemption applies	30		
Continuing to work in the same occupation for the same Sponsor	30		

Resident labour market test (RLMT)

All posts to be filled by a Tier 2 (General) migrant must satisfy the resident labour market test (RLMT), unless an exemption applies.

Where the test does apply, the employer must first advertise the job in the UK in accordance with the relevant provisions in Appendix A (tables 11B and 11C).

An exemption from the RLMT will apply;

➤ where the employee is continuing to work in the same job for which they were sponsored in their last grant of leave, or
➤ the post is on the shortage occupation list at Appendix K to the Immigration Rules, or
➤ where the migrant seeks to switch from the Tier 1 (Post-Study Work) route, or has graduated whilst in the U.K. under Tier 4 leave.

Maintenance

The requisite 10 points will be awarded for maintenance where the applicant has.

➤ £945 in savings held for a consecutive 90 day period before the application is made

➤ plus a further £630 for each dependant (Appendix E of the Immigration Rules)

➤ or a maintenance undertaking from an A-rated sponsor, which must be endorsed on the CoS

English language skills

10 points will be awarded for knowledge of English at or above level B1 of the CEFR.

The migrant will need to show competence in the English language by:

➢ passing a specified test at the appropriate level;

➢ coming from a majority English speaking country; or

➢ having been awarded a degree taught in English

Genuineness

From 6 November 2014, applicants under Tier 2 (General) (and Tier 2 (ICT)) will have to show (under paragraphs 74G-74J and 81H-81I of Appendix A);

➢ there exists a genuine vacancy,
➢ that has not been exaggerated to meet the Tier 2 skills threshold, or
➢ tailored to exclude resident workers from being recruited, or
➢ where there are reasonable grounds to believe that the applicant is not qualified to do the job.

Additionally, the applicant cannot be sponsored to fill a position, undertake an ongoing routine role or to provide an ongoing routine service for a third party who is not the sponsor.

Switching

The detailed rules for switching into Tier 2 at rule 245HD(b), and the points requirements under Appendix A for switching, including exemptions to the Resident Labour Market Test (RLMT), are now too complex to lay out here in full.

In a nutshell, applicants can switch into Tier 2 from Tier 1 and Tier 2 and their predecessor categories, from Tier 4 in limited circumstances, and Tier 5 (professional footballers only). A partner of a Tier 4 migrant can also switch into Tier 2. There are substantial restrictions on Tier 2 (ICT) and Tier 4 migrants switching into Tier 2 (General). Where those switching have previously studied in the UK, the job may be exempt from the RLMT (see paragraph 78B of Appendix A).

Period and conditions of leave, and curtailment

Entry will be granted for the shorter of the period of engagement plus 1 month, or 5 years and 1 month. The Tier 2 migrant must work in the employment for which they have been sponsored, but can also take supplementary employment and do voluntary work. 'Supplementary employment' is narrowly defined in paragraph 6 of the Immigration Rules. Similar provisions apply to those who have switched into this category.

Where a person granted leave under Tier 2 (General) seeks to extend their stay to continue their employment, they will be granted leave to bring them up to the maximum period of 6 years that they can spend in the UK this category, unless an exception applies.

Those not restricted to the 6 year maximum period under Tier 2 (General) will include those who were granted leave under the Tier 2 rules as they were prior to 6 April 2011 and who have not subsequently been granted entry clearance under Tier 2 or any other category.

Settlement

Those granted leave under Tier 2 on the basis of an application made before 6 April 2011 can settle after 5 years of continuous lawful residence, providing their employer still holds a sponsor licence and still requires the applicant for the employment in question. Time spent in the UK under Tier 1 and in pre-PBS employment categories can be aggregated with the time spent under Tier 2.

For those who arrived in the UK on or after 06 April 2011, they will only be able to apply for settlement after 5 years if they are earning a minimum sum (dependent on their date of application, around £35,000), or are in a job that has at some time whilst they have occupied it been on the shortage occupation list, or are in a PhD-level job. The rules as they will apply from 06 April 2016 are in Appendix I to the rules. Those not meeting these requirements will be able to spend a maximum period of 6 years in the U.K. and will not then be able to return to the U.K. under Tier 2 for a minimum period of 12 months (the 'cooling off' period).

Additionally, the applicant will need a letter from the existing sponsor confirming that:

(i) he still requires the applicant for the employment in question, and

(ii) in the case of a Tier 2 (General) Migrant applying for settlement, that they are paid at or above the appropriate rate for the job as stated in the Codes of Practice in Appendix J, or where the applicant is not paid at that rate only due to maternity, paternity or adoption leave, the date that leave started and that the applicant was paid at the appropriate rate immediately before the leave.

Additional specified evidence must be submitted, including payslips and bank statements, a letter from the employer detailing any absences from work, and further evidence in cases where the applicant is not being paid the appropriate rate in Appendix J due to maternity, paternity or adoption leave.

There is nothing in the Tier 2 Policy Guidance concerning settlement under Tier 2, but there is guidance to Home Office caseworkers in the Modernised guidance (see above link). It is particularly important to make sure the employee is earning the requisite salary at the time of application, and that the specified evidence is provided exactly as stated in the rules.

Tier 2 (Intra-Company Transfer)

Beginning at rule 245G, this route enables multinational employers to transfer their existing employees from outside the EEA to their UK branch for training purposes or to fill a specific vacancy that cannot be filled by a British or EEA worker.

Given the myriad of sub-categories under this route, the many transitional provisions, and the detailed evidential requirements, we lay out here only the bare bones of the scheme.

There are four sub-categories within the Intra Company Transfer route:

> **Long-term staff** - for established, skilled employees to be transferred to the UK branch of their organisation for more than 12 months to fill a post that cannot be filled by a new recruit from the resident workforce. The salary must be at least £41,000. 5 or 9 years leave can be granted.
> As there is no current route to settlement under Tier 2 (ICT), the limit has been set at 9 years to prevent an application for settlement being made on the basis of lawful long residence.

> **Short-term staff** - for established, skilled employees to be transferred to the UK branch of their organisation for 12 months or less to fill a post that cannot be filled by a new recruit from the resident workforce. Salary must be at least £24,500. Up to 12 months leave can be granted.

> **Graduate trainee** - this route allows the transfer of recent graduate employees to a UK branch of the same organisation, as part of a structured graduate training programme which clearly defines progression towards a managerial or specialist role. Salary must be at least £24,500. Up to 12 months leave can be granted.

> **Skills transfer** - this route allows the transfer of new graduate employees to a UK branch of the same organisation to learn the skills and knowledge required to perform their job overseas, or to impart their specialist skills or knowledge to the UK workforce. Salary must be at least £24,500. Up to 6 months leave can be granted.

The requisite points for Attributes will be awarded for a Certificate of Sponsorship and for the appropriate salary being paid. As from 1 October 2013, there has been no English language requirement. Applicants will need savings of £945.00. For migrants entering under the post-6 April 2010 rules, there is no route to settlement. For those applying before that date, a settlement application can be made after 5 years.

There is a 12 month cooling off period for those whose leave has expired and who have returned home.

Tier 2 (Sportsperson)

Beginning at rule 245H, this category is for sportsperson who are internationally established at the highest level; and will make a significant contribution to the development of their sport at the highest level in the United Kingdom.

Tier 2 sportsperson applicants require a valid certificate of sponsorship, which will give them the 50 points they require for Attributes. The employer must show that the potential employee;

➤ is qualified to do the job in question;

➤ intends to base themselves in the United Kingdom;

➤ has been endorsed by the governing body for his/her sport (listed in Appendix M). The endorsement must confirm that the player or coach is internationally established at the highest level whose employment will make a significant contribution to the development of his sport at the highest level in the UK, and that the post could not be filled by a suitable settled worker;

➤ will comply with the conditions of their permission to stay and leave the United Kingdom when their leave expires.

Funds of £945 are required, and basic English at level A1 – enough to say 'bloody ref' or 'on me'ed' when necessary.

Tier 2 (Ministers of Religion)

Also beginning at rule 245H, this category is intended for ministers of religion undertaking preaching and pastoral work, missionaries or members of religious orders. Those applying under the minister of religion category need to:

➤ be qualified to do the job in question;

➤ intend to base themselves in the United Kingdom;

➤ intend to comply with the conditions of permission to stay and leave the United Kingdom when their leave expires.

For applications made on or after 1 October 2013, the applicant must also show that they genuinely intend to undertake, and are capable of undertaking, the role for which they have been employed.

The maintenance requirement is £945, and English language, a minimum of Level B2.

Leave is granted for 3 years and 1 month. A Minister of Religion can apply for ILR after 5 years, which can include a period spent under Tier 1 (other than PSW), in pre-PBS categories, or in other Tier 2 categories.

Tier 4: students

Tier 4 is for migrants who want to study in the UK. It consists of two categories; Tier 4 (General) Student and Tier 4 (Child) Student.

Remember though that students coming for study of up to 6 months (or up to 11 months if learning English) can come under the student visitor category. The prospective student route that used to exist under Part 3 of the Immigration Rules is now closed.

Tier 4 has turned into something of a battleground in recent years. As the largest group of migrants from outside the EEA, students have been at the centre of the government's policy to reduce net migration into the UK. Hundreds of colleges, including publically funded universities, previously granted sponsor licences to recruit overseas students have seen their sponsor licences revoked for failure to comply with the requirements of the scheme. Sponsors have been made wholly responsible for ensuring those they sponsor comply with the Tier 4 scheme, and will now lose their licence if more than 10% of their sponsored students are refused leave by the Home Office. Measures have also been introduced which require students to show their intention to study in the UK is genuine, replicating very much the provisions of the pre-PBS student rules; which provide for maximum time limits to study in the UK, reducing the numbers who qualify for settlement under the 10-year long residence rule; and which allow the Home Office to test the English language ability of overseas students, even where the sponsor has certified the English language to be at the appropriate level.

In both categories, a student applicant must gain 40 points, made up of 30 points for a valid sponsorship arrangement (i.e. they must have been issued by their sponsor with a 'Certificate of Acceptance for Studies' (CAS)), and 10 points for funds.

The policy guidance for applicants is at:
https://www.gov.uk/government/publications/guidance-on-application-for-uk-visa-as-tier-4-student
Modernised guidance is at:
https://www.gov.uk/government/collections/studying-modernised-guidance

Tier 4

General

- Most adult students will fall into this category
- Sponsorship is mandatory
- Minimum academic levels
- Maximum time limits for studies
- Variable maintenance provisions

Child students

- For sponsored students under the age of 18 studying at a fee-paying independent school in the UK

Requirement to have a sponsor

Before a student can apply to come to the UK to study under Tier 4, he or she must be sponsored. The sponsor will be the education provider in the UK that has accepted the student for a course of study. The education provider must have a Home Office sponsor licence. They will issue the students they sponsor a CAS, essentially a reference number from the Sponsor Management System.

The Home Office states that sponsorship plays two main roles in the application process:

(i) It provides an assurance that the education provider is confident that the student is capable of doing the particular course of study; and

(ii) It involves a pledge from the sponsoring education provider that it will accept responsibility for the student whilst he is in the UK.

The Tier 4 register of sponsors is at:
https://www.gov.uk/government/publications/register-of-licensed-sponsors-students

Licensing of sponsors

Guidance for Tier 4 sponsors, including guidance for making sponsor licence applications, is at:
https://www.gov.uk/government/publications/sponsor-a-tier-4-student-guidance-for-educators

All education providers need a Home Office sponsor licence if they want to recruit students from outside the EEA. To get a licence, education providers need to show they are inspected or audited or hold valid accreditation with one of the Home Office approved accreditation bodies.

All Tier 4 sponsors must apply for Highly Trusted Sponsor (HTS) status within 12 months of being granted their licence. Sponsors who do not apply for or are refused HTS status will have their licence suspended, and will not be able to sponsor further students.

To comply with the licence requirements, sponsors must:

(i)   Keep a copy of all their non-EEA students' passports and biometric residence permits;

(ii)   Keep each student's contact details and update them as necessary;

(iii)   Report to the Home Office any unauthorised student absences including a student who;

- Fails to enrol with them by no later than 10 working days after the end of their prescribed enrolment period;
- Misses 10 consecutive expected contacts. For students in schools, Further Education (FE) and English Language Colleges this will normally be where the student has missed 2 weeks of a course. In the Higher Education (HE) sector, where daily registers are not kept the Home Office will accept this reporting where the student has missed 10 expected interactions (e.g. Tutorials, submission of coursework etc);
- Stops attending either because they have withdrawn them from the course or because the student has said they are leaving, within 10 working days of this being confirmed;
- Defers their studies after their arrival in the UK. In such cases the student's permission to be in the UK will cease to be valid as they will no longer be actively studying. The sponsor will need to notify the Home Office of the deferral and advise the student to leave the UK. When the student is ready to resume their studies they will need to make a fresh visa application.

(iv)   Report to the Home Office any students who discontinue their studies (including any deferrals of study);

(v)   Report to the Home Office any significant changes in students' circumstances, (e.g. if the duration of a course of study shortens);

(vi)   Maintain any appropriate accreditation;

(vii)   Offer only those courses to international students which comply with the Home Office conditions;

(viii) Comply with applicable PBS rules and the law; and

(ix)   Co-operate with the Home Office as to the sponsorship requirements generally.

Should more than 20% (10% as from 1 November 2014) of the sponsor's students be refused leave following the issue of a CAS, or drop out or fail to enrol in the course, this will raise concerns about the sponsor's recruitment processes and their overall suitability as a sponsor. In these circumstances the Home Office state they will investigate and can suspend or revoke HTS status or the licence itself.

Tier 4 (General)

Beginning at rule 245ZT, this is the category under which most applications for the purpose of study in the UK are made.

Eligibility

When the student applies for their entry clearance or an extension, they will need a valid CAS from a licensed sponsor, and evidence of meeting the maintenance requirement. Unusually under the PBS, the English language requirements are under Appendix A. It is for the sponsor to assess that the English language requirements are met when issuing the CAS. A failure by the sponsor to properly do so could render the CAS invalid.

The student may also need to satisfy the Home Office as to their English language proficiency and that they are a genuine student. Applicants may be interviewed for this purpose. Failure to attend an interview without a reasonable explanation is a new mandatory ground of refusal (r.320(7D)).

If refused a visa, applicants can apply to the entry clearance post for Administrative Review of the decision. Those refused an extension of stay can usually appeal to the First-tier Tribunal (IAC) (until Part 2 of the Immigration Act 2014 is commenced). In either case, applicants will not be able to rely on evidence not submitted with their application. It is therefore important to get the application right first time.

Visas are granted for the full duration of the course, and a little bit extra.

There are a number of general requirements and restrictions under Tier 4 (General). These are laid out in Part 6A and relate to;

➢ Age
➢ Security clearance
➢ Maximum time limits for studying in the UK
➢ Particular requirements for postgraduate doctors or dentists on a recognised Foundation Programme
➢ And for those currently being sponsored by a Government or international scholarship agency
➢ The Entry Clearance Officer must be satisfied that the applicant is a genuine student

In addition to these Part 6A provisions, some of which we will look at below, many additional requirements under Tier 4 are provided for in Appendix A, and relate to the validity of the CAS. We look at the Appendix A provisions under the 'CAS' section further down.

Applicants will be expected to provide specified evidence of meeting the maintenance requirement, and of the qualifications they relied on when applying to the education provider for sponsorship, so that they can be verified by the UKVI.

Low risk countries

However, students from specified countries considered low risk and who are sponsored by a Highly Trusted Sponsor will receive light-touch scrutiny and will not have to produce documentary evidence to support their application unless requested to do so. Students of low risk countries can though be interviewed to test their genuineness.

The list of low risk nationalities, in Appendix H to the Immigration Rules, at the time of writing was as follows:

- Argentina
- Australia
- Barbados
- Botswana
- Brunei
- Canada
- Chile
- Hong Kong
- Japan
- Malaysia
- New Zealand
- Oman
- Qatar
- Singapore
- South Korea
- Taiwan (for some passport holders)
- Trinidad and Tobago
- UAE
- United States of America
- a British National (Overseas)

Age restrictions

The applicant must be at least 16 years old. If under 18, the applicant must have the support and consent of their parent(s).

Security clearance

Where the applicant wishes to undertake a course in a discipline listed in Appendix 6, they will need a valid Academic Technology Approval Scheme (ATAS) clearance certificate from the Counter-Proliferation Department of the Foreign and Commonwealth Office. Appendix 6 includes courses involving various sciences, maths and engineering which might provide the necessary skills for would-be terrorists (and vets). As an example, a student applying from Iran to do post-doctoral research in plutonium enrichment may not be welcomed with open arms by the FCO.

Maximum length of stay as a student

If the course is below degree level, the grant of leave the applicant is seeking must not lead to the applicant having spent more than 3 years in the UK as a Tier 4 Migrant since the age of 18 studying courses that did not consist of degree level study. Degree level study is defined in paragraph 6 as;

'A course which leads to a recognised United Kingdom degree at bachelor's level or above, or an equivalent qualification at level 6 or above of the revised National Qualifications Framework, or levels 9 or above of the Scottish Credit and Qualifications Framework'.

There is also a 5-year time limit for those studying at degree level or above. This provision was designed to make it more difficult for a student to meet the requirements of the 10-year rule, the 'holy grail'. Exceptions to the 5-year rule include;

➢ Migrants studying for a Master's degree at a Higher Education Institution (HEI), following successful completion of an undergraduate degree where the course duration was 4 or 5 years. For these students the limit will be set at 6 years in total instead of 5. This will cover the typical situation in Scottish universities (but applies also to the rest of the UK).

➢ Those studying for a PhD at an HEI. However if on completion of the PhD the time spent in Tier 4 (General) exceeds 8 years, no further leave will be granted in Tier 4.

➢ Those following courses in:

  o Architecture;

  o Medicine;

  o Dentistry;

  o Law, where the applicant has completed a course at degree level in the UK and is progressing to:

    ▪ a law conversion course validated by the Joint Academic Stage Board in England and Wales, a Masters in Legal Science (MLegSc) in Northern Ireland, or an accelerated graduate LLB in Scotland; or

    ▪ the Legal Practice Course in England and Wales, the Solicitors Course in Northern Ireland, or a Diploma in Professional Legal Practice in Scotland; or

    ▪ the Bar Professional Training Course in England and Wales, or the Bar Course in Northern Ireland

  o Veterinary Medicine & Science; or

  o Music at a music college that is a member of Conservatoires UK (CUK).

197

The 5 year limit, and exceptions, operates in addition to time permitted in Tier 4 (General) at below degree level (3 years) and any time spent in the Tier 4 (Child) route.

Genuine student provision

This provision applies both to applications for entry clearance and for in-country applicants. It allows for students to be interviewed by the decision maker in order that their English language skills can be tested, and to satisfy them that the applicant is a genuine student.

The ECO should interview the applicant in accordance with their policy as laid out in the <u>Entry Clearance Guidance</u> (ECG);

> 4. In assessing whether the applicant is a genuine student, ECOs must take into account all the evidence available from the application and from the interview. If, having reviewed the application, they have one or more reasonable doubts that the applicant is a genuine student and an interview has been conducted, ECOs should take into account all the following factors insofar as they are relevant, and any other relevant matters before deciding whether they consider, based on their expertise in assessing entry clearance applications and the evidence available to them (including any omissions in such evidence), that the applicant meets the requirement of paragraph 245ZV(k).
>
> The following issues are not a checklist and must not be used as such. They are a guide to assessing whether an applicant satisfies paragraph 245ZV(k). These examples will not be appropriate to all cases and ECOs may consider other relevant matters that arise in the particular circumstances of each case.
>
> i) The immigration history of the applicant and any dependant, in the UK and other countries, for example:
> - Previous visa applications for the UK and other countries, including reasons for any visa refusals;
> - The amount of time the applicant has spent in the UK or other countries on previous visas, and for what purpose; or
> - Whether the applicant has complied with the terms of previous visas for the UK and other countries.
>
> ii) The applicant's education history, study and post study plans, for example:
> - The amount of time that has elapsed since the applicant last studied, and whether the applicant has sound reasons for returning to, or commencing, formal study in this area, particularly after any significant gap;
> - Whether the applicant demonstrates sufficient commitment to the course;
> - Whether the course represents academic progression;
> - The credibility of the applicant's rationale for, knowledge of, and level of research undertaken into, the proposed course of study and sponsoring institution, and living arrangements in the UK;
> - The relevance of the course to post-study plans in the UK or overseas; or
> - How the circumstances of any dependant may affect the ability or motivation of the applicant to study.

iii) The personal and financial circumstances of the applicant and any dependant, for example:

- The economic circumstances of the applicant and any dependant in their region in their home country;
- Whether the applicant has credible funds to meet course fees, and living costs for himself / herself and any dependants for the duration of the course in a UK city, with limited or no ability to work in the UK;
- How the applicant was able to acquire the necessary funds for course fees, as well as accommodation in a UK city and living expenses in a UK city for themselves and any dependant;
- The distance between the applicant's place of study and their proposed accommodation in the UK:
- The average monthly expenditure for the applicant and any dependant in a UK city; or
- The applicant's personal circumstances, where these would make it difficult to complete a full-time course of study.

The ECO should take account of the fact that the applicant will need to make a considerable investment in gaining a qualification from the UK.

iv) The qualification, course provider and agents, for example:

- If the applicant is applying to study towards a qualification or attend an institution that is under investigation or has been identified by the Home Office as an institution of concern in relation to immigration compliance; or
- where the application is being managed by an agent about which there are concerns, that may be an indication the applicant is not a genuine student.

v) Where an applicant will be accompanied by a dependant or dependants and it appears that the one of the main applicant's reasons for applying for a Tier 4 (General) Student visa is employment, education or health care benefits to the dependants, the case-worker should consider particularly carefully whether they are satisfied that the applicant is a genuine student.

The interview may be short and brutal. The decision maker may well be looking for reasons to refuse the application and will take no prisoners. It will be a key part of the adviser's role to prepare their clients for their interview, and vital for the applicant to be well prepared for any questions that may be asked. They will be well advised, for instance, to find out the opening times of their college's library before their interview!

The CAS

Under Appendix A, the only way to earn the requisite 30 points for Attributes is to hold a valid CAS. Paragraphs 116 - 120 of Appendix A lay out the detailed requirements that need to be met for the CAS to be valid. These include requirements that;

➢ The CAS must have been issued by a Tier 4 (General) licenced sponsor, and no more than 6 months before the application is made, and the offer must not have been withdrawn;

➢ The sponsor must be A-rated or HTS status (unless the CAS is being issued for the completion of a course already commenced)

➢ The application for entry clearance or leave to remain is made no more than 3 months before the start date of the course of study;

➢ The CAS cannot have been used for a previous decided (i.e. valid) application;

➢ The CAS must contain mandatory information concerning the applicant and the course (e.g. the study address, the course fees, any work placements involved, how the applicant's English language skills were assessed);

➢ The student must provide specified documents unless exempt (see paragraph 120-SD);

➢ If not issued for studies, the CAS must be issued to a student union sabbatical officer or person on the doctorate extension scheme;

➢ The applicant must have met the English language requirements (see below);

➢ Is for a single course of study, or for a pre-sessional course followed by a degree;

➢ If the sponsor is not a HTS, the applicant must not previously have re-sat the same examination or repeated the same module more than once;

The CAS must be issued for a course which;

➢ leads to an 'approved qualification' (see below); and

➢ is at NQF Level 3, or Level 6 SCQF in Scotland, or above if the sponsor is an HTS, or NQF4/SCQF7 or above if not; or

➢ at minimum Level B2 CEFR if for an English language course; or

➢ if for a person studying at an overseas HEI, is a short term Study Abroad Programme at degree level;

➢ or the course must be a recognised Foundation Programme for postgraduate doctors or dentists; and

➢ must be for a full time course at degree level, or otherwise be a full time course of study involving a minimum of 15 hours per week organised daytime study; and

➢ the course must represent genuine academic progress i.e. (i) be above the level of the previous course for which the applicant was granted leave as a Tier 4 (General) Student or as a Student, or (ii) involve further study at the same level, which the Tier 4 Sponsor confirms as complementing the previous course for which the applicant was granted leave as a Tier 4 (General) Student or as a Student.

Restrictions also apply to courses where there is a work placement involved.

An approved qualification is one that is:

(1) validated by Royal Charter,

(2) awarded by a body that is on the list of recognised bodies produced by the Department for Business, Innovation and Skills,

(3) recognised by one or more recognised bodies through a formal articulation agreement with the awarding body,

(4) in England, Wales and Northern Ireland, on the Register of Regulated Qualifications (http://register.ofqual.gov.uk/) at National Qualifications Framework (NQF) / Qualifications and Credit Framework (QCF) level 3 or above,

(5) in Scotland, accredited at Level 6 or above in the Scottish Credit and Qualifications Framework (SCQF) by the Scottish Qualifications Authority,

(6) an overseas qualification that UK NARIC assesses as valid and equivalent to National Qualifications Framework (NQF) / Qualifications and Credit Framework (QCF) level 3 or above, or

(7) covered by a formal legal agreement between a UK-recognised body and another education provider or awarding body.

English language

The detailed rules setting out the English language requirements under Tier 4 are in Appendix A (and not in Appendix B as might be expected). The substantive and evidential requirements are complex.

It will be for the sponsor to ensure they are met, and they will need to certify on the CAS that they have assessed the student and that they meet the requirements.

For degree level study the requirement is a minimum level of B2 CEFR in all four components (reading, writing, speaking and listening), and for below degree level a minimum level of B1.

The evidential requirements differ depending on the level of the course and type of provider. Particularly, where the course is at degree level and provided by a publically funded sponsor, there is no requirement for the student to provide a test certificate.

Funds and maintenance

Students will be expected to show that they hold sufficient funds to cover the full costs of their course fees (or for the first academic year if the course is for a year or more) plus £1020 per month for maintenance (£820 per month for those studying outside London) for each month of the course up to a maximum of 9 months.

Students with an 'established presence studying in the United Kingdom' need only show the £1020 or £820 requirement for a maximum of 2 months rather than 9 months.A student is considered to have an established presence if:

➢ He/she has completed a course that was at least six months long within their last period of leave, and this leave finished within the last four months; or

➢ He/she is applying for continued study on a course where he/she has studied at least six months of that course and has been studying within the last four months; or

➢ He/she is applying to continue in Tier 4 as a sabbatical officer or as a Postgraduate Doctor or Dentist and he/she has completed a course that was at least six months long within his/her last period of leave, and this leave finished within the last four months; and

➢ Must have current leave at the time of application. There is no disregard of up to 28 days of overstaying here. If the applicant becomes an overstayer, they will need to meet the full maintenance requirement.

The money must be held in the relevant account at the date of the application and for a consecutive 28 day period beforehand.

Example

For a course lasting 12 months or more for a student with no established presence, an applicant must have the course fees for the first year of the course plus £9180 for maintenance (£7380 if outside London). They must have held this amount for 28 days prior to the date of application.

Study is considered to be in London if more than 50% of the applicant's study time is in any of the following London boroughs: Camden, City of London, Hackney, Hammersmith and Fulham, Haringey, Islington, Kensington and Chelsea, Lambeth, Lewisham, Newham, Southwark, Tower Hamlets,

Wandsworth and Westminster. The address given in the visa letter is used by the Home Office to determine the main study site.

The funds must consist of one or more of;

➢ Cash in an account in the applicant's name (including a joint account)

➢ Cash in an account in an account owned by the parents or legal guardians of the student where the relationship can be proven and permission to use the funds is demonstrated by specified evidence

➢ For child students, cash in an account in their parent's name (with prescribed additional evidence such as a birth certificate and a letter from the parent).

➢ A loan in the applicant's name

➢ Official financial or government sponsorship.

Length and conditions of leave

Leave will be granted for the duration of the course. The following table sets out the extra leave that is granted on top of this period:

Type of course	Period of entry clearance to be granted before the course starts	Period of entry clearance to be granted after the course ends
12 months or more	1 month	4 months
6 months or more but less than 12 months	1 month	2 months
Pre-sessional course of less than 6 months	1 month	1 month
Course of less than 6 months that is not a pre-sessional course	7 days	7 days
Postgraduate doctor or dentist	1 month	1 month

Those completing a PhD in the UK can apply for an additional 12 months leave under the doctorate extension scheme (245ZX(n)).

The no recourse to public funds condition will always be applied. Employment is forbidden except as follows:

(1) employment during term time of no more than 20 hours per week for those studying at degree level and above

(2) employment during term time of no more than 10 hours per week for those studying below degree level (including Foundation degrees), but only at certain colleges

(3) employment (of any duration) during vacations

(4) employment as part of a course-related work placement which forms an assessed part of the applicant's course and provided that any period that the applicant spends on that placement does not exceed half of the total length of the course undertaken in the UK

(5) employment as a Student Union Sabbatical Officer, for up to 2 years, provided the post is elective and is at the institution which is the applicant's Sponsor

(6) employment as a postgraduate doctor or dentist on a recognised Foundation Programme.

Additionally, a Tier 4 (General) student may not be self-employed, or employed as a Doctor in Training other than a vacancy on a recognised Foundation Programme, professional sportsperson (including a sports coach) or an entertainer, and must not fill a full time vacancy other than a vacancy on a recognised Foundation Programme.

Extensions

To apply for an extension as a Tier 4 (General) student, a person must have, or have last been granted, entry clearance, leave to enter or leave to remain in one of the following categories (taken from paragraph 245ZX(b)):

(i) as a Tier 4 (General) Student,
(ii) as a Tier 4 (Child) Student,
(iii) as a Tier 1 (Post-study Work) Migrant,
(iv) as a Tier 2 Migrant,
(v) as a Participant in the International Graduates Scheme (or its predecessor, the Science and Engineering Graduates Scheme),
(vi) as a Participant in the Fresh Talent: Working in Scotland Scheme,
(vii) as a Postgraduate Doctor or Dentist,
(viii) as a Prospective Student,
(ix) as a Student,
(x) as a Student Nurse,
(xi) as a Student Re-sitting an Examination,
(xii) as a Student Writing-Up a Thesis,
(xiii) as a Student Union Sabbatical Officer, or
(xiv) as a Work Permit Holder.

Paragraph 245ZX(l) requires that the applicant must be applying for leave to remain for the purpose of studies which would commence no more than 28 days after the applicant's current entry clearance or leave to remain (including 3C leave) expires or, where the applicant has overstayed, within 28 days of when that period of overstaying began. Where the gap between the leave running out and the new course is more than 28 days, the student is expected to return home and apply for entry clearance.

For applications made from 20 October 2014, a refusal will no longer attract a right of appeal to the Tribunal. Instead, an Administrative Review will be available (see section on Administrative Review under the chapter on Appeals). Students (and those facing deportation) will be the first victims of the cull in appeals rights introduced in stages by the Immigration Act 2014.

Tier 4 (Child)

Beginning at rule 245ZZ, this route is for children at least 4 years old and under the age of 18 who wish to be educated in the UK.

The following forms of study will be permitted with the following forms of assessment:

➤ **Residential Independent Schools**
For a child studying and boarding at a residential independent school the Home Office will require evidence of sufficient funds to pay school fees for a year plus any additional accommodation fees required by the school. Access to funds will need to be demonstrated through either money in the child's own name or money in accounts held by a parent or legal guardian.

➤ **Non-Residential Independent School (private foster care arrangement)**
For a child studying at a non-residential independent school in a private foster care arrangement, the Home Office will require evidence of sufficient funds to pay school fees for one year plus an undertaking from a UK resident or citizen to provide maintenance and accommodation for the duration of the course. The undertaking must set out the nature of the relationship with the child and the child's parent(s). In addition, the individual providing maintenance and accommodation will need to be able to demonstrate that they have accommodation and the funds to support a child in addition to their own existing commitments (available income of at least £500 per month will be required).

➤ **Independent School (Parent accompanying a child under 12)**
The Home Office will continue to allow children studying at independent schools under the age of 12 to be accompanied to the UK by a parent who will be responsible for their care. In this case, the Home Office will require evidence of funds required to pay school fees for one year plus £1335 per month for each month up to a maximum of 12 months. If more than one child is studying then as well as evidence of ability to pay annual fees for each additional child, evidence of a further £535 per month will need to be shown to be available for each additional child.

The following periods of leave will be granted:

Category	Leave
Child of primary school age at an independent fee paying school.	Leave may be granted for the duration of studies to the end of the academic year in which the child is 11, then to 31 October.
Child aged 11-16 studying pre/ for GCSEs at an independent fee-paying school.	Leave may be granted for the duration of studies to the end of the academic year in which the child is 16, then to 31 October.
Child aged 16 or over studying for A-levels at an independent fee-paying school.	Leave may be granted for the duration of studies to the end of the academic year in which child is 18, then to 31 October.

Tier 5: youth mobility and temporary workers

This two-part tier of the PBS collected together and replaced a range of schemes and programmes that formerly existed both inside and outside the immigration rules, the best known being the working holiday maker scheme.

Entry clearance is mandatory under Tier 5.

Tier 5

Youth Mobility Scheme	Temporary Workers
• Two year visa • Open to young people aged 18 to 31 • from Australia, Canada, New Zealand, Japan, Monaco Taiwan, Hong Kong and S. Korea • and British nationals who are not British citizens	• Creative and sporting • Charity worker • Religious • Government authorised exchange • International agreement

Tier 5 (Youth Mobility Scheme)

Beginning at rule 245ZI, this scheme is for young people from participating countries and territories who wish to live and work temporarily in the UK. The successful applicant will be able to spend a maximum of two years in the UK doing pretty much as they wish (subject to some restrictions on self-employment). It is open to nationals of the following countries, as listed in Appendix G:

- Australia
- Monaco
- Canada
- Taiwan
- Japan
- South Korea
- New Zealand
- Hong Kong

An annual quota of places is available for each of the above countries (see Appendix G for the current quotas). In addition to the Appendix G countries, the scheme is also open (without quotas) to British Overseas Citizens, British Overseas Territories Citizens or British Nationals (Overseas).

Countries who wish to join the scheme must have a reciprocal arrangement for granting young British citizens a similar visa.

Entry clearance is mandatory. There is no facility to switch into this category. The maximum stay is for 2 years. An applicant must be 18 or over when his or her entry clearance becomes valid for use and under the age of 31 on the date his or her application is made. The applicant must have no children under the age of 18 who are either living with him or her or for whom he or she is financially responsible.

But for Hong Kong, Taiwan, and South Korea, sponsorship is deemed on the basis that the applicant holds the appropriate passport (and so is a bit of a myth, really). Nationals of Hong Kong, Taiwan, and South Korea must apply to their governments for a certificate of sponsorship (COS). The GOV.UK website provides links to the relevant country's COS application process at: https://www.gov.uk/tier-5-youth-mobility/eligibility

In addition to sponsorship, deemed or actual, the applicant must show that they have £1890 available in funds (held for 90 day continuous period prior to the date of application). Specified documents under paragraph 1B of Appendix C must be submitted as proof of the availability of these funds.

The applicant must not previously have spent time in the UK as a Working Holidaymaker or a Tier 5 (Youth Mobility Scheme) Temporary Migrant.

If all of these requirements are met, entry clearance will be granted for a period of 2 years subject to the following conditions:

(a) no recourse to public funds,

(b) registration with the police, if this is required by paragraph 326 of these Rules,

(c) no employment as a professional sportsperson (including as a sports coach), and

(d) no employment as a Doctor or Dentist in Training, unless the applicant has obtained a degree in medicine or dentistry at bachelor's level or above from a UK institution that is a UK recognised or listed body, or which holds a sponsor licence under Tier 4 of the Points Based System, and provides evidence of this degree.

(e) no self employment, except where the following conditions are met:

    (i)   the migrant has no premises which he owns, other than his home, from which he carries out his business,

    (ii)   the total value of any equipment used in the business does not exceed £5,000, and

    (iii)   the migrant has no employees.

Tier 5 (Temporary worker)

This route (245ZM et seq) is for certain types of temporary worker whose entry helps to satisfy cultural, charitable, religious or international objectives including volunteering and job shadowing.

The scheme provides for temporary workers in the following categories (some of which have sub-categories);

- creative and sporting
- government authorised exchange
- charity workers
- religious workers
- international agreement

Guidance for sponsors is at:
https://www.gov.uk/government/publications/sponsor-a-tier-2-or-5-worker-guidance-for-employers

Modernised guidance is at:
https://www.gov.uk/government/publications/points-based-system-tier-5-temporary-worker

The principle requirement for a Tier 5 (Temporary Worker) is the obtaining of a Certificate of Sponsorship. Unlike Tier 2, the sponsor need not necessarily be the migrant's employer, but must have a sponsor licence.

The maximum length of leave will depend on the particular purpose of entry. Maximum lengths of stay range from 6 to 24 months (and up to 5 years for a private servant in a diplomatic household under the international agreement category.

Prior entry clearance will usually be required for Tier 5 temporary workers. The only exception being for those who are non-visa nationals sponsored under the creative and sporting category where the total period of engagement (including any gaps between consecutive engagements) is for no more than three months.

In addition to points for Attributes and maintenance, a 'genuineness' requirement was added to the Tier 5 (Temporary Worker) category from 1 October 2013. The applicant must genuinely intend and be capable of undertaking the role for which they have been sponsored.

There is no English language requirement.

For maintenance the applicant will need £945 or an undertaking from an A rated sponsor.

We outline the categories below.

Creative and sporting category

This category is for migrants who want to come to the United Kingdom to work as sports people for up to 12 months, or to perform as entertainers or creative artists for up to 24 months. The requirements are then sub-divided into sporting and creative requirements.

Sporting

This subcategory is aimed at sportspeople who are internationally established at the highest level in their sport and/or whose employment will make a significant contribution to the development and operation of that particular sport in the United Kingdom and for coaches who must be suitably qualified to fulfil the role in question. Whether such requirements are met is for the sponsor to decide, notably.

Sporting sponsors must be a sporting body, sports club, events organiser or other organiser operating, or intending to operate in the sporting sector. An agent cannot be a sponsor under Tier 5 sporting sub-category. The prospective sponsor must submit an endorsement from the Home Office recognised governing body for the sport. A governing body is one that is recognised by one of the home country sports councils (for example Sport England). A list of the approved governing bodies is at Appendix M to the Immigration Rules. If there is no recognised governing body, the Home Office can be contacted.

A migrant who has already been granted leave under Tier 5 (Creative and Sport) for a job as a footballer may switch into Tier 2 (Sportsperson) provided they will still be employed as a footballer and he/she can meet the Tier 2 (Sportsperson) migrant requirements.

Creative

In order to gain a licence as a sponsor of creative and sporting workers and their entourage, the prospective sponsor must be operating, or intend to operate, in the creative or sporting sector. Examples include a national body, event organiser, producer, venue, agent or other similar organisation. Where applicable, the prospective sponsor must prior to issuing each certificate of sponsorship commit to having applied the Home Office codes of practice for taking into account the needs of the resident labour market in that field. The codes of practice will operate in three specific areas: dance, theatre, and film & television.

Charity worker category

Migrants coming to work temporarily in the United Kingdom as charity workers should only be undertaking voluntary activity and not paid employment. The migrant should intend to carry out fieldwork directly related to the purpose of the sponsoring organisation.

Migrants entering the United Kingdom under the charity workers sub-category will be given a maximum of 12 months' permission to stay. Their dependants will be allowed to work if they are accompanying or joining them in the United Kingdom.

Religious worker category

The religious worker category is for people coming to the United Kingdom to work temporarily. Religious workers can:

- do preaching, pastoral work and non-pastoral work;

- work in the United Kingdom in the same way that they are working in an overseas organisation (although their duties in the United Kingdom may be different). The job should be done in their holiday from their job overseas; or

- work in a religious order with a community which involves a permanent commitment, such as a monastery or convent. The work in a religious order must be in the order itself or be outside work directed by the order. A migrant can apply if he or she is a novice whose training means taking part in the daily community life of the order.

The work of a member of a religious order must be within the order itself, or outside work directed by the order. Teachers working in schools not maintained by their order must apply as a teacher under Tier 2 (General). Novices whose training consists of taking part in the daily community life of their order may apply under this category, but anyone studying for a qualification, on a formal full-time course of study or training in an academic institution not maintained by the order should apply as a student under Tier 4. People who are not members of a religious order, but who are working or studying within such a community, are not eligible to apply under this category and must satisfy the requirements of the relevant work or study category.

Migrants entering the United Kingdom under this category will be given a maximum of 24 months' permission to stay. Their dependants will be allowed to work if accompanying or joining them in the United Kingdom.

Sponsors wishing to apply for a licence under this category must be a bona fide religious institution, which is defined as follows:

(i)   Is a registered, excepted or exempt United Kingdom charity or is an ecclesiastical corporation established for charitable purposes. Charities who are not registered according to the relevant charity legislation must explain the reason for non-registration in their application for a sponsor licence

(ii)   It must be the structure for a faith-based community with a common system of belief and spiritual goals, codes of behaviour and religious practice, which exists to support and/or propagate those common beliefs and practices and where such beliefs
- include any religious belief or similar philosophical belief in something transcendental, metaphysical or ultimate
- exclude any philosophical or political belief concerned with man, unless that belief is similar to religious belief

(iii)   Does not exclude from its community on the basis of gender, nationality or ethnicity

(iv)   Receives financial and material support for its core religious ministry from its congregation or community on a voluntary basis only, without promise or coercion

(v)   Does not breach, or encourage others to breach, any United Kingdom legislation and

(vi)   Does not operate against the public interest, or in a way that has a detrimental effect on personal or family life as these are commonly understood in the United Kingdom.

Government authorised exchange category

A list of approved government authorised exchanged schemes is at Appendix N to the Immigration Rules.

The government authorised exchange category is for people coming to the United Kingdom through approved schemes that aim to share knowledge, experience and best practice. This category must not be used to fill job vacancies or to bring unskilled labour to the United Kingdom.

Migrants entering the United Kingdom under the government authorised exchange category will be given a maximum of 12 or 24 months' permission to stay, depending on the scheme. Their dependants are allowed to work if they are accompanying or joining them in the United Kingdom.

Usually there will have to be an overarching body to administer an exchange scheme under this category. This overarching body will be the sponsor and must apply for a licence. The scheme and the overarching body must have the support of a United Kingdom government department or one of its executive agencies. The overarching body will assign certificates of sponsorship to migrants who meet the requirements of the scheme.

Tier 4 graduates undertaking corporate internships can apply for an Extension under Tier 5.

International agreement category

This category is for migrants who are coming to the United Kingdom under contract to provide a service that is covered under international law, including:

- the General Agreement on Trade in Services (GATS);

- similar agreements between the United Kingdom and another country;

- employees of overseas governments and international organisations; and

- private servants in diplomatic households.

Migrants entering the United Kingdom under the international agreement sub-category can apply for leave as follows:

- GATS and similar agreements, up to a maximum of 24 months;

- Employees of overseas governments and international organisations, up to an initial maximum of 24 months, with the option to make in-country extensions for periods of 12 months at a time up to a total maximum of 72 months

- Private servants in diplomatic households, or households of employees of international organisations, up to an initial maximum of 24 months, with the option to make in-country extensions for periods of 12 months at a time up to a total maximum of 72 months.

Their dependants will be allowed to work if they are accompanying or joining them in the United Kingdom.

Family members of PBS migrants

Provision is made at Part 8 of the Immigration Rules for the entry of dependent family members of most PBS migrants (rules 319AA-319J), though severe restrictions apply to the dependents of Tier 4 migrants. Relevant family members are spouses, civil partners, unmarried partners and minor children.

Modernised Guidance is at:
https://www.gov.uk/government/publications/family-members-of-points-based-system-migrants

Policy Guidance is at:
https://www.gov.uk/government/publications/guidance-for-dependants-of-uk-visa-applicants-tiers-1-2-4-5

Applications can be made for entry clearance and, for those with leave other than as a visitor, from within the UK.

Under Tier 4, only students applying to study at postgraduate level for a year or more can now be accompanied or joined by dependants. Those dependants of students who were granted leave prior to this restriction being imposed are able though to continue to extend their leave in line with the Tier 4 migrant.

The PBS migrant or dependant, other than in the Tier 1 (Exceptional Talent) and Tier 1 (Investor categories) must show the availability of additional funds as laid out in Appendix E to the Immigration Rules.

Leave will be granted to expire on the same day as that of the PBS migrant.

To qualify for a grant of ILR following or at the same time as the PBS migrant, those granted leave as a partner of the PBS migrant will have to have been in the U.K. for a minimum of two years. For applicants applying to join this category on or after 9 July 2012 the qualifying period of settlement will be five years. The PBS dependant will be able to extend their stay in the same capacity to bring them up to the five year point, rather than switch into Appendix FM, even though the PBS migrant may already by then have been granted ILR or British citizenship.

Dependants, but for those of some Tier 4 migrants, can work in the U.K.

Challenging PBS decisions

Those refused a visa under Part 6A of the Immigration Rules have no right of appeal. At the outset of the PBS, the government argued that the new rules were so simple and transparent, and the criteria so completely objective, that the right of appeal was unnecessary. That was never true, but as the requirements of the PBS have become increasingly complex, and particularly with the addition of very subjective genuineness requirements, it is difficult to see how the government can reasonably sustain that argument.

There is currently a right of appeal to the First-tier Tribunal for those refused an extension of stay under the PBS, though provisions added to the Nationality

Immigration and Asylum 2002 Act restrict a judge to considering only those documents submitted with the PBS application.

Under s85A of the 2002 Act, the Tribunal may consider evidence adduced by the appellant only if it:

> ➤ was submitted in support of, and at the time of making, the application to which the immigration decision related, or

> ➤ relates to the appeal in so far as it relies on grounds such as asylum, human rights, EEA law, and race discrimination

> ➤ is adduced to prove that a document is genuine or valid, or

> ➤ is adduced in connection with the Secretary of State's reliance on a discretion under immigration rules, or her compliance with a requirement not related to the acquisition of "points".

This latter provision allows for new evidence concerning a general ground of refusal under Part 9 or, arguably, where the application is refused on 'genuineness' grounds. In Ahmed and Another (PBS: admissible evidence) [2014] UKUT 365 (IAC), the Upper Tribunal said that new evidence is not permitted where it goes to a refusal on genuineness grounds, but that might not be the last word on the matter.

Administrative review

For those applying from abroad, there is no right of appeal. The remedy is the right of administrative review (i.e review by the Home Office).

This is invoked by submitting an Administrative Review Request Notice to the entry clearance post. An applicant must provide a full description of the claimed error regarding Age, Qualifications, Previous Earnings, UK Experience, English Language, Maintenance, or the General Refusal Grounds. Then the form is signed (electronic signature suffices) and handed back to the relevant Visa Application Centre or Visa Section.

An application for Administrative Review is made if the subject of the decision believes that the refusal was incorrect. An Entry Clearance Manager who was not involved in the original decision will conduct the review. In some cases, the Entry Clearance Manager may be located at a different entry clearance post to where the original entry clearance application was considered.

There is a right to apply only for one Administrative Review of the decision to refuse an application. No new or further information/documents in support of the request for Administrative Review can be submitted, unless the refusal is under paragraphs 320(7A) or 320(7B) or the new evidence goes to the provenance of the documents previously relied on. The objective is that, where new information or documents are available, a fresh application must be made. Administrative Reviews are to be conducted within 28 days. Written notice will be provided if it is not possible to achieve this. The Administrative Review process is non-statutory and the only guidance available is in the PBS Policy Guidance for each route.

Chapter 8: International Protection

We consider in this chapter the regimes for refugee protection under the Refugee Convention and humanitarian protection under the EU Qualification Directive.

The Refugee Convention

The fundamental provision of the UN Convention Relating to the Status of Refugees 1951 (read with the 1967 New York Protocol), usually referred to as the Refugee Convention, is Article 1(A)(2). A refugee is defined therein as a person who:

> Owing to well-founded fear of being persecuted for reasons of race, religion, nationality, membership of a particular social group or political opinion is outside the country of his nationality and is unable or owing to such fear, is unwilling to avail himself of the protection of that country; or who, not having a nationality and being outside the country of his former habitual residence is unable or, owing to such fear, unwilling to return to it.

This provision deals with the situation of both persons with a nationality and those without (i.e. the "stateless"). The courts have interpreted the requirements of the definition to be the same in both cases.

The definition can be broken down into its constituent parts:

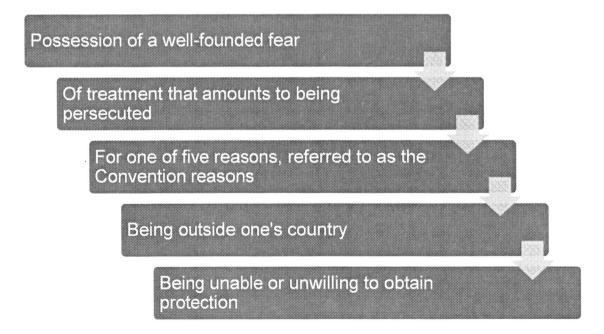

Sources of refugee law

The Refugee Convention has existed for over sixty years and inevitably there are various authorities that provide guides to the meaning and construction of the Convention principles including, most importantly;

➤ The 'EC Council Directive 2004/83/EC of 29 April 2004 on minimum standards for the qualification and status of third country nationals or stateless persons as refugees or as persons who otherwise need international protection and the content of the protection granted' is one of the most important (and certainly the longest titled) of these guides to Refugee Convention construction. This is usually referred to for reasons of convenience as the Qualification Directive as it sets out the definitions of those who qualify for protection.

➤ The Qualification Directive has been transposed into UK law through The Refugee or Person in Need of International Protection (Qualification) Regulations 2006 and modifications to the asylum section of the immigration rules at Part 11.

➤ The Handbook on Procedures and Criteria for Determining Refugee Status, published by UNHCR in 1978 in Geneva, is a fundamental text for any practitioner, particularly in the paragraphs (193 onwards) where it concentrates on the processes for determination of the facts of the case.

➤ UNHCR also gives guidance beyond the UNHCR Handbook, in terms of occasional statements on best practice (there has been an influential one on detention, for example); in the UK they intervene in individual cases only occasionally, increasingly doing so via legal interventions in test cases; they also provide guidelines on risks in particular countries. Their online facility Refworld is a very impressive and useful database of national and international legal authority relevant to refugee law.

➤ The Preamble to the Convention is a useful reminder that the Convention is related to other international legal materials such as other human rights instruments (e.g. the Universal Declaration of Human Rights, the International Covenant on Civil and Political Rights).

➤ Case law: Judicial decisions from the Immigration and Asylum Chamber of the Upper Tribunal (and its predecessors), the Court of Appeal, the House of Lords and Supreme Court, the European Court of Human Rights and the Court of Justice of the European Union provide additional guidance. Because the Convention is international in nature, it is also possible to look further afield, to e.g. case law of the highest courts of Canada, America, New Zealand and Australia

➤ The works of legal scholars have often cast light upon the proper approach to the Convention. See e.g. the works of Professors Hathaway and Guy Goodwin-Gill

Top tip

HJT strongly recommends reading the following ILPA best practice guides, which are essentially asylum skills guides. They are written by skilled, experienced practitioners who have distilled their learning into readable and accessible form. Aspiring practitioners should not pass by the opportunity to learn from them! They are available for free download at http://www.ilpa.org.uk/pages/publications.html.

- Best practice guide to asylum and human rights appeals, Mark Henderson (2003). The second edition was published in 2003 but an **updated version** (2012) has been made available electronically via the Electronic Immigration Network. A brand new edition is to be published soon by Legal Action.

- Making an asylum application: a best practice guide, Jane Coker, Garry Kelly, Martin Soorjoo (2002)

Asylum seekers

An asylum seeker is a person who has left their country of nationality or habitual residence, and has made a claim in a signatory country (i.e. an asylum claim or application) to the effect that they are entitled to protection there under the provisions of the Convention. The asylum seeker will hold that status until the asylum application is finally decided by that country.

If the asylum application is refused on the basis that the asylum seeker is not entitled to that protection, as they do not meet the definition of a refugee in Article 1(A)(2), the Home Office (presuming the asylum claim is made in the UK) will then be obliged to consider whether they are entitled to humanitarian protection under EU Qualification Directive.

If the asylum seeker is refused under both protection regimes, and not entitled to stay in the UK on any other basis, they will no longer be an asylum seeker. In some circumstances they may be able to make a further claim on asylum on human rights grounds under what is called in the UK, the 'fresh claim' procedure. If they are not able to establish their claim for protection, they will generally be removable to their own country.

Well-founded fear

There are two aspects to the possession of a well-founded fear: well foundedness and fear.

Fear

The fear test requires the asylum seeker to establish that they fear returning to their own country. It is a subjective test as it concerns the emotions of the claimant.

That being said, a person who cannot or does not show subjective fear, perhaps due to age (see e.g. rule 351) or mental illness, or bravado, may be presumed to have that fear if the risks they may be subjected to can be shown to have objective foundation.

Procedurally, the asylum seeker will have an opportunity to establish that they do have a genuine fear of returning to their country in their asylum interview, with a detailed statement of their claim (if they are properly represented), and any corroborative evidence they may be able to submit to the Home Office. On the basis of this information, the Home Office will make an assessment of the truthfulness (or as the Home Office likes to call it 'credibility') of the asylum seeker. They will ask themselves if the asylum seeker is telling the truth about their profile or about what happened to him or her in the past?

The Home Office sometimes need reminding that an asylum seeker may lie about some or all of their claim, or exaggerate their fear, but may still have a well-founded fear of persecution. Liars are not immune to persecution. For example, if they are a member of a class or group of persons who are at risk (e.g. members of Somali minority clans or Eritrean military service evaders) an asylum seeker might succeed in showing an entitlement to refugee status, notwithstanding the rejection of their own account. A person may also be at risk if forced to return to a particular country, not because of anything they have said in their asylum claim, but because of the view taken by the authorities of that country of asylum seekers returning from abroad in general or from the UK in particular, as has been found from time to time regarding countries such as Sudan and Zimbabwe, and currently Syria. Merely claiming asylum or even merely having been in the UK can put a person at risk on return (see e.g. KB (Failed asylum seekers and forced returnees) Syria CG [2012] UKUT 426 (IAC). Of course, it is easier to succeed if you are telling the truth but many asylum seekers do not, usually because they are poorly advised (not usually in this case by poor advisers, but by agents, interpreters, members of their community or others they come across before or during the asylum process).

Well-foundedness

This is an objective test and concerns, in part, the claimant's account being looked at in the light of the conditions in the applicant's country of origin. It also requires a consideration of future risk. The claimant might fear return, but is that fear well founded in the sense of there being a sufficient likelihood of those fears being realised?

As the UNHCR Handbook puts it;

42. As regards the objective clement, it is necessary to evaluate the statements made by the applicant. The competent authorities that are called upon to determine refugee status are not required to pass judgement on conditions in the applicant's country of origin. The applicant's statements cannot, however, be considered in the abstract, and must be viewed in the context of the relevant background situation. A knowledge of conditions in the applicant's country of origin--while not a primary objective--is an important element in assessing the applicant's credibility. In general, the applicant's fear should be considered well-founded if he can establish, to a reasonable degree, that his continued stay in his country of origin has become intolerable to him for the reasons stated in the definition, or would for the same reasons be intolerable if he returned there.

43. These considerations need not necessarily be based on the applicant's own personal experience. What, for example, happened to his friends and relatives and other members of the same racial or social group may well show that his fear that sooner or later he also will become a victim of persecution is well-founded. The laws of the country of origin, and particularly the manner in which they are applied, will be relevant. The situation of each person must, however, be assessed on its own merits. In the case of a well-known personality, the possibility of persecution may be greater than in the case of a person in obscurity. All these factors, e.g. a person's character, his background, his influence, his wealth or his outspokenness, may lead to the conclusion that his fear of persecution is "well-founded".

So these are the two key questions in status determination, although they can be broken down further:

Historic fact

- Standard of proof
- Credibility/Plausibility

Future risk

- Country information
- Past persecution
- Specific or general risk
- Activities in the United Kingdom
- Future behaviour

Standard of proof

The standard of proof for both aspects of well-founded fear is that of 'a reasonable degree of likelihood', which is lower than the civil standard of the balance of probabilities and is sometimes expressed as 'substantial grounds for believing' or 'real risk'. The leading case is Ravichandran [1996] Imm AR 97.

This was further elaborated on by the Court of Appeal in an important and often misunderstood case, Karanakaran [2000] Imm AR 271. Effectively, the Court of Appeal found that the concept of a legal standard of proof akin to the balance of probabilities, where probabilities are artificially elevated to certainties once a threshold is crossed, is redundant in asylum cases. Instead, a decision-maker should simply evaluate the risk on the basis of relevant evidence. The Court held that the first three of the following four categories of evidence identified by a decision maker are relevant for this purpose:

(i)   evidence they are certain about

(ii)   evidence they think is probably true

(iii)   evidence to which they are willing to attach some credence, even if they could not go so far as to say it is probably true

(iv)   evidence to which they are not willing to attach any credence at all.

See also the comments of Brooke LJ in Karanakaran:

> ... when considering whether there is a serious possibility of persecution for a Convention reason if an asylum seeker is returned, it would be quite wrong to exclude matters totally from consideration in the balancing process simply because the decision-maker believes, on what may sometimes be somewhat fragile evidence, that they probably did not occur.

The requirement to give the benefit of the doubt applies only where the account is generally credible (UNHCR Handbook paras 196, 204 and the Qualification Directive at Art.4(5)). The low standard of proof operates for the benefit of asylum seekers, and should never be employed to their detriment. Thus it is unacceptable to make a finding based on the chance that an alternative explanation for certain matters to that put forward by the applicant is 'reasonably likely'.

Credibility

The assessment of past facts in asylum cases is a complex process. There are statutory provisions that have an impact on the assessment of credibility as well as immigration rules and case law.

Qualification Directive

Due to the Qualification Directive, the immigration rules now include at paragraph 339L the following guidance for decision-makers in assessing credibility:

> 339L. It is the duty of the person to substantiate the asylum claim or establish that he is a person eligible humanitarian protection or substantiate his human rights claim. Where aspects of the person's statements are not supported by documentary or other evidence, those aspects will not need confirmation when all of the following conditions are met:
> (i) the person has made a genuine effort to substantiate his asylum claim or establish that he is a person eligible humanitarian protection or substantiate his human rights claim;

(ii) all material factors at the person's disposal have been submitted, and a satisfactory explanation regarding any lack of other relevant material has been given;
(iii) the person's statements are found to be coherent and plausible and do not run counter to available specific and general information relevant to the person's case;
(iv) the person has made an asylum claim or sought to establish that he is a person eligible for humanitarian protection or made a human rights claim at the earliest possible time, unless the person can demonstrate good reason for not having done so; and
(v) the general credibility of the person has been established.

This should be the starting point for the assessment of credibility. The rider that the applicant must be generally credible enables decision makers to attach appropriate weight to inconsistencies and other credibility issues, but this paragraph provides a useful reminder that corroborating evidence is not always required and that the benefit of the doubt should be given where it is not. But an asylum seeker must, where possible, corroborate a claim, and where attempts to do so have been made, but have failed, these should also be explained to the decision maker.

Example

Irene was a journalist in Zimbabwe writing under a pseudonym. She cannot easily prove that it was she who wrote the articles in question, nor is it easy for her to obtain copies of the articles from Zimbabwe.

To an extent, she can address this is a witness statement and explain everything she remembers about the articles she wrote and the process of getting them published. However, her case would be much stronger if she could obtain copies of the articles or something that links her to the pseudonym she used, such as a letter from the publisher.

Failing that, most immigration judges would view her case more sympathetically if she could at least demonstrate that she has tried very hard to obtain the relevant evidence and show copies of letters written, calls made and so on, and explain in her statement what steps she has taken to try to obtain the evidence. This would distinguish her case from someone who makes a claim but makes no attempt to substantiate it, at least as far as the judge can see. Immigration Rules 339L(i) and (ii) lend support to this approach.

Asylum and Immigration (Treatment of Claimants etc) Act 2004

Section 8 of the 2004 Act introduced a mandatory requirement that specific types of 'behaviour' by an asylum seeker after they left their own country be treated by decision makers, including judges, as damaging credibility: reliance on false documents, destruction of documents, claiming asylum after receiving an immigration decision or after arrest, and not claiming asylum despite having had a reasonable opportunity to do so in a "safe" third country (safe third country is given a specific meaning later in the section).

A number of criticisms have been made of what many consider to be a crass attempt to impose un-evidenced assumptions about the norms of refugee behaviour. The judiciary has proven jealous of its role in assessing credibility and in SM (Section 8: Judge's process) Iran [2005] UKAIT 00116 the Asylum and Immigration Tribunal found that even where section 8 applies, the tribunal should look at the evidence as a whole and decide which parts are more important and which less and that section 8 does not require the behaviour to which it applies to be treated as the starting-point of the assessment of credibility.

The legally controversial principle has also been the subject of significant criticism from the Court of Appeal. Thus in ST (Libya) v Secretary of State for the Home Department [2007] EWCA Civ 24 (12 January 2007) Sedley LJ thought there should at least be some link between, for example, a failure to claim asylum in a safe third country and the substantive case for asylum before an adverse inference could be drawn.

Nevertheless, the types of behaviour falling within section 8 should as far as possible be addressed in individual claims. Both the HO and the courts will be obliged to take them into account.

Failure to Claim Asylum in a Safe Third Country

Regarding the safe country assumption in s8, first of all check that the any countries through which the claimant has passed are actually defined as safe in section 8(7) itself, i.e. whether they are countries listed at Part 2 of Schedule 3 of the 2004 Act. Even if the country concerned is on this list, there is no principle in international law to the effect that an asylum seeker should seek asylum in the first available country they pass through, though the authors of Home Office decision letters often speak as if there was one. That they are incorrect is shown by the decision of the Divisional Court in R v Uxbridge Magistrates Court ex parte Adimi, & Ors [1999] Imm AR 560:

> ... I am persuaded by the applicants' contrary submission, drawing as it does on the travaux préparatoires, various Conclusions adopted by UNHCR's Executive Committee ('ExCom'), and the writings of well-respected academics and commentators (most notably Professor Guy Goodwin-Gill, Atle Grahl-Madsen, Professor James Hathaway, & Dr Paul Weis), that some element of choice is indeed open to refugees as to where they may properly claim asylum.

However, an explanation should always be sought as to a failure to claim asylum abroad, particularly if there has been a lengthy stay in a country. A desire to join relatives in the UK, or a pre-arranged journey with only transit stops abroad, might be possible explanations; as might an ability to speak English, so might conditions in the third country (e.g. colonial or diplomatic relationships with the asylum seeker's country of origin might encourage or discourage an asylum claim).

Regarding delays in claiming asylum, much depends on the individual circumstances. Many asylum seekers who attempt to enter the country before making their claims will do so for the good reasons laid out by agencies such as the UNHCR, e.g. the effects of trauma, language problems, lack of information, previous experiences with authority and feelings of insecurity, rather than with a view to falsifying their claims with the assistance of contacts in this country – see Simon Brown LJ in R v Uxbridge Magistrates Court, ex p Adimi [1999] Imm AR 560.

Entering the Country

The capacity in which a person enters the country ought not to carry decisive weight in the analysis of their claim to need international protection. Someone might claim asylum having entered as a visitor: the UNHCR has warned that this will often arise out of an understandable desire to secure some form of temporary stay in a country, to avoid simply being returned home from the border.

Simon Brown stated in Adimi "Most asylum seekers who attempt to enter the country before making their claims will do so for the reasons suggested by UNHCR rather than with a view to falsifying their claims with the assistance of friends and contacts here."

Inconsistencies

Although there are lots of possible explanations for discrepancies, inconsistencies can properly found a finding of a lack of credibility. For this reason one of the practitioner's most important functions is taking full and accurate instructions, in order to avoid matters which seem like discrepancies appearing in the account.

One area in which reliance upon inconsistencies to found a finding that an asylum seeker's account lacks credibility will be particularly objectionable will be where the individual is giving an account of traumatic past events: Jakitay (12658; 15 November 1995). On an appeal in a case where a lack of self-confidence in relating traumatic factors is present, you might wish to advise your client to give evidence in private. The specialist international Tribunal regarding torture, the United Nations Committee against Torture (UNCAT), has warned that complete accuracy is seldom to be expected from victims of torture: Alan v Switzerland (UNCAT) [1997] INLR 29.

Top tip

There is no such thing as perfect recall and no human being is capable of giving a completely consistent account of the same events on different occasions. The reasons for this lie in the way that memories are made.

Firstly memories must be <u>recorded</u>. Bystanders to the same events always perceive the same events differently and attach significance to different aspects of those events. The human brain searches for patterns and where information is absent (or even where it is present sometimes) the brain completes the 'picture' by filling in blanks.

Secondly, memories must be <u>stored</u>. Sometimes memories are simply lost or partially lost and blanks filled in. Minor aspects of events, such as sensations, may be recalled long after the event even though major events are forgotten. The passage of time generally degrades memories.

Thirdly, memories must then be <u>recalled and recounted</u>. There is ample opportunity for memories to be recalled differently on different occasions. For example, the use of leading questions will often change the way that memories are recalled, particularly in children.

Despite this, the fact is that in many asylum cases the only evidence is the witness' own testimony. If it is perceived as flawed, it will be rejected.

Due allowance must be made for the different stages of the asylum process, and the various ways in which information is elicited - the nature of the process is such that a single perfectly consistent telling of the story is unlikely. Whilst the Tribunal has agreed that inconsistencies between accounts given at different times can properly be referred to for the purpose of assessing credibility, 'adjudicators should always bear in mind the circumstances in which these interviews take place and the, often, somewhat amateurish nature of the questioning techniques'.

Top tip

Not all additional information is necessarily inconsistent with an earlier account. It is the very nature of the process that further questions are asked later on about an account that has already been given. Indeed, this is the whole purpose of a Home Office asylum interview. It would be truly absurd, then, to say that the provision of additional information is an elaboration of an account that is in some way not credible.

However, providing additional information is not the same as making changes to an account or adding new events, which are likely to cause significant credibility issues.

Failure to read back the contents of the interview to its subject may make it a very unreliable basis for criticising an account, though see DA (Unsigned interview notes) Turkey [2004] UKIAT 00104 (14 May 2004) for the fact that an objection to an interview's conduct plus a mere failure to sign does not of itself mean an interview should be disregarded without analysing the circumstances of that interview. Contemporaneous complaints about unsatisfactory interviews will be more telling than late challenges at appeal. The screening interview is not intended to be a vehicle for exploring the substance of the asylum claim.

Some claimants fail to satisfy the Secretary of State or an immigration judge of the truth of their account because they cannot provide adequate detail to the decision maker. Others may be unable to meet the burden not because their accounts are false, but because they simply do not possess the relevant detail, or because their level of their education deprives them of the opportunity to convey the story in the requisite structured and measured fashion. Vagueness should always be identified, though, see B (DR Congo) [2003] UKIAT 00012 (12 June 2003).

Plausibility

A person who advances an account which falls outside the realms of possibility is unlikely to be able to establish themselves as a refugee. However, when judging questions of plausibility, the particular nature of the asylum seeker's evidence must be taken into account, and it must be adjudicated upon by the standards of the country of origin. As the Tribunal wrote in Suleyman (16242; 11 February 1998):

> It is clear to us that a repressive regime ... may well act in ways which defy logical analysis. A person who is genuinely a victim of such a regime may well find that the partial account he is able to give of its activities as they have affected him is not something which will stand up to a strictly logical analysis. The regime may seem to govern by confusion; it may engage in other activities, of which the Appellant knows

> nothing; it may simply behave in a way which a person sitting in safety in the United Kingdom might regard as almost beyond belief.

Country information and understanding of the conditions and culture in a given country is absolutely crucial when assessing plausibility. There are many quotations from case law to this effect, but one of the most frequently cited is from Horvath [1999] INLR 7:

> One cannot assess a claim without placing that claim into the context of the background information of the country of origin. In other words, the probative value of the evidence must be evaluated in the light of what is known about the conditions in the claimant's country of origin.

Unfortunately the message that plausibility must be assessed through the prism of country information (and expert evidence) and not based on the life experiences of the immigration judge has not been taken on board by all immigration judges. In the case of HK v SSHD [2006] EWCA Civ 1037 the Court of Appeal was critical of the tribunal's approach to expert evidence and to the issue of plausibility and Neuberger LJ held as follows at paragraph 29:

> Inherent probability, which may be helpful in many domestic cases, can be a dangerous, even a wholly inappropriate, factor to rely on in some asylum cases. Much of the evidence will be referable to societies with customs and circumstances which are very different from those of which the members of the fact-finding tribunal have any (even second-hand) experience. Indeed, it is likely that the country which an asylum-seeker has left will be suffering from the sort of problems and dislocations with which the overwhelming majority of residents of this country will be wholly unfamiliar.

Chadwick LJ agreed:

> On analysis of the tribunal's reasoning, I am unable to avoid the conclusion that the applicant's account has been rejected simply because the facts that he describes are so unusual as to be thought unbelievable. But, as Lord Justice Neuberger has pointed out, that is not a safe basis upon which to reject the existence of facts which are said to have occurred within an environment and culture which is so wholly outside the experience of the decision maker as that in the present case. There is simply no yardstick against which the decision maker can test whether the facts are inherently incredible or not. The tribunal's failure to confront that problem must lead to the conclusion that they erred in law.

The application of tests of likelihood based upon any form of presumption as to how a "reasonable man" would act is particularly unreliable in the refugee context. See Bingham MR in (1985) 38 Current Legal Problems 14 cited as relevant in this area of law in Kasolo (13190; 1 April 1996):

> No judge worth his salt could possibly assume that men of different nationalities, educations, trades, experience, creeds and temperaments would act how he might think he would have done or even – which may be quite different – in accordance with his concept of what a reasonable man would have done.

As has been pointed out by the Court of Appeal (*Y v SSHD* [2006] EWCA Civ 1223), this does not mean that an account must be accepted at face value or that the decision maker must suspect their own judgment entirely. It will be for an adviser to anticipate and identify areas where an account may be found to be implausible and then take sufficient further instructions to show as far as possible how and why the events happened as claimed. Where necessary country information can be found to help corroborate the account or at least show it is consistent with what happens in that country.

Dishonesty

Proven, or admitted, dishonesty inevitably counts against any person who seeks to demonstrate their story's truthfulness, but a lack of veracity on one issue does not necessarily disprove the remainder of the account. Any acts of dishonesty must be specifically explained (for example entering the country on false documents). The core of an account may be credible even though some elements are not made out: Chiver (10758; 24 March 1994). However, see also *K (DR Congo)* [2003] UKIAT 00014 (23 June 2003) for the fact that an account may be found lacking in credibility notwithstanding discrepancies only being found in peripheral details.

Demeanour

An immigration judge who hears oral evidence from an asylum seeker will have the opportunity to assess their demeanour. If such is to be relied upon, then caution should be exercised, for cultural reasons: Kasolo (13190); B (DR Congo) [2003] UKIAT 00012 (12 June 2003). Whatever the role given to demeanour, it would be wrong to presume that a witness would necessarily give evidence in a particular emotional state: see the Tribunal in M (Yugoslavia) [2003] UKIAT 00004 (29 May 2003):

> Given the adjudicator's apparent awareness of the medical evidence that the appellant suffered from Post Traumatic Stress Disorder one of whose symptoms is emotional numbness, we do not think the adjudicator was justified in counting against the appellant at paragraph 26 his failure at the hearing to "show emotional distress when the traumatic events were raised...

Future risk

The asylum applicant must demonstrate that there is a serious possibility of the events which he fears actually occurring. Thus Lord Keith in Sivakumaran [1988] 1 AC 958 stated:

> ...protection ... does not extend to the allaying of fears not objectively justified, however reasonable these fears may appear from the point of view of the individual in question...

Future risk is sometimes referred to as objective risk. The applicant must demonstrate that something bad will happen to them if they are sent to their country of origin. The question of how bad these future experiences must be before the protection of the Refugee Convention is engaged is addressed below in the section on persecution.

Since the advent of the Country Guideline system in the immigration tribunal, it has become essential to check whether an applicant falls within guidance previously given by the tribunal. A list of Country Guideline ('CG') cases is kept on the MoJ's website and is regularly updated. Cases are both added and removed from this list. A list of pending country guidance cases and issues is also available. For both see: http://www.judiciary.gov.uk/tribunal-decisions/immigration-asylum-chamber/. For those wanting an update on CG cases currently awaiting listing or determination, or being challenged in the higher courts, the Refugee Legal group (RLG) is an essential forum. For details of how to join the RLG, see:
http://www.asylumaid.org.uk/pages/refugee_legal_group.html.

Most CG cases include clear pointers as to future risk for various categories of asylum claimants.

Criticisms have been made of the CG system (see e.g. IAS report Country Guideline cases: benign and practical? available for download from http://www.freemovement.org.uk). If an appellant does fall within a group dealt with in a current CG case, it will be very difficult to persuade an immigration judge to depart from that guidance. Failure to follow it may amount to an error of law by the judge unless the appellant can somehow distinguish their case from it (see e.g. the Practice Directions of the immigration tribunals at paragraph 12.4). The production of recent country material not previously considered in the CG case may assist (for example an expert report), although the starting point is likely to be whether this is new material is sufficient to displace the previous guidance.

Country information

Country information is an essential tool for demonstrating future risk. It is often referred to as 'objective' evidence. It may or may not be objective, but unless it is from a respected source its objectivity must be established by the party relying on it.

There are many different sources of country information, and each source has its advantages and disadvantages. A high quality source to which weight is likely to be attached would possess the following qualities:

➢ **Up to date**: the source would be a recent one, or failing that there would be information that suggested the situation or subject matter of the report was unlikely to have changed.

➢ **Objective**: there is no such thing as an entirely objective source, but clearly biased sources or sources more likely to have an agenda of some kind may be considered less reputable. However, even a biased source might include useful factual information: much depends on how the information is used and presented.

> **Origins**: the sources used by a report would be as well-informed as possible and their research methodology would be clear.

Common types of information source include:

> **Government reports**. E.g. the UKVI's Country Information and Guidance reports (CIGs) reports, US Department of State reports may reflect the agenda of the government or government department concerned but subject to public review. Tend to be infrequently updated.

> **Inter-governmental reports**. E.g. UNHCR, African Union. May be compromised by the agendas of different constituent governments or by the organisation's own agenda or remit. Tend to be infrequently updated.

> **Non-governmental reports**. E.g. Amnesty International, Human Rights Watch. May reflect campaigning agenda of the organisation concerned, but research methodology may be clear and the organisations have their reputations to protect. Annual reports are infrequent but updates are sometimes published.

> **Press**. E.g. national or international newspapers and websites. Some articles may be the product of good quality journalism, others less so. Tends to be very recent.

Example

The suitability of a source depends on the context in which it is used. Normally, a blog post from an anonymous blogger in the country of origin would be given little weight. However, if the blog is long standing and appears unconnected personally to the asylum seeker, it might be useful corroboration of a claimed fact of some sort, particularly if backed up directly or indirectly by other sources.

An opposition newspaper might be expected by the reader to be highly critical of the government it opposes and to contain 'biased' information that suggests the opposition is badly treated. However, it may be corroborated by other sources and may contain specific facts or details that have a direct bearing on the account of a given asylum seeker.

Unusual sources should not lightly be discarded merely because they can be said to be biased, but they should be used with care and further corroboration should always be sought.

In the case of Sufi and Elmi v United Kingdom (Application no 8319/07 and 11449/07) [2011] ECHR 1045, the European Court of Human Rights deprecated the use of anonymous sources:

> In the present case the Court observes that the description of the sources relied on by the fact-finding mission is vague. As indicated by the applicants, the majority of sources have simply been described either as "an international NGO", "a diplomatic source", or "a security advisor". Such descriptions give no indication of the authority or reputation of the sources or of the extent of their presence in southern and central Somalia. This is of particular concern in the present case, where it is accepted that the presence of international NGOs and diplomatic missions in southern and central Somalia is limited. It is therefore impossible for the Court to carry out any assessment of the sources' reliability and, as a consequence, where their information is unsupported or contradictory, the Court is unable to attach substantial weight to it.

The ECtHR's position on anonymous sources in Sufi and Elmi was considered by the Upper Tribunal in CM (EM country guidance; disclosure) Zimbabwe CG [2013] UKUT 00059(IAC) which had been remitted from the Court of Appeal on this and other issues. The Upper Tribunal distinguished the case from Sufi and Elmi and decided that country evidence from unnamed NGOs would be allowed in certain circumstances.

The Home Office produces Country Information and Guidance reports (CIGs) on the top 20 asylum intake countries. These have replaced the Country of Origin Information (COI) reports and Operational Guidance Notes (OGNs) of old.

The CIGs can be found at: https://www.gov.uk/government/publications/uganda-country-information-and-guidance

The OGNs used to set out the policy position of the Home Office towards protection issues in particular countries. As policy documents they were never meant to be objective, often drawing very selectively from the available country information. The new CIGs may simply be repackaged OGNs, but have not been subjected to any detailed critique as yet (by e.g. the Independent Advisory Group on Country Information), so the jury is still out as to how objective they are.

Nevertheless, those representing asylum seekers will need to read the relevant CIGs as, objective or not, they certainly contain relevant and useful country information, a resume of relevant case law, and lay out the policy position of the Home Office with respect to risk groups in the countries they cover.

Many of the OGNs have been subjected to a detailed critique by the Still Human Still Here organisation. The reports can be found at:
http://stillhumanstillhere.wordpress.com/resources/

For the view of some senior members of the tribunal on the use of country information and expert evidence see, for example, the case of TK (Tamils - LP updated) Sri Lanka CG [2009] UKAIT 00049.

Relevance of past experiences to future risk

The fact of past ill-treatment, be it severe enough to be deemed persecution or not (although the more severe the better from the viewpoint of making a good case), is a matter to be strongly taken into account when assessing the risk of any recurrence. Professor Hathaway's test was approved by Stuart Smith LJ in the Court of Appeal in Demirkaya v Secretary of State for the Home Department [1999] Imm AR 498:

> Where evidence of past maltreatment exists, however, it is unquestionably an excellent indicator of the fate that may await an applicant on return to her home. Unless there has been a major change of circumstances within that country that makes prospective persecution unlikely, past experience under a particular regime should be considered probative of future risk ... In sum, evidence of individualised past persecution is generally a sufficient, though not a mandatory, means of establishing prospective risks.

However, it is not the only relevant consideration, as there may have been a change in circumstances in the country in question. Past persecution is therefore useful as an indicator of future risk, but it would be wise to seek to demonstrate that the causes of that past persecution continue to be active now.

This principle is now embedded in the immigration rules, thanks to the Qualification Directive. See rule 339K:

> The fact that a person has already been subject to persecution or serious harm, or to direct threats of such persecution or such harm, will be regarded as a serious indication of the person's well-founded fear of persecution or real risk of suffering serious harm, unless there are good reasons to consider that such persecution or serious harm will not be repeated.

Specific individual risk

It is always important in an asylum case to look at individual risk factors thrown up in the individual case.

For example, if the claimant possesses a passport, this will be noted by the authorities in the UK, and an explanation needs to be sought as to why an individual travelled on their own documentation as this might suggest that the authorities of his or her home country allowed him or her to leave. An asylum seeker may be a person of whom the authorities are pleased to be rid, or one who is a member of a class of persons at risk albeit that as an individual he is not being actively sought at the time of departure, or one coming from a country where inefficient or corrupt security services cannot be relied upon to routinely enforce the will of their superiors.

See also Collins J in the Administrative Court in R v Secretary of State for the Home Department, ex p Q [2003] EWHC 195 (Admin):

> The UNHCR Handbook makes it clear that 'possession of a passport cannot ... always be considered as evidence of loyalty on the part of the holder, or ... of the

absence of fear' and that passports are often 'issued to a person who is undesired in his country of origin [for] the sole purpose of securing his departure.

Generic risk cases

Where an individual is relying for their claim of persecution not on a desire by officials or non-state actors to target them as an individual, but rather from general problems (e.g. poor prison conditions: see Batayav v SSHD [2003] EWCA Civ 1489 and again at [2005] EWCA Civ 366), then it will be necessary to show that the matters complained of are truly endemic. See the Court of Appeal in Hariri v SSHD [2003] EWCA Civ 807:

> 'The point is one of logic. Absent evidence to show that the appellant was at risk because of his specific circumstances, there could be no real risk of relevant ill-treatment unless the situation to which the appellant would be returning was one in which such violence was generally or consistently happening. There is nothing else in the case that could generate a real risk. In this situation, then, a "consistent pattern of gross and systematic violation of fundamental human rights", far from being at variance with the real risk test is, in my judgment, a function or application of it.'

This test, requiring gross and systematic violation of fundamental human rights before a case based on generic risk can succeed, has itself been criticised, and the Tribunal has increasingly referred to the test being whether there is "a consistent pattern of such mistreatment". Thus in AA (Risk for involuntary returnees) Zimbabwe CG Rev 1 [2006] UKAIT 00061 the Tribunal stated:

> The appellant does not need to show a certainty or a probability that all failed asylum seekers returned involuntarily will face serious ill-treatment upon return. He needs to show only that there is a consistent pattern of such mistreatment such that anyone returning in those circumstances faces a real risk of coming to harm even though not everyone does.

Generic risk arguments have been attempted for Iraq, Somalia and Zimbabwe and have succeeded in the case of the latter two countries. There is interesting overlap here with Article 15(c) of the Qualification Directive, which is dealt with in the section on humanitarian protection, where a consistent pattern of mistreatment is not a requirement for entitlement to protection.

Activities in the United Kingdom and claims made in bad faith

Activities in the United Kingdom

Refugees can base their claim for asylum on their own activities that post-date their departure from their country of origin, or in changes in the situation there (e.g. a coup that places all those holding their political affiliation at risk; or it may be that whereas they might not have been at risk had they never left the country, the increased attention they will attract on a return at the border will itself create a risk of persecution). These are known as "sur place" claims.

Immediate risk on return at an airport has been explored in considerable detail for some countries, such as Zimbabwe and Turkey, and is also argued for other countries, such as Eritrea and Sri Lanka. Compelling evidence is usually needed to succeed with such arguments as they affect a large number of asylum applicants. The latest Country Guideline cases should always be checked.

Returnees cannot be expected to lie about their beliefs or how they have spent their time in the UK – see IK (Returnees - Records – IFA) Turkey CG [2004] UKIAT 00312 – re Turkey, but of interest in any "questioning on return" case: "It will be for an Adjudicator in each case to assess what questions are likely to be asked during such investigation and how a returnee would respond without being required to lie. The ambit of the likely questioning depends upon the circumstances of each case." This principle was more considered more recently and upheld in the Supreme Court's judgment in RT (Zimbabwe) & Ors [2012] UKSC 38.

If a claimant has engaged in activities directed against his or her own government while in the UK, it will be difficult to obtain evidence that the government in question (a) monitors UK based opposition activities, (b) communicates that information to the domestic authorities and (c) that those authorities make use of that information to target the individuals concerned.

In YB (Eritrea) v SSHD [2008] EWCA Civ 360 the Court of Appeal dealt with this question in the context of Eritrea and concluded that a common sense approach should be followed where the emphasis was on consequences rather than solidity of evidence:

> 17. As has been seen (§7 above), the tribunal, while accepting that the appellant's political activity in this country was genuine, were not prepared to accept in the absence of positive evidence that the Eritrean authorities had "the means and the inclination" to monitor such activities as a demonstration outside their embassy, or that they would be able to identify the appellant from photographs of the demonstration. In my judgment, and without disrespect to what is a specialist tribunal, this is a finding which risks losing contact with reality. Where, as here, the tribunal has objective evidence which "paints a bleak picture of the suppression of political opponents" by a named government, it requires little or no evidence or speculation to arrive at a strong possibility – and perhaps more – that its foreign legations not only film or photograph their nationals who demonstrate in public against the regime but have informers among expatriate oppositionist organisations who can name the people who are filmed or photographed. Similarly it does not require affirmative evidence to establish a probability that the intelligence services of such states monitor the internet for information about oppositionist groups. The real question in most cases will be what follows for the individual claimant.

Bad faith activities

The issue of the wilful creation of an asylum claim through activities found to be conducted in "bad faith" outside the country of origin (for example, cynical attendance at demonstrations outside an embassy) has occasionally arisen. In Danian v SSHD [2000] Imm AR 96 the Court of Appeal held that the motive behind activities is irrelevant, the only questions is whether there is a well-founded fear of being persecuted for a Convention reason.

The question of an asylum claim made in "bad faith" was canvassed in the Zimbabwe litigation, in the case of AA and LK v SSHD [2006] EWCA Civ 401. There the argument for the asylum seekers was that the security forces in Zimbabwe would persecute returnees because of the political opinion they would attribute to them for having claimed asylum in the UK, regardless of how opportunistic their motivation. The Court of Appeal did not overturn the reasoning in Danian, but did find that a person who could safely make a voluntary return to their country of origin even though a forced return would put them at risk is not a refugee because that person is not outside his or her country of origin for reason of a well-founded fear of being persecuted.

Under rule 339J(iv), the immigration rules now state that the Secretary of State must take into account in making an asylum decision '*whether the person's activities since leaving the country of origin or country of return were engaged in for the sole or main purpose of creating the necessary conditions for making an asylum claim or establishing that he is a person eligible for humanitarian protection or a human rights claim, so as to assess whether these activities will expose the person to persecution or serious harm if he returned to that country*'. This rule reflects the Refugee Qualification Directive, but it does not suggest how the asylum seeker's motivation for their activities should affect the assessment of risk. Implicitly, the rule suggests that where the motivation for the activities is solely to create a situation of risk, the asylum seeker's national authorities will somehow know this and refrain from subjecting them to persecution as an opponent.

This position was disapproved in *KS (Burma) & Anor v SSHD* [2013] EWCA Civ 67 where the Court of Appeal found in a case concerning political 'hangers-on' from Burma [30];

> The second flaw is the underlying assumption that the Burmese authorities in Rangoon operate a rational decision-making process which can reliably be trusted to distinguish between a genuine political opponent and a hanger-on. There is no evidence of how the authorities, faced with a person identified and photographed participating in an anti-government demonstration outside the Embassy in London, might go about satisfying themselves that the person in question is simply an opportunistic hanger-on. The general evidence about the behaviour of the authorities does not support a tendency to rational, careful assessment. The accepted evidence is of a repressive, arbitrary regime. A presumption of rational assessment – which is what paragraph 93 amounts to – is, in my judgment, counter-intuitive in the context of the rest of the accepted evidence. The confidence placed in the Burmese authorities is not supported by evidence.

The Court of Appeal also stated that the CG case on Burma would benefit from the approach taken by the Tribunal in BA (Demonstrators in Britain – risk on return) Iran CG [2011] UKUT 36 (IAC). BA pointed to a number of factors and "a spectrum of risk". The non-exhaustive list of factors in BA is grouped under a number of headings: nature of sur place activity; identification risk; factors triggering inquiry/action on return; consequences of identification; and identification risk on return. Each heading is then illustrated and amplified.

In TS (Political opponents – risk) Burma CG [2013] UKUT 00281 (IAC), which followed KS, the Tribunal accepted new evidence from an expert which purported to show exactly how the Burmese regime *would* assess such activities and, in any case, found that demonstrating by itself, even if for genuine motives, would not lead to persecution.

Future activities

In the case of HJ (Iran) and HT (Cameroon) v Secretary of State for the Home Department [2010] UKSC 31 the Supreme Court fundamentally changed the approach of the UK courts to the issue of how future behaviour will be considered relevant to the assessment of entitlement to refugee status. The previous legal settlement on this issue, established by the case of Iftikar Ahmed [2000] INLR 1, was a very British and pragmatic one. Essentially, the question of whether future behaviour could make a person a refugee became a simple question of fact: would the person in question in fact, despite the dangers, behave in a way that would expose him or her to risk of persecution?

HJ (Iran) establishes that where a person would in future refrain from behaving in a way that would expose them to danger because of the risk of persecution that behaviour brings, that person is a refugee.

The context in HJ (Iran) is famously homosexuality — would a gay man or lesbian woman have to conceal aspects of their sexuality in order to avoid persecution — but the legal principle is a wider one of profound significance. If a political or religious activist would want to continue his or her activities in future but would not be able to because of the fear of persecution, it is no answer to say that person can move to another part of the country and remain effectively gagged and bound there as well. See, for example, the subsequent Court of Appeal case of TM (Zimbabwe) v Secretary of State for the Home Department [2010] EWCA Civ 916.

The leading judgment in HJ (Iran) is that of the late Lord Rodgers, who gives guidance on the proper approach as follows:

> When an applicant applies for asylum on the ground of a well-founded fear of persecution because he is gay, the tribunal must first ask itself whether it is satisfied on the evidence that he is gay, or that he would be treated as gay by potential persecutors in his country of nationality.
>
> If so, the tribunal must then ask itself whether it is satisfied on the available evidence that gay people who lived openly would be liable to persecution in the applicant's country of nationality.
>
> If so, the tribunal must go on to consider what the individual applicant would do if he were returned to that country.

> If the applicant would in fact live openly and thereby be exposed to a real risk of persecution, then he has a well-founded fear of persecution – even if he could avoid the risk by living "discreetly".
>
> If, on the other hand, the tribunal concludes that the applicant would in fact live discreetly and so avoid persecution, it must go on to ask itself why he would do so.
>
> If the tribunal concludes that the applicant would choose to live discreetly simply because that was how he himself would wish to live, or because of social pressures, e g, not wanting to distress his parents or embarrass his friends, then his application should be rejected. Social pressures of that kind do not amount to persecution and the Convention does not offer protection against them. Such a person has no well-founded fear of persecution because, for reasons that have nothing to do with any fear of persecution, he himself chooses to adopt a way of life which means that he is not in fact liable to be persecuted because he is gay.
>
> If, on the other hand, the tribunal concludes that a material reason for the applicant living discreetly on his return would be a fear of the persecution which would follow if he were to live openly as a gay man, then, other things being equal, his application should be accepted. Such a person has a well-founded fear of persecution. To reject his application on the ground that he could avoid the persecution by living discreetly would be to defeat the very right which the Convention exists to protect – his right to live freely and openly as a gay man without fear of persecution. By admitting him to asylum and allowing him to live freely and openly as a gay man without fear of persecution, the receiving state gives effect to that right by affording the applicant a surrogate for the protection from persecution which his country of nationality should have afforded him.

The judgment is also significant for what it says about internal relocation in these cases. At paragraph 84 Lord Rodgers goes on:

> I add a comment on the case of HT. The tribunal rejected his application on the ground that, on his return to Cameroon, he could go to live in another part of the country and live discreetly there. In that event he would have no real fear of persecution. But there appears to have been nothing in the evidence to suggest that there was any area of Cameroon where gay men could live openly without any fear of persecution. So in no sense would the applicant be returning to a part of the country where the state would protect him from persecution. In effect, therefore, the tribunal was simply saying that his application should be rejected because, on return, he could take steps to avoid persecution by conducting himself discreetly. For the reasons which I have given, that approach is inconsistent with the very aims of the Convention.

Following the principles in HJ (Iran), the Supreme Court held in the case of RT (Zimbabwe) v SSHD [2012] UKSC 38 that asylum seekers cannot be expected to lie or dissemble in order to achieve safety in their own country. This principle applies equally to a committed political activist and to a person with no politician convictions: neither can be expected to lie.

The issue arose from the Country Guidance case of RN (Zimbabwe) [2008] UKAIT 00083, in which the immigration tribunal held that, in the febrile atmosphere before and following the 2008 elections, any Zimbabwean returned from the UK would have a well-founded fear of persecution unless he or she could prove loyalty to the ZANU-PF party. The Secretary of State had suggested in subsequent appeals that a person with no political allegiance could reasonably be expected to lie about being loyal to ZANU-PF to avoid persecution.

The leading judgment is delivered by Lord Dyson. He observes at paragraphs 36 and 45 that established international law protects the right to hold opinions and not to do so as well:

> Under both international and European human rights law, the right to freedom of thought, opinion and expression protects non-believers as well as believers and extends to the freedom not to hold and not to have to express opinions. The rights to freedom of thought, opinion and expression are proclaimed by articles 18 and 19 of the Universal Declaration of Human Rights 1948. As Lord Hope said in HJ (Iran) at para 15: "The guarantees in the Universal Declaration are fundamental to a proper understanding of the Convention"...
>
> ...There is no support in any of the human rights jurisprudence for a distinction between the conscientious non-believer and the indifferent non- believer, any more than there is support for a distinction between the zealous believer and the marginally committed believer. All are equally entitled to human rights protection and to protection against persecution under the Convention. None of them forfeits these rights because he will feel compelled to lie in order to avoid persecution.

Being persecuted

There are two main elements to examine in the context of the requirement to show a risk of being persecuted:

Actors

- State
- Non-state

Acts

- Human rights analysis
- Subjective element
- Role of Convention reasons

Actors of persecution

The Refugee or Person in Need of International Protection (Qualification) Regulations 2006 which transpose the Qualification Directive specify at regulation 3 that the following actors can act as persecutors for the purposes of assessing cases under the Refugee Convention:

(a) the State;

(b) any party or organisation controlling the State or a substantial part of the territory of the State;

(c) any non-State actor if it can be demonstrated that the actors mentioned in paragraphs (a) and (b), including any international organisation, are unable or unwilling to provide protection against persecution or serious harm.

This broadly reflects the position under UK law.

Acts of persecution

The Qualification Directive sets out a minimum definition of what might constitute acts of persecution at Art.9, which has been transposed into the Refugee or Person in Need of International Protection (Qualification) Regulations 2006 as follows:

Act of persecution

5. (1) In deciding whether a person is a refugee an act of persecution must be:

(a) sufficiently serious by its nature or repetition as to constitute a severe violation of a basic human right, in particular a right from which derogation cannot be made under Article 15 of the Convention for the Protection of Human Rights and Fundamental Freedoms(1); or

(b) an accumulation of various measures, including a violation of a human right which is sufficiently severe as to affect an individual in a similar manner as specified in (a).

(2) An act of persecution may, for example, take the form of:

(a) an act of physical or mental violence, including an act of sexual violence;

(b) a legal, administrative, police, or judicial measure which in itself is discriminatory or which is implemented in a discriminatory manner;

(c) prosecution or punishment, which is disproportionate or discriminatory;

(d) denial of judicial redress resulting in a disproportionate or discriminatory punishment;

(e) prosecution or punishment for refusal to perform military service in a conflict, where performing military service would include crimes or acts falling under regulation 7.

(3) An act of persecution must be committed for at least one of the reasons in Article 1(A) of the Geneva Convention.

Key to this definition is a requirement that the act must be sufficiently serious to amount to a non-derogable right under the ECHR. The non-derogable rights are Article 2 (right to life, except for deaths resulting from lawful acts of war), Article

3 (torture and inhuman or degrading treatment or punishment), Article 4(1) (slavery and servitude), and Article 7 (retrospective conviction).

Whilst Regulation 5(1) may be considered to be restrictive in its definition, Regulation 5(2) appears to be quite expansive.

Acts of persecution can be rendered serious by their nature or their repetition, meaning a sufficiently serious one-off act is capable of amounting to persecution. This construction was endorsed by Keene LJ in the Court of Appeal in BA (Pakistan) v Secretary of State for the Home Department [2009] EWCA Civ 1072: '[21] That phrase "by their nature or repetition" is disjunctive. It emphasises that there need not be repeated acts if an act is sufficiently serious.'

In the Court of Appeal case of MA (Ethiopia) v Secretary of State for the Home Department [2009] EWCA Civ 289 (02 April 2009) Elias LJ commented as follows regarding deprivation of nationality and persecution:

> 60 ... if the appellant were able to establish that she has been arbitrarily refused the right to return to Ethiopia for a Convention reason, that would in my view amount to persecution. It would negate one of the most fundamental rights attached to nationality, namely the right to live in the home country and all that goes with that. Denial of that right of abode would necessarily prevent the applicant from exercising a wide range of other rights - if not all - typically attached to nationality, as well as almost inevitably involving an interference with private and/or family life in breach of Article 8 of the ECHR.

The case is an illustration of the cross over between the refugee and human rights conventions, and indicates that a broader approach to the definition of persecution than that provided in Regulation 5(1) may be appropriate in particular cases.

Human rights analysis

The Qualification Directive clearly links the concept of persecution to human rights law principles. This is not an entirely new approach in UK case law. In the case of Gashi [1997] INLR 97, as approved by the House of Lords in Ullah [2004] UKHL 26, the Tribunal adopted the following approach:

> In aid of this sometimes difficult assessment, UNHCR generally agrees with Professor Hathaway's formulation that persecution is usually the "sustained and systemic denial of core human rights" (J Hathaway at p.112). Clearly, some human rights have greater pre-eminence than others and it may be necessary to identify them through a hierarchy of relative importance. This can be achieved by reference to the International Bill of Rights as the universal measure of appropriate standards.
>
> (a)The first category includes inviolable human rights such as the right of life and the prohibition against torture, cruel, inhuman or degrading punishment or treatment. A threat to these rights would always be a serious violation amounting to persecution, as referred to in paragraph 51 of the Handbook.'
>
> (b)The second category includes rights where limited derogation or curtailment by the state in times of public emergency can be justified. They would include, inter

> alia, the rights to be free from arbitrary arrest and detention, and the right to freedom of expression. A threat to these rights may amount to persecution if the state cannot demonstrate any valid justification for their temporary curtailment. In any event, the measures will usually be accompanied by other forms of discrimination treatment which if assessed cumulatively, could amount to persecution.'
>
> (c) The third category are rights which although binding upon states, reflect goals for social, economic or cultural development. Their realisation may be contingent upon the reasonable availability of adequate state resources. But the state must nonetheless act in good faith in the pursuit of these goals and otherwise in a manner which does not violate customary norms of non-discrimination. This category would include, inter alia, the right to basic education and the right to earn a livelihood. In appropriate circumstances, a systemic and systematic denial of these rights may lead to cumulative 'consequences of a substantially prejudicial nature for the person concerned' of such severity as would amount to persecution within the meaning and spirit of the Convention. This would be particularly so where the state has adequate means to implement the rights but applies them in a selective and discriminatory manner.

The Qualification Directive and implementing regulations certainly affirm this approach to the interpretation of persecution regarding first and second category rights, as can be seen from Article 5 of the regulations quoted above. Whether the Directive embraces third category rights is less clear, but the Preamble, Recital (11), holds "With respect to the treatment of persons falling within the scope of this Directive, Member States are bound by obligations under instruments of international law to which they are party and which prohibit discrimination."

Subjective nature of being persecuted

The threshold at which ill-treatment becomes persecution is undoubtedly a high one. However, the threshold is not identical in all cases, as being persecuted is in part a subjective concept: what amounts to persecution for one person does not necessarily for another. The UNHCR Handbook states as follows at paragraph 55:

> Whether other prejudicial actions or threats would amount to persecution will depend on the circumstances of each case, including the subjective element to which reference has been made in the preceding paragraphs. The subjective character of fear of persecution requires an evaluation of the opinions and feelings of the person concerned. It is also in the light of such opinions and feelings that any actual or anticipated measures against him must necessarily be viewed. Due to variations in the psychological make-up of individuals and in the circumstances of each case, interpretations of what amounts to persecution are bound to vary.

In Katrinak v SSHD [2001] EWCA Civ 832 the Court of Appeal endorsed this approach:

> [21] ...the attacks also potentially evidence the appellants' vulnerability in the future. An activity which would not amount to persecution if done to some people may amount to persecution if done to others. It is easier to persecute a husband whose

> wife has been kicked in a racial attack whilst visibly pregnant than one whose family has not had this experience. What to others may be an unbelievable threat may induce terror in such a man.

The Qualification Directive reiterates this approach at Article 9 (regulation 5 of the UK regulations). Acts of a gender specific or child specific nature are specifically mentioned in the Directive as examples of acts that might constitute persecution (although these references are not transposed into national law and are omitted from the Refugee or Person in Need of International Protection (Qualification) Regulations 2006), as is mental as well as physical violence. The reference at Article 9(1)(b) of the Directive to the effect on an individual suggests a proper focus on the subjective aspect of persecution.

Role of Convention reasons

In the course of his judgment in the case of Sepet and Bulbul v SSHD [2001] EWCA Civ 681, Lord Justice Laws provided a very useful exposition of the role of a Convention reason in defining persecution:

> 63. There are some classes of case in which the threatened conduct is of such a kind that it is universally condemned, by national and international law, and always constitutes persecution: torture, rape (though of course it is not necessarily persecution for a Convention reason). In those instances, the question whether or not there is persecution is straightforwardly a matter of fact. But it is not always so; and Kagema [1997] IAR 137 (relied on by Mr Macdonald in reply) is no authority that it is. There are other classes of case in which the threatened conduct is by no means necessarily unjustified at the bar of law or opinion: imprisonment is a plain instance (where its length is not disproportionate and its conditions are not barbarous). In such a case some further factor is required to turn the treatment in question into persecution. Torture is absolutely persecutory; imprisonment only conditionally so.
>
> 64. What is the further factor that may turn imprisonment into persecution? It can only be that the claimant is liable to be imprisoned for a Convention reason. There can be no other way in to the regime of Convention protection. In this case, then, the existence of a Convention reason is what defines the treatment as persecutory.
>
> 65. See where this leads. The putative act of persecution - imprisonment - is only such if it is inflicted for a Convention reason. (I leave aside all the uncontentious possibilities: that the military service involves acts or conditions which are barbarous, or that the punishment for draft evasion is barbarous or disproportionate). It is the why and wherefore of the punishment's infliction that alone can transform the imprisonment suffered into persecution. But then it must constitute persecution according to the Convention's common standard, within and according to the autonomous international meaning of the Convention.

The House of Lords later gave judgment in the same case (neutral citation [2003] UKHL 15), but this passage from the Court of Appeal judgment stands as both a masterful exposition and a useful starting point for further exploration of the role of Convention reasons in determining what is and is not an act of persecution. In making apparently difficult judgments about whether a criminal offence (e.g. homosexual acts or exercise of the right to protest) are 'reasonably' defined as crimes in a given country, the starting point is international human rights law. If international standards as defined in the UN Conventions prohibit certain laws or State actions then that will be a useful guide to whether a punishment is capable of being an act of persecution.

Prosecution and persecution

Straightforward fugitives from justice are not refugees. However to suggest that anyone who flees forms of harm that arise via prosecution is a criminal rather than a refugee is to over-simplify the question and it is clear from the Qualification Directive that there are circumstances where prosecution will amount to persecution: where it is disproportionate or discriminatory.

The UNHCR Handbook similarly suggests, at paragraph 57, that excessive punishment upon conviction imposed for a Convention reason would be persecutory:

> A person guilty of a common law offence may be liable to excessive punishment, which may amount to persecution within the meaning of the definition.

The question of proportionality must be determined according to international human rights and criminal law standards, as set out in the various international treaties.

That which is apparently prosecution may be rendered persecutory by a discriminatory manner of application: e.g. directing prosecution for public order offences only against supporters of the political opposition. See the UNHCR Handbook, paragraph 59 showing that it will be necessary to examine whether there is discriminatory application of the law for political offences:

> More often, however, it may not be the law but its application that is discriminatory. Prosecution for an offence against 'public order', e.g. for distribution of pamphlets, could for example be a vehicle for the persecution of the individual on the grounds of the political content of the publication.

Prosecution may also be heightened to persecution by the absence of due process within the justice system, so long as the procedural deficiencies are directed on Convention grounds (e.g. convicting opposition political supporters without a fair trial).

States which punish people for the exercise of fundamental human rights may be persecuting individuals rather than simply prosecuting them, see the Court of Appeal in Tientchu v Immigration Appeal Tribunal (C/2000/6288; 18 October 2000):

> ...having accepted ... certain parts of her evidence ... in my judgment he could only properly have refused her claim for asylum, given the wealth of evidence before him of the gravest human rights abuses in Cameroon, had there been some evidence truly pointing towards this applicant having committed a non-political offence, rather than having acted in a way which the international community would surely regard as involving the legitimate expression and advancement of a political view.

In fact this principle extends beyond narrow political opinion cases into those cases where it is the loss of the ability to give expression to one's sexual identity (because doing so would expose the individual to prosecution) that forms the basis of the persecution, see Jain v Secretary of State for the Home Department [2000] Imm AR 76 (as where a homosexual faces prosecution simply for consensual actions committed in private).

Military service

It has been found that there is no international human right to conscientious objection. See Sepet and Bulbul [2001] EWCA Civ 681:

> [T]here is no material to establish a presently extant legal rule or principle which vouchsafes a right of absolute conscientious objection, such that where it is not respected, a good case to refugee status under the Convention may arise. No such putative rule or principle is to be found in the Convention's international autonomous meaning or common standard.

The necessary implication is that prosecution for refusal to perform military service is therefore, at least potentially, legitimate prosecution for breach of a state's criminal law. The act of imprisonment would not therefore amount to being persecuted as there is no Convention reason behind the punishment in question.

This approach was upheld by the House of Lords on appeal ([2003] UKHL 15). Lord Bingham commented that there are, though, circumstances where a conscientious objector might succeed in a claim for refugee status:

> There is compelling support for the view that refugee status should be accorded to one who has refused to undertake compulsory military service on the grounds that such service would or might require him to commit atrocities or gross human rights abuses or participate in a conflict condemned by the international community, or where refusal to serve would earn grossly excessive or disproportionate punishment...

In Krotov v SSHD [2004] EWCA Civ 69 the Court of Appeal held that "a genuine conscientious refusal to participate in a conflict in order to avoid participating in inhumane acts required as a matter of state policy or systemic practice [amounts] to an (implied or imputed) political opinion as to the limits of governmental authority". However, the asylum seeker will have to show that they would personally be associated with actions whose "defining characteristic and hallmark is service in a military which breaches international standards."

This approach was effectively transposed to peace-time atrocities as well, in the case of BE (Iran) v SSHD [2008] EWCA Civ 540. Sedley LJ gave the judgment of the court and concluded as follows:

> 40. In our judgment, on the limited facts before the tribunal, this appellant was entitled to succeed in his claim for international protection. It is common ground that, once it is established that the individual concerned has deserted rather than

commit a sufficiently grave abuse of human rights, whatever punishment or reprisal consequently faces him will establish a well-founded fear of persecution for reasons of political opinion.

41. For the reasons we have given, we hold that what this appellant was seeking to avoid by deserting was the commission of what this country and civilised opinion worldwide recognise as an atrocity and a gross violation of human rights – the unmarked planting of anti-personnel mines in roads used by innocent civilians. He is consequently entitled to asylum, and his appeal accordingly succeeds.

The Qualification Directive and regulations specifically refer in the examples of possible acts of persecution (Article 9 or regulation 5) to "prosecution or punishment for refusal to perform military service in a conflict, where performing military service would include crimes or acts falling under [the exclusion provisions". There is no reference here to disproportionate acts of punishment, but this need not prevent such cases being argued as (a) the directive imposes minimum requirements and that level of protection can be exceeded and (b) a disproportionate punishment case can be pursued under a more conventional analysis, where there must be a Convention reason (e.g. race or religion) behind the disproportionate punishment and that punishment must amount to being persecuted.

Civil war

In relation to civil war victims, see also the later section on Humanitarian Protection. As can be seen below, the Refugee Convention has not proven helpful to many victims of civil war, and the Qualification Directive fills some of the resulting protection gap (see further below).

In order to secure refugee status, persons fleeing civil war must demonstrate that they face a differential impact over and above the general risks of a civil war in which law and order has broken down completely: the House of Lords in R v Secretary of State for the Home Department ex parte Adan [1998] Imm AR 338. The reasoning is essentially that of 'collateral damage': the ordinary victims of civil war are not being specifically targeted, rather they are simply in the way of the opposing factions and are accidentally caught in the crossfire. Civilians who can show that they are specifically targeted for a Convention reason or who suffer a differential impact in related activities such as looting and robbery following the breakdown of law and order can potentially make out a claim for refugee status.

However, egregious breaches of international humanitarian law are not part of the ordinary risks of civil war: the Tribunal in Rudralingam (00/TH/02264; 24 November 2000). So if people suffer torture, or civilians are killed, or hospitals attacked, on "Convention" grounds, then persecution may still be found, even in a civil war.

Example

In the case of Adan, it was found that there was a general state of civil war and lack of law and order in Somalia. All or many citizens of Somalia could be said to be victims of the civil war in a wide sense. In the leading judgment Lord Lloyd cited a number of authorities, including Hathaway: "victims of war and conflict are not refugees unless they are subject to differential victimisation based on civil or political status."

The same reasoning would not necessarily apply in a country such as 1994 Rwanda, where victims of genocide were being targeted for the very specific Convention reason of race. This went far beyond the normal threat from a general civil war.

The Convention reasons

The Convention reasons are central to the Refugee Convention. A refugee is a person with a 'well-founded fear of being persecuted for reasons of...'. There must therefore be a causal link between the harm suffered and one of the five Convention reasons.

In addition, as described above, the Convention reasons can have a transformative effect on certain types of harm. For example, imprisonment as a result of criminal behaviour does not amount to persecution, whereas imprisonment for reasons of a Convention reason would amount to persecution.

The Convention reasons are as follows:

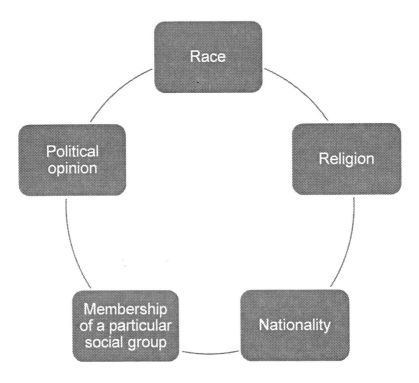

Race

"Race" is interpreted to include "...all persons of identifiable ethnicity" (quote from Professor Hathaway's The Law of Refugee Status). The Qualification Directive states that 'the concept of race shall in particular include considerations of colour, descent or membership of a particular ethnic group'.

Religion

The Qualification Directive offers a very inclusive definition of religion:

> the concept of religion shall in particular include the holding of theistic, non-theistic and atheistic beliefs, the participation in, or abstention from, formal worship in private or in public, either alone or in community with others, other religious acts or expressions of view, or forms of personal or communal conduct based on or mandated by any religious belief

Cases of religious conversion can be controversial, and are best prepared by anticipating possible Home Office objections to the credibility of any conversion. However, the depth of religious conviction of the apostate should not be permitted to obscure the fact that the agents of persecution may not be overly concerned about the theological commitment of the convert.

Whether or not one has a well-founded fear of persecution on the basis of future activities will be governed by the principle in Iftikar Ahmed (discussed above): will the appellant in reality carry out the threatened activities, and will those actions lead to a well-founded fear of persecution?

Nationality

The Qualification Directive definition of nationality is an interesting one that extends conventional understanding of the concept:

> "the concept of nationality shall not be confined to citizenship or lack thereof but shall in particular include membership of a group determined by its cultural, ethnic, or linguistic identity, common geographical or political origins or its relationship with the population of another State".

Membership of a particular social group

Discrimination is the focal point of determining whether a person is a member of a particular social group. Other relevant criteria are whether the discrimination is on the basis of an immutable characteristic of the individual: i.e. one that is either beyond the power of an individual to change (i.e. is innate) or one that it would be contrary to their fundamental human rights for them to forgo (i.e. is non-innate).

Innate characteristic

- e.g. gender, sexuality

Common background that cannot be changed

- e.g. being a former teacher or policeman

Fundamental belief or characteristic

- e.g. home schooling

The House of Lords held in Shah and Islam [1999] UKHL 20 that women in Pakistan constituted a particular social group. This was because they share the common immutable characteristic of gender, they were discriminated against as a group in matters of fundamental human rights and the State gave them no adequate protection because they were perceived as not being entitled to the same human rights as men.

The Qualification Directive adopts the Shah and Islam approach but also elevates societal attitude to a strict requirement; both have to be shown to establish that there is a social group. This is also reflected in the Refugee or Person in Need of International Protection (Qualification) Regulations 2006 at regulation 6(d) and (e):

> (d) a group shall be considered to form a particular social group where, for example:
>
> (i) members of that group share an innate characteristic, or a common background that cannot be changed, or share a characteristic or belief that is so fundamental to identity or conscience that a person should not be forced to renounce it, and
>
> (ii) that group has a distinct identity in the relevant country, because it is perceived as being different by the surrounding society;
>
> (e) a particular social group might include a group based on a common characteristic of sexual orientation but sexual orientation cannot be understood to include acts considered to be criminal in accordance with national law of the United Kingdom

The Qualification Directive is therefore be more restrictive than the current UK case law position, as societal identification of the group is not a requirement in Shah and Islam. Indeed, it would be difficult to argue that Pakistani society regarded women as a distinct social group. In SSHD v K; Fornah v SSHD [2006] UKHL 46 the House of Lords ruled that it is the more generous UK approach that should prevail.

A social group cannot be defined by the persecution which a potential member is experiencing. It has to exist independently of the persecution, although the persecution may play a role in the group becoming identifiable. This does not prevent future victims of Female Genital Mutilation constituting a particular social group: SSHD v K; Fornah v SSHD.

In SM (PSG, Protection Regulations, Regulation 6) Moldova CG [2008] UKAIT 00002 the Tribunal found that "Former victims of trafficking" and "former victims of trafficking for sexual exploitation" are capable of being members of a particular social group within regulation 6(1)(d) because of their shared common background or past experience of having been trafficked. This recognition that historical experience can give rise to membership of a particular social group is important: hitherto cases had succeeded only on the basis of some characteristic that the individual was born with, or was fundamental to their identity.

In K and Fornah (above) the Law Lords accepted that the family was a particular social group. This enables, for example, individuals whose fears arise from a family involvement in blood feuds to make good their claims for asylum. .

Political opinion

Express political opinion is perhaps the most often cited Convention reason. Most obviously it will reflect a political opinion against the interests of the state itself, but the Qualification Directive (as transposed) does not limit the definition

> 'the concept of political opinion shall include the holding of an opinion, thought or belief on a matter related to the potential actors of persecution mentioned in regulation 3 [see actors of persecution, above] and to their policies or methods, whether or not that opinion, thought or belief has been acted upon by the person'

The definition appears wider than that offered in the previous leading case on political opinion, Guteirrez Gomez (00/TH/02257; 20 November 2000; Starred:

> 'To qualify as political the opinion in question must relate to the major power transactions taking place in that particular society. It is difficult to see how a political opinion can be imputed by a non state actor who (or which) is not itself a political entity.'

The Qualification Directive definition would encompass groups such as feminists and single issue campaigners, which were arguably excluded from Refugee Convention protection by the Gomez approach.

Many claimants will be able to demonstrate a fear of persecution based on what they have already done, or are thought to have done. Whether or not one has a well-founded fear of persecution on the basis of activities that are intended in the future will be governed by the principle in Iftikar Ahmed (discussed above): will the appellant in reality carry out the threatened activities, and will those actions lead to a well-founded fear of persecution?

Attributed Convention reasons

Regulation 6(2) of the Qualification Regulations demonstrates that a characteristic may be externally ascribed (i.e. imputed or attributed) to an individual by the persecutor, even if it does not in fact exist. It states:

'In deciding whether a person has a well-founded fear of being persecuted, it is immaterial whether he actually possesses the racial, religious, national, social or political characteristic which attracts the persecution, provided that such a characteristic is attributed to him by the actor of persecution.'

Protection and relocation

Protection from non-state persecution

The issue of the availability of protection arises most acutely in non-state persecution cases. In Horvath, the House of Lords held that persecution by non-state actors is only persecution within the meaning of the Refugee Convention if the state is unable to provide a system of protection.

This approach is also followed in the Qualification Directive, as transposed in the Refugee or Person in Need of International Protection (Qualification) Regulations 2006 at regulations 3 and 4 read together:

3. In deciding whether a person is a refugee or a person eligible for humanitarian protection, persecution or serious harm can be committed by:

(a) the State;

(b) any party or organisation controlling the State or a substantial part of the territory of the State;

(c) any non-State actor if it can be demonstrated that the actors mentioned in paragraphs (a) and (b), including any international organisation, are unable or unwilling to provide protection against persecution or serious harm.

4. (1) In deciding whether a person is a refugee or a person eligible for humanitarian protection, protection from persecution or serious harm can be provided by:

(a) the State; or

(b) any party or organisation, including any international organisation, controlling the State or a substantial part of the territory of the State.

(2) Protection shall be regarded as generally provided when the actors mentioned in paragraph (1)(a) and (b) take reasonable steps to prevent the persecution or suffering of serious harm by operating an effective legal system for the detection, prosecution and punishment of acts constituting persecution or serious harm, and the person mentioned in paragraph (1) has access to such protection.

(3) In deciding whether a person is a refugee or a person eligible for humanitarian protection the Secretary of State may assess whether an international organisation controls a State or a substantial part of its territory and provides protection as described in paragraph (2).'

Horvath is a difficult judgment to read as none of their Lordships offer a clear definition of what is meant by a system of protection. The consensus among asylum lawyers and judges is that the Horvath test is:

(i)   whether or not there is a system in place to offer protection and

(ii)   whether there is a reasonable willingness in the country to operate such a system.

All of the judgments differ in emphasis but perhaps the most practical test is that adopted by Lord Lloyd, actually that of Stuart-Smith LJ in the Court of Appeal below (paragraphs 20, 22, & 44 of Stuart-Smith's judgment):

"... the state may be unwilling to afford protection to a certain class of its citizens if there is widespread and systemic indifference to their plight on the part of the law enforcement agencies such as the police and the courts

...No state can guarantee the safety of its citizens. And to say that the protection must be effective suggests it must succeed in preventing attacks, which is something that cannot be achieved. Equally to say that the protection must be sufficient, begs the question, sufficient for what? In my judgment there must be in force in the country in question a criminal law which makes the violent attacks by the persecutors punishable by sentences commensurate with the gravity of the crimes. The victims as a class must not be exempt from the protection of the law. There must be a reasonable willingness by the law enforcement agencies, that is to say the police and courts to detect, prosecute and punish offenders. It must be remembered that inefficiency and incompetence is not the same as unwillingness, unless it is extreme and widespread. There may be many reasons why criminals are not brought to justice including lack of admissible evidence even where the best endeavours are made; they are not always convicted because of the high standard of proof required, and the desire to protect the rights of accused persons. Moreover, the existence of some policemen who are corrupt or sympathetic to the criminals, or some judges who are weak in the control of the court or in sentencing, does not mean that the state is unwilling to afford protection. It will require cogent evidence that the state which is able to afford protection is unwilling to do so, especially in the case of a democracy...

...In some cases where individuals are targeted by terrorists or dissidents it may be possible for the state to provide special police protection, for example by an armed guard or the provision of a new identity in a different part of the territory. But these attacks are unpredictable as to victims, time and location, and it is clear that the only form of protection which can be provided is in the form of deterrence through detection, prosecution, convictions and sentencing of criminals."

As can be seen, the Qualification Directive test is simpler, and it refers explicitly to the protection being both available to the person concerned and the system of protection including an 'effective legal system for the detection, prosecution and punishment of acts constituting persecution'. At the time of writing there is no case law on whether there is any difference between the two tests.

In both tests, the focus should be on the plight of the individual, and whether they can avail themselves of the protection of their country. Past failures of protection may assist an applicant in establishing that the protection supposedly available in the future would not be adequate (Haddadi (00/TH/02141)).

The greater the link between the authors of harm and the state itself, then the more attention must be paid to the efforts made by the state to provide protection – the steps that can be taken to rein in "uniformed persecutors" may be more extensive than those possible for individuals with no association with the state, see Svazas v Secretary of State for the Home Department [2002] EWCA Civ 74.

Example

Leroy is from Jamaica. He witnessed a murder and has been targeted by the criminal gang responsible.

Jamaica is a democracy and although there are serious problems with crime and organised crime, the criminal justice system does broadly function, albeit not very well. The case of AB (Protection - criminal gangs - internal relocation) Jamaica CG [2007] UKAIT 00018 deals with this subject and states that cases have to be decided on their own facts; some asylum claimants will be able to show inadequate protection is available given their particular circumstances. Depending on what has already happened to Leroy, he might well have a strong claim for protection.

Internal relocation

Situations arise where an individual may face persecution in a particular part of their country of origin but will be expected to relocate to a different part of their country where they can live in safety. This usually arises in non-state persecution cases, as it is difficult to imagine where a person might be able to relocate within the territory of a state while fearing persecution by that state. In Januzi v SSHD [2006] UKHL 5, the House of Lords held that there is, however, no legal presumption that internal relocation is not viable in state persecution cases.

The immigration rules refer to the concept of internal relocation and transpose the requirements of the Qualification Directive at rule 339O:

(i) The Secretary of State will not make:
   (a) a grant of asylum if in part of the country of origin a person would not have a well-founded fear of being persecuted, and the person can reasonably be expected to stay in that part of the country;
or
   (b) a grant of humanitarian protection if in part of the country of return a person would not face a real risk of suffering serious harm, and the person can reasonably be expected to stay in that part of the country.

> (ii) In examining whether a part of the country of origin or country of return meets the requirements in (i) the Secretary of State, when making his decision on whether to grant asylum or humanitarian protection, will have regard to the general circumstances prevailing in that part of the country and to the personal circumstances of the person.
>
> (iii) (i) applies notwithstanding technical obstacles to return to the country of origin or country of return

The rule (and the Directive) does not provide much practical guidance on approaching the question of whether internal relocation is applicable in a given case. Logically, there should be three stages of reasoning:

(i) Is there persecution in the 'home area'?

- If there is no persecution in the home area then the question of internal relocation does not arise. However, in other cases it is still important to start with this question because you cannot properly assess whether an applicant will be safe after return in another area if you have not examined the nature and severity of the threat they face in their home area.

(ii) Is there a 'safe place' to which the person can relocate?

- In cases of state persecution the answer to this question will often be 'no' but cases might arise where a person has been targeted by local government and could relocate to another area. In cases of non-state persecution, the influence and reach of the non-state actors will need to be assessed, particularly though country information.

(iii) Is it reasonable to require the person to relocate there?

- If there is a safe place, the last and most difficult question is whether it is reasonable to expect a person to relocate there. There may be inhospitable jungle or desert in a given country where a person would be free from persecution, but it would be unduly harsh to expect the person to live there.

This last question was the main subject of the major House of Lords decision in Januzi v SSHD [2006] UKHL 5, which effectively replaces R v Secretary of State for the Home Department & Immigration Appeal Tribunal ex parte Robinson [1997] Imm AR 568 as the principal authority on internal relocation. Januzi itself was then the subject of further explanatory litigation in AH Sudan in the Court of Appeal ([2007] EWCA Civ 297) and again in the House of Lords ([2007] UKHL 49).

In this last case, the House of Lords upheld an immigration tribunal decision finding that relocation to refugee camps around Khartoum by Darfuri refugees was reasonable. The House of Lords did however stress that it would be an error of law to impose the standard of breaches of Article 3 ECHR for the reasonableness threshold and that both the conditions in the home area and in the proposed area of relocation were relevant to the question of whether relocation was reasonable. The approach was summarised thus, by Lord Bingham, citing himself in Januzi:

> The decision-maker, taking account of all relevant circumstances pertaining to the claimant and his country of origin, must decide whether it is reasonable to expect the claimant to relocate or whether it would be unduly harsh to expect him to do so... The decision-maker must do his best to decide, on such material as is available, where on the spectrum the particular case falls... All must depend on a fair assessment of the relevant facts.

He then went on:

> Although specifically directed to a secondary issue in the case, these observations are plainly of general application. It is not easy to see how the rule could be more simply or clearly expressed. It is, or should be, evident that the enquiry must be directed to the situation of the particular applicant, whose age, gender, experience, health, skills and family ties may all be very relevant. There is no warrant for excluding, or giving priority to, consideration of the applicant's way of life in the place of persecution. There is no warrant for excluding, or giving priority to, consideration of conditions generally prevailing in the home country.

Baroness Hale alongside him:

> As the UNHCR put it in their very helpful intervention in this case,
>
> "...the correct approach when considering the reasonableness of IRA [internal relocation alternative] is to assess all the circumstances of the individual's case holistically and with specific reference to the individual's personal circumstances (including past persecution or fear thereof, psychological and health condition, family and social situation, and survival capacities). This assessment is to be made in the context of the conditions in the place of relocation (including basic human rights, security conditions, socio-economic conditions, accommodation, access to health care facilities), in order to determine the impact on that individual of settling in the proposed place of relocation and whether the individual could live a relatively normal life without undue hardship."

Note that the position in Sudan has changed since this judgment and the Home Office's current position at the time of writing was that it was not reasonable to expect a Darfuri refugee to relocate to the refugee camps around Khartoum.

Example

In the case of AA (Uganda) v SSHD [2008] EWCA Civ 579 the Court of Appeal held that it was not reasonable to expect a particularly vulnerable single young woman to relocate from her home area to the capital, where she had no connections and an expert had concluded she would be forced to make a living as a prostitute. There is therefore scope to argue internal relocation is

254

unreasonable, but evidence rather than generalised assertions is necessary.

Non Refoulement

The previous sections have all dealt with Article 1A of the Refugee Convention, which sets out the definition of a refugee. Other clauses set out the rights that a refugee should enjoy. Article 33 sets out the most important right for refugees, the right not to be returned to the frontiers of territories where they fear persecution (note there is no absolute right to non-return to other territories).

> 1. No Contracting State shall expel or return ("refouler") a refugee in any manner whatsoever to the frontiers of territories where his life or freedom would be threatened on account of his race, religion, nationality, membership of a particular social group or political opinion.

Even this fundamental right has limitations however, see below. The word 'refouler' is used because it implies return to the frontier of a territory where life or freedom would be threatened – this means that returns to third countries where there would be no persecution are not prohibited.

Article 32 requires states not to expel a refugee lawfully in their territory save on grounds of national security or public order. This offers more generous protection than Article 33 which only protects against refoulement. In *R (on the application of ST (Eritrea)) v SSHD* [2012] UKSC 12, the Supreme Court found that there was nothing to prevent the Home Office from making a decision to remove a women of Eritrean descent to Ethiopia, despite the fact that her asylum appeal against a decision to remove her to Eritrea had been allowed on Refugee Convention grounds. As she remained on temporary admission it was found that she was not yet lawfully present in the UK and could not therefore benefit from Article 32.

Cessation Clauses

Refugee status is not necessarily permanent as the Refugee Convention includes several cessation clauses governing the circumstances in which a recognised refugee's status as a refugee ceases. A person under this Article may cease to be recognised a refugee if they have:

(i) • Voluntarily availed themselves of the protection of the country of their nationality

(ii) • Voluntarily re-acquired a lost nationality

(iii) • Acquired the nationality of a country (including the UK) and availed themselves of the protection of that country

(iv) • Voluntarily established themselves in a country in respect of which they were a refugee

(v) • If the circumstances in their country of origin have changed such that the person no longer has a well-founded fear of persecution there.

It can be seen that the Refugee Convention does not oblige States to offer settlement to refugees. Indeed, refugee status appears as a temporary form of protection in the Convention itself.

In the United Kingdom, a successful asylum claimant will be recognised as a refugee and five years leave to remain will be granted. In the past ILR was granted but this policy was altered in August 2005.

If the refugee reaches the end of the five year period without his or her case having been reviewed, ILR will normally be granted, subject to the absence of criminal convictions. If, during the five year period, a Minister has issued a ministerial declaration that a particular country is now considered to be generally safe, all refugees of that nationality will have their cases individually reviewed, with a right of appeal against any decision to revoke refugee status. The burden will rest with the Home Office to establish that the individual is no longer a refugee. Assurances have been given that there will be few declarations, but this remains to be seen in practice. There have been none as yet.

Detailed guidance is provided to Home Office caseworkers in the API on Cessation, Cancellation and Withdrawal of Refugee Status. A person's refugee status can be revoked, or not renewed, in accordance with the refugee convention, under rule 339A.

Where there has been a grant of refugee status abroad, the asylum seeker should not have their claim addressed in the UK without regard to that fact. Thus the Tribunal's consideration is only on the basis that (as per *LW (Cancellation refugee status: UNHCR Note) Ethiopia* [2005] UKIAT 00042);

> Refugee status, once granted, should not be reviewed or annulled except on the most substantial and clear grounds.

This is very important – it effectively puts the burden of proof on the Home Office to show a change of circumstances, which is very important, given the tendency to inertia in Home Office advocacy and case preparation.

Exclusion clauses

It will be noted that the Convention has several forms of exclusion clause within it, for example Article 1E for possession of rights akin to nationality, the second limb of Article 1A(2) for dual nationals, the better known Article 1F exclusions for crimes against international law and serious criminal activity of a non-political nature. But even those accepted to be refugees may face limitations as to the duties owed to them under Article 33(2).

> 33(2). The benefit of the present provision may not, however, be claimed by a refugee whom there are reasonable grounds for regarding as a danger to the security of the country in which he is, or who, having been   convicted by a final judgment of a particularly serious crime, constitutes a danger to the community of that country.

The UK has chosen to automatically declare offences of certain kinds as meeting these criteria under the 2002 Act; this is dealt with below. Rules 334 and 339A contain provisions which allow the Secretary of State to exclude a person from protection under the Convention.

Article 1(D)

Applicable to Palestinian refugees receiving UNWRA assistance.

In Said (Article 1D : meaning) Palestinian Territories [2012] UKUT 413 (IAC) the Tribunal found that a Palestinian forced out of the protection of the UNRWA region by virtue of circumstances beyond their control, such as armed conflict in their refugee camp, may well be entitled to the benefits of the Refugee Convention, regardless of whether or not they also possess a well-founded fear of persecution for a Convention reason. The Tribunal also had to acknowledge in Said that the right to protection under 1D, as now enshrined in the Qualification Directive, applied to all those Palestinians who had received the protection of UNWRA, and not just those who were receiving it at the date the Refugee Convention was concluded (I.e. in 1951).

Article 1(F)

The following forms of behaviour lead to a person who would otherwise be a refugee being excluded from the Convention by virtue of Article 1F:

- Has committed a crime against peace, a war crime, or a crime against humanity, as defined in the international instruments drawn up to make provision in respect of such crimes

- Has committed a serious non-political crime outside the country of refuge prior to his admission to that country as a refugee

- Has been guilty of acts contrary to the purposes and principles of the United Nations.

The exclusion clauses are part of the Refugee Convention (similar ones appear in the Refugee Qualification Directive) and so can be considered by the immigration tribunal even where the Secretary of State has not raised them, subject to giving an opportunity to an Appellant to deal with such issues – the foreseeability of the issue arising will be relevant to the need for an adjournment.

The Refugee Qualification Directive has added words to its interpretation of the Refugee Convention, so that regarding Art 1F(b) cases, "prior to his admission" means prior to "the time of issuing a residence permit based on the granting of refugee status" (Art 12(2)(b) of Directive).

Discussion of Art 1F cases has often concentrated on whether a crime is political or non-political in nature. The House of Lords in 'T' (T v Secretary of State for the Home Department [1996] Imm AR 443) rejected the idea that any crime that was incidental to a political cause could be insulated from categorisation as 'non-political'. Acts of terrorism, being incidents of depersonalised and abstract violence coldly indifferent to the human rights of the victims, are sufficiently divorced from the objectives they are thought to serve to sever them of true political content.

Nexus to acts falling within Article 1F

The question of guilt by association has recurred in case law over the exclusion clauses. In the starred case of Gurung [2002] UKIAT 04870, the Tribunal suggested that membership of an organisation that committed terrorist acts might well lead to one's exclusion from the Refugee Convention. It also suggested locating the organisation in question on a continuum, where some organisations carry out both legitimate and terrorist activities and that some members of terrorist organisations would not be excluded from refugee status. The implication was that the nature of an organisation was an important indicator of whether a member should be excluded from refugee status for commission of war crimes.

The Court of Appeal revisited this issue in two cases in 2009 and the Supreme Court gave judgment again on the issue in 2010.

In KJ (Sri Lanka) v SSHD [2009] EWCA Civ 292 the Court of Appeal held that acts of a military nature committed by an independence movement (such as the LTTE) against the military forces of the government are not themselves acts contrary to the purposes and principles of the United Nations and suggested that an armed campaign against a government would not necessarily constitute acts contrary to the purposes and principles of the United Nations.

The Court went on to find that that mere membership of an organisation that, among other activities, commits acts of terrorism does not suffice to bring the exclusion into play. In contrast, where an organisation's activities are only acts of terrorism and a claimant is an active member, Article 1F is likely to apply. The Court then goes on to hold as follows:

> 38. However, the LTTE, during the period when KJ was a member, was not such an organisation. It pursued its political ends in part by acts of terrorism and in part by military action directed against the armed forces of the government of Sri Lanka. The application of Article 1F(c) is less straightforward in such a case. A person may join such an organisation, because he agrees with its political objectives, and be willing to participate in its military actions, but may not agree with and may not be willing to participate in its terrorist activities. Of course, the higher up in the organisation a person is the more likely will be the inference that he agrees with and promotes all of its activities, including its terrorism. But it seems to me that a foot soldier in such an organisation, who has not participated in acts of terrorism, and in particular has not participated in the murder or attempted murder of civilians, has not been guilty of acts contrary to the purposes and principles of the United Nations.

In the case of R (on the application of JS (Sri Lanka)) v SSHD [2010] UKSC 15 the Supreme Court explicitly rejected the approach of the tribunal in Gurung:

> 29... In the first place, it is unhelpful to attempt to carve out from amongst organisations engaging in terrorism a sub-category consisting of those "whose aims, methods and activities are predominantly terrorist in character", and to suggest that membership of one of these gives rise to a presumption of criminal complicity: "very little more will be necessary" (Gurung para 105).

The Supreme Court suggests a different approach:

> 30. Rather, however, than be deflected into first attempting some such sub-categorisation of the organisation, it is surely preferable to focus from the outset on what ultimately must prove to be the determining factors in any case, principally (in no particular order) (i) the nature and (potentially of some importance) the size of the organisation and particularly that part of it with which the asylum-seeker was himself most directly concerned, (ii) whether and, if so, by whom the organisation was proscribed, (iii) how the asylum-seeker came to be recruited, (iv) the length of time he remained in the organisation and what, if any, opportunities he had to leave it, (v) his position, rank, standing and influence in the organisation, (vi) his knowledge of the organisation's war crimes activities, and (vii) his own personal involvement and role in the organisation including particularly whatever contribution he made towards the commission of war crimes.

There should be no presumption, rebuttable or not, of individual liability, and the nature of an organisation and its aims and objectives are irrelevant to the question of whether a particular individual is guilty of war crimes.

In the Court of Appeal judgment under appeal in JS, the ambit of the exclusion clauses was very narrowly drawn with reference to the concept of criminal liability. The Supreme Court considered that this was too narrow an approach and lay down a different, rather wider analysis:

> 38... Put simply, I would hold an accused disqualified under article 1F if there are serious reasons for considering him voluntarily to have contributed in a significant way to the organisation's ability to pursue its purpose of committing war crimes, aware that his assistance will in fact further that purpose.

Evidence

In YS (Egypt) v SSHD & Anor [2009] EWCA Civ 222 the Court of Appeal finds unequivocally that in assessing whether there are 'serious reasons for considering' that a claimant has committed acts covered by the exclusion clauses, no weight whatsoever should be attached to a criminal conviction in another country based on evidence obtained by torture.

Relevance and definition of terrorist acts

Two Court of Appeal cases deal with this question: KJ (Sri Lanka) v SSHD [2009] EWCA Civ 292 and Al-Sirri v SSHD & Anor [2009] EWCA Civ 222. Both allow for a distinction between military activities against a government and terrorist activities against civilians. Insofar as there is a conflict, Al-Sirri is probably to be preferred as the argument on this question was far fuller than in KJ (Sri Lanka).

Section 54 of the Immigration, Asylum and Nationality Act 2006 seeks to add domestic definition to the exclusion clauses and provides as follows:

> **Refugee Convention: construction**
>
> (1) In the construction and application of Article 1(F)(c) of the Refugee Convention the reference to acts contrary to the purposes and principles of the United Nations shall be taken as including, in particular—
> > (a) acts of committing, preparing or instigating terrorism (whether or not the acts amount to an actual or inchoate offence), and
> > (b) acts of encouraging or inducing others to commit, prepare or instigate terrorism (whether or not the acts amount to an actual or inchoate offence).
>
> (2) In this section—
> "the Refugee Convention" means the Convention relating to the Status of Refugees done at Geneva on 28th July 1951, and
> "terrorism" has the meaning given by section 1 of the Terrorism Act 2000 (c. 11).

Section 1 of the Terrorism Act 2000 as amended then provides as follows:

Terrorism: interpretation

(1) In this Act "terrorism" means the use or threat of action where—
(a) the action falls within subsection (2),
(b) the use or threat is designed to influence the government [or an international governmental organisation] or to intimidate the public or a section of the public, and
(c) the use or threat is made for the purpose of advancing a political, religious, [racial] or ideological cause.

(2) Action falls within this subsection if it—
(a) involves serious violence against a person,
(b) involves serious damage to property,
(c) endangers a person's life, other than that of the person committing the action,
(d) creates a serious risk to the health or safety of the public or a section of the public, or
(e) is designed seriously to interfere with or seriously to disrupt an electronic system.

(3) The use or threat of action falling within subsection (2) which involves the use of firearms or explosives is terrorism whether or not subsection (1)(b) is satisfied.

(4) In this section—
(a) "action" includes action outside the United Kingdom,
(b) a reference to any person or to property is a reference to any person, or to property, wherever situated,
(c) a reference to the public includes a reference to the public of a country other than the United Kingdom, and
(d) "the government" means the government of the United Kingdom, of a Part of the United Kingdom or of a country other than the United Kingdom.

(5) In this Act a reference to action taken for the purposes of terrorism includes a reference to action taken for the benefit of a proscribed organisation.

However, the Qualification Directive gives effect to the Refugee Convention in UK law and in setting out the exclusion clauses it specifically refers to 'acts contrary to the purpose and principles of the United Nations as set out in the Preamble and Articles 1 and 2 of the Charter of the United Nations'. Articles 1 and 2 cannot be construed as being as wide as the definition of terrorism in the Terrorism Act 2000. In the case of YS (Egypt) v SSHD & Anor [2009] EWCA Civ 222 the Court of Appeal held that the Terrorism Act 2000 therefore had to be 'read down' to be compatible with the Qualification Directive. The Court goes on to define terrorism as 'the use for political ends of fear induced by violence' and also finds that there must be an international element to the terrorism in order to bring it within the scope of the exclusion clauses.

Procedure

In asylum appeals, the Home Office may certify that the appellant is not entitled to the protection of the Convention because Article 1F applies. The Tribunal (or SIAC) is required first to decide whether it agrees with the certificate. If it does, the appeal must be dismissed on asylum grounds (though the hearing will need to continue to consider whether removal will breach Article 3).

In Gurung [2002] UKIAT 04870, the Tribunal held that issues of exclusion may arise on appeal even though the point was not taken in the refusal letter. They cannot though be raised after an appeal has been allowed.

Article 33(2)

Article 33(2) of the Refugee Convention lifts the ban on return to the frontiers of territories where they fear persecution ("non-refoulement") for refugees for whom there are reasonable grounds for regarding as a danger to the security of the country in which he is, or who have been convicted of a particularly serious crime. It is not limited to crimes committed outside the country of asylum, which is a difference between it and Art 1(F)(b).

It had long been thought that this provision would only operate with respect to individuals who committed serious crimes either after obtaining asylum, or in the course of their asylum claim being considered.

However, NIAA 2002, section 72, which brings Article 33(2) into domestic law, in effect excludes from refugee status those deemed to fall within the terms of that Article in advance of an immigration judge considering their asylum claim.

Section 72 has the effect of creating a presumption that a person convicted of certain criminal offences for which he was sentenced to a period of imprisonment of 2 years either in or outside the UK is a danger to the community. The presumption also arises if he was convicted of a certain crime in the UK, specified by an order, or if the SSHD certifies that a conviction abroad is of a crime similar to one specified in the order. If the SSHD issues a certificate asserting that the presumption is engaged, unless that appellant persuades the immigration judge at the start of the hearing that the presumption should not apply to him, or is rebutted, the appellant's appeal on the grounds that his removal would breach the Refugee Convention must be dismissed.

The Court of Appeal in EN (Serbia) v SSHD [2009] EWCA Civ 630 found that the presumptions in section 72 of the NIA 2002 both in relation to the seriousness of the crime and in relation to danger to the community were rebuttable.

The applicant retains the right to establish that his removal would be in breach of the ECHR, so this provision prevents people becoming refugees and (presently) obtaining indefinite leave to remain rather than condemning them to a return abroad to face torture or inhuman treatment etc). So there would be no inhibition on their arguing their human rights grounds before an Immigration judge if the Secretary of State did not accept their 'well foundedness'.

The SSHD passed an order setting out certain offences, which, under section 72(4) and (5), gave rise to the presumption that the appellant is a danger to the community, regardless of the sentence. However, this order was declared unlawful by the Court of Appeal in the case of EN (Serbia) (see above) and at the time of writing the position remains that the entire order is ultra vires and therefore ineffective.

Humanitarian Protection

Under the Refugee Convention, a person whose removal from the territory would threaten their life or freedom is entitled to remain in the country of asylum, and to various other rights to be enjoyed for the course of stay as a refugee (including non-discrimination). However, the European Convention on Human Rights, which has since 2 October 2000 been effective in domestic law to supplement the Refugee Convention as a way of receiving protection, did not give any rights to those who benefit from its provisions to the extent of removing return to their country of origin – in essence the only right is to be free from torture, etc, not to other rights regarding the form of leave to remain, family reunion or travel documents.

From 1 April 2003 it became Home Office policy to give some formal rights to asylum seekers who were staying for "human rights" reasons. These forms of leave were known either "Humanitarian Protection" or "Discretionary Leave". Formerly, with some variations in practice, general policy was to grant Exceptional Leave to Remain.

From 10 October 2006 the EC Qualification Directive entered force. It brought a new era of protection and includes both refugee status and Humanitarian Protection under its wing. It is important to realise that Humanitarian Protection prior to that date was no more than a form of leave to remain given by virtue of Home Office policy – i.e. an administrative discretion. Humanitarian Protection after that date is a form of international protection given under directly effective European Community law (in EC law it is known as Subsidiary Protection, but the UK has chosen to keep the name for the pre-existing form of leave). Whilst the name may be the same, the legal basis is quite different.

Serious harm

Humanitarian Protection is received by those who face a risk of 'serious harm'. The forms of serious harm are as follows, see Article 15(a) of the Directive:

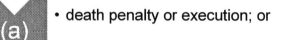
- death penalty or execution; or

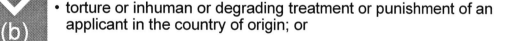
- torture or inhuman or degrading treatment or punishment of an applicant in the country of origin; or

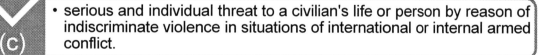
- serious and individual threat to a civilian's life or person by reason of indiscriminate violence in situations of international or internal armed conflict.

This has been incorporated into the immigration rules (Rule 339C) thus:

> **Grant of humanitarian protection**
>
> 339C. A person will be granted humanitarian protection in the United Kingdom if the Secretary of State is satisfied that:
> ...
> (iii) substantial grounds have been shown for believing that the person concerned, if he returned to the country of return, would face a real risk of suffering serious harm and is unable, or, owing to such risk, unwilling to avail himself of the protection of that country; and
>
> Serious harm consists of:
>
> (i) the death penalty or execution;
> (ii) unlawful killing;
> (iii) torture or inhuman or degrading treatment or punishment of a person in the country of return; or
> (iv) serious and individual threat to a civilian's life or person by reason of indiscriminate violence in situations of international or internal armed conflict."

Basically, then, the question is whether the individual faces a real risk of "serious harm" for one of this quartet of reasons.

It will be noted that the forms of harm are reminiscent of the some of the more basic protections afforded by the ECHR (rule 339C(ii) is like Article 2 ECHR; rule 339C(iii) resembles Article 3 ECHR). However there are numerous differences. European Community law has its own maxims of interpretation that are different to international or domestic law: it is significantly more purposive.

In addition, it is accepted in Strasbourg and domestically that ECHR Art 6 (the right to fair trial) does not apply in immigration proceedings. However because there is now a right under European Community law to refugee status or Humanitarian Protection, this may well have to be revisited. The Court of Appeal have resisted the temptation to do in R (on the application of MK (Iran)) v Secretary of State for the Home Department [2010] EWCA Civ 115 finding that this was a matter for the Strasbourg Court alone.

The right to refugee status and Humanitarian Protection demands that the Secretary of State determine applications on those grounds (rather than leaving them to the immigration tribunal as has often been done in recent years regarding those earmarked for deportation on criminal grounds), and requires a fully effective right of appeal for those seeking Humanitarian Protection (section 83 of the Nationality Immigration and Asylum Act 2002 only gives an upgrading appeal on refugee grounds): the Court of Appeal found that in fact it was necessary to read words into the Nationality Immigration and Asylum Act 2002 such that the appeal provisions addressing refugee law rights of appeal extended to Humanitarian Protection ones too: FA (Iraq) v Secretary of State for the Home Department [2010] EWCA Civ 696 (18 June 2010).

Article 15(c)

These differences aside, it will be seen that Article 15(c) (immigration rule 339C(iv)) finds no obvious reflection in human rights law. The issue has been investigated by the Tribunal and Courts in a string of cases now, starting from the ill-fated first foray by the Tribunal in KH (Article 15(c) Qualification Directive) Iraq CG [2008] UKAIT 00023. Whilst many of the decisions recognise that this is a new form of international protection, collectively they severely limit the extra scope the provision offers beyond that of the Refugee and European Conventions.

"Conflict"

In KH Iraq the Tribunal found that the matters to be investigated in determining whether there is an "internal armed conflict" are;

➢ firstly, whether there can be said to be "parties to the conflict";

➢ secondly, their "degree of organization";

➢ thirdly, the "level of intensity" of the conflict (which has to be higher than "situations of internal disturbances and tensions, such as riots, isolated and sporadic acts of violence, or other acts of a similar nature"); and

➢ fourthly, the "protraction" of the conflict.

However, it is doubtful whether this form of analysis remains necessary: because the Court of Appeal in *QD Iraq* [2009] EWCA Civ 620find in the special sense of Article 15(c), "armed conflict" has "an autonomous meaning broad enough to capture any situation of indiscriminate violence, whether caused by one or more armed factions or by a state." The third and fourth factors will be relevant to the rest of the Article 15(c) enquiry though, because they are relevant to whether there are sufficient dangers as to amount to a "real risk" of "indiscriminate violence".

Standard of Proof

Some respectable commentators and judges have thought the critical issue that differentiates Article 15(c) from the other forms of international protection is that the provision was built around a form of harm other than that where a "real risk" was present, i.e. that the provision's aim was to address a bare threat of harm. Certainly this fits with the language of "real risk ... of a threat". This would have represented a broader form of protection than for the more familiar parts of human rights and refugee law, where there must actually be a "real chance" of ill-treatment or persecution.

However, this idea seems to have been rejected by the Court of Appeal in QD Iraq v Secretary of State for the Home Department [2009] EWCA Civ 620 which found that 15(c) "seeks to cover ... real risks and real threats presented by the kinds of endemic act of indiscriminate violence."

The big remaining question will be when it can be said that civilians face real risks: some authorities have spoken, in other contexts, of a "well-founded fear" of persecution equating to a 10% chance of persecution, or that there might be a "real risk" of a human rights breach there was a one in ten chance of it happening (Batayav v Secretary of State for the Home Department [2003] EWCA Civ 1489). There can be few conflicts in history that have produced such casualty rates.

"Indiscriminate violence"

The European Court of Justice in Elgafaji (Justice and Home Affairs) [2009] EUECJ C-465/07 (17 February 2009) decided that "indiscriminate violence" refers to a high intensity of violence: so high, in fact, that the side effects of armed conflict "may extend to people irrespective of their personal circumstances." In addition:

> ➢ There may be classes of individual at enhanced risk due to personal factors. In UK case law, examples given in GS Afghanistan were the disabled person who cannot flee shellfire as swiftly as the able-bodied civilians around them, and members of groups who might be sought out by parties to the conflict, or taking advantage of the conflict, for special attention;

> ➢ Past exposure to violence in a conflict might show a likelihood of a repetition of such experiences absent a change of circumstances.

In GS (Existence of internal armed conflict) Afghanistan CG [2009] UKAIT 00010 the Tribunal found that "indiscriminate violence" would include that meted out by criminals taking advantage of the law and order vacuum created by the conflict.

"Life or Person"

However, the personal interests threatened, according to both the KH and GS Tribunals, must be of the most extreme variety: thus "life and person" might be murder, mutilation, cruel treatment and torture, but not "mere" inhuman or degrading treatment. In Elgafaji, however, followed by the Court of Appeal in QD Iraq, and the Upper Tribunal in AMM and others (conflict; humanitarian crisis; returnees; FGM) Somalia CG [2011] UKUT 445, a person could benefit from Article 15(c) protection from types of harm that are less severe than those encompassed by Article 3.

So, Article 15(c) presently requires the following:

> ➢ a real risk of a threat

> ➢ perhaps, the threat being of dangers to life and person narrowly construed as death or serious physical injury

> ➢ in circumstances where there is a high intensity of violence such that civilians

can be said to be at risk on an "indiscriminate basis" (subject to "enhanced risks")

The critical question

The conclusion of the Court of Appeal in QD was that "the critical question" was:

> Is there in Iraq or a material part of it such a high level of indiscriminate violence that substantial grounds exist for believing that an applicant ... would, solely by being present there, face a real risk which threatens his life or person?

At the time of writing internal armed conflicts had been found by the tribunal to exist in Iraq (as above), Somalia (AMM and others (conflict; humanitarian crisis; returnees; FGM) Somalia CG 2011] UKUT 445 (IAC)) and Afghanistan (GS Afghanistan). However, civilians in Afghanistan and Iraq were found not to be at sufficient risk to enliven Article 15(c); only in Somalia has the violence been found to be such that a person might be entitled to protection under Article 15(c).

Victims of trafficking

Victims of trafficking will often have protection needs, and can apply for asylum where necessary, where they, for example, fear retribution from their traffickers, or being re-trafficked (see e.g. PO (Nigeria) v SSHD [2011] EWCA Civ 132). Additionally, victims of trafficking may benefit from services, and be granted short periods of discretionary leave under the convention against trafficking.

Trafficking victims may need medical help, both physical and psychological, assistance in respect of their current circumstances, and the need for immediate protection, with matters of criminal law, with immigration status and detention issues, and other matters, all of which may new to many immigration advisers. Assisting trafficking victims is a specialist area and advisers who have concerns that their clients may be victims of trafficking should seek specialist advice. An extremely useful resource for those who are interested in this area is the Human Trafficking Handbook: Recognising Trafficking and Modern-Day Slavery in the UK, edited by Parosha Chandran, a barrister at 1 Pump Court.

The convention against trafficking

The Government ratified the Council of Europe Convention on Action against Trafficking in Human Beings on 17 December 2008 and implemented it from 1st April 2009.

Two Home Office guidance documents outline the policies and practices of the Home Office in regard to the U.K.'s obligations under the Convention:

Victims of Trafficking: guidance for frontline staff:

https://www.gov.uk/government/uploads/system/uploads/attachment_data/file/27 5239/Human_trafficking.pdf

Victims of Trafficking: guidance for the competent authorities: https://www.gov.uk/government/uploads/system/uploads/attachment_data/file/29 8421/traffickingcompetent.pdf

The website of the Anti-Trafficking Legal Project (ATLeP) (http://www.atlep.org.uk/) hosts a great deal more useful information for those representing victims of trafficking.

Definition of trafficking

The convention defines trafficking under Article 4;

> a "Trafficking in human beings" shall mean the recruitment, transportation, transfer, harbouring or receipt of persons, by means of the threat or use of force or other forms of coercion, of abduction, of fraud, of deception, of the abuse of power or of a position of vulnerability or of the giving or receiving of payments or benefits to achieve the consent of a person having control over another person, for the purpose of exploitation. Exploitation shall include, at a minimum, the exploitation of the prostitution of others or other forms of sexual exploitation, forced labour or services, slavery or practices similar to slavery, servitude or the removal of organs;
>
> b The consent of a victim of "trafficking in human beings" to the intended exploitation set forth in subparagraph (a) of this article shall be irrelevant where any of the means set forth in subparagraph (a) have been used;
>
> c The recruitment, transportation, transfer, harbouring or receipt of a child for the purpose of exploitation shall be considered "trafficking in human beings" even if this does not involve any of the means set forth in subparagraph (a) of this article;
>
> d "Child" shall mean any person under eighteen years of age;
>
> e "Victim" shall mean any natural person who is subject to trafficking in human beings as defined in this article.

Many victims will not understand themselves to have been trafficked, or be willing to disclose their true story. The two Home Office policy documents referred to above provide useful indicators of trafficking and should be consulted where there is concern that a client might be a victim of trafficking.

Referral Process

All agencies and organisations who find themselves with grounds for concern that a person may be a victim of human trafficking have a responsibility for ensuring the safeguarding needs of the child are assessed and addressed and for reporting their trafficking concerns to a first responder.

First responders are the agencies who will refer the child onto the National Referral Mechanism. A first responder may be:

- a local authority
- UK Visas and Immigration (UKVI)
- the police
- the National Crime Agency (NCA)
- Barnardo's
- the NSPCC's Child Trafficking Advice Centre (CTAC)
- an agency who deals predominantly with adults who have been trafficked (such as Gangmasters Licensing Authority, The Poppy Project, TARA, Migrant Help, the Medaille Trust, Kalayaan and the Salvation Army).

Where a *First Responder* finds themselves with grounds for concern that a person may be a victim of human trafficking, a formal referral is made into the *National Referral Mechanism*, a victim identification and support process which is designed to make it easier for all the different agencies that could be involved in a trafficking case – e.g. police, Home Office, local authorities and NGOs – to co-operate; to share information about potential victims and facilitate their access to advice, accommodation and support.

Competent Authorities

Decisions about who is a victim of trafficking are made by one of the two *Competent Authorities* - the UK Human Trafficking Centre, where the person is a UK or EEA national, or where there is an immigration issue but the person is not yet known to Home Office, and the Home Office for situations where trafficking is raised as part of an asylum claim or in the context of another immigration process.

The decision making process has two stages. Within 5 days of a referral, the Competent Authority should apply a 'reasonable grounds' test to consider if the statement "I suspect but cannot prove" that the person is a victim of trafficking holds true. If the answer is positive, the person will be granted a minimum of 45 calendar days for recovery and reflection. No detention or removal action will be taken against the subject during this time.

Following a positive *reasonable grounds* decision, Competent Authorities are required to make a second identification decision, on 'conclusive grounds', which is to conclusively decide if the individual is a victim of trafficking. The expectation is that a conclusive grounds decision will be made in 45 calendar days.

Those found, in a *conclusive grounds* decision, to be victims of trafficking may be granted a period of 12 months and 1 day discretionary leave (DL) either to assist with police enquiries, or due to their personal circumstances, unless they are entitled to a more generous form of leave (e.g. as a Refugee). The DL can be extended where necessary.

The entitlement to grant of leave of 12 months and 1 day can be found in the DL policy in the Asylum Policy section of the Operational Guidance. The grant of leave, where granted following the refusal of an asylum claim, allows for an appeal against the refusal of asylum under s83 of the 2002 Act. The relevant section is at 4.5 which states as follows;

4.5 Trafficking cases

Where the UK Competent Authority has conclusively identified the applicant as a victim of trafficking and the personal circumstances of the case are so compelling that a grant of leave is considered appropriate, Discretionary Leave should be granted. The period of leave will depend on the individual facts of the case but must not be less than 12 months and 1 day and no more than 30 months (2.5 years). The minimum period of leave ensures that a victim of trafficking who is refused asylum but granted Discretionary Leave has a right of appeal against the rejection of their asylum claim by virtue of Section 83(1)(b) of the Nationality, Immigration and Asylum Act 2002

Where the UK Competent Authority has conclusively identified the applicant as a victim of trafficking and the individual is cooperating with the police in an ongoing police investigation into their trafficking case and their presence is required in the UK by the police for this purpose, they should be granted 12 months and 1 day Discretionary Leave. A further period of leave may be granted where appropriate.

The only means of challenging a negative NRM decision is by way of Judicial Review. A judicial review application is made to the Administrative Court (part of the High Court), and must be made by a solicitor.

A decision to remove however can be challenged in the Tribunal on the basis of a failure by the Home Office to properly consider their duties under the Convention, and on the basis that removal would breach Article 4 of the ECHR: see EK (Article 4 ECHR: Anti-Trafficking Convention) Tanzania [2013] UKUT 00313.

Chapter 9: Asylum process and practice

Claiming asylum

An 'asylum claim' is legally defined at section 113 of the Nationality, Immigration and Asylum Act 2002;

> "asylum claim" means a claim made by a person to the Secretary of State at a place designated by the Secretary of State that to remove the person from or require him to leave the United Kingdom would breach the United Kingdom's obligations under the Refugee Convention,

Asylum claims must be made in person at the port of entry or by appointment at the Asylum Screening Unit in Croydon.

From April 2013, the Home Office has been implementing its new Asylum Operating Model 'designed to deliver more conclusions, faster, at lower cost and higher quality than ever before'. Sadly, as stated by The Independent Chief Inspector of Borders and Immigration;

> A poorly managed change programme for asylum casework had resulted in the rapid loss of experienced staff, which led to a backlog of over 13,000 cases by the end of 2013[1].

Detailed guidance on asylum policies and processes is provided for Home Office staff, and is available on the GOV.UK website, in the Asylum Policy section of the Operational Guidance.

Simply put, the process for most asylum seekers is broadly as follows:

---

[1] http://icinspector.independent.gov.uk/poorly-managed-organisational-change-leads-to-backlog-of-asylum-casework/

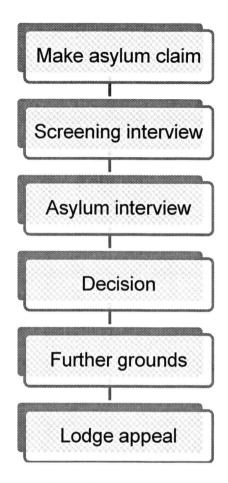

Excluded from this process, following the screening interview, will be those asylum seekers for whom the UK is not responsible for assessing their asylum claim, i.e. those who may be returned to another EU country which has that duty under EU law.

Screening interview

Once a claim has been made, the next step is the screening process. This includes fingerprinting of the applicant and the entry of those fingerprints into the EURODAC database to detect any multiple applications (including applications made in other EU countries).

A screening interview takes place, which concentrates on personal details and mode of entry and travel to the United Kingdom, said by the Home Office to be intended to address identity and nationality. This questioning will also address whether the applicant has potentially committed a criminal offence under s.2 of the 2004 Act (see later chapter on criminal offences). If the answers given by the applicant suggest the offence may have been committed, a referral to the police and CPS will be considered by the Home Office.

Applicants are given a form of induction during which they receive an Application Registration Card (ARC) which contains their personal details and acts as a form of identity. The immigration rules (rule 359) require the Secretary of State to provide to an asylum seeker a document certifying their status as such, within 3 days of their arrival.

Under immigration rule 358, the Secretary of State must now inform asylum seekers, "within fifteen days after their claim for asylum has been recorded of the benefits and services that they may be eligible to receive and of the rules and procedures with which they must comply relating to them."

Routing

Having been screened, and all things being equal, the asylum case will be referred, via the Asylum Routing Team (ART), to a regional asylum team where their case will be allocated to a case owner. The regional asylum teams are situated in Cardiff, Glasgow, Leeds, Liverpool, Central London, West London and Solihull.

Those not immediately referred to the ART will be previous absconders, children, those convicted of a serious offence, those with damaged fingerprints, cases suitable for the Detained Fast Track, EEA nationals, medical cases, prosecution cases, repeat applications, Third Country Unit cases, and those who appear to be Victims of Trafficking. All of these will be dealt with in accordance with the relevant policies.

The role of the representative

Unless the asylum seeker is to be removed from the UK without a decision being made on their asylum application under the Safe Third Country procedure, the asylum seeker will need help in preparing their asylum claim. Legal aid remains available for this purpose. Where the asylum seeker is in the Detained Fast Track, a representative from a legal aid firm will be available on site. Otherwise, the asylum seeker will need to find their own representative.

The adviser will need to take instructions from the asylum seeker to establish the basis for and the merits of the asylum claim, and to give appropriate advice. The adviser will then take more detailed instructions with a view to drafting a statement of the claim and preparing the asylum seeker for their interview.

The process of taking a detailed statement from the asylum seeker should help prepare them for the asylum interview. An experienced adviser will close question the asylum seeker, challenging them (in a friendly manner) where potential issues arise as to plausibility and consistency, and ensuring that the asylum seeker is aware of the level of detail they will need to provide as to their background and fears. The ILPA best practice guides on asylum applications and appeals remain essential reading for advisers on taking their clients instructions and drafting representations.

The statement will usually be completed post-interview and given to the case owner with detailed representations and any corroborative evidence available, before the asylum decision is made.

Asylum interview

Having been screened and accepted into the asylum procedure, the next big step in the decision making process will be the asylum interview. The HO policy on the asylum interview process is at: https://www.gov.uk/government/publications/conducting-the-asylum-interview-process.

Representatives are not funded to attend interviews unless the asylum seeker is a minor or particularly vulnerable. As a consequence of this funding bar, the Home Office should, on request, tape record the interview: see the case of R (Dirshe) v SSHD [2005] EWCA Civ 421. It is strongly advisable that asylum applicants make use of this facility, which is available on demand but is not automatic.

Decision

Decisions follow quite quickly from asylum interviews, although the time taken by individual case owners varies, depending on their working speed and whether they agree to wait for additional evidence or submissions. Home Office policy is to conclude new asylum claims within 6 months of the application being made.

Asylum seekers can apply for permission to take up employment, although only in shortage occupations, and excluding self-employment, if a decision at first instance has not been taken on their asylum application (or fresh asylum claim) within one year of the date on which it was recorded – so long as the delay is not attributable to them (rule 360).

Further grounds: Section 120 statement

When a person makes an application to enter or remain in the UK, the SSHD or an immigration officer may serve a notice on him asking for him to state in writing:

➢ his reasons for wishing to enter or remain in the United Kingdom,

➢ any grounds on which he should be permitted to enter or remain in the United Kingdom, and

➢ any grounds on which he should not be removed from or required to leave the United Kingdom.

Where a person has an immigration decision within the meaning of section 82 of the 2002 Act made in respect of them, the SSHD may serve a similar notice on the applicant asking for the same information.

There is no requirement for a repetition of reasons or grounds contained in the original application or that have already been considered in the immigration decision (2002 Act, s120).

Lodging the appeal

The deadline for the submission of an asylum appeal varies depending on the exact circumstances of the appellant:

> In-country, not detained: 10 business days

> In-country, detained: 5 business days

> Out of country: 28 calendar days

These time limits originate in the Asylum and Immigration Tribunal Appeal (Procedure) Rules 2005. Appeals law is covered in more detail in a later chapter, including business and calendar days, time for postage and submission of late appeals.

An asylum appeal will normally be lodged with the immigration tribunal directly, but detainees have the option of lodging an appeal with their custodian.

Asylum Support

Asylum support, often still referred to as NASS support, a reference to the now defunct National Asylum Support Service, is available to asylum seekers (and those who have made a claim under Article 3 ECHR) aged over 18 and their dependants who would otherwise be homeless and/or destitute. Unaccompanied children will be supported by their local authority under Section 20 of the Children Act 1989 and not by the Home Office.

Asylum support can be claimed immediately on claiming asylum. The application will be processed by the same officials involved in considering the asylum application.

Information on asylum support can be found on the GOV.UK website at: https://www.gov.uk/government/collections/asylum-support-asylum-instructions. Very useful advice for advisers is provided by the Asylum Support Appeals Project (ASAP: http://www.asaproject.org/about-asap/).

Support is provided under s95 Immigration and Asylum Act 1999. It is subject to a means assessment and takes the form of allocated accommodation, if the asylum seeker requires it, and a weekly income equivalent to approximately 70% of income support. Emergency accommodation will be provided if necessary. The asylum seeker will then be dispersed somewhere outside of London.

Asylum support can be denied to an asylum seeker who has not made a claim as soon as reasonably practicably after arriving in the UK, generally 3 days, (a "section 55 decision"). An asylum seeker cannot though be left destitute as a result (see 'Limbuela' [2005] UKHL 66). Compliance with the strict terms of asylum support is essential, as a failure to do so can lead to termination of support.

Where an asylum claim is finally determined, their asylum support will come to an end unless they have a dependent child. If the claim is successful, the asylum seeker (now a refugee) will be able to apply for mainstream benefits. Their asylum support will continue for four weeks to allow them to do so.

If an asylum seeker is refused asylum support, or support is withdrawn, they can appeal to the First-tier Tribunal (Asylum Support).

Those who are destitute and refused asylum, in cases where there are practical obstacles to them returning home, which can include an outstanding fresh claim, or judicial review proceedings where permission has been granted, or no viable route of return, can claim 'section 4 support' (i.e. under s4 of the 1999 Act). S4 support consists of accommodation, and a weekly sum via a payment card.

Those asylum seekers who, because of age, mental or physical ill health, disability or any other circumstances, are in need of care and attention which they cannot access anywhere else (i.e. which cannot be met by the provision of s95 or s4 support) may be entitled to support from a local authority under Section 21(1) of the National Assistance Act 1948. This is a complex area of law and advice should be sought from a community care specialist adviser or lawyer.

Age disputes

Relevance of age

Where an asylum seeker is under 18 years of age, that will impact on many things – most importantly how the asylum seeker is to be supported in the UK, how their asylum claim will be assessed, and what will happen to them if their asylum claim is refused.

There has been considerable litigation around disputed age assessments of young asylum seekers. Home Office policy is to treat a person claiming to be a minor as an adult *only where their physical appearance / demeanour very strongly suggests that they are significantly over 18 years of age*. The initial assessment process is often carried out by untrained and inexpert Home Office staff simply on the basis of a visual assessment.

If children are wrongly assumed to be adults, this will lead to their applications for asylum and other international protection being assessed by processes designed for adults rather than children.

This could lead to them being detained within the fast track system with adults. They may also be detained because the doubt about their age has damaged their overall credibility. If they are relying on having been subjected to child specific forms of persecution their applications may be fatally undermined. Age is also a central part of a child's identity and a failure to believe that they are children could lead to them losing all confidence in the decision making system and failing to disclose further and necessary details about their past persecution and future fears.

They will also be refused accommodation under Section 20 of the Children Act 1989 and will be dispersed to NASS accommodation as adults.

Because of the additional care and rights that a child in the asylum process has over an adult, it is therefore important to challenge a Home Office assessment that means the child will be treated as an adult.

The Home Office policy, after dealing with those who it finds to be significantly over 18, then states;

> 'All other applicants should be afforded the benefit of the doubt and treated as children, in accordance with the 'Processing an asylum application from a child AI [asylum instruction], until a careful assessment of their age has been completed. This policy is designed to safeguard the welfare of children. It does not indicate final acceptance of the applicant's claimed age, which will be considered in the round when all relevant evidence has been considered, including the view of the local authority to whom unaccompanied children, or applicants who we are giving the benefit of the doubt and temporarily treating as unaccompanied children, should be referred.

Having been given the benefit of the doubt, an unaccompanied minor will be put under the care of a local authority which should then carry out a 'Merton complaint' age assessment. The assessment carried out by the local authority will usually then be accepted by the Home Office.

Challenging an age assessment

The sequence of challenges will normally be as follows:

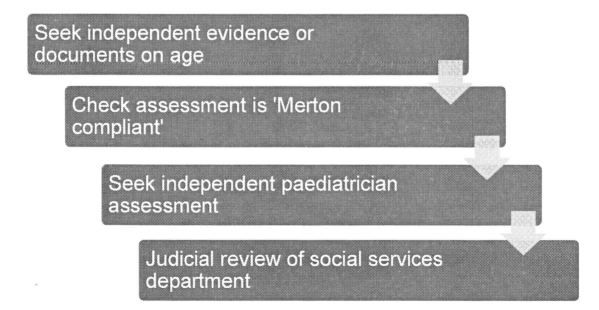

Seek independent evidence or documents on age

Check assessment is 'Merton compliant'

Seek independent paediatrician assessment

Judicial review of social services department

Before seeking to challenge a Home Office age assessment it is important to obtain any independent evidence available as to a person's age. Any such evidence will carry weight with whoever conducts an age assessment. Attempts should therefore be made to verify any documentation the child may have with them in the form of passports, national or school identity cards, family records or similar. Schools, doctors, hospitals, local officials, NGOs in the field and other objective sources of data about their age will need to be followed up. Statements and affidavits from family and community members should also be sought.

The first avenue for challenge is to approach the local social services department, which has a duty to conduct an age assessment in order to determine whether the person is a child and if so a child in need. This social services age assessment must be 'Merton compliant', i.e. comply with the standards set down in the case of R (on the application of B) v London Borough of Merton Council [2003] EWHC 1689 (Admin), in which it was held that:

> ...the decision maker cannot determine age solely on the basis of the appearance of the applicant. In general, the decision maker must seek to elicit the general background of the applicant, including his family circumstances and history, his educational background, and his activities during the previous few years. Ethnic and cultural information may also be important. If there is reason to doubt the applicant's statement as to his age, the decision maker will have to make an assessment of his credibility, and he will have to ask questions designed to test his credibility.

In R (on the application of T) v London Borough of Enfield [2004] EWHC 2297 (Admin), Jackson J held in addition that it was necessary to ask the individual why they believed that they were a minor and take into account any evidence which indicates that they are suffering from trauma and/or have any special educational needs.

If the social services age assessment is unfavourable, there are different courses of action that can be pursued, including:

1.   Seeking alternative independent evidence of age as suggested above.

Should new evidence become available social services will need to conduct a new age assessment.

2.   Seeking a paediatrician age assessment.

This is simply one form of independent evidence, but it is a controversial one because of the case of A v London Borough of Croydon & SSHD (Interested Party), WK v SSHD and Kent County Council [2009] EWHC 939 (Admin). In this case Collins J held that paediatrician age assessments are unreliable and do not have to be given any particular weight by social services.

3.   Judicial review of social services.

In the case of R (on the application of A) v London Borough of Croydon [2009] UKSC 8 the Supreme Court held that an age assessment by social services is subject to a full appeal in the courts, rather than being a matter simply for the social services department. The question whether or not a person is a child for the purposes of section 20 of the 1989 Children Act is a question of fact which must ultimately be decided by the court. This is very helpful when it comes to challenging a social services department. The Supreme Court case came after the judgment of Mr Justice Collins (they are related but distinct cases) and undermines key parts of the reasoning of the earlier case, so it may prove to be the case that paediatrician assessments will be considered more acceptable again in future.

The fact is that deciding someone's age is an extremely difficult exercise and it is not possible to be completely accurate. The most honest assessments include a margin of error of around two years either way. Any relevant evidence is therefore highly relevant to the assessment.

As with asylum support issues, disputing age assessments has become a specialist area of the law, and advice should be sought from a community care specialist. Age assessment JRs are usually heard now by the Upper Tribunal and are reported at https://tribunalsdecisions.service.gov.uk/utiac/decisions with an 'AAJR' prefix to the citation.

Fast-track appeals

The detained 'fast track' procedure is one whereby the asylum decision and appeal takes place in a very short time frame. In order to ensure compliance with this process, the subject is detained throughout.

The key features of fast track appeals are as follows:

As can be seen, everything about the fast track process points to the need to extract one's client from it if at all possible. The success rate of cases going through the fast track process is very low indeed, at around a 1%. Whether this is because Home Office is spectacularly successful at selecting low merit cases for the process or because any case that goes through the process thereby becomes low merit is a question many practitioners have posed.

Those who are allocated to the fast track processes at Harmondsworth and Yarl's Wood receive a decision on their claim within 3 days of arrival and are subjected to an expedited appeals procedure.

As from 20 October 2014, the new Fast Track procedure rules are to be found in a Schedule to the Tribunal Procedure (First-tier Tribunal) (Immigration and Asylum Chamber) Rules 2014. The Schedule governs appeals under the accelerated regime where the appellant is in immigration detention at a place specified in the rule 2(3) (presently Harmondsworth, Yarls Wood, and Colnbrook) on the date they are served with the appealable decision, and remain in detention.

➢ The notice of appeal must be served not later than 2 working days after the appellant receives the appealable decision (rule 5(1)). Time will be extended only if it is in the interests of justice to do so

➢ the HO must provide the Tribunal with specified documents within 2 days of receiving the notice of appeal from the Tribunal (rule 7).

➢ The Tribunal must fix the date of hearing not later than 3 working days after the day on which the documents are provided by the Home Office (rule 8).

The Tribunal must provide notice of the date, time and place of the hearing to every party as soon as practicable, and in any event not later than noon on the working day before the hearing.

➢ The Tribunal must conclude the hearing of the appeal on the date fixed under the Fast Track Rules (9) unless adjourned under rule 12.

➢ The Tribunal can adjourn the hearing of the appeal only where the Tribunal is satisfied that the appeal could not justly be decided if the hearing were to be concluded on the date fixed under the Fast Track Rules, and where there is an identifiable future date, not more than 10 working days after the date so fixed, upon which the Tribunal can conclude the hearing and justly decide the appeal within the timescales provided for in the Fast Track Rules (rule 12).

There is a power in the immigration tribunal to order removal of the appeal from the fast track procedure:

➢ if all the parties consent (rule 14(1)(a)); or

> if the Tribunal is satisfied that the case cannot justly be decided within the timescales provided for in the Fast Track Rules (rule 14(1)(ab)).

A case turning on authenticity of documents would be one example unsuitable for treatment under this procedure, see Lord Phillips MR in the Court of Appeal in *ZL and VL v Secretary of State for the Home Department and Lord Chancellors Department* [2003] EWCA Civ 25.

In *SH (Afghanistan) v SSHD* [2011] EWCA Civ 1284, the Court of Appeal found that the decision of the tribunal to refuse an adjournment in order to await an expert age assessment was unfair and unlawful, even in circumstances where the adjournment would have necessitated the appeal being removed from the fast track process.

On a removal from the process, any time periods for acts to be done which are then running are to be replaced by their equivalent in the principal rules (rule 31).

In <u>Detention Action</u> v Secretary of State for the Home Department [2014] EWHC 2245 (Admin), Ouseley J found that the Detained Fast-Track system was unlawful as it was being being operated, because lawyers were not involved at an early enough stage. The Court of Appeal decided though that measures the HO had put in place since the judgment – particularly the provision of a 4 day period prior to the asylum interview for the asylum seeker to receive appropriate legal advice was adequate to render the system now lawful.

Safe Third Country Cases

An asylum applicant cannot normally be removed from the UK whilst their claim is pending a decision upon it (2002 Act, section 77). An exception to this is where the Home Office intends to remove the asylum applicant to a safe third country. Thus asylum claims may be refused without substantive consideration of the claim if the applicant can be returned to a safe third country.

Dublin 3

EC Council Regulation Number No <u>604/2013</u> ("Dublin 3") is the instrument which now generally governs the procedures by which one European Union Member State only will be identified as responsible for a particular asylum claim. In practice this tends to be the State where they were first detected as entering the European Union territory subject to having relatives or family members present in other countries, or other special circumstances such as having been granted a visa for another country.

There is more subsidiary legislation that it is necessary to look at alongside Dublin 3, for example addressing the identification of relatives of an unaccompanied minor and their ability to care for the minor, establishing family links, dependency and care (Recital 35): see for example the Implementing Regulation No 118/2014 of 30 January 2014.

Procedurally, the Dublin process will begin when a Eurodac hit determines that the asylum seeker has already claimed asylum elsewhere in the EU. The Secretary of State will then tell the asylum seeker that they are suitable for the third country process, and will write to the third country to invite them to take responsibility. The third country will then accept responsibility. If they fail to do so, this is "tantamount to accepting the request" and so they are deemed to have taken responsibility (see Articles 22(7) and 25(2) of Dublin 3) where the requested Member State does not reply in time. The Secretary of State certifies that their case is eligible for the third country process under Schedule 3 to the Asylum and Immigration (Treatment of Claimants, etc.) Act 2004. This will serve to deny the asylum seeker an in-country right of appeal. The only remedy at this stage will be for the asylum seeker to make a human rights claim. It is likely that the Secretary of State will then certify the human rights claim as 'clearly unfounded', and the asylum seeker will have to then challenge the certificate by way of judicial review.

A very experienced lawyer will be needed to challenge the certificate and it will only be in rare cases that such a challenge can succeed, usually on the basis that the reception conditions will breach the asylum seekers Article 3 rights. Both the European courts have found such to be the case in respect of Greece. The European Court of Human Rights is currently considering a similar challenge in respect of Italy (see more on challenges below).

Below is the hierarchy set out in Chapter 3 of Dublin 3: taking aside special cases of minors, those where family members are present, and questions of visa requirements and issue, most asylum seekers will face return to the country where they first entered the European Union. Cases are to be assessed "on the basis of the situation obtaining when the applicant first lodged his or her application for international protection with a Member State" (Article 7(2)).

1. Minors have their claim determined where they have a family member (spouse, unmarried partner, father, mother or guardian: Article 2(g)) or sibling and if the minor is married with no legally resident spouse in the European Union, in the State where their father, mother or other adult is responsible for them or their spouse: Article 8(1)) (all this is subject to a "best interests" consideration (Article 8(1) and (2));

2. Accompanied minors have their situation treated as "indissociable" from their family member provided this in their best interests (Article 20(3));

3. Unaccompanied minors should have their claim considered where they have a legally present "relative" (uncle, aunt, or grandparent, regardless of wedlock: Article 2(h) who can care for them (Article 8(2)) – and if there are relatives in different States then their "best interests" should be used to resolve the forum (8(3));

4. Unaccompanied minors without relatives have their claim determined in the State "where the unaccompanied minor has lodged his or her application" – ie in the place they claim asylum (ie there is no power to return a minor to a country where they merely transited without claiming asylum) and this must

be read consistently with the interpretation of the CJEU in <u>MA & Ors</u> v Secretary of State for the Home Department [2013] EUECJ C-648/11 of the similar provision in Dublin 2 that this meant the State where an asylum application was most recently lodged, ie usually their present location;

5. In the Member State where there is a family member (as defined in Article 2(i) as spouse, unmarried partner, minor unmarried dependent children) with international protection status, regardless of whether the family was previously formed in the country of origin (Article 9));

6. In the Member State where there is a family member with a pending claim for asylum that has so far not been the subject of a first decision (Article 10);

7. There is a specific "Family procedure" which operates where minor unmarried siblings or family members "submit applications for international protection in the same Member State simultaneously, or on dates close enough for the procedures for determining the Member State responsible to be conducted together" who would normally face separation under the hierarchy's operation, in that the responsible Member State is that responsible under the Regulation for the greatest number of them or the elder (Article 11):

8. In the Member State which has issued a residence document or visa (even if it was "issued on the basis of a false or assumed identity or on submission of forged, counterfeit or invalid documents" unless the (Article 12(5));

9. In the Member State into which "an asylum seeker has irregularly crossed the border … by land, sea or air having come from a third country" as established on the basis of "proof or circumstantial evidence" including Eurodac hits (Article 13);

10. In a Member State which the asylum seeker has entered where visa requirements are waived unless they subsequently enter a further country where visa requirements are also waived, in which case the latter has responsibility (Article 14);

11. In a Member State where an asylum claim has been lodged in the transit area of an airport (Article 15);

12. Where no other Member State is responsible, the first country where an asylum claim has been lodged (Article 3(2));

13. If at any time a Member State issues a residence document to an asylum seeker, responsibility switches to them (Article 19(1)).

There is a time scale for the various administrative actions to take place (see Articles 20 to 22). The request to take charge must be made within 2 months where there has been a Eurodac hit, and 3 months in other cases. The reply must be made by the requested Member State within two months of receipt of the request. Where there is no reply, it will be treated as that state having accepted the request. Timescales will be reduced in detention cases.

Safe third country certificates

The concept of designating some countries as automatically 'safe' and thereby depriving their citizens of a right of appeal has been around since the 1990s. The current incarnation of the list of safe third countries is set out in the Asylum and Immigration (Treatment of Claimants') Act 2004 ("the 2004 Act").

The 2004 Act creates four lists of safe countries:

(1) EEA countries

(2) Non EEA countries safe for the purposes of the Refugee Convention and human rights

(3) Non EEA countries safe for the purposes of the Refugee Convention only

(4) Any country considered safe for the purposes of the Refugee Convention on the facts of the particular case

The countries on the first three lists can be amended by order. No countries have yet been designated under lists (3) and (4) above.

Returns to EEA countries

Part 2 of Schedule 3 of the 2004 Act specifies that EEA countries 'shall be treated' as places:

(a) where a person's life and liberty are not threatened by reason of his race, religion, nationality, membership of a particular social group or political opinion,

(b) from which a person will not be sent to another State in contravention of his Convention rights, and

(c) from which a person will not be sent to another State otherwise than in accordance with the Refugee Convention.

In theory there can be no tenable claim that an EU country will either ill-treat an individual themselves, or that they will send a person onwards to face Article 3 mistreatment or persecution elsewhere. The provisions themselves state that they apply 'for the purposes of the determination by any person, tribunal or court' and therefore appear to bind the tribunal and courts as much as to the officials of the Secretary of State.

Inevitably, the courts did not take this ouster lightly and challenges to removal to supposedly safe third countries have been entertained and have ultimately succeeded, but only in respect of Greece (see further below).

Substance of safe third country challenges

In the case of *TI v United Kingdom* [2000] INLR 211 the European Court of Human Rights held that Dublin II (the predecessor to Dublin III) did not absolve the United Kingdom from responsibility to ensure that a decision to expel an asylum seeker to another Member State did not expose that asylum seeker, once removed, to treatment contrary to article 3 of the Convention.

Building on this Strasbourg case there were a number of domestic UK cases in which claimants sought to establish that removal to a number of countries, including Greece and Italy, would breach their human rights and/or lead to refoulement back to their home country without examination of their asylum claim. These domestic cases ultimately failed. However, on 21 January 2011 the European Court of Human Rights sent shockwaves through the Dublin II system when it held in the case of M.S.S. v Greece and Belgium (Application no. 30696/09) [2011] ECHR 108 that conditions for asylum seekers in Greece were so appalling that return there from Belgium under Dublin II arrangements did amount to a breach of Article 3 ECHR. Damages of 24,900 Euros were awarded against Belgium, the State that had conducted the removal, and 1000 Euros against Greece, where the inhuman and degrading treatment had actually occurred.

Removals to Greece from the UK were subsequently suspended and remain so.

In NS (European Union law) [2011] EUECJ C-411/10, the Court of Justice of the European Union followed the decision of the ECtHR in MSS by finding that returns to Greece under Dublin II would breach the Charter of Fundamental Rights of the European Union.

Current challenges continue in respect of a number of EU countries including Italy, Cyprus, Hungary and Malta.

In respect of minors though, in MA & Ors v SSHD [2013] EUECJ C-648/11 the CJEU found that where an unaccompanied minor with no member of his family legally present in the territory of a Member State has lodged asylum applications in more than one Member State, the Member State in which that minor is present after having lodged an asylum application there is to be designated the 'Member State responsible'. Taking as its starting point Article 6 of the Regulation, and that a primary consideration in any decision involving a child should be the best interests of the child, a minor cannot now be returned to another country under the Dublin procedure.

Those keen to find out more about challenges to Dublin 3 are recommended to take the online CPD training course designed by Mark Symes, the barrister that has led many of the challenges to Dublin, available on the Free Movement website.

'Clearly unfounded' certificates

An appellant cannot normally be removed from the UK whilst an asylum application or appeal is pending (2002 Act, s.78 and 79). However, the SSHD has the power to certify asylum or human rights claims as clearly unfounded. If the SSHD issues such a certificate the applicant cannot appeal under s.82 of the 2002 Act whilst he is in the UK.

Section 94 of the 2002 Act creates a presumption that all claims where the applicant is entitled to reside in listed countries (the 'white list') are "clearly unfounded" for reason that there was in general no serious risk of persecution there. The Home Office must certify such claims as clearly unfounded unless satisfied that they are not so. The list in the statute is frequently changed but at the time of writing includes;

Albania	Mauritius	Gambia (men)
Bolivia	Moldova	Kenya (men)
Bosnia Herzegovina	Mongolia	Kosovo
Brazil	Montenegro	Liberia (men)
Ecuador	Peru	Malawi (men)
India	Serbia	Mali (men)
Jamaica (see JB	South Africa	Nigeria (men)
below)	Ukraine	Sierra Leone (men)
Macedonia	Ghana (men)	South Korea

Bangladesh was added to the list but has been removed, as was Sri Lanka. In R v SSHD, ex parte Husan [2005] EWHC 189 (Admin), Wilson J concluded that the inclusion of Bangladesh on the list was unlawful:

> ...whether in July 2003, when it was added to the list, or at any time since then, no rational decision-maker could have been satisfied that there was in general in Bangladesh no serious risk of persecution of persons entitled to reside there or that removal of such persons thither would not in general contravene the UK's obligations under the Human Rights Convention. The objective material drove and drives only one rational conclusion; and it is to the contrary.

In JB (Jamaica), R (on the application of) v SSHD [2013] EWCA Civ 666, the Court of Appeal found that the designation of Jamaica as a country in which there is in general no risk of persecution was unlawful.

There are two kinds of "clearly unfounded" case. As well as the white list countries, there are those where the claim is viewed by the SSHD as so hopeless as to merit certification even without the general presumption, i.e. cases that are weak on their own facts, so it is not the designation of the country which is determinative. For example, Mr Husan, the claimant whose judicial review succeeded in establishing that Bangladesh should not have appeared on the list, still lost his case on its being clearly unfounded in its own terms.

Decision makers should be slow to find a claim to be clearly unfounded, especially on grounds of credibility – in fact some judges have recommended that the case be taken at its highest for the purposes of considering whether it is unfounded. As the test was put in R v SSHD ex parte Thangarasa; Yogathas [2002] UKHL 36:

> The question to which the Secretary of State had to address his mind....is whether the allegation is so clearly without substance that the appeal would be bound to fail.

On judicial review, the judge will look to see whether the SSHD correctly applied the tests set out above. In ZT (Kosovo) v SSHD [2009] UKHL 6 the House of Lords held that an Administrative Court Judge reviewing a clearly unfounded certificate must (i) ask the questions which an immigration judge would ask about the claim and (ii) ask itself whether on any legitimate view of the law and the facts any of those questions might be answered in the claimant's favour.

Prohibition on further appeals or raising grounds late

As well as clearly unfounded certificates, a certificate can be issued on s96 grounds. If a matter (whether legal or factual) is not raised in the "One Stop" Notice, or otherwise pre-decision or on appeal, and then an attempt is made to raise it later after the appeal against a refusal of the original application has been dealt with, then the decision maker may issue a certificate that prevents any further appeal. This power arises under NIA 2002 section 96.

This provision is seldom used as it only arises where the migrant has the possibility of sequential appeals (i.e. for example, an appeal against a refusal of an extension application followed some time later by an appeal against removal). These decisions are usually now made together and a single appeal will therefore deal with both decisions simultaneously.

Certification is likely to follow

➤ where the claim or application to which the new decision relates relies on a matter that could have been raised in an appeal against the old decision, and

➤ where, in the opinion of the Secretary of State or the immigration officer, there is no satisfactory reason for that matter not having been raised in an appeal against the old decision.

Example

Ahmed is facing deportation. He was given a notice of decision to deport him under the non-automatic deportation provisions. He fails to mention that he has two children and an arguable family life in the UK. He does not lodge an appeal against the decision.

> Ahmed is in a difficult situation. If he puts forward his family life arguments now in an application to revoke the deportation order, he risks certification. He would need to show instead that he meets the test for a fresh claim. It might also be worth investigating whether to make a late appeal to the Tribunal, if Ahmed had difficulty obtaining legal representation in detention, was not given appeal forms at the time of the immigration decision or something similar that led him to not appeal the earlier decision.

The only remedy against these a decision to certify under s96 will be judicial review, i.e. an application to the Administrative Court showing that the certificate is wrongly made on grounds such as an error of law within it, or because of a failure to take account of all relevant evidence.

The provisions are designed to catch all circumstances, whether or not an appeal was brought, or if one was brought, whether or not it has been determined. Once an appeal has been instituted, however, there can be no certification (section 96(7) as amended by the 2004 Act, which suggests that if there is no certification in the fresh refusal letter, an appeal cannot be cut off by a subsequent certificate).

These provisions apply whether or not the appellant has been outside the UK since the requirement to state additional grounds arose or since the right of appeal arose (2002 Act, s96(5)).

Fresh claims

It may sometimes be possible to make a further asylum or human rights claim if a previous claim has failed. A 'fresh claim' is essentially a new claim for protection or on human rights grounds that differs substantially from the previous claim.

A fresh claim is made by way of 'further submissions', i.e. written representations accompanied by any documentary evidence available to support the representations. A form is available from the GOV.UK website, but is not mandatory. Rule 353A prevents a person being removed from the U.K. whilst the fresh claim is being considered.

When the further submissions are considered by the Home Office, a decision maker must first decide whether or not to grant leave on the basis of the representations and new evidence. It is only on deciding not to do so that the decision maker must then go on to consider the fresh claim test in r.353.

Legal test

The Immigration Rules set out the circumstances in which 'further submissions' will be accepted as constituting a fresh claim for asylum or human rights protection.

p913

353. When a human rights or asylum claim has been refused and any appeal relating to that claim is no longer pending, the decision maker will consider any further submissions and, if rejected, will then determine whether they amount to a fresh claim. The submissions will amount to a fresh claim if they are significantly different from the material that has previously been considered. The submissions will only be significantly different if the content:

(i) had not already been considered; and

(ii) taken together with the previously considered material, created a realistic prospect of success, notwithstanding its rejection.

This paragraph does not apply to claims made overseas.

The key elements are that:

➢ The material upon which the fresh claim is based has not already been considered by the Home Office

➢ It is significantly different from any previous material that has been considered

➢ It should then be considered together with and in the light of the previous claims and decisions that have been made in the case

➢ and, everything considered together, must now create a realistic prospect of success on appeal

To support the contention that the legal test has been met, it will usually be necessary to show that;

1. there is new evidence relating to a claim, such as evidence of a new threat to safety, or

2. there is new evidence that suggests that the previous decision or appeal was incorrectly decided, or

3. there are new grounds, such as the person now having established family life in the UK, or

4. the law has changed requiring, for instance, a different approach to be taken to the claim (e.g. HJ (Iran))

Further submissions that meet these requirements will be treated as a fresh claim and, if so, the Home Office will make a fresh immigration decision. The immigration decision will trigger a right of appeal to the immigration tribunal in accordance with s.82 of the 2002 Act.

The decision under r.353 is not therefore a substantive decision on whether leave is to be granted or not, as the Home Office will have refused to grant status before considering the fresh claim test, but a decision as to whether the further submissions entitle the migrant to a further appeal or not. That will depend on the extent to which the decision maker concludes that any appeal would have a reasonable prospect of succeeding.

Many 'further submissions' are rejected as fresh claims by the Home Office. The only remedy in these circumstances is judicial review. Judicial reviews on fresh claim decisions are heard by the Upper Tribunal (IAC).
The main stages of the process are as below;

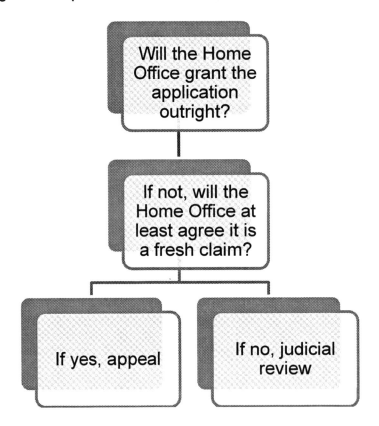

Exceptional circumstances

Further submissions will often be made at the last minute i.e. when the Home Office has set removal directions or has detained a person with a view to doing so. Until that point the asylum seeker may be getting on with their lives and not considering the necessity or possibility of getting further legal advice.

When considering whether the further submissions amount to a fresh claim, or in cases where there are no outstanding further submissions and appeal rights are exhausted, the Home Office will consider whether there are any exceptional circumstances which mean that removal is no longer appropriate. This is the procedure set out in r.353B, in the Home Office guidance on further submissions (in the APG: Post-decision representations), and in the Enforcement Instructions and Guidance at chapter 53. It will be a similar process to that which used to be carried out under the deleted r.395C.

The onus is on the failed asylum seeker to put forward any exceptional circumstances that they want to be considered at this final stage before removal.

Following the changes made on 9 July 2012, when Article 8 considerations were brought into the rules, it is unlikely that the Home Office will grant leave on Article 8 grounds outside the rules other than on the bases laid out in the policy in the EIG at chapter 53. Where the further submissions are made on asylum grounds, the Home Office position will often be that the new material does not amount to a fresh claim, either because it fails to dislodge an earlier finding that the asylum seeker lacked credibility, or is not sufficiently different to previous material relied on. It will be important therefore to ensure the further submissions are as well prepared and well evidenced as possible as, if a judicial review application is made, they will end up in front of a senior Upper Tribunal judge who will be reviewing the Home Office's decision to reject them as a fresh claim.

Fresh claims and clearly unfounded certificates

In ZT (Kosovo) v SSHD [2009] UKHL 6, the House of Lords considered the interaction of the tests for a fresh human rights claim and a clearly unfounded certificate imposed under s.94 of the 2002 Act.

The two tests are similar sounding to the layman:

Section 94

- Does the claim exceed the relatively modest 'clearly unfounded' threshold?

Rule 353

- Does the claim have a realistic prospect of success?

The Lords held that the rule 353 procedure does apply where a person's asylum or human rights claim is certified under s.94 certificate, but they have not yet left the UK to exercise their out of country right of appeal, and then they make new representations to the Home Office.

They also held that there is a potential difference between the outcomes of considering a case under s.94 and rule 353. In R (on the application of YH) v Secretary of State for the Home Department [2010] EWCA Civ 116 though, the Court of Appeal held that for all intents and purposes the tests are indistinguishable. Nevertheless, an asylum seeker who is certified under s.94 can put forward a fresh claim which must be considered by the Home Office under the rule 353 criteria.

Example

Mirza claims asylum and his claim is certified as 'clearly unfounded' under section 94 of the 2002 Act. However, he is not immediately removed from the UK. In the meantime, he manages to acquire documentary evidence that assists his case.

The new evidence is put forward as a fresh human rights claim.

The fresh claim must be assessed by the Home Office under rule 353 and the 'realistic prospect of success' test applied. Assuming the Home Office decide that the test was not passed, no immigration decision (under s.82(2)) will be made and there is no right of appeal to the tribunal. The only remedy would be an application for judicial review.

Case law on fresh claims

The original case on the circumstances where a fresh claim must be accepted is ex p. Onibiyo [1996] Imm AR 370 in the Court of Appeal. Sir Thomas Bingham held as follows in relation to the question 'what constitutes a fresh claim?';

> The acid test must always be whether, comparing the new claim with that earlier rejected, and excluding material on which the claimant could reasonably have been expected to rely in the earlier claim, the new claim is sufficiently different from the earlier claim to admit of a realistic prospect that a favourable view could be taken of the new claim despite the unfavourable conclusion reached on the earlier claim.

In the case of WM (DRC) v SSHD [2006] EWCA Civ 1495 the Court of Appeal gave guidance on the task of the Secretary of State under the modern rule and held that the Secretary of State should consider whether an immigration judge on a future appeal would consider that the test was satisfied, bearing in mind that the test was a 'somewhat modest' one. The reliability of any new material is an important consideration, as are any findings by a previous judge as to the claimant's honesty and reliability as a witness. The Court went on to suggest that the role of the court in judicially reviewing such a decision is confined to the principles of judicial review, i.e. a Wednesbury unreasonable test applies, although the principle of anxious scrutiny means that the decision will be unreasonable if not reached with most anxious scrutiny.

Since then in R (on the application of TR (Sri Lanka)) v Secretary of State for the Home Department [2008] EWCA Civ 1549 and R (on the application of YH) v Secretary of State for the Home Department [2010] EWCA Civ 116 the Court of Appeal has held that on an application for judicial review it was for the court to decide for itself whether the relevant threshold is met rather than to apply Wednesbury principles in conducting the review.

Although the test is in law a 'relatively modest' one and little or no deference is due to the Home Office view, it can nevertheless be an uphill struggle to engage the interest of a High Court (or now, Upper Tribunal) judge in a fresh claim application for judicial review. This is particularly the case where the claimant was previously found to be dishonest. The challenge is therefore obtaining good quality evidence on which to base the claim.

Example

Dinu is from Sri Lanka and made an unsuccessful claim for asylum in 2009 on the basis of his involvement with the LTTE. His claim was rejected at that time both on the basis that it was fabricated and on the basis that even if it was not, there was no risk on return because of the peace process.

Even at the height of the conflict between the Sri Lankan government and the LTTE it would have been very hard for Dinu to make out a successful fresh claim on the basis of his own evidence or deterioration in the country situation because of the earlier adverse credibility findings. He would have needed independent evidence to suggest that the credibility findings were in fact wrong, such as compelling documentary evidence, or evidence that notwithstanding his poor credibility, his profile is such that he would now be at risk (perhaps because of the regime's current attitude to failed asylum seekers).

Evidence

Previously available evidence

There is no legal bar to reserving or failing or omitting to put forward evidence or submissions as part of a previous application and appeal and then seeking to institute a later fresh claim on the basis of such evidence or submissions (although as discussed earlier this may lead to certification under s.96 of the 2002 Act, meaning no right of appeal).

This, after all, is what happens where a person is very poorly represented by a previous adviser, who makes simple but highly prejudicial mistakes, and the case is then put forward afresh by a more competent adviser. In FP (Iran) v SSHD [2007] EWCA Civ 13 the Court of Appeal held that "there is no general principle of law which fixes a party with the procedural errors of his or her representative", particularly in asylum cases.

However, there being no legal bar does not mean that relying on old and available evidence is straightforward. Part of the context to any discussion of this subject has to be the old case of Ladd v. Marshall [1954] 1 WLR 1489. There the principles governing admission of new evidence into appeal proceedings were said to be previous unavailability, significance and apparent credibility, or, more fully:

(1) the fresh evidence could not have been obtained with reasonable diligence for use at the trial

(2) if given, it probably would have had an important influence on the result

(3) it is apparently credible although not necessarily incontrovertible.

The Ladd v Marshall test does not strictly apply in a fresh claim situation, but it is very likely to be in the mind of any judge and common sense dictates that due heed is given. Very good reasons will need to be given as to why the material was not previously submitted.

The way in which the Home Office and perhaps the court will reject newly submitted evidence that was previously available is by suggesting that it is not credible that such evidence would not have been forward sooner if it was available. Essentially, it is to allege that the evidence is forged or at least that even the claimant sets little store by it.

Example

Takunda made a claim for asylum in 2008 and it was dismissed. He was found to have fabricated his account. At that time, he had no documentary evidence to support his claim.

He later makes a fresh claim, having in the meantime acquired some documentary evidence that supports important parts of his case, including his claimed identity. He did not seek to acquire this earlier because his representative did not suggest it and he had not realised it could be important.

If this evidence is from an independent source and cannot be easily dismissed as itself being fabricated then he may well have a good case for why the evidence should be considered and a good fresh claim.

Good reasons for departing from the general principles could, as discussed above, include negligence or omission by a previous representative. In R (Gungar) v Secretary of State [2004] EWHC 2117 (Admin) 7 September 2004 Collins J stated in respect of Rule 346 (which still applied at that time and is differently worded to rule 353 in respect of old evidence):

> The effect of all that, as I see it, is that, as the court said in E, Ladd v Marshall is the starting point and availability is a factor to be taken into account and certainly will be

given considerable weight because it is important that there should be finality. It seems to me that in cases of availability the court should look with care to see whether in reality the evidence could have affected the result and if ignored would mean that there was a risk that human rights would be breached. I also bear in mind that it is said forcibly in this case, and I have no reason to doubt it since complaints have been made to the OSS about the conduct of the previous solicitors, that they did not prepare and so present the claimant's case as competently as they ought to have done and in particular they did not obtain, as they should, some material which would have assisted his claim. (para 19)

As should be clear from this quote, care needs to be taken in making such allegations against a representative. Unless a complaint is made to the relevant regulator (the Solicitor Regulation Authority or the OISC, depending on the firm or organisation) then the courts are not likely to be interested in intervening. Without such a formal complaint the allegation will look like hot air. See BT (Former Solicitors' alleged misconduct) Nepal [2004] UKIAT 00311 for further guidance on how to address this issue. The Home Office may prove to be more flexible, however, as proved to be the case with one of the above scenario examples.

Another good reason might be that the issue was never raised or the claimant thought that sufficient evidence had already been submitted. For example, if a First-tier Tribunal judge finds against a claimant on credibility and truthfulness grounds – particularly where the RFRL did not raise the issue in question – that claimant might well be able to obtain more evidence substantiating that, for example, he was a lawyer, teacher or political activist.

Sur place style arguments

Many fresh claims rely on new evidence that has been obtained regarding risk on return. Examples might include:

➢ New documents that post-date the previous case that have been obtained from the home country, such as an arrest warrant, a witness statement or a newspaper article

➢ New witness evidence from within the UK, such as from representatives of the claimant's political party or family members who have recently arrived

➢ New expert evidence of some kind

The problem with any new evidence is that if the claimant has already been found to be untruthful and capable of deceit, any new evidence put forward will probably need to come from an independent source to stand much chance of being accepted by the Home Office or a judge.

It is also worth taking note of Mr Justice Collins' comments in the case of R (on the app. of Rahimi) v SSHD [2005] EWHC 2838 (Admin). Collins J outlined the test to be applied by the Secretary of State in deciding whether any new material is credible and therefore sufficient to found a fresh asylum claim and found that it is a low test of whether the evidence is capable of belief.

In practical terms, it is important to be careful about how any new evidence is presented. For example, an original document with good, certified translation and an authentication report by an expert is more likely to work than a badly faxed and poorly translated document.

As well as new evidence, there may well be new developments in the country of proposed removal that mean the case must be looked at afresh. These may be flagged up by new news from the country or by a new CG case pointing to changes in the relevant risk factors.

One contemporary example is to be found with Sri Lanka. During the peace process many claims for asylum failed, but when that broke down and then ended, many Sri Lankans successfully put forward fresh claims. The situation changed again with the military defeat of the LTTE, potentially undermining those fresh claims. Subsequently new information came to light that notwithstanding the end of the civil war, the regime were continuing to torture those who they saw as separatists.

These Sri Lankan claims often illustrate the potential problem with putting forward a new claim based on a change of circumstances (or on new evidence for that matter). If the claimant was previously found to be dishonest and, for example, was found not really to have been a member of the LTTE or not really to have been harassed and detained by the authorities, then a fresh claim is unlikely to get far. The Home Office and then a High Court judge will find that there is still no risk as there is no reason for the authorities to be interested in the claimant.

However, where there have been positive findings of fact, for example in a case where it was found that the claimant was detained and that there might be a record of that detention, but that there was no risk because of the peace process, then the claimant might have a sound fresh claim.

Example

In the earlier example of Dinu from Sri Lanka, his first asylum claim had been dismissed on both credibility and future risk grounds.

If it has been accepted that he had been telling the truth about several detentions he had suffered then his claim might still have been rejected at the time that the peace process was going on.

Assuming he was not removed in the meantime, the breakdown of the peace process might well have been sufficient change of circumstances that a fresh claim could have succeeded.

Article 8 private and family life

Many fresh claims rely on Article 8, where the 'failed' asylum seeker has established family and/or private life. Many asylum seekers do not or cannot voluntarily depart the UK when their cases are concluded. They can remain in the UK for sometimes many years and then either step forward voluntarily to put forward a new case or come to the attention of the immigration authorities in some way.

Any fresh claim made on Article 8 grounds will now be decided under the private and family life provisions in the Immigration Rules (i.e. at rule 276ADE(1), and in Appendix FM, where EX1 applies – see rules 276A0 and GEN1.9). If it fails to meet the requirements of the relevant rule, the Home Office should then consider whether there are exceptional circumstances why leave should be granted outside the rules. For more on the relevant law, go to the sections on rule 276ADE(1), Appendix FM and Article 8.

With fresh claims based on family life relationships, whether or not the circumstances appear to meet the requirements of the Immigration Rules, it is crucial to put forward good evidence of the relevant family relationships. As well as the parties to the relationship, friends and family can give witness statements, and utility bills or correspondence placing the parties at the same address is very helpful as a form of objective proof.

Example

Victor entered the UK many years ago and claimed asylum. He failed to attend his hearing and his case was dismissed. The Home Office made no attempt to remove him.

He comes to the attention of the police and is detained for removal as an illegal entrant.

His solicitors assert in representations that Victor has a long term relationship with a British lady and is joint carer for a stepson and a child of the relationship. However, Victor is removed because the solicitors failed to include any evidence of family life.

Evidence to consider putting forward includes:

> ➢ Witness statement from claimant including history of relationship, meaning of relationship to him/her, why he/she likes the partner, activities together,

> ➢ Witness statement from partner as above and, if possible, including plans for the future should the claimant be removed

> ➢ Witness statement from family members of the partner

> ➢ Witness statements from mutual friends or others who have seen the parties together and can confirm and describe the relationship

> ➢ Correspondence placing the parties at the same address

> ➢ Photographs of the parties together

> ➢ Receipts, tickets, bank statements or other evidence of expenditure on activities together (ask the parties to empty their handbags, coat pockets, wallets and drawers to search for any such material)

> ➢ Telephone bills showing calls to each other (with proof of the owner of the respective telephone numbers)

> ➢ Correspondence between the parties such as letters, emails, texts, cards

> ➢ Any local press coverage of the case. Local newspapers can be sympathetic in these cases, particularly where the claimant has been detained.

Where there are children affected by a decision (whether the biological children or step children of the claimant), the House of Lords cases of Beoku-Betts and EM (Lebanon) require that the immigration authorities consider the rights of all those affected by an immigration decision but also give careful separate consideration to the rights of affected children. This approach is all the more important in light of the Home Office's s.55 duties and ZH (Tanzania). Evidencing the effect on children is not straightforward but the following may help:

> ➢ Witness statement from the UK-based parent (and others, potentially) describing the relationship between the claimant and affected children, including how the child regards the claimant, describing activities together and claimant's role in upbringing and day to day care

> ➢ Photographs of the claimant and child together

> ➢ Report of an Independent Social Worker

The latter can be expensive but can also be invaluable in providing qualitative evidence of the nature of the relationship.

Benefits of recognition as a refugee

Refugees and immigration status

When an asylum claim succeeds under the Refugee Convention, the applicant will be recognised as a refugee and five years leave to remain will be granted (rule 339Q(i)). Prior to 30 August 2005, ILR was granted. The grant of refugee status will be made by way of a Biometric Residence Permit. There will be no conditions on the grant of leave.

Settlement protection

Where the refugee reaches the end of the five year period, they can apply for settlement under the Settlement protection route (rule 339R). The UKVI will then consider whether there are any grounds to revoke or not renew the status under rules 339A, and if not, any reasons to refuse or delay ILR for reasons of criminal conduct (339R(iii)). If not, ILR will be granted without an active review of the applicant's circumstances or consideration of current risk.

If, during the five year period, a Minister has issued a ministerial declaration that a particular country is now considered to be generally safe, all refugees of that nationality will have their cases individually reviewed, with a right of appeal against any decision to revoke refugee status. The burden will rest with the Home Office to establish that the individual is no longer a refugee. Assurances have been given that there will be few declarations, and there has been none to date. Given existing Home Office workloads, it seems unlikely that any such declarations will be made in the near future.

Applications for settlement for refugees (and for those granted humanitarian protection) who have completed their 5 years of limited leave are made on form SET(P). There are no requirements (e.g. under Appendix KOLL) to meet or fees to pay.

The Settlement Protection modernised guidance is at: https://www.gov.uk/government/publications/settlement-protection-asylum-policy-instruction. The policy also provides guidance on applications for settlement for the dependants of refugees and those granted humanitarian protection.

Refugee family reunion

The origin of the Home Office policy on family reunion lies in the Final Act of the United Nations Conference on the Status of Refugees and Stateless Persons. As set out at Annex I of the UNHCR Handbook, the Conference, considering that the family was "the natural and fundamental group of society" and that unity of the family was "an essential right of the refugee" recommended that "Governments… take the necessary measures for the protection of a refugee's family, especially with a view to … ensuring that the unity of the refugee's family is maintained particularly in cases where the head of the family has fulfilled the necessary conditions for admission to a particular country".

Pre-existing family

The refugee family reunion rules in Part 11 promote the reunion of a recognised refugee (and those granted humanitarian protection) with family members that were left behind at the time that the refugee fled his or her country of origin (sometimes referred to as the pre-flight family). The principal benefit of these rules is that there are no English language, maintenance and accommodation requirements to meet. There is no exemption however in respect of the general grounds of refusal.

The rules cover the following pre-flight family members:

> ➢ Spouses or civil partners (paragraphs 352A)

> ➢ Unmarried or same sex partner (paragraph 352AA)

> ➢ Children (paragraph 352D)

There are various requirements applying to these rules, including that the applicant must not fall under the exclusion clauses and in the case of children that they are under 18, are not leading an independent life and were part of the family unit of the refugee at the time that the refugee fled. The sponsor must remain a refugee at the time of decision, so should not prematurely apply to naturalise.

In the case of MS (Somalia) v SSHD [2010] EWCA Civ 1236, the Court of Appeal held that a family member granted leave under the family reunion rules is not automatically recognised as a refugee. Where a person granted leave under the want themselves to sponsor a family reunion application for other family members, they will have to first apply for asylum and be recognised as a refugee by the UKVI.

Visas issued under these rules are often wrongly endorsed with a condition that the person has no recourse to public funds. The rules do not allow for such a prohibition. Errors can be corrected by writing to RCU EC Errors, 15th Floor, Apollo House, 36 Wellesley Road, Croydon CR9 3RR (see ECB19 in the ECGs).

The British Red Cross can assist where necessary with family tracing, and in making arrangements for the family to travel to the UK, including help with travel costs.

'Post flight' and other family members

New and existing family members not entitled to family reunion can be sponsored under provisions in Appendix FM. These will include new partners, and adult dependent relatives. Where a family member cannot meet the requirements of Appendix FM, it may be possible to make an application outside the rules relying on exceptional circumstances (see sections on Appendix FM and Article 8).

Travel documents

Recognised refugees are entitled to a Refugee Convention Travel Document (CTD), under Article 28 of the Convention.

These CTDs are blue in colour and resemble a passport in appearance. They can be used for travel to any country that is a signatory to the Convention other than the country from which the holder is a refugee.

Applications, which now include an application for a biometric residence permit, are made on form TD112. The cost is £72.50 (£46 for a child under 16). The document will be valid for the length of the refugee's leave, or for 10 years if the refugee is settled (5 years for a child).

Pre-existing family members of refugees are often issued a CTD on request but this does not constitute recognition as a refugee and does not entitle the bearer to bring in other further family members under refugee family reunion rules.

Refugees and work, benefits and education

Any person with refugee status, indefinite leave to remain (ILR), exceptional leave to remain (ELR), humanitarian protection, or discretionary leave has the right to work in the UK and does not need to ask permission from, nor inform the Home Office, before taking up employment or setting up a business.

A refugee or person granted humanitarian protection may apply for a loan to assist with their integration into the community; for a rent deposit, household items, or for education and training for work: see https://www.gov.uk/refugee-integration-loan/overview for more details.

Refugees will be treated as home students for the purpose of tuition fees and student support, as will their dependants who were pre-flight family members. Those granted discretionary leave will be treated as overseas students. They will have to pay higher fees and will not be entitled to student support.

Benefits of Humanitarian Protection

Immigration status

'Subsidiary protection' status (as it is called in the Qualification Directive) or Humanitarian Protection (HP) as it is called in the UK is in most practical respects equivalent to refugee status. A person who qualifies for HP will be granted leave for 5 years.

Holders of Humanitarian Protection who have completed 5 years of leave will be eligible to apply for ILR under the Settlement Protection route as for refugees (see above). The individual should apply for settlement shortly before the expiry of their Humanitarian Protection leave.

→ Exclusion

Persons who face a real risk of treatment which meets the criteria for Humanitarian Protection will not be granted leave if they fall under the exclusion criteria set out in EC Qualification Directive and Immigration Rules. These criteria include:

> ➤ Those whose presence in the UK is not conducive to the public good, for example because of their criminal behaviour and/or their threat to security of the United Kingdom.

> ➤ Those falling under the exclusion criteria for the Refugee Convention in Articles 1F and 33(2) (i.e. those of whom there are serious reasons for considering them to have committed war crimes etc, serious non-political crimes, crimes against purposes of United Nations; and those convicted of serious crimes in the UK or abroad, regardless of motive, one for which a custodial sentence of at least 12 months has been imposed in the United Kingdom).

> ➤ Those considered to be a threat to national security.

> ➤ Those whose character, conduct or associations counts against them. For example, where deportation action has been considered and has only not been pursued or has been abandoned because Article 2 or Article 3 considerations render removal impossible for the time being.

A "serious crime" for these purposes is or a crime considered serious enough to exclude the person from being a refugee in accordance with Article 1F(b) of the Convention. For the purposes of Humanitarian Protection, those who commit serious crimes are excluded whether or not they have a political motive. The ability of the state to exclude an asylum seeker for a "serious crime" for Humanitarian Protection is much more extensive than their ability to do so for Refugee Convention purposes.

There are provisions for the ending of Humanitarian Protection if an individual takes actions such as re-availing themselves of their country's protection that mirror the Cessation Clauses within the Refugee Convention. There is also provision for revocation where it comes to light that the exclusion criteria are satisfied, or where dishonesty is discovered to have founded the grant of HP.

Family reunion and travel documents

Those with subsidiary protection are entitled to family reunion on the same terms as refugees.

A person with Humanitarian Protection can obtain travel documents "where that person is unable to obtain a national passport or other identity documents which enable him to travel, unless compelling reasons of national security or public order otherwise require": rule 334A(ii). If such a person can theoretically obtain such documents but has not done so, then a travel document may be issued if "he can show that he has made reasonable attempts to obtain a national passport or identity document and there are serious humanitarian reasons for travel": rule 334A(iii).

The document issued will be a Certificate of Travel, which does not carry the weight of a Convention Travel Document. A number of countries, currently including Austria, Belgium, Denmark, France, Germany, Greece, Iceland, Italy, Luxembourg, the Netherlands, Portugal, South Africa, Spain, Switzerland, do not accept Certificates of Travel.

Chapter 10: Human rights law

Human Rights Act 1998

The Human Rights Act 1998 came into force in the United Kingdom on 2 October 2000. It brought the European Convention of Human Rights and Fundamental Freedoms (ECHR) into domestic law and made the rights protected by the ECHR directly enforceable in the British courts.

The Act has had a very important impact on immigration and asylum law.

Mechanisms for protection of human rights

- Interpretation of statute and rules
- Binding on public authorities
- Damages and compensation for breaches
- Ground on which immigration appeals can be allowed

Interpretation of statute

Decisions and other material emanating from the European Court of Human Rights (ECtHR, often referred to by the shorthand 'Strasbourg' as this is where the court sits) must be taken into account by judges here (section 2(1) HRA). The English judiciary has indicated that they will not deviate from the Strasbourg approach. Lord Slynn of Hadley in R (Alconbury Developments Ltd) v Secretary of State for the Environment [2001] 2 WLR 1389 at paragraph 26:

> In the absence of some special circumstances it seems to me that the court should follow any clear and constant jurisprudence of the European Court of Human Rights.

Section 3(1) of the HRA is the key to the interpretation of English statute that must be taken in future by the judiciary:

> So far as it is possible to do so, primary legislation and subordinate legislation must be read and given effect in a way which is compatible with the Convention rights.

The Immigration Rules must, in line with section 3(1), be read to conform with human rights obligations. See Mr Justice Collins in Arman Ali [2000] INLR 89, finding that the (then) interpretation of the immigration rules did not seem to be so compatible (because it potentially forbade reliance on third party support):

> The interference may be justified under Article 8(2), but it must be proportionate to the legitimate aim concerned, which in this case is the maintenance of the economic well-being of the state: see Beldjoudi v France (1992) 14 EHRR 801. Thus it is, as it seems to me, justifiable to avoid any recourse to public funds. But the barrier must not be greater than necessary. Accordingly, the Rules would not in my view be in

> accordance with Article 8 if they were construed so as to exclude a spouse when his or her admission would not affect the economic well-being of the country because there would be no recourse to public funds or any other detriment caused by it.

This approach was endorsed by the Supreme Court in the case of Mahad [2009] UKSC 16.

Effect on public authorities

Section 6(1) of the HRA demonstrates that the ambit of the Act is in no way limited to the review of statutory material - rather, any acts of a public authority may be challenged if they conflict with the fundamental rights and freedoms recognised in the ECHR:

> It is unlawful for a public authority to act in a way which is incompatible with a Convention right.

This includes the Home Office and also the courts and tribunals, including the Immigration tribunal.

Under the HRA 1998 itself, section 7(1), a person who claims that a public authority has acted (or proposes to act) incompatibly with the European Convention on Human Rights brings proceedings against the authority under the HRA 1998 in the appropriate court or tribunal, or may rely on the Convention right or rights concerned in any legal proceedings (that is to say, the immigration tribunal will normally be the appropriate venue; otherwise the ECHR may be relied on in any judicial review proceedings). Such an individual has to demonstrate that they would be a victim of the act to have standing (section 7(3) HRA 1998). As will be explored below, this provides a free standing right of judicial review of an act that will breach human rights, but this represents a fall-back level of protection in many immigration and asylum situations. The first port of call will be an appeal to the immigration tribunal, where a right of appeal exists (see further below).

Damages and compensation

Under section 8(2) HRA 1998 damages may be awarded only by a court which has power to award damages, or to order the payment of compensation, in civil proceedings. The immigration tribunal lacks powers of this kind: however, the High Court and the Court of Appeal do possess them.

Section 9(3) HRA indicates that the opportunity to obtain damages for judicial errors regarding human rights will be limited, except, perhaps, in bail cases:

> In proceedings under this Act in respect of a judicial act done in good faith, damages may not be awarded otherwise than to compensate a person to the extent required by Article 5(5) of the Convention.

Under section 9(1) HRA 1998, proceedings under section 7(1)(a) in respect of a judicial act may be brought only by exercising a right of appeal, on an application for judicial review, or in such other forum as may be prescribed by rules. Whereas challenges to removal will be brought via the immigration tribunal (i.e. the "right of appeal" route), challenges to breaches of human rights in the UK (e.g. regarding conditions of detention in reception centres, NASS withdrawal leading to destitution sufficiently severe to raise Article 3 issues, etc) will go via the judicial review route. Occasionally there may be two avenues for challenge for the same kind of decision (as where some human rights affected by an immigration decision belong to individuals not subject to immigration control: see Kehinde below).

Section 9(5) defines a "judicial act" as including an act done by a "judge". A "judge" includes a member of a tribunal "or other officer entitled to exercise the jurisdiction of a 'court'" which includes a tribunal. So the members of the immigration tribunal are potentially caught by this provision. In general, complaints about human rights that relate to removal, or possibly the manner in which a decision has been taken, will be challenged via the statutory appeal in the immigration tribunal (see generally section 7 below). But complaints about other treatment by public authorities, relating to detention, welfare, and human rights interferences suffered by individuals outside the appeals process, will be brought by way of judicial review.

Human rights as a ground of appeal

The above passages relate to the Human Rights Act itself. Where a right of appeal to the immigration tribunal exists, though, the main mechanism for preventing breaches of human rights is to appeal the immigration decision relying on the ground that the decision will breach human rights. This ground of appeal is specified at section 84(c) and also (g).

European Convention on Human Rights

Articles of the ECHR

The ECHR has a very useful website with the full texts of the Convention and Protocols and the Rules of Court along with all of the judgments and admissibility decisions of the Court and the old Commission. It is found at http://www.echr.coe.int. It includes a search engine, known as HUDOC.

Section 1 of the Human Rights Act explains which Convention rights are incorporated. The rights and fundamental freedoms protected are, in summary:

Article 2	• Right to life
Article 3	• Prohibition of torture or inhuman or degrading treatment of punishment
Article 4	• Prohibition of slavery and forced labour
Article 5	• Right to liberty and security of the person
Article 6	• Right to a fair trial
Article 7	• Freedom from retrospective criminal offences and punishment - "no punishment without law"
Article 8	• Right to respect for private and family life
Article 9	• Freedom of thought, conscience and religion
Article 10	• Freedom of expression
Article 11	• Freedom of assembly and association
Article 12	• Right to marry and found a family
Article 14	• Prohibition of discrimination in the enjoyment of Convention Rights
1st Protocol	• Art 1: Protection of property; Art 2: Right to education; Art 3: Right to free elections
13th Protocol	• Art 1: Prohibition on death penalty

Article 1 of the European Convention on Human Rights requires the contracting states to secure to everyone 'within their jurisdiction' the Convention rights and freedoms. This was not actually incorporated into domestic law by the Human Rights Act 1998.

Top tip

Although it is important to know about all the rights enshrined in the ECHR, the most useful and frequently relied on by immigration lawyers are Articles 3 and 8.

The other rights are frequently relied on but very rarely successfully so.

Categories of rights

The rights and freedoms dealt with by the European Convention on Human Rights can be categorised in three ways:

Unqualified rights

- Those rights which apply absolutely without qualification and from which there can be no derogation by the state party even in time of war or public emergency threatening the life of the nation.
- e.g. the right to life, the right not to be condemned to the death penalty or executed except in time of war, the right not to be subjected to torture or to inhuman or degrading treatment or punishment, the right not to be held in slavery or servitude and the right not to be punished by retrospective laws.

Limited rights

- Those rights which display some limitation on their face (and which when read in context with the whole of the European Convention on Human Rights are subject to exceptions and which in time of war or public emergency threatening the life of the nation may be the subject of derogations).
- e.g. the right to liberty and security, the right to fair trial, the right to freedom of thought, conscience and religion, the right to education and the right to enjoy Convention rights and freedoms without discrimination.

Qualified rights

- Rights which are expressly qualified on their face and which must be balanced against, and may have to give way to, other competing public interests.
- e.g. the rights to respect for private and family life, home and correspondence, freedom to manifest one's religion and beliefs, freedom of expression and to hold opinions, freedom of peaceful assembly and association, and freedom of movement.

Standard of Proof

The standard of proof for assessing whether the likelihood of a human rights breach is sufficient for the ECHR to be engaged is whether there is a 'real risk' of the claimed problem actually happening, or 'substantial grounds for believing' a breach will occur. The test is essentially the same as the 'reasonable degree of likelihood' test in refugee cases.

However, in some cases, the claimant may assert that she will be subject to a generalised risk of a breach of her rights, for example by being exposed to poor environmental conditions in a country's prisons system or generalised problems in military service in a given country. In such cases the Tribunal is of the view that it is necessary to show gross, flagrant and systematic breaches of human rights before all members of the category can be accepted as being at risk. The leading case on this subject is generally acknowledged to be Hariri v SSHD [2003] EWCA Civ 807.

ECHR and immigration law

Applicability of ECHR in immigration cases

The protected Convention rights are universal and intended to apply to everyone within the United Kingdom's jurisdiction, not just to British nationals. Furthermore, the preamble of the ECHR describes the rights as having a universal quality - they apply to all persons regardless of nationality, race, sex or other "status".

There are two broad categories of case where the ECHR has an impact in the field of immigration and asylum law, identified by the House of Lords in Ullah and Do:

Domestic cases

- Acts or omissions by the UK authorities
- e.g. breach of private and family life established in the UK
- e.g. catastrophic deterioration of medical condition owing to absence of treatment after removal

Foreign cases

- Acts or omissions by a foreign state after removal
- e.g. detention in breach of Article 5
- e.g. total deprivation of contact with child

It was the House of Lords case of Ullah and Do that established definitely in UK law that all of the articles of the ECHR can potentially be relied on in foreign cases. The Strasbourg cases of Soering v UK (1989) 11 EHRR 439 and Chahal v UK (1996) 23 EHRR 413 had already established that Article 3 could operate to prevent removal where there was a real risk of a future breach of human rights. However, for articles other than article 3, it is necessary to show that there would be a 'flagrant breach' of the right or rights in question, or that the right or rights would be completely nullified. This is sometimes referred to as the Devaseelan test after the starred determination that first set out this test, later approved by the House of Lords in EM (Lebanon) v SSHD [2008] UKHL 64.

Article 2

Article 2 of the ECHR is as follows:

> 1. Everyone's right to life shall be protected by law. No one shall be deprived of his life intentionally save in the execution of a sentence of a court following his conviction of a crime for which this penalty is provided by law.

> 2. Deprivation of life shall not be regarded as inflicted in contravention of this article when it results from the use of force which is no more than absolutely necessary:
> (a) in defence of any person from unlawful violence;
> (b) in order to effect a lawful arrest or to prevent the escape of a person lawfully detained;
> (c) in action lawfully taken for the purpose of quelling a riot or insurrection.

So far, in immigration cases, the article tends to be argued in addition to Article 3, for the simple reason that death or execution would be rather likely to be considered in the modern world to cross the threshold for Article 3 ill treatment in any event. There has not yet been a removal case in the UK or at Strasbourg that has succeeded on Article 2 but not on Article 3. It is worth remembering that in Soering the claimant feared execution and the experience of 'death row', and his case succeeded on the latter ground only.

Protocol 13, Article 1 contains an absolute prohibition on the death penalty. Following UK ratification of the 13th Protocol reference to Article 13 has now been inserted into the HRA 1998, see SI 2004/1574, in force from 22 June 2004). Thus, where there are "substantial grounds for believing" that following a removal from this country a person will be condemned to death or executed, even if for murder, such removal would be to breach their human rights. The Article reads:

> The death penalty shall be abolished. No-one shall be condemned to such penalty or executed.

Article 3

The right is expressed in these terms, and is notably unqualified:

> No one shall be subjected to torture or to inhuman or degrading treatment or punishment.

There are therefore three forms of ill treatment, but each is afforded the same level of protection in immigration proceedings:

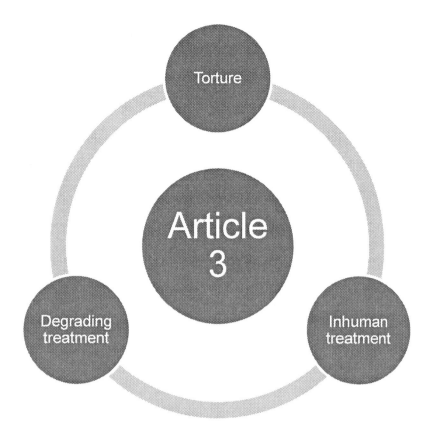

Outside an immigration context, these three forms of ill treatment can be seen as a spectrum, with torture at the most serious end, going through inhuman treatment and then degrading treatment. However, for ill treatment to amount to torture it would probably always have to be deliberately inflicted and intentional, whereas, as is discussed below, inhuman and degrading treatment can potentially be passive in nature.

Absolute nature of Article 3

Article 3 is absolute in nature, meaning that there are no circumstances in which it can be derogated from, nor can there be any justification for failure to observe it. This means that even very unpleasant individuals who have committed very serious crimes can benefit from its protection.

In Soering, the claimant was mentally ill and had horribly murdered two people in the United States. His extradition to stand trial there was being sought. Strasbourg held that he could not be extradited because of the real risk of exposure to the death row experience, which would breach Article 3.

In Chahal, the claimant was accused of being a terrorist extremist and a danger to the national security of the United Kingdom, but the ECtHR in Chahal v United Kingdom (1997) 23 EHRR 413 found that because right is absolute his removal to India was not permitted because 'the activities of the individual in question, however undesirable or dangerous, cannot be a material consideration' (para 80).

Whether Article 3 is breached or not in an individual case is a question of fact, based on measuring up all the relevant considerations – so it is always necessary to examine the impact of the feared future treatment on this individual. The courts say that (e.g. Ireland v United Kingdom (1978) 2 EHRR 25 at para 162):

> ...ill-treatment must attain a minimum level of severity if it is to fall within the scope of Article 3. The assessment of this minimum is, in the nature of things, relative; it depends on all the circumstances of the case, such as the nature and context of the treatment or punishment, the manner and method of its execution, its duration and its physical or mental effects.

The right operates so as to prevent removal of a person within a country's territory to another territory in which there would be a breach of Article 3 of the ECHR. It is, therefore, irrelevant from an immigration perspective whether the breach of which the claimant complains will be one that amounts to torture, inhuman treatment or degrading treatment. For the purposes of understanding Article 3 is it is nevertheless important to explore the nature of each type of ill treatment.

Torture

In Ireland v UK (1978) 2 EHRR 167 torture was defined as "deliberate inhuman treatment causing very serious and cruel suffering". This was a thought to be a very high threshold, and very few cases were found to reach this high level.

In Selmouni v France (1999), the ECtHR revised this approach and derived assistance from the UN Convention against Torture, and ultimately adopted a definition which could be summarised as the situation where "physical and mental violence, considered as a whole, committed against the applicant's person caused 'severe' pain and suffering and was particularly serious and cruel". Although still high, the threshold at which torture is set is now lower than before the Selmouni case.

In the case of Aydin v Turkey (1998) 25 EHRR 251 the ECtHR found that rape amounted to torture.

Inhuman treatment or punishment

Ireland v UK (1978) 2 EHRR 167 saw the European Court finding that a combination of forms of ill-treatment of detainees (deprivation of food, drink and sleep, hooding, subjection to noise and being stood up against a wall) amounted to inhuman and degrading treatment.

> 167. The five techniques were applied in combination, with premeditation and for hours at a stretch; they caused, if not actual bodily injury, at least intense physical and mental suffering to the persons subjected thereto and also led to acute psychiatric disturbances during interrogation. They accordingly fell into the category of inhuman treatment within the meaning of Article 3 (art. 3).

Pretty v United Kingdom (2002) 35 EHRR 1 at para 52 shows that natural illness, if made worse by certain conditions, may cross the threshold:

> As regards the types of 'treatment' which fall within the scope of Article 3 of the Convention, the Court's case law refers to 'ill-treatment' that attains a minimum level of severity and involves actual bodily injury or intense physical or mental suffering... Where treatment humiliates or debases an individual showing a lack or respect for, or diminishing, his or her human dignity or arouses feelings of fear, anguish or inferiority capable of breaking an individual's moral and physical resistance, it may be characterised as degrading and also fall within the prohibition of Article 3.... The suffering which flows from naturally occurring illness, physical or mental, may be covered by Article 3, where it is, or risks being, exacerbated by the treatment, whether flowing from conditions of detention, expulsion or other measures, for which the authorities can be held responsible...

The death row phenomenon can constitute inhuman punishment, see Soering v United Kingdom (1989) 11 EHRR 439.

Degrading treatment or punishment

In Ireland v UK the court said the following about the nature of degrading treatment:

> The techniques were also degrading since they were such as to arouse in their victims feelings of fear, anguish and inferiority capable of humiliating and debasing them and possibly breaking their physical or moral resistance.

The ECHR has held that prison conditions can amount to degrading treatment, and even inhuman treatment. See for example Kalashnikov v Russia (2002) 36 EHRR 587:

> ...The suffering and humiliation involved must in any event go beyond that inevitable element of suffering or humiliation connected with a given form of legitimate treatment or punishment.
>
> Measures depriving a person of his liberty may often involve such an element. Yet it cannot be said that detention on remand in itself raises an issue under Article 3 of the Convention...
>
> Nevertheless, under this provision the State must ensure that a person is detained in conditions which are compatible with respect for his human dignity, that the manner and method of the execution of the measure do not subject him to distress or hardship of an intensity exceeding the unavoidable level of suffering inherent in detention and that, given the practical demands of imprisonment, his health and well-being are adequately secured.
>
> When assessing conditions of detention, account has to be taken of the cumulative effects of those conditions, as well as the specific allegations made by the applicant.

Munby J, in the Court of Appeal in Batayav v Secretary of State for the Home Department [2003] EWCA Civ 1489, found that it was dangerous for the Tribunal to find that Article 3 was not engaged by Russian prisons when the European

Court had disagreed so recently. However, on the presumption that this complaint is raised on the basis of general prison conditions in a country rather than any particular feature of the applicant's account, when considering this kind of case it is necessary for the individual to show a generic risk (in the sense of showing that all individuals in prisons face a real risk of human rights abuses). The Tribunal accordingly says that it is necessary to demonstrate a consistent pattern of gross and systematic violations of the human rights of those detained before it will be satisfied of the extent of the risk. Nevertheless, cases have been successful on this basis. See, for example, PS (prison conditions; military service) Ukraine CG [2006] UKAIT 00016.

Top tip

While the law says that a person cannot be removed if he or she is going to be detained in conditions that would be contrary to Article 3 ECHR, it is not at all easy to prove that the conditions will in fact be so bad as to meet this threshold. A line from a US Department of State report will not be sufficient.

Expert evidence will be needed, and/or specific reports on detention conditions in that country by a relevant international NGO or monitoring organisation of some sort, such as Penal Reform. ECHR signatories are monitored by the Committee for the Prevention of Torture, an official organ of the Council of Europe. The reports of the CPT were instrumental in the Ukrainian case. Unfortunately, such detailed and influential reports do not generally exist outside Council of Europe countries, so other forms of evidence must be sought.

In Tyrer v United Kingdom (1978) EHRR 1 the ECtHR held that corporal punishment of a minor amounted to degrading treatment or punishment, but said that the punishment must exceed the usual element of humiliation involved in the criminal justice system, and that "a punishment does not lose its degrading character just because it is believed to be, or actually is, an effective deterrent or aid to crime control":

> 30. In the Court's view, in order for a punishment to be "degrading" and in breach of Article 3 (art. 3), the humiliation or debasement involved must attain a particular level and must in any event be other than that usual element of humiliation referred to in the preceding subparagraph. The assessment is, in the nature of things, relative: it depends on all the circumstances of the case and, in particular, on the nature and context of the punishment itself and the manner and method of its execution.
>
> ...As regards their belief that judicial corporal punishment deters criminals, it must be pointed out that a punishment does not lose its degrading character just because it is believed to be, or actually is, an effective deterrent or aid to crime control.

> Above all, as the Court must emphasise, it is never permissible to have recourse to punishments which are contrary to Article 3 (art. 3), whatever their deterrent effect may be.

In Ocalan v Turkey (2003) 37 EHRR 10 at para 220 the Court took the object of the punishment or treatment into account, so that if the object of the ill-treatment is humiliation or debasement, it will be easier to find that the threshold has been crossed into Article 3 territory:

> Furthermore, in considering whether a punishment or treatment is "degrading" within the meaning of Art. 3, the Court will have regard to whether its object is to humiliate and debase the person concerned and whether, as far as the consequences are concerned, it adversely affected his or her personality in a manner incompatible with Art. 3.

In East African Asians v UK (1981) 3 EHRR 76 the court concluded that discrimination based on race could, in certain circumstances, of itself amount to degrading treatment

> [207] ... that discrimination based on race could, in certain circumstances, of itself amount to degrading treatment within the meaning of Article 3 ... The Commission recalls in this connection that, as generally recognised, a special importance should be attached to discrimination based on race; that publicity [sic] to single out a group of persons for differential treatment on the basis of race might, in certain circumstances, constitute a special form of affront to human dignity; and that differential treatment of a group of persons on the basis of race might therefore be capable of constituting degrading treatment when differential treatment on some other ground would raise no such question.

The Tribunal in S&K [2002] UKIAT 05613 (3 December 2002) (starred) found that racial motivation could cause the threshold to be crossed, for example where ill-treatment is motivated by racial grounds.

> We do not doubt that discrimination on the ground of race is a factor that should be taken into account in deciding whether a breach of Article 3 has been established. It may in some circumstances tip the balance.

Specific types of Article 3 case

Absence of exclusion clauses

Article 3 is subject to no limitation, and unlike the Refugee Convention, there are no exclusion clauses to deprive an individual of the rights which it recognises, see Chahal v UK (1996) 23 EHRR 413. Nevertheless whilst the Secretary of State cannot remove some individuals, he can treat them differently vis-à-vis the form of leave to remain he gives them – so an individual who can establish a risk of a human rights breach on removal but who has committed serious criminal offences may well find that they receive Discretionary Leave to Remain rather than Humanitarian Protection. Even a person who can establish the inclusion requirements for refugee status may suffer the same fate if they are excluded under the Refugee Convention.

In the most serious cases Home Office policy is to grant six months Discretionary Leave at a time, which a review on each occasion until the individual has attained 10 years of residence.

Absence of Convention reasons

It will be obvious that, unlike the Refugee Convention, there is no requirement under the ECHR that the harm feared be linked to the individual's race, religion, nationality, membership of a particular social group or political opinion. In cases where the individual faces serious ill treatment or harm on return but behind which there is no Convention reason, the individual may not be entitled to refugee status but may not nevertheless be removed.

Sufficiency of protection test

In the case of Bagdanavicius [2005] UKHL 38 the House of Lords held that although there was some difference in wording between the Horvath formulation of the standard of protection required by the Refugee Convention and the Strasbourg formulation in HLR v France (1998) 26 EHRR 29, the tests were to all intents and purposes the same.

It is therefore not possible to argue that the 'sufficiency of protection' test does not apply in human rights cases or that it is a different test to that which applies under the Refugee Convention.

Destitution in the UK

A number of cases explored the circumstances in which the problems that ensue from blocking support might engage Article 3 of the ECHR, which are discussed in the chapter on benefits.

Unavailability of medical treatment abroad

It is argued in some cases that a difference in medical treatment between the UK and the country to which a person is to be removed will cause suffering or death and that removal would therefore breach the person's human rights and engage the UK's responsibilities.

Such arguments can be pursued in two ways, although these are not mutually exclusive. One is to argue the suffering will be so serious as to amount to a breach of Article 3, relying on a principle established in the case of D v UK (1997) 24 EHHR 423. The other is to argue that although the suffering would not be so serious as to engage Article 3, the suffering allied to other issues may engage Article 8, relying on the case of Bensaid v UK (2001) 33 EHRR 205.

In N v UK (Application no. 26565/05) [2008] ECHR 453 Strasbourg examined the case of a Ugandan woman known as N who had contracted HIV/AIDS and was receiving treatment in the UK. The case was an appeal from the House of Lords, who had earlier ([2005] UKHL 31) examined N's case and rejected it. The Strasbourg court rejected it too.

Before going on to consider the reasoning of the European Court of Human Rights, it is worth examining the House of Lords judgment to see how unwavering it is. For example, it was accepted that the claimant would die in unpleasant circumstances within approximately one year if removed, as Lord Hope made abundantly clear at paragraph 20 of the judgment:

> The decision which your Lordships have been asked to take in this case will have profound consequences for the appellant. The prospects of her surviving for more than a year or two if she is returned to Uganda are bleak. It is highly likely that the advanced medical care which has stabilised her condition by suppressing the HIV virus and would sustain her in good health were she to remain in this country for decades will no longer be available to her. If it is not, her condition is likely to reactivate and to deteriorate rapidly. There is no doubt that if that happens she will face an early death after a period of acute physical and mental suffering. It is easy to sympathise with her in this predicament.

At paragraph 50 Lord Hope outlines the circumstances that would have to be satisfied of a case were to be successful:

> For the circumstances to be, as it was put in Amegnigan v The Netherlands, "very exceptional" it would need to be shown that the applicant's medical condition had reached such a critical stage that there were compelling humanitarian grounds for not removing him to a place which lacked the medical and social services which he would need to prevent acute suffering while he is dying.

So dying in unpleasant circumstances within approximately one year if removed did not make for a very exceptional case, but allowing someone to stay here to die to prevent acute suffering whilst dying does. It is a thin line.

At Strasbourg the reasoning of the court is not easy to discern because of the discursive nature of the judgment. However, at paragraph 42 the test appears to boil down to whether 'the humanitarian grounds against the removal are compelling'. The words 'very exceptional case' are also used, or whether this is a predictor of the number of cases that will meet the test or is part of the test itself is a moot point.

Conceivably the Strasbourg decision in N is moderately better for claimants than was that of the House of Lords, which effectively limited success to deathbed cases. The European Court placed significant weight on the element of speculation that attended the predictions for the future of Ms N, whereas some immigrants might be able to put forward more concrete materials. Strasbourg also seems to have based its findings on the premise that the necessary treatment is widely available in Uganda (paragraph 48), although expensive such that N was unlikely to be able to afford it.

Strasbourg declined to examine the case under Article 8. However, in the case of KH (Afghanistan) v SSHD [2009] EWCA Civ 1354 the Court of Appeal held that the high threshold in N is also to be applied in cases of mental illness considered under Article 3. The Court went on to dismiss the Article 8 case as well, suggesting it would be very rare for a medical case of this nature to succeed under Article 8 if it failed under Article 3.

There has been discussion around the continued applicability of the approach taken by the Court of Appeal in the case of CA v SSHD [2004] EWCA Civ 1165. In CA the Court of Appeal found that return of a mother and child to a country where there would be inadequate medical treatment would breach Article 3 because of the effect on the mother of watching her child suffer and die: "It seems to me obvious simply as a matter of humanity that for a mother to witness the collapse of her new-born child's health and perhaps its death may be a kind of suffering far greater than might arise by the mother's confronting the self-same fate herself" (Laws LJ). It has been suggested that this reasoning, which has been applied in a number of other cases, cannot survive N in Strasbourg.

There is some Strasbourg authority behind the argument that a parent can be the victim of a breach of the human rights of the child. Although the case is a detention case, see Mubilanzila Mayeka and Kaniki Mitunga v. Belgium, no. 13178/03, ECHR 2006:

> The Court reiterates, secondly, that the issue whether a parent qualifies as a "victim" of the ill-treatment of his or her child will depend on the existence of special factors which gives the applicant's suffering a dimension and character distinct from the emotional distress which may be regarded as inevitably caused to relatives of a victim of a serious human rights violation. Relevant elements will include the proximity of the family tie – in that context, a certain weight will attach to the parent-child bond –, the particular circumstances of the relationship and the way in which the authorities responded to the parent's enquiries. The essence of such a violation lies in the authorities' reactions and attitudes to the situation when it is brought to their attention. It is especially in respect of this latter factor that a parent may claim directly to be a victim of the authorities' conduct (see, mutatis mutandis, Çakıcı v. Turkey [GC], no. 23657/94, ECHR 1999-IV, § 98; and Hamiyet Kaplan and Others v. Turkey, no. 36749/97, § 67, 13 September 2005).

It has also been successfully argued that a lower threshold of suffering should apply to children than adults as they are less able to bear it than adults. There is considerable authority behind the proposition that treatment or punishment that would not breach the rights of an adult may nevertheless breach the rights of a child.

In RS (Zimbabwe) v SSHD [2008] EWCA Civ 839, the Court of Appeal found that "humanitarian considerations" recognised by the ECtHR in N meant that a health case could succeed notwithstanding that it was not a deathbed case, and that problems caused by a deliberate withholding of medical care or food were not caught by the high threshold in N

In GS and EO (Article 3 - health cases) India [2012] UKUT 397 (IAC), the Tribunal held that the fact that life expectancy is dramatically shortened by withdrawal of medical treatment in the host state is in itself incapable of amounting to the highly exceptional case that engages the Article 3 duty but that there are recognised departures from the high threshold approach in cases concerning children, discriminatory denial of treatment, absence of resources through civil war or similar human agency. The Tribunal also held that Article 8 cases may also require a different approach and will do so where health questions arise in the context of obstacles to relocation.

Following the Court of Appeal case of JA (Ivory Coast) v SSHD [2009] EWCA Civ 1353 there is hope too for some in the UK who were previously granted leave on the basis of their medical condition. Although this relates to Article 8, it is convenient to deal with it here. The Court allowed the appeal (albeit only to the extent of remitting it to the tribunal) of a woman with HIV/AIDS on the basis that she was a lawful entrant, had previously been granted leave on the basis of her medical condition and had been lawfully resident in the UK for quite some time on that basis. When considering proportionality, a continuously lawful entrant was not required to demonstrate exceptional circumstances as compelling as those in D v United Kingdom.

The co-appellant was unsuccessful on the basis that the immigration judge had found that she could find work in her home country and support her treatment costs. Giving the leading judgment, Sedley LJ went on:

> JA's is a markedly different case. Her position as a continuously lawful entrant places her in a different legal class from N, so that she is not called upon to demonstrate exceptional circumstances as compelling as those in D v United Kingdom. There is no finding by the AIT that she has much if any hope of securing treatment if returned to Ivory Coast, or therefore as to the severity and consequences of removal (see Razgar [2004] UKHL 27). Depending on these, the potential discontinuance of years of life-saving NHS treatment, albeit made available out of compassion and not out of obligation, is in our judgment capable of tipping the balance of proportionality in her favour.

The Court found that it was possible for JA to succeed on the basis of Article 8. Whether on the facts of an individual case a particular appellant does so succeed will be at the discretion of the individual immigration judge.

One such recent case, where the decision of the First-tier judge to allow the appeal on Article 8 grounds was upheld by the Upper Tribunal, is Akhalu (health claim: ECHR Article 8) [2013] UKUT 00400 (IAC). Here, the Appellant had arrived in the UK legally in 2004 to study, but was then diagnosed in the UK as suffering from end stage kidney failure. It was accepted that she was not aware of the illness prior to arriving in the UK. After successfully completing her studies, she received a kidney transplant and thereafter required carefully monitored medication to ensure that the transplanted organ is not rejected. It was accepted that she could not afford such treatment in Nigeria and would therefore die soon after returning there. In upholding the allowed appeal, the Upper Tribunal concluded;

> 49. It cannot be said that this was an appeal allowed simply because of a disparity in the treatment available. That is to misrepresent what the judge has said. He plainly concluded that this was one of the "very rare cases" contemplated by the Tribunal in GS and EO (India) that could succeed under article 8 where the claim relies in part upon the need to continue with medical treatment being received here.

> 50. Correctly understood, in our judgement, the judge did not allow the appeal simply because the claimant could continue to receive medical treatment here that she would not have access to in Nigeria. His was a holistic assessment, drawing on the truly exceptional level of engagement with her local community that was disclosed by the evidence he alluded to and which he did not need to set out extensively in his determination and a comparison of her ability to enjoy any private life at all in Nigeria, as well as the foreseeable consequences for her health should she be removed to Nigeria.

Effect of the act of removal

Circumstances might be different where medical problems ensue other than from a want of resources, however, where the human rights interference is caused not by the difference in treatment between here and abroad and the medium term repercussions of that difference, but where the act of removal actually causes a deterioration in physical or mental health. See J v SSHD [2005] EWCA Civ 629 where it was the trauma of removal bringing with it an enhanced risk of suicide rather than any "want of resources" that led to the human rights interference.

Successful Article 2, 3 and 8 claims and leave to remain

A person succeeding on the basis that their Article 2 or 3 rights would be breached in the country of return would be entitled to humanitarian protection under r.339C. Those succeeding on the basis that the removal would breach their Article 3 or 8 rights on medical grounds, due to suicide risk or their inability to access suitable treatment at home, would be entitled to 30 months leave on a 10 year route to settlement. For more, see the Home Office guidance on Humanitarian Protection (APG/Considering and deciding the claim) and on Human rights claims on medical grounds (Modernised guidance/Other cross-cutting information).

Article 4

Article 4 (1) is the only absolute right amongst the parts of this Article, which could capture cases involving the future threat of trafficking, forced prostitution, or bonded labour:

> 1. No one shall be held in slavery or servitude.
>
> 2. No one shall be required to perform forced or compulsory labour.
>
> 3. For the purpose of this article the term "forced or compulsory labour" shall not include:
>   (a) any work required to be done in the ordinary course of detention imposed according to the provisions of Article 5 of this Convention or during conditional release from such detention;
>   (b) any service of a military character or, in case of conscientious objectors in countries where they are recognised, service exacted instead of compulsory military service;
>   (c) any service exacted in case of an emergency or calamity threatening the life or well-being of the community;

(d) any work or service which forms part of normal civic obligations.

In Rantsev v Cyprus and Russia (Application no. 25965/04), the European Court of Human Rights held that trafficking falls within the scope of Article 4 of the Convention and that there is a procedural obligation under Article 4 to investigate alleged trafficking. Following Rantsev, the Tribunal in EK (Article 4 ECHR: Anti-Trafficking Convention) Tanzania [2013] UKUT 00313 allowed an appeal against removal largely on the basis of a breach of the Appellant's Article 4 rights.

Article 5

Article 5 ECHR is as follows:

> 1. Everyone has the right to liberty and security of person. No one shall be deprived of his liberty save in the following cases and in accordance with a procedure prescribed by law:
> (a) the lawful detention of a person after conviction by a competent court;
> (b) the lawful arrest or detention of a person for non-compliance with the lawful order of a court or in order to secure the fulfilment of any obligation prescribed by law;
> (c) the lawful arrest or detention of a person effected for the purpose of bringing him before the competent legal authority on reasonable suspicion of having committed an offence or when it is reasonably considered necessary to prevent his committing an offence or fleeing after having done so;
> (d) the detention of a minor by lawful order for the purpose of educational supervision or his lawful detention for the purpose of bringing him before the competent legal authority;
> (e) the lawful detention of persons for the prevention of the spreading of infectious diseases, of persons of unsound mind, alcoholics or drug addicts or vagrants;
> (f) the lawful arrest or detention of a person to prevent his effecting an unauthorised entry into the country or of a person against whom action is being taken with a view to deportation or extradition.
>
> 2. Everyone who is arrested shall be informed promptly, in a language which he understands, of the reasons for his arrest and of any charge against him.
>
> 3. Everyone arrested or detained in accordance with the provisions of paragraph 1.c of this article shall be brought promptly before a judge or other officer authorised by law to exercise judicial power and shall be entitled to trial within a reasonable time or to release pending trial. Release may be conditioned by guarantees to appear for trial.
>
> 4. Everyone who is deprived of his liberty by arrest or detention shall be entitled to take proceedings by which the lawfulness of his detention shall be decided speedily by a court and his release ordered if the detention is not lawful.
>
> 5. Everyone who has been the victim of arrest or detention in contravention of the provisions of this article shall have an enforceable right to compensation.

Article 5 applies in the UK scheme of detention for the purposes of immigration control.

However, R v Secretary of State for the Home Department ex parte Saadi & Ors [2001] EWCA Civ 1512 (and the House of Lords then Strasbourg case that followed) shows that short-term detention of asylum seekers is permissible, even absent any risk of their absconding.

As mentioned above, damages are available under section 9(3) of the HRA, even for judicial acts carried out in good faith. There have been a number of successful claims for damages in immigration detention cases.

The requirement that liberty be lost only pursuant to "a procedure prescribed by law" has the consequence that the Secretary of State must reveal any policies which underlie detention decisions. For example, in Nadarajah v Secretary of State for the Home Department [2003] EWCA Civ 1768 the Court of Appeal found that, given that the ECtHR had held that the phrase "prescribed by law" in Article 10(2) required that the law must be adequately accessible, those subject to the law must have an indication which is adequate in the legal circumstances of the legal rules which are applicable to the given case. This means that any Home Office policies that underlie detention should be accessible.

As discussed above, a flagrant breach of Article 5 can inhibit removal. Given that only the authorities of a country can presumably deprive of an individual of their liberty pursuant to law, there must be a strong argument that loss of liberty at the hands of non-state actors constitutes a fundamental breach of the Article.

Article 6

Article 6 ECHR reads as follows:

> 1. In the determination of his civil rights and obligations or of any criminal charge against him, everyone is entitled to a fair and public hearing within a reasonable time by an independent and impartial tribunal established by law. Judgment shall be pronounced publicly but the press and public may be excluded from all or part of the trial in the interests of morals, public order or national security in a democratic society, where the interests of juveniles or the protection of the private life of the parties so require, or to the extent strictly necessary in the opinion of the court in special circumstances where publicity would prejudice the interests of justice.
>
> 2. Everyone charged with a criminal offence shall be presumed innocent until proved guilty according to law.
>
> 3. Everyone charged with a criminal offence has the following minimum rights:
>   (a) to be informed promptly, in a language which he understands and in detail, of the nature and cause of the accusation against him;
>   (b) to have adequate time and facilities for the preparation of his defence;
>   (c) to defend himself in person or through legal assistance of his own choosing or, if he has not sufficient means to pay for legal assistance, to be given it free when the interests of justice so require;
>   (d) to examine or have examined witnesses against him and to obtain the attendance and examination of witnesses on his behalf under the same conditions as witnesses against him;

> (e) to have the free assistance of an interpreter if he cannot understand or speak the language used in court.

The Tribunal in MNM (00/TH/02423; 1 November 2000) (starred) confirms that, consistently with the decision of the ECHR in Maaroui v France, Article 6 does not apply in immigration appeals in the UK because immigration rights are not "private" in nature and therefore do not amount to civil rights and obligations. However the Tribunal took the view that the common law would guarantee everything that Article 6 would provide, anyway, so this should not matter very much. Article 6 may also have some limited applicability in preventing removal if a lack of fair trial would be the gateway to article 3 breaches.

> 16...The fact is that the IAA provides an independent and impartial tribunal established by law. The hearing is in public and the procedures are designed to ensure that it is fair. If there is any unfairness, the tribunal or the Court of Appeal will correct it. Thus any complaints that the special adjudicator conducted an unfair hearing fall to be considered by us and we apply the same tests as would be applicable if Article 6 (1) applied. The only advantage which Article 6(1) might confer is the requirement that the hearing be held within a reasonable time. That does not arise in this case and should not, unless some disaster occurs, arise in any case having regard to the timetables and procedures laid down by the adjudicators and the tribunal.

Their Lordships confirmed in Ullah that "It can be regarded as settled law that where there is a real risk of a flagrant denial of justice in the country to which an individual is to be deported article 6 may be engaged."

The issue was revisited in practice in RB (Algeria) v SSHD [2009] UKHL 10. Lord Phillips in the House of Lords held that the Court of Appeal's statement of the test for a flagrant breach of Article 6 was the correct one – a real risk of a total denial of the right to a fair trial -- but went on:

> 136. This is neither an easy nor an adequate test of whether article 6 should bar the deportation of an alien. In the first place it is not easy to postulate what amounts to "a complete denial or nullification of the right to a fair trial" That phrase cannot require that every aspect of the trial process should be unfair. A trial that is fair in part may be no more acceptable than the curate's egg. What is required is that the deficiency or deficiencies in the trial process should be such as fundamentally to destroy the fairness of the prospective trial.
>
> 137. In the second place, the fact that the deportee may find himself subject in the receiving country to a legal process that is blatantly unfair cannot, of itself, justify placing an embargo on his deportation. The focus must be not simply on the unfairness of the trial process but on its potential consequences. An unfair trial is likely to lead to the violation of substantive human rights and the extent of that prospective violation must plainly be an important factor in deciding whether deportation is precluded.

Because there is now a right under European Community law to refugee status or Humanitarian Protection, it may be that ECHR Art 6 applies to asylum appeals brought under the Refugee Qualification Directive – see the Court of Appeal recognising this as arguable in HH (Iran) v Secretary of State for the Home Department [2008] EWCA Civ 50.

Article 8

Article 8 provides as follows:

> (1) Everyone has the right to respect for his private and family life, his home and his correspondence.
> (2) There shall be no interference by a public authority with the exercise of this right except such as is in accordance with the law and is necessary in a democratic society in the interests of national security, public safety or the economic well-being of the country, for the prevention of disorder or crime, for the protection of health or morals, or for the protection of the rights and freedoms of others.

On 9 July 2012, the Secretary of State amended the immigration rules to introduce Article 8 considerations into the new private and family life routes, and in respect of deportation decisions. This section should be read in conjunction with the sections on private life rule 276ADE(1), Appendix FM, and deportation.

As we have seen, the Upper Tribunal and Court of Appeal (in cases such as MF, Izuazu, and Ogundimu) has decided that if an Article 8 claim on appeal is found not meet the requirements of the new immigration rules, the judge must continue on to consider the claim outside the rules under the binding principles set in the light of Strasbourg jurisprudence by the UK courts. In this litigation, the Home Office did not seek to argue that the new rules covered all the instances in which Article 8 might be in play. Indeed, its own guidance sets out clearly the need to consider exceptional circumstances in cases where the rules are not met.

It was suggested in R (on the application of) Nagre v SSHD [2013] EWHC 720 (Admin), that in a case which fell to be refused under the rules, the judge need not go on in every case to then consider Article 8 principles outside the rules. Sales J argued that there was a gateway to be crossed before doing so, essentially that the appellant would need to show arguably good grounds for doing so. That approach was rejected by the Court of Appeal in MM & Ors, R (On the Application Of) v SSHD (Rev 1) [2014] EWCA Civ 985 where Aikens LJ stated [129];

> I cannot see much utility in imposing this further, intermediary, test. If the applicant cannot satisfy the rule, then there either is or there is not a further Article 8 claim. That will have to be determined by the relevant decision-maker.

It is the established principles under Article 8 that we look to now, those that must be considered if the Article 8 claim fails under the rules. As a word of warning though, before we do so, it will not be easy to succeed on Article 8 grounds on this basis. There will need to be, at least, some compelling circumstances which the rules do not take into account.

In paragraph 17 of the important case of Razgar [2004] 2 AC 368, Lord Bingham set out five questions that must be posed in assessing whether an act of removal from the UK would breach Article 8 in a given case:

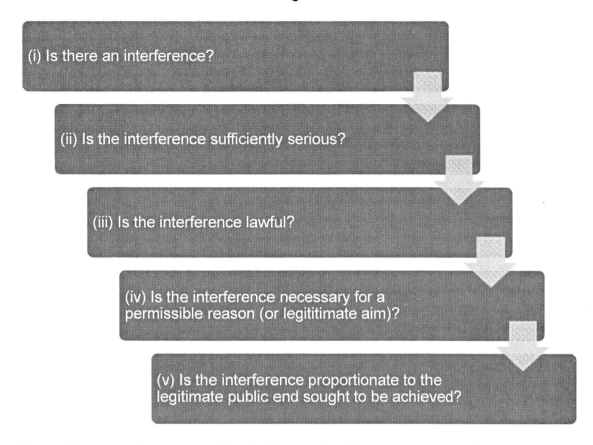

(i) Is there an interference?

(ii) Is the interference sufficiently serious?

(iii) Is the interference lawful?

(iv) Is the interference necessary for a permissible reason (or legititimate aim)?

(v) Is the interference proportionate to the legitimate public end sought to be achieved?

These five questions are critical. Firstly, the five step approach provides an essential tool for analysing any Article 8 factual scenario. Secondly, it has been recognised that it may well amount to an error of law for an immigration judge to fail to follow the five step approach.

Interference with Article 8 rights

In order to establish that that there will be an interference with an Article 8 right, it is first necessary to show that there is an Article 8 relationship (or relationships) in place.

Family relationships

Family life can include various relationships. Marckx v Belgium (1979) 2 EHRR 330:

> The Court concurs entirely with the Commission's established case-law on a crucial point, namely that Article 8 (art. 8) makes no distinction between the 'legitimate' and the 'illegitimate' family. Such a distinction would not be consonant with the word 'everyone', and this is confirmed by Article 14 (art. 14) with its prohibition, in the enjoyment of the rights and freedoms enshrined in the Convention, of discrimination grounded on 'birth.'

> ...'[F]amily life', within the meaning of Article 8 (art. 8), includes at least the ties between near relatives, for instance those between grandparents and grandchildren, since such relatives may play a considerable part in family life.

In Sen v Netherlands (2003) 36 EHRR 81, the European Court of Human Rights made it very clear that a biological parent-child relationship will almost always give rise to family life:

> The respondent Government acknowledges that the existence of "family life" between the applicants has been established. The Court reiterates in this regard that a child born of a marital union is ipso jure part of that relationship; hence from the moment of the child's birth and by the very fact of it, there exists between him and his parents a bond amounting to family life (Gul v. Switzerland (1996) 22 EHRR 93, para 32; Boughanemi v. France (1996) 22 EHRR 228, para 35) which subsequent events cannot break save in exceptional circumstances (Berrehab v. Netherlands (1989) 11 EHRR 322, para 21; Ahmut v. Netherlands (1997) 24 EHRR 62, para 60).

In Singh v ECO New Delhi [2004] EWCA (Civ) 1075 the Court of Appeal examined Strasbourg case law which shows that family and private life is a question of fact and can cover a range of diverse situations:

> ...the starting point of the law is a tolerant indulgence to cultural and religious diversity and an essentially agnostic view of religious beliefs ... such is the diversity of forms that the family takes in contemporary society that it is impossible to define, or even to describe at anything less than almost encyclopaedic length, what is meant by "family life" for the purposes of Article 8. The Strasbourg court, as I have said, has never sought to define what is meant by family life. More importantly for present purposes, and this is a point that requires emphasis, the Strasbourg court has never sought to identify any minimum requirements that must be shown if family life is to be held to exist. That is because there are none...
>
> The existence or non-existence of "family life" for the purposes of Article 8 is essentially a question of fact depending upon the real existence in practice of close personal ties

Those close personal ties might though, in certain circumstances, be ones that have yet to be formed. The obligations under Article 8 require a state not only to refrain from interference with existing life, but also from inhibiting the development of a real family life in the future (R (Ahmadi) v Secretary of State for the Home Department [2005] EWCA Civ 1721).

The ECHR in Berrehab v Netherlands (1988) 11 EHRR 322 held that cohabitation, whilst strong evidence, is not an essential feature of family life:

> The Court likewise does not see cohabitation as a sine qua non of family life between parents and minor children. It has held that the relationship created between the spouses by a lawful and genuine marriage – such as that contracted by Mr. and Mrs. Berrehab – has to be regarded as 'family life' (see the Abdulaziz, Cabales and Balkandali judgment of 28 May 1985, Series A no. 94, p. 32, § 62). It follows from the concept of family on which Article 8 (art. 8) is based that a child born of such a union is ipso jure part of that relationship; hence, from the moment of the child's birth and by the very fact of it, there exists between him and his parents a

> bond amounting to 'family life', even if the parents are not then living together ... Subsequent events, of course, may break that tie ...

But family life will not necessarily be accepted to be established between adults (e.g. adult children and their parents, adult siblings), see Advic v United Kingdom 00025525/94 (6 September 1995):

> Although this will depend on the circumstances of each particular case, the Commission has already considered that the protection of Article 8 (Art. 8) did not cover links between adult brothers who had been living apart for a long period of time and who were not dependent on each other (No. 8157/78, Dec. 5.12.79, unpublished). Moreover, the relationship between a parent and an adult child would not necessarily acquire the protection of Article 8 (Art. 8) of the Convention without evidence of further elements of dependency, involving more than the normal, emotional ties (No. 10375/83, Dec. 10.12.84, D.R. 40 p. 196).

However, in ZB (Pakistan) v SSHD [2009] EWCA Civ 834 the Court of Appeal held that Advic and other cases should not be seen as precluding the existence of family life between adults in cases involving extended families. The Court was highly critical of the tribunal's determination in the case, finding that it did not show a proper appreciation for the need to respect family life or the importance of family life to those who have one and then that the tribunal had artificially compartmentalised individual relationships within the family group rather than looking at the family as a whole. In deciding whether there is a family life between adults, the Court held that the relevant question is how dependent is the older relative on the younger ones in the UK and does that dependency create something more than the normal emotional ties?

Private life

The concept of private life as protected by Article 8 has repeatedly been held to be a very broad one. In Niemietz v Germany (1992) 16 EHRR 97 the EctHR said as follows at para 29:

> The Court does not consider it possible or necessary to attempt an exhaustive definition of the notion of "private life". However, it would be too restrictive to limit the notion to an "inner circle" in which the individual may live his own personal life as he chooses and to exclude therefrom entirely the outside world not encompassed within that circle. Respect for private life must also comprise to a certain degree the right to establish and develop relationships with other human beings.

In the House of Lords case of Razgar, Lord Bingham said the following about the nature of private life (paragraph 9):

> This judgment establishes, in my opinion quite clearly, that reliance may in principle be placed on article 8 to resist an expulsion decision, even where the main emphasis is not on the severance of family and social ties which the applicant has enjoyed in the expelling country but on the consequences for his mental health of removal to the receiving country. The threshold of successful reliance is high, but if

the facts are strong enough article 8 may in principle be invoked. It is plain that "private life" is a broad term, and the Court has wisely eschewed any attempt to define it comprehensively. It is relevant for present purposes that the Court saw mental stability as an indispensable precondition to effective enjoyment of the right to respect for private life. In Pretty v United Kingdom (2002) 35 EHRR 1, paragraph 61, the Court held the expression to cover "the physical and psychological integrity of a person" and went on to observe that

> "Article 8 also protects a right to personal development, and the right to establish and develop relationships with other human beings and the outside world."

Elusive though the concept is, I think one must understand "private life" in article 8 as extending to those features which are integral to a person's identity or ability to function socially as a person. Professor Feldman, writing in 1997 before the most recent decisions, helpfully observed ("The Developing Scope of Article 8 of the European Convention on Human Rights", [1997] EHRLR 265, 270):

> "Moral integrity in this sense demands that we treat the person holistically as morally worthy of respect, organising the state and society in ways which respect people's moral worth by taking account of their need for security."

The concept is clearly an exceedingly broad one.

As to the threshold for establishing a private life that engages Article 8(1), in AG (Eritrea) v Secretary of State for the Home Department [2007] EWCA Civ 801, a case concerning the private life of an unaccompanied minor, Sedley LJ stated [28];

> It follows, in our judgment, that while an interference with private or family life must be real if it is to engage art. 8(1), the threshold of engagement (the "minimum level") is not a specially high one. Once the article is engaged, the focus moves, as Lord Bingham's remaining questions indicate, to the process of justification under art. 8(2). It is this which, in all cases which engage article 8(1), will determine whether there has been a breach of the article.

And at [40];

> The private life established in this country by a lone 14-year old whose asylum claim is not processed for four years, who has no known family in Eritrea and cannot speak the language, and who has acquired an education, psychological support and a social circle here, not only brings him very plainly within art. 8(1) but raises an obvious question about the necessity and proportionality of removing him notwithstanding the legality and proper objects of immigration control.

In Janjanin v Secretary of State for the Home Department [2004] EWCA Civ 448 the Court of Appeal did not refuse to recognise that valuable and responsible work in the National Health Service could constitute private life. Equally someone who made a great contribution to the community outside work (see UE (Nigeria) [2010] EWCA Civ 975), or who has close relationships in the UK such as being someone's carer, might be able to build a case.

Article 8 may also prevent a person's removal where their private life in terms of their mental (or perhaps physical) health would be affected seriously whilst falling short of Article 3 ill-treatment. However, such a breach would need to be flagrant - see Ullah (HL):

> Another possible field of application could be the expulsion of an alien homosexual to a country where, short of persecution, he might be subjected to a flagrant violation of his article 8 rights. In Z v Secretary of State for the Home Department [2002] Imm AR 560 this point came before the Court of Appeal. Schiemann LJ (with whom the other members of the court agreed) was not prepared to rule out such an argument. In my view he was right not to do so. Enough has been said to demonstrate that on principles repeatedly affirmed by the ECtHR article 8 may be engaged in cases of a real risk of a flagrant violation of an individual's article 8 rights.

See also for example the Strasbourg court in Bensaid v UK (2001) 33 EHRR 10.

> Not every act or measure which adversely affects moral or physical integrity will interfere with the right to respect to private life guaranteed by Article 8. However, the Court's case-law does not exclude that treatment which does not reach the severity of Article 3 treatment may nonetheless breach Article 8 in its private life aspect where there are sufficiently adverse effects on physical and moral integrity. Private life is a broad term not susceptible to exhaustive definition. The Court has already held that elements such as gender identification, name and sexual orientation and sexual life are important elements of the personal sphere protected by Article 8. Mental health must also be regarded as a crucial part of private life associated with the aspect of moral integrity. Article 8 protects a right to identity and personal development, and the right to establish and develop relationships with other human beings and the outside world. The preservation of mental stability is in that context an indispensable precondition to effective enjoyment of the right to respect for private life...

See the more abbreviated definition from the House of Lords in Razgar [2004] UKHL 27 quoted above: "those features which are integral to a person's identity or ability to function socially as a person."

For more on Article 8 and health cases, see the section above on Article 3 and the unavailability of medical treatment abroad.

In EM (Lebanon) v SSHD [2008] UKHL 64 one of the points made in the course of judgment is that it is the existing family and/or private life right that has to be considered, not some future alternative relationships that might or might not be developed in the future (paragraph 39 of judgment). This may go some way to defeating the standard Home Office submission in Article 8 cases that an alternative family or private life is available to the person in their country of origin, but as ever much depends on the facts of the case.

Threshold for interference in foreign cases

In 'foreign cases' (a term used in Ullah and Do), i.e. cases where there is argued to be a breach of rights that will take place in the future, after removal from the UK rather than inside the UK itself by the action or inaction of the UK authorities, it has to be shown that there will be a 'flagrant denial' of the right in question if it is not an absolute right.

The leading case is EM (Lebanon) v SSHD [2008] UKHL 64, in which the House of Lords holds that the 'complete nullification' and 'flagrant denial' tests, which seemed in the lower courts to have been understood to represent different thresholds, are simply reflections of the same test. EM (Lebanon) is believed to have made European legal history by being the first significant decision in which this very high test was made out.

Relocating the family

The Home Office may argue in Article 8 cases that turn on a relationship that was formed in the UK, that it is not the decision of the Home Office to remove the illegal immigrant that would sunder the relationship, but the refusal of the UK-based person to relocate to the foreign country in question. The right of a state to regulate immigration control is often cited, and the fact that couples do not have an automatic right to choose their country of residence together.

Based on a misunderstanding of an early case on Article 8, R (Mahmood) v SSHD [2001] 1 WLR 840, the Home Office and many immigration judges considered that the test for whether a UK-based person could be expected to relocate abroad was whether there were any 'insurmountable obstacles' to their doing so. Taken literally, this test was impossible to satisfy. No obstacle is insurmountable in this context.

This inaccurate interpretation of Mahmood was laid to rest, at least until 09 July 2012, by Lord Bingham at paragraph 12 of his judgment in EB (Kosovo) v SSHD [2008] UKHL 41, in which there is no reference at all to an 'insurmountable obstacles' test:

> ...it will rarely be proportionate to uphold an order for removal of a spouse if there is a close and genuine bond with the other spouse and that spouse cannot reasonably be expected to follow the removed spouse to the country of removal...

The correctness of a simple reasonableness test was confirmed by the Court of Appeal in VW (Uganda) v SSHD [2009] EWCA Civ 5. However, it remains a difficult test to satisfy, even if not literally an insurmountable one. As an example, in Amrollahi v Denmark (Appl no 56811/00; 11 October 2002), where the applicant was a convicted drug trafficker, the Court did find that it was not reasonable to pursue family life abroad, but on the following compelling facts:

> 41. The applicant's wife, A, is a Danish national. She has never been to Iran, she does not know Farsi and she is not a Muslim. Besides being married to an Iranian man, she has no ties with the country. In these circumstances the Court accepts even if it is not impossible for the spouse and the applicant's children to live in Iran that it would, nevertheless, cause them obvious and serious difficulties. In addition, the Court recalls that A's daughter from a previous relationship, who has lived with A since her birth in 1989, refuses to move to Iran. Taking this fact into account as well, A cannot, in the Court's opinion, be expected to follow the applicant to Iran.

The current government's attempt to revive the insurmountable obstacles test in EX1 of Appendix FM has so far been given short shrift by the Upper Tribunal (see e.g. MF (Article 8 - new rules) Nigeria [2012] UKUT 393 (IAC) where the headnote states, *'When considering Article 8 in the context of an appellant who fails under the new rules, it will remain the case, as before, that "exceptional circumstances" is not to be regarded as a legal test and "insurmountable obstacles" is to be regarded as an incorrect criterion'.*

The HO has been compelled to amend the rules (as from 28 July 2014) to define 'insurmountable obstacles' as, in fact, only "very significant difficulties which would be faced by the applicant or their partner in continuing their family life together outside the UK and which could not be overcome or would entail very serious hardship for the applicant or their partner (see paragraph EX.2 inserted into Appendix FM as from 28 July 2014).

In recent years greater respect has been shown to the right of British citizens to reside in their country of nationality. In AB (Jamaica) v SSHD [2007] EWCA Civ 1302 the Court of Appeal was very critical of the 'cavalier' consideration of the possibility of relocation abroad by a British citizen by both the Home Office and the immigration tribunal:

> In substance, albeit not in form, Mr Brown was a party to the proceedings. It was as much his marriage as the appellant's which was in jeopardy, and it was the impact of removal on him rather than on her which, given the lapse of years since the marriage, was now critical. From Strasbourg's point of view, his Convention rights were as fully engaged as hers. He was entitled to something better than the cavalier treatment he received not only from the Home Office but, I regret to say, from the AIT. It cannot be permissible to give less than detailed and anxious consideration to the situation of a British citizen who has lived here all his life before it is held reasonable and proportionate to expect him to emigrate to a foreign country in order to keep his marriage intact. One finds no consideration given to any of these matters by the AIT at either stage.

See also ZH (Tanzania) v SSHD [2011] UKSC 4 on the importance of citizenship. The context in ZH is of children, but the point made about the 'intrinsic importance of citizenship' is valid for adults also.

Building on the principles outlined in ZH (Tanzania), and in Ruiz Zambrano, and in the context of a deport case, the Secretary of State conceded in Sanade and others (British children - Zambrano - Dereci) India [2012] UKUT 48 (IAC) that;

> The respondent properly accepts that [the Appellant's British wife and children] cannot be required to leave the Union as a matter of law, and that as a matter of relevant consideration they cannot reasonably be expected to relocate outside of the European Union. Accordingly, the question is whether Mr Sanade's conduct is so serious as to make it proportionate to the legitimate aim in his case to require him to leave his wife and young children for an indefinite period unless and until the deportation order can be revoked?

The most recent word on this though was in the Court of Appeal's decision in MM & Ors, R (On the Application Of) v SSHD (Rev 1) [2014] EWCA Civ 985, where Aikens LJ made the point that despite the fact that a UK national has a statutory right to reside in the UK "without let or hindrance", and the right of that person to marry and found a family and the right to respect of the private and family life created as a result of the exercise of the previous rights;

> There is nothing in the 1971 Act or the common law that grants a "constitutional right" of British citizens to live in the UK with non-EEA partners who do not have the right of abode in the UK and who are currently living outside the UK [138].

In investigating whether the UK-based party to the relationship can move abroad, it will clearly be a relevant consideration if they have refugee status or humanitarian protection in the United Kingdom. However, in such cases, it is not illegitimate for the decision maker to consider if they have a current protection need, particularly if the protection status was granted some time ago.

Applying for entry clearance from abroad

Another Home Office argument on the question of whether there is a real interference with the Article 8 rights of a person facing removal is that the person who is in the UK irregularly can apply to return to the UK for entry clearance in the normal way.

However, the House of Lords effectively rejected this approach in the case of Chikwamba v SSHD [2008] UKHL 40, holding that it was more sensible to assess human rights at the point of application:

> 40. ... it seems to me that only comparatively rarely, certainly in family cases involving children, should an article 8 appeal be dismissed on the basis that it would be proportionate and more appropriate for the appellant to apply for leave from abroad. Besides the considerations already mentioned, it should be borne in mind that the 1999 Act introduced one-stop appeals. The article 8 policy instruction is not easily reconcilable with the new streamlined approach. Where a single appeal combines (as often it does) claims both for asylum and for leave to remain under article 3 or article 8, the appellate authorities would necessarily have to dispose substantively of the asylum and article 3 claims. Suppose that these fail. Should the article 8 claim then be dismissed so that it can be advanced abroad, with the prospect of a later, second section 65 appeal if the claim fails before the ECO (with the disadvantage of the appellant then being out of the country)? Better surely that in most cases the article 8 claim be decided once and for all at the initial stage. If it is well-founded, leave should be granted. If not, it should be refused.

The Home Office have been slow to recognise the ratio of Chikwamba and it is standard for the Home Office to argue that Chikwamba applies only in situations such as that pertaining in Zimbabwe at the time of the judgment. This confusion of fact with law should be resisted. For its wider remit, the principle was considered in Zhang, R (on the application of) v SSHD [2013] EWHC 891 (Admin), in which a High Court judge found that it would be disproportionate for a PBS migrant to have to return to China to rejoin her husband here as a PBS dependent. He found;

> It must follow from this that the application of the blanket requirement to leave the country imposed by paragraph 319C(h)(i) of the immigration rules is unsustainable.

It is simply not consistent with the ratio of the decision in <u>Chikwamba</u> that this paragraph, as presently worded, should continue to form part of the rules.

As a consequence of this decision, the rules were amended as of 1 October 2013 to allow in-country switching into dependant categories.

In accordance with the law

Immigration control is in accordance with the law for Article 8 purposes, in relation to interference with family and private life as well as in relation to moral and physical integrity cases. Strasbourg tends to construe "in accordance with the law" as meaning there is a power in law to make the decision in question: and most would-be immigrants are the subject of lawful decisions in this sense, e.g. a person who does not fit into the immigration rules and is rejected as a refugee will not be able to establish any basis to come enter the country, and hence there will be a power in law to refuse them leave to enter.

For a legitimate aim

The potential legitimate aims listed at Article 8 (2) are as follows:

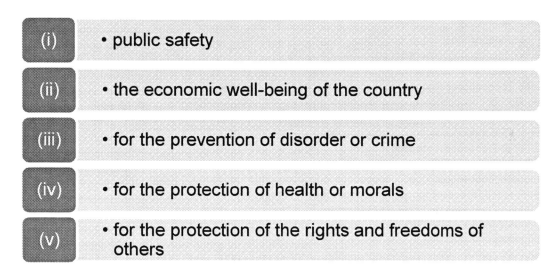

(i) • public safety

(ii) • the economic well-being of the country

(iii) • for the prevention of disorder or crime

(iv) • for the protection of health or morals

(v) • for the protection of the rights and freedoms of others

As indicated already, this tends to be automatically answered against the immigrant. Lord Bingham in Razgar in the House of Lords [2004] UKHL 27:

> 19. Where removal is proposed in pursuance of a lawful immigration policy, question (4) will almost always fall to be answered affirmatively. This is because the right of sovereign states, subject to treaty obligations, to regulate the entry and expulsion of aliens is recognised in the Strasbourg jurisprudence (see Ullah and Do, para 6) and implementation of a firm and orderly immigration policy is an important function of government in a modern democratic state. In the absence of bad faith, ulterior motive or deliberate abuse of power it is hard to imagine an adjudicator answering this question other than affirmatively.

The European Court in Bensaid v United Kingdom (E. Ct. H.R. 6 February 2001): speaking of interferences compelled by the consequences of immigration control:

> ... the Court considers that such interference may be regarded as complying with the requirements of the second paragraph of Article 8, namely as a measure 'in accordance with the law', pursuing the aims of the protection of the economic well-being of the country and the prevention of disorder and crime, as well as being 'necessary in a democratic society' for those aims.

This approach as upheld more recently by the Upper Tribunal in Shahzad (Art 8: legitimate aim) Pakistan [2014] UKUT 85 (IAC).

Necessary in a democratic society

Having shown a legitimate aim for the interference, the Home Office must also show that it is necessary in a democratic society. This is Razgar's 5th question and had been transposed by the courts into an assessment of the proportionality of the decision.

The concept of proportionality is central to the application of Article 8, although it is very important to follow the five-step approach and not jump straight to proportionality.

Proportionality in the context of the exercise of immigration control usually boils down to a question of identifying those cases where the adverse effect on the individual is so disproportionate to the need to maintain an effective system of immigration control that it is unlawful. A series of Court of Appeal and House of Lords decisions have examined the test for proportionality. For a time it was thought by the Immigration tribunal that a case had to be found to be 'truly exceptional', seizing on a phrase used by Lord Bingham in the case of Razgar, in order to succeed. However, the House of Lords held that this was incorrect in the later case of Huang [2007] UKHL 11 and observed that Lord Bingham's earlier comments were merely predictive of the numbers of cases that might succeed. They did not amount to a legal test. There is no requirement to show that there are exceptional circumstances.

In the case of AG (Eritrea) v SSHD [2007] EWCA Civ 801 the Court of Appeal at paragraph 31 comments on this as follows:

> The fact that in the great majority of cases the demands of immigration control are likely to make removal proportionate and so compatible with art.8 is a consequence, not a precondition, of the statutory exercise. No doubt in this sense successful art.8 claims will be the exception rather than the rule; but to treat exceptionality as the yardstick of success is to confuse effect with cause.

Assessing proportionality is sometimes compared to a balancing exercise. The scales and the weights on each side of the fulcrum can be represented thus:

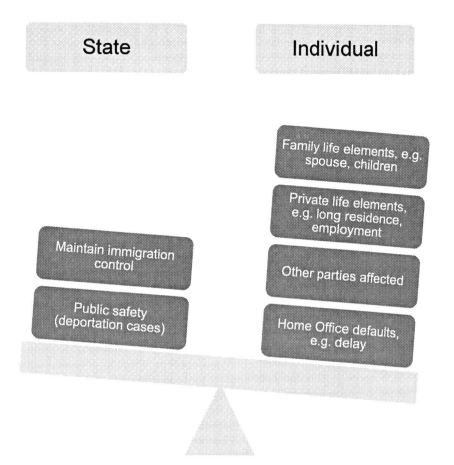

Effect on children

The effect of an immigration decision on any affected child or children has to be given special consideration, and this is often now incorporated into the assessment of Article 8 proportionality. A number of legal factors become relevant.

The first is the decision of the United Kingdom Government to lift what was known as the 'immigration reservation' to the UN Convention on the Rights of the Child 1989 ('UNCRC'). This previously purported to exempt the United Kingdom from the obligations of the UNCRC in respect of children subject to immigration control. The reservation was formally lifted on 4 December 2008. Perhaps the most important part of the UNCRC is Article 3:

> In all actions concerning children, whether undertaken by public or private social welfare institutions, courts of law, administrative authorities or legislative bodies, the best interests of the child shall be a primary consideration

The lifting of the immigration reservation can be linked to the passage of section 55 of the Borders, Citizenship and Immigration Act 2009, the duty to have regard to the need to safeguard and promote the welfare of children in the UK. The wording of section 55 replicates that in section 17 of the Children Act 1989 and section 11 of the Children Act 2004 and for the first time applied the same duty to the Home Office and those carrying out immigration functions. In addition, under statutory guidance issued under s.55(3), the Secretary of State has explicitly recognised that the best interests of a child are a primary consideration.

Case law has also played an important part. In LD (Article 8 best interests of child) Zimbabwe [2010] UKUT 278 (IAC) the President of the Immigration and Asylum Chamber of the Upper Tribunal found that the UN Convention on the Rights of the Child is highly relevant to Article 8 ECHR:

> 27. The two younger children of the appellant have lived in the UK continuously for eleven years and for most of their lives. Previously Home Office policy tended to identify seven years of residence of a child as one that would presumptively require regularisation of immigration status of child and parents in the absence of compelling countervailing factors. That was really an administrative way of giving effect to the principle of the welfare of the child as a primary consideration in such cases and when it was considered that those interests normally required regularisation of the immigration position of the family as a whole. The policy may have been withdrawn but substantial residence as a child is a strong indication the judicial assessment of what the best interests of the child requires. The UN Convention on the Rights of the Child 1989 Art 3 makes such interests a primary consideration.
>
> 28. Although questions exist about the status of the UN Convention on the Rights of the Child in domestic law, we take the view that there can be little reason to doubt that the interests of the child should be a primary consideration in immigration cases. A failure to treat them as such will violate Article 8 (2) as incorporated directly into domestic law.

This case was followed by ZH (Tanzania) v SSHD [2011] UKSC 4 in the Supreme Court. The judgment is a seminal one for children's rights in an immigration context. Delivering the leading judgment, Lady Hale demonstrates how the UNCRC had influenced Strasbourg case law and prompted the passage of section 55 and then goes on to stress the importance of properly considering the impact of immigration decisions on children, the need to consult with children or at least give separate consideration to the impact on them, the meaning of best interests being a primary consideration (no other consideration can be given more weight) and the right of British children to grow up in their country of nationality.

The Statement of Intent: Family Migration published in June 2012 states that where a child's best interests are relevant to a removal or deportation decision, or raised in an Article 8 claim, they will be determined in line with the private and family life provisions in the Immigration Rules.

The new Part 5A provisions should not affect the assessment and weight given to the best interests of any children affected by an immigration decision as is made explicit in s71 of the Immigration Act 2014.

Home Office delay

The definitive case on delay by the Home Office as a factor in assessing proportionality is that of the House of Lords in EB (Kosovo) v Secretary of State for the Home Department [2008] UKHL 41. In summary, the three ways in which Lord Bingham says that delay may affect an Article 8 claim are as follows:

(i)   The Article 8 family and/or private life rights will develop and grow during a period of delay.

(ii)   Delay reduced the weight to be attached to the consideration that a relationship was entered into in the knowledge of its precariousness owing to immigration control considerations. To put it another way, delay allows Article 8 rights to become established and entrenched, and the decision-maker must show appropriate recognition of this reality.

(iii)   Delay reduces the significance of the Article 8 (2) consideration of the need to maintain immigration control because delay gives rise to 'a dysfunctional system which yields unpredictable, inconsistent and unfair outcomes'.

The Home Office policy on delay is set out in Chapter 53 of the Enforcement Instructions. This requires its decision makers to give weight to its own delay in making a decision on an asylum or human rights claim or in setting removal directions following refusal of such a claim of 3 years or more in the case of children or 6 years or more in the case of adults. See earlier section on Home Office policies for details. In Okonkwo (legacy/Hakemi; health claim) Nigeria [2013] UKUT 401 (IAC), the Tribunal made it clear that this does not equate to a principle that those who have been in the UK for 6 years or more should be given leave under the policy

Example

Deidre has been waiting for five years for a decision on her application to remain in the UK as the spouse of Barry. She originally entered the UK several years before that as a visitor and she overstayed her visa. She met and married Barry and they have two children now. They made an application under DP3/96 after they had been married for two years.

Deidre has not suffered any procedural prejudice by the delay she has experienced, as she was unlawfully present when she made the application and had overstayed her original visa with no expectation of being allowed to remain. Unlike earlier case law, EB (Kosovo) does not require there to be any procedural prejudice, however.

She has a very strong case even aside from EB (Kosovo). Although DP3/96 has been abolished (see section on immigration policies), consideration under the policy had begun and the Home Office say they will apply DP3/96 to any cases already under consideration.

If the application was ultimately rejected for some reason, Deidre would have a good case on appeal for the tribunal to apply the policy itself in accordance with AG and others (Policies; executive discretions; Tribunal's powers) Kosovo [2007] UKAIT 00082 (see further below). In addition, a delay of five years is a very long one and is a relevant factor, and the couple have established a very strong family life in the UK during that time.

Failure to apply a policy

If the facts of the case bring the claimant within a policy that has not been properly considered in their case, this is very likely to render disproportionate a failure to apply that policy. For example, in AA (Afghanistan) v SSHD [2007] EWCA Civ 12 Keene LJ said the following at paragraph 15:

> This court has held more than once that for the Secretary of State to fail to take account of or give effect to his own published policy renders his decision not "in accordance with the law": see, for example, Secretary of State for the Home Department v. Abdi [1996] Imm. AR 148 at 157. Likewise the AIT should have concluded that the adjudicator had made an error of law.

Where an individual fits within a policy that will suggest that a decision inconsistent with the policy will be disproportionate: for the existence of the policy will strongly suggest where the public interest lies.

However, the tribunal are reluctant to make decisions for itself under policies that retain a degree of Home Office discretion. Where a policy is found by the tribunal to apply to a person and the outcome is clear-cut, the appeal should be allowed. Where it is not clear-cut that the policy should be applied, the tribunal will allow an appeal as being not in accordance with the law (because the policy has not been considered), but expect the Home Office to make their own decision about whether the policy does in fact apply: AG and others (Policies; executive discretions; Tribunal's powers) Kosovo [2007] UKAIT 00082.

The fact that on arrival in the United Kingdom the applicant had a legitimate claim to enter can also be a determinative factor in assessing the proportionality of a decision to refuse status. In the related cases of SSHD v R (on the app. of Rashid) [2005] EWCA Civ 744 and R (on the app. of A, H and AH) v SSHD [2006] EWHC 526 (Admin), it was held that the Home Office had acted unlawfully in concealing a policy from the applicants and then denying status once that policy had been ended.

Third party rights

In Strasbourg cases, such as Berrehab v Netherlands (1989) 11 EHRR 322, Beldjoudi v France (1992) 14 EHRR 801 and Amrollahi v Denmark [2002] ECHR 585 (arguably, at least), the European Court of Human Rights considers the rights of the family as a whole, including the rights of the family members with a right to reside in the country concerned. Whatever the final outcome of these cases, many of which are successful, it is clear from the judgments that the collective rights of the family as a whole have been considered.

For some years the Tribunal maintained a restrictive approach to third party rights. However in Beoku-Betts v Secretary of State for the Home Department [2008] UKHL 39 (25 June 2008) the House of Lords reversed this, in the context of the right of appeal set out in the Immigration and Asylum Act 1999 but which will demand the same approach in appeals brought under the Nationality Immigration and Asylum Act 2002.

> Once it is recognised that ... "there is only one family life", and that, assuming the appellant's proposed removal would be disproportionate looking at the family unit as a whole, then each affected family member is to be regarded as a victim, section 65 seems comfortably to accommodate the wider construction.

The implications for practice and evidence are considerable. Evidence from family members may now prove crucial, particularly in relation to:

(i) Strength and depth of relationship and/or attachment, and what the applicant means to the family member concerned.

(ii) Reasons why the family member(s) cannot or should not be expected to relocate to the country concerned.

(iii) Information regarding the effect on any children affected, ideally from family court proceedings (permission will be needed), child psychologist or from an Independent Social Worker.

Beoku-Betts was followed by another landmark House of Lords case, EM (Lebanon) v SSHD [2008] UKHL 64. The Lords held that the rights of the child in this case had to be considered separately to the mother (both were facing removal) and also suggested that separate representation for a child might be appropriate in some cases.

Part 5A, 2002 Act considerations

When considering proportionality a judge must, in addition to established principles, have regard to the considerations laid out under Part 5 of the 2002 Act, inserted as from 28 July 2014 by the Immigration Act 2014 (s19).

According to Part 5, it is in the public interest and in the interest of the economic well-being of the United Kingdom that those seeking to enter or remain in the UK are able to speak English, and are financially independent. Also that little weight should be given to a private or family life established at a time when the person was in the UK illegally or precarious. But depending on the facts of the case, these factors may go to either side of the balance. Helpfully, Part 5A also states that the public interest does not require a person who is not liable to deportation to be removed from the UK where they have a genuine and subsisting parental relationship with a qualifying child, and it would not be reasonable to expect the child to leave the United Kingdom.

For a detailed analysis of these new statutory provisions see the Free Movement blog at:
http://www.freemovement.org.uk/new-statutory-human-rights-considerations-take-immediate-effect/ and http://www.freemovement.org.uk/weighing-the-public-interest-in-deportation-cases/#more-16296

There is no case law on these provisions as yet and it remains to see how they will impact on judicial decision making. The judge must have regard to them but they must still go on and weigh the public interest against the rights of affected individuals.

Article 8 and the Immigration Rules

As a result of the introduction of private and family life categories into the Immigration Rules on 9 July 2012, we effectively have two Article 8 regimes running in parallel – firstly, as provided for in the rules and secondly, in the binding precedents of the UK courts and in the jurisprudence from Strasbourg. On 13 June 2012, the Home Office issued a lengthy statement, Immigration Rules on Family and Private Life (HC194): Grounds of Compatibility with Article 8 of The European Convention on Human Rights, setting out its view that the two are not incompatible.

The argument was, essentially, that the approach taken by the Court of Appeal in Huang & Others v SSHD [2005] EWCA Civ 105 (the Court of Appeal judgment which preceded that of the HoL, see below), represents the correct approach that a Tribunal or court should now take in considering a refusal of an Article 8 claim, i.e. a position of deference to parliament. As the statement says, quoting from Huang in the CA;

> 8. The approach the Courts initially adopted in immigration cases when considering proportionality and the Rules is demonstrated in the following passage (emphasis added):
>
> "In such a case the adjudicator is not ignoring or overriding the Rules. On the contrary it is a signal feature of his task that he is bound to respect the balance between public interest and private right struck by the Rules with Parliament's approval. That is why he is only entitled on Article 8 grounds to favour an appellant outside the Rules where the case is truly exceptional. This, not Wednesbury or any revision of Wednesbury, represents the real restriction which the law imposes on the scope of judgment allowed to the adjudicator. It is not a question of his deferring to the Secretary of State's judgment of proportionality in the individual case. The adjudicator's decision of the question whether the case is truly exceptional is entirely his own. He does defer to the Rules; for this approach recognises that the balance struck by the Rules will generally dispose of proportionality issues arising under Article 8; but they are not exhaustive of all cases. There will be a residue of truly exceptional instances. In our respectful view such an approach is also reflected in Lord Bingham's words in Razgar, which we have already cited"

The statement acknowledges that the House of Lords rejected that approach, but reasons that it did so because the Immigration Rules did not at that time purport to reflect Article 8, and Parliament had not been given an opportunity to debate how proportionality assessments under Article 8 should be undertaken. The courts therefore had no option but to carry out a proportionality assessment on a case by case basis. Now that Parliament, following the debate on the new rules, has made its view as to where the proportionality balance should normally lie, the democratic deficit no longer exists, and the courts should now defer to Parliament's position as reflected in the rules.

As so much of the Article 8 case law since the House of Lord's judgement in Huang has taken that judgement as its starting point, it was the government's view that the new rules will require the courts to relook at its approach, in effect roll back its case law to pre-Huang (HL) days. That is why the Home Office felt entitled to explicitly resurrect long dead principles such as 'exceptionality' and 'insurmountable obstacles'. Essentially, the government's argument was that now parliament had approved Article 8 compliant immigration rules, Article 8 no longer existed outside the rules and that the courts could now ignore all its prior jurisprudence.

But until such time as the Supreme Court decides that it does need to revisit its own established principles, and no Article 8 cases have yet reached the Supreme Court since the new rules came into force, the court's position remains as it was laid out EB (Kosovo). Lord Bingham's warns at paragraph 12 that an overly prescriptive approach is incompatible with the Article 8 assessment exercise, and that Article 8 is an important and fundamental human right worthy of genuine respect:

> Thus the appellate immigration authority must make its own judgment and that judgment will be strongly influenced by the particular facts and circumstances of the particular case. The authority will, of course, take note of factors which have, or have not, weighed with the Strasbourg court. It will, for example, recognise that it will rarely be proportionate to uphold an order for removal of a spouse if there is a close and genuine bond with the other spouse and that spouse cannot reasonably be expected to follow the removed spouse to the country of removal, or if the effect of the order is to sever a genuine and subsisting relationship between parent and child. But cases will not ordinarily raise such stark choices, and there is in general no alternative to making a careful and informed evaluation of the facts of the particular case. The search for a hard-edged or bright-line rule to be applied to the generality of cases is incompatible with the difficult evaluative exercise which article 8 requires.

In the most recent litigation on Article 8 and the new rules, the government has to an extent pulled back from its earlier position that the new rules are a complete code where an Article 8 claim is made. It has had to accept that exceptionally a case can succeed outside the rules.

Article 14

Article 14 prohibits discrimination only in when it can be linked with a lack of respect for one or more of the rights otherwise set out in the European Convention on Human Rights – it is the enjoyment of those rights which must be secured without discrimination. There is very little in the way of helpful case law on the issue so far.

Discretionary Leave

This is a residual form of leave to remain given to some individuals who do not qualify for other forms of leave to remain.

As of 9 July 2012, there is a new <u>Discretionary Leave (DL) policy</u> (in the Asylum Instructions section of the Operational Guidance) narrowing the group to whom DL will be granted, but saving the position of those granted DL before that date.

The policies, old and new, are difficult to follow, referring as they do to DL, Restricted Leave and Leave outside the rules – 3 different types of leave granted in similar but slightly different circumstances.

Old DL

The most common situation where you would, pre-9 July 2012, have expected to see a grant of discretionary leave to remain was in Article 8 cases where removal would breach the person's or their family's right to a private and family life in the United Kingdom, or where a person's medical condition would render their removal in breach of Article 3 or 8.

In those circumstances, a person would normally have been granted 3 years DL, followed by an active review, a further 3 years DL if successful, and then ILR. Those on that route under the old policy will continue on that route.

New DL

Those who would previously have been granted DL on Article 8 grounds will now be granted 30 months LTR on a ten-year route to settlement. Such leave will not be called discretionary leave as it is ostensibly granted under the private and family life provisions of Appendix FM.

New grants of DL will also usually be for 30 months. An application for extension can be made where there is a continued need for DL. A person with DL under the new policy will not usually be able to apply for ILR until they have had DL for 10 years. As each application for an extension will be subject to an active review, the course to settlement will be uncertain.

Discretionary leave will be granted under the current policy;

➢ where removal would breach Article 3 in medical and other cases which would not give rise to a grant of Humanitarian Protection,

> if having considered the factors set out in Paragraph 353B of the Immigration Rules and the guidance in Chapter 53.1 of the Enforcement Instructions and Guidance (EIG), removal is no longer considered appropriate. Some cases in this category will be entitled to an immediate grant of ILR under the pre-20 July 2011 policy,

> where a UK Competent Authority has conclusively identified that person as a victim of trafficking within the meaning of Article 4 of the Council of Europe Convention on Action Against Trafficking in Human Beings and the individual's personal circumstances, although not meeting the criteria of any of the other categories listed, are so compelling that it is considered appropriate to grant some form of leave in line with the Duration of Grants of Leave [policy] below,

>> where the victim has lodged a legitimate compensation claim against the trafficker and a grant of leave would help secure justice for the trafficked person and assist in ensuring the trafficker faces the consequences of their actions. The fact that someone is seeking compensation will be relevant to the consideration but does not, in itself, merit a grant of leave. Leave must only be granted where it would be unreasonable for them to pursue that claim from outside of the UK,

>> if an individual is cooperating with an ongoing police investigation in relation to their trafficking case and their presence is required for this purpose it may be appropriate to grant leave.

Unaccompanied minors refused asylum used to be granted DL until they were aged 17½ years, but that policy was incorporated into the rules with effect from 6 April 2013, so they will now be granted leave under the rules (r.352ZC).

The Home Office APIs state as follows:

> There are likely to be very few other cases in which it would be appropriate to grant Discretionary Leave to an unsuccessful asylum seeker. However, it is not possible to anticipate every eventuality that may arise, so there remains scope to grant Discretionary Leave where individual circumstances, although not meeting the criteria of any of the other categories listed above, are so compelling that it is considered appropriate to grant some form of leave.

Individuals who would have qualified for Refugee status or Humanitarian Protection but for committing activities that have caused their exclusion will usually receive Restricted Leave for periods of 6 months at a time. They can apply for ILR only after 10 years. In R (on the application of AO) v Secretary of State for the Home Department [2011] EWHC 3088 (Admin), the High Court found that the 10 year policy for exclusion cases was an unlawful fettering of the Secretary of State's discretion. In an exceptional case, it will therefore be possible to argue that a person should not have to wait 10 years before ILR will be considered.

Those liable to deportation, but have made out a successful claim under Article 8 (as transposed into Immigration Rules 399-399A), will be entitled to 30 months leave within the Immigration Rules.

There are provisions for revocation of DL. However, given that discretionary leave to remain does not normally result from any "protection" need but rather is based on relationships or care in the UK, travel to the country of origin and use of their own national passport does not bring with it the same negative connotations as in asylum and humanitarian protection cases.

There are no provisions which entitle a person with DL to sponsor family members to join them in the U.K. They can of course rely on Article 8 to make an application outside the Immigration Rules.

Travel documents

A person granted DL will be expected to travel on their national passport. They can apply to the Home Office for a certificate of travel, but only if they have been unreasonably and formally (i.e. by letter) refused a national passport.

A refusal of a national passport will not be unreasonable if on the grounds of a failure to complete military service, a failure to provide evidence to confirm identity, or due to having a criminal record in their country.

Children need to apply for their own travel document. All applicants will now have to enroll their biometrics with the Home Office.

The GOV.UK website sets out the requirements for amendments to applications and travel documents. In virtually all cases a full further application form (and full fee) needs to be sent together with extrinsic evidence (e.g. on a change of name, the relevant legal documentation must be produced; if documents are lost or stolen, a police report must be provided). If details on the travel document that is issued are incorrect, and the Home Office are at fault, then there will be no further fee. The documents are not extendable, and if they expire whilst the holder is abroad, then it will be necessary to apply to the nearest British Embassy or High Commission for advice.

There will be an investigation into the loss and so the Home Office warns that applications to replace lost documents can take considerably longer than the usual period.

Chapter 11: European Community law

Underlying legal principles

When discussing this area of law, the formally correct terminology is to refer to European Community ('EC') law as this is the relevant treaty framework. However, it is more commonly referred to as European Economic Area or EEA law, as it is to nationals of the EEA (and Switzerland) that the relevant laws apply. It is also sometimes referred to as European Union or EU law.

The founding purpose of the European Economic Community was to create a common market and guarantee the four freedoms: freedom of goods, capital, services and people. That purpose has been set out in various Treaty and subordinate provisions of EC law since 1957 and currently resides in the Treaty on the Functioning of the European Union (TFEU) and Directive 2004/38/EC, commonly referred to as the Citizens' Directive[9]. These provisions allow EEA nationals and their family members to move freely among Member States to work, and study. The rights are not wholly unrestricted, particularly regarding the ability to secure stay for family members, but they are powerful nonetheless.

In simple terms, EC law on free movement of persons is intended to, and usually does, make it as easy to move from Bilbao to London as it is from Birmingham to London. As such it is the antithesis of immigration control.

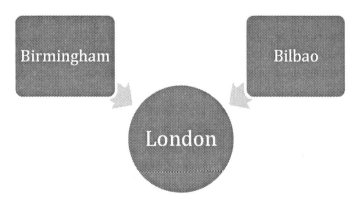

Free movement rights also apply to the family members of EEA nationals, whether those family members are EEA nationals or not. Sometimes too, those rights might apply in the UK to the non-EEA national family members of UK

---

[9] Directive 2004/38/EC of the European Parliament and of the Council of 29 April 2004 on the right of citizens of the Union and their family members to move and reside freely within the territory of the Member States

nationals, where the UK national has exercised their free movement rights elsewhere in the EEA and have returned to the UK.

As will be seen below, the principal advantage of reliance on EEA law rather than UK immigration law is that EEA law is designed to encourage movement and UK immigration law to restrict it.

Countries to which EC law applies

The free movement regime applies to nationals of the Member States of the EEA, and Switzerland.

The EEA is made up of the 28 EU member countries plus Iceland, Norway and Liechtenstein. Switzerland has a bilateral agreement with the EU adding it to the free movement regime. A recent referendum in Switzerland though may require the government to sever the bilateral agreement by 2018.

The countries whose nationals now enjoy rights of free movement around the European Economic Area and Switzerland are as follows:

Austria	Latvia
Belgium	Lithuania
Croatia	Lichtenstein
Cyprus	Luxembourg
Bulgaria	Malta
Czech Republic	The Netherlands
Denmark	Norway
Estonia	Poland
Finland	Portugal
France	Romania
Germany	Slovakia
Greece	Slovenia
Hungary	Spain
Iceland	Sweden
Ireland	Switzerland
Italy	The United Kingdom

It is important to remember though that the rights are enjoyed by those moving or who have moved within the EEA, so will not normally be enjoyed by UK nationals (even if dual UK/EEA nationals) in the UK.

Interaction of UK and EC law

Rights not privileges

There is a very important difference of principle between UK immigration law and EC freedom of movement rights. In UK law, if a foreign national wishes to come to the UK, he or she must first make an application and await a positive decision. There is no pre-existing 'right' to enter the UK. Entry and stay in the UK is contingent on it being permitted by the Secretary of State: see section 1(2) of the Immigration Act 1971.

The position is very different under EC law. Certain individuals have a right to reside in the UK by virtue of their citizenship of another EEA country and their economic activities, or through their family relationship with such a person. The UK is bound by EC law to recognise and promote this right.

A great deal flows from this distinction between inherent rights and discretionary privileges, and for those schooled in UK immigration law many aspects of EEA free movement law may seem counterintuitive. The fact that family permit applications are free, that no particular application form (or indeed any form at all) is necessary, that EEA documents (i.e. family permits and residence documents) are unnecessary for the exercise of free movement rights, and that immigration officers cannot stamp the passports of EEA nationals are all natural consequences of the nature of pre-existing free movement rights in EC law.

That being said, the current coalition government has decided to make free movement rights a major focus for its policy of reducing migration into the UK. Consequently, several recent amendments have been made to the Immigration (European Economic Area) Regulations 2006, the domestic version of EC law, all of which are of dubious legality. Some are being investigated by the EC or are subject to infringement proceedings.

Also consequent on the government's attitude to free movement is the fact that UKVI policy and decision makers often ignore, in practice, one of the explicit purposes of the Citizens Directive, to 'simplify and strengthen the right of free movement and residence of all Union citizens' (Recital 3). The Home Office, for example, require far more evidence be provided than is either lawful or necessary (see Article 8 and 10 of the Citizens Directive) when EEA nationals and their family members seek to document their status. They regularly refuse applications for documents that are clearly made in accordance with the provisions of the Directive.

Those refused EEA entry and residence documents normally have a right of appeal to the First-tier Tribunal, though it will often make more sense in terms of time and cost to apply again with better evidence, than to appeal.

Implementation of EC law

In UK law, EEA free movement rights are laid out in the **Immigration (European Economic Area) Regulations 2006** ('the Regulations'). The Regulations are designed to implement the changes to EC free movement law that were introduced by the Citizens' Directive. However, EC law, in the form of the Treaties, the Citizens Directive and the judgements of the Court of Justice of the European Union (CJEU), is directly effective in the UK, and will therefore trump any provision or practice contrary to their strictures. So, where the Regulations are more restrictive than the principles they supposedly enshrine, then it is the EC law principles which will triumph.

The other side of the coin is that the UK's implementation of EEA law may occasionally be more generous than that of the EU. The EU does not prohibit a more generous approach than it provides for. This appears to be the view of the Tribunal regarding dependent family members in AP and FP (Citizens Directive Article 3(2); discretion; dependence) India [2007] UKAIT 00048 (13 June 2007) and the Court of Appeal in relation to spouses entering the UK from outside the EEA in KG (Sri Lanka) v Secretary of State for the Home Department [2008] EWCA Civ 13 (25 January 2008). So if a client fits into the terms of the UK's EEA Regulations, their rights therein should be respected, but they cannot necessarily show that European law demands the grant of residence unless provided for in the Directive itself or in the case law of the CJEU.

In cases of doubt over the proper interpretation of EU provisions, the UK courts (including the immigration tribunal) can make a reference to the CJEU (previously the European Court of Justice) to seek clarification.

For most (but certainly not for all) practical purposes, the Regulations, as amended several times, provide a reasonable exposition of the way that the British government gives access to Treaty rights for the three categories of individual that benefit from Community law:

➢ "qualified persons", usually being the EEA nationals themselves

➢ their family members

➢ their extended/other family members, i.e. those in a durable relationship with the EEA national, those relatives who are dependent on them or were previously part of their households

There are particular concerns though in respect of more recently introduced provisions of the EEA Regulations concerning dual UK/EEA nationals, the Surinder Singh principle, the definition of job-seeker, and the cancellation of EEA rights.

The government has not consolidated its plethora of recent amendments into an up to date version of the Immigration (EEA) Regulations 2006. An unofficial but useful consolidated version can be found at:
http://www.eearegulations.co.uk/versions/latest.php

Operational Guidance on the free movement regime is available at:

➢ https://www.gov.uk/government/collections/eea-swiss-nationals-and-ec-association-agreements-modernised-guidance and

➢ https://www.gov.uk/immigration-operational-guidance/european-casework-instructions

It is not always up to date and certainly not comprehensive.

Choice of method of entry/residence

An EEA citizen who is settled (i.e. permanently resident under Regulation 15) in the UK may have a choice as to whether to pursue an application for a family member under the rules or under EC law. This was much more of a live issue before Appendix FM was introduced as the old spouse/civil partner/unmarried partner category was a quicker route to settlement than under EEA law. Now the time periods are the same under UK and EU law. There may still be an advantage though for a settled EU national to bring children under 18 into the UK under UK law as they will be entitled to settlement immediately on entry and will not have to remain financially dependent on their parent once they reach the age of 21 if they have not yet become permanently resident by that age.

The benefits of relying on EC over UK law are myriad and include, non-exhaustively;

➢ the absence of any requirement for prior entry clearance,
➢ the absence of suitability, English language, maintenance and accommodation requirements,
➢ the chance to be reunited with children and grandchildren at any age (subject to showing financial dependence if they are over 21), and with dependent parents, grandparents and extended family,
➢ the absence of conditions restricting work and recourse to public funds,
➢ and in respect of appeal rights.

Conversely, the fact that a person is here under UK law will not detract from rights they will also have under EC law. In some cases it may be appropriate to pursue both simultaneously (e.g. an application as a parent under Appendix FM and an application for a 'Ruiz Zambrano' Derivative Residence Card (DRC)). These provisions are not mutually exclusive. The DRC application is cheaper, and carries with it a right of appeal, but the parent application provides for a route to settlement (which the DRC does not).

Where necessary, a person relying on their EU right to reside may switch into the partner category of Appendix FM. This might assist a dependent child of an EU national who loses their dependency, and therefore their EU right to reside, on marriage to a person present and settled in the U.K.

EC law and the ECHR

Article 6 (2) TEU provides:

> The Union shall respect fundamental rights, as guaranteed by the European Convention for the Protection of Fundamental Freedoms signed in Rome .... And as they result from the constitutional traditions common to the Member States, as general principles of Community law.

Whilst the EC is not yet a signatory to the ECHR, its own EU Charter of Fundamental Rights became part of the EU Treaties on 1 December 2009.

Who benefits from free movement?

Below, we take the following approach to explaining the effect of the freedom of movement provisions:

(i)   Who benefits from EC free movement rights?
(ii)   What are those rights?
(iii)   When can those rights be removed?
(iv)   Accession State workers and the Association Agreements

EEA nationals exercising Treaty rights

The Citizens' Directive allows for an unconditional right of admission (Regulation 11) and residence for an initial period of three months (Regulation 13) for all EEA nationals and their family members. There will be an extended right to reside (Regulation 14) thereafter for students and those who have entered the UK to seek work, who are economically active as workers or self-employed, or the self-sufficient:

Those entitled to an extended right of residence are referred to in the Immigration (European Economic Area) Regulations 2006 as 'qualified persons'. The definitions are set out at regulations 4 and 6.

Those who have had a continuous right to reside for 5 years (and some others, e.g retired workers under Regulation 5) will be permanently resident (Regulation 15). Permanently residence provides a right to reside in itself (i.e. the person no longer needs to be a qualified person). Permanent residence can only be lost by an absence from the UK for a continuous period of 2 years or exclusion.

As you can see, the term 'exercising Treaty rights' will often be inadequate to accurately define the status of an EEA national or family member. A person exercising Treaty rights will have a right of admission, an initial right to reside, an extended right to reside or be permanently resident. Each type of status has different requirements and will give rise to different rights.

Qualified persons

Jobseekers

A jobseeker is defined in Regulation 6 (a very difficult provision to wade through) as a person who entered the United Kingdom in order to seek employment, or a person who is seeking employment following a period of residence in the UK in one of the other categories of qualified person. Note though that a worker who is involuntary unemployed may continue to be a worker under the provisions in Regulation 6(2), and does not therefore revert to being a jobseeker on losing their job (see 'Workers' below).

To establish a right to reside as a jobseeker, the person must be able to provide evidence that they are seeking employment and have a genuine chance of being engaged. They can remain a jobseeker for no longer than 182 days. After that period, they will lose their right to reside as a jobseeker unless they are able to show 'compelling evidence that they are continuing to seek employment and have a genuine chance of being engaged'. If the jobseeker leaves the UK at the end of the 182 day period, they will not be able to return as a job-seeker within 12 months of having left unless they can meet the 'compelling evidence' test. If they return home before they have exhausted their 182 days of job-seeking, they will have right to reside as a job-seeker on return for the remainder of the 182 days.

The 182 day period is being reduced to 91 days as from 10 November 2014, under The Immigration (European Economic Area) (Amendment) (No. 3) Regulations 2014. When combined with the initial three months of residence conferred by regulation 13 of the 2006 Regulations, a jobseeker who entered the United Kingdom in order to seek employment will be able to enjoy a right to reside for six months.

This restriction on the period a person can remain a jobseeker is designed to reduce the period EU nationals can claim unemployment benefits in the UK. Both the cut off period and the enhanced evidential burden at the end of that period are of dubious legality under EU law.

In determining whether an individual is a jobseeker or not, it is necessary to evaluate the merits of the case looking at the individual's intentions in entering the host Member State, his job seeking history vis-à-vis the labour market and his chances of getting employment: AG & Ors (EEA-jobseeker-self-sufficient person-proof) Germany [2007] UKAIT 00075.

Workers

In the case of Lawrie Blum (1986) ECR 2121 the ECJ (the predecessor to the CJEU) defined a "worker" as:

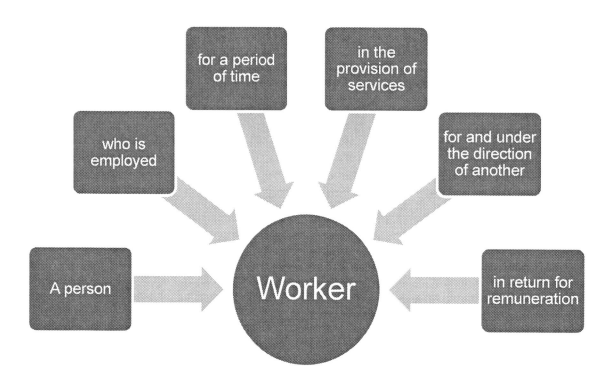

The definition is very broad indeed. The work need not be well paid nor full time so long as it is "effective and genuine" and not marginal or ancillary. If the work falls to be so defined it does not matter if the individual has to claim social assistance to top up their earnings, Article 7(2) of Regulation 1612/68 guarantees the right to do so on a non-discriminatory basis.

> **Article 7**
>
> A worker who is a national of a Member State may not, in the territory of another Member State, be treated differently from national workers by reason of his nationality in respect of any conditions of employment and work, in particular as regards remuneration, dismissal, and should he become unemployed, reinstatement or re-employment.
>
> He shall enjoy the same social and tax advantages as national workers.
>
> He shall also, by virtue of the same right and under the same conditions as national workers, have access to training in vocational schools and retraining centres.

On this basis a part-time music teacher giving 12 lessons a week topped up with Dutch Social Security payments was a worker for Community purposes and entitled to a residence permit even if he was also receiving public funds (Kempf v Staatsecretaris van justitie 1987 1 C.M.L.R 764 ECJ).

There is no minimum period an EEA citizen must work in order to be a worker.

Temporary inability to work owing to illness or accident does not cause a worker to cease being considered a worker for the purposes of EC law (Regulation 6(2)(a)). Nor does leaving a job to have a baby, and for the reasonable aftermath of childbirth (Saint Prix [2014] EUECJ C-507/12).

Under Regulation 6(2), where a person is in duly recorded involuntary unemployment after a period of employment in the UK, they remain a worker whilst they look for work, so long as they register as a jobseeker and can provide evidence that they seeking employment and have a genuine chance of being engaged. For those who had been employed for less than one year prior to losing their job, they can retain their right to reside as a worker for only 6 months. For those employed for a year or more, they can retain their status as a worker for more than 6 months, but with the heightened evidential burden of showing *compelling* evidence as for jobseekers (see above).

Under EU law (rather than under the UK's legally contentious version of it), where a person has been unemployed for 6 months, the onus shifts to them to show that they remain active in the labour market (Antonissen (Case 292/89) 26 February 1991).

A worker or self-employed person becomes permanently resident under regulation 15(1)(c) if he or she ceases activity in one of the following specified circumstances:

➤ Retirement, if resident in the UK for at least three years and working for at least a year prior to retirement and having reached state retirement age or having taken early retirement if a worker: regulation 5(2)

➤ Permanent incapacity to work, if resident in the UK for at least two years prior to this incapacity and the incapacity is the result of an accident at work or an occupational disease that entitles him or her to a pension payable in full or in part by an institution in the United Kingdom: regulation 5(3)

➤ Resident in the UK as a worker or self-employed person for at least three years and has retained a place of residence, to which he or she returns as a rule at least once a week: regulation 5(4), but also see regulation 5(5) which states that prior residence in the UK is not necessary to benefit from this provision

In addition, regulation 5(6) states that the above rules on periods of residence and activity do not apply where the person is married to or the civil partner of a UK national.

Posted workers

Some third country workers may derive rights under the provision of services rubric; because the ECJ has taken the view that companies have their own legal personality which itself deserves free movement rights. The ECJ in Van der Elst determined that an employer based in one European Economic Area ("EEA") state providing services in another, may transfer third country nationals, i.e. non-EEA nationals who are lawfully in their employment to service such contracts on a "temporary basis". Such a worker can apply for a 'Van der Elst visa'.

Self-employed persons

Article 43 Treaty of the European Union (TEU) covers those who wish to set themselves up in business or become self-employed. Article 49 TEU covers those who wish to provide or receive services.

Differentiating between employed and self-employed status is relatively straightforward. An activity is regarded as self-employed where it is carried out under an agreement with other commercial operators or consumers, but there is absent the subordination of one party or another into a relationship of salaried employment, which is the key element in the Lawrie Blum test of who is a worker (see above).

Self-employed persons who cease activity enjoy very similar protection as workers, as described above. See regulation 5 of the Immigration (EEA) Regulations 2006.

Self-sufficient persons

The self-sufficient enjoy unrestricted rights of residence for as long as they can show that they have sufficient funds not to become dependent on benefits and that they have comprehensive private health insurance (Regulation 4(1)(c) see further below).

In Chen v the United Kingdom (C-200/02; 20 October 2004), the ECJ recognised the right of a particularly youthful EU citizen (a baby only a few months old) to reside in the host Member State and to be looked after by her mother, a third country national, her primary carer, the latter of whom accordingly acquired a right of residence in order to deliver the requisite care, so long as the parent had sufficient resources for that minor not to become a burden on the public finances of the host Member State, and provided that the minor was covered by appropriate sickness insurance. The fact that the family specifically went to the Member State where the child was born for the express purpose of the child's acquiring citizenship of the Union was irrelevant to the child's right to exercise her free movement and residence in the EU.

'Chen' has now been incorporated into the EEA Regulations 2006 at regulation 15A(2), providing for a 'derivative' right of residence for the parents of a self-sufficient EU child. A Chen parent will now be entitled to a derivative residence card under regulation 18A.

The child's right to be in the UK is founded on its self-sufficiency which must, therefore pre-date its entry GM and AM (EU national; establishing self-sufficiency) France [2006] UKAIT 00059.

The self-sufficiency requirement cannot be met by the income of a parent working unlawfully in the UK, or where they are working lawfully only by reason of having 3C leave pending the conclusion of any proceedings relating to their right to reside.

Essentially, on one view, a Chen child will only have a right to reside where they are self-sufficient at the point of admission and remain so otherwise than by reliance on their parent's employment in the UK. On another view, lawful employment in the UK might sustain the child's self-sufficiency in some circumstances, where the parent's right to employment derives other than from their right to reside under Chen. This issue was discussed at length in Seye (Chen children; employment) France [2013] UKUT 178 (IAC), though was left unresolved.

Students

Those seeking to enter another Member State solely for the purposes of study must be enrolled at a recognised education establishment for the principal purpose of following a vocational training course, and must provide an assurance, in the form of a declaration or such like, that they are economically self-sufficient. They must also have comprehensive sickness insurance cover. If such an assurance is provided admission is unrestricted and there is no requirement to demonstrate means through the production of objective evidence. Spouses and children of a student also enjoy a right of entry and/or residence, but will also need to be economically self-sufficient.

EEA students studying in the UK can apply for loans to pay tuition fees and other forms of student support in some circumstances. The rules differ depending on whether the person is studying in England, Wales, Scotland or Northern Ireland. Detailed information is provided on the UKCISA website.

It is important to remember that students, whose rights are somewhat restricted under the Directive (e.g. on being joined by family members and requiring comprehensive sickness insurance cover), might also be workers or self-sufficient people without such restrictions.

Comprehensive sickness insurance cover

Under the Regulations, students (unless they are also qualified on another basis, e.g. as workers) and the self-sufficient require comprehensive sickness insurance cover (CSIC). Family members of self-sufficient EEA nationals, but not students, will also require CSIC.

The European Casework Instructions at Chapter 4 state that the Home Office will accept an EHIC card issued abroad as amounting to comprehensive sickness insurance cover, but only for those who certify themselves as being here only on temporary basis.

Where a student was issued a Registration Certificate before 20 June 2011, they will be able to apply for a document certifying permanent residence without needing to show that they have held CSIC for the relevant period (see Annex B to Chapter 6 of the European Casework Instructions)

The issue as to whether access to free NHS care amounts to comprehensive sickness insurance cover remains a moot point.

Sedley LJ in the Court of Appeal in W (China) & Anor v Secretary of State for the Home Department [2006] EWCA Civ 1494) has questioned whether this necessarily means private health insurance rather than access as of right to free NHS treatment, although the general view in the UK is that it does. In April 2012, the EU Commission started infringement proceedings against the U.K. for refusing to accept that those who are entitled to free treatment by the NHS do not need private health insurance. The Court of Appeal in Ahmad v SSHD [2014] EWCA Civ 988 remains of the view that CSIC is mandatory.

British citizens exercising Treaty rights

By a huge margin, an EEA national in the UK is generally in a better position than a UK national in the UK when it comes to the rights of their non-EEA family members. So there are clear benefits to a UK national in the UK being 'treated as holding a valid passport issued by an EEA State' (Regulation 9(4)) in this regard.

So how does a UK national in the UK become an EEA national? Essentially, by exercising their Treaty rights in the EEA and then returning to the UK.

In the case of Surinder Singh, a UK national married an Indian national living in the UK. They then spent a period of time living and working together in Germany. They later decided to relocate back to the UK. When the couple began divorce proceedings in the UK, the Home Office tried to remove Mr Singh as no longer meeting the requirements of the immigration rules. He argued before the ECJ that the right to go and work in other EEA countries must necessarily include a right to return to the UK afterwards on the same basis, and therefore that EC freedom of movement law applied to his return and re-entry, not UK immigration law. The court accepted this argument. The principle thereafter kept his name.

The Immigration (EEA) Regulations 2006 incorporate the Surinder Singh judgment (C-370/90, [1992] ECR I-4265) at Regulation 9.

Regulation 9 was amended as from 1 January 2014 to make the Surinder Singh route tougher. But a subsequent case in the CJEU, O v The Netherlands (Case C-456/12) set out principles which are inconsistent with the domestic version. Regulation 9 does not therefore conform to EEA law. So, we effectively have two versions of Surinder Singh, the lawful EU version, and the dodgy one. The EU version has primacy, of course, except for one part of Regulation 9 which is arguably more generous (relating to whether family members have to join the EEA national in the other Member state).

For the amended version of Regulation 9 to apply, the British citizen must have been residing in the EEA state as a worker or self-employed person. The EEA national's spouse or civil partner (but not other family members) must have been living with them in that EEA state. There is no minimum time limit as to how long the British citizen has to be economically active in that EEA state, but the centre of the UK national's life must have transferred there. Factors relevant to whether the centre of the UK national's life has transferred to another EEA State include;

> the period of residence in the EEA State as a worker or self-employed person;

> the location of their principal residence; and

> their degree of integration in the EEA State.

UKVI operational guidance on the new transferring the centre of life test can be found on the WhatDoTheyKnow[10] website, but has not yet made its way to the UKVI website. The test does not exist under EU law. In O v The Netherlands (Case C-456/12), the CJEU decided that;

> A residence period of three months is required (para 54)

> Weekend visits and holidays do not count as residence for this purpose (para 59)

> Any citizen of the Union exercising their Treaty rights can potentially benefit from this right, not just workers and the self-employed (references to Article 7 of Citizens Directive 2004/38 , e.g. para 56, and to Article 21 of the TFEU, e.g. para 54)

> During the period of residence family life must have been "created or strengthened" (para 51)

> Abuse is impermissible (para 58)

In order to meet the requirement under 'O' that during the period of residence in the EEA state family life must have been created or strengthened, it might be presumed, though the court did not explicitly state it to be so, that the family members that wish to join or accompany the UK national back the UK must first have spent time together with the UK national in the EEA state. That requirement only applies to spouses under the Regulations.

The interpretation of the concept of 'abuse' will be critical in cases relying on O v Netherlands. The subject of abuse in this context has been considered in detail in the Free Movement blog at http://www.freemovement.org.uk/abuse-of-eu-law-and-surinder-singh/.

---

[10] See link from the Free Movement blog article at:
http://www.freemovement.org.uk/surinder-singh-immigration-route/

Two other judgments bear mention;

In OB (EEA Regulations 2006 - Article 9(2) - Surinder Singh spouse) Morocco [2010] UKUT 420 (IAC), the Tribunal found that a 13 month gap between the UK national's end of employment in another Member state and their return to the UK did not break the link between the exercise of a treaty right and their return.

In Eind (C-291/05), the ECJ found that there was no requirement that the family member (in this case a daughter) had lived with the EU national in their home state prior to the exercise of their Treaty rights, nor that the EU national had to continue to exercise a Treaty right on their return to their own country.

Family members of qualified persons

Family members of EEA nationals who enjoy free movement rights under the Regulations include both EEA nationals that are not themselves exercising Treaty rights and non-EEA nationals. Both groups are entitled to accompany, or join and reside with an EEA national who has a right to reside in the UK.

There are two tiers of family member. They must be related as described to either the EEA national (who must have a right to reside in the UK) or to their spouse or civil partner.

The first tier (Regulation 7) comprises immediate (sometimes called 'ordinary' or 'direct') family members, described fully below. The benefit of being an immediate family member is that free movement rights are innate and can be evidenced in any suitable way, i.e. they do not rely on the possession of a particular EU entry or residence document.

The second tier is the 'extended' or 'other' family member under Regulation 8. This group benefit from the same rights of freedom of movement as immediate family members, but only if they have applied for and been granted the relevant entry or residence document. Their rights are therefore subject to a successful application (and, according to the Tribunal in AP and FP(Citizens Directive Article 3(2); discretion; dependence) India [2007] UKAIT 00048 (see more below), their substantive rights of entry are a matter of domestic legal provision alone, their European law rights being only procedural ones of extensive examination.

Ordinary family members

Family members are defined at Article 2.2 of the Citizens' Directive thus:

'Family member' means:

(a) the spouse;

(b) the partner with whom the Union citizen has contracted a registered partnership, on the basis of the legislation of a Member State, if the legislation of the host Member State treats registered partnerships as equivalent to marriage ... ;

(c) the direct descendants who are under the age of 21 or are dependants and those of the spouse or partner as defined in point (b);

(d) the dependant direct relatives in the ascending line and those of the spouse or partner as defined in point (b).

These provisions are faithfully transposed into the domestic regulations at regulation 7(1).

Note that there is no provision under Regulation 7 for unmarried partners or fiancés. They must apply under Regulation 8 as durable partners. The Immigration Rules suggest (see definition of "present and settled") that the fiancé of an EEA national who is permanently resident in the UK should apply under Appendix FM, but it must be arguable that they should treated instead as durable partners.

For students (unless also qualified on another basis e.g. as a self-sufficient person or worker) however,

> children (regardless of their age) must be dependent in order to be family members and

> there is no provision for dependent direct relatives in the ascending line.

In the case of SM (India) v Entry Clearance Officer [2009] EWCA Civ 1426, the Court of Appeal held, following the case of Jia in the ECJ, that dependency is a simple question of fact. It can be dependency of choice and need not be of necessity. This means that an enquiry is limited to whether a person is in fact dependent rather than why that person is dependent. Voluntary dependency is not therefore excluded, if for example a person chooses to give up their job to become dependent. In Lim (EEA -dependency) Malaysia [2013] UKUT 437 (IAC), the Tribunal found that a relationship of dependency could exist where a dependent has savings but chooses not to live on them.

Also following Jia, 'dependency' must be in regard to the relative's material needs, generally taken to mean financial dependency.

Free movement rights for a spouse or civil partner will not extend to a party to a marriage or civil partnership of convenience (i.e. a "sham"). In IS (marriages of convenience) Serbia [2008] UKAIT 00031 the Tribunal found that the appellant's general duty to prove his case includes a duty to prove that his marriage is not one of convenience. The later case of Papajorgji (EEA spouse - marriage of convenience) Greece [2012] UKUT 38 (IAC) made it clear though that the duty only applied where there was evidence justifying reasonable suspicion that the marriage was entered into for the predominant purpose of securing residence rights.

It is worth noting that, but for spouses and civil partners, other non-EEA family members do not have any right under EC law to be accompanied by their own family members (e.g. a non-EEA child of an EEA national does not have a right to be joined in the UK by their own non-EEA spouse unless the spouse has an ordinary or extended family relationship as defined under the Regulations with the EEA national themselves or their spouse or civil partner). They would need to rely on the UK immigration rules once they have acquired the right of permanent residence, usually after five years, or Article 8, or wider EU law principles such as non-discrimination.

Case of Metock

- Right of residence of family member not conditional on prior lawful residence in another Member State
- Need not physically accompany EU citizen from one country to another
- Does not matter if relationship post-dates entry of EU citizen

In the landmark case of Metock and Ors v Ireland (Case C-127/08) the European Court of Justice held that the right of a national of a non-member country who is a family member of a Union citizen to accompany, join or remain with that citizen cannot be made conditional on prior lawful residence in the EEA, nor can the right be said to be conditional on physically accompanying a Union citizen from one country to another. It is the exercise of the rights of free movement in the wider sense (rather than physically moving between countries) by the Union citizen that triggers the right to be accompanied by the spouse.

The Court goes on to hold specifically that a non-Community spouse of a Union citizen who accompanies or joins or seeks to remain with that citizen can benefit from the directive, irrespective of when and where their marriage took place and of how that spouse entered the host Member State. The Court further considers that it makes no difference whether nationals of non-member countries who are family members of a Union citizen have entered the host Member State before or after becoming family members of that citizen; the host Member State is, however, entitled to impose penalties, in compliance with the directive, for entry into and residence in its territory in breach of the national rules on immigration.

Those who are in the UK irregularly – even those removable under UK law and facing imminent removal – will gain a right to reside immediately on becoming a genuine family member of an EEA national (who must themselves have a right to reside in the UK).

Example

Clare is French and permanently resident in the UK. She met and married Carl here in the UK. Carl is a failed asylum seeker who entered the UK unlawfully from a 3rd country outside the EEA.

Following Metock, Carl ought to obtain residence on the basis of his relationship with Clare. The only provisions that might stop him obtaining residence would be the public policy, public security or public health clauses, which are unlikely to apply in most cases.

Other family members

The Directive provides as follows at Article 3:

1. This Directive shall apply to all Union citizens who move to or reside in a Member State other than that of which they are a national, and to their family members as defined in point 2 of Article 2 who accompany or join them.

2. Without prejudice to any right to free movement and residence the persons concerned may have in their own right, the host Member State shall, in accordance with its national legislation, facilitate entry and residence for the following persons:

(a) any other family members, irrespective of their nationality, not falling under the definition in point 2 of Article 2 who, in the country from which they have come, are dependants or members of the household of the Union citizen having the primary right of residence, or where serious health grounds strictly require the personal care of the family members by the Union citizen;

(b) the partner with whom the Union citizen has a durable relationship, duly attested.

The host Member State shall undertake an extensive examination of the personal circumstances and shall justify any denial of entry or residence to these people.

To implement this part of the Directive, the Home Office included at regulation 7(3) a provision that a person falling under regulation 8 and who has been issued with an EEA family permit, a registration certificate or a residence card would be considered a full family member.

Regulation 8, now amended to take account of Metock, is subtitled 'Extended family member' and defines the following as such:

> A relative of the EEA national, their spouse or civil partner who resides or resided in the same country, other than the United Kingdom, as the EEA national and is dependent on the EEA national, or a member of his household (see regulation 8(2) for full definition).

> A relative of the EEA national, their spouse or civil partner who on serious health grounds strictly requires the personal care of the EEA national, spouse or civil partner. The use of the word "serious" requires the "health grounds" to be well beyond ordinary ill health and as a matter of practice to require detailed medical evidence in support of any claim, reinforcing the need for personal care (regarding the daily physical tasks and needs of the person cared for) to be provided on a day to day basis: TR (regulation 8(3) EEA Regulations 2006) [2008] UKAIT 00004.

> A partner of an EEA national in a durable relationship with the EEA national. The Home Office applies a rule of thumb of two years cohabitation but at least imply in their policy (see European Casework Instructions) that this is not a prerequisite. There is no definition of 'durable' so each case can be argued on its facts. In YB (EEA reg 17(4), proper approach) Ivory Coast [2008] UKAIT 00062, the Tribunal held that national law must not seek to define terms which are Community law terms (such as "durable relationship", which does not mean, in Community law, "living together in a relationship akin to marriage which has subsisted for two years or more"). It does not even necessarily entail cohabitation (Dauhoo (EEA Regulations - reg 8(2)) Mauritius [2012] UKUT 79 (IAC) at [19])

> A relative of the EEA national, their spouse or civil partner who would meet the requirements of the adult dependent relative category in Appendix FM of the Immigration Rules. It's hard to see how this adds anything to the second category above.

The extent of the rights of extended or 'other' family members has been a matter of considerable legal controversy. Some decisions of the Upper Tribunal (IAC) though have made their plight somewhat easier.

In the case of MR and Others (EEA extended family members) Bangladesh [2010] UKUT 449 (IAC) the President of the Upper Tribunal's Immigration and Asylum Chamber referred a comprehensive range of questions to the Court of Justice of the European Union regarding the meaning, extent and application of Article 3 of the Directive. The CJEU, in SSHD v Islam & Anor [2012] EUECJ C-83/11, did little to resolve those issues, allowing a wide discretion to Member states in the criteria they use to determine how their discretion in respect of

EFMs be exercised, so long as those criteria were consistent with the normal meaning of the term 'facilitate'.

In AP and FP (Citizens Directive Article 3(2); discretion; dependence) India [2007] UKAIT 00048 the Tribunal ruled that the grant of EEA family permits is subject to the provision in Regulation 12(2)(c) – if "in all the circumstances, it appears to the entry clearance officer appropriate to issue the EEA family permit." This means that grant of the application is discretionary notwithstanding the fact that the criteria for entry are satisfied, which perhaps opens the door for the injection of criteria such as immigration history, maintenance and accommodation.

The position of the Upper Tribunal (IAC) towards Regulation 8(2) extended family members has been helpfully refined and summarised in Dauhoo (EEA Regulations - regulation 8(2)) Mauritius [2012] UKUT 79 (IAC). Regulation 8(2) provides for two categories of relative of the EEA national, his spouse or civil partner; those who were a member of the EEA national's household before coming to the UK, and those who were dependent on the EEA national. Note here that the prior membership of household or prior dependency must be in respect of the EEA national (and not their spouse or civil partner). The Tribunal found that a person can succeed in establishing that he or she is an "extended family member" under regulation 8(2) in any one of four different ways, each of which requires proving a relevant connection both prior to arrival in the UK and in the UK:

> ➤ prior dependency and present dependency
> ➤ prior membership of a household and present membership of a household
> ➤ prior dependency and present membership of a household
> ➤ prior membership of a household and present dependency

The Tribunal also confirmed that there is also no requirement to show that the EEA national and their family member were in the same country during the period of dependency.

Benefits of the exercise of Treaty rights

The key benefits of free movement laws dealt with below are as follows:

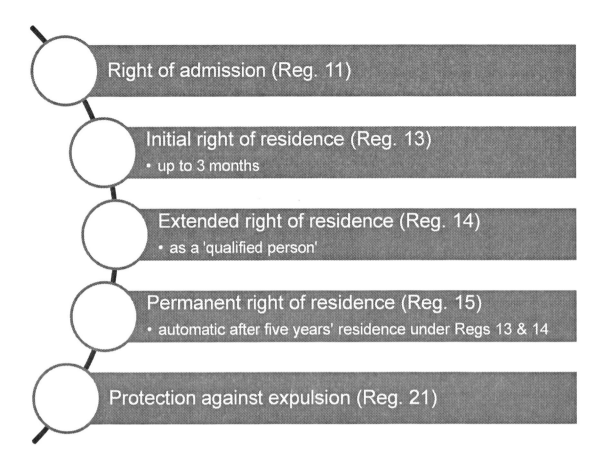

Right of admission (Reg. 11)

Initial right of residence (Reg. 13)
• up to 3 months

Extended right of residence (Reg. 14)
• as a 'qualified person'

Permanent right of residence (Reg. 15)
• automatic after five years' residence under Regs 13 & 14

Protection against expulsion (Reg. 21)

Admission

All EEA nationals and EEA family members have a right of admission (without requiring leave to enter or remain: section 7 of the Immigration Act 1988). The domestic regulations at first glance appear to require possession of a passport or valid national identity card for EEA nationals and a passport and EEA family permit, residence card or permanent residence card for family members (see regulation 11(1) and (2)). However, as should be clear from the discussion earlier regarding rights not privileges, as there is an inherent right of entry, it would be surprising if any such documentary prerequisite could be imposed. Reading on in the regulations, one indeed finds that there are alternatives to possession of the above formal documents, as the EEA national or family member must be given the opportunity to 'prove by other means' their entitlement to admission (Regulation 11(4)).

There is no requirement for the family member (whether a direct or extended family member) to have lawfully resided in another EEA state prior to entry: Metock and Bigia. Further, the family relationship with the EEA citizen need not pre-date either party's entry to the UK.

A family member wishing to travel to the UK can apply to an Entry Clearance Officer for a family permit (Regulation 12), which will considerably ease passage into the UK. The application is free and the permit must be issued as soon as possible if the person qualifies. As is discussed above in relation to the distinction between immediate and extended family members, an extended family member is subject to an extensive examination by the ECO, whereas an immediate family member need only furnish evidence of the qualifying relationship with the EEA national and of the fact that the EEA national is entitled to reside in the UK under the terms of the Directive, which includes the initial right of residence, the extended rights of residence which accrue to a qualified person, or a permanent right of residence. The Tribunal in AP and FP found "the procedure for application, reasoned refusal and right of appeal provided under our own legislation" was sufficient to count as "extensive examination".

In CO (EEA Regulations: family permit) Nigeria [2007] UKAIT 00070 the tribunal held that a family member who is unable to meet the requirements of regulation 12, or chooses not to obtain an EEA family permit, is at liberty to present himself to the Immigration Officer and prove his eligibility under regulation 11(4).

Example

Klara is German and resident in the UK. She met and married Teddy whilst on holiday in Trinidad. She wants to bring Teddy back to the UK with her at the end of her holiday.

Teddy can apply for a family permit, online, to the British High Commission in Trinidad. He does not have to. As a non-visa national, he may not find it too difficult to fly here without a visa, so can assert his right of admission on entry to the UK.

Whether applying for a family permit or seeking admission at the border without one, Teddy will need to evidence his right of admission. He will need a passport, evidence of the marriage, and that Klara is an EEA citizen currently residing in the UK as a worker.

An EU national, and accompanying family members, can exercise their right of admission purely for the purpose of a holiday in the UK. There is no requirement that they intend to at some stage to become a qualified person.

Initial right of residence

All EEA citizens and their family members enjoy what is referred to in the Immigration (EEA) Regulations 2006 as an 'initial right of residence' (regulation 13). This enables an EEA citizen to travel to the UK and reside here for three months as if he or she were a qualified person (which therefore includes being accompanied by family members) but without having to establish that he or she is yet a qualified person.

This provision enhances the possibilities of free movement around Europe by allowing for an unchallenged right to reside in order to become established (i.e. begin to earn money, start the course etc).

Extended right of residence

Qualified persons have a right to reside in the UK as long as they remain qualified persons (Regulation 14). In addition, in some circumstances, they are permitted to retain a right of residence even though their qualifying activity has ceased, as is discussed above (i.e. temporary incapacity, temporary unemployment, retirement, permanent incapacity or retention of a place of residence: regulations 5 and 6).

During 'extended right of residence', qualified persons can apply for and must immediately be granted a Registration Certificate on production of a valid identity card or passport plus proof that the person is a qualified person (regulation 16). The application is made on form EEA1 and costs £55.00. This certificate is not necessary and it merely evidences the right, it does not create it. Nevertheless, such certificates can be useful, particularly for EEA citizens likely to be travelling in and out of the UK who might otherwise suffer the inconvenience of regular questioning by HM Immigration Officers.

Similarly, the right to extended residence for family members is set out at regulation 14. However, the document to evidence their status and right of residence is referred to as a residence card, the details of which are set out at regulation 17. The application is made on form EEA2 and costs £55.00.

Qualified persons can carry out qualifying activities and must not be subject to any form of discrimination compared to the national workforce. This means that rights to benefits and other advantages enjoyed by the national workforce have to be enjoyed in equal measure.

As long as a family member falls within the definitions of family members set out in the Citizens' Directive and transposed into national law by the Immigration (EEA) Regulations 2006, that family member has a right to reside in the UK with the qualified person. There are no additional limitations relating to maintenance and accommodation, intention to live permanently with the other or subsisting marriage. The family members of qualified persons enjoy the same rights to take up activities in Member States.

The children of nationals of a Member State who are or who have been employed in the territory of another Member State are entitled to that State's general educational, apprenticeship and vocational training courses under the same conditions as a national.

These rights have to be respected in an extremely proactive way by Member States. The rights are derived from the Treaty and are innate, meaning that it is for Member States to protect and promote these rights as far as possible. For example, when an EEA citizen or family member enters a Member State, the authorities must merely check that their documents are in order. The authorities are not entitled to ask further questions about intention, availability of funds, sponsors or the like – although, so long as they have a reasonable belief that there may be grounds for it, they may investigate exclusion on the grounds of public policy, public security or public health.

Example

Anya is German and has been working in the UK for two years. She has never applied for a registration certificate. Nevertheless, by virtue of her work, she has automatically acquired a right to reside.

Herman is Canadian. He entered the UK as a visitor and overstayed his visa. He married Anya a year ago but has done nothing about his immigration status since then. Nevertheless, he has automatically acquired a right of reside by virtue of his family relationship with Anya and Anya's position as a qualified person. Herman can apply for a residence card if he wants to but he does not have to. After five years of marriage he will automatically acquire a right to reside permanently, presuming Anya retains her right to reside for that period, whether or not he applies for the relevant paperwork.

Permanent residence

Under the Regulations (Regulation 15), EEA citizens and family members automatically acquire a permanent right of residence in the UK after five years continuous residence in accordance with the Regulations (i.e. with a right to reside other than a Derivative right to reside).

Also acquiring permanent residence under Regulation 15 will be;

➤ a worker or self-employed person who has ceased activity (defined under Regulation 5), and their family members; and
➤ family members of a worker or self-employed person who has died, where the family member resided with him immediately before his death, and where he had lived in the UK for at least the two years immediately before his death or the death was the result of an accident at work or an occupational disease

Continuity of residence is not broken by periods of absence from the UK for six months or less per year, absence due to military service, or one absence not exceeding twelve months for an important reason (e.g. child birth, serious illness, study or an overseas posting) (Regulation 3).

Residence under previous Directives will count towards permanent residence (Schedule 4: Transitional Provisions of the Regulations).

The right of permanent residence, which in all respects is equivalent to ILR, brings with it enhanced protection from removal, as is discussed below. A permanently resident person, whether an EEA national or a family member, will have that status unconditionally. It will not depend on whether the EEA national remains a qualified person or not, or whether the non-EEA family member remains a family member of the EEA national.

As under U.K. law, permanent residence will lapse with two years continuous absence from the U.K. (Regulation 15(2)).

An EEA citizen can apply for a Document Certifying Permanent Residence (form EEA3) and the non-EEA family member, a Permanent Residence Card (form EEA4), both £55.00, issued under Regulation 18. This is not necessary but may prove to be convenient.

Evidencing permanent residence is not always easy. An EEA national may have had periods of economic inactivity in the relevant five year period, through illness, childbirth or unemployment, or through none of those things. Careful attention must be had to Regulations 4 – 15 to ensure the relevant provisions are met throughout the period and are fully evidenced.

The non-EEA family member's application will depend on the evidence that the EEA national had a continuous right to reside in the UK during the same five year period; and that the family relationship, including where necessary, financial dependency, continued throughout; or on establishing a retained right of residence (see below) for some of the period.

The Home Office will require substantial evidence to support an application for a permanent residence document, essentially requiring clients to prove their case to the criminal standard, or go to appeal. Little authoritative case law comes from the CJEU on rights of residence, the court being weary of seeming to bind member states to detailed rules covering every eventuality, and much of the law in this area therefore remains subject to aregument.

Retained rights of residence

In some circumstances, family members of EEA citizens might acquire independent rights of admission or residence in the UK where they have lost their family connection to the EEA national of whom they were a family member, by e.g. death, divorce, or the EEA national leaving the UK.

As an example, in the case of Baumbast [2002] EUECJ C-413/99 (17 September 2002), an EEA citizen had been living and working in the UK but then returned to his own country. In the meantime, his wife and child had effectively settled in the UK and the child was attending an educational course. The mother did not want to leave the UK. The ECJ held that the child had acquired a right to reside in the UK to pursue their education and, in addition, that this right would be ineffective if the child's mother was not permitted to remain in the UK to care for the child.

These rights have been enshrined in the Regulations in the form of 'retained rights' (regulation 10) and 'derivative rights' (regulation 15A). We consider derivative rights in the next section.

In the following situations, the family member will have retained their rights of residence despite ceasing to be the family member of a qualified person:

➢ Where the qualified person dies but the family member has resided in the UK for at least one year and is either him or herself employed, self-employed or self-sufficient or is the family member of such a person (i.e. the child or dependent relative) (regulation 10(2))

➢ Where the family member is the child of qualified person who has died or left the UK where the family member has been attending an educational course (or the child of the qualified person's spouse or civil partner in the same circumstances) (regulation 10(3))

➢ Where the family member is a parent with actual custody of a child as described immediately above (regulation 10(4))

➢ Where the family member ceased to be a family member of a qualified person on the termination of the marriage or civil partnership of the qualified person and was residing in the UK under the Directive at that time and is him or herself employed, self-employed or self-sufficient (or is the family member of such a person, i.e. the child or dependent relative) and either:

  ▪ prior to the initiation of the proceedings for the termination of the marriage or the civil partnership the marriage or civil partnership had lasted for at least three years and the parties to the marriage or civil partnership had resided in the United Kingdom for at least one year during its duration (regulation 10(5)(d)(i)), or

  ▪ the former spouse or civil partner of the qualified person has custody of a child of the qualified person (regulation 10(5)(d)(ii)), or

  ▪ the former spouse or civil partner of the qualified person has the right of access to a child of the qualified person under the age of 18 and a court has ordered that such access must take place in the United Kingdom (regulation 10(5)(d)(iii)); or

  ▪ the continued right of residence in the United Kingdom of the person is warranted by particularly difficult circumstances, such as he or another family member having been a victim of domestic violence while the marriage or civil partnership was subsisting (regulation 10(5)(d)(iv)).

It is important to note that the spouse (this also applies to civil partners) of an EEA citizen continues to be a spouse and a family member as long as the marriage legally persists. Separation does not dissolve this relationship for the purposes of EC law, nor does a decree nisi. It is only when a decree absolute has been issued that the relationship is considered no longer to qualify (Diatta v Land Berlin 1986 2 CMLR 164).

As well as being difficult to construe legally, these Regulation 10 provisions often give rise to evidential problems for those family members who need to establish the whereabouts and activity of the relevant EEA national to show they have retained rights. Where, for instance, the person claiming a retained right of residence is relying on their divorce from the EEA national, they will need to show that they continued to have a right to reside up until the date of the decree absolute (or they will have nothing to retain). If they have lost contact with their ex-spouse, or the ex-spouse refuses to assist them, it will be difficult to provide evidence that their ex-spouse was in the UK with a right to reside on the relevant date. They will need to do everything they can to find that evidence, up to and including the hiring of a private detective, but what if their efforts draw a blank?

The Tribunal has found that the burden of proof on establishing that the qualified person has left the UK lies upon the applicant, not the government: MJ and others (Art.12 Regulation 1612/68, self-sufficiency?) [2008] UKAIT 00034. The same applies to the question as to whether the EEA national is exercising his Treaty rights on the date of the decree absolute. In Amos v SSHD [2011] EWCA Civ 552 the Court of Appeal agreed that the burden does rest with the claimant but left open the possibility that the Home Office might assist a claimant if requested to do so or if directed to do so by the tribunal. Under s.40(1)(j) of the UK Borders Act 2007, the Home Office has the power to obtain a person's National Insurance and other HMRC records if desired. Home Office policy is to generally refuse to assist the applicant in evidencing the position of the EEA national, unless there has been domestic violence, but they will do so in the event a Direction is issued by the Tribunal.

So it may be necessary to make an application for a residence or permanent residence card that is bound to fail for lack of evidence, but then to apply to the First-tier Tribunal for a Direction in the appeal that the Home Office provide any information that they have access to as to the whereabouts and activities of the EEA national.

Examples

Robert and Steve became civil partners in the Netherlands six years ago. Robert is South African and Steve is Dutch. They lived in the Netherlands for two years and came to the UK four years ago when Steve was posted to the UK by the oil company he works for. The two of them have now separated and are going to dissolve their civil partnership. As long as Robert is employed, self-employed or self-sufficient, and continues to have a right to reside up to the point that the civil partnership is finally dissolved, he can choose to remain in the UK after this occurs if he wants to, as the situation falls within regulation 10(5)(d)(i). He will retain his right of residence.

Proving that Robert has a right to reside on the date of the dissolution will entail proving Steve has a right to reside on that date as well. Hopefully, Steve will assist him with that!

Marie and Peter were married four years ago. Marie is French and Peter is from Cameroon. Marie was already living and working in the UK when they got married and Peter came to the UK directly. They have one child, Cecile, who is four years old and has just started attending school. Marie now wants to return to France but Peter does not want to leave his part-time job in the UK and he wants Cecile to grow up in the UK. They decide to separate and Marie returns to France, leaving Peter to care for Cecile in the UK. Cecile will retain a right of residence under regulation 10(3) and Peter will retain his right of residence under regulation 10(4). In addition, it appears that both Cecile and Peter will soon qualify for a permanent right of residence in the UK.

Derivative right of residence

Further to the decisions in;

➢ Chen [2004] EUECJ C-200/02,

➢ Ibrahim [2010] EUECJ C-310/08 and Teixeira [2010] EUECJ C-480/08, and

➢ Ruiz Zambrano [2011] EUECJ C-34/09,

the Immigration (European Economic Area) Regulations 2006 were amended (twice) in 2012 to include a new derivative right to reside. The new provisions are at regulation 15A. A person with a derivative right to reside under regulation 15A will be entitled to apply for a derivative residence card under regulation 18A.

Those entitled to a derivative residence card are;

➢ The primary carer of a self-sufficient EEA national child (i.e. Chen)

➢ A child of an EEA national who resided in the United Kingdom at a time when the EEA national parent was residing in the United Kingdom as a worker; and Is in education in the United Kingdom and was in education there at a time when the EEA national parent was in the United Kingdom (i.e. Teixeira and Ibrahim)

➢ The primary carer of the above

➢ The primary carer of a British citizen who would be unable to reside in the UK if the primary carer were required to leave (Ruiz Zambrano)

> ➤ The siblings of the Chen, Teixeira and Ibrahim, and Ruiz Zambrano children

The regulations require the relevant children and their to be under 18, which is contentious as generally under EC law a child is considered to be under 21.

To understand these provisions it is helpful to understand the cases that gave birth to them.

Chen

We have already looked at the case of Chen (see above under 'Self-sufficient persons'). The non-EEA parent(s) of a self-sufficient EEA national child will have a derivative right of residence under regulation 15A(2), and any non-EEA siblings of the child will have the same right under regulation 15A(5).

Teixeira and Ibrahim

In the cases of Teixeira and Ibrahim, the Appellants had initially applied to their local authorities for housing under the UK's homelessness legislation. Ms Teixeira was a Portuguese woman living in the UK, had worked here previously, but was not working at the relevant time. Ms Ibrahim was a Somali national, whose Danish husband had worked in the UK but had then stopped work and later left the country. Both had children in the UK in school. The local authorities made decisions in both cases that the mothers did not have a right to reside in the UK, and therefore no right to housing. It was those decisions which eventually arrived at the CJEU. It was accepted that neither the children nor their parents met the requirements of regulation 10 (retained rights) as they had not lost their right to reside as a result of their parents dying or leaving the UK. It was the case rather that they had lost their right to reside on Ms Teixeira and Mr Ibrahim ceasing to work as they were no longer qualified persons and had not become permanently resident.

In both cases, the mothers relied on the fact that their children were the children of EEA nationals who had worked in the UK, and were education. They relied directly on Article 12 of Regulation No 1612/68 which continued to have effect notwithstanding the entry into force of Directive 2004/38. Article 12 provided;

> 'The children of a national of a Member State who is or has been employed in the territory of another Member State shall be admitted to that State's general educational, apprenticeship and vocational training courses under the same conditions as the nationals of that State, if such children are residing in its territory.
>
> Member States shall encourage all efforts to enable such children to attend these courses under the best possible conditions.'

Similar arguments had succeeded in Baumbast (see above), but in that case the parents were self-sufficient. In allowing the appeals of Ms Teixeira and Ms Ibrahim, it was expressly stated that in order to confer on a child a right of residence it is only required that he has lived with his parents or either one of them in a Member State while at least one of them resided there as a worker; a parent caring for the child of a migrant worker who is in education in the host Member State has a right of residence in that State and that right is not conditional on the parent having sufficient resources not to become a burden on the social assistance system.

The derivative right to reside pursuant to the principles in Teixeira and Ibrahim are at regulation 15A(3) for the children in education, and at regulation 15A(4) for their parent(s).

Education excludes nursery education, but includes attendance in a reception class (Shabani v SSHD (EEA - jobseekers; nursery education) [2013] UKUT 315).

To meet the requirements of regulation 15A(3), it is not necessary for the child to have been in school at the time the EEA national parent was working in the UK (Ahmed (Amos; Zambrano; reg 15A(3)(c) 2006 EEA Regs) [2013] UKUT 00089 (IAC)).

Ruiz Zambrano

Until the case of *Ruiz Zambrano v Belgium*, immigration lawyers were entirely focused on free movement provisions within EC law as provided for by the Citizens' Directive. In *Ruiz Zambrano*, though, a Belgian social security tribunal referred to the CJEU the question of whether the *citizenship* provisions of EC law might also impart the right of residence and the right to work to citizens of the EU and indirectly to their third country national family members.

The judgment of the Court is brief and it seems likely that there was disagreement between the judges on the reasons the Court should give. The judgment relies entirely on Article 20 TFEU, which provides as follows:

> 1. Citizenship of the Union is hereby established. Every person holding the nationality of a Member State shall be a citizen of the Union. Citizenship of the Union shall be additional to and not replace national citizenship.
>
> 2. Citizens of the Union shall enjoy the rights and be subject to the duties provided for in the Treaties. They shall have, inter alia:
>
> (a)　　the right to move and reside freely within the territory of the Member States...

Mr Ruiz Zambrano and his wife had arrived in Belgium as asylum seekers from Colombia, but failed in their asylum applications and ostensibly had no further claim to reside in Belgium. However, two of their children were born in Belgium and through a quirk (now historic) of Belgian nationality law were born as Belgian citizens and also therefore citizens of the EU. Neither child had resided anywhere except Belgium and neither child had exercised any Treaty rights (employment, self-employment, etc), so they were unable to benefit from conventional free movement law and the Citizens' Directive.

The court held that the children had a right to reside in Belgium by virtue of Article 20 TFEU, even though they had not moved within the EU; that there is a right to reside that is independent of the right to move freely. The Court also held Mr and Mrs Ruiz Zambrano, the parents and carers of the children, must be given a right to reside in Belgium and a right to work to support their children. Without the parents having such rights, the children's right of residence in the EU would not be effective as they were too young to look after themselves.

The ground-breaking principle in Ruiz Zambrano has been considered further by the CJEU and UK courts, with nearly 100 such judgments listed on BAILII. The principle has been found to apply only in limited circumstances; the key issue being whether the EU citizen will be denied the genuine enjoyment of the substance of the rights conferred by virtue of his status as a citizen of the Union if a parent or carer is not entitled to live with them in the EU (see e.g. Dereci [2011] EUECJ C-256/11). The principle is not about family unity, so where the EU citizen has a parent or carer entitled to live in the EU, the provision will not give rights to other parent. For instance, where a father is refused entry to the UK, or is facing deportation to a country outside the EU, that in itself will not deny the children a right to live in the EU if someone else is available to care for them (Sanade and others (British children - Zambrano - Dereci) India [2012] UKUT 48 (IAC)). Whether there is any other person able to care for the dependent EU citizen in the EU will be a question of fact. Whether Article 8 rights apply to the situation is an entirely separate legal argument.

The derivative right to reside for the parent or carer pursuant to the principle in Ruiz Zambrano is at regulation 15A(4A).

Notwithstanding the wording of regulation 15A(4A), Ruiz Zambrano has potential application where the child in the UK is a citizen of another EEA country: the test in all cases is whether the adverse decision would require the child to leave the territory of the Union (Ahmed (Amos; Zambrano; reg 15A(3)(c) 2006 EEA Regs) [2013] UKUT 00089 (IAC)).

Ruiz Zambrano and Appendix FM

Many cases which might succeed under regulation 15A(4A), or might not in the light of later case law, may well meet the requirements of the Parent of a child in the U.K. category under Appendix FM. Where the applicant has a genuine parental relationship with a British citizen child, Section EX: Exception will apply, and the only requirement to meet will be in respect of 'suitability'. It is Home Office policy to consider Parent applications under both EU and UK law. That can cause problems to applicants where the application is rejected under EU law by the European Caseworking team, with an appealable decision being made, prior to the application being considered in a different section under UK law. Common sense would suggest that the two decisions be made simultaneously and served together.

General considerations

Where reference is made in paragraph 15A to the 'primary carer' of a person, that term is defined in Regulation 15A(7). A 'primary carer' may be a person with sole or primary responsibility for providing care, or a person who shares responsibility for that person's care with one other person who is not an exempt person. An 'exempt person' is defined in Regulation 15A(6)(c) as one has a right to reside under any other provision of the Regulations, or is a British citizen or settled in the UK. So essentially, a derivative right to reside is for a single parent, or both parents where they both require a derivative right to stay in the UK. Where care is shared with a person who is a British citizen, a settled person, or has a right to reside under other provisions in the Regulations, the parent with no right to reside or leave will not have a derivative right to reside. The presumption will be that the child will be able to remain in the UK with that the exempt parent. The other parent will have to find another route to enter or stay in the UK, possibly under the parent or partner provisions in Appendix FM or outside the rules.

Regulations 11 and 12 provide for a right of admission and a right to a family permit for those who benefit from a derivative right of residence.

Those with a derivative right to reside are excluded from becoming permanently resident (regulation 15(1A)). At the point where the child reaches the age of 18, or in the case of regulation 15A(4A) is able to live independently, the parents/carers will lose their right to reside.

Ruiz Zambrano and Chen parents will be denied recourse to public funds, under revised benefits regulations. Teixeira and Ibrahim parents however will be entitled to recourse to public funds.

When considering derivative rights for a parent, particularly in a case where the person does not appear to meet the exacting requirements of Regulation 15A or of the partner category in Appendix FM, it will be useful to remember the provision in s117B(6) of the 2002 Act which states that the public interest does not require the parent's removal where they have a genuine and subsisting parental relationship with a qualifying child, and it would not be reasonable to expect the child to leave the United Kingdom. Where such an argument succeeds on Article 8 grounds, the parent will be entitled to leave under UK law. That may be preferable both in providing the parent with a possible route to settlement, and with the possibility of claiming public funds.

Dual nationals and McCarthy

The Court of Justice of the European Union returned to the issue of EU citizenship shortly after Ruiz Zambrano, in the case of McCarthy v United Kingdom (Case C-434/09) Once again, the reasoning of the Court is virtually non-existent, which makes it very difficult to extract transferable or general legal principles from the case.

Mrs McCarthy in this case was a British citizen who married a foreign national with no immigration status. She was not a worker and she had never exercised her free movement rights to reside in another EEA state. Mrs McCarthy had Irish heritage and applied for and received recognition as an Irish citizen. She argued that as an Irish citizen in the U.K, regardless of the fact that she was also a British citizen, she should have the benefit of free movement rights, entitling her husband to a right to reside,

The Court held that in this case the refusal to grant residence to Mr McCarthy did not have the effect of depriving Mrs McCarthy of the genuine enjoyment of the substance of the rights conferred by virtue of her status as a Union citizen. The Court does not really explain why there is no genuine interference, though. It was at least arguable that Mrs McCarthy was going to have to leave the UK in order to reside with her husband, and that this was comparable to the effect on the Ruiz Zambrano children.

The principle in McCarthy, that a British citizen in the UK who is a dual national of another EEA Member cannot rely on that other nationality to invoke Treaty rights, has now been implemented in U.K. law by way of the Immigration (European Economic Area) (Amendment) Regulations 2012 (see definition of 'EEA national' in Regulation 2).

It is more than arguable though that the implementation of McCarthy under the Regulations goes much further than the judgment allows. It denies Treaty rights to all UK/EEA dual nationals in the UK. In doing so, were it lawful, it would take away those rights from an EEA citizen in the UK who had come to the UK to exercise their Treaty rights in the UK and then naturalises as a British citizen. One consequence would be that their family members would also lose their right to reside. Unlike Mrs McCarthy, that person would have exercised their Treaty rights and cannot be prejudiced by gaining a new nationality.

Accession countries

Between 1 May 2004, when they joined the European Union, and 1 May 2011, nationals of the Czech Republic, Estonia, Hungary, Latvia, Lithuania, Poland, Slovakia and Slovenia were required to register in the UK under the Workers Registration Scheme for the first 12 months of their employment. In all other respects they enjoyed free movement rights.

Two further countries, Bulgaria and Romania, (the 'A2') then joined the EU on 1 January 2007 and, again, were not immediately granted full access to the UK labour market. They were treated even less generously than the A8 countries, restricting those entitled to be employed in the UK to those granted work permits.

The restrictions on A8 and A2 nationals no longer exist as the maximum period the UK could apply them was for 7 years from the date of their country's accession. Failure to comply with those restrictions however may still have implications for A8 and A2 nationals who are seeking permanent residence documentation from the Home Office.

Croatia joined the EU on 1 July 2013. Their nationals have free movement rights but, unless they are exempt, will require sponsorship under the Tiers 2 or 5 of the PBS for the first 12 months of their employment in the UK. The accession rules for Croatian workers and their family members are in the Accession of Croatia (Immigration and Worker Authorisation) Regulations 2013. The sponsored Croatian will not need to apply for visas or extensions under the PBS, but will require a Certificate of Sponsorship reference number and a purple registration.

Modernised guidance for Croatians is at:
https://www.gov.uk/government/collections/eea-swiss-nationals-and-ec-association-agreements-modernised-guidance

Association Agreements

Association Agreements are signed between the EU and third countries, usually states interested in becoming members. All of the Accession States had entered into EC Association Agreements before joining. The only current agreement with meaningful immigration consequences is now with Turkey.

The EU-Turkey Association Agreement gives self-employed persons a right to establish themselves in business in the EEA, and allows for some Turkish workers lawfully employed in the UK to extend their stay to continue their employment. The idea is to promote integration of the economy prior to full membership.

The Turkish agreement, often referred to as the Ankara Agreement, was signed between Turkey and the EEC before Britain joined in 1973. The effect of the agreement is that the UK cannot impose additional restrictions on workers or the self-employed over and above those that were in place in 1973. This is by virtue of the 'standstill' clause of the agreement. This subject is explored in more detail below.

Application forms

Although there is no requirement for an application form to be used, the Home Office has issued forms that can conveniently be used to make applications:

> Form EEA1 can be used by an EEA or Swiss national to apply for a registration certificate (Regulation 16)

> Form EEA2 can be used by a non-EEA or non-Swiss national family member of an EEA or Swiss national to apply for a residence card (Regulation 17)

> Form EEA3 can be used by an EEA or Swiss national to apply for a document certifying permanent residence (Regulation 18)

377

> ➤ Form EEA4 can be used by a non-EEA or non-Swiss national family member of an EEA or Swiss national to apply for permanent residence.

> ➤ DRF1 for a Derivative Residence Card

> ➤ Various CR forms for Croatians and their family member

> ➤ Various ECAA forms for the Turkish Association Agreement

Applications for these documents now cost £55.00.

Family permits remain free. The application will normally be made on line, but if a hard copy application is made, it will be on form VAF5.

Excluding and removing EEA nationals from UK

Ceasing to be qualified

A person who no longer satisfies the requirements of the Regulations ceases to have a right to reside and faces possible removal, though must not be removed as the automatic consequence of having recourse to the social assistance system of the United Kingdom (Regulation 19).

EEA nationals are rarely removed though under this provision as they would simply be able to return to the UK. Recent the amendments to Regulation 6, designed to lock out indigent EEA nationals for a period of 12 months, are of dubious legality though currently remain untested.

Non-EEA family members who lose their right to reside will need to find a route under UK law or Article 8 if they want to stay in the UK.

Public policy removals and exclusions

The Citizens' Directive enhanced the protection afforded to EEA citizens and their family members. The Secretary of State may refuse to issue, revoke or refuse to renew a registration certificate, a residence card, and a document certifying permanent residence or a permanent residence card if the refusal or revocation is justified on grounds of public policy, public security or public health. Similarly, an Immigration Officer may revoke a family permit on a person's arrival in the UK on the same grounds.

Under regulation 21, different periods of residence are rewarded with different levels of protection against expulsion:

Children under 18
- Imperative grounds of public security
- Unless decision is in child's best interests

10 years +
- EEA nationals only
- Imperative grounds of public security

Permanent residence
- Serious grounds of public policy or public security

1st five years or on initial entry
- Grounds of public policy, public security, public health

Note that there are two ways in which the protection given by EEA law is enhanced with the length of stay in the UK: there is firstly a narrowing of the grounds, from "public policy, public security or public health", to "public policy and public security", to "public security" alone; secondly there is a raising of the threshold, from bare "grounds", to "serious grounds", to "imperative grounds".

The thorny question as to whether and to what extent residence in prison counts as residence for the purposes of determining which of the regulation 21 legal tests applies continues to be batted around the courts with none coming up with an authoritative conclusion. The issue was considered by the Court of Appeal in Secretary of State for the Home Department v FV (Italy) [2012] EWCA Civ 1199. The court held that in determining whether accrued residence rights are lost by virtue of a period of absence or imprisonment, the test to be applied is an integration test. A period of imprisonment does not of itself prevent a person accruing ten years residence and therefore engaging the imperative grounds of public security test. Similarly, once ten years of residence has been acquired, a period of imprisonment does not necessarily cause the person to lose the safeguard against deportation. The Court opined obiter that a period of imprisonment would disrupt the acquisition of permanent residence, but makes clear that once permanent residence is acquired it will not be lost through a period of imprisonment. This view was upheld by the Tribunal in Essa (EEA: rehabilitation/integration) [2013] UKUT 00316 (IAC).

As is made clear though in MG (prison-Article 28(3) (a) of Citizens Directive) [2014] UKUT 392 (IAC), the latest word on the issue, the case law conflicts in its approach to this question and the conflict remains to be resolved.

The meaning of "imperative grounds of public security" awaits resolution. Although in MG and VG Ireland [2006] UKAIT 00053 it was said that the Secretary of State's considered view was that the phrase "public security" was directed to the risk of "terrorist offences", by the time of LG (Italy) v Secretary of State for the Home Department [2008] EWCA Civ 190 (18 March 2008)) it was noted that "Public security" was not to be equated with "national security", and that the words might equate to a "risk to the safety of the public or a section of the public". However in any event there was a need to show an actual risk to public security, so compelling that it justifies the exceptional course of removing someone who has become "integrated" by "many years" residence in the host state. That test was not met in regard to an Appellant sentenced to 8 years imprisonment for manslaughter in the case of SSHD v FV (Italy) [2012] EWCA Civ 1199.

Regardless of which test is to be applied, the following factors must be considered when reaching any decision based on public policy, public security or public health:

➢ the decision must comply with the principle of proportionality

➢ the decision must be based exclusively on the personal conduct of the person concerned

➢ the personal conduct of the person concerned must represent a genuine, present and sufficiently serious threat affecting one of the fundamental interests of society

➢ matters isolated from the particulars of the case or which relate to considerations of general prevention do not justify the decision

➢ a person's previous criminal convictions do not in themselves justify the decision

➢ in public policy and public security (not public health) cases, account must also be taken of considerations such as the age, state of health, family and economic situation of the person, the person's length of residence in the United Kingdom, the person's social and cultural integration into the United Kingdom and the extent of the person's links with his country of origin.

In GW (EEA regulation 21: "fundamental interests") Netherlands [2009] UKAIT 00050 the tribunal held that the term 'fundamental interests' of a society is a question to be determined by reference to the legal rules governing the society in question, and that it is unlikely that conduct that is subject to no prohibition can be regarded as threatening those interests. The case concerned the attempt by the Secretary of State to exclude Geert Wilders from visiting the UK on the grounds of his unpleasant views about Islam. Mr Wilder's appeal was upheld.

A person who is subject to an attempted exclusion has the same legal remedies in respect of any decision concerning entry, or refusing the issue or renewal or a residence permit, or ordering expulsion from the territory, as are available to nationals of the State concerned in respect of acts of the administration. Additional procedural guarantees are provided for in specific cases (e.g. where there is no right of appeal to a court of law, or where the appeal cannot have a suspensive effect, etc.).

Any national of a Member State who wishes to seek employment in another Member State may re-apply for a residence permit, even after having previously been expelled or refused.

Rights of appeal

EEA decisions, as defined in Regulation 2 below, attract a right of appeal under Regulation 26. Until the appeal provisions of the Immigration Act 2014 come into force, the available grounds of appeal are those in section 84 of the 2002 Act (i.e. as for those with a right of appeal under UK law). EU law grounds may also be raised in a s82 appeal against a decision made under UK law.

> "EEA decision" means a decision under these Regulations that concerns—
>
> (a) a person's entitlement to be admitted to the United Kingdom;
>
> (b) a person's entitlement to be issued with or have renewed, or not to have revoked, a registration certificate, residence card, derivative residence card, document certifying permanent residence or permanent residence card;
>
> (c) a person's removal from the United Kingdom; or
>
> (d) the cancellation, pursuant to regulation 20A, of a person's right to reside in the United Kingdom;
>
> but does not include decisions under regulations 24AA (human rights considerations and interim orders to suspend removal) or 29AA (temporary admission in order to submit case in person)

To establish a right of appeal under the Regulations, a person claiming to be an EEA national must produce a valid national identity card or passport issued by an EEA State, and a person claiming to be the family member or relative of an EEA national must produce evidence of that relationship.

Appeals under the Regulations are from abroad where the decision is:

➢ to refuse to admit him to the United Kingdom;

➢ to make an exclusion order against him

➢ refuse to revoke a deportation order made against him;

> to refuse to issue him with an EEA family permit;

> to revoke, or to refuse to issue or renew any document under these Regulations where that decision is taken at a time when the relevant person is outside the United Kingdom; or

> to remove him from the United Kingdom after he has entered or sought to enter the United Kingdom in breach of a deportation order (unless asylum or human rights grounds are raised, and not certified: regulation 27(3)).

However such appeals can still be brought "in country", despite being of the nature just described, where:

> the person held an EEA family permit, a registration certificate, a residence card, a document certifying permanent residence or a permanent residence card on his arrival in the United Kingdom or can otherwise prove that he is resident in the United Kingdom;

> the person is deemed not to have been admitted to the United Kingdom under regulation 22(3) but at the date on which notice of the decision to refuse to admit him is given he has been in the United Kingdom for at least 3 months;

> the person is in the United Kingdom and a ground of the appeal is that, in taking the decision, the decision maker acted in breach of his rights under the Human Rights Convention or the Refugee Convention, unless the Secretary of State certifies that that ground of appeal is clearly unfounded.

The procedures are those applying to the immigration tribunal generally.

Where the SSHD certifies that the decision under challenge was taken 'wholly or partly' in the interests of national security or relations with a foreign State the right of appeal lays to the Special Immigration Appeals Commission (regulation 28).

Additionally, the SSHD may bar reliance on particular grounds of appeal by certifying that the ground had been previously considered (regulation 26(5)).

The Ankara Agreement

Under the European Community Association Agreement (ECAA) with Turkey, the 'Ankara Agreement', a Turkish national may apply to enter or stay in the UK to establish and run a business, and in some circumstances for an extension of stay to continue employment in the UK.

The Ankara Agreement is the oldest Association Agreement, dating back to 1963, with an Additional Protocol of 1970. The rights granted to Turkish nationals are not reflected either in the Immigration Rules or in the Immigration (European Economic Area) Regulations 2006 and anybody seeking to benefit from them will therefore have to refer directly to EC law and the provisions of the ECAA.

However to the extent that the Ankara Agreement and its Protocol themselves refer to the free movement of workers provisions in the EC Treaty itself, interpretation of the Ankara is guided by the ECJ's extensive jurisprudence on free movement of EC workers. Article 12 of the Ankara Agreement states:-

> The Contracting Parties agree to be guided by Articles 48, 49 and 50 of the Treaty establishing the Community for the purpose of abolishing restrictions on freedom of establishment between them.

The Additional Protocol includes a so-called "stand-still" provision which has the effect of requiring Member States, including the United Kingdom, not to introduce any new restrictions, after its entry into force in 1973, on the rights of Turkish nationals to set up in business as self-employed persons. Although it does not provide the Turkish national with a directly effective right of establishment (as is enjoyed by EEA nationals) it means that the Immigration Rules that should be applied to them are not those in force now but, in effect, the Immigration Rules in force in 1973, which imposed much less stringent requirements on being allowed to set up in business (see further: Self-Employed, below).

Workers

The rights of Turkish workers are laid down in a Decision of the Association Council, Decision 1/80 (unpublished). This provides Turkish workers who have been in 'legal employment' in a Member State for a certain period of time with a right to have their permission to work renewed and to have their right of residence renewed in line with the right to work.

The rights provided for in Article 6(1) only benefit those workers who fulfil the requirements in terms of legal employment, belonging to the labour force and time. These are the requirements:

➢ He is a worker and legally employed

➢ He is duly registered as belonging to the labour force

➢ He has been legally employed for one of three possible time periods.

A worker and legally employed

"Turkish worker" connotes the Community law definition. The requirement that the worker is legally employed within the territory of the Member State does not necessarily presuppose the possession of residence documents or even a work permit. The legality of employment is determined in the light of the legislation of the Member State governing the conditions under which the Turkish worker entered the national territory and is employed there. The worker cannot be working in breach of any legal conditions of stay or have entered on false documentation and thereby entered into employment as the result of fraudulent conduct.

The legality of employment "presupposes a stable and secure situation". There must be an undisputed right of residence, for any dispute as to that right leads to an instability in the worker's situation. Working pending an appeal against refusal of a residence permit is not sufficient, unless the appeal ultimately succeeds. This means that a Turkish worker needs prior leave to remain in order to set off their Ankara rights.

In Payir and Ozturk v Secretary of State for the Home Department (Case C-294/06; 24 January 2008) the European Court of Justice accepted that students and au pairs were workers and duly registered as part of the labour force, so that the benefits of this agreement were available to them.

The reasons for a Member State allowing a Turkish national to work and reside in its territory are not relevant to the question of whether the employment was "legal". Even the fact that a Turkish worker expressly accepted restrictions on his length of stay does not deprive him of the rights acquired under Article 6(1) unless it was demonstrated that he had been deliberately deceiving the national authorities.

Duly registered as belonging to the labour force

Relevant concerns are whether the worker:

➢ **Is in an employment relationship or available for employment**

The question narrows down to whether or not the individual is in "genuine and effective employment".

The mere fact that the employment in question was solely designed to qualify the worker for work elsewhere in the undertaking, did not deprive it of the character of "employment". Additionally the level of pay, and temporary nature of the employment are not determining factors.

➢ **Is engaged in employment which can be located within the territory of the Member State or retains a sufficiently close link with that territory**

Breaks in employment. Temporary breaks in employment, annual holidays, absences for reason of maternity or an accident at work or short periods of sickness, will not disqualify an applicant. An "inactive" period cannot be treated as a period of legal employment, although the rights of the worker acquired as a result of previous employment cannot be affected.

In the case of permanent incapacity, the worker can no longer be considered as available for work and there is no objective justification for guaranteeing him the right of access to the labour force and an ancillary right of residence.

Retirement age will be that defined by the Member State's national legislation, regardless of capacity to work.

Unemployment: In the case of involuntary unemployment, Article 6(2) provides that like in the case of long periods of absence due to sickness, the inactive period cannot be treated as periods of legal employment for the purposes of Article 6(1) although they do not affect the rights which the worker acquired as the result of preceding employment.

With regards voluntary unemployment applicants will be given a reasonable amount of time in which to find work. The ECJ has left it to the discretion of the Member States to determine how long a reasonable period for seeking employment would be but it may not deprive Article 6 of its substance by effectively jeopardising prospects of obtaining work.

Links with the territory: The Court of Justice has held that factors such as place of hire, the location of paid employment, and national legislation on social security and employment law should be taken into account.

➢ **Has completed the applicable formalities required by national law**

The requirement to fulfil formalities laid down in national law would include the payment of income tax, contributions for health, pension and unemployment insurance.

"Legal employment" for one of three possible time periods

In order to qualify under Article 6 (1) of Decision 1/80 specifies time periods of legal employment which must have been fulfilled. See the Ankara Agreement:

> Article 6.1
> A worker shall, after one year's legal employment, be entitled to have his permit to work extended to continue to work for the same employer if a job is available.
> A worker shall be entitled to change employers within the same occupation after three years subject to EC nationals having priority.
> A worker shall be free to take any employment after 4 years.
>
> Article 6.2
> The rights at 6.1 are not affected by annual holidays, maternity leave, accidents at work or short periods of sick leave

One year's legal employment gives the Turkish worker a right to have his or her right to work renewed for the same employer and to have his or her leave to remain renewed in line. A Turkish national can only benefit from this right if he or she has been employed with the same employer for the whole year.

The GOV.UK website states "We would interpret this as the applicant remaining in the same job when a different employer takes over and keeps him on, since the spirit of the agreement is to benefit Turkish workers established in employment rather than United Kingdom firms."

Three years' legal employment with the same employer entitles a Turkish worker to a further renewal. At this stage the employer may be altered, however the occupation pursued must remain the same. Again, there is an entitlement to have the right of residence renewed in line with the right to work. In order to benefit from this right the Turkish national must have been employed with the same employer for three continuous years. If the Turkish worker has changed employment within the three years, she or he will either have to rely on the 'one year' rule, if one year has been achieved or, if not, will fall outside the benefit provided by Decision 1/80.

The GOV.UK website says:

> After 3 years with the same employer an applicant is entitled to change employers but only when the new employer cannot recruit from EC labour and if the new employment is in the same occupation. Caseworkers should therefore ask for evidence that the employer cannot fill the post from EC labour before granting leave to remain on Code 4 for 12 months at a time.

After **four years' legal employment**, a Turkish worker is entitled to free access to the labour market, which includes a right to give up his or her job and to be a job-seeker for a reasonable period of time, probably similar to that allowed for job seeking EEA nationals.

The GOV.UK website says

> The Agreement does not provide for the removal of time limit, only for the freedom to take any employment after 4 years. Applications for indefinite leave to remain should be refused and further leave to remain granted on Code 1 for 12 months at a time.

Rights of residence

The rights that the Decisions give to Turkish workers re employment bring with them residence rights.

There is no requirement that lawfulness of employment be attested to by possession of any particular administrative document e.g. work permits – these would be "declaratory" of the existence of the worker's rights, they would not be the foundation of them.

Expulsion

Decision 1/80 makes the expulsion criteria of the Ankara arrangements reflective of those with which we are already familiar in EC law – i.e. public policy, public security or public health. The focus must be on the personal characteristics of the offender.

Family members

Family members qualify for entry or leave to remain under the ECAA on the same basis as dependants of PBS migrants as outlined in the Home Office guidance (Modernised Guidance/working/ECAA Turkish employed applications)

Their right to work however is contingent on the ECAA which states at Article 7;

> The members of the family of a Turkish worker who have been authorised to join him in a Member State may take jobs in that Member State after 3 years lawful residence subject to EC nationals having priority; and may freely take jobs in that Member State after 5 years lawful residence;
>
> The children of Turkish parents, one of whom has been legally employed in a Member State for 3 years, may, if they have completed a course of vocational training, take any job in that Member State, irrespective of how long they (the children) have resided there.

Home Office guidance states that;

> The criteria are based on those used for family members of points-based system (PBS) migrants. To build up rights under article 7, a family member must cohabit with the main applicant for three years, during which time they must continue to meet the criteria for family members of PBS migrants.

Self-employed

Rights of Establishment

The ECJ in Case C-37/98 Savas held that the 'standstill clause in Article 41(1) of the Additional Protocol of the Association Agreement was not in itself capable of conferring upon a Turkish national the benefit of the right of establishment and the right of residence which is its corollary. This means that a Turkish national's first admission to the territory of a Member State is governed exclusively by that State's own domestic law.

The standstill clause in Article 41(1) of the Additional Protocol precludes a Member State from adopting any new measure having the object or effect of making the establishment, and, as a corollary, the residence of a Turkish national in its territory subject to stricter conditions than those which applied at the time when the Additional Protocol entered into force with regard to the Member State concerned.

The UK became party to the European Community 1st January 1973 (and therefore party to the Agreement and the Additional Protocol). It is therefore the Immigration Rules HC 510 and 509 which were in force at the time that are applicable to Turkish nationals who wish to establish in business in the UK

In general HC510 and 509 are considerably more favourable than the current immigration rules pertaining to business people (HC395). The principal differences are:

➢ There was no minimum level of investment under HC510 or 509

➢ There was no requirement to offer employment to a minimum number of people under HC510 or 509

➢ There was no mandatory entry clearance requirement under HC510 and 509 and passengers arriving without entry clearance would be given a period of leave to enter to have their application examined by the Home Office

The main requirement under the 1973 Immigration Rules is for business people to demonstrate that they can maintain and accommodate themselves and any dependants from the profits of their business. If they are buying into an existing business they need to demonstrate that their investment is needed and they will have a controlling and active interest in the business.

Lawful entry

The Home Office had sought to distinguish between those lawfully and those illegally in the UK when applying Savas. The Home Office contended that where a person had committed a major illegality the current Immigration Rules HC 395 will be applied to them.

In R (Veli Tum) v Secretary of State the Secretary of State [2004] EWCA Civ 788, a case concerning Turkish asylum seekers who had sought to exercise his rights under the Ankara Agreement, the SSHD contended that if a person has lawfully entered this country, and, having done so, sought to establish himself here and to operate a business, he could rely on the law as it was in 1973. It was argued that this only applied to those who had so entered. In Tum it was contended that section 11 of the Immigration Act 1971, meant the Appellants were treated for legal purposes as having not entered the country, and therefore the position was that they are governed by the current domestic law.

The Administrative Court rejected this argument, stating that the "standstill" provisions are to apply to "a person whatever his status so far as his right to remain in this country or his right to enter this country is concerned". There was one caveat, regarding those obtaining entry via fraud:

> 23. The one exception that I would make to that clear position is with regard to a person who achieves entry to this country by the use of fraud. It has long been the situation that those who enter by fraud cannot benefit from the point of view of immigration status by so doing.

The European Court of Justice has upheld the approach of the English courts, in Tum and Dari v Secretary of State for the Home Department (C16-05; 20 September 2007). The mere fact of a prior unsuccessful asylum claim could not constitute abuse or fraud.

Thus only in instances of clear deception or fraud (this would include instances where an asylum claim was determined to be completely false or incredible) should a Turkish port of entry applicant for asylum be denied access to the Ankara Agreement. However, the Administrative Court in Aldogan (R on the application of) v Secretary of State for the Home Department [2007] EWHC 2586 (Admin) suggested that an application based on conduct whilst the individual was here unlawfully or while the business was carried on in breach of Immigration Rules was not to be encouraged.

In EK (Ankara Agreement - 1972 Rules-construction) Turkey [2010] UKUT 425 (IAC), overturning an earlier decision (LE(Turkey)), the Tribunal found that HC510 did not prohibit switching into business status for anyone but a visitor. HC510 did not preclude the possibility of anyone switching into that status, and therefore now, the Ankara Agreement.

Applications

Applications are considered on the basis of the guidance in the IDIs at Chapter 6 Section 6.

Where all of the considerations are decided in favour of the applicant leave to enter/remain should be granted for two years in the first instance (immigration rule 215). It will then be for the applicant to apply for further leave to remain before the end of that two year period. If successful the next period of leave to be granted will be 3 years (r.220). There is provision for settlement after 4 years continuous leave in this category (r.222).

Appeals

The GOV.UK website acknowledges, with reference to the "not in accordance with the law" jurisdiction, that "an adjudicator would have jurisdiction to consider whether a person qualified by virtue of a directly enforceable right under the [Ankara] Agreement."

However appeals may be brought from within the UK only where there is a human rights claim or asylum claim made alongside them (as where there is an independent Article 8 claim regarding family or private life in the UK, possibly related to the importance of the business to the applicant's private life). The Tribunal in SS & Ors (Ankara Agreement, no in-country right of appeal) Turkey [2006] UKAIT 00074 (29 September 2006) found that an historic asylum or human rights claim would suffice, but in Etame v Secretary of State for the Home Department & Anor [2008] EWHC 1140 (Admin) (23 May 2008) the Administrative Court has said that in general, the suspension on removal brought by such claims is predicated on a link between the present application and human rights or asylum grounds. This is a complicated area that is not yet finally settled.

Additional agreements

In addition to the above Association Agreements, the EU has concluded a series of Association Agreements and Co-operation Agreements with countries such as Algeria, Tunisia and Morocco. The significance of these agreements in immigration terms is extremely limited in that they merely provide for non-discrimination clauses akin to those included for workers in the Europe Agreements. As was said there, the provisions do not create either a right of entry or residence nor do they create a right to have your leave to remain extended until the expiry of your employment contract.

Chapter 12: British Nationality Law

Broadly, the subject of nationality law covers too central questions; firstly, am I a British citizen and, secondly, if I am not, how do I become one?

A brief history of nationality law

It is useful briefly to review the historical development of different forms of British nationality to ensure familiarity with the key terminology of nationality law. Also an old passport, or the passport of someone who has died, may be for a category of British nationality that is no longer current but may be useful to establish a person's current entitlements.

The key stages of development are broadly as follows:

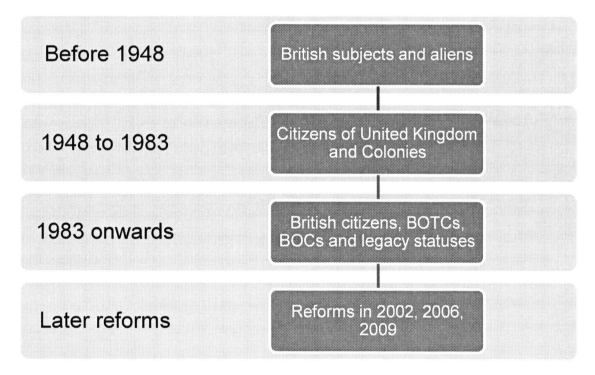

Before 1948	British subjects and aliens
1948 to 1983	Citizens of United Kingdom and Colonies
1983 onwards	British citizens, BOTCs, BOCs and legacy statuses
Later reforms	Reforms in 2002, 2006, 2009

Pre 1948

Until 1948 the terminology used in law was "British Subject". The world was divided into British subjects, who were in the UK and overseas, and aliens, with the exception of British protected persons who were connected not to colonies but to British protectorates. They were not subject to immigration control.

1948 to 1983

The British Nationality Act 1948 created the status of a "**Citizen of the UK and Colonies**", often abbreviated to CUKC. All CUKCs had a right of abode in the UK. They were also, at the same time, British Subjects.

Citizens of colonies which had become independent were not CUKCs but they retained the status of British Subject and with it the right of abode. The term Commonwealth Citizen was also used for this group.

No change was made to British Protected Persons and the status of British Subject Without Citizenship was created for those for those who had not acquired the citizenship of the independent country, but were not CUKCs either.

As more colonies became independent after 1948 their citizens lost their CUKC status if they gained citizenship of the new country, and became British Subjects/Commonwealth citizens.

From the 1960s onwards, some CUKCs and some British subjects began to lose their right of abode. The IA 1971 introduced the term "patriality". Patrial citizens were those who had a right of abode and thus were not subject to immigration control:

➢ **Patrial CUKCs** – who had acquired their CUKC citizenship in the UK (by birth, registration or naturalisation) had a parent or grandparent who had similarly acquired CUKC status in the UK, or had lived in the UK for five years or more; or CUKCs .

➢ **Non-patrial CUKCs** – all CUKCs not in the category above.

The right of abode was also withdrawn from certain British Subjects and Commonwealth citizens during this period.

In summary, the following people born before 1 January 1983 are British Citizens:

➢ Those born in the UK pre 1 January 1983 (save the children of diplomats)

➢ Those born abroad pre 1 January 1983 whose father was born in the UK

➢ Those born abroad pre 1 January 1983 whose father was registered or naturalised as British before their birth

➢ Those adopted in the UK by a British father.

1983 onwards

With the coming into force of the British Nationality Act 1981 on 1 January 1983, what mattered primarily was parentage, rather than place of birth. The Act created three new categories of British nationals:

➢ **British Citizens** – these were people who, on 31 December 1982, were patrial CUKCs. As British citizens they retained their rights of abode, and are recognisable as the British Citizens of today.

> **British "Dependent" Territories Citizens** (renamed "**Overseas**" in the British Overseas Territories Citizens Act 2002) for people who, on 31 December 1982, were CUKCs because of their connection with a British Dependent Territory (e.g. Bermuda). Those who had the right of abode retained it.

> **British Overseas Citizens** for non-patrial CUKCs who did not fit into the category of British Dependent (Overseas Territories) Citizens.

Meanwhile,

> **British Protected Persons** retained their status.

> **Commonwealth Citizens'** status did not change. Those who had the right of abode retained it.

> **British Subject** changed its meaning. It became the new name for British Subjects without Citizenship as defined in the BNA 1948.

Section 11 of the BNA 1981 made provision for certain CUKCs to become British citizens on passage of the Act. The principle requirements were that a person, on 31 December 1982:

> Was a citizen of the UK and colonies

> Had a right of abode in the UK

From 1 January 1983, under the British Nationality Act 1981 nationality could be obtained in three ways:

> As of right, by operation of law. This nationality will be operative regardless of any further actions.

> As of entitlement, by taking the step of registering. If the step is not taken, the entitlement can be lost. In some cases the application must be made whilst the applicant is still a minor: it is only those born and living in the UK for the first ten years of their life who enjoy a lifelong chance to register.

> By discretion, by obtaining naturalization, or in some cases by registering, as the Secretary of State has a discretion to register any child as a British citizen if the circumstances impress her sufficiently.

2002 legislation

In 2002, the British Overseas Territories Act 2002 was passed. This Act renamed British Dependent Territories, British Overseas Territories. People became British Overseas Territories Citizens automatically on 26 February 2002 and on the 21 May 2002 they all became British Citizens with a right of abode in the UK, with the exception of those connected with the Sovereign bases.

In the same year, the Nationality, Immigration and Asylum Act 2002 were passed. It did not change the list of categories of citizen, but enlarged some and did make changes to entitlements to move between categories. It also finally abolished the partial-centric approach of previous nationality laws and in section 9 of the Act made unmarried fathers the transmitters of British nationality just as much as unmarried mothers. This provision came into force on 1 July 2006.

At the moment there are therefore a number of types of British national currently in existence:

This manual is intended as an introductory text and therefore focuses on British citizens.

2006 legislation

The Immigration, Asylum and Nationality Act 2006 made further changes to nationality law, widening the power to deprive a person of citizenship (s.56) or the right of abode (s.57) to include 'conducive to public good' and also removes registration as a British citizen as of right by inserting a good character test for all applicants. An Order passed in January 2010 also includes children aged 10 and over in the 'good character requirement'.

2009 legislation

Some sections of the Borders, Citizenship and Immigration Act 2009 came into force 13 January 2010. These sections are what might be described as the nice not naughty bits of the Act. The changes are as follows:

➢ Enables registration as British of the children born outside the UK of members of the armed forces and confirms automatic British citizenship of children born in the UK of members of the armed forces.

➢ Allows registration of children born outside the UK under s.3(2) of the BNA 1981 up to their 18th birthday (extended from 12 months after their birth or 6 years in exceptional circumstances).

➢ Permits registration of otherwise stateless BN(O)s.

➢ Enables registration of those born before 7 February 1961 with British mothers, if they would have become a British citizen at birth had women been able to pass on citizenship in the same way as men.

2014 legislation

When brought into force, s65 of the Immigration Act 2014 will provide for the registration as a British citizen of all those who missed out on being a British citizen at birth because their mother was not married to their father.

Birth or adoption in the UK

The routes by which a child born in the UK is a British citizen by birth or can become so by registration under s1 of the BNA 1981 are as follows:

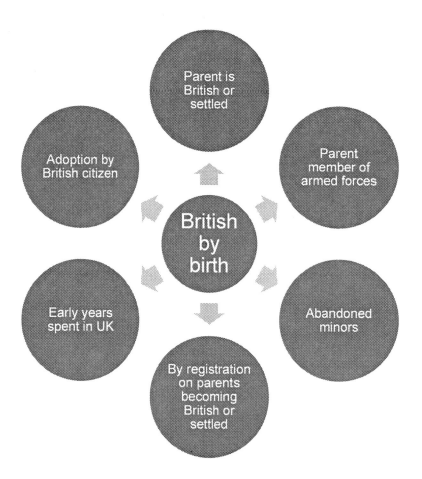

Parent is British or settled

The plain fact of birth in the United Kingdom since 1 January 1983 does not usually create any entitlement to citizenship unless it is combined with a parental link to a person settled in the United Kingdom:

> s.1(1) A person born in the United Kingdom after commencement, or in a qualifying territory on or after the appointed day, shall be a British citizen if at the time of the birth his father or mother is--
> (a) a British citizen; or
> (b) settled in the United Kingdom or that territory.

This form of acquisition of citizenship operates by law, so no registration or other forms need be completed. However, proof that a person meets the above criteria may be required to prove citizenship.

Settlement is defined in the Immigration Act 1971 as "being ordinarily resident in the United Kingdom ... without being subject under the immigration laws to any restriction on the period for which he may remain." Effectively this means that the parent in question had indefinite leave to remain or a permanent right of residence under EC law.

Until 1 July 2006, a child could establish his right to nationality via either parent so long as he was born within marriage. 'Illegitimate' children (for this was the effect of this provision) could trace entitlement only via their mother. Pursuant to section 47 of the British Nationality Act 1981, a person born out of wedlock is to be treated as legitimate for the purposes of nationality law if their parents subsequently marry.

Under a policy articulated in March 2000, Home Office practice was to register the illegitimate child of a British citizen father where (a) paternity is not in doubt (b) no reasonable objections have been lodged by those with parental responsibility; (c) there are no objections on grounds of character.

This old fashioned and discriminatory approach finally came to a partial end as of 1 July 2006 with the coming into force of section 9 of the 2002 Act. However, the change did not apply retrospectively, only to children born on or after 1 July 2006.

Provisions in s65 the Immigration Act, when brought into force, will provide the right to register for all those who missed out on British citizenship by reason of their mother not being married to their father (see Guidance at: https://www.gov.uk/government/publications/children-of-british-citizen-fathers-become-a-british-citizen).

Example

Beatrice was born in the UK in 2005 to a French national mother and British father. The mother had only been present in the UK for 18 months. The parents were not married. Beatrice was not automatically therefore born British, although she could almost certainly later have been registered as British (see below).

Bertie was born in the UK in 2007 to the same French mother and British father. The mother was still not resident and the parents were not married. Bertie, however, was automatically born British because of the change in the law effective from 2006.

Under s50(9A) of the BNA 1981 the father is presumed to be;

➢ the husband of the mother, or

➢ the person treated as the father under s28 of The Human Fertilisation and Embryology Act 1990, or

➢ the person treated as the father under s35, 36, 42 or 43 of The Human Fertilisation and Embryology Act 2008, or

➢ the person who satisfies the requirements of The British Nationality (Proof of Paternity) Regulations 2006 – either the person named as the father of the child in a birth certificate issued within one year of the date of the child's birth, or the person who otherwise satisfies the Secretary of State that he is the father (e.g. by way of a DNA test report)

The references to qualifying territories throughout the Act are not of great importance for our purposes, being references to specific entitlements for those born on or after 21 May 2002 in a "Qualifying territory" – which means a British overseas territory other than the Sovereign Base Areas of Akrotiri and Dhekelia in Cyprus, if a parent is a British citizen and settled in the UK or that qualifying territory.

Children born inside UK to members of the armed forces

Section 42 of the Borders, Citizenship and Nationality Act 2009 provides a statutory basis for the acquisition of British citizenship for children born in the UK to members of the armed forces. This removes the need to treat as settled parents of such children, which was a somewhat legally suspect 'work around' previously in place.

A new section 1(1A) was inserted into the BNA 1981, which provides that a person born in the United Kingdom or a qualifying territory on or after the relevant day shall be a British citizen if at the time of the birth his father or mother is a member of the armed forces.

Abandoned minors

Under s.1(2), a new born infant found abandoned in the United Kingdom on or after 1 January 1983 can be regarded, for the purposes of s.1(1), as having been:

➢ born in the United Kingdom on or after 1 January 1983; and

➢ born to a parent who at the time of the birth was a British citizen or settled in the United Kingdom,

unless the contrary can be proven by the Home Office. So the presumption will be that such a child is a British citizen.

Registration on parents becoming British or settled

Minors are entitled to registration under s.1(3) of the British Nationality Act 1981 if:

➢ they were born in the United Kingdom on or after 1 January 1983; and

➢ they were not British citizens at birth because at the time neither parent was a British citizen or settled here; and

➢ while they are minors, either parent becomes a British citizen or becomes settled in the United Kingdom; and

➤ they are minors on the date of application

Example

To continue with the example of Beatrice, above, if her mother becomes settled in the UK after five years of residence under EC law, Beatrice could be registered as British. Unlike with Bertie, this is a positive step that must be taken and it must be taken before Beatrice turns 18.

Alternatively, Beatrice could probably have been registered under s.1(3) after 1 July 2006, once her father was recognised in law as her father for nationality purposes, i.e. when one of her 'parents' became British.

Registration due to early years spent in UK

Adults or minors are entitled to registration under s.1(4) of the BNA 1981 if they:

➤ were born in the United Kingdom on or after 1 January 1983; and

➤ were not a British citizen at birth because at the time neither parent was a British citizen or settled here; and

➤ were aged 10 years or more on the date of application; and

➤ have lived in the United Kingdom for the first 10 years of their life; and

➤ during that 10 years have not been out of the United Kingdom for more than 90 days in any one of those years

The lawfulness of residence is irrelevant for this provision. The statute (s.1(7)) gives a discretion to extend this latter requirement. This statutory discretion receives a gloss from the Nationality Instructions, which indicate that non-intentional longer absences may be permitted, and also other absences within limited parameters.

Schedule 2 of the 1981 Act makes some provision for reducing statelessness. Paragraph 3 enables a person born in the UK after commencement who is and has always been stateless to be registered as a British citizen if under the age of 22 and resident in the UK for a period of five rather than ten years (as long as absent for no more than 450 days during that period).

Minors adopted by British citizens

Section 1(5) of the British Nationality Act 1981, as amended, explains which children adopted on or after 1 January 1983 acquired British citizenship automatically because of their adoption. Under s.1(5), a child who is not already a British citizen becomes a British citizen from the date of an adoption order if **EITHER**:

> ➢ the adoption is authorised by order of a court in the United Kingdom on or after 1 January 1983 or, on or after 21 May 2002, by an order of a court in a qualifying territory; and

> ➢ the adopter or, in the case of a joint adoption, one of the adopters is a British citizen on the date of the adoption order

OR

> ➢ it is a Convention adoption under the 1993 Hague Convention on Intercountry Adoptions; and

> ➢ the adoption is effected on or after 1 June 2003; and

> ➢ the adopter or, in the case of a joint adoption, one of the adopters is a British citizen on the date of the Convention adoption; and

> ➢ the adopter or, in the case of a joint adoption, both of the adopters is habitually resident in the United Kingdom on the date of the Convention adoption

Birth outside the UK

The routes by which a child born outside the UK can become British are as follows:

At birth

- To a parent who is a British citizen otherwise than by descent

On registration

- Any time up to age of 18
- On residence in UK with British citizen parents for 3 years
- If parent is or becomes a member of the armed forces

Acquisition by descent

Section 2(1) of the BNA 1981 reads as follows:

> A person born outside the United Kingdom after commencement shall be a British citizen if at the time of the birth his father or mother:
> (a) is a British citizen otherwise than by descent; ...

This form of transmission of nationality operates by law, so no registration form need be completed, but evidence may be required that the person does meet the above requirements.

Example

Chris is a British citizen who emigrates to Australia with his Australian girlfriend, Clarissa. They do not get married. They have a baby boy, Clarence, in 2005. Clarence has no entitlement to British nationality because he was born before the law changed on 1 July 2006.

Chris and Clarissa have another child, a baby girl called Carrie, who is born in 2007. Carrie is automatically born British and does not need to take any further steps to become British. She is likely to be entitled to dual nationality, depending on the nationality laws of the country in which she is born and the nationality laws of the country of the other parent.

Acquisition by registration

Some minors have an entitlement to register as British citizens (save for exceptions not relevant for this overview). The intention of sub-sections 3(2) and 3(5) is to remedy harshness created by section 2(1), with its limitation of transmission of nationality to a single generation.

Section 3(1), which is a very wide discretion, can be used to register a variety of problem cases (it is known to be used sometimes to deal with an illegitimate child where the Secretary of State accepts the relationship of the child to the British citizen father).

> 3(1) If while a person is a minor an application is made for his registration as a British citizen, the Secretary of State may, if he thinks fit, cause him to be registered as such a citizen.

Section 3 permits registration where there is a sufficiently strong link with the UK, looking back across the generations, as to make it unfair to decline to permit access to full British citizenship. The requirements, in the normal case, are as follows:

➤ As of 13 January 2010, the child to be registered must be under the age of 18. The previous rule until the relevant section of the Borders, Citizenship and Immigration Act 2009 came into effect was that registration had to take place within 12 months of birth or six years in exceptional circumstances.

➤ The child's parent has the weak form of nationality ('by descent') but whose grandparent has the strong form of nationality (otherwise than by descent').

➤ The child's parent has a geographical link with the UK, in that they lived there for a three year period some time prior to the birth of the child, and did not leave the UK for more than 270 days within that period (however, for a child born stateless, this requirement is waived).

➤ With effect from 13 January 2010, as a result of the Borders, Citizenship and Immigration Act 2009, certain children born in the UK to a parent who becomes member of the UK armed forces before the child reaches 18, or born outside the UK to a parent serving overseas in the UK armed forces.

Section 3(5) permits of another form of registration. This does not require the grandparent connection that we saw in section 3(2), nor does it require the historic 3 year stay in the UK that that section entertains – however, it does require that the family including the child were in the UK for the 3 years leading up to the application for registration, and did not leave the UK for more than 270 days within that period. The application can only be made whilst the child is a minor.

Example

To continue with the story of the family of Chris and Clarissa, we saw earlier that Carrie was born British by descent by virtue of section 2(1) of the Act. Section 14 of the Act sets out a definition of a British citizen 'by descent' and Carrie falls within that definition.

When Carrie grows up she has a child of her own, Colin, who is born in Australia. Colin is not automatically born British citizens under the same section as Carrie, because section 2(1) states that the parent must be a British citizen 'otherwise than by descent'.

However, Colin could be registered as British citizens under section 3(2) if the proper procedures are followed, or could be registered under section 3(5) if they were later to qualify (see below).

When Colin grows up, he has two children, Claude and Cedric. They have no entitlement at all to British citizenship by descent.

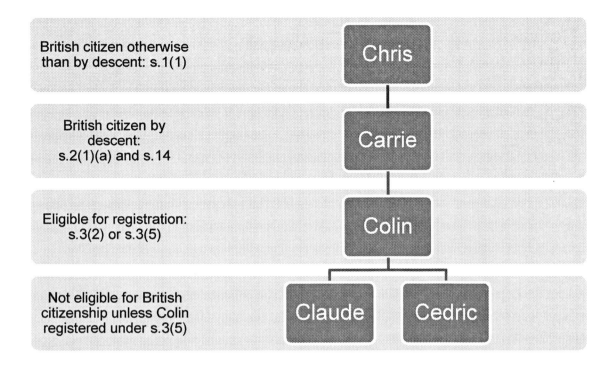

British citizen otherwise than by descent: s.1(1)	**Chris**
British citizen by descent: s.2(1)(a) and s.14	**Carrie**
Eligible for registration: s.3(2) or s.3(5)	**Colin**
Not eligible for British citizenship unless Colin registered under s.3(5)	**Claude** **Cedric**

Acquisition by registration as an adult

Certain adults are also able or entitled to register as British citizens:

➢ A person who is a British overseas territories citizen, British National (Overseas), a British Overseas citizen, a British subject or a British protected person may register as a full British citizen if he or she meets the same residence requirement as for naturalisation and, since the advent of the 2006 Act, a good character requirement.

➢ There is a discretion to register as a British citizen the above persons, even if the residence requirements are not met (s.4(4) of 1981 Act).

➢ When s65 of the Immigration Act 2014 is commenced, those would have become British citizens automatically under the 1981 Act provisions had their parents been married, and those who would currently have an entitlement to registration under the 1981 Act provisions but for the fact that their parents are not married (see Guidance at: https://www.gov.uk/government/publications/children-of-british-citizen-fathers-become-a-british-citizen).

Registration applications involve the completion of a form. There is a fee. Applications for the registration of people living abroad will normally be made through a British Diplomatic Post; consult the Foreign and Commonwealth Office website. Applications for people living in the UK are made to the Home Office. Registration is evidenced by a certificate and the person can subsequently apply for a British passport.

If on receipt of an application the Home Office detect that a person does not need to register because they are already a British Citizen, they will inform the applicant of this and refund the application fee.

The Nationality, Immigration and Asylum Act 2002 amended the BNA 1981 so that those wishing to acquire British Citizenship will now do so at a public ceremony. This applies also to applicants for registration.

Naturalisation

Section 6(1) deals with naturalisation cases based on a UK connection other than marriage, and makes reference to Schedule 1 of the BNA 1981. In addition to length and continuity of residence and immigration status, the requirements therein are that an individual is of good character, has sufficient knowledge of the English, Welsh or Scottish Gaelic language; and that they intend to make their principal home in the United Kingdom, or, if they intend to live abroad, that they work in Crown service or for a UK enterprise.

Provisions in the 2009 were set to change the route to naturalisation in a major way. They were enacted but never commenced, and the current government has scrapped them. Advisers should be careful though as some textbooks might include the 2009 amendments as if they are law.

The criteria for naturalisation are as follows:

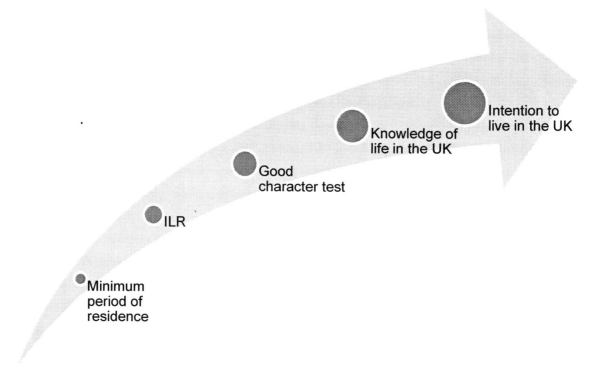

Period of residence

Non-spouse cases

The requirements of residence for those not applying as spouses are set out at Schedule 1 paragraph 2.

> (a) subject to subsection (3), that he was in the United Kingdom at the beginning of the period of five years ending with the date of the application and that the number of days on which he absent from the United Kingdom in that period does not exceed 450; and
> (b) that the number of days on which he was absent from the United Kingdom in the period of twelve months so ending does not exceed 90; and
> (c) that he was not at any time in the period of twelve months so ending subject under the immigration laws to any restriction on the period for which he might remain in the United Kingdom;
> (d) that he was not any time in the period of five years so ending in the United Kingdom in breach of the immigration laws.

However, there is discretion to treat these conditions as satisfied despite insufficient periods of time being accumulated.

Spouse cases

Section 6(2) deals with applications of persons "married to a British citizen". The required residence period is 270 days, with the references to 5 years replaced by 3 years, in sub-paragraphs (a) and (d).

The restriction at 3(c) is lifted, so that there is no requirement to be free from immigration control (i.e. to have indefinite leave to remain) for 12 months prior to the date of application, with the practical consequence that a spouse can apply from the grant of indefinite leave to remain without waiting for a further year.

There is no requirement to make the UK their permanent home, though they are expected to meet the good character requirement, and the language requirement or to comply with the language test.

Naturalisation is a discretionary power. There is no right of appeal against a refusal of naturalisation. However, reasons must be given and, subsequent to the amendments effected to the BNA 1981 (s.1 and s.44) by s.7 of the Nationality, Immigration and Asylum Act 2002, there is no limit on the scope of judicial review of such a refusal.

In breach of the immigration laws

Where there are qualifying periods to be met, periods spent in the relevant territory "in breach of the immigration laws" do not count. The meaning of "in breach of the immigration laws" for the specific purpose of calculating residence is set out in s.11 of the NIA 2002.

The section is not as clear as it could be, especially in subs. (3). The government has explained that subs. (3) means that periods people (usually refugees) who have not been illegal entrants or overstayers spent on temporary admission or in detention before the decision to grant their application will not be treated as periods in the UK in breach of immigration control for the calculations. The policy is that time taken from the application (not entry to the UK) to the Home Office decision to allow the application is not treated as time spent "in breach of the immigration laws" for the purposes of the calculation. Time spent in the UK without leave prior to making the application will not count.

EU nationals and their families used only to be treated as having been in the UK in breach of the immigration laws if they had remained here after a deportation order or removal directions had been made. From 7 November 2002 onwards, as a result of s.11, the broader grounds that they do not have either an entitlement to be here under European Community law nor permission to be here will apply.

The good character requirement

This is not tightly defined. All criminal convictions, including motoring offences have to be declared. Checks are made on financial solvency and a bankrupt is unlikely to be considered of good character. Security risks will be taken into account and there can be a police check.

Detailed guidance to Home Office caseworkers is provided in Annex D to Chapter 18 of the Nationality Instructions. This states, *inter alia*;

3.1.1 From the 1 October 2012, certain immigration and nationality decisions were exempt from s4 of the Rehabilitation of Offenders Act 1974. As a result, the concept of a conviction becoming "spent" no longer applies when making an assessment of good character. Therefore, when dealing with nationality applications made on or after 13 December 2012, caseworkers should refuse an individual who has a conviction within the relevant sentence based threshold as detailed in the table below.

	Sentence	Impact on Nationality applications
1.	4 years or more imprisonment	Application should be refused, regardless of when the conviction occurred.
2.	Between 12 months and 4 years imprisonment	Application should be refused unless 15 years have passed since the end of the sentence.
3.	Up to 12 months imprisonment in the last 7 years	Applications should be refused unless 7 years have passed since the end of the sentence.
4.	A non-custodial offence	Applications should be refused if the conviction occurred in the last 3 years.

The guidance on good character needs to be read as a whole however as some minor convictions may be disregarded, and useful advice is given, for example, as to the effect of receiving a fixed penalty notice.

The good character requirement has been extended to include children aged 10 and over.

Sufficient knowledge of language and life in the UK

Under Schedule 1 of the BNA 1981, all applicants for naturalisation must show sufficient knowledge of English, Welsh or Scottish Gaelic, and 'sufficient knowledge about life in the UK'.

The British Nationality (General) (Amendment) Regulations 2013 provide that the language and life in the UK tests are met in pretty much the same way as under Appendix KOLL for a person applying for settlement. Where the Appendix KOLL provisions have been met, an applicant for naturalisation will not have to meet them again.

To pass the English language requirement, applicants will need to come from an English speaking country listed in Schedule 2A to the Regulations, have a degree taught in English, or pass a test specified in Schedule 2A (excluding those provided by the Educational Testing Service). For the life in the UK element, the applicant must have passed the Life in the UK test.

The Home Office possesses a discretion to waive the language requirement where it would be unreasonable to expect the applicant to fulfil it because of age or physical or mental condition. The language requirement will normally be waived where the applicant is aged 65 or over.

The grounds for exemption of younger people need to be compelling, such as where the applicant:

(i)   is suffering from a long term illness or disability which severely restricts mobility and ability to attend language classes; or

(ii)   suffers from a speech impediment which limits ability to converse in the relevant language; or

(iii)   has a mental impairment which means that they are unable to learn another language.

Guidance on these tests and the exercise of discretion is in Annex E to Chapter 18 of the Nationality Instructions

Intention to live in the UK

If a person is abroad or about to go abroad it may be important to explain this. For example, caring for a person overseas who is ill or dying is likely to be a temporary absence and should not be treated as evidence that a person has no intention to live in the UK.

Citizenship ceremonies

The Nationality, Immigration and Asylum Act 2002 substitutes a new s.42 to 42B and Schedule 5 into the BNA 1981 so that anyone over the age of 18 who wish to acquire British Citizenship, whether by registration or naturalisation, will now do so at a public ceremony and are required to take the Oath of Allegiance (there is an affirmation to be used by people of different religions and of none) and now a new pledge as set out in these provisions. Full details of the ceremonies can be found on a special website uknationality.gov.uk which is also a convenient portal to use to access the relevant information from the Home Office site. Ceremonies are normally held in groups, although arrangements can be made (at a price) to have individual ceremonies. People can invite guests. A fee is payable.

Some people are exempted from the requirement by Section 42(2) of the 1981 Act. These are:

a. those not of full age; or

b. those who are already:

- British citizens; or
- British overseas territories citizens; or
- British Nationals (Overseas); or
- British Overseas citizens; or
- British subjects under the 1981 Act; or
- citizens of any country of which Her Majesty is Queen (Antigua and Barbuda, Australia, the Bahamas, Barbados, Belize, Canada, Grenada, Jamaica, New Zealand, Papua New Guinea, St Christopher and Nevis, St Lucia, St Vincent and the Grenadines, Solomon Islands and Tuvalu.)

Where an applicant is required to take an oath of allegiance s/he must normally do so within the time limit of 3 months prescribed by the British Nationality (General) Regulations 1982 (or the British Nationality (General) Regulations) 2003, as appropriate). Otherwise the applicant cannot be registered or naturalised unless the Home Secretary decides to extend the period. Notification letters will advise the applicant to contact the local authority to arrange a ceremony. The Home Office will also notify the local authority.

If a person does not attend a citizenship ceremony within the time limit permitted, the Home Office should notify them that it will not be possible to become a British citizen because the Home Secretary is not able to register or naturalise a person who has not attended a ceremony and taken an oath/pledge. If the applicant still wishes to become a British citizen, and had an entitlement at the date of application, a certificate may be issued at any time on the basis of the original application on payment of the balance of fee and attending a citizenship ceremony and making an oath/pledge. In all other cases, the applicant will need to re-apply under an appropriate provision of the legislation.

In exceptional circumstances an exemption may be made in respect of any or all of the following:

➢ the requirement to attend a citizenship ceremony

➢ the requirement to make an oath of allegiance and pledge

> ➤ the time limit for attending a ceremony

Challenging nationality decisions

Section 7 of the NIA 2002 amends s.44 of the BNA 1981 and the British Nationality (Hong Kong) Act 1990 so that the Home Office must now give at least broad reasons for a refusal of citizenship (in practice, its policy has been to do so since 1997). There are no limits on the scope of a judicial review of such a refusal. In practice however, the High Court will generally defer to the very wide discretion that the Secretary of State has to refuse applications on good character grounds and there is no requirement that she discloses to any serious extent the basis of the reasons for that refusal.

There is still no right of appeal against refusal to register or naturalise a person as a British Citizen, despite the confusing title of the section in the 2002 Act. Thus nationality decisions are not included in the list of immigration decisions set out in s.82 of the NIA 2002 and providing an exhaustive list of appealable decisions. A review of a decision can be requested for a fee.

There are specific rights to challenge decisions to deprive a person of their British citizenship and these are set out below under the consideration of deprivation of citizenship.

Stopping being British

The different ways in which a person can stop being a British national or citizen fall into three categories:
> ➤ Loss

> ➤ Renunciation

> ➤ Deprivation

Loss of British nationality

British Citizens cannot simply lose their nationality. However, as described above, when looking at the history of British nationality law, other categories of British national have lost their status at different points in the history of nationality law. To this must be added those who have lost rights and entitlements previously attendant on their status (as for example with the abolition of special voucher quota schemes described above). As noted above, British Citizens by descent do not pass on their nationality to their children born outside the UK.

Other forms of British national can still lose their British nationality. A British subject who gains any other citizenship or nationality after 1 January 1983 will no longer be a British subject unless they used to be a citizen of Eire and have made a claim to remain a British subject under section 2 of the British Nationality Act 1948 or under the 1981 Act. Similarly, a British Protected Person will no longer be a British Protected Person on acquiring any other nationality or citizenship.

Renunciation of British nationality

A person can renounce their form of British nationality. People are likely to want to renounce British nationality if they wish to become or remain the national of a country that does not allow them to hold another nationality.

The requirements are that a British citizen, British Overseas Territories Citizen (see note below), British Overseas citizen, British subject, British National (Overseas) or British Protected Person may renounce that nationality if:

➢ s/he has a nationality other than the one it is sought to renounce; or

➢ can show that s/he will get another citizenship or nationality; and

➢ is over 18 (or under 18 but have been married); and

➢ is of full capacity (i.e. not of unsound mind).

The procedure is that a declaration of renunciation must be filled in. The date of registration of the declaration is the date at which nationality is lost but if the person does not obtain another citizenship within six months, the declaration does not take effect and is considered to have kept their British nationality.
If a person renounced their British citizenship or British overseas territories citizenship to keep or get another citizenship, they have a right to register and resume the citizenship they renounced. They can make use of this only once. Any subsequent attempt to resume following a second registration will be at the discretion the Home Secretary (for British citizenship) or the Governor of a British overseas territory (for British overseas territories citizenship) will decide whether you can resume it again.

Section 5 of the NIA 2002 amended the BNA 1981 to give men the (superior) rights previously enjoyed only by women, who had renounced their UK and colonies citizenship before 1983 to qualify for registration on the basis of a connection with the UK or a British Overseas Territory by marriage. It is still necessary to meet all the qualifying requirements.

All other forms of British nationality cannot be resumed following renunciation.

Deprivation of nationality

Powers to deprive people of their citizenship are set out under the Section 40 and 40A of the BNA 1981 as amended.

There are powers to deprive people of the different forms of British nationality on the following grounds:

> If the Secretary of State is satisfied that deprivation is conducive to the public good: s.40(2). This is no usually applicable if the person would thence be made stateless under s.40(4), but see amendments brought in by the Immigration Act 2014 below).

> If the Secretary of State is satisfied that nationality obtained by registration or naturalisation was in fact obtained by fraud, false representation or concealment of a material fact (there is no protection here in respect of statelessness): s.40(3)

Section 40A, inserted by the 2002 Act, gives a right of appeal against deprivation of nationality. This is to the immigration tribunal or to the Special Immigration Appeals Commission (SIAC). The Secretary of State must notify a person of the intention to deprive them of their nationality and the deprivation will not take effect until any appeal has been finally determined (s.40A(6)) or the time for appealing has expired.

Section 66 of the Immigration Act 2014 (brought into force on 28 July 2014) amends s40 of the BNA 1981 to allow for revocation in certain circumstances even where the person might thereby be rendered stateless, so long as 'the Secretary of State has reasonable grounds for believing that the person is able, under the law of a country or territory outside the United Kingdom, to become a national of such a country or territory'.

In Deliallisi (British citizen: deprivation appeal: Scope) Albania [2013] UKUT 439 (IAC), the Upper tribunal decided that an appeal against deprivation of citizenship might engage Article 8 of the ECHR where as a foreseeable consequence of deprivation the Appellant may have to leave the UK. The Tribunal also decided that a person deprived of citizenship does not automatically revert to having ILR if that was their status before becoming a British citizenship.

In Kaziu & Ors v Secretary of State for the Home Department [2014] EWHC 832 (Admin), the Administrative Court found that where British citizenship had been gained by impersonation (i.e. by providing a false name, date of birth, nationality or place of birth) that citizenship was a nullity i.e. the person was not a British citizen and so there was no issue as to revocation on the basis of deception. The earlier grant of ILR would therefore continue to be effective.

Chapter 13: Enforcement: detention, removal and deportation

Operational Guidance on detention, removal and deportation issues can be found in the Enforcement instructions and guidance at: https://www.gov.uk/government/collections/enforcement-instructions-and-guidance and in the Modernised Guidance at: https://www.gov.uk/government/collections/criminality-and-detention-modernised-guidance

Detention

Power to detain

There are four circumstances in which a person may be detained as set down in Schedules 2 and 3 of the Immigration Act 1971 (as amended by the Immigration and Asylum Act 1999):

Examination

- During examination by an immigration officer to decide whether or not to grant leave to enter, including those previously granted entry clearance (Schedule 2, paragraph 16(1) and (1A) of the Immigration Act 1971 (IA 1971) as amended by paragraph 57, 60 Schedule 14 IAA 1999); includes the asylum detained fast-track cases

Pending removal directions

- Pending the giving of removal directions and removal for those refused leave to enter and for those determined to be illegal entrants (Schedule 2, paragraph 8,9 and 16(2) IA 1971 as amended by section 140(1) of the IAA 1999); and under s62 of the NIA 2002.

Pending deportation

- Pending removal of those served with notice of intention to deport under s.3(5) of 71 Act, in respect of whom a deportation order has been signed and those recommended for deportation (Schedule 3, paragraph 2 of the IA 1971); and under section 36 of the UK Borders Act 2007 (automatic deportation)

Crew members

- Crew members who overstay pending the giving of removal directions and pending removal or are reasonably suspected of intending to do so (Schedule 2, paragraph 12,13 and 16(2) of IA 1971)

It can be seen that the power to detain is very extensive, in the sense that almost any person subject to immigration control can potentially be detained. However, there are limitations on the power to detain. The most important of these in a practical sense is the Secretary of State's policies on detention; exercise of the power to detain contrary to a policy is very likely to be unlawful. These policies are examined in detail below. In addition, the power to detain will lapse in lengthy detention cases if there is no realistic prospect of removal.

This principle was established by Woolf J in R v Governor of Durham Prison ex parte Hardial Singh [1984] 1 WLR 704:

> "First, the power can only be exercised during the period necessary, in all the circumstances of the particular case, to effect removal. Secondly, if it becomes clear that removal is not going to be possible within a reasonable time, further detention is not authorised. Thirdly, the person seeking to exercise the power of detention must take all reasonable steps within his power to ensure the removal within a reasonable time."

If it is proving impossible to actually remove or deport the person from the United Kingdom then the detention would become unlawful, something that might be demonstrated by lengthy detention whilst unsuccessful attempts are made to remove an individual: see Wasfi Suleman Mahmod [1995] Imm AR 311. In the case of R (I) v SSHD [2003] INLR 196, Dyson LJ summarised the law as follows:

1. The Secretary of State must intend to deport the person and can only use the power to detain for that purpose

2. The deportee may only be detained for a period that is reasonable in all the circumstances

3. If, before the expiry of the reasonable period, it becomes apparent that the Secretary of State will not be able to effect deportation within that reasonable period, he should not seek to exercise the power of detention

4. The Secretary of State should act with the reasonable diligence and expedition to effect removal

However, the actions of the detainee, both past and present, can have an impact on whether it is reasonable to exercise the power to detain. In R (on the application of A) v SSHD [2007] EWCA Civ 804 the Court of Appeal found that a risk of absconding was relevant to the period before which detention becomes unreasonable, as was a refusal of voluntary departure from the UK and risk of re-offending. More recent case law has found detention for several years not to be unlawful whilst the Home Office held out before the court that there remained some real prospect of removal, despite several years of trying.

See further below regarding bringing a challenge to the lawfulness of detention.

Example

Rahul is from Algeria. He is to be deported and his appeal rights were exhausted 18 months ago. However, he has been detained now for 21 months, allegedly pending removal.

The Home Office insist that they are doing everything in their power to remove Rahul, but the Algerian authorities are not co-operating. A face to face interview between Rahul and the Algerians took place 20 months ago in detention in order to obtain an Emergency Travel Document. The Algerians stated that they did not accept Rahul was Algerian. The Home Office asked Rahul to provide some written proof of his Algerian nationality. Being in detention in a foreign country, Rahul was unable to do so.

A second interview was arranged and took place 15 months ago. The Algerians maintained their position. It is not clear whether any new information was submitted by the Home Office.

A third telephone interview took place 3 months ago with the same result.

Rahul has applied for bail five times in the last 21 months and has been refused each time because he is a high absconding risk. There is strong support for this view, as Rahul has a very poor criminal and immigration record.

Rahul's detention may well be unlawful and probably has been for some time; arguably since the first interview, almost indisputably since the second. Tribunal bail applications have failed him so he must apply for habeas corpus and/or judicial review. On the claim form he should also specify that he seeks a declaration of unlawful detention and damages. Quantum could easily be tens of thousands of pounds in a case such as this.

The detainee will be detained in a place in which the SSHD designates as appropriate, usually at an Immigration Removal Centre, although prisons are still used, and Reception Centres, with a less regimented environment, have been introduced.

The original powers regarding removal, which are the foundation for the powers to award temporary admission, or detention, are found in the 1971 Act, although subsequent legislation also addresses bail. The 2002 Act extended the rights to apply for bail to those against whom there had been a recommendation to deport or a signed deportation order, therefore filling the vacuum that had prevented universal access to release.

The 2002 Act also extended the power to detain. Section 62 permits detention even where a decision is being considered as to whether or not to make removal directions. Section 67 of the Act provides for detention where an individual cannot currently be removed and certain factors exist because of a legal impediment connected with the UK's obligations under an international agreement, where practical difficulties are impeding or delaying the making of arrangements, or where practical difficulties or demands on administrative resources are impeding or delaying the taking of a decision in respect of him.

Criteria for detention

The initial reasons for detention will be provided in Form IS91R; there should be regular reviews of detention (see below), the reasons for subsequent detention being given in Form IS93. These procedures are set out in the Immigration Service's Enforcement Instructions and Guidance. There is a duty promptly to provide reasons for detention and a failure to do so renders the detention unlawful (although, controversially, this is not necessarily the same as qualifying the detainee for release from detention): Saadi v UK 13229/03 [2008] ECHR 80.

There will be a temptation for initial reasons for detention to be built upon at a later stage should bail be sought, because at that point a bail summary will have to be prepared. Those representing detainees may therefore wish to seek disclosure of the initial reasons for detention. Sometimes the Immigration Service will reveal these on application; on other occasions, it may be necessary to seek disclosure via other measures, such as a Subject Access Bureau request under the Data Protection Act.

Guidance on detention policy can be found in chapter 55 of the Enforcement Instructions and Guidance (EIG). This includes extremely useful instructions on the factors to be taken into account in assessing whether a person is as an absconding risk and on re-detention of bailees. Chapter 55 also incorporates commitments given by the Government in the 1998 White Paper and subsequently that detention is a tool of last resort and alternatives would be used whenever possible.

Presumption of liberty

There is a presumption of liberty, meaning that the starting point must be that a person should not be detained unless there are good reasons for doing so. The potential reasons for detention are explored below.

This presumption exists in common law and is also enshrined in Article 5 of the ECHR.

The presumption of liberty is also reflected in Home Office policy. EIG chapter 55.1.1 states that there is a presumption of liberty and this is reiterated at other points in the EIG. For foreign national offenders the presumption can be displaced by the risk of absconding or re-offending (55.1.2).

Top tip

In a bail application, if the Home Office cannot prove to the civil standard that detention is necessary for one of the above reasons, the person ought to be released on bail. This is certainly how a bail application should work. Some immigration judges tend to require the bail applicant to prove that they are reliable, however, which can be very difficult to evidence.

Reasons to detain

The basic justifications for detention are as follows:

1. To effect removal

2. Establish identity or basis of claim

3. Reason to believe will fail to comply with conditions

These justifications are set out in Enforcement Instructions and Guidance (EIG) 55.1.1.

There are implied limitations to these justifications, which are explored below. For example, a person cannot really be detained to effect removal if there is no real prospect of their removal in a reasonable timescale.

The EIG lists the factors to be taken into account in decisions to detain at 55.3, albeit specifically stating that CCD cases are excluded from these considerations:

➢ There is a presumption in favour of temporary admission or temporary release - there must be strong grounds for believing that a person will not comply with conditions of temporary admission or temporary release for detention to be justified.

➢ All reasonable alternatives to detention must be considered before detention is authorised.

➢ Each case must be considered on its individual merits.

Home Office policy also states that the following factors must be taken into account when considering the need for initial or continued detention (although notably no steer is given as to whether an answer in the affirmative will suggest suitability or non-suitability for detention):

- What is the likelihood of the person being removed and, if so, after what timescale?

- Is there any evidence of previous absconding?

- Is there any evidence of a previous failure to comply with conditions of temporary release or bail?

- Has the subject taken part in a determined attempt to breach the immigration laws? (e.g. entry in breach of a deportation order, attempted or actual clandestine entry)

- Is there a previous history of complying with the requirements of immigration control? (e.g. by applying for a visa, further leave, etc)

- What are the person's ties with the United Kingdom? Are there close relatives (including dependants) here? Does anyone rely on the person for support? Does the person have a settled address/employment?

- What are the individual's expectations about the outcome of the case? Are there factors such as an outstanding appeal, an application for judicial review or representations which afford incentive to keep in touch?

- Is there a risk of offending or harm to the public (this requires consideration of the likelihood of harm and the seriousness of the harm if the person does offend)?

- Is the subject under 18?

- Does the subject have a history of torture?

- Does the subject have a history of physical or mental ill health?

Factors militating against detention

The following factors were announced as future detention policy in the 2002 White Paper, Fairer, Faster, Firmer – A Modern Approach to Immigration and Asylum and have been incorporated into the EIG:

(i) Detention will normally be justified (especially where there has been a systematic attempt to breach immigration control) where there is a reasonable belief that the individual will fail to keep the terms of temporary admission; initially to clarify a person's identity and the basis of their claim; or where removal is imminent.

(ii) Evidence of torture should weigh strongly in favour of temporary admission whilst an asylum claim is being considered.

(iii) Detention of families with young children should be planned to be effected as close to removal as possible so as to ensure that families are not normally detained for more than a few days.

(iv) Unaccompanied minors should never be detained other than in the most exceptional circumstances and then only overnight with appropriate care if they, for example, arrive unaccompanied at an airport. In all cases children under the age of 18 should be referred to the Refugee Council Children's Panel. Where reliable medical evidence indicates that a person is under 18 years of age they will be treated as minors.

In relation to children the EIG states that:

Detention involving or impacting on children under 18 must demonstrably comply with the statutory duty under section 55 of the Borders, Citizenship and Immigration Act 2009 which requires UKBA to have regard to the need to safeguard and promote the welfare of children whilst carrying out its functions.

The EIG also incorporates at 55.1.4.1 the lawfulness factors identified in leading case law on detention, particularly from the case of R (on the app of I) v SSHD [2003] INLR 196. (see earlier).

Deportation cases

At the time of writing the modification to the presumption of liberty in deportation cases is set out at EIG 55.1.2 and is worth quoting in full:

'Cases concerning foreign national prisoners – dealt with by the Criminal Casework Directorate (CCD) - are subject to the general policy set out above in 55.1.1, including the presumption in favour of temporary admission or release. Thus, the starting point in these cases remains that the person should be released on temporary admission or release unless the circumstances of the case require the use of detention. However, the nature of these cases means that special attention must be paid to their individual circumstances.

In any case in which the criteria for considering deportation action (the "deportation criteria") are met, the risk of re-offending and the particular risk of absconding should be weighed against the presumption in favour of temporary admission or temporary release. Due to the clear imperative to protect the public from harm from a person whose criminal record is sufficiently serious as to satisfy the deportation criteria, and/or because of the likely consequence of such a criminal record for the assessment of the risk that such a person will abscond, in many cases this is likely to result in the conclusion that the person should be detained, provided detention is, and continues to be, lawful. However, any such conclusion can be reached only if the presumption of temporary admission or release is displaced after an assessment of the need to detain in the light of the risk of re-offending and/or the risk of absconding.'

While it can be seen that the draughtsman of this policy hopes that the policy incorporates the presumption of liberty, later parts of the EIG (e.g. 55.3) suggest that in reality the presumption of liberty is not applied in deportation cases.

In the case of Lumba v SSHD [2011] UKSC 12 the Supreme Court considered the consequences of a modification of detention policy in cases of foreign national detained prisoners following on from the revelation in 2006 that foreign prisoners were being released from prison without being considered by the

Home Office for deportation. The ensuing scandal cost the then Home Secretary, Charles Clarke, his job and had far reaching consequences for the Home Office, leading to the creation of the UK Border Agency out of the old Immigration and Nationality Directory and the 'backlog clearance exercise', commonly known as the Legacy programme.

The modification to detention policy after the 2006 scandal was that a presumption of detention was secretly introduced for foreign national prisoners facing deportation. The old policy, which clearly stated that there was a presumption in favour of release, remained the publicly declared policy, however.

The Supreme Court held in Lumba that the application of a secret policy was unlawful. However, in common with the Kambadzi judgment, below, only nominal damages were awarded as it was held that the detention would have been justified and inevitable under the publicly declared policy anyway.

Families and children

There is specific guidance in the Enforcement Instructions and Guidance about the detention of families, at chapter 55.9.4. The guidance reiterates that there is a presumption in favour of temporary release and includes the following passage on family unity:

> As a matter of policy we should aim to keep the family as a single unit. However, it will be appropriate to separate a child from its parents if there is evidence that separation is in the best interests of the child. The local authority's social services department will make this decision.

In section 5 of the Immigration Act 2014, brought into force on 28 July 2014, substantial restrictions are put in place regarding the detention of unaccompanied children (by way of an amended schedule 2 to the 1971 Act.

Detained fast track

The Home Office also exercises the power to detain in order to operate the fast track processes at Harmondsworth, Yarl's Wood, Colnbrook and Campsfield (see EIG 55.4). Detention in these circumstances is effectively for the purpose of administrative convenience but it has been upheld as acceptable by Strasbourg (Saadi v UK 13229/03 [2008] ECHR 80).

In Detention Action v Secretary of State for the Home Department [2014] EWHC 2245 (Admin), however, Ouseley J found that the Detained Fast-Track system is unlawful as it is currently being operated, because lawyers are not involved at an early enough stage, thus removing a crucial safeguard. The court decided though that the system could continue to operate whilst the Secretary of State brought about improvements aimed at giving detainees a sufficient time to give proper instructions to their lawyers.

The following categories of applicants should not, according to the APG on Detained Fast Track Processes, be detained in any detained fast track process:

- Women who are 24 or more weeks pregnant;
- Family cases;
- Children (whether applicants or dependants), whose claimed date of birth is accepted by the UK Border Agency;
- Those with a disability which cannot be adequately managed within a detained environment;
- Those with a physical or mental medical condition which cannot be adequately treated within a detained environment, or which for practical reasons, including infectiousness or contagiousness, cannot be properly managed within a detained environment
- Those who clearly lack the mental capacity or coherence to sufficiently understand the asylum process and/or cogently present their claim. This consideration will usually be based on medical information, but where medical information is unavailable, officers must apply their judgement as to an individual's apparent capacity;
- Those for whom there has been a reasonable grounds decision taken (and maintained) by a competent authority stating that the applicant is a potential victim of trafficking or where there has been a conclusive decision taken by a competent authority stating that the applicant is a victim of trafficking;
- Those in respect of whom there is independent evidence of torture.

A failure to follow the DFT policy may render the detention unlawful, leading to a claim for damages. In the case of R (on the application of D) v SSHD & Ors [2006] EWHC 980 (Admin), for example, Davis J held the detention centre rules required a medical examination to take place that had not in fact taken place, that if it had taken place the Home Office would have accepted that the detainee was a victim of torture, and had this happened the detainee would have been released in accordance with policy. Damages were awarded.

Similar unlawful detention cases have been brought in respect of minors and age dispute cases, such as R (on the application of I & O) v SSHD [2005] EWHC 1025 (Admin). In R (on the application of AA) (FC) v SSHD [2013] UKSC 49, where the Supreme Court found that the Home Office had adhered to its policy in detaining a person assessed as being over 18, who was later assessed to be a child. Consequently, the detention was not unlawful.

Detention reviews

The Enforcement Instructions and Guidance requires at 55.8 that a decision to detain or maintain detention must be reviewed at certain times and at a certain level of seniority. In the case of Shepherd Masimba Kambadzi v SSHD [2011] UKSC 23 the Supreme Court held that a failure to conduct these reviews at the required frequency and level of seniority rendered the detention unlawful. However, the Court also held that it would not have been appropriate to order release from detention because the claimant would have been detained in any event, had the reviews been properly conducted. The Court also found that only nominal damages would be appropriate in such a case.

Reference, below, is made to various Civil Service roles. It will be useful to explain their titles to help contextualise their functions.

Managerial positions follow a grading structure for both 'functions'. An Executive Officer (EO) is a junior management grade. The equivalent in the Enforcement arm is the Immigration Officer (IO). A Chief Immigration Officer (CIO) is a middle management grade in Enforcement and the Higher Executive Officer (HEO) is the equivalent grade on the administrative arm. Her Majesty's Inspector (HMI) is a senior manager in Enforcement and the Senior Executive Officer (SEO) is the administrative equivalent. After HMI/SEO the management grades convert to Executive grades at Director level, the lowest being Assistant Director, then Deputy Director and finally Director, who will be the most senior Civil Servant at 'regional' level.

When making decisions relating to detention, the initial decision must be made by a CIO/HEO or Inspector/SEO. The requirements are for reviews to take place after:

> 24 hours
> 7 days
> 14 days by an Inspector
> 21 days
> 28 days by an Inspector

Thereafter the reviews are to take place monthly at the following levels of seniority:

> Months 1 and 2: EO
> Months 3 and 4: SEO or HMI
> Months 5, 6 and 7: Assistant Director or Grade 7
> Months 8, 9, 10 and 11: Deputy Director
> Month 12 and every three months at Director level, within intervening monthly reviews at Deputy Director level

Release and bail

There are a number of steps to be pursued in order to seek release of a client from detention:

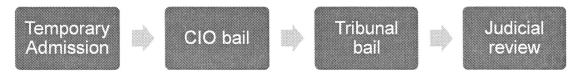

Temporary admission and CIO bail

If a client is detained under the Immigration Acts then consideration must always be given to how they can be released. In the first place verbal communications with the Immigration Service may yield some results, though representations should also be put in writing by way of a request for Temporary Admission ('TA').

Then representations can be made to the Chief Immigration Officer, which is effectively a request for CIO bail. Unlike immigration tribunal bail, there is no prescribed form for CIO bail.

It is unusual for CIO bail to be granted if Temporary Admission has been refused. However, CIO bail enables some additional powers, including demand for a recognisance and sureties. A CIO bail application can be a useful tactical step; if CIO bail is agreed in principle but an unreasonably high recognisance is demanded or it is said that sureties are necessary, these are issues that can sometimes more sensibly be argued and debated with a First-tier Tribunal Judge on an application for immigration tribunal bail. Once the Home Office has agreed bail in principle the only debate should be over conditions.

The local enforcement team responsible for detaining the person should be contacted by phone or fax and reasons obtained if these have not already been provided and representations made as to Temporary Admission. Contact details should be on any IS96 the person has been given. If the representations are unsuccessful then the request should be followed up in writing. Written reasons are presently provided to detainees and interpreted in the form of a checklist. They are reiterated on a monthly basis.

If the detainee is released they will usually be required to comply with conditions. The usual conditions are:

1) Residence at a specified address.

2) Reporting to Police Station or /Immigration Service.

3) Sureties. These conditions can be varied by an application to an IO or immigration judge.

4) Regarding work, he can work so long as there is no restriction on this imposed by the immigration judge (the Home Office does not have power to impose work conditions on an immigration judge's grant of bail).

The Immigration and Asylum Act 1999 enables the making of regulations which can prohibit those granted Temporary Admission from residing in a particular area. In addition the Home Secretary has the power to provide accommodation to those granted Temporary Admission. Where he does so, he is empowered to place conditions on their Temporary Admission requiring them to reside in that accommodation and to impose restrictions on the individual's absence from it.

Information, advice and forms for detainees wanting to get out of detention is available from Bail for Immigration Detainees at:
http://www.biduk.org/433/how-to-get-out-of-detention/useful-forms-and-the-bid-bail-handbook.html
A factsheet on Section 4 support for bail applicants is available from the Asylum Support Appeals Project at:
http://www.asaproject.org/research-publications/factsheets/

Tribunal bail

Power to grant bail

The right to seek bail is contained mainly in Schedule 2 of the 1971 Act as modified over the years since 1971. The right to bail arises in the following circumstances:

i)   new arrivals detained for more than 7 days pending examination (Schedule 2 paragraph 22(1)(a)(1b) as amended by Schedule 2 paragraph 11(1)-(3) of 96 Act);

ii)   those whose leave to enter is cancelled or leave to enter is refused (paragraph 22(1)(aa), Schedule 14 para 63 of the 99 Act);

iii)   suspected illegal entrants and overstayers pending the giving of directions (22(1)(b));

iv)   following a decision to deport (22(1)(b);

v)   following a recommendation for deportation or a deportation order: s.54 of 1999 Act;

vi)   on an application for judicial review as part of interim relief;

vii)   by the Court of Appeal on appeal from the Upper Tribunal.

Bail applications may be made to a Chief Immigration Officer, or to the immigration tribunal.

Under provisions in s7 of the Immigration Act 2014, amending Schedule 2 of the 1971 Act, a person cannot be released on bail without the permission of the Secretary of State, where removal directions have been set and require the person to leave the UK within 14 days of the date of the bail decision. S7 also requires the Tribunal procedure rules to be amended to exclude repeat bail applications within a 28 day period from the previous bail decision unless there has been a material change of circumstances.

Part IV of the Asylum and Immigration Tribunal (Procedure) Rules 2005 (as explained in the appeals chapter, these are now the procedure rules for the Immigration and Asylum Chamber in the First-tier Tribunal) makes specific provision for bail applications before the immigration tribunal. The rules require detailed grounds in support, together with advanced service of a bail address and surety details (though the provision of the latter is not a pre-requisite under the rules), and similarly envisages service of the Respondent's Bail summary by 2.00pm the day prior to the bail application provided adequate notice was given.

An immigration tribunal bail application must be made on a prescribed form, a B1.

An immigration judge may release a bail subject to conditions similar to those an Immigration Officer may impose but with the additional power to require recognisance from the client and any sureties. This will include reappearing before the immigration judge at a later hearing usually the full appeal hearing. Immigration judges can be expected to be sympathetic to clients not attending every further hearing especially where they have to travel some distance – but you may need to make clear at the hearing that your client has maintained contact with you. The exception is where the hearing is a bail variation or extension.

Scottish bail cases are very different to those in England and Wales. This chapter addresses the English and Welsh variety of bail application only.

Factors relevant to bail

The bail guidance issued by the President of the Immigration and Asylum Chamber of the First-tier Tribunal in relation to bail hearings in July 2011 (and amended June 2012) is very useful reading for anyone participating in bail hearings.

The bail guidance starts with a call to arms at paragraph 1:

> The right to liberty is a fundamental right enjoyed by all people in the United Kingdom, whether British citizens or subject to immigration control.

Bail itself is a restriction on liberty, it should be remembered. In bail applications there is a presumption in favour of bail and therefore the burden of proof in justifying detention lies on the Secretary of State. The standard of proof is the balance of probabilities.

The guidance states that there are three broad considerations to be taken into account in making a decision on bail:

> a. The reason or reasons why the person has been detained.
> b. The length of the detention to date and its likely future duration.
> c. The likelihood of the person complying with conditions of bail.

The lawfulness of detention is not something that an Immigration Judge can make a finding on. However, if it appears that a successful claim to habeas corpus or judicial review of the detention could be made then this will be a relevant factor for the Immigration Judge:

> …it will be a good reason to grant bail if for one reason or another continued detention might well be successfully challenged elsewhere.

Some very approximate guidance is given at paragraph 18 as to what is considered a long period of detention:

> ...it is generally accepted that detention for three months would be considered a substantial period of time and six months a long period. Imperative considerations of public safety may be necessary to justify detention in excess of six months.

Where a detainee has difficulty providing an address it is possible to arrange accommodation through the Home Office. A protocol exists between the Home Office and the tribunal and is attached to the tribunal bail guidance.

The guidance includes a section on bail in principle, whereby bail might be granted in principle but release is dependent on certain information being provided to the Immigration Judge. This might arise, for example, where an address for release needs to be provided or information provided by a surety.

Other features of the guidance include the desire to avoid hearings for bail condition variations and the restrictions to be imposed on hearings where a previous bail application was refused in the last 28 days and the fresh application contains no new evidence and no new ground. In these cases the hearing will be shortened as will the opportunity for the applicant to confer with his or her legal representative over the video link before the hearing.

The immigration judge must give a reasoned decision in writing.

Sureties and recognisance

Sureties are put forward as potential guarantors that a person will answer their bail.

There is no requirement in law that sureties or a recognisance be provided (Glowacka), nor that there be any particular sum of money, nor that the money be in especially liquid form (hence one might offer to stand on the basis of property rather than cash deposits in a bank). The UNHCR in their 1999 Guidelines on Criteria and Standards Relating to the Detention of Asylum Seekers make the point that asylum seekers should not be expected to produce sureties willing to offer prohibitively high sums of money.

The standard Bail Form, the B1, has spaces for two sureties, though there is no requirement that there are two: more could be made available, or none. The details of any sureties must be provided to the immigration tribunal and Home Office so that the individuals in question, and their addresses, can be the subject of investigation via the Police National Computer (PNC). Two days' notice should be given to the Home Office for this purpose.

Those with criminal convictions or insecure immigration status, or whose addresses have in the past been associated with absconding, are unlikely to make good sureties.

The sureties should always attend court – it will rarely be the case that non-attendance will be accepted (though it is not completely unknown for a formal declaration to suffice, taken before an establishment figure). The surety should have proof of ID, address occupation, financial status, immigration status (ideally British citizenship or Indefinite Leave to Remain) and evidence of the address that is available to the detainee. Immigration judges tend to prefer a surety who is living with or near an applicant to ensure that are able to exercise a measure of control over them. The surety should explain their relationship to the detainee, and what level of contact they have had with them in the past, and intend to maintain in the future.

For renewals and variations it may be possible to avoid attendance by the sureties and it may even be possible to avoid a hearing. The current bail guidance allows for no hearing to take place where the Home Office have no objection to the renewal or variation.

If the bailee breaches the bail conditions in any way the sureties risk forfeiting all or part of their recognisance at a forfeiture hearing at the tribunal. It is important that the sureties fully understand this risk as they may be liable even though they have done their best to avoid such an event.

Large sums have sometimes been required by immigration judges and adjudicators (or CIOs) sums of several thousands of pounds are not unknown. In order to ascertain the surety's appreciation of the situation, the immigration judge may question the sureties to see if their confidence in the applicant meeting his bail conditions was well founded, whether they monitored compliance with bail conditions and whether they suspected any failure to comply.

Top tip

Parents and partners are often not powerful sureties. This is because of their close relationship with the applicant for bail: many immigration judges will have had the unpleasant task of conducting forfeiture hearings with such sureties and will consider them not best able to judge a bail applicant's character because of their closeness, or alternatively too much under the influence of the bail applicant or willing to do anything to get the bail applicant out of detention, including forfeit large amounts of money.

Close friends or colleagues willing to put up substantial sums and who can explain that they understand the risk may make better sureties.

Generally, Bail Circle volunteers or detention visitors are not considered good sureties by most immigration judges.

Bail conditions

Immigration Judges will usually be anxious to avoid a situation arising where a grant of bail or conditions conflict with a <u>licence for release</u> from prison following a criminal sentence. To that end, information from the probation service may well be required. The Criminal Casework Directorate should hold the details of any licence so this information can usually be provided by the Home Office.

Where an immigration appeal is pending, the primary conditions for bail are usually as follows:

➢ to attend the next and every subsequent hearing of the appeal at such places and times as shall be notified or as otherwise varied in writing by the Tribunal; and

➢ following final determination of the appeal, unless bail is revoked by the Tribunal or by operation of law, to appear before an Immigration Officer at such time and place as directed by the Tribunal; and

➢ the terms of bail may be varied at any time during their currency by application or at the Tribunal's own motion.

An Immigration Judge is also likely to impose secondary conditions such as relating to the place of residence of the person to be released on bail and how the person released on bail should maintain contact with the immigration authorities.

Preparing bail applications

Bail summaries provided by the Home Office are, unfortunately, often accurate and/or misleading, sometimes woefully so. For example, the Home Office may allege that a person was an absconder when in fact they were not or may fail to record that a person has complied with previous conditions for bail or temporary admission. It is therefore crucial to take instructions on the accuracy of a bail summary.

It can be very helpful to prepare a witness statement by a bail applicant. Such statements need not be long, but it should be borne in mind that live evidence at a bail hearing, particularly one by video link, is often unhelpful to the applicant. Any applicant for bail can be expected to state that he or she will comply with conditions, for example, and such assurances therefore carry little weight. Cross examination of a bail applicant is often a productive exercise for the Home Office, though, particularly with an unprepared witness.

The following are suggestions for instructions to consider taking from a client who is applying for bail:

➤ The detention criteria issues listed already, in so far as relevant to the facts of the case in hand.

➤ Ensure that the facts that are said to give rise to a power to detain are truly established – e.g. was the person working in breach of conditions, and/or are the Home Office right to say they have overstayed their leave? Do they have an entitlement to remain in the UK under a Home Office policy?

➤ Ensure that any referrals are made that are shown to be necessary by the instructions – e.g. for mental or physical health care.

➤ Ensure that instructions are taken in a way that recognises any vulnerability of the client.

Top tip

It is an unfortunate fact that bail summaries are often woefully inaccurate and/or highly misleading. For example, the underlying facts are sometimes wrong, or important facts are omitted – such as difficulties the Home Office has had in obtaining an EDT. Sometimes a person will be accused of failing to report when in fact they did report, or were in immigration or criminal detention at the relevant time.

It is crucial not to assume bail summaries are accurate and to take full instructions on them.

It is also important to prepare the sureties. A criminal records check and also an address check against immigration records and past bail cases may be conducted with sureties. Therefore, it is important that sureties are aware this will happen; otherwise they will get an unpleasant surprise they will not welcome at the hearing. Also seek instructions on the following information pertaining to the sureties:

➤ Any criminal convictions (especially offences of dishonesty or related to immigration)

➤ Financial situation, including expenses and income – any recent large transactions into their account should be explained. Liquidity of assets – they may have to deposit the money in question; and can they deal with its forfeiture.

➤ Evidence of support and accommodation arrangements. Ensure any money comes from sources that do not raise questions of ethics or criminal immigration offences

> Plans regarding any trips abroad or other engagements which might impact on the effectiveness of their being surety, or their ability to support subsequent extensions of bail.

> How they know, and how they intend to maintain contact with, or control over, the applicant

> What they would do in the event that the bailee did breach bail conditions.

National security cases

Under the NIAA 2002, the SSHD may certify that it is believed that the person's presence in the United Kingdom is a "risk to national security" and that it is suspected that the person is connected to international terrorism. On certifying an individual is such a person the Home Office may take removal action.

Applications for bail are brought before the SIAC. Under the Asylum & Immigration (Treatment of Claimants Etc.) Act 2004, section 32 gives a right of appeal regarding the grant of bail, on a point of law, to the Court of Appeal, to which the normal SIAC processes then apply, i.e. an appeal may be brought only with the leave of the Commission or, if such leave is refused, with the leave of the appropriate appeal court.

Challenges to lawfulness of detention

Detention can be challenged on Hardial Singh principles, essentially whether the length of detention is reasonable, and on the grounds that the detention is not in accordance with Home Office policies. It would be unusual directly to challenge lawfulness of detention before applying for temporary release and/or bail (bail is covered in the next section), as these are the simplest ways to secure a detainee's release from detention, which is likely to be the detainee's main priority. However, an understanding of lawfulness of detention can inform such applications, and can be important in securing compensation for a detainee after release.

Applications in such cases may be run by way of habeas corpus application, but more normally by way of judicial review proceedings in the Administrative Court. Judicial review has the advantage of being able to pursue damages as part of the proceedings (although the case will be referred to the Queen's Bench Division or a county court for assessment). Habeas corpus can only be used where it is the power to detain that is under challenge, but it has the advantage of a quick listing in the Administrative Court.

There is judicial support for the notion that whereas immigration judges are to consider the correctness of the exercise of the power to detain (via the factors set out above, paragraph 3.1 onwards), the lawfulness of the exercise of the power is a matter for the Administrative Court alone. Thus Collins J stated in R v Secretary of State for the Home Department ex parte Konan [2004] EWHC 22 Admin:

> An adjudicator in considering a bail application is not determining (indeed, he has no power to determine) the lawfulness of the detention.

However many arguments may be relevant under both the lawfulness of detention and its correctness – e.g. a lengthy detention is something which might eventually make detention unlawful, but it is also a relevant consideration as to the correctness of detention in all the circumstances and according to Home Office detention policy. Nevertheless, many immigration judges are reluctant to consider length of detention as a relevant factor and will allow detention to continue considerably beyond a reasonable period on the grounds that lawfulness is not for the immigration tribunal to decide.

In addition, unlawful detention can be grounds for compensation: see ID and Others v The Home Office [2005] EWCA Civ 38. Where lawfulness arises as an issue, it may be in the client's best interests to make an application for an Order to the High Court. This can be done simultaneously with an immigration tribunal bail application, as the bail application is the fastest way to try to secure release for a client, but it is not a challenge to lawfulness and is not a basis for securing compensation.

Where the issue is one of lawfulness of the detention a writ of habeas corpus can be applied for. This has a higher priority over judicial review with respect to listing of the hearing and a refusal of the writ is potentially appealable to the House of Lords whereas a refusal by the Court of Appeal, on a renewed application, to grant permission to apply for JR is not.

For an excellent and thorough lesson in all aspects of Unlawful detention, go to: http://www.freemovement.org.uk/training/training-courses/

Administrative removal

Most forcible removals of foreign nationals from the UK take place by way of 'administrative removal'. Once outside the UK, the removed person will be prevented from applying for re-entry for a 10 year period (rule 320(7B)) unless the applicant is seeking to return under an Appendix FM category rule A320). This distinguishes administrative removal from deportation, as a deportation order excludes the person forever unless the deportation order is revoked.

The power of administrative removal is currently provided for in;

➢ Schedule 2 of the 1971 Act, particularly at paragraph 8. This applies to illegal entrants, as defined at s.33 of the 1971 Act.

➢ Section 10 of the Immigration and Asylum Act 1999 extends the power to those who become present in the UK illegally, including those
   o who have overstayed their leave
   o who have otherwise breached the conditions of their stay in the UK

- o using deception in seeking (whether successfully or not)leave to remain
- o whose indefinite leave to remain has been revoked under s76(3) of the 1999 Act,
- o and family members of the above

Service of the decision to remove cancels any leave the person may have had prior to that date.

Provisions under the Immigration Act 2014 change the statutory power to deport and will have important procedural consequences which we will look at below.

Challenging removal decisions

Currently, removing an illegal entrant or a person who has breached the conditions of their stay is a two-part process.

Firstly, a removal decision has to be made and served in accordance with the requirements of the Immigration (Notices) Regulations 2003 (as amended). That decision will be appealable under s82 of the NIA 2002 and, where an asylum or human rights claim has already been made, will (unless the human rights claim or asylum claim has been certified as clearly unfounded, see below) give rise to an in-country right of appeal. Where an appeal is lodged, removal will be suspended pending the conclusion of the appeal process (s78 of the NIA 2002).

Where the decision gives rise to an in-country right of appeal it should be served with a Notice of Appeal (Regulation 5(4)). Where human rights claim is made after the service of the decision, the decision-maker should withdraw the decision and, if the claim is to be refused, re-serve it in accordance with the Regulations (i.e. accompanied by a Notice of Appeal).

Secondly, if no appeal is lodged, or the appeal is finally determined against the appellant, or where the right of appeal is to be exercised out of country, the Home Office will then set removal directions (RDs). RDs will determine the date and time of removal.

Where a person facing removal has exhausted all rights of appeal, the Secretary of State used to be required (under the notorious and now deleted rule 395C) to consider all relevant circumstances of the person facing removal, to determine whether there were any exceptional circumstances which suggested removal was not now the appropriate course. The position now, under rule 353B, is that the onus is on the person facing removal to bring any reasons why they should not face removal to the attention of the Home Office. Where those reasons engage Article 8 of the ECHR, the various private and family life provisions in the rules will be applied.

An Article 8 claim can be made by way of a valid application under Rule 276ADE(1) or Appendix FM, but a valid application will not have to be made in the circumstances outlined in GEN 1.9;

> GEN.1.9. In this Appendix:
>
> (a) the requirement to make a valid application will not apply when the Article 8 claim is raised:
>
> (i) as part of an asylum claim, or as part of a further submission in person after an asylum claim has been refused;
>
> (ii) where a migrant is in immigration detention. A migrant in immigration detention or their representative must submit any application or claim raising Article 8 to a prison officer, a prisoner custody officer, a detainee custody officer or a member of Home Office staff at the migrant's place of detention; or
>
> (iii) in an appeal (subject to the consent of the Secretary of State where applicable); and
>
> (b) where an application or claim raising Article 8 is made in any of the circumstances specified in paragraph GEN.1.9.(a), or is considered by the Secretary of State under paragraph A277C of these rules, the requirements of paragraphs R-LTRP.1.1.(c) and R-LTRPT.1.1.(c) are not met.".

In such cases, a fee can be saved by making the claim by way of representations and accompanying evidence.

If the Article 8 claim gets nowhere, it is highly unlikely that the factors referred to in 353B will change the Home Office's mind. Chapter 53 of the EIG, 'Extenuating circumstances' lays out the considerations that must be applied at this stage.

Where a person has made an in-time application for an extension of stay, Section 47 of the 2006 Act allows the Secretary of State to make simultaneous decisions to refuse to extend a person's leave and to remove them from the UK.

As you will see in the section on appeals however, where a decision is made to refuse an application made by an overstayer, there is no requirement on the Home Office in refusing the application to generate an appealable decision at all (i.e. a decision to remove). Such a person may remain in limbo indefinitely.

Those caught in the limbo situation may be able to seek judicial review of their human rights claim, but an appeal is preferable. In certain circumstances[11], the Home Office will respond positively to a request for a removal decision, made by way of a pre-action protocol letter, particularly where;

---

[11] Modernised Guidance: Requests for removal decisions

- the refused application for leave to remain included a dependant child under 18 resident in the UK for three years or more
- the applicant has a dependant child under the age of 18 who is a British citizen
- the applicant is being supported by the Home Office or has provided evidence of being supported by a local authority (under section 21 of the National Assistance Act 1948 or section 17 of the Children Act 1989), or
- there are other exceptional and compelling reasons to make a removal decision at this time.

Under the provisions in Part 2 of the Immigration Act 2014 though, the right of appeal will not be in respect of the removal decision itself, but against the decision to refuse a human rights claim. That should end the current situation of people waiting in limbo, potentially for many years, awaiting the removal decision and therefore the right of appeal.

Removal under the Immigration Act 2014

Section 1 of the Immigration Act 2014 repeals and replaces section 10 of 1999 Act, removing the need for a removal decision to be made before removal directions are set. The purpose of the new provisions is to streamline the removal process, requiring just one decision to refuse or curtail leave before the person can be removed.

The new section 10 applies, as of 20 October 2014, to students and their dependants.

A person with no leave who is required to have it may simply be removed from the United Kingdom with no further notice or legal step being required. Consequently, presumably, the Immigration (Notices) Regulations will be repealed or substantially amended when the new s10 comes into force.

Related provisions apply to family members as defined (see below). If a notice of removal is served on such a family member, the notice invalidates any leave that the family member previously possessed: s10(6). The Home Office stated early in the passage of the Bill that it was intended that the new power be a feature of a single decision which will apply to:

- people who make applications to the Home Office for leave to remain in the UK
- people who have not made an application, but where the Home Office receives information (e.g. from a sponsor) that leads to the person's leave being curtailed or revoked, and
- people unlawfully in the UK who are encountered by immigration officers

Essentially, this new power removes the need for a separate decision to remove prior to removal directions being set, as well as doing away with the very considerable administrative problems caused by section 47 of the Immigration, Asylum and Nationality Act 2006.

The new removal power applies to any person who 'requires leave to enter or remain in the United Kingdom but does not have it': s.10(1). Those who do have it, but are caught in breach (e.g. working in breach of a restriction or prohibition), will presumably have their leave curtailed first.

The new provision should be seen as a power to remove rather than a type or species of immigration decision as we are used to under the Immigration (Notices) Regulations 2003 and s82 of the 2002 Act. There is no right of appeal removal under the new appeal provisions because there will be no decision as such under the new section 10. However, the service of removal directions might well lead a person making a human rights or asylum claim (or applying for judicial review if they have other grounds to challenge their removal).

The power also applies to a member of family of the person facing removal: s.10(2). Member of family is fairly widely defined to include partner, parent, adult dependent relative or child or child living in the same household where the person facing removal has care of the child: s.10(3).

The member of the family must either have leave to enter or remain on the basis of family life with the person facing removal or, in the opinion of the Secretary of State or immigration officer, if making an application for leave would not be granted leave in his or her own right but would be granted leave on the basis of family life with the person facing removal if the person facing removal themselves had leave: s.10(4). The removal power does not apply if the family member is a British citizen or has an enforceable EU right to reside: s.10(5).

Section 2 inserts a new s.78A into 2002 Act to provide protection from removal where a child is to be removed and a parent or person with care of the child or a person in the child's household is also to be removed.

The new provision provides for a 28 day grace period from exhaustion of appeal rights in which actual removal is forbidden for the child and for the adult where 'if, as a result, no relevant parent or carer would remain in the United Kingdom'. Preparatory steps towards removal such as the setting of removal directions or making of a deportation order are not prohibited.

Section 3 inserts a new s.54A into the 2009 Act immediately before s.55 to provide statutory footing for the Independent Family Returns Panel ('the panel').

The panel must be consulted by the Secretary of State 'on how best to safeguard and promote the welfare of the children of the family':

> (a) in each family returns case and

> (b) in each case where the Secretary of State proposes to detain a family in pre-departure accommodation, on the suitability of so doing, having particular regard to the need to safeguard and promote the welfare of the children of the family.

A 'family returns case' is a case where removal of a child is going to take place along with removal of a person who:

(i) is a parent of the child or has care of the child, and

(ii) is living in a household in the United Kingdom with the child

There is no duty on the Secretary of State to abide by any recommendations, only to consult. Recommendations or comments could therefore be disregarded by the Secretary of State, although that would obviously call into question whether the Secretary of State was abiding by the duty imposed by s.55 of the 2009 Act and reiterated by s.71 of this Act, which provides:

> For the avoidance of doubt, this Act does not limit any duty imposed on the Secretary of State or any other person by section 55 of the Borders, Citizenship and Immigration Act 2009 (duty regarding the welfare of children).

Deportation

Power to deport

A person who is not a British citizen is liable to deportation from the United Kingdom if "the Secretary of State deems his deportation to be conducive to the public good", or if he is the family member of such a person (section 3(5)(a) Immigration Act 1971 refers). By section 5(1) of the 1971 Act the Secretary of State may make a deportation order against a person liable to deportation under section 3(5).

A deportation order requires the person to leave and prohibits such person from entering the UK whilst such order is extant. Before attempting to apply to return to the UK, the deportee must first apply for the deport order to be revoked.

Section 3:

> (5) A person who is not a British citizen is liable to deportation from the United Kingdom if-
> (a) the Secretary of State deems his deportation to be conducive to the public good; or
> (b) another person to whose family he belongs is or has been ordered to be deported.
> (6) Without prejudice to the operation of subsection (5) above, a person who is not a British citizen shall also be liable to deportation from the United Kingdom if, after he has attained the age of seventeen, he is convicted of an offence for which he is punishable with imprisonment and on his conviction is recommended for deportation by a court empowered by this Act to do so.

Section 5:

> (1) Where a person is under section 3(5) or (6) above liable to deportation, then subject to the following provisions of this Act the Secretary of State may make a deportation order against him, that is to say an order requiring him to leave and

> prohibiting him from entering the United Kingdom; and a deportation order against a person shall invalidate any leave to enter or remain in the United Kingdom given him before the order is made or while it is in force.
>
> (2) A deportation order against a person may at any time be revoked by a further order of the Secretary of State, and shall cease to have effect if he becomes a British citizen.

Section 7 of the 1971 Act provides for exemption from deportation for long term residents who:

> ➢ are Commonwealth or Irish citizens and were such on 1 January 1971 when the 1971 Act came into force
>
> ➢ were ordinarily resident in the UK on 1 January 1973
>
> ➢ have been resident in the UK for five years at the time of either a court or the Secretary of State considering whether to make a deportation order.

'Ordinarily resident' has no statutory meaning but has been held to exclude unlawful residence.

Procedure for deportation

Deportation decisions can be made on discretionary grounds, based on the recommendation of a criminal court judge or a decision of the Secretary of State, or automatic grounds under the provisions of s32 of the UK Borders Act 2007.

The procedures for discretionary and automatic deportation decisions are slightly different, though the differences have few practical implications. In either case, the Secretary of State identifies a person subject to deportation, and then gives them an opportunity to make representations as to why they should not be deported.

With the commencement of parts of the Immigration Act 2014 on 20 October 2014, those defined under s117D(2) of 2002 Act as a foreign criminal will no longer have an automatic right of appeal.

> (2) In this Part, "foreign criminal" means a person—
>
> (a) who is not a British citizen,
>
> (b) who has been convicted in the United Kingdom of an offence, and
>
> (c) who—
> (i)   has been sentenced to a period of imprisonment of at least 12 months,
> (ii)   has been convicted of an offence that has caused serious harm, or
> (iii)   is a persistent offender.

They will be served with a s120 notice giving them an opportunity to raise a human rights or asylum claim. The refusal of the asylum or human rights claim will give rise to a right of appeal.

The new procedure is laid out in 'Appeals guidance annex A: appeals transitional guidance' at: https://www.gov.uk/government/publications/appeals

Amendments to the 2002 Act, by s17 of the Immigration Act 2014, and brought into force on 28 July 2014, allow the HO to remove a deportee prior to their appeal (see further below).

Discretionary deportation

Notification of the decision to deport and the procedure to be followed is described at rules 381 to 384:

> 381. When a decision to make a deportation order has been taken (otherwise than on the recommendation of a court) a notice will be given to the person concerned informing him of the decision and of his right of appeal.
>
> 382. Following the issue of such a notice the Secretary of State may authorise detention or make an order restricting a person as to residence, employment or occupation and requiring him to report to the police, pending the making of a deportation order.
>
> 383. ...
>
> 384. If a notice of appeal is given within the period allowed, a summary of the facts of the case on the basis of which the decision was taken will be sent to the appropriate appellate authorities, who will notify the appellant of the arrangements for the appeal to be heard.

The implication that notice of a decision to deport need not be given to a person if the decision is made on the recommendation of a court is incorrect. It reflects the position prior to the coming into force of NIAA s. 82 which for the first time introduced a right of appeal against decisions to deport following the recommendation of a court. The Immigration (Notices) Regulations 2003 (SI 2003/658) require written notice to be given to a person of any appealable immigration decision. A decision to deport following a recommendation of the Court remains appealable (albeit usually out of country) and therefore a decision of which written notice must be given.

Security cases

Where the SSHD certifies that the decision to make a deportation order was taken on the grounds that the person's removal from the UK would be in the interests of national security (NIAA 2002 s. 97A). Such a person will be able to appeal against the decision to deport only to SIAC and only from outside the country.

If the person then makes a human rights claim, he or she can appeal in country unless the SSHD certifies that removal would not breach the person's human rights. In such a case, the person can appeal, in country, to SIAC against that certificate.

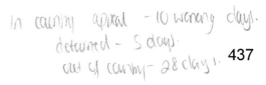

In country appeal - 10 working days.
detained - 5 days.
out of country - 28 days.

Automatic deportation — *no need for notice of intention*

'Automatic' deportations were introduced in the wake of the foreign prisoner scandal in 2006. In fact such deportations are not completely automatic as the traditional human rights defence still operates.

Perhaps the most notable procedural difference, described below, is that the deportation order itself is made very early in the process without the need for a notice of intention to deport or a notice of a decision to make a deportation order. However, the making of an 'automatic' section 32 deportation order does not prevent an appeal; the appeal in such a case actually lies against the deportation order itself.

Section 32 of the UK Borders Act 2007, which partially came into force on 1 August 2008, places a duty on the Secretary of State to make a deportation order in respect of a person who is not a British citizen and who has been convicted in the UK of an offence and sentenced to a period of imprisonment of at least 12 months (i.e. 'Condition 1). Condition 2, for serious criminals not imprisoned for 12 months or more, has not yet been brought into force.

Imprisonment for 12 months or more does not include suspended sentences, or shorter consecutive sentences which only meet the test when aggregated (see s38).

Section 32(4) introduces a statutory presumption that a deportation to which section 32 applies is conducive to the public good for the purpose of s.3(5)(a) 1971 Act. This duty applies to all foreign criminals except where they fall within one of the exceptions in section 33. Where an exception does apply, deportation may still be appropriate under the existing discretionary deportation provisions of the Immigration Act 1971 or, in the case of EEA nationals and their family members who are exercising Treaty rights, under the Immigration (European Economic Area) Regulations 2006.

The exceptions in s.33 are as follows:

(1) Where deportation would breach human rights or the refugee convention

(2) Age (under 18 at date of conviction)

(3) EC treaty rights would be breached

(4) Extradition – where the person is the subject of extradition proceedings

(5) Mental health grounds – but only where specific sections of the Mental Health Act 1983 apply to the person

(6) Recognised victim of trafficking – this is not yet in force but protects where the SSHD take the view removal would breach the Council of Europe trafficking convention

The applicability of one of the exceptions does not render a section 32 deportation unlawful, but can lead to revocation of the deportation order if made out.

Appeal rights under the 2014 Act

The new appeals regime for deportees, brought into force on 28 July 2014, enables the Secretary of State to require any appeal against deportation to be brought from abroad only, both in UK law and EU law cases. To create this new power, a new section 94B of the Nationality, Asylum and Immigration Act 2002 has been created. This provides as follows:

> **94B Appeal from within the United Kingdom: certification of human rights claims made by persons liable to deportation**
>
> (1) This section applies where a human rights claim has been made by a person ("P") who is liable to deportation under—
>
> (a) section 3(5)(a) of the Immigration Act 1971 (Secretary of State deeming deportation conducive to public good), or
>
> (b) section 3(6) of that Act (court recommending deportation following conviction).
>
> (2) The Secretary of State may certify the claim if the Secretary of State considers that, despite the appeals process not having been begun or not having been exhausted, removal of P to the country or territory to which P is proposed to be removed, pending the outcome of an appeal in relation to P's claim, would not be unlawful under section 6 of the Human Rights Act 1998 (public authority not to act contrary to Human Rights Convention).
>
> (3) The grounds upon which the Secretary of State may certify a claim under subsection (2) include (in particular) that P would not, before the appeals process is exhausted, face a real risk of serious irreversible harm if removed to the country or territory to which P is proposed to be removed.

It can be seen that this section only creates the power to issue a certificate. The effect of the certificate is in the new amended version of section 92 NIAA 2002 when that is brought into force, and in the meantime by a modified version of section 92 brought into effect by a Commencement Order. New guidance from the Home Office addresses the circumstances in which these new certificates will be issued. Separate guidance exists for non EEA and EEA cases:

> ➤ <u>Section 94B certification guidance for Non European Economic Area deportation cases.</u>

The guidance on non EEA cases suggests that the Home Office will be enthusiastic about use of the new power:

> The Government's policy is that the deportation process should be as efficient and effective as possible and therefore case owners should seek to certify a case using the section 94B power in all cases meeting these criteria where doing so would not result in serious irreversible harm.

However, the new power will apparently be tested on a limited group of cases where:

➢ the individual is aged 18 or over at the time of the deportation decision, and
➢ does not have a parental relationship with a dependent child or children. It will be possible to certify cases involving children where there is no evidence that the FNO [Foreign National Offender] has any parental relationship with the dependent child or children

Further guidance is given on cases that might be considered to involve children, including that where there is evidence of an individual who is being considered for certification playing an active role in a child's life, then certification would not normally be appropriate in this initial test phase.

The Home Office accepts that Article 3 and refugee cases should not be certified under this new power:

> It is not appropriate to certify protection claims made on the basis of the Refugee Convention and/or ECHR Article 2 and Article 3 because there will arguably be a real risk of serious irreversible harm.

➢ <u>Guidance on certification for non-suspensive appeals in EEA deportation cases</u>

The Immigration (European Economic Area)(Amendment)(No.2) Regulations 2014 (SI 2014/1976) came into force on 28 July 2014. They amend the Immigration (European Economic Area) Regulations 2006 so that an appeal against a deportation decision under Regulation 19(3)(b) can still be lodged in the UK but no longer suspends removal proceedings, except where:

➢ The Secretary of State has not certified that the person would not face a real risk of serious irreversible harm if removed to the country of return before the appeal is finally determined.
➢ The person has made an application to the courts for an interim order to suspend removal proceedings (e.g. by judicial review) and that application has not yet been determined, or a court has made an interim order to suspend removal.

Where an interim order to suspend removal proceedings is initiated, the guidance states that removal will not be suspended where:

➢ the notice of a decision to make a deportation order is based on a previous judicial decision;
➢ or the person has had previous access to judicial review;
➢ or the removal decision is based on imperative grounds of public security.

In addition, a person removed from the UK under this new regime can apply to re-enter the UK under Regulation 29AA to make submissions at his own appeal hearing. This is because Article 31(4) of Directive 2004/38/EC states that:

> Member States may exclude the individual concerned from their territory pending the redress procedure, but they may not prevent the individual from submitting his/her defence in person, except when his/her appearance may cause serious troubles to public policy or public security or when the appeal or judicial review concerns a denial of entry to the territory.

Serious and irreversible harm

The Home Office guidance on the test applies in both non EEA and EEA cases. The guidance observes that the test relates to the period between deportation and the conclusion of any appeal, after which the person will return to the UK if successful, and that the test requires that the harm be serious AND irreversible. Next, the guidance goes on to suggest situations that in the opinion of the Home Office would <u>not</u> meet the test:

➤ A person will be separated from their child/partner for several months while the individual appeals against a human rights decision
➤ A family court case is in progress
➤ A child/partner is undergoing treatment for a temporary or chronic medical condition that is under control and can be satisfactorily managed through medication or other treatment and does not require the person liable to deportation to act as a full time carer
➤ The FNO has a medical issue which does not lead to an Article 3 breach
➤ A person has strong private life ties to a community that will be disrupted by deportation (e.g. they have a job, a mortgage, a prominent role in a community organisation etc.)

It might be thought that the family court case suggestion is clearly wrong. A person usually needs to be physically present in the UK in contested family court proceedings as various assessments are often needed which will be impossible if the person is not present in the UK.

The guidance then goes on to give examples of situations that in the view of the Home Office would meet the test:

➤ The person has a genuine and subsisting parental relationship with a child who is seriously ill, requires full-time care, and there is no one else who can provide that care
➤ The person has a genuine and subsisting long-term relationship with a partner who is seriously ill and requires full-time care because they are unable to care for themselves, and there is no one else who can provide that care

The guidance concludes:

> The onus is on the Secretary of State to demonstrate that there is not a real risk of serious irreversible harm. However, if a person claims that a non-suspensive appeal

would result in serious irreversible harm, the onus is on that person to substantiate the claim with documentary evidence, preferably from official sources, for example a signed letter on letter-headed paper from the GP responsible for treatment, a family court order, a marriage or civil partnership certificate, documentary evidence from official sources demonstrating long-term co-habitation, etc. Case owners should expect to see original documents rather than copies.

Example

Mehmet was convicted of a crime and sentenced to 14 months' imprisonment. Irrespective of whether a recommendation for deportation is made by the sentencing judge, the sentence should trigger the automatic deportation process.

If the Home Office take the view that none of the 2007 Act s.33 exceptions apply, Mehmet will be served with a Deportation Order at a time of the Home Office's choosing. We would expect this to occur while Mehmet is serving his criminal sentence, or shortly afterward when brought into immigration detention.

The serving of the Deportation Order currently triggers a right of appeal, because of s.82(3A) of the 2002 Act. The right of appeal will be out of country (i.e. Mehmet will have to await deportation before the appeal hearing can go ahead). A human rights claim will not help to bring the appeal back in-country unless Mehmet is able to show that he faces a real risk of serious irreversible harm if removed to the country or territory to which P is proposed to be removed.

The only arguments available to Mehmet on appeal are whether any of the s.33 exceptions apply to him. If the appeal is successful, the Deportation Order will be revoked and he will be able to return to the UK if he has the leave to do so. If the appeal is dismissed, the Deportation Order will remain in force and he will not be able to return to the UK.

Revocation of deportation order

Immigration rule 390 provides as follows:

390. An application for revocation of a deportation order will be considered in the light of all the circumstances including the following:

(i) the grounds on which the order was made;

(ii) any representations made in support of revocation;

(iii) the interests of the community, including the maintenance of an effective immigration control;

(iv) the interests of the applicant, including any compassionate circumstances.

390A. Where paragraph 398 applies the Secretary of State will consider whether paragraph 399 or 399A applies and, if it does not, it will only be in exceptional circumstances that the public interest in maintaining the deportation order will be outweighed by other factors.

Immigration rules 391-392 then go on to set out the circumstances where revocation may be appropriate and the effect of revocation:

391. In the case of a person who has been deported following conviction for a criminal offence, the continuation of a deportation order against that person will be the proper course:

(a) in the case of a conviction for an offence for which the person was sentenced to a period of imprisonment of less than 4 years, unless 10 years have elapsed since the making of the deportation order, or

(b) in the case of a conviction for an offence for which the person was sentenced to a period of imprisonment of at least 4 years, at any time,

Unless, in either case, the continuation would be contrary to the Human Rights Convention or the Convention and Protocol Relating to the Status of Refugees, or there are other exceptional circumstances that mean the continuation is outweighed by compelling factors.

391A. In other cases, revocation of the order will not normally be authorised unless the situation has been materially altered, either by a change of circumstances since the order was made, or by fresh information coming to light which was not before the appellate authorities or the Secretary of State. The passage of time since the person was deported may also in itself amount to such a change of circumstances as to warrant revocation of the order.

392. Revocation of a deportation order does not entitle the person concerned to re-enter the United Kingdom; it renders him eligible to apply for admission under the Immigration Rules. Application for revocation of the order may be made to the Entry Clearance Officer or direct to the Home Office.

A refusal to revoke a deportation order is appealable to the immigration tribunal (see NIAA s. 82(2)(k)). Such an appeal will usually be an out of country appeal by virtue of s.92 2002 Act. However, where a fresh asylum or human rights claim is made as part of the application for revocation then this qualifies the claimant for an in-country right of appeal under s.92(4)(a) irrespective of whether the fresh claim qualifies under immigration rule 353 (R (on the app of BA (Nigeria)) v SSHD [2009] UKSC 7). The Home Office can however certify the claim as clearly unfounded, or now under the new s94B, removing the in-country right of appeal.

Substantive considerations

Operational Guidance on criminality and Article 8 is in the IDIs (Chapter 13) at: https://www.gov.uk/government/publications/chapter-13-criminality-guidance-in-article-8-echr-cases

The immigration rules in respect of deportation have changed substantially over the years to reflect the ever-growing level of political attention given to foreign national prisoners.

The Immigration Rules governing deportation decisions were amended on 9 July 2012 to incorporate the government's view of how Article 8 considerations should be applied to a person facing deportation, and again on 28 July 2014 to reflect various judgments of the Upper Tribunal and the Court of Appeal on the new rules.

The new rules as amended apply to all ECHR Article 8 claims from foreign criminals which are decided on or after 28 July 2014. The unamended new rules applied to those facing deportation on or after 9 July 2012 regardless of when the notice of intention to deport or the deportation order was served.

Article 8 claims made in the context of a deport decision will now be assessed in line with rules 398 to 399C.

Deportation and Article 8

A398. These rules apply where:

(a) a foreign criminal liable to deportation claims that his deportation would be contrary to the United Kingdom's obligations under Article 8 of the Human Rights Convention;
(b) a foreign criminal applies for a deportation order made against him to be revoked

398. Where a person claims that their deportation would be contrary to the UK's obligations under Article 8 of the Human Rights Convention, and

(a) the deportation of the person from the UK is conducive to the public good and in the public interest because they have been convicted of an offence for which they have been sentenced to a period of imprisonment of at least 4 years;
(b) the deportation of the person from the UK is conducive to the public good and in the public interest because they have been convicted of an offence for which they have been sentenced to a period of imprisonment of less than 4 years but at least 12 months; or
(c) the deportation of the person from the UK is conducive to the public good and in the public interest because, in the view of the Secretary of State, their offending has caused serious harm or they are a persistent offender who shows a particular disregard for the law,

the Secretary of State in assessing that claim will consider whether paragraph 399 or 399A applies and, if it does not, the public interest in deportation will only be

---

outweighed by other factors where there are very compelling circumstances over and above those described in paragraphs 399 and 399A.

399. This paragraph applies where paragraph 398 (b) or (c) applies if –
(a) the person has a genuine and subsisting parental relationship with a child under the age of 18 years who is in the UK, and
    (i) the child is a British Citizen; or
    (ii) the child has lived in the UK continuously for at least the 7 years immediately preceding the date of the immigration decision; and in either case
    (a) it would be unduly harsh for the child to live in the country to which the person is to be deported; and
    (b) it would be unduly harsh for the child to remain in the UK without the person who is to be deported; or

(b) the person has a genuine and subsisting relationship with a partner who is in the UK and is a British Citizen or settled in the UK, and
    (i) the relationship was formed at a time when the person (deportee) was in the UK lawfully and their immigration status was not precarious; and
    (ii) it would be unduly harsh for that partner to live in the country to which the person is to be deported, because of compelling circumstances over and above those described in EX.2. of Appendix FM; and
    (iii) it would be unduly harsh for that partner to remain in the UK without the person who is to be deported.

399A. This paragraph applies where paragraph 398(b) or (c) applies if –
(a) the person has been lawfully resident in the UK for most of his life; and
(b) he is socially and culturally integrated in the UK; and
(c) there would be very significant obstacles to his integration into the country to which it is proposed he is deported.

399B. Where an Article 8 claim from a foreign criminal is successful:
(a) in the case of a person who is in the UK unlawfully or whose leave to enter or remain has been cancelled by a deportation order, limited leave may be granted for periods not exceeding 30 months and subject to such conditions as the Secretary of State considers appropriate;
(b) in the case of a person who has not been served with a deportation order, any limited leave to enter or remain may be curtailed to a period not exceeding 30 months and conditions may be varied to such conditions as the Secretary of State considers appropriate;
(c) indefinite leave to enter or remain may be revoked under section 76 of the 2002 Act and limited leave to enter or remain granted for a period not exceeding 30 months subject to such conditions as the Secretary of State considers appropriate;
(d) revocation of a deportation order does not confer entry clearance or leave to enter or remain or re-instate any previous leave.

399C. Where a foreign criminal who has previously been granted a period of limited leave under this Part applies for further limited leave or indefinite leave to remain his deportation remains conducive to the public good and in the public interest notwithstanding the previous grant of leave.

399D. Where a foreign criminal has been deported and enters the United Kingdom in breach of a deportation order enforcement of the deportation order is in the public interest and will beimplemented unless there are very exceptional circumstances.

> 400. Where a person claims that their removal under paragraphs 8 to 10 of Schedule 2 to the Immigration Act 1971, section 10 of the Immigration and Asylum Act 1999 or section 47 of the Immigration, Asylum and Nationality Act 2006 would be contrary to the UK's obligations under Article 8 of the Human Rights Convention, the Secretary of State may require an application under paragraph 276ADE(1) (private life) or Appendix FM (family life) of these rules. Where an application is not required, in assessing that claim the Secretary of State or an immigration officer will, subject to paragraph 353, consider that claim against the requirements to be met under paragraph 276ADE(1) or Appendix FM and if appropriate the removal decision will be cancelled.

So the starting point for the consideration of a claim made on Article 8 grounds, by a criminal sentenced to less than 4 years imprisonment, will be that the public interest in deporting foreign criminals will outweigh the individual's right to respect for their family and private life rights unless the circumstances in outlined in rule 399 (family life) and rule 399A (private life) apply.

Where the circumstances do not apply, or the person is sentenced to 4 years or more imprisonment, the public interest in deportation will only be outweighed by other factors where there are very compelling circumstances over and above those described in paragraphs 399 and 399A.

A person whose Article 8 claim is made out will be granted 30 months leave, regardless of the leave they had (or lack of it) prior to the deport proceedings.

In respect of deport decisions, Article 8 considerations have now been fully brought into the Immigration Rules. Where the deportee is found not to meet the requirements of 399 and 399A, the decision maker, whether the Home Office or Tribunal must go on to consider whether there are very compelling circumstances over and above those described in paragraphs 399 and 399A. Prior to the amendments of 28 July 2014 the term 'exceptional circumstances' was used for the same process.

When considering the reference to 'exceptional circumstances' the Court of Appeal found in MF (Nigeria) v Secretary of State for the Home Department [2013] EWCA Civ 1192 that;

> 42. .·. in approaching the question of whether removal is a proportionate interference with an individual's article 8 rights, the scales are heavily weighted in favour of deportation and something very compelling (which will be "exceptional") is required to outweigh the public interest in removal. In our view, it is no coincidence that the phrase "exceptional circumstances" is used in the new rules in the context of weighing the competing factors for and against deportation of foreign criminals.
>
> 43. The word "exceptional" is often used to denote a departure from a general rule. The general rule in the present context is that, in the case of a foreign prisoner to whom paras 399 and 399A do not apply, very compelling reasons will be required to outweigh the public interest in deportation. These compelling reasons are the "exceptional circumstances".
>
> 44.   We would, therefore, hold that the new rules are a complete code and that the exceptional circumstances to be considered in the balancing exercise

> involve the application of a proportionality test as required by the Strasbourg jurisprudence. We accordingly respectfully do not agree with the UT that the decision-maker is not "mandated or directed" to take all the relevant article 8 criteria into account (para 38)."

That brings Strasbourg jurisprudence and the case law of the domestic courts which has been developed in the light of that jurisprudence into play in cases where the provisions of paragraphs 399 and 399A do not apply.

Additionally, we now have the statutory public interest considerations placed into the 2002 Act by s19 of the Immigration Act. These state;

> **117C   Article 8: additional considerations in cases involving foreign criminals**
>
> (1) The deportation of foreign criminals is in the public interest.
>
> (2) The more serious the offence committed by a foreign criminal, the greater is the public interest in deportation of the criminal.
>
> (3) In the case of a foreign criminal ("C") who has not been sentenced to a period of imprisonment of four years or more, the public interest requires C's deportation unless Exception 1 or Exception 2 applies.
>
> (4) Exception 1 applies where—
>
> (a) C has been lawfully resident in the United Kingdom for most of C's life,
> (b) C is socially and culturally integrated in the United Kingdom, and
> (c) there would be very significant obstacles to C's integration into the country to which C is proposed to be deported.
>
> (5) Exception 2 applies where C has a genuine and subsisting relationship with a qualifying partner, or a genuine and subsisting parental relationship with a qualifying child, and the effect of C's deportation on the partner or child would be unduly harsh.
>
> 6) In the case of a foreign criminal who has been sentenced to a period of imprisonment of at least four years, the public interest requires deportation unless there are very compelling circumstances, over and above those described in Exceptions 1 and 2.
>
> (7) The considerations in subsections (1) to (6) are to be taken into account where a court or tribunal is considering a decision to deport a foreign criminal only to the extent that the reason for the decision was the offence or offences for which the criminal has been convicted.

So the government have made it clear to judges, by the introduction of primary legislation, that certain considerations will have to be taken account of when considering the weight to be given to the public interest when assessing proportionality. That weight will be very great. That does not mean that the public interest will always outweigh the person's individual rights where they cannot meet the requirements of the rules, but it will be only in exceptional cases that it does not.

We turn therefore to some of the case law pre-dating the immigration rules-based Article 8 regime which might remain relevant in such cases. Saying that, a recent decision of the Court of Appeal LC (China) v Secretary of State for the Home Department [2014] EWCA Civ 1310, at paragraph 26, suggests that that case law itself has been subsumed into the Immigration Rules and the decision maker does not therefore need to give it further thought. If that is the case, it is going to be very difficult indeed to make a case on a legal case on Article 8 grounds on the basis of very compelling circumstances.

In a case involving previous criminal offences, there is a need to address the likelihood of the Appellant's re-offending, as is stated in N (Kenya) v Secretary of State for the Home Department [2004] EWCA Civ 1094 at paragraph 45. However, in the same judgment it is made clear that re-offending is not the whole picture:

> 64 ... Essentially the same balance is expressed as that between the appellant's right to respect for his private and family life on the one hand and the prevention of disorder or crime on the other. Where a person who is not a British citizen commits a number of very serious crimes, the public interest side of the balance will include importantly, although not exclusively, the public policy need to deter and to express society's revulsion at the seriousness of the criminality. It is for the adjudicator in the exercise of his discretion to weigh all relevant factors, but an individual adjudicator is no better able to judge the critical public interest factor than is the court. In the first instance, that is a matter for the Secretary of State. The adjudicator should then take proper account of the Secretary of State's public interest view.
>
> 65. The risk of re-offending is a factor in the balance, but, for very serious crimes, a low risk of re-offending is not the most important public interest factor. In my view, the adjudicator's decision was over-influenced in the present case by his assessment of the risk of re-offending to the exclusion, or near exclusion, of the other more weighty public interest considerations characterised by the seriousness of the appellant's offences.

Most deportation cases will turn on Article 8 ECHR considerations, and reference can be made to the sections of this manual covering Article 8 (i.e. on private and family life applications, and the separate section on Article 8).

The case of Üner v. The Netherlands (Application No. 46410/99) is the leading judgment on the Article 8 ECHR considerations that arise in a deportation case. The claimant had been convicted of violent assaults on previous occasions and the incident that triggered his deportation involved him shooting one man in the leg and injuring him and another man in the head and killing him. The claimant was sentenced to seven years in jail. The Court ultimately concluded that in expelling the claimant, a correct balance had been struck in this case.

The following factors are set out by the court at paragraphs 57 and 58:

1. The nature and seriousness of the offence committed by the applicant;
2. The length of the applicant's stay in the country from which he or she is to be expelled;

3. The time elapsed since the offence was committed and the applicant's conduct during that period;

4. The nationalities of the various persons concerned;

5. The applicant's family situation, such as the length of the marriage, and other factors expressing the effectiveness of a couple's family life;

6. Whether the spouse knew about the offence at the time when he or she entered into a family relationship;

7. Whether there are children of the marriage, and if so, their age; and

8. The seriousness of the difficulties which the spouse is likely to encounter in the country to which the applicant is to be expelled.

9. The best interests and well-being of the children, in particular the seriousness of the difficulties which any children of the applicant are likely to encounter in the country to which the applicant is to be expelled; and

10. The solidity of social, cultural and family ties with the host country and with the country of destination.

Uner is itself then supplemented by another later case, Maslov v Austria 1638/03 [2008] ECHR 546:

> 74. Although Article 8 provides no absolute protection against expulsion for any category of aliens (see Üner, cited above, § 55), including those who were born in the host country or moved there in their early childhood, the Court has already found that regard is to be had to the special situation of aliens who have spent most, if not all, their childhood in the host country, were brought up there and received their education there (see Üner, § 58 in fine).
>
> 75. In short, the Court considers that for a settled migrant who has lawfully spent all or the major part of his or her childhood and youth in the host country very serious reasons are required to justify expulsion. This is all the more so where the person concerned committed the offences underlying the expulsion measure as a juvenile.

Maslov re-emphasises that cases involving long-settled migrants, particularly who entered the UK as children, involve very substantial interferences with Article 8 which must be properly weighed in the balance.

The Court of Appeal in D v SSHD [2012] EWCA Civ 39 found that as a matter of law the Maslov approach does not apply to a case where the deportee has spent his time in the country unlawfully.

Top tip

It is important to consider what arguments and evidence might be available in a deportation case. It is not easy to acquire good evidence in deportation cases but this will be decisive on appeal. Of course getting detailed testimony from your client, and expert evidence, will be far more difficult if they are to be outside the UK when preparing their appeal.

Evidence to seek might include:

- Sentencing judge remarks. Ensure a complete copy is obtained and do not leave it to the Home Office to do so. The Home Office often quote very selectively and a full copy may be helpful to the client.
- Up to date probation report. Some probation officers are helpful, some are not. Whether an up to date report on risk of re-offending can be obtained might be critical.
- Copies of all pre-sentence reports. There may have been a psychological or psychiatric assessment as well as a pre-sentence probation report.
- Solid and incontrovertible evidence of family life. The Home Office will question everything in a deportation case, including even the existence of children or a partner. Whether the client can get out on bail and therefore re-establish a current and strong family life before the appeal hearing can be a critical factor.

Chapter 14: The law of appeals

This chapter concerns the statutory right of appeal provided for by Part 5 of the Nationality, Immigration and Asylum Act 2002.

Under the 2002 Act, certain immigration decisions of the Home Office give rise to an independent right of appeal before a judge of the First-tier Tribunal (Immigration and Asylum Chamber). The First-tier Tribunal judge has the power to allow or refuse an appeal, subject only to a further challenge on legal grounds to the Upper Tribunal (Immigration and Asylum Chamber).

The trajectory of this government and the last has been to gradually take away appeal rights under the 2002 Act. Appeal rights were lost to students, workers, and businesspersons refused entry clearance alongside the introduction of the PBS from 2008. In 2011, substantial limitations were placed on the evidence a PBS appellant could rely on in an appeal against a refusal of an extension of stay. In 2013, the government took away the full right of appeal for those refused family visit visas.

The 14th edition of this manual was prepared at the point that the new appeals provisions of Part 2 of the Immigration Act 2014 were being partially brought into force. These aim to take away a whole tranche of appeal rights, leaving only those whose human rights or asylum claim with a right of appeal. For others there will be a right of Administrative Review, an internal review of a decision by Home Office caseworkers, or judicial review to the Upper Tribunal. Judicial review is only undertaken by solicitors and barristers and remains largely beyond the scope of this manual.

On 20 October 2014, students and their families refused an extension of stay in the UK lost their right of appeal to the First-tier Tribunal, as did deportees unless they have made a human rights or asylum claim. This effectively leaves us with two versions of Part 5 of the 2002 Act, one for students and deportees as amended for those groups by s15 of the Immigration Act 2002, and the old Part 5 as unamended for all others.

What follows covers the current appeals regime, as it appears on 20 October 2014, with sections on Administrative Review and impending further changes at the end.

It should be noted that the Tribunal itself transforms its own structure from time to time. In early days it was referred to as the Immigration Appellate Authorities (IAA), with challenges to the IAA made to the Immigration Appeals Tribunal (IAT). Under provisions in the Immigration and Asylum (Treatment of Claimants Etc) Act 2004, the two tribunals were combined to form the Asylum and Immigration Tribunal. That was then split into two again by the Tribunals, Courts and Enforcement Act 2007 (TCEA 2007), and that structure remains; the First-tier Tribunal (Immigration and Asylum Chamber) and the Upper Tribunal (Immigration and Asylum Chamber).

Right of appeal

It is not always easy (and does not get easier) to determine whether there is a right of appeal, what the grounds of appeal might be and whether the appeal should be determined inside the UK or outside. These three issues provide the framework for the first part of this chapter:

Is there an immigration decision?
- See sections 82, 83, 83A

Does a limitation apply?
- See sections 88, 88A, 88A, 90, 91, 96

Is the appeal in or out of country?
- See sections 92 and 94

Decisions attracting a right of appeal

Section 82 of the 2002 Act outlines the main rights of appeal generated under the 2002 Act. Sub-section 82(2) exhaustively defines which immigration decisions are potentially appealable under s.82:

82 Right of appeal: general

(1)   Where an immigration decision is made in respect of a person he may appeal to the Tribunal.

(2)   In this Part "immigration decision" means—
(a)   refusal of leave to enter the UK

(b)   .refusal of entry clearance

(c)   refusal of certificate of entitlement under section 10 of this Act

(d)   refusal to vary a person's leave to enter or remain in the UK if the result of the refusal is that the person has no leave to enter or remain;

(e)   variation of a person's leave to enter or remain in the UK if when the variation takes effect the person has no leave to enter or remain;

(f)   revocation under section 76 of this Act of indefinite leave to enter or remain in the UK;

(g)   a decision that a person is to be removed from the UK by way of directions under section [10(1)(a), (b), (ba) or (c)]** of the IAA 1999

(h)   a decision that an illegal entrant is to be removed from the UK by way of directions under paragraphs 8-10 of Schedule 2 to the Immigration Act 1971 (control of entry: removal)

[ha)   a decision that a person is to be removed from the United Kingdom by way of directions under section 47 of the Immigration, Asylum and Nationality Act 2006 (removal: persons with statutorily extended leave)]**

(i)   a decision that a person is to be removed from the UK by way of directions given by virtue of paragraph 10A of that schedule (family)

[ia)   a decision that a person is to be removed from the United Kingdom by way of directions under paragraph 12(2) of Schedule 2 to the Immigration Act 1971 (c. 77) (seamen and aircrews)]*

[ib)   a decision to make an order under section 2A of that Act (deprivation of right of abode)]**

(j)   a decision to make a deportation order under section 5(1) of that Act, and

(k)   refusal to revoke a deportation order under section 5(2) of that Act

(3A)   Subsection (2)(j) does not apply to a decision to make a deportation order which states that it is made in accordance with section 32(5) of the UK Borders Act 2007; but—
(a)   a decision that section 32(5) applies is an immigration decision for the purposes of this Part, and
(b)   a reference in this Part to an appeal against an automatic deportation order is a reference to an appeal against a decision of the Secretary of State that section 32(5) applies.

(4)   The right of appeal under subsection (1) is subject to the exceptions and limitations specified in this Part.

A right of appeal is also generated by section 83 and 83A of the 2002 Act. These rights of appeal are specific to asylum and humanitarian protection appeals and are addressed in greater detail below. There is also a right of appeal against a decision to revoke British citizenship under s40A of the British Nationality Act 1981, and against an EEA decision in regulation 26 of the Immigration (EEA) Regulations 2006.

To determine whether a particular non-EEA immigration decision gives rise to a right of appeal or not, it is always necessary to consider the Notice of Immigration Decision and to discern from that whether it is a decision described in ss82, 83 or 83A.

Some decisions which might be expected to attract appeal rights do not do so, or the right of appeal may be restricted to limited grounds, often rendering the right largely worthless:

➢ Refusal of asylum where leave to enter or remain is granted for one year or less: see section 83(1). However where successive grants in combination succeed one year, they will attract an asylum appeal right from the grant that lead to the period exceeding 12 months;

➢ Decisions on applications made when the applicant is an overstayer or illegal entrant. The applicant will have to await a decision to remove before they have a right of appeal.

➢ Destination specified in the removal directions – it is only the original, underlying decision that a person is to be removed by way of removal directions that attracts a right of appeal, not a complaint about the country to which the person is to be removed.

➢ Refusal of entry clearance under the Points Based System – restricted to race discrimination or human rights grounds only (see limitations on right of appeal, below)

Top tip

It is crucial to understand that the list of immigration decisions that generate a right of appeal is exhaustive. If a decision is one that does not appear on the list, there is no right of appeal. For example, there is no right of appeal against the refusal of an out of time application for leave to remain, or where the application is made by an illegal entrant. It cannot be described as an application to vary leave (which might in some circumstances attract a right of appeal under s.82(2)(d)) as there is no current leave that could be varied.

There is no right of appeal against a decision to refuse leave to remain if the application is made by an overstayer or illegal entrant, even where the applicant relies on human rights grounds. In fact, it is commonplace for human rights applications to be refused, but with no appealable immigration decision being made thereby depriving the applicant of a right of appeal, leaving the applicant effectively in limbo, and leaving judicial review as the only potential remedy, until and unless an appealable removal decision is made.

That will change when Part 2 of the Immigration Act 2014 is brought fully into force. When that happens, the only appealable decisions will be to refuse an asylum or human rights claim, or to revoke leave granted for those reasons.

Validity of the notice of decision

As required by the *Immigration (Notices) Regulations 2003* (SI 2003/658), the Home Office issues a Notice of Decision with an accompanying statement declaring whether that decision is appealable or not. Where there is an in country right of appeal, the notice must be accompanied by a Notice of Appeal. A Notice of Decision which does not conform to the Notices Regulations may be invalid. Regardless of the validity of the notice though, if the Home Office has in fact made an appealable immigration decision under the terms of section 82, an immigration judge will have jurisdiction to deal with the appeal (subject to the exceptions and limitations in the Act).

If the Home Office wrongly assert that there is a right of appeal when in law there is not, the immigration tribunal must normally decline to hear the case'

The Immigration (Notices) Regulations 2003 are an important safeguard to ensure that a migrant is properly informed of the reasons for the decision made against them and the extent of their appeal rights (i.e. whether the appeal is to be in-country or not, or on restricted grounds only or not). It can be argued that an incorrect notice of decision, where no reasons are given for the decision or where wrong information is given as to appeal rights, is invalid. The deadline for lodging an appeal will not start to run from the date of service of such a notice. An applicant could either choose to lodge an appeal in any case, where they have a right of appeal, waiving the right to a valid notice, or simple await service of a valid notice.

Example

A particular problem has arisen in relation to those who arrive in the UK as visitors and then claim asylum. On arrival such people will usually have been granted 6 months leave to enter/remain as a visitor. If they still possess such leave at the time of the refusal, they are not in the position described in section 82(2)(d) - because they still have current leave to remain. Home Office practice is to curtail the existing leave. The right of appeal in such a situation is actually against the curtailment (a variation of leave) rather than the original refusal to vary leave. If the Home Office do not curtail leave and do not set removal directions, however, there would be no right of appeal.

It would not be acceptable to advise an applicant to delay applying for asylum in such circumstances because the delay in claiming could then be held against them when assessing the credibility of their account, it may also have implications for their eventual ability to access support and accommodation through NASS pursuant to the requirement in section 55 NIAA 2002 that asylum applicant's claim 'as soon as reasonably practicable' or risk losing access to support.

This problem will also go away when Part 2 of the Immigration Act 2014 comes into force, as there will be a right of appeal against the refusal of an asylum claim.

Limitations on the right of appeal

There are miscellaneous exceptions to the right to appeal. Where there appears to be a right of appeal under s82 it may be taken away or limited by the provisions in ss88 to 91 of the 2002 Act, and now by the partially introduced provisions of s15 of the Immigration Act 2014.

S88 limits the right of appeal (i.e. restricts the available grounds of an appeal) to those and their dependants who do not;

- ➢ satisfy a requirement as to age, nationality or citizenship specified in immigration rules (e.g. a person below the age of 18 applying as a partner, or over the age of 31 under Tier 5 (Youth Mobility), or a non-commonwealth citizen applying for an ancestry visa;

- ➢ have a visa, where the requirement is mandatory, or those without a passport or any other kind of acceptable travel document;

- ➢ provide a medical document where required (e.g. a TB test certificate);

- ➢ or who are seeking leave for longer than permitted under the rules (e.g. applying for an extension of a 6 month visit visa); or

- ➢ for a purpose other than one for which entry or remaining is permitted in accordance with immigration rules (e.g. to care long-term for a sick relative).

Section 88A similarly limits the right of appeal against the refusal of a visit or PBS visa.

S89 gives a right of appeal against refusal of leave to enter only to those who arrive in the UK with a visa and seek to enter for the purpose stated in their visa application.

Where there is a limited right of appeal, as under ss88 and 88A, the person can only rely on race discrimination, human rights or asylum grounds.

Race discrimination is not discussed elsewhere in this manual. Suffice it to say that an appeal allowed on race discrimination grounds has no effect on a person's leave to enter or remain, and is therefore of limited use.

Generally too, as most of the limitations apply to those seeking to enter the UK in non-family categories, it will be very unlikely that human rights grounds will assist them. So in most cases, a limited right of appeal is tantamount to no right of appeal.

Exceptionally though, an appeal against the refusal of a visit visa might succeed on human rights grounds where, for instance, it was being sought to visit a close family member in the UK, particularly where the UK based family member is unable to visit the applicant in another country. If, in an appeal on human rights grounds, the tribunal judge finds that the visit visa application met the requirements of the rules, the refusal decision will not have been made in accordance with the law (i.e. Razgar's 3rd step), and may also be disproportion to the needs of maintaining immigration control[12].

Students and deportees

The Immigration Act 2014 (Commencement No. 3, Transitional and Saving Provisions) Order 2014 is almost impossible to understand, even by very experienced lawyers. Essentially, it brings into force s1 and s15 of the Immigration Act 2014, amending the removal power in s10 of the 1999 Act, and the appeals provisions in the 2002 Act, but only for Tier 4 students and deportees.

Students who apply to extend their stay from 20 October 2014 will have a right to administrative review (see end of this chapter) if refused, but no right of appeal. The right applies to both those who apply when they have current leave, and to those who apply within the 28 day period of overstaying, so to that extent only may be a good thing for some students.

If the administrative review does not succeed, the student and their family will be removable without the Home Office needing to make a removal decision. They will be removable simply because they no longer have permission to be in the UK.

The guidance on the new appeals provisions at https://www.gov.uk/government/publications/appeals states in paragraph 4.3 that;

> All persons liable for removal or deportation will normally receive a section 120 notice at some point in the process. Once a notice has been served it will not be re-issued, however a person may be reminded of their ongoing duty.

Annex A to the appeals guidance states that a student will be given the s120 notice when the deadline for bringing an application for Administrative Review has passed and no application has been made, or when the Administrative Review is decided and the original decision maintained. A deportee will be given the s120 notice when the foreign criminal is notified of the intention to deport.

---

[12] For more on visit appeals on human rights grounds, buy the Free Movement eBook, *Visit visa refusals: how to challenge decisions*

The section 120 notice will give the person facing deportation or who has been refused an extension of stay under Tier 4 the opportunity to raise human rights or asylum grounds as to why they should not be removed. Where they raise such grounds, and are refused, the person will then have a right of appeal unless the grounds are certified as clearly unfounded.

In-country and out-of-country appeals

Section 92 establishes a presumption that an appeal can only be pursued from outside the UK unless s92 says otherwise. The trigger for the hearing of the appeal from inside the UK is either (or both) the type of decision appealed against and type of claim made:

In-country appeal - immigration decisions

- refusal of certificate of entitlement
- refusal to vary leave if refusal leaves person with no leave
- variation of leave if variation leaves person with no leave
- revocation of ILR under s.76 2002 Act

Or the appellant is in the UK

- and has made an asylum claim
- or a human rights claim
- whilst in the UK
- or a claim that the decison breaches their EEA Treaty rights

A decision to remove, will be out of country unless the person has made an asylum or human rights claim or invoked their EEA rights whilst in the UK.

An asylum claim must be made in person. A human rights or EEA claim must be made in writing to the Secretary of State. It will not suffice therefore, to gain an in-country appeal, simply to raise asylum, human rights or EEA rights grounds on the Notice of Appeal.

It does not matter when the asylum, human rights or EEA claim is made, so long as it is *before* the appeal is lodged. Where the claim is made after the decision is served, the claim, when made, renders the Notice of Decision invalid as it will now contain incorrect information about the right of appeal (i.e. the notice states it is out-of-country whereas it is now in-country). If the claim is then refused, and not certified as clearly unfounded under s94, the Home Office must serve a new Notice of Decision accompanied by a Notice of Appeal, and the appeal will now be in-country.

In addition, there is an in-country right of appeal where a person with entry clearance is refused leave to enter on arrival in the UK, unless the refusal is for an attempt to enter for a purpose other than that specified in the entry clearance.

Perhaps the most arresting feature of the modern appeal system is that some asylum seekers do not enjoy a right of appeal from within the UK at all. These are those subject to 'clearly unfounded' certification procedures, set out at s.94 of the 2002 Act. We deal with this phenomenon in our asylum chapter.

We also have now the new provisions relating to deportation. As can be seen from the section on deportation and appeal rights under the 2014 Act (see Chapter on deportation), where a human rights claim is raised in response to a decision to deport, the appeal can be certified on the basis that removal will not breach a person's human rights, thus rendering the appeal out of country.

Grounds of appeal

The potential grounds of appeal are set out at section 84 of the 2002 Act as follows:

(a)   not in accordance with immigration rules

(b)   that the decision is unlawful by virtue of 19(b) Race Relations Act 1976 (discrimination by public authorities)

(c)   decision is unlawful by virtue of section 6 Human Rights Act incompatible with A's convention rights;

(d)   appellant is EEA national or family member and decision breaches the appellant's rights under Community Treaties in respect of entry to or residence in the UK;

(e)   decision otherwise not in accordance with the law;

(f)   person taking decision should have exercised differently a discretion conferred by immigration rules;

(g)   removal of A from UK in consequence of the immigration decision would breach UK's obligations under the Refugee Convention or would be unlawful under section 6 HRA.

At least one of these grounds of appeal must be relied upon, though often several will be relevant. It is best to include on the Notice of Appeal all those grounds that *might* be argued at the hearing as at this early stage of the appeal process it may not be clear exactly what the case will look like by the date of hearing.

The exception to this is in s.83 appeals, which are limited to Refugee Convention and Humanitarian Protection grounds (see FA (Iraq) v SSHD [2010] EWCA Civ 696 in respect of HP grounds).

Statement of additional grounds

The 'one stop procedure' is a key element of the appeals system. It allows the Tribunal judge in an appeal to consider all available grounds and facts that might allow a person to stay in the UK in one hearing. Section 120 of the 2002 Act requires an appellant who is given a *Statement of Additional Grounds* (also called 's120 notice') by the Home Office to declare any additional grounds for being allowed to stay in the UK other than those raised in their application.

Commonly, asylum seekers are given a s120 notice soon after claiming asylum and can raise, for example, Article 8 issues, or their right to stay in the UK under other provisions of the rules. By completing the s.120 notice before a decision is made on the substantive application, the Home Office will then have to make a decision on all the issues raised in it alongside the decision on the asylum claim. Those grounds and reason can then be raised again in an appeal if the application is refused on all grounds.

A s120 notice is also given to a person who the Home Office has decided to remove from the UK. They are asked in the decision letter to now state any other basis upon which they think they may be entitled to stay in the UK. Where the s120 notice is completed, and that can be done by completing the appropriate box on the Notice of Appeal, the tribunal on appeal are required to consider all the stated grounds that an appellant has for remaining in the UK, whether or not the appropriate applications have been made to the Home Office and indeed whether or not these issues have been raised with the Home Office before the appeal at all.

The issue of when and whether the Home Office is required to give a person a s.120 notice was considered by the Court of Appeal in *Lamichhane v Secretary of State for the Home Department* [2012] EWCA Civ 260. The Court of Appeal found that s.120 was permissive only. Although the court stated 'that good and efficient administration is furthered by the service of a section 120 notice', that did not amount to a legal requirement that a s.120 notice be served on an applicant, or even that one should be served unless there was a good reason not to.

The new appeals guidance does suggest a s120 notice should be served to all those who may be removed or deported as a consequence of a decision.

The person must state on the s120 notice:

➢ His reasons for wishing to enter or remain

➢ Any grounds on which he should be permitted to enter or remain in the UK, and

➢ Any grounds on which he should not be removed from the UK

The statement need not repeat reasons or grounds set out in the application to which the immigration decision relates.

It is absolutely essential to keep up to date with a client's circumstances and take full and detailed instructions when matters arise. The client, if refused, will have one chance to put arguments before an immigration judge. If this chance is lost, it will be very difficult to have the arguments considered at all before or after the person is removed.

Preparation for appeals MUST include consideration of:

➢ Any human rights issues arising pre or post decision;

➢ Any home office policy or concession applicable to the case;

➢ Any immigration rule applicable

If a s.120 notice has not been served on the client at any time before the decision is received, or with the decision, and there are issues to raise before the tribunal in respect of which a s.120 will have to be submitted, an adviser might sensibly consider whether to request the immediate service of a s120 notice.

Examples:

➢ An asylum seeker facing removal registers a civil partnership with an EEA national with a right to reside in the UK. By completing a s120 notice, the removal decision can be challenged on asylum and EEA grounds.

➢ A student who has been refused an extension of stay under Tier 4 has a British citizen child with his ex-girlfriend. By completing a s120 notice, after or instead of going through the Administrative Review process in connection with the Tier 4 refusal, the UKVI will then have to consider whether he has a right to leave under Appendix FM. If they decide that he does not, he should then have a right of appeal against the human rights decision.

In *SZ (Applicable immigration rules) Bangladesh [2007] UKAIT 00037*, the Tribunal found that there is no general duty on the Tribunal to consider whether a claimant's case if differently presented or if made the subject of a different application might have succeeded on a different basis from that on which the application or claim was made. It will only be exceptionally that the facts of a case or the terms of a notice of decision may require the Tribunal to consider the appeal on a number of alternative bases. Using the s120 procedure will therefore be vital to ensure that all relevant facts and potential avenues for succeeding on appeal are considered by the judge.

Appeals structure

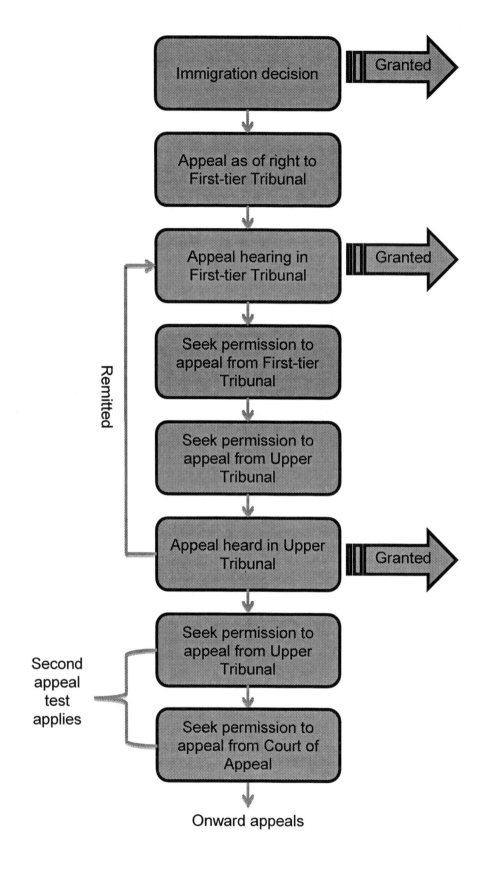

Sources of law, practice and procedure

The legislation setting out the process for immigration appeals is the Tribunals, Courts and Enforcement Act 2007. It provides for the multi-stage process described in the diagram above.

In addition to the primary legislation itself there are several other sources of practice and procedure, as follows:

The Tribunal Procedure (First-tier Tribunal) (Immigration and Asylum Chamber) Rules 2014

- Replace, as from 20 October 2014, the Asylum and Immigration (Procedure) Rules 2005 and the Asylum and Immigration Tribunal (Fast Track Procedure) Rules 2005 for the First-tier Tribunal (IAC)

Tribunal Procedure (Upper Tribunal) Rules 2008

- The Upper Tribunal (IAC) procedure rules are for all chambers of the Upper Tribunal, though accommodate the particular features of immigration appeals in various places.

Immigration and Asylum Chamber Practice Directions

- Practice Directions for both Tribunals, supplementing the Procedure Rules.

Guidance notes

Including (but not limited to);
- Child, vulnerable adult and sensitive appellants
- Unaccompanied children
- Fee awards in immigration appeals
- Anonymity Directions in the FtT(IAC)

Immigration and Asylum Chamber Practice Statements

- The Practice Directions are now supplemented by Practice Statements, again in the form of a unified document for the Immigration and Asylum Chambers of both the First-tier and Upper Tribunals

Immigration and Asylum Chamber Practice Statements

- Similar to practice directions, supplement the procedure rules.

First-tier Tribunal

Immigration appeals in the First-tier Tribunal (IAC) are, as from 20 October 2014, governed by the Tribunal Procedure (First-tier Tribunal) (Immigration and Asylum Chamber) Rules 2014 (the 'Rules').

The new Rules replaced the Asylum and Immigration Tribunal (Procedure) Rules 2005 and the Asylum and Immigration Tribunal (Fast Track Procedure) Rules 2005 from that date in respect to any outstanding or future immigration appeal.

Fast Track appeals are dealt with in the Asylum chapter.

Immigration appeals to the Immigration and Asylum Chamber of the Upper Tribunal are governed by the amended Tribunal Procedure (Upper Tribunal) Rules 2008, addressed below.

The procedure rules are supplemented by both Practice Directions, Practice Statements and Guidance Notes.

For the First-tier rules etc, go to:
http://www.justice.gov.uk/tribunals/immigration-asylum/rules-and-legislation
For the Upper Tribunal, go to:
http://www.justice.gov.uk/tribunals/immigration-asylum-upper/rules-and-legislation

The new Rules for the First-tier are slimmed down and much less prescriptive than those they replace. They also differ in important respects; with, for instance new deadlines for lodging appeals, and by providing the possibility of an award of 'wasted' costs, where a party has acted improperly, unreasonably or negligently.

Overriding Objective

The overriding objective of the Rules, and therefore the Tribunal, is to deal with cases fairly and justly (rule 2(1)). This replaces the old maxim of 'fairly, quickly and efficiently as possible'. Gone too is a reference to 'the public interest'. This all sounds good, particularly for appellants seeking directions against the Home Office, or adjournments. Rule 2(1) interprets 'fairly and justly' as including;

(a) dealing with the case in ways which are proportionate to the importance of the case, the complexity of the issues, the anticipated costs and the resources of the parties and of the Tribunal;
(b) avoiding unnecessary formality and seeking flexibility in the proceedings;
(c) ensuring, so far as practicable, that the parties are able to participate fully in the proceedings;
(d) using any special expertise of the Tribunal effectively; and
(e) avoiding delay, so far as compatible with proper consideration of the issues.

Lodging appeals

The notice of appeal must be sent, faxed, or submitted online to the First-tier Tribunal (Immigration and Asylum Chamber) itself, though detainees can serve their notice of appeal on their custodian if in detention.

Information about submitting appeals, and to submit them online, go to: http://www.justice.gov.uk/tribunals/immigration-asylum/appeals

The notice of appeal must, if reasonably practicable, be accompanied by the notice of decision, and the reasons for that decision, against which the appellant is appealing (rule 19).

Rule 19 also requires the Notice of Appeal to set out the grounds of appeal (but not, as under the old rules, the reasons), and lists the additional information that must be provided with the Notice.

A fee is payable for appeals before the tribunal, under the provisions of the *First-tier Tribunal (Immigration and Asylum Chamber) Fees Order 2011*, unless the appellant is exempt. Those exempt include those appealing a removal decision, those in receipt of legal aid, and minors being cared for by a local authority. The fee is £140 for an oral hearing and £80 for the appeal to be decided on the papers.

Detailed guidance on fees is available at:
http://www.justice.gov.uk/downloads/tribunals/immigration-and-asylum/lower/online-fees-guidance.pdf including guidance on applying for a fee remission if there are exceptional circumstances (i.e. you cannot afford to pay the fee).

Deadline for appeal

The **new** deadlines for receipt by the Tribunal of the Notice of Appeal are specified at rule 19:

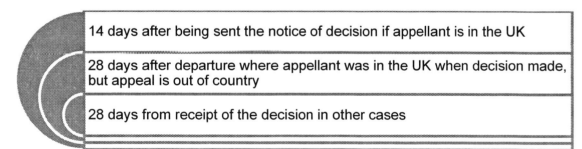

14 days after being sent the notice of decision if appellant is in the UK

28 days after departure where appellant was in the UK when decision made, but appeal is out of country

28 days from receipt of the decision in other cases

The distinction between business and calendar days has largely disappeared, as have the deemed receipt provisions. Days are calendar days, finishing at midnight; but where a deadline falls on a day other than a working day, the act is done in time if it is done on the next working day (rule 11).

Extension of time for lodging notice of appeal

There is provision at rule 20 for lodging an appeal outside the time limit in rule 19. The notice of appeal must include an application for such an extension of time and the reason why the notice of appeal was not provided in time.

Where the tribunal believes that an appeal has not been lodged in time, but there has been no application for an extension, the Tribunal must notify the person in writing to give them an opportunity for either contending that it was lodged in time or to apply to extend time.

Under rule 21, which deals with "imminent removal" cases, where the respondent informs the tribunal that it is proposed to remove the individual within 5 days of the date on which notice of appeal was given, the extension of time procedure is to be expedited.

There is no legal test in rule 20 to govern the exercise of the Tribunal's discretion (under rule 4(3)(a)) to extend time. The Tribunal will make a decision that is fair and just as per its overriding objective.

Any application for an extension should therefore give reasons why it is fair and just in the particular case to extend time – explaining, with evidence, the reason for the delay, and showing why justice requires a hearing. Justice will usually depend on the purpose and merit of the appeal. If there is some real purpose to the hearing, justice suggests it should be allowed to go ahead.

Case management powers

Under the new Rules, at rules 4 and 14 particularly, the Tribunal has wide-ranging case management powers.

Under rule 4, the Tribunal may give a direction in relation to the conduct or disposal of proceedings at any time, including a direction amending, suspending or setting aside an earlier direction. A party can request or challenge a direction under rule 5.

The Tribunal may, inter alia;

(a)	extend or shorten the time for complying with any rule, practice direction or direction;
(b)	consolidate or hear together two or more sets of proceedings or parts of proceedings raising common issues;
(c)	permit or require a party to amend a document;
(d)	permit or require a party or another person to provide documents, information, evidence or submissions to the Tribunal or a party;
(e)	provide for a particular matter to be dealt with as a preliminary issue;
(f)	hold a hearing to consider any matter, including a case management issue;
(g)	decide the form of any hearing;
(h)	adjourn or postpone a hearing;
(i)	require a party to produce a bundle for a hearing;

(j)	stay (or, in Scotland, sist) proceedings;
(k)	transfer proceedings to another court or tribunal if that other court or tribunal has jurisdiction in relation to the proceedings and—
	(i) because of a change of circumstances since the proceedings were started, the Tribunal no longer has jurisdiction in relation to the proceedings; or
	(ii) the Tribunal considers that the other court or tribunal is a more appropriate forum for the determination of the case; or
(l)	suspend the effect of its own decision pending the determination by the Tribunal or the Upper Tribunal of an application for permission to appeal against, and any appeal or review of, that decision.

There is no longer a specific provision relating to the holding of Case management review hearings, but the Tribunal can hold a hearing on a case management issue if it so directs.

Directions as to issues, evidence, expert evidence, and witnesses can be given under rule 14. Witnesses can be summoned to attend, or answer questions or produce documents on application of either party or on the Tribunal's own volition under rule 15.

Rule 6 allows the Tribunal to take what action as it considers just where there has been non-compliance with a rule or direction, including referring the matter to the Upper Tribunal to exercise its powers under section 25 of the 2007 Act (which are the same as those exercised by the High Court (i.e. scary ones)).

In practice, standard directions issued with the notice of hearing sent to the parties will include a date by which directions must be complied with, and require the Appellant to produce;

➢ witness statements of the evidence to be called at the hearing, such statements to stand as evidence in chief at the hearing;
➢ a paginated and indexed bundle of all the documents to be relied on at the hearing with a schedule identifying the essential passages;
➢ a skeleton argument, identifying all relevant issues including human rights claims and citing all the authorities relied upon; and
➢ a chronology of events;

The respondent will be required to serve on the Tribunal and the appellant a paginated and indexed bundle of all the documents to be relied upon at the hearing, with a schedule identifying the relevant passages, and a list of any authorities relied upon.

Practice Direction 7.7 slightly softens the steer given regarding witness statements standing as evidence in chief:

Although in normal circumstances a witness statement should stand as evidence-in-chief, there may be cases where it will be appropriate for appellants or witnesses to have the opportunity of adding to or supplementing their witness statements.

The power of the tribunal to issue directions was circumscribed by the Court of Appeal in Mwanza v SSHD (C/2000/0616; 3rd November 2000), which ruled that directions could be given only pursuant to "the conduct of the appeal" – this ruled out orders that the Secretary of State re-interview someone, or make a new decision with a new refusal letter, for these were matters that were prior to the appeal process, and substantive rather than procedural in nature.

The tribunal may also make directions pursuant to the outcome of an appeal, in order to give effect to that appeal (under s87 of the 2002 Act). Such directions could, for instance, include a direction that leave be granted, in addition to the appeal being allowed. Such directions form part of the determination and if the respondent is discontented with the directions, they must be appealed as normal (LS (Gambia) [2005] UKAIT 00085).

In R v SSHD (ex parte Boafo) [2002] 1 WLR 1919 the Court of Appeal held that the Secretary of State is bound by the factual findings of the tribunal and must normally give effect to an appeal, irrespective of whether directions have been given at the conclusion of that appeal. There are, however, some limited circumstances where the Secretary of State might re-open a decision, such as where the circumstances have changed since the appeal was decided.

Documents to be sent to tribunal by the Home Office

When the notice of appeal is sent to the Home Office, rules 23 (for entry clearance cases) and 24 (for other cases) require the Home Office to provide to the Tribunal;

➢ the notices of decision to which the appeal relates,
➢ any document giving reasons for the decisions,
➢ any statement or application form, and
➢ interview records relevant to the decisions,
➢ any other unpublished documents referred to in the decision or reasons for refusal,
➢ the notice of any other appealable decision made in relation to the appellant

This gives some power to the tribunal to extract documents from the Home Office. The Appellant can additionally request directions and/or the issue of a witness summons to get further disclosure.

Response

Under rule 23, for entry clearance appeals, the Home Office must provide to the Tribunal a statement of whether the respondent opposes the appellant's case and, if so, the grounds for such opposition.

The equivalent provision under rule 24, for other appeals, requires the Home Office, if they intend to change or add to the grounds or reasons relied upon' to provide the Tribunal and the other parties with a statement of whether the respondent opposes the appellant's case and the grounds for such opposition.

Variation of grounds of appeal

Grounds of appeal may be varied only with the permission of the Tribunal (Rule 19(7)). An application to vary should be made as soon as possible as permission may not be given if the Tribunal perceive that any delay was deliberate or careless.

Adjournments

Applications for adjournments are not specifically provided for in the new Rules. The power to adjourn or postpone a hearing is at rule 4(3)(h), and the power will presumably be exercised when it is fair and just to do so.

The considerations raised in R v Kingston-upon-Thames Magistrates ex parte Martin [1994] Imm AR 172) will be relevant to the decision;

> 1. The importance of the proceedings and their likely consequences to the party seeking the adjournment.
> 2. The risk of the party being prejudiced in the conduct of the proceedings if the application were refused.
> 3. The risk of prejudice or other disadvantage to the other party if the adjournment were granted.
> 4. The convenience of the court.
> 5. The interests of justice generally in the efficient dispatch of court business.
> 6. The desirability of not delaying future litigants by adjourning early and thus leaving the court empty.
> 7. The extent to which the party applying for the adjournment had been responsible for creating the difficulty which had led to the application.

The Upper Tribunal in Nwaigwe (adjournment: fairness) [2014] UKUT 418 (IAC) posit the main consideration to be one of 'fairness';

> If a Tribunal refuses to accede to an adjournment request, such decision could, in principle, be erroneous in law in several respects: these include a failure to take into account all material considerations; permitting immaterial considerations to intrude; denying the party concerned a fair hearing; failing to apply the correct test; and acting irrationally. In practice, in most cases the question will be whether the refusal deprived the affected party of his right to a fair hearing. Where an adjournment refusal is challenged on fairness grounds, it is important to recognise that the question for the Upper Tribunal is not whether the FtT acted reasonably. Rather, the test to be applied is that of fairness: was there any deprivation of the affected party's right to a fair hearing? See SH (Afghanistan) v Secretary of State for the Home Department [2011] EWCA Civ 1284.

Applications must be made not later than 17:00 hours one full working day before the hearing – that is to say, more than 24 hours before the hearing (Practice Direction 9.1, 9.2). Later applications require the attendance of the applicant at the hearing.

Conduct of the appeal

The tribunal is free to regulate procedure as it sees fit (Rule 4), no doubt having regard to "the overriding objective" identified above (Rule 2). The Rules particularise the matters upon which directions may be made, although the list is not exhaustive. The directions are now standard in nature. Parties must provide the other party copies of any documents served under directions.

The order of proceedings is normally approximately as follows:

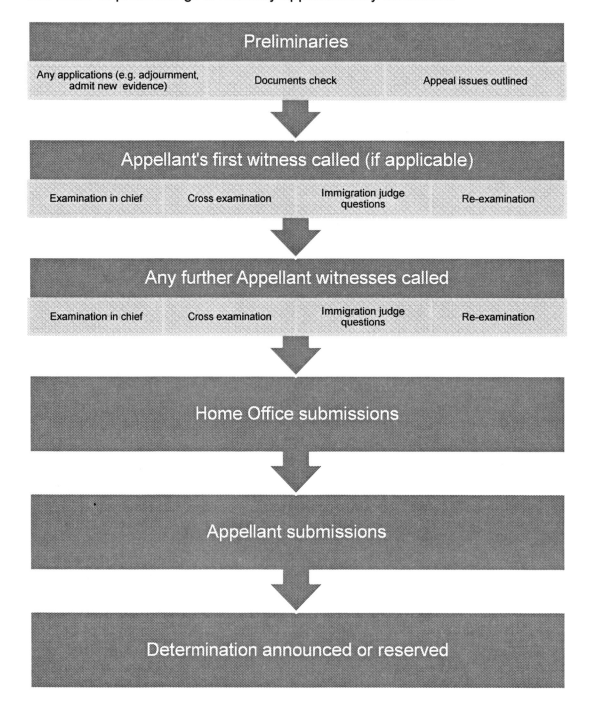

Concessions by the Home Office

In a determination intended to be followed in preference to any others on the issue, the Tribunal in Carcabuk & Bla (00/TH/01426; 18 May 2000) authoritatively ruled that an immigration judge should not seek to go behind concessions of fact ('for example that a particular document is genuine or that an event described by the appellant or a witness did occur') although the immigration judge might wish to raise doubts as to the correctness of a concession. The issue of withdrawing concessions was revisited in the case of NR (Jamaica) v SSHD [2009] EWCA Civ 856. It was held that the Tribunal had discretion to permit withdrawal but that it should not prejudice the affected party: an adjournment may well be necessary.

It is to be noted that Practice Direction 7.8 states that concessions and agreed issues are to be recorded at the Case Management Review Hearings, suggesting that these interlocutory hearings may be used to steer the proceedings.

Natural justice

If a refusal is based on one element of the Immigration Rules, but by the time of the hearing it becomes apparent that there was some other requirement of the Immigration Rules which the appellant could not meet, that matter must be dealt with on appeal, and the parties must be allowed any appropriate adjournment in order to avoid the injustice of being taken by surprise: see RM (Kwok On Tong: HC395 para 320) India [2006] UKAIT 00039

Asylum appeals are supposed to receive 'the most anxious scrutiny'. Thus an immigration judge should give the parties a chance to make submissions upon any research the immigration judge themselves might enter upon, or upon the immigration judge's own accumulated specialist knowledge of a particular country's history; so too the immigration judge should give an opportunity to be addressed upon decisions of factual relevance of which the immigration judge is aware, including their own, and equally upon authorities the immigration judge considers relevant. The general rule is that an opportunity should be given to address any material said to be adverse to the appellant's case.

An immigration judge is entitled to probe evidence where it contains apparent improbabilities in order to satisfy themselves of the account's reliability. The immigration judge should enter the arena, however, only where it is absolutely necessary to enable them to ascertain the truth and without giving any impression of being partisan.

For a rare example of a challenge to the conduct of proceedings by an immigration judge being seriously entertained by the higher courts, see R (on the application of AM (Cameroon)) v Asylum and Immigration Tribunal [2007] EWCA Civ 131.

Public hearing

In general, hearings take place in public (Rule 27). Where allegations of forgery are made with respect to which it would be contrary to the public interest if the detection methods were exposed, then that element of the proceedings which addresses this must be carried out in the absence of the appellant and their representatives; any members of the public must also be excluded. This procedure is provided for at s.108 of the NIAA 2002 and is also addressed in the case of OA (Alleged forgery; section 108 procedure) Nigeria [2007] UKIAT 00096:

> 1. Each application on behalf of the respondent for the section 108, Nationality, Immigration and Asylum Act, 2002 procedure to be invoked must be decided on its own merits.
>
> 2. Immigration Judges should first consider whether it is being alleged that the document concerned is a forgery, or whether it is simply asserted that it is a document which cannot be relied upon (Tanveer Ahmed [2002] UKIAT 00439*).
>
> 3. Applications must be heard in camera, in the absence of the appellant and the appellant's representatives.
>
> 4. The Home Office Presenting Officer should be ready to identify precisely what documents the respondent contends are forged and the evidence which it is claimed relates to the detection of the forgery and which is to be the subject of the section 108 application. Explaining why disclosure of this evidence would be contrary to the public interest.
>
> 5. A careful note should be taken by the judge. The respondent may, if he wishes to, withdraw the allegation and in doing so withdraw the evidence relied upon.
>
> 6. Clear evidence will be necessary; if RP (Proof of Forgery) Nigeria [2006] UKAIT 00086 is not satisfied, then the application will fail.
>
> 7. If the judge grants the application, he should say so in public and clearly identify which document or documents or other evidence is the subject of the section 108 application.

The public generally, or particular individuals, may be excluded from the hearing under rule 27.

Hearing in the absence of a party

Where appropriate, the tribunal may hear the appeal in the absence of a party, where the parties have been given notice of the hearing, and the Tribunal considers that it is in the interests of justice to proceed with the hearing.

Determination without a hearing

Rule 25 sets out that every appeal must be considered at a hearing before an immigration judge, subject to certain exceptions.

Combined hearings

The tribunal may determine that two or more pending appeals are to be heard together where they raise common issues (rule 4(3)(b)).

Evidence

Immigration appeals are intended to be an informal procedure, in which the forms of material which may constitute evidence of facts (especially in asylum and human rights cases regarding the well-foundedness of the appellant's fears) are broader than might support a case in other jurisdictions, see Rule 14(2): The Tribunal may admit evidence whether or not the evidence would be admissible in a civil trial in the United Kingdom or, subject to section 85A(4) of the 2002 Act, the evidence was available to the decision maker.'

Forgery and authenticity of documents

Given the variety of documents that face the tribunal, it is difficult to contend that all are entitled to a presumption of genuineness. The approach now is that the asylum seeker bears the burden of proof (albeit to the same low standard as regards the rest of their claim) in establishing the genuineness of documents in support of their appeal; where such a person does so, which they might do so either on account of their intrinsic cogency or via extraneous evidence, the Secretary of State bears the burden of showing that they are nevertheless forged. This has the consequence that is permissible for an immigration judge to make findings on the documents based on findings on the oral evidence (*Tanveer Ahmed* [2002] UKIAT 00439 (20 February 2002; starred), at least so long as they do not rule out the chance that the documents themselves would have an impact on their initial credibility assessment.

Where the respondent alleges forgery, it is for the respondent to make out this allegation. See *RP (proof of forgery) Nigeria* [2006] UKIAT 00086:

> 14. In judicial proceedings an allegation of forgery needs to be established to a high degree of proof, by the person making the allegation. This is therefore a matter on which the respondent bears the burden of proof. Immigration Judges decide cases on evidence, and in the absence of any concession by the appellant, an Immigration Judge is not entitled to find or assume that a document is a forgery, or to treat it as a forgery for the purposes of his determination, save on the basis of evidence before him. In the present case the evidence was limited to the Entry Clearance Officer's assertion of his own view and the defect in the document identified in the notes on the application form – that is to say, the mismatch between the run date and the date stamp on one of the remittance documents. That evidence is wholly insufficient to establish that that document is a forgery. There is no reason to suppose that it is not a simple mistake. As it happens, "petroleum" is misspelt in the Notice of Refusal. Although we would be inclined to suppose that Entry Clearance Officers can spell this word, we do not automatically assume that the Notice of Refusal is a forgery: there is no reason to suppose that it was not simply a mistake.

See *OA (Alleged forgery; section 108 procedure) Nigeria* [2007] UKIAT 00096, above, regarding the section 108 procedure for excluding the appellant from a hearing while certain forms of evidence regarding forgery are considered by the tribunal.

Burden and standard of proof in allegations

When an allegation is made by an ECO or the Home Office, the burden proof shifts to them, under the principle of 'he who asserts must prove'. As to the standard of proof that applies, this has proven to be contentious. In *NA & Others (Cambridge College of Learning) Pakistan* [2009] UKAIT 00031, the Tribunal disapprove an earlier decision which finds that the required standard of proof is "at the higher end of the spectrum of balance of probability" as it wrongly suggests the civil standard of proof is a variable one. NA concludes rather that *the only way in which the greater seriousness of the allegation or of the consequences is of relevance is in relation to the necessary quality of the evidence.*

Evaluating country reports

The Country Guideline case of TK (Tamils – LP updated) Sri Lanka CG [2009] UKAIT 00049 represents the tribunal's considered view on the assessment of country reports and expert evidence. The tribunal urges judges to adopt the approach of Strasbourg in NA v UK App. no. 25904/07:

> 5. …it seems to us that, at least within the context of Article 3 jurisprudence, judges should now be assessing COI by the standards set out by the Court at paras 132-135 of NA (which can be summarised as accuracy, independence, reliability, objectivity, reputation, adequacy of methodology, consistency and corroboration). Indeed, within the closely related context of asylum and humanitarian protection claims, very much the same standards have now become, by virtue of EU legislation, legal standards: see the Refugee Qualification Directive (2004/83/EC), Article 4(1), 4(3)(a), 4(5),4(5)(a) and 4(5)(c) and the Procedures Directive (2005)85/EC), Article 8(2)(a)and (b) and 8(3).

The tribunal then goes on to decry the use of the term 'objective evidence':

> 7. The emphasis we place on assessment based on objective merit prompts us to make one further comment. It is still widespread practice for practitioners and judges to refer to "objective country evidence" when all they mean is background country evidence. In our view, to refer to such evidence as "objective" obscures the need for the decision-maker to subject such evidence to scrutiny to see if it conforms to the COI standards just noted. This practice appears to have had its origin in a distinction between evidence relating to an individual applicant (so-called "subjective evidence") and evidence about country conditions (so-called "objective evidence"), but as our subsequent deliberations on the appellant's case illustrate (see below paras 153-9), even this distinction can cause confusion when there is an issue about whether an appellant's subjective fears have an objective foundation. We hope the above practice will cease.

Abandonment of appeals

The tribunal possesses the power to declare an appeal abandoned where the statute deems it to be so (rule 16), referring to s104(4A) of the Nationality,

Immigration and Asylum Act 2002, where an appeal the appellant has left the UK or been granted leave to remain in the course of the appeal.

It is important to note that the regime governing abandonment of appeals has been altered by the 2006 Act, which allows racial discrimination appeals and upgrade Refugee Convention appeals to continue despite leave to enter being granted or the appellant leaving the UK. Where in such cases the Appellant wants the appeal to continue, they must give notice within 28 days of having received notice of the grant of leave.

Decisions by the Home Office to withdraw the decision

In recent times, perhaps due to the imposition of targets on HOPOs to succeed in a specified percentage of appeals, appellants have frequently found that the HOPO simply withdraws the decision appealed against the day before or at the hearing itself. This exasperates the judges as much as the appellants and their representatives, but there has been nothing that can be done to challenge the decision outside of seeking permission to judicially review it. Particularly exasperating is the fact that in many cases the refusal is then remade sometime later with different reasons given. The appellant will have the wasted the costs of the preparation of the first appeal (and may not now be entitled to legal aid if they were beforehand due to the provisions in LASPO) and months may pass before the appeal gets to be heard again.

A provision at rule 17(2) appears to give the First-tier Tribunal some discretion to continue with an appeal, notwithstanding the withdrawal of the decision, though it remains to be seen how and whether this happens in practice.

There is also provision for the first time for a wasted costs order to be made against a party if a person has acted unreasonably in bringing, defending or conducting proceedings (rule 9). The Tribunal may make an order under this rule on an application or on its own initiative. The rule also contains the procedure for making such an application, and for a detailed assessment of the costs.

Authority to represent

At appeal, the Secretary of State may be represented by any person authorised to act on her behalf. The appellant may be represented by any person not prohibited from providing legal services under s84 of the Immigration and Asylum Act 1999.

Under rule 10;

➢ Anything permitted or required to be done by a party under these Rules, a practice direction or a direction may be done by the representative of that party, except signing a witness statement.

➢ A person who receives notice of the appointment of a representative must provide to them any document which is required to be provided to the represented party, and need not provide that document to the represented party.

> As from the date on which a person has notified the Tribunal that they are acting as the representative of an appellant and has given an address for service, if any document is provided to the appellant a copy must also at the same time be provided to the appellant's representative.

A party is not though responsible for the errors of his or her representative, and should not be prejudiced by them. In *FP (Iran) v SSHD* [2007] EWCA Civ 13, the appellant had lost touch with the tribunal through the fault of his representative. The immigration judges had in both cases proceeded to hear the appeals in the absence of the parties, as was required by the procedure rules. The Court of Appeal held that (i) there is no general principle of law that a party is fixed with the faults of his representative and (ii) the procedure rules were unlawful because of the absence of discretion not to proceed without a party being present.

Irregularities and corrections

Clerical errors, accidental slips and omissions in a determination may be corrected by the tribunal (rule 31). Under rule 32, the Tribunal can also set aside a decision, or part of such a decision, and re-make the decision, or the relevant part of it, if the Tribunal considers that it is in the interests of justice to do so, where certain conditions apply.

> The conditions are—
>
> (a) a document relating to the proceedings was not provided to, or was not received at an appropriate time by, a party or a party's representative;
>
> (b) a document relating to the proceedings was not provided to the Tribunal at an appropriate time;
>
> (c) a party, or a party's representative, was not present at a hearing related to the proceedings; or
>
> (d) there has been some other procedural irregularity in the proceedings.

Second or subsequent appeals

Notwithstanding the one-stop provisions, some may have more than one appeal (e.g. after a fresh claim has succeeded).

The Tribunal in *Devaseelan* [2004] UKIAT 000282 gave guidance on this situation. The first immigration judge's determination should always be the starting-point for consideration of a later application, for it is the authoritative assessment of the appellant's status at the time it was made. Facts happening prior to the original determination, but of no relevance to the issues it decided, and facts happening since the original determination, can be considered by the second immigration judge afresh.

476

Facts said to have been relevant to the original determination, but not raised, should be treated with circumspection in so far as they are particular to the individual appellant; country material tending to undermine the original determination will be of limited relevance to the later appeal.

Where there is no material difference between the facts relied upon at the second appeal to the first, the immigration judge charged with the later consideration of the case should treat matters as settled by his predecessor. The later decision-maker should only countenance an allegation that an error of a representative undermines the earlier decision where satisfied that such is genuinely the case, and should ensure that such a state of affairs is reported to those responsible for the regulation of immigration advice. Lack of representation on the first occasion is not determinative.

This approach was approved by the Court of Appeal in *AA (Somalia) v SSHD [2007] EWCA Civ 1040,* and it is clear that although Devaseelan concerned one specific set of subsequent appeals (so-called Pardeepan appeals), the same principles can be applied in other subsequent appeal situations and even between appeals of a witness, e.g. where a witness was found credible in a previous appeal that witness must still be evaluated on giving evidence in a later appeal, which necessarily may mean their evidence might not be accepted, even though the earlier determination should be a starting point.

Decisions

First-tier judges are now encouraged to give an oral determination at the end of the hearing. A written notice of decision and notice of any right of appeal must be given.

Where the appeal concerns an asylum or humanitarian protection claim, the Tribunal must provide, with the notice of decision, written reasons for its decision. In any other matter, the Tribunal can choose whether or not to provide written reasons. If they do not, a party may make a written application to the Tribunal for a statement of the reasons. The application must be made within 28 days of the date the party was sent the notice of decision. The written statement of reasons to each party as soon as reasonably practicable.

The special procedure under the old rules, whereby asylum decisions were served only on the Respondent, no longer exists.

Seeking permission to appeal to the UT from the FTT

A decision of the First-tier Tribunal can be challenged by either party on a point of law. To do so the complaining party must make an application to the First-tier Tribunal for permission to appeal to the Upper Tribunal. If permission is refused, the application for permission to appeal can be made directly to the Upper

Tribunal. The process chart earlier in this chapter sets out the various stages in applying for permission to appeal and pursuing such an application further.

Basis of application

Applications for permission to appeal are made only on the basis of an error of law. Such errors might consist of:

(i)   Making perverse or irrational findings on a matter or matters that were material to the outcome ("material matters");

(ii)   Failing to give reasons or any adequate reasons for findings on material matters;

(iii)   Failing to take into account and/or resolve conflicts of fact or opinion on material matters;

(iv)   Giving weight to immaterial matters;

(v)   Making a material misdirection of law on any material matter;

(vi)   Committing or permitting a procedural or other irregularity capable of making a material difference to the outcome or the fairness of the proceedings;

(vii)   Making a mistake as to a material fact which could be established by objective and uncontentious evidence, where the appellant and/or his advisers were not responsible for the mistake, and where unfairness resulted from the fact that a mistake was made.

See *R (Iran) & Ors v SSHD* [2005] EWCA Civ 982 for a detailed consideration of what amounts to 'an error of law'. The Court of Appeal in *E v SSHD* [2004] EWCA Civ 49 explains the circumstances in which error of fact could be an error of law:

> First, there must have been a mistake as to an existing fact, including a mistake as to the availability of evidence on a particular matter. Secondly, the fact or evidence must have been 'established', in the sense that it was uncontentious and objectively verifiable. Thirdly, the appellant (or his advisers) must not have been responsible for the mistake. Fourthly, the mistake must have played a material (not necessarily decisive) part in the Tribunal's reasoning.

Application to the First-tier Tribunal

An application form is provided on the First-tier Tribunal (IAC) section of the Justice website:

IAFT–4: Application to the First–tier Tribunal for permission to appeal to the Upper Tribunal

478

The *new* deadline for receipt of the application by the First-tier Tribunal is '14 days after the date on which the party making the application was provided with [i.e. sent] written reasons for the decision' and 28 days where the appellant is outside the UK.

Where no request for written reasons has been received, the Tribunal will treat the application for permission as such an application. The Tribunal must then decide whether the application for permission to appeal is also to be treated as an application for permission to appeal, or not.

Presumably, the Tribunal will expect a party seeking to challenge the First-tier decision to first request the written reasons, if not provided with the notice of decision, and then to make the application for permission to appeal on the basis of those reasons.

The application must;

(i)   identify the decision of the Tribunal to which it relates,

(ii)   identify the alleged error or errors of law in the decision, and

(iii)   state the result that the party seeks.

An application for an extension of time can be made if necessary.

As will be seen below, there are two different possible routes to a FTT decision being overturned: self-review and appeal. If the party does have a preference, submissions could be made on this point in the grounds of appeal.

Decisions made in the First-tier Tribunal on review and permission to appeal are made by a select band of experienced First-tier judges. Those made in the Upper Tribunal are made by Upper or deputy-Upper Tribunal judges

Review process

FTT considers whether to review the decision

The first thing the FTT has to do on receipt of an application for permission to appeal is decide whether it should itself review the decision against which an appeal is sought. This is provided for at new rule 34, and the review procedure is detailed at new rule 35. The statutory authority to review a decision of the FTT is contained in section 9 of the TCEA 2007. In order to undertake a self-review, the FTT has to be satisfied that there was an error of law in the decision. If the FTT decides not to review or having reviewed the decision decides to leave it substantively the same, the FTT then has to go on and decide whether to grant permission to appeal to the UT. The FTT rarely self-reviews itself.

Seeking permission to appeal from the UT

If the First-tier Tribunal refuses permission, or refuses to extend time for the application for permission, a further application can be made directly to the Upper Tribunal.

Applications to the Upper Tribunal are governed by the Tribunal Procedure (Upper Tribunal) Rules 2008 as in force on 20th October 2014. They are available at:
http://www.justice.gov.uk/downloads/tribunals/general/consolidated-upper-tribunal-procedure-rules-20-october-2014.pdf

The application to the UT must be received no later than 14 days after the date on which notice of the First-tier Tribunal's refusal of permission was sent to the appellant (or 4 working days in fast track cases). The time limit is one month where the appellant is outside the UK (see UT rule 21).

Rule 5(3)(a) imparts the UT with discretion to vary any time limits, so if an application is made late reasons should be included.

The form provided (although not specified as compulsory in the rules) for applications to the UT for permission to appeal to the UT is:

> IAUT–1 Application to the Upper Tribunal for permission to appeal to the Upper Tribunal

If permission to appeal to the UT is granted by the UT, written notice must be given to both parties.

Status and race relations appeals

There is a specific procedure laid out at UT rule 17A and Practice Direction 5 for pursuing an appeal where leave has been granted and the appeal would otherwise be treated as abandoned i.e. where refugee status is sought or the appellant wants a finding made on their race discrimination grounds.

Pursuing an Upper Tribunal appeal

Procedure in the UT is dictated by the amended Tribunal Procedure (Upper Tribunal) Rules 2008 in combination with the joint Practice Directions and Practice Statements of the FTT and UT Immigration and Asylum Chambers.

Non-compliance in the UT

Non-compliance with UT rules is explicitly dealt with at UT rule 7 and also rules 8 (strike out of case), 10 (wasted costs) and 5 (case management). However, rules 8 and 10 do not apply in immigration and asylum cases, leaving the UT with very limited powers.

In a speech to the new tribunal shortly before commencement, President Mr Justice Blake said as follows regarding compliance with directions:

> We must expect that the legal profession and UKBA representatives will respond to these directions and be imaginative in sanction if they don't. Although this chamber of the UT may not have the power to strike out cases for non-compliance, there are other measures available in terms of identifying the issues and how they will be determined that may sorely disadvantage defaulting parties [whoever] they are.

In practice, the UT rarely applies sanctions against the HO for its very poor conduct before it.

Respondent's response to appeal

Rule 24(1A) states that, subject to any directions from the tribunal, the respondent 'may' (not must) lodge a response to a notice of appeal. However, the information required in such a response strongly suggests that these responses will considered important documents and failure to lodge one may have consequences for a respondent:

(a) the name and address of the respondent;

(b) the name and address of the representative (if any) of the respondent;

(c) an address where documents for the respondent may be sent or delivered;

(d) whether the respondent opposes the appeal;

(e) the grounds on which the respondent relies, including [(in the case of an appeal against the decision of another tribunal)] any grounds on which the respondent was unsuccessful in the proceedings which are the subject of the appeal, but intends to rely in the appeal; and

(f) whether the respondent wants the case to be dealt with at a hearing.

Sub-rule 24(4) suggests by its very existence that non-compliance may be taken seriously:

> If the respondent provides the response to the Upper Tribunal later than the time required by paragraph (2) or by an extension of time allowed under rule 5(3)(a) (power to extend time), the response must include a request for an extension of time and the reason why the [response] was not provided in time.

The failure to lodge a response may give the UT the green light to find an error of law without a hearing. Should there be a hearing though, the failure to lodge a response does not preclude the Respondent from arguing that there is no error of law.

Further evidence

The Upper Tribunal may consider fresh evidence not previously relied on in the FTT. A specific provision was inserted into the general UT procedure rules to deal specifically with immigration and asylum appeals, however, at rule 15(2A):

New evidence

> (2A) In an asylum case or an immigration case
>
> (a) if a party wishes the Upper Tribunal to consider evidence that was not before the First-tier Tribunal, that party must send or deliver a notice to the Upper Tribunal and any other party
>   (i)   indicating the nature of the evidence; and
>   (ii)   explaining why it was not submitted to the First-tier Tribunal; and
>
> (b) when considering whether to admit evidence that was not before the First-tier Tribunal, the Upper Tribunal must have regard to whether there has been unreasonable delay in producing that evidence.

Practice Direction 4 addresses evidence in the UT and emphasises that rule 15(2A) must be complied with in every case where a party wishes to rely on further evidence. In addition, the Practice Directions specifies that a party seeking to adduce new evidence must make it clear in the rule 15(2A) notice whether the evidence is:

> (a) in connection with the issue of whether the First-tier Tribunal made an error of law, requiring its decision to be set aside; or
>
> (b) in connection with the re-making of the decision by the Upper Tribunal, in the event of the First-tier Tribunal being found to have made such an error.

In asylum and human rights cases where the facts have to be decided at the date of hearing, it will be normal for fresh country information evidence to be admitted. Evidence as to other matters will normally be subject to the test set out by the Court of Appeal in *E v SSHD* [2004] EWCA Civ 49:

> The Ladd v Marshall principles are, in summary: first, that the fresh evidence could not have been obtained with reasonable diligence for use at the trial; secondly, that if given, it probably would have had an important influence on the result; and, thirdly, that it is apparently credible although not necessarily incontrovertible. As a general rule, the fact that the failure to adduce the evidence was that of the party's legal advisers provides no excuse: see Al-Mehdawi v Home Secretary [1990] 1AC 876.

As the Tribunal recognized in the starred appeal of MA (Fresh evidence) Sri Lanka [2004] UKIAT 00161 (21 June 2004):

> Of course there may be exceptional factors in an asylum or human rights case, which mean that evidence which could and should have been before the Adjudicator can be admitted on appeal.

Hence the test for admission of fresh evidence has three stages:

(1) Prior availability taking into account the need for reasonable diligence;

(2) Materiality;

(3) Apparent Credibility;

With a fourth, doubtless rare, get out clause:

(4) With a residual possibility of exceptional factors being present in an asylum and human rights case albeit that the above criteria are not met.

The tribunal cannot give permission to appeal, nor consider whether to allow an appeal, on the grounds of fresh evidence, unless an error of law is present in the determination of the immigration judge; see the Court of Appeal in CA v Secretary of State for the Home Department [2004] EWCA Civ 1165.

Initial hearing

The first issue to be decided in the Upper Tribunal will be whether there was in fact an error of law in the decision of the First-tier Tribunal. This test is a prerequisite to an appeal to the UT and must be satisfied in all cases, whether permission was granted by the FTT or the UT. The possible grounds for asserting that there is an error of law are addressed briefly above.

It will be unusual for new evidence to be relied on at this stage in the proceedings because the focus must be the material that was before the decision maker who it is contended committed an error of law.

The procedure to be followed on appeal is set out in Practice Direction 3. There is a clear steer towards the UT retaining cases for final decision rather than remitting them to the FTT, though in practise this appears to be shifting more towards remittal.

Since the inception of the Asylum and Immigration Tribunal in 2005, representatives have faced considerable difficulties in assessing whether full evidence should be prepared in advance of an initial error of law hearing. This is because any such preparation could be a colossal waste of time and money because the tribunal might decide there was no error of law, meaning the evidence would not be called upon.

This dilemma very much continues in the TCEA 2007 tribunal structure. Practice Direction 3 provides as follows:

3.2 The parties should be aware that, in the circumstances described in paragraph 3.1(c), the Upper Tribunal will generally expect to proceed, without any further hearing, to re-make the decision, where this can be undertaken without having to hear oral evidence...

3.3 In a case where no oral evidence is likely to be required in order for the Upper Tribunal to re-make the decision, the Upper Tribunal will therefore expect any documentary evidence relevant to the re-making of the decision to be adduced in accordance with Practice Direction 4 so that it may be considered at the relevant hearing; and, accordingly, the party seeking to rely on such documentary evidence will be expected to show good reason why it is not reasonably practicable to adduce the same in order for it to be considered at that hearing.

It therefore seems safe to assume that where the error of law asserted is such that oral evidence would be necessary for a re-decision, witnesses need not attend the initial UT hearing and full up-to-date evidence need not be prepared. In all other cases, representatives have to assess whether it is 'reasonably practicable' to prepare and adduce any necessary further evidence.

It is impossible to give firm guidance. Common sense and experience will be required in assessing whether to prepare on the basis that the Upper Tribunal may immediately re-hear the case.

Consider the following examples:

Credibility challenge in asylum case

- It is unlikely that the case can be re-decided without oral evidence, adjournment very likely

Failure to consider relevant evidence

- Oral evidence may not be needed, adjournment unlikely

Legal error such as Convention reason

- Oral evidence unlikely to be needed, adjournment very unlikely. In AH (Scope of s103A reconsideration) Sudan [2006] UKAIT 00038, under the old regime, but with clear analogies to the new, the Tribunal said that on reconsideration the Tribunal should adopt any parts of the earlier determination that are not vitiated by error of law.

It should be noted that consent orders are now specifically provided for, at UT rule 39. This would obviate the need for an error of law hearing where the error is clear – should the Home Office prove to be capable of responding to correspondence.

Appeals to the Court of Appeal

Seeking permission from the UT

An Upper Tribunal decision can, exceptionally, be challenged in the Court of Appeal. An application must be made to the UT for permission to appeal to the Court of Appeal which, if refused, can be renewed directly to the Court of Appeal.

The deadline is set out at UT rule 44(3B) and is 12 days from the sending of the determination, or 7 working days if the person is detained or 38 days if the person is outside the UK. Different time limits apply where the person was served personally or by electronic means.

An appeal to the Court of Appeal must be on a point of law (s.13 TCEA 2007) and must also satisfy a new hurdle created by the TCEA 2007 and show:

(a) that the proposed appeal would raise some important point of principle or practice, or

(b) that there is some other compelling reason for the relevant appellate court to hear the appeal.

These criteria are sometimes referred to as the 'second tier appeals test'. The Court of Appeal considered the nature and effect of the criteria in the case of *PR (Sri Lanka) & Ors v SSHD* [2011] EWCA Civ 988. A restrictive approach was adopted and the Court took the view that the prospects of success should normally be very high or the case should be one that cries out for consideration by the court. If an appeal in the Upper Tribunal involved a wholly exceptional collapse of fair procedure then permission should be granted, or where it is clear that the decision was perverse or plainly wrong. 'Compelling' was held by the court to mean 'legally compelling'. The second appeals test was considered again in *JD (Congo) v SSHD [2012] EWCA Civ 327*, in which the Court found that the fact that an appellant has succeeded before the FTT and failed before the UT, or the fact that the FTT's adverse decision has been set aside, and the decision has been re-made by the UT, were relevant factors when the court is considering whether there is some other compelling reason to grant permission to appeal.

UT self-review

The possibility of the UT reviewing its own decision is allowed for in detail at section 10 of TCEA 2007, either of the UT's own initiative or on application by a party with a right of appeal.

This is dealt with at UT rules 41 to 47, although not all of those rules will be relevant in immigration and asylum cases.

Unlike some previous historic slip rules in immigration cases, s.10 allows the UT to set aside its own decision. However, there are limited circumstances in which the UT can review an UT decision, however. UT rule 45(1) provides that a review can only occur on receiving an application for permission to appeal (this may allow review in the unlikely scenario that an application for permission to appeal is not made) where either

(a) when making the decision the Upper Tribunal overlooked a legislative provision or binding authority which could have had a material effect on the decision; or

(b) since the Upper Tribunal's decision, a court has made a decision which is binding on the Upper Tribunal and which, had it been made before the Upper Tribunal s decision, could have had a material effect on the decision.

In addition, the decision can only be set aside where the UT considers that it would be in the interests of justice to do so AND one of four conditions applies:

(a) a document relating to the proceedings was not sent to, or was not received at an appropriate time by, a party or a party's representative;

(b) a document relating to the proceedings was not sent to the Upper Tribunal at an appropriate time;

(c) a party, or a party's representative, was not present at a hearing related to the proceedings; or

(d) there has been some other procedural irregularity in the proceedings.

Tribunal determinations as precedents

Reported tribunal cases

The senior tribunal judiciary identify those decisions of the UT which are 'reportable'. These are anonymised where a request has been made by the Appellant to do so. Only reported decisions can be cited before the tribunal (aside for a caveat for the determinations of family members and for proceedings to which the present appellant was a party), though exceptionally a party may manage to persuade the decision maker of the authoritativeness of a non-reported decision through a predefined, and rather onerous, mechanism (see Practice Direction).

There is no bar on citing Tribunal decisions from the era before the new regime, though from 1 May 2004 those relying on them must be able to certify there is no more modern authority on the point:

The Tribunal's practice of issuing 'starred' i.e. legally binding decisions, has fallen into disuse.

'Country Guideline' decisions

Unusually in the legal field, because of the need for consistency in determining asylum appeals, it is necessary to recognize some need for factual precedent, see Laws LJ in the Court of Appeal in S and Others [2002] EWCA Civ 539:

While in our general law this notion of a factual precedent is exotic, in the context of the IAT's responsibilities it seems to us in principle to be benign and practical. Refugee claims vis-à-vis any particular State are inevitably made against a political backdrop which over a period of time, however long or short, is, if not constant, at any rate identifiable. Of course the impact of the prevailing political reality may vary as between one claimant and another, and it is always the appellate authorities' duty to examine the facts of individual cases. But there is no public interest, nor any

> legitimate individual interest, in multiple examinations of the state of the backdrop at any particular time. Such revisits give rise to the risk, perhaps the likelihood, of inconsistent results; and the likelihood, perhaps the certainty, of repeated and therefore wasted expenditure of judicial and financial resources upon the same issues and the same evidence.

The Tribunal regularly issues 'Country Guideline' decisions on risks relating to various groups in various countries. The Country Guideline (CG) case system has grown increasingly important and it is now essential to be familiar with relevant CG cases. Indeed, the tribunal states in the Practice Directions that it expects practitioners to be familiar with relevant CG cases. They are available at:

http://www.judiciary.gov.uk/tribunal-decisions/immigration-asylum-chamber/

Appeals under the Immigration Act 2014

Rights of appeal

Section 15 of the Immigration Act 2014 repeals and replaces sections 82, 83, 83A and 84 of the 2002 Act. This is a very major change in appeal rights.

S15 has been partially bought into force, as of 20 October 2014, but only in respect of students and their families and deportees.

The current unamended version of s.82 provides that there is a right of appeal to the tribunal where one of a long list of immigration decisions (e.g. removal, refusal to vary stay, curtailment) is made. If there is an appeal, s.84 then sets out a range of legal arguments or grounds that can be relied on. That system, which ties appeals to the service of a formal immigration decision of a particular type, is being replaced with a system that only permits an appeal if a decision regarding international protection or human rights is made.

In fact, the whole concept of an 'immigration decision' against which lies a right of appeal has been done away with. The only types of decisions that can be appealed are those that raise refugee or human rights protection issues.

Under the new s82, currently a person may appeal to the Tribunal only where the Secretary of State has decided to refuse a protection or human rights claim or has decided to revoke protection status.

A "protection claim" is a claim that removal of from the United Kingdom would breach the United Kingdom's obligations under the Refugee Convention or obligations in relation to eligibility for a grant of humanitarian protection.

A "human rights claim" means a claim made by a person that to remove him from or require him to leave the United Kingdom or to refuse him entry into the United Kingdom would be unlawful under section 6 of the Human Rights Act 1998 (c. 42) (public authority not to act contrary to Convention) as being incompatible with his Convention rights.

There will be no right of appeal against decisions to curtail or refuse to extend leave, unless human rights or asylum grounds have been raised in the application or by way of a claim made on those grounds.

As now, the right of appeal is subject to the exceptions and limitations specified in that part of the Act. The Home Office also retains, and will surely overuse, the power to certify an asylum or human rights claim as clearly unfounded, thus preventing the appeal happening until the person leaves the UK.

The right of appeal against adverse EU rights decisions is being separately preserved. This right of appeal currently originates in the Immigration (EEA) Regulations 2006 as amended and the Government has indicated (Hansard 3 Mar 2014 : Column 1190) that the right of appeal will be preserved.

Applications for extensions that do not raise asylum or human rights issued will be subject to a regime of Administrative Reviews to replace the loss of appeal rights. See look at Administrative Reviews below.

Grounds of appeal

Section 84 of the 2002 Act, which provides the grounds (or legal reasons or basis) for an appeal, is also repealed and replaced by s.15 of the new Act. The new version provides:

84 Grounds of appeal

(1) An appeal under section 82(1)(a) (refusal of protection claim) must be brought on one or more of the following grounds—

(a) that removal of the appellant from the United Kingdom would breach the United Kingdom's obligations under the Refugee Convention;
(b) that removal of the appellant from the United Kingdom would breach the United Kingdom's obligations in relation to persons eligible for a grant of humanitarian protection;
(c) that removal of the appellant from the United Kingdom would be unlawful under section 6 of the Human Rights Act 1998 (public authority not to act contrary to Human Rights Convention).

(2) An appeal under section 82(1)(b) (refusal of human rights claim) must be brought on the ground that the decision is unlawful under section 6 of the Human Rights Act 1998.

(3) An appeal under section 82(1)(c) (revocation of protection status) must be brought on one or more of the following grounds—

(a) that the decision to revoke the appellant's protection status breaches the United Kingdom's obligations under the Refugee Convention;
(b) that the decision to revoke the appellant's protection status breaches the United Kingdom's obligations in relation to persons eligible for a grant of humanitarian protection.

It can be seen that this change removes a considerable number of previous grounds of appeal, including that the decision was not in accordance with the law, was not in accordance with the immigration rules, was racially discriminatory, that a discretion conferred by the immigration rules should have been exercised differently or that the decision was not in accordance with European Union obligations. In line with the new section 82 the only available appeals are ones raising refugee or human rights issues.

Family and private life applications and claims under the rules will carry a right of appeal under Article 8, as presumably will applications made under the bereaved partner and domestic violence rules. Applications on Article 8 grounds that are clearly outside the rules are likely to be certified as clearly unfounded, challengeable only by way of a judicial review application being lodged with the Upper Tribunal (IAC).

In all Article 8 appeals under the new regime, judges will have to have regard to the statutory considerations in the new Part 5A of the 2002 Act.

Where applications are made that might engage Article 8, under categories of the rules that do not specifically refer to Article 8 (e.g. for settlement under the Points-based system, the 10-year rule or the UK Ancestry provisions), applicants will have to make the case in their accompanying representations that the application is also being made on Article 8 grounds if they are to have any chance of engaging the new rights of appeal if refused. As it stands, it looks like the Home Office are intending to make such applications solely subject to the Administrative Review regime.

Examples

Christophe enters the UK as a student under Tier 4. He is granted leave for three years. After two years, he applies for leave to remain as a spouse, specifying in his application that he believes that he meets the requirements of the Immigration Rules but also that he relies on Article 8 of the ECHR.

Under the old appeal system, Christophe would not have a right of appeal. Under the new system, he would have a right of appeal on human rights grounds.

Danielle entered the UK several years ago and claimed asylum. Her claim was dismissed and her appeal rights exhausted but no steps were taken to remove her and she has remained in the UK. She is now in a serious relationship with a British citizen and has two British citizen children by her partner. She applies for leave to remain on human rights grounds but her application is refused.

> *Under the old system Danielle would not normally have been granted a right of appeal by the Home Office, at least initially. She would have needed to pursue protracted, expensive and uncertain judicial review proceedings to obtain a right of appeal. Under the new system, she would have a right of appeal on human rights grounds.*

Eric entered the UK under Tier 1 of the Points Based System as an Entrepreneur. He applied to extend his leave. The application was refused, Eric believes on incorrect and spurious grounds because a document was not read properly.

> *Under the old appeal system, Eric would have had a right of appeal. Under the new system, Eric does not have a right of appeal. He must rely instead on 'administrative review' and/or an application for judicial review.*

Section 85 of the 2002 Act, already fairly recently amended, is to be further amended to prevent the consideration of new grounds of appeal after the decision has been made unless the Secretary of State has given the Tribunal consent to do so. This substantially undermines the scope of the s120 procedure, though how much effect this will have in practice, given the culling of appeal rights, may be minimal.

From where may appeals be brought?

Section 17 repeals and replaces s.92 of the 2002 Act, and introduces a new s.94B, on the issue of from where an appeal might be brought, i.e. whether from inside the UK or from outside. These include, particularly, new provisions requiring most deportation appeals to be brought from outside the UK (see section on Deportation). Otherwise they are largely to be expected.

Section 92(4) explicitly provides for out of country human rights appeals where a human rights claim is made from outside the UK, and subsection (5) provides that where revocation occurs the appeal is brought from inside the UK if the person was in the UK at the time of revocation or must be brought from outside the UK if the person was outside the UK at the time of revocation. Subsection (8) provides for appeals brought from within the UK to be treated as abandoned if the person leaves the UK and section 104 of the 2002 Act on pending appeals receives consequential amendments (see paragraph 47 of Schedule 9 for details).

Administrative Review

For those people whose immigration applications are refused and who would formerly have had a right of appeal, and for some who would not have had that right, an 'administrative review' (AR) will be available. This will be modelled on, but separate from, the existing administrative review process for challenging the refusal of a PBS application.

The new AR regime was partially brought into effect on 20 October 2014.

Looking at *Commencement No. 3, Transitional and Saving Provisions) Order 2014* (SI 2014/2711), a very complex commencement provision, it appears that only students (and their partners and children) applying to extend their stay under Tier 4 from 20 October 2014 will be brought under the new AR regime for the time being. Tier 4 refusals of such applications will be amenable to challenge only by way of AR (or judicial review where the AR process is inappropriate). Other groups will presumably be brought under the new regime in due course.

Deportees also lose their right to an appeal to the Tribunal on 20 October 2014 (unless they have made an asylum or human rights claim), but have not been brought within the AR regime.

As explained in the Explanatory Statement to Statement of Changes HC693, published on 16 October 2014,

> The new administrative review process will resolve case-working errors and will do so more quickly than the appeals process it replaces. The reviewer will be a different person from the original decision maker. The Home Office service standard is to determine an administrative review application within 28 days whereas the average time for a Points Based System appeal to be concluded is 12 weeks.

The new AR process is provided for in the new Administrative Review Immigration Rules (ARIR) in HC693; procedurally by way of rules 34L-34Y, and substantively in Appendix AR. HO modernised guidance is at: https://www.gov.uk/government/publications/administrative-review

Amendments to section 3C of the Immigration Act 1971 (see Part 4, Schedule 9 to the Immigration Act 2014) provide for continuing leave whilst an administrative review can be brought or is pending. Paragraph AR2.8 of the ARIR confirms the Home Office will not seek to remove the applicant from the United Kingdom where administrative review is pending (as defined in AR2.9).

The ARIR define an Administrative Review as;

> 'the review of an eligible decision to decide whether the decision is wrong due to a case working error'.

An AR will be available where an 'eligible decision' has been made. Eligible decisions are listed in AR3.2, currently only relating to applications from Tier 4 Migrants and their dependants. An eligible decision will be a refusal of leave, or a grant of leave where the period granted is being challenged.

AR3.4 provides a complete list of *'Case working errors'* (as below);

> (a) Where the original decision maker applied the wrong Immigration Rules;
>
> (b) Where the original decision maker applied the Immigration Rules incorrectly;

(c) Where the original decision maker incorrectly added up the points to be awarded under the Immigration Rules;

(d) Where there has been an error in calculating the correct period of immigration leave either held or to be granted;

(e) Where the original decision maker has not considered all the evidence that was submitted as evidenced in the eligible decision;

(f) Where the original decision maker has considered some or all of the evidence submitted incorrectly as evidenced in the eligible decision;

(g) Where the Immigration Rules provide for the original decision maker to consider the credibility of the applicant in deciding the application and the original decision maker has reached an unreasonable decision on the credibility of the applicant;

(h) Where the original decision maker's decision to refuse an application on the basis that the supporting documents were not genuine was incorrect;

(i) Where the original decision maker's decision to refuse an application on the basis that the supporting documents did not meet the requirements of the Immigration Rules was incorrect;

(j) Where the original decision maker has incorrectly refused an application on the basis that it was made more than 28 days after leave expired; and

(k) Where the original decision maker failed to apply the Secretary of State's relevant published policy and guidance in relation to the application."

This should allow for most challenges to incorrect refusal decisions, but perhaps not all. It should provide for arguments over the meaning of the rules, including the possibility that the interpretation of the rules does not conform to principles established by case law. It should provide to for challenges over the admissibility of evidence, which may include arguments on procedural unfairness, but it may not. Certainly, the 'otherwise not in accordance with the law' ground available before the Tribunal has a larger remit than AR3.4.

Paragraph AR2.4 of Appendix AR prohibits new evidence from being considered when applying for administrative review except where evidence that was not before the original decision maker is submitted to demonstrate that a case working error as defined in paragraph AR3.4 (e), (g), (h) and (j) has been made. A procedure at AR2.5 provides that 'the Reviewer' can contact the applicant to request relevant evidence where such a case working error has been identified.

An application cannot be varied by way of an AR application (AR2.6).

Procedure

Paragraph 34L provides that written notice of an eligible decision must be given. As with an appealable decision under the Immigration (Notices) Regulations 2003, it must be accompanied by a statement of reasons, and information about how to apply for AR, including the time limit.

Only one valid application for administrative review may be made in respect of an eligible decision, unless the administrative review does not succeed, but for different or additional reasons to those specified in the decision under review (34M).

To be a *valid* application, it must conform to the following requirements.

The application must be made in relation to an eligible decision (34P), while the applicant is in the UK (34Q).

Dependants can be include in the AR application where they were dependants on the application which resulted in the eligible decision (34S).

The application must be made (34R):

(a) where the applicant is not detained, no more than 14 calendar days after receipt by the applicant of the notice of the eligible decision; or

(b) where the applicant is in detention under the Immigration Acts, no more than 7 calendar days after receipt by the applicant of the notice of the eligible decision.

Where notice of the eligible decision is sent by post to an address in the UK, it is deemed to have been received, unless the contrary is shown, on the second working day after the day on which it was posted.

The AR application is treated as being made on the marked date of posting, or on the date it is delivered by a courier or submitted online.

The AR application may be accepted out of time if the Secretary of State is satisfied that it would be unjust not to waive the time limit and the application was made as soon as reasonably practicable.

It must be made in accordance with 34U if made online, or 34V if made by post.

The guidance states that Tier 4 AR applications must be made online. The paper form will only be available where the initial application was made on a paper form, and will only apply to Tier 4 migrant who has more than 10 dependants, or used the super-premium route.

Where an application is made online any specified fee must be paid, any section of the online application which is designated as mandatory must be completed as specified; and documents specified as mandatory on the online application or in the related guidance must be submitted in the specified manner (34U).

The current fee for an AR is £80.00 (see Schedule 6 of The Immigration and Nationality (Cost Recovery Fees) (Amendment) Regulations 2014.

A notice of invalidity informing an applicant that their application is invalid must be given in writing.

It remains to be seen how effective the AR regime will be, but the simultaneous loss of the right of appeal to an independent tribunal will certainly not help to inspire confidence in the internal AR process.

Chapter 15: Criminal offences

Introduction

Immigration legislation contains a plethora of offences. In addition the practitioner will find a range of other penalties, for examples the fines and civil penalties that can be imposed upon carriers under Part II of the Immigration and Asylum Act 1999. It is also important to note that the new Asylum and Immigration (Treatment of Claimants etc) Act 2004, increases the range of offences considerably, for example creating a new offence of failure to cooperate, without reasonable excuse, in one's documentation for removal or deportation; or failing to possess a valid passport or similar document without reasonable excuse on arrival.

It is also important to be aware that there are general offences of aiding and abetting the commission of a criminal offence, which can broaden the scope of who can be caught by an offence.

Top tip

If sitting the accreditation examinations, it is important to bear in mind that criminal offences will be examined, but questions raising such issues may not be immediately obvious. As with the ethical dimension to the exams, practitioners are expected to identify when problems might arise without a specific 'pointer' to this effect.

Immigration officers and police powers

Part VII of the Immigration and Asylum Act 1999, modelled to a large extent of the Police and Criminal Evidence Act 1984, amended the Immigration Act 1971 to give immigration officers powers of arrest and search, previously the sole province of the police force. These powers have been extended by subsequent legislation. Section 145 of the 1999 Act provides for immigration officers to have regard to Codes of Practice in exercising these powers. Code of Practice Directions have been issued. These take as their starting point the PACE codes, and take the form of a series of instructions modifying those Codes. However it is also notable that some safeguards that apply to police officers do not apply to them, for example the requirement to give one's name when conducting certain searches.

Section 14 of the Asylum and Immigration (Treatment of Claimants etc) Act 2004 considerably broadens the powers of arrest, and ancillary powers of entry, search and seizure, of immigration officers. Once in force, they will possess powers of arrest when in the course of exercising a function under the immigration acts they form a reasonable suspicion that one of a wide range of offences under the general criminal law have been committed, including conspiracy to defraud under the common law, bigamy under the Offences Against the Person Act 1861, offences under s.3 or s.4 of the Perjury Act 1911, as well as aiding and abetting offences; a range of offences pertaining to obtaining by deception, false accounting and handling stolen goods under the Theft Acts and a range of offences under the Forgery and Counterfeiting Act. Perhaps this represents the development of a separate policing of persons under immigration control.

The Act also contains proposals to allow the DPP to give immigration officers advice on criminal offences.

Article 31 defence against prosecution

During the passage of the Immigration and Asylum Act 1999, judgement was given in R v Uxbridge Magistrates Court ex p Adimi [1999] INLR 490, [1999] EWHC Admin 765, [2001] QB 667. The case examined the United Kingdom's obligations under Article 31 of the UN Convention on the Status of Refugees. Article 31(1) states:

> The contracting States shall not impose penalties, on account of their illegal entry or presence, on refugees who, coming directly from a territory where their life or freedom was threatened in the sense of Article 1, enter or are present in their territory without authorisation, provided they present themselves without delay to the authorities and show good cause for their illegal entry or presence.

As a result, s.31 was introduced into the 1999 Act. Section 31, by contrast, requires the refugee to have:

 ➢ presented him/herself to the authorities in the UK without delay

 ➢ made a claim for asylum as soon as was reasonably practicable after his arrival in the UK (interesting cases have arisen where refugees have been deemed to have presented early enough not be caught by the denial of support for late claims under s.55 of the NIA 2002 but have nonetheless been prosecuted with the view being taken that they delayed in presenting themselves to the authorities)

 ➢ shown good cause for the illegal entry or presence

The Adimi case has led to successful applications for compensation for those imprisoned in violation of the UK's obligations under Article 31. Such cases are brought by first quashing the conviction and then making a claim for compensation, which has been paid for the Home Office's ex gratia scheme.

In R v Afsaw [2008] UKHL 31 the House of Lords considered the extent to which Article 31 and section 31 IAA 1999 afford protection against prosecution. The majority held that it was an abuse of process to prosecute offences not explicitly covered by the section 31(3) exclusions from prosecution but which nonetheless fell within the scope of Article 31.

Lessons were not learnt though by defendant's representatives, prosecutors, and judges. The Court of Appeal had to revisit the issue again in R v Mateta & Ors, [2013] EWCA Crim 1372 where, perhaps unfairly, it was only the defence representatives that were admonished for their failures.

Trafficking

Criminalising of trafficking straddles immigration legislation and other laws.

In sections 145 (and 146) of the Nationality, Immigration and Asylum Act 2002, the offence of Traffic in Prostitution was created. This criminalised those who arranged or facilitated the arrival in the UK, or departure from the UK, of a person intending that the trafficker, or another person, would exercise control over the prostitution of the person moved, whether in the UK or in another country. It also criminalised arranging or facilitating travel within the UK of a person who had been brought into the country, where it was intended that the trafficker, or another person, would exercise control over the person moved. The maximum penalty is 14 years.

In the Sexual Offences Act 2003, the government revisited the 2002 Act and produced a whole part of the Act on trafficking (sections 57 to 60). Section 57 criminalised trafficking into the UK for sexual exploitation; section 58 trafficking within the UK, section 59 trafficking from the UK. Sexual exploitation is defined by reference to criminal offences within UK law. Intentionally arranging or facilitating travel was criminalised. The maximum sentence was again 14 years.

Section 4 of the Asylum and Immigration (Treatment of Claimants, etc.) Act criminalises other forms of trafficking: acts in contravention of Article 4 of the European Convention on Human Rights (slavery or forced labour); trafficking in human organs, and the use of force, threats or deception to induce a person to provide services, provide another person with benefits of any kind or to enable another person to acquire benefits of any kind. Again the maximum penalty is 14 years.

Section 4 was amended as of 10 November 2009 whereby a person is exploited under AITCA 2004, s 4(4)(d) in circumstances where a person uses or attempts to use him for any purpose listed in s 4(4)(c)(i)–(iii), having chosen him for that purpose on the ground that:

(i) he is mentally or physically ill or disabled, he is young or he has a family relationship with a person; and

(ii) a person without the illness, disability, youth or family relationship would be likely to refuse to be used for that purpose.

497

Offences under the Immigration Act 1971

This is one of the main sources of offences under immigration law. The key offences are as follows:

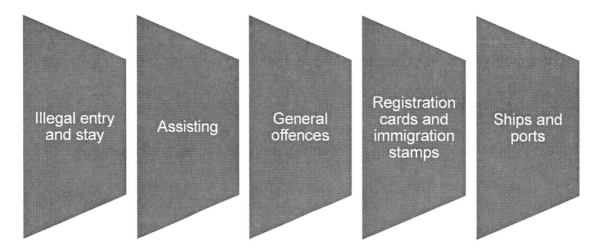

Illegal entry and stay: s.24 to 24A

Section 24 criminalises entry into the UK in breach of a deportation order or without leave; overstaying and failing to comply with the conditions on which leave if granted without reasonable excuse. By s.24(1A) an overstayer is committing an offence throughout the period of overstaying, but can only be prosecuted once in respect of overstaying the same leave. It is for the defence to prove that the person did in fact have leave, or that a stamp in a passport or travel document is wrong.

The s.24 offence as a whole is subject to an extended time limit for prosecution as set out in s.28. The offence can be tried if information is laid within 3 years of the commission of the offence provided that a senior police officer certify that this is within 2 months of the date on which there is sufficient evidence to justify proceedings. Otherwise, the more usual 6 month time limit for trial in the magistrates' court applies.

Section 24A, inserted by the Immigration and Asylum Act 1999, again applies to a person who is not a British citizen. It criminalises obtaining or seeking to obtain leave to enter or remain, or securing or seeking to secure avoidance postponement or revocation of the giving of removal directions, making a deportation order, or actual removal, by deception. It can be tried either way and before the Crown Court the maximum penalty is two years imprisonment and a fine.

Assisting: s.25 to 25D

These offences were substantially amended by the NIAA 2002. Section 25 means that it is an offence to do anything

> to facilitate

> the entry, transit or stay in the UK

> of a person who is not an European Union national

> in breach of the immigration law of any member State of the EU (the Asylum and Immigration (Treatment of Claimants etc) Act gives the Secretary of State powers to add states to the list covered if it is necessary to do so to comply with UK obligations under EU law)

> if you know, or have reasonable cause to believe that the person is not an EU national

AND

> if you know or have reasonable cause to believe that your act facilitates a breach of immigration law.

Anyone can be prosecuted for an act done in the UK. All forms of British nationals can be prosecuted for acts done outside the UK and so can corporate bodies incorporated under UK law. The maximum penalty is 14 years in prison and a fine.

It is not an offence to make an application to regularise a person's status where that person is an overstayer, or has entered illegally. Such an application would assist the person to attempt to stop being in the UK in breach of immigration law. Nor does the section override normal duties of confidentiality. If a person comes to you and you advise them that they are, or may be, in the UK in breach of immigration law, you have not facilitated their stay by giving them that advice. Nor would you do so if you took action on behalf to regularise their stay. Nor would you do so if you gave your advice and they said "thank you very much" and disappeared. Where you would be in trouble would be if you took steps to facilitate their remaining in the UK in breach of immigration law.

Section 25A makes it an offence to

> facilitate the arrival in the UK of a person

> knowingly

> and for gain

> if you know or have reasonable cause to believe that the person is an asylum-seeker (the definition of an asylum seeker also covers those who say that their removal would be contrary to the Human Rights Act 1998).

There is an exception to 25A. To benefit from the exception you must be

- ➢ acting on behalf on an organisation

- ➢ which aims to assist asylum-seekers and

- ➢ and which does not charge for its services.

Gain is not limited to financial gain. The exception is narrowly drafted. It will not help a person who is working for a "not for profit" organisation if they are not acting in the course of their employment, and it will not help a person who works for an organisation existing to help people seeking asylum if the organisation charges for its services.

Section 25B means that it is an offence to do anything

- ➢ to facilitate a breach of a deportation order

- ➢ by an EU national

- ➢ if you know or have reasonable cause to believe that your act facilitates a breach of a deportation order.

OR

- ➢ to assist a person who has been excluded from the UK

- ➢ on the grounds that this is conducive to the public good

- ➢ to arrive in, enter, or remain in the UK

- ➢ if you know or have reasonable cause to believe that your act assists the person to arrive in, enter or remain in the UK

- ➢ and if you know or have reasonable cause to believe that the person is excluded from the UK because this is considered conducive to the public good.

All three offences carry a maximum sentence of 14 years in prison. Section 25D deals with related powers to detain ships aircrafts and vehicles.

General offences: s.26

Section 26 lists a whole series of offences, all of which carry a maximum sentence of six months imprisonment and a fine, and to all of which the extended time limit for prosecution (s.28) applies (see note above to s.24). The offences are all linked to the administration of the immigration acts.

Those under examination under Schedule 2 to the 1999 Act (i.e. clients) are criminalised if:

- ➢ they fail to submit to such examination without reasonable excuse

> they fail without reasonable excuse, or refuse, to produce documents in their possession or control which they are under examination to produce

> they fail to complete and produce a landing or embarkation card in accordance with an order made under Schedule 2 of the 1971 Act

> without reasonable excuse they fail to comply with reporting restrictions (or certificates of registration or payment of fees for same – i.e. requirements of regulations made under s.4(3) of the IA 1971).

The last two offences in the section could catch anybody:

> Altering without lawful authority a certificate of entitlement, entry clearance, work permit or other document issued or made under or for the purposes of any of the Acts named; or (this later part for clients and third parties, probably under immigration control) using or having in one's possession for a document for such use which one knows or has reasonable cause to believe to be false.

> Obstructing an immigration officer or other person acting lawfully in the execution of one of the named Acts, without reasonable excuse.

Registration cards and immigration stamps

Section 26A provides for a whole range of criminal offences in connection with ARC (Asylum Registration Card) issued to people seeking asylum including forgery etc. Penalties vary with the offence to a maximum of two years in prison or a fine.

Section 26B criminalises having in one's possession an "immigration stamp" – not the impression it leaves in a passport or on a document, but the device used to make that impression – or a replica of the same, without reasonable excuse. The maximum penalty is two years in prison and a fine.

The Asylum and Immigration (Treatment of Claimants etc) Act proposes corresponding amendments to the Forgery and Counterfeiting Act 1981.

Offences connected with ships or ports

Criminalising captains, owners and agents of ships or aircraft for offences in connection with embarkation and disembarkation, including making arrangements in connection with a removal: highly specialist work.

Powers of entry and search

As detailed above, there are broad powers for both the police and immigration officers, of arrest and to enter and search premises, with or without a warrant, in connection with immigration offences. These are broad powers but there is a protection for items subject to legal privilege. However, there is no protection for a solicitor's firm, voluntary organisation or other body, from searches for people taking place, and arrests being made, on the premises.

The Asylum and Immigration (Treatment of Claimants etc) Act extends the search powers of immigration officers, providing powers under sections 28C, 28E, 28F and 28I in relation to the general criminal offences for which immigration officers will now have powers of arrest.

S.28G (inserted by the IAA 1999 s.134) allows searches, excluding strip searches but including searches of a person's mouth, at places other than a police station.

Failure to comply with a written notice to attend for fingerprinting makes a person liable to arrest without warrant under s.142 of the Immigration Act 1999, and although no provision is made for a corresponding offence the person could no doubt be caught by the provisions of Part III of the IAA 1971, for example s.26.

Offences under the 2004 Act

Immigration document offence: s.2

There are a new set of criminal provisions regarding those who (or whose dependants) are unable to produce an "immigration document" (passport or document of similar function) at an interview on arrival; for those already within the UK, they have three days grace to produce such a document (see section 2 of the Asylum & Immigration (Treatment Of Claimants Etc.) Act 2004).

There are defences: viz being an EEA national; or having a reasonable excuse for so doing, or proving that the document was used as an immigration document for all purposes en route to the UK, or proving that no immigration document was used on the journey at all.

Reasonable excuses will not include the fact that a document has been deliberately destroyed or disposed of, unless the disposal or destruction was for a reasonable cause or beyond the control of the person charged with the offence. Reasonable excuses do not include following an agent's instructions, unless in the circumstances of the case it is unreasonable to expect non-compliance with the instructions or advice. The burden of proof is on the applicant in these cases.

In Thet v Director of Public Prosecutions [2006] EWHC 2701 (Admin) the Lord Chief Justice held that the section applies to genuine immigration documents, and if a genuine document is not held then the person has a reasonable excuse for not possessing it and can make out the defence at s.2(6)(b). This decision drastically curtailed the number of s.2 prosecutions.

Duty to co-operate: s.35

The government says that currently more than 60 per cent of asylum seekers have no documents and this is the single biggest barrier to dealing with their claim and, if their claim is rejected, to returning them to their country of origin.

There is provision for certain steps to be taken to facilitate removal, by an enforced duty of co-operation with endeavours to obtain travel documents: see Asylum & Immigration (Treatment Of Claimants Etc.) Act 2004 section 35. Under this section a person commits an offence if he fails without reasonable excuse to comply with a requirement of the Secretary of State relating to arrangements for removal, including making arrangements with third parties, the provision of information, complying with identification procedures.

In R v Tabnak [2007] EWCA Crim 380 the Court of Appeal held that the 'reasonable excuse' had to render a person unable to comply with requests, rather than simply unwilling, and that fear of the consequences of removal was not sufficient to render the person unable to comply.

Offences in Nationality Acts

Section 46(1) makes it an offence for a person, for the purpose of procuring anything to be done or not done under the Act, to:

> ➢ make a statement which s/he knows to be false in a material particular

> ➢ recklessly make a statement is false in a material particular

The offence carries a maximum penalty of three months imprisonment and a fine. It is subject to extended time limits for prosecution on the same terms as those contained in the IA 1971 s.28.

Section 46(2) criminalises failure without reasonable excuse to comply with requirements the Act imposes on delivering up certificates of naturalisation. The maximum penalty is a level 4 fine, and there is no extended time limit for prosecution.

Employer and financial institution offences

Civil penalties

Sections 15 to 25 of the 2006 Act introduced a scheme of civil penalties for employers, with a criminal offence of knowingly employing someone who does not possess permission to work. The maximum fine per employee went up on

16 May 2014 to £20000. There is a system of appeals first to the government then to the county court against the level or imposition of a fine.

The Home Office had issued fines totalling almost £80m as of summer 2013, though had collected only about £25m of that.

The Points Based System has radically increased the risk to persons involved with immigrants, namely education providers and employers. There is a concerted drive to transfer responsibility for policing migrants to these categories of person. It is now possible to be sentenced to up to two years for failure to make proper checks and keep records on non-EEA employees/ students. Employers and education providers also risk breaching discrimination legislation if they target foreign workers only, for record keeping purposes. See the Chapter on Race Discrimination, above, for information about a recent decision at the Employment Tribunal.

Sections 135 to 139 of the 2002 Act

Employers or financial institutions can be required to provide information relevant to determining whether a person has committed an immigration offence, or an offence of fraud in relation to asylum support. Section 136 provides that employers or banks must reply to a notice issued by the Secretary of State requiring the information. Failure to do so, without reasonable excuse, is made a criminal offence under s.137 for which a range of responsible people in the company (see s.138) can be held responsible.

Information provided in a response to a s.136 notice could be used in a criminal prosecution for a s.137 offence. However, it cannot be used in other criminal proceedings against the person providing the information

Giving immigration advice: The OISC

Section 91 of the Immigration and Asylum Act 1999

Section 91 states as follows:

> 91(1) A person who provides immigration advice or immigration services in contravention of s.84 or of a restraining order is guilty of an offence

Immigration advice" is defined in s.82 as advice which:

➢ Relates to a particular individual

➢ Is given in connection with one or more relevant matters

➢ Is given by a person who knows that he is giving it in relation to a particular individual and in connection with one or more relevant matters

➢ By a person in the UK (wherever the client is)

> In the course of a business carried on whether or not for profit, by him or another

AND

> Is not given in connection with representing an individual before a court in criminal proceedings or in matters ancillary to criminal proceedings.

Immigration services are defined as the making of representations on behalf of a particular individual:

> In connection with one or more relevant matters

> In civil proceedings before a judicial decision maker in the United Kingdom or

> In correspondence with a Minister of the crown or government department

> By a person in the UK (wherever the client is)

> In the course of a business carried on whether or not for profit, by him or another

Section 84 of the Immigration and Asylum Act 1999

Section 84 provides that no person may provide immigration advice or immigration services unless s/he is a qualified person. Qualified people are defined in s.84 to include those registered with the Immigration Services Commissioner, or employed by them or working under their supervision. They also include those authorised by a "designated professional body" to and those working under their supervision. The bodies designated in the Act are the Solicitor Regulation Authority, ILEX and the Bar Council.

The Asylum and Immigration (Treatment of Claimants etc) Act inserts a new s.92A into the 1999 Act to give the OISC a power to enter and search premises, with a warrant where there are reasonable grounds for suspecting that immigration advice or services are being provided by someone thereby committing a criminal offence under s.91 of the 1999 Act and that material likely to be "of substantial value (whether by itself or together with other material) to the investigation of the offence" is on the premises. Material subject to legal privilege is expressly included.

The Act also creates, by inserting a new s.92B into the 1999 Act, a new offence of advertising or offering to provide immigration or services when unqualified, with a maximum penalty of a fine.

Offences connected with support

Provisions connected with asylum support can fall within the general scope of offences relating to all immigration acts, as detailed in the discussion of Part III of the IA 1971 above. However, there are also specific offences related to asylum support.

False and dishonest representations, delay or obstruction

Sections 112 and 113 of the 1999 Act address the means by which the Secretary of State may recover expenditure on support following misrepresentation or a sponsor's failure to support and maintain.

Section 105 provides that a person is guilty of an offence if with a view to obtaining support under Part VI of the 1999 Act for him/herself and any other person s/he:

- makes a statement which s/he knows to be false in a material particular

- Gives or causes to be given to a person exercising functions under Part VI a document s/he knows to be false in a material particular

- Fails, without reasonable excuse to notify a change of circumstances when required to do so in accordance with support provisions or knowingly causes another person so to fail.

Section 106 relates to a more serious offence. It contains all the same provisions as s.105, but with the aggravating circumstance that the person does what they do dishonestly. In this case the maximum sentence is seven years imprisonment, or a fine. The provision is modelled on the Social Security Administration Act 1992. Although they are not part of the statute or an official statement of the law, it is interesting to note that the Explanatory Notes to the Act specify:

> "This section is directed at cases of serious and calculated fraud, such as where a person makes a plan to extract as much from the Home Office as possible by deception."

Section 107 of the 1999 Act

Section 107 provides that a person is guilty of an offence if without reasonable excuse s/he intentionally delays or obstructs a person exercising functions conferred by or under Part VI refuses or neglects to answer a question, give any information or produce a document when required to do so in accordance with support provisions. The maximum penalty is a level three fine. The provision is modelled on s.111 of the Social Security Administration Act 1992.

Failure of a sponsor to maintain

Section 108 criminalises a sponsor who, having given a written undertaking to support and maintain under the immigration rules "persistently refuses or neglects" without reasonable excuse, to maintain the person in accordance with that undertaking, where a consequence of that refusal or neglect is that support under Part VI of the 1999 Act has to be provided for that person.

Offences under Schedule 3 of the NIA 2002

Schedule 3 of the NIA 2002 makes provision for withdrawal of support for different categories of person under immigration control. Its overriding philosophy is "if you cannot afford to support yourself here and you can leave – please leave". There are provisions to assist people to leave the UK, and to accommodate them pending their departure. Paragraph 13 of the Schedule makes it an offence to leave the UK in accordance with arrangements made under the Schedule and then return to ask for assistance in leaving again, or for support during the period pending departure. It is also an offence to request such support without disclosing that one has made a previous request. The penalty is 6 months in prison.

Chapter 16: Professional ethics

Ethical issues are pervasive in immigration practice, and questions on ethics will always be asked in OISC and IAAS assessments. An understanding of ethics is such a central and critical part of an adviser's knowledge that a failure to answer correctly the questions on ethical issues may lead to the paper being failed for gross professional error, regardless of the overall test result.

In this section we consider various documents where mention is made of ethical issues, and where the duties of advisers are laid out. Solicitors are now bound by the SRA Code of Conduct 2011, and OISC advisers by the Code of Standards and Commissioners Rules 2012. Some of the older documents referred to in this section are for illustrative purposes only.

General duties

The following is an extract from the Guidelines for Immigration Practitioners issued by the Law Society and approved by its immigration law committee in June 2001. Its salient requirements are to:

> ➢ Be aware of vulnerability of clients;

> ➢ Use appropriate interpreters;

> ➢ Avoid deceit or active misleading of the immigration authorities;

> ➢ Limit work in terms of competence and capacity;

> ➢ Maintain records.

General duties

1. Solicitors are expected to maintain the highest traditions of professional service in the conduct of activities as advisers and representatives in the field of immigration, nationality and asylum law and practice related matters. In particular:

(a) They should give sound advice having familiarised themselves with the relevant law, the immigration rules (including details of any published concessions outside the rules), and the principal published materials that relate to the issue in question (e.g. the best practice guides published from time to time by the Immigration Law Practitioners' Association/the Law Society/Refugee Legal Group, and the published determinations of the Immigration Appeal Tribunal, etc).

(b) They should at all times show sensitivity to the particularly vulnerable position of those seeking immigration advice. Practitioners should pay due regard to the related difficulties faced by such a client, and should ensure that the client fully understands the implications for his or her position of any decision or proposed course of action, making full use of an appropriate interpreter, who should be appropriately monitored and used for translation purposes only, as necessary.

(c) They must not deceive or deliberately mislead the immigration authorities or the courts or knowingly allow themselves to be used in any such way.

(d) They should consider whether, by virtue of their knowledge, skills and experience, they are competent to act in the particular case, and must not take on cases outside their area of competence or beyond their caseload capacity.

(e) They must maintain proper records of their professional dealings, including records of the matters set out below [costs and appeals]."

Basic principles

The 10 mandatory principles of the Solicitor Regulation Authority Code of Conduct are that you must:

1. uphold the rule of law and the proper administration of justice;
2. act with integrity;
3. not allow your independence to be compromised;
4. act in the best interests of each *client*;
5. provide a proper standard of service to your *clients*;
6. behave in a way that maintains the trust the public places in you and in the provision of legal services;
7. comply with your legal and regulatory obligations and deal with your regulators and ombudsmen in an open, timely and co-operative manner;
8. run your business or carry out your role in the business effectively and in accordance with proper governance and sound financial and risk management principles;
9. run your business or carry out your role in the business in a way that encourages equality of opportunity and respect for diversity; and
10. protect *client* money and *assets*.

The guidance to the code states that 'where two or more core duties come into conflict, the factor determining precedence must be the public interest, and especially the public interest in the administration of justice. Compliance with the core duties, as with all the rules, is subject to any overriding legal obligations.' The guidance as to the meaning of best interests specifically refers to the duty of confidentiality, obligations with regards to conflicts of interest and not taking unfair advantage of the client.

The professional advisor may be forced to withdraw in a case where the client's conduct threatens compromise or impairment of any of the foregoing. On the other hand, so long as the client accepts advice that will prevent the problem arising, there will be no difficulty in continuing to act.

False representations

Where a client indicates that they wish to represent a state of affairs to the Home Office which is not correct, including reliance on false documents, the advisor will find their duty not to mislead to be in conflict with the usual duty to act in accordance with the client's instructions. It is the duty of honesty which prevails.

This may also be relevant where it is apparent to the advisor from the client's general conduct or from other information which comes to light that the facts of the case are not in truth consistent with the client's express instructions. In this scenario you should advise the client that you are unable to act unless you can be satisfied that their instructions accord with the reality of the situation. An adviser cannot inform the immigration authorities of dishonesty as this is not one of the scenarios which attracts the waiver of confidentiality (see generally below): the solution for the professional advisor is to cease acting.

Remember too that the will be a potential breach of the criminal law by an adviser who assists a client to apply for leave by deception.

Appeals

This too emanates from the Guidelines for Immigration Practitioners issued by the Law Society and approved by its immigration law committee in June 2001:

> ➤ Take all reasonable steps to comply with Rules and Directions of the tribunal;

> ➤ Determine the retainer only for good reason and with reasonable notice;

> ➤ Deal with issues surrounding merits tests, funding, arrangements for the advocate, in good time before the hearing - it is unacceptable to end the retainer shortly before an appeal hearing.

Appeals

5. In the conduct of appeals a solicitor must take all reasonable steps to comply with the rules of procedure and with practice and court directions both to protect the interests of the client and to meet obligations to the court which includes the immigration appellate authorities.

6. A solicitor must not terminate a retainer except for good reason and upon reasonable notice, recording the reasons for terminating the retainer. Where, for good reason, whether the client has Community Legal Service funding or otherwise, the solicitor determines his/her retainer, it must be with as much notice to the client as possible in all the circumstances. Issues of merits, funding and arrangements to provide advocacy must be addressed at the earliest possible date so as to avoid damage either to the client's interests or to the effective operation of the court. Such advice as may be appropriate should be given to the client for alternative representation. Notice of withdrawal from representation must be promptly given to the court in such manner as to minimise prejudice to the client and to avoid misallocation of resources to the court.

7. If a practitioner is without funds to cover a hearing it is unacceptable for the solicitor to terminate the retainer so close to the date of the hearing as to prevent the client having any opportunity of seeking to find alternative representation, or to hinder the court in adequately disposing of matters pending."

Costs and client care

The same June 2001 guidance note has this to say about costs, in essence:

> ➢ Costs information and complaints handling should be given out at the outset of taking instructions;

> ➢ Public funding eligibility should be addressed and the availability of free legal advice mentioned;

> ➢ Costs estimates should be given, and revised, throughout the proceedings, including VAT and disbursements.

Costs information

2. Solicitors must observe Practice Rule 15 and the Solicitors' Costs Information and Client Care Code in relation to the giving of advance costs information, general information for clients and complaints handling (see Chapter 13 p.265 - 275 in 'The Guide to the Professional Conduct of Solicitors 8th edition' - the Guide).

3. At the outset, the question of whether the client is eligible for any level of Community Legal Service funding (Legal Help/Controlled Legal Representation/Legal Representation) must be explored and discussed with the client. It is good practice to make the client aware of the existence and range of any services for free representation.

4. Where a charge is to be made to a client for the provision of legal services, a written estimate of the costs should be supplied to the client at the outset of the matter to which the charge relates, with a description of the work to be done to a specified stage and the method of calculation of such fee (unless the fee is fixed) and the likely overall cost including disbursements and VAT. Where the fee is likely to exceed the estimate given or requires variation, a written revision of the estimate and mode of calculation should be given as soon as it becomes apparent that the original estimate is likely to be exceeded or requires revision, and in any event before it is in fact exceeded.

Addressing status of the fee earner in the client care letter

There is a specific requirement to inform the client of the status (especially of unqualified staff) of the fee earner who would be carrying out their work and to give the name of the supervising principal where the fee earner is not a partner.

Supervision

There follows an extract from the Law Society's note of September 2002 regarding Supervision and Obtaining Work, in which it warns against providing nominal supervision to non-solicitor businesses:

3.1 The Society is concerned by reports of solicitors being requested to supervise the work of non-qualified immigration advisers in circumstances where it appears that this is merely a device to avoid the immigration adviser needing to register with

OISC. The Society considers that the purpose of the Act was to exempt from a requirement to register with OISC solicitors and staff supervised as part of their practice. It was not intended to allow solicitors to provide nominal supervision to non-solicitor businesses. Supervision of immigration work for the purpose of the Act must be an internal function and form part of the management structure of the firm. It is not possible for a supervisor to fulfil this task properly unless that person works as a part of the firm. The Society takes a similar view regarding the provision of other "reserved" activities – e.g. conveyancing, and probate.

3.2 Solicitors need to be aware, therefore, that this kind of involvement with a non-solicitor organisation is likely to involve a breach of the Solicitors' Practice Rules 1990, in particular:

- practice rule 1 (basic principles)
- practice rule 4 (employed solicitors) and/or
- practice rule 5 (providing services other than as a solicitor).

Practice rule 1 sets out a solicitor's fundamental duties which include preserving his or her integrity and the good repute of the profession. Practice rule 4, broadly, prevents a solicitor working in a non-solicitor firm doing, or taking responsibility for, work for the public. Practice rule 5 prevents a practising solicitor from becoming involved in the running of a non-solicitor business which provides legal services.

Liens – retention of documents

A client is entitled to the papers on his file which belong to him unless the solicitor can exercise a lien for unpaid costs.

> However, best practice is that the solicitor should transfer papers even though financial issues remain unresolved, obtaining undertakings from the new representatives as appropriate;

> The client should, if now acting for themselves, be given copies of material on file at their own expense, and be given access to the file.

Lien (privately funded)

8. If the client terminates the retainer just before a hearing date and a successor solicitor is appointed, the Society recommends the papers be released to the successor solicitor, subject to a satisfactory undertaking as to costs being given in lieu of the exercise of a lien.
Lien (CLS funded)

9(a) Subject to the need to comply with the requirements of the General Civil Contract in relation to Legal Help and Controlled Legal Representation, a solicitor who has acted in a CLS funded matter may call for an undertaking from a successor solicitor either:

to return the papers promptly at the end of the matter to enable a bill of costs to be drawn up; or that the successor solicitor will include the former solicitor's costs in a bill to be assessed, collect those costs and then pay them over to the former solicitor.

(b) If the client subsequently acts for himself or herself, it is not misconduct for a solicitor to retain the file to get a bill drawn and assessed, but the client must be allowed access to the file and to take copies of the papers at the client's expense.

Under the OISC Code of Standards the position is even clearer. As stated in OISCNews, July 2013;

Codes 47 and 88 explain an adviser's obligations when a client requests their file. They make it clear that advisers should not place any unreasonable obstacles in the way of clients being given their files such as refusing to hand a file over until photocopy fees are paid.

Further, where a client needs to take quick action such as lodging an appeal, no delay in handling over the file is acceptable.

Advisers are also reminded that they do not have a lien over a client's file. The client's file must be given to the client or sent to their new representative on request, and advisers should seek to recover any outstanding fees using civil remedies, as necessary.

Standard of work

In an urgent case, it is permissible to take on a client simply for the purpose of seeking an adjournment. However if that is refused, and if continuing to act will do more harm than good, then representation at the hearing should be curtailed (which is not to say that the firm should not continue to act).

Standard of work

10. A solicitor should not normally agree to represent a client where adequate preparation of a case is not possible, but in cases of urgency the solicitor may agree to act or continue to act for the purpose of applying for an adjournment. Where an adjournment is refused, the solicitor must consider whether continuing to act compromises effective standards of representation. If so, the solicitor should then not participate further in the hearing.

This is therefore a limited caveat to the general rule 12.03 of the Professional Conduct rules which states:

"A solicitor must not act, or continue to act, where the client cannot be represented with competence or diligence."

The Rules stipulate that this applies where a solicitor has insufficient time, experience or skill to deal with the instructions.

Supervision of staff

There follows an extract from the Law Society's note of September 2002 regarding Supervision and Obtaining Work:

4. Supervision of staff in a solicitors' practice

4.1 The Society is also asked, from time to time, for advice concerning the supervision requirements when a solicitors' practice employs staff, whether qualified or unqualified, who deal with immigration work. The staff may be employed under a contract of service or a contract for services. Solicitor principals must comply with practice rule 13 with regard to the supervision and management of their practice. See also principle 3.07 and Annexes 3C and 21G in The Guide to the Professional Conduct of Solicitors (8th edition, 1999). Solicitor principals, as a matter of professional conduct, must ensure that staff (whether employed under a contract of service or a contract for services):

- are competent to carry out the work; and
- are appropriately supervised.

4.2 "Supervision" in the context of practice rule 13 refers to the professional overseeing of staff and the professional overseeing of clients' matters. Operationally, supervision may be delegated within an established framework for reporting and accountability. However, ultimate responsibility remains with the principals. The Society acknowledges that work may properly take place away from the office (e.g. when staff visit clients, attend court etc., or if a person normally works away from the office, such as a teleworker) but it is important that systems of supervision and management encompass these situations.

4.3 Practice rule 13, however, also prohibits a non-solicitor immigration practitioner from operating, as a member of a solicitors' practice, from a separate office, unless a solicitor who is qualified to supervise is employed at that office.

4.4 In addition, solicitors should be aware that unqualified staff working on immigration matters must be supervised by a solicitor (or by an RFL principal or by a person registered with OISC) in order to comply with the requirements of the Act. This can only be done if the unqualified staff, even if employed under a contract for services, are working within the firm's practice, and not if they are working independently."

Conflict of interest

The relevant parts of rule 3 of the Solicitor Code of Conduct read as follows:

'3.01 Duty not to act

(1) You must not act if there is a conflict of interests (except in the limited circumstances dealt with in 3.02).

(2) There is a conflict of interests if:
(a) you owe, or your firm owes, separate duties to act in the best interests of two or more clients in relation to the same or related matters, and those duties conflict, or there is a significant risk that those duties may conflict; or
(b) your duty to act in the best interests of any client in relation to a matter conflicts, or there is a significant risk that it may conflict, with your own interests in relation to that or a related matter.

(3) For the purpose of 3.01(2), a related matter will always include any other matter which involves the same asset or liability.

3.02 Exceptions to duty not to act

(1) You or your firm may act for two or more clients in relation to a matter in situations of conflict or possible conflict if:
(a) the different clients have a substantially common interest in relation to that matter or a particular aspect of it; and
(b) all the clients have given in writing their informed consent to you or your firm acting.

(2) Your firm may act for two or more clients in relation to a matter in situations of conflict or possible conflict if:
(a) the clients are competing for the same asset which, if attained by one client, will make that asset unattainable to the other client(s);
(b) there is no other conflict, or significant risk of conflict, between the interests of any of the clients in relation to that matter;
(c) the clients have confirmed in writing that they want your firm to act in the knowledge that your firm acts, or may act, for one or more other clients who are competing for the same asset; and
(d) unless the clients specifically agree, no individual acts for, or is responsible for the supervision of, more than one of those clients.

(3) When acting in accordance with 3.02(1) or (2) it must be reasonable in all the circumstances for you or your firm to act for all those clients.

(4) If you are relying on the exceptions in 3.02(1) or (2), you must:
(a) draw all the relevant issues to the attention of the clients before agreeing to act or, where already acting, when the conflict arises or as soon as is reasonably practicable, and in such a way that the clients concerned can understand the issues and the risks involved;
(b) have a reasonable belief that the clients understand the relevant issues; and
(c) be reasonably satisfied that those clients are of full capacity.

3.03 Conflict when already acting

If you act, or your firm acts, for more than one client in a matter and, during the course of the conduct of that matter, a conflict arises between the interests of two or more of those clients, you, or your firm, may only continue to act for one of the clients (or a group of clients between whom there is no conflict) provided that the duty of confidentiality to the other client(s) is not put at risk.

3.04 Accepting gifts from clients

Where a client proposes to make a lifetime gift or a gift on death to, or for the benefit of:
(a) you;
(b) any manager, owner or employee of your firm;
(c) a family member of any of the above,
and the gift is of a significant amount, either in itself or having regard to the size of the client's estate and the reasonable expectations of the prospective beneficiaries, you must advise the client to take independent advice about the gift, unless the client is a member of the beneficiary's family. If the client refuses, you must stop acting for the client in relation to the gift.'

Additional guidance is given on conflict of interests between clients. While it is clearly aimed principally at criminal law solicitors the principles are clearly transferrable:

> 'Co-defendants
>
> 23. In publicly funded cases, regulations require that one solicitor be appointed to act for all co-defendants in a legal aid case unless there is, or is likely to be, a conflict. The purpose of this is to ensure economy in the use of public funds by ensuring that a single solicitor represents co-defendants where it is proper to do so. The professional conduct obligations which deal with conflicts of interest have always prevented a solicitor or firm acting for two or more clients where there is a conflict or significant risk of a conflict arising between the interests of two or more clients. A solicitor can act, however, for co-defendants where conflict is not a factor. The difficulty often lies, however, in spotting potential conflict and deciding whether it is sufficiently real to refuse instructions.
>
> 24. Your starting point should always be your fundamental professional obligation to act in each client's best interests. Can you discharge this obligation to each client? This means first asking each client if they are aware of any actual or potential conflict between them and then, if they indicate that there is no such conflict, asking yourself whether you feel there are any constraints on the advice you would want to give to one client, or on the action you would want to take on that client's behalf, which are likely to arise because you act for another co-defendant.
>
> 25. A conflict of interest arises wherever there is a constraint of that sort, for example where it is in the best interests of client A:
> (a) to give evidence against client B;
> (b) to make a statement incriminating client B;
> (c) to implicate client B in a police interview;
> (d) to provide prejudicial information regarding client B to an investigator;
> (e) to cross-examine client B in such a manner as to call into question his or her credibility;
> (f) to rely upon confidential information given by client B without his or her consent; or
> (g) to adopt tactics in the course of the retainer which potentially or actually harm client B.
>
> 26. If these obligations actually come into conflict when acting for two or more clients you will have to cease to act for one and often both. This can cause considerable disruption and expense, which is why the rules require that you should not accept instructions if there is a significant risk of this happening.
>
> ...
>
> 29. When considering accepting instructions from more than one client in the same matter you need to assess not only whether there is a conflict at the outset, but whether events are likely to arise which will prevent you from continuing to act for one or both at a later stage in the proceedings. In almost all cases there will be some possibility of differences in instructions between the clients but the rules do not prevent you acting unless the risk of conflict is significant. Assessing the risk is

often not easy. It is also important that where you have accepted instructions from co-defendants you remain alert to the risk of conflict arising as the case progresses.

30. When considering whether there is an actual conflict there are obvious indicators such as whether the clients have differing accounts of the important relevant circumstances of the alleged crime or where one seems likely to change his or her plea. There are also less obvious indicators. These would include situations where there is some clear inequality between the co-defendants which might, for example, suggest that one client is acting under the influence of the other rather than on his or her own initiative. If you are acting for both this may make it difficult for you to raise and discuss these issues equally with them. In trying to help one, you might be undermining the other. If you believe you are going to be unable to do your best for one without worrying about whether this might prejudice the other you should only accept instructions from one.

31. The risk of future conflict can be an even more difficult issue to assess. It may be that you have two clients who are pleading not guilty and who are apparently in total agreement on the factual evidence. Should they both be found guilty, you need to consider at the outset whether you would be able to mitigate fully and freely on behalf of one client without in so doing harming the interests of the other. It may be that one has a long list of convictions and is considerably older than the other. If so, it may be that the younger client with a comparatively clean record was led astray or pressurised into committing the crime and would want you to emphasise this in mitigation. If there is a significant risk of this happening you should not accept instructions from both.

32. Even where care is taken when accepting instructions from more than one client in the same matter there will inevitably be situations where a conflict subsequently arises. This will commonly happen where one defendant changes his or her plea or evidence. A decision will then have to be taken as to whether it is proper to continue to represent one client or whether both will have to instruct new firms. In making this decision you need to consider whether in the changed circumstances your duty to disclose all relevant information to the retained client will place you in breach of your duty of confidentiality to the other client. In other words, you need to decide whether you hold confidential information about the departing client which is now relevant to the retained client. If you do have such information then you cannot act for either client.

...

34. For the avoidance of doubt, you cannot resolve a conflict by instructing another firm or counsel to undertake the advocacy on behalf of one client. Neither can you pass one of the clients to another member of your firm. The rules make it quite clear that your firm cannot act for clients whose interests conflict.

35. Any decision to act, or not to act, for co-defendants should be recorded with a brief note of the reasons.

Your interests conflicting with the client's – 3.01(2)(b)

39. There are no circumstances where you can act for a client whose interests conflict with your own interests. The situations outlined in 3.02 where you can act for two or more clients whose interests conflict have no application in this situation. This is because of the fiduciary relationship which exists between you and your

client which prevents you taking advantage of the client or acting where there is a conflict or potential conflict of interests between you and your client...

...

54. Where you discover an act or omission which would justify a claim against you, you must inform the client, and recommend they seek independent advice. You must also inform the client that independent advice should be sought in cases where the client makes a claim against you, or notifies an intention to do so. If the client refuses to seek independent advice, you should not continue to act unless you are satisfied that there is no conflict of interest. See 20.09 (Dealing with claims).'

In the case of Kaur (01/TH/02438; 26 September 2001) the tribunal noted that in the case of a solicitor whose firm practises in the same centre as that in which he or she is an Adjudicator, actual interest, not merely appearance of interest, arises if a member of the firm appears before him or her. It is essential that in such cases the Adjudicator disqualifies himself or herself at once. For that reason it is no doubt better if the centre where the Adjudicator sits is not the one at which the firm practises, thus avoiding possible problems of last-minute relisting.

Confidentiality

Basic duty

The duty of confidentiality is fundamental to the relationship of solicitor and client. It exists as an obligation both in law, having regard to the nature of the contract of retainer, and as a matter of conduct. See rule 4 of the solicitors code of conduct:

4.01 Duty of confidentiality

You and your firm must keep the affairs of clients and former clients confidential except where disclosure is required or permitted by law or by your client (or former client).

4.02 Duty of disclosure

If you are a lawyer or other fee earner you must disclose to a client for whom you are personally acting on a matter, whether individually or as one of a group, or whose matter you are personally supervising, all information of which you are aware which is material to that client's matter regardless of the source of the information, subject to:
(a) the duty of confidentiality in 4.01 above, which always overrides the duty to disclose; and
(b) the following where the duty does not apply:
    (i) where such disclosure is prohibited by law;
    (ii) where it is agreed expressly that no duty to disclose arises or a different standard of disclosure applies; or
    (iii) where you reasonably believe that serious physical or mental injury will be caused to any person if the information is disclosed to a client.

> 4.03 Duty not to put confidentiality at risk by acting
>
> If you are a lawyer or other fee earner and you personally hold, or your firm holds, confidential information in relation to a client or former client, you must not risk breaching confidentiality by acting, or continuing to act, for another client on a matter where:
> (a) that information might reasonably be expected to be material; and
> (b) that client has an interest adverse to the first-mentioned client or former client, except where proper arrangements can be made to protect that information in accordance with 4.04 and 4.05 below.

The rule receives is supplemented by the following guidance:

> 3. Rule 4.01 sets out your fundamental duty to keep all clients' affairs confidential. It is important to bear in mind the distinction between this duty and the concept of law known as legal professional privilege. The duty of confidentiality extends to all confidential information about a client's affairs, irrespective of the source of the information, subject to the limited exceptions described below. Legal professional privilege protects certain communications between you and your client from being disclosed, even in court. However, not all communications are protected from disclosure and you should, if necessary, refer to an appropriate authority on the law of evidence.
>
> 4. The duty of confidentiality continues after the end of the retainer. After the client dies the right to confidentiality passes to the personal representatives, but note that an administrator's power dates only from the grant of the letters of administration.
>
> 5. Information received in the context of a joint retainer must be available between the clients. They must, however, all consent to any confidential information being disclosed to a third party. Information communicated to you when acting for one of the clients in relation to a separate matter must not be disclosed to the other client(s) without the consent of that client.
>
> 6. If you obtain information in relation to a prospective client you may still be bound by a duty of confidentiality, even if that prospective client does not subsequently instruct your firm. There may be circumstances, however, where you receive information where there is no real or genuine interest in instructing your firm and that information is unlikely to be confidential.

In summary:

> ➢ Even aside from legal professional privilege (which applies to communications between solicitor and client), there is a duty to maintain confidentiality;
>
> ➢ It applies regarding any source of information;
>
> ➢ It applies after the client's death or the end of the retainer;
>
> ➢ A duty may arise even regarding a prospective client.

Guidance specifically states that a client's address should not be disclosed without the client's consent.

Exceptions to the rule on confidentiality

This is the Solicitor Regulation Authority's guidance on this issue:

12. You may reveal confidential information to the extent that you believe necessary to prevent the client or a third party committing a criminal act that you reasonably believe is likely to result in serious bodily harm.

13. There may be exceptional circumstances involving children where you should consider revealing confidential information to an appropriate authority. This may be where the child is the client and the child reveals information which indicates continuing sexual or other physical abuse but refuses to allow disclosure of such information. Similarly, there may be situations where an adult discloses abuse either by himself or herself or by another adult against a child but refuses to allow any disclosure. You must consider whether the threat to the child's life or health, both mental and physical, is sufficiently serious to justify a breach of the duty of confidentiality.

14. In proceedings under the Children Act 1989 you are under a duty to reveal experts' reports commissioned for the purposes of proceedings, as these reports are not privileged. The position in relation to voluntary disclosure of other documents or solicitor-client communications is uncertain. Under 11.01, an advocate is under a duty not to mislead the court. Therefore, if you are an advocate, and have certain knowledge which you realise is adverse to the client's case, you may be extremely limited in what you can state in the client's favour. In this situation, you should seek the client's agreement for full voluntary disclosure, for three reasons:
(a) the matters the client wants to hide will probably emerge anyway;
(b) you will be able to do a better job for the client if all the relevant information is presented to the court; and
(c) if the information is not voluntarily disclosed, you may be severely criticised by the court.
If the client refuses to give you authority to disclose the relevant information, you are entitled to refuse to continue to act for the client if to do so will place you in breach of your obligations to the court.

...

16. Occasionally you may be asked by the police or a third party to give information or to show them documents which you have obtained when acting for a client. Unless the client is prepared to waive confidentiality, or where you have strong prima facie evidence that you have been used by the client to perpetrate a fraud or other crime and the duty of confidence does not arise, you should insist upon receiving a witness summons or subpoena so that, where appropriate, privilege may be claimed and the court asked to decide the issue.

In summary:

➢ A solicitor should not permit themselves to be used as an instrument of crime or fraud;

➢ The client may consent to the duty being waived;

> ➢ Information can be passed on if relevant to a reasonable belief that the client or a third party will commit a criminal act resulting in serious bodily harm.

> ➢ Information can be passed on where there is a threat to a child's physical or mental health.

Money Laundering

The Solicitor Regulation Authority warns that if solicitors do not take steps to learn about the provisions of the Criminal Justice Act 1993, they may commit criminal offences, by assisting someone known or suspected to be laundering money generated by any serious crime, by telling clients or anyone else that they are under investigation for an offence of money laundering, or by failing to report a suspicion of money laundering in the case of drug trafficking or terrorism.

Accordingly, attention should be paid to: Unusual settlement requests, unusual instructions, large sums of cash, secretive clients (particularly where you do not meet them in person) and dealings with suspect territories where production of drugs or drug trafficking may be prevalent.

As at late 2004, the Law Society indicated that the problems that might ensue from the Home Office demanding that the lodging of the surety money is a condition of bail, given that the Proceeds of Crime Act 2003 can disadvantage a bail applicant who is unrepresented and can pose problems for solicitors with regard to the Law Society's conduct rules. The Home Office is therefore issuing revised instructions to staff that indicate that they should no longer impose a condition of bail requiring the lodging of monies and that they should not seek such a condition from an adjudicator.

Terrorism, Money Laundering and Confidentiality

It is an offence to provide assistance to a money launderer to retain the benefit of funds if that person should have known or suspected that those funds were the proceeds of terrorism. It is also an offence for any person who acquired knowledge or a suspicion of money laundering of terrorist funds in the course of their profession, not to report it.

Section 19 of the Terrorism Act 2000 creates a duty to disclose to the police any information where a person suspects that another person has committed a terrorist offence outlined in sections 15 to 18 (involving funding terrorist purposes and money laundering). This section is triggered where the belief or suspicion is based on information gathered "in the course of a trade, profession, business or employment". The duty comprises disclosing (a) the belief or suspicion in question and (b) the information on which it is based. The maximum penalty for the failure to disclose such information is five years imprisonment. There is a defence if the person charged establishes he had a "reasonable excuse" for not disclosing the information. The Anti-Terrorism

Crime and Security Act 2001 has introduced a further level of liability by developing this offence so as to require disclosure of "information about acts of terrorism" in general. It is now an offence if the individual does not disclose "as soon as reasonably practicable" information which can be of "material assistance" in preventing an act of terrorism, or lead to the apprehension, prosecution, or conviction of a person involved in acts of terrorism. Once again there is a defence of "reasonable excuse."

Duties to the Court

There is a fundamental duty not to deceive or mislead the court (Rule 11):

11.01 Deceiving or misleading the court

(1) You must never deceive or knowingly or recklessly mislead the court.

(2) You must draw to the court's attention:
(a) relevant cases and statutory provisions;
(b) the contents of any document that has been filed in the proceedings where failure to draw it to the court's attention might result in the court being misled; and
(c) any procedural irregularity.

(3) You must not construct facts supporting your client's case or draft any documents relating to any proceedings containing:
(a) any contention which you do not consider to be properly arguable; or
(b) any allegation of fraud unless you are instructed to do so and you have material which you reasonably believe establishes, on the face of it, a case of fraud.

11.02 Obeying court orders

You must comply with any court order requiring you or your firm to take, or refrain from taking, a particular course of action.

11.03 Contempt of court

You must not become in contempt of court.

11.04 Refusing instructions to act as advocate

(1) You must not refuse to act as an advocate for any person on any of the following grounds:
(a) that the nature of the case is objectionable to you or to any section of the public;
(b) that the conduct, opinions or beliefs of the prospective client are unacceptable to you or to any section of the public; or
(c) that the source of any financial support which may properly be given to the prospective client for the proceedings is unacceptable to you.

(2) You are not required to act as an advocate:
(a) under a conditional fee agreement; or
(b) if you reasonably consider that you are not being offered a proper fee having regard to:
(i) the circumstances of the case;
(ii) the nature of your practice; or

(iii) your experience and standing.

11.05 Appearing as an advocate

If you are appearing as an advocate:
(a) you must not say anything which is merely scandalous or intended only to insult a witness or any other person;
(b) you must avoid naming in open court any third party whose character would thereby be called into question, unless it is necessary for the proper conduct of the case;
(c) you must not call into question the character of a witness you have cross-examined unless the witness has had the opportunity to answer the allegations during cross-examination; and
(d) you must not suggest that any person is guilty of a crime, fraud or misconduct unless such allegations:
    (i) go to a matter in issue which is material to your client's case; and
    (ii) appear to you to be supported by reasonable grounds.

11.06 Appearing as a witness

You must not appear as an advocate at a trial or act in the litigation if it is clear that you, or anyone within your firm, will be called as a witness, unless you are satisfied that this will not prejudice your independence as an advocate, or litigator, or the interests of your client or the interests of justice.

The duty encompasses;

➢ advising the court of cases or provisions that state the law;

➢ advising the adjudicator of relevant materials filed in the proceedings that would assist the opponent;

➢ calling a witness whose evidence is untrue to their knowledge (not belief);

There is specific guidance on the distinction between misleading the court and deceiving the court and how to reconcile one's duty to the client and duty to the court:

12. Rule 11.01 makes a distinction between deceiving the court, where knowledge is assumed, and misleading the court, which could happen inadvertently. You would not normally be guilty of misconduct if you inadvertently misled the court. However, if during the course of proceedings you become aware that you have inadvertently misled the court, you must, with your client's consent, immediately inform the court. If the client does not consent you must stop acting. Rule 11.01 includes attempting to deceive or mislead the court.

13. You might deceive or mislead the court by, for example:
(a) submitting inaccurate information or allowing another person to do so;
(b) indicating agreement with information that another person puts forward which you know is false;
(c) calling a witness whose evidence you know is untrue;
(d) not immediately disclosing a document you have become aware of during the course of a case, which should have been, but was not, disclosed;

(e) attempting to influence a witness, when taking a statement from that witness, with regard to the contents of their statement; and

(f) tampering with evidence or seeking to persuade a witness to change their evidence. To avoid such allegations it would be wise, when seeking to interview a witness for the other side, to offer to interview them in the presence of the other side's representative.

14. Whilst a person may call themselves by whatever name they choose, you must (in the context of court proceedings) be satisfied that the client is not adopting a different name or date of birth to avoid previous convictions becoming known to the court, or to deceive the court in any other way.

15. If you are acting for a defendant, you need not correct information given to the court by the prosecution or any other party which you know may allow the court to make incorrect assumptions about the client or the case, provided you do not indicate agreement with that information.

16. Where a client admits to having committed perjury or having misled the court in any material matter relating to ongoing proceedings, you must not act further in those proceedings unless the client agrees to disclose the truth to the court.

17. If, either before or during the course of proceedings, the client makes statements to you which are inconsistent, this is not of itself a ground for you to stop acting. Only where it is clear that the client is attempting to put forward false evidence to the court should you stop acting. In other circumstances it would be for the court, and not for you, to assess the truth or otherwise of the client's statement.

18. There are some types of information which you are obliged to disclose to the court, whether or not it is in the best interests of the client to do so. Failure to disclose such information could amount to a breach of 11.01. For example:

(a) The advocates on both sides must advise the court of relevant cases and statutory provisions. If one of them omits a case or provision or makes an incorrect reference to a case or provision, it is the duty of the other to draw attention to it even if it assists the opponent's case.

(b) Except when acting or appearing for the prosecution, if you know of facts which, or of a witness who, would assist the adversary you are not under any duty to inform the adversary, or the court, of this to the prejudice of your own client. However, if you know that a relevant document has been filed in the proceedings and is therefore notionally within the knowledge of the court, you must inform the judge of its existence.

Complaints procedures

The LSC give certain guidance on complaints. A complaint should be defined as any expression of client dissatisfaction, however it is expressed. This might be in writing, over the telephone or in person.

The firm's approach to complaints should be positive, as they alert you to problems that your clients have about the service and thereby provide an opportunity for service.

Practice Rule 15, the "client care" rule provides that all private firms must operate a complaints system and must make their clients aware of it. Although the client does not need to be advised of the entire system when given one-off advice (including police station advice and court duty solicitor advice), they must at least be advised of the name of the person with whom they should raise any problems. Compliant practice would therefore include telling the client whom to approach in the event of dissatisfaction and/or providing them with a prepared letter/leaflet containing a brief explanation, and supplementing that with a more detailed written explanation if/once a file is opened and further work is done for them.

The Solicitor Regulation Authority has recommended that firms consider having face to face meetings earlier in the process to discuss concerns given the potential needs of immigration clients.

Responsibility for complaints

Ensure that the client is aware of the names of individuals who are authorised to handle complaints (e.g. those to whom specific training has been given), or the level at which all complaints should first be handled (e.g. by the caseworker initially, with guidance from the supervisor or a manager). This will include the name of the individual who has ultimate responsibility in the organisation for tracking and monitoring complaints (this is often, but not always, the same person to whom complaints escalate if they cannot be resolved initially).

It is imperative that the firm has a system to report and record centrally every complaint made: so ensure complaints are passed onto this system, for analysis and review of all complaints at least annually by an appropriate person.

Ensure that you respond appropriately to any complaint. This will include identifying the cause of any problem of which a client has complained, offering any appropriate redress and correcting any unsatisfactory procedure.

Practical solutions

Make sure that you explain the circumstances behind any problem clearly to a client, and explain what practical steps are available to remedy whatever problems have arisen (obtaining statements from delinquent interpreters or colleagues or third parties, writing representations, admitting one's error to the immigration authorities).

Third party instructions

The client is the individual for whom you are providing legal services. This is from the old Law Society Professional Conduct Guide:

> **12.05 Third party instructions**
>
> Where instructions are received from a third party, a solicitor should obtain written instructions from the client that he or she wishes the solicitor to act. In any case of doubt the solicitor should see the client or take other appropriate steps to confirm instructions.

1. This principle applies to a joint retainer, e.g. when acting for a husband and wife in a conveyancing transaction.

2. The solicitor must advise the client without regard to the interests of the introducer. See also 11.05 (p.224), 11.07 (p.227) and the Solicitors' Introduction and Referral Code (Annex 11B, p.238).

3. When acting for a client who has language or other communication difficulties, and instructions are given through an interpreter, the solicitor should take reasonable steps to ensure that the interpreter is appropriate for the client's needs. Guidelines for solicitors dealing with immigration cases are set out in Annex 12C, p.262.

4. In the case of elderly clients, a solicitor is sometimes put under pressure by the client's family to accept instructions which are not in accordance with the client's own intentions. In this case the solicitor should see the client.

There is no obvious equivalent in the new Code of Conduct. Rule 2 (client relations) touches on the subject as follows:

2.01 Taking on clients

(1) You are generally free to decide whether or not to take on a particular client. However, you must refuse to act or cease acting for a client in the following circumstances:
(a) when to act would involve you in a breach of the law or a breach of the rules of professional conduct;
(b) where you have insufficient resources or lack the competence to deal with the matter;
(c) where instructions are given by someone other than the client, or by only one client on behalf of others in a joint matter, you must not proceed without checking that all clients agree with the instructions given; or
(d) where you know or have reasonable grounds for believing that the instructions are affected by duress or undue influence, you must not act on those instructions until you have satisfied yourself that they represent the client's wishes.

(2) You must not cease acting for a client except for good reason and on reasonable notice.

2.02 Client care

(1) You must:
(a) identify clearly the client's objectives in relation to the work to be done for the client;
(b) give the client a clear explanation of the issues involved and the options available to the client;
(c) agree with the client the next steps to be taken; and
(d) keep the client informed of progress, unless otherwise agreed.

(2) You must, both at the outset and, as necessary, during the course of the matter:
(a) agree an appropriate level of service;
(b) explain your responsibilities;
(c) explain the client's responsibilities;

(d) ensure that the client is given, in writing, the name and status of the person dealing with the matter and the name of the person responsible for its overall supervision; and

(e) explain any limitations or conditions resulting from your relationship with a third party (for example a funder, fee sharer or introducer) which affect the steps you can take on the client's behalf.

(3) If you can demonstrate that it was inappropriate in the circumstances to meet some or all of these requirements, you will not breach 2.02.'

Top tip: accreditation exams

If there is a question with an ethics dimension to which you are unsure of the answer in the exam, you may wish to indicate that you would consult a supervisor and/or the Solicitor Regulation Authority Professional Conduct telephone line. A note on examination technique previously posted on the CLT website suggested this was a possible way of trying to extract a mark and it would seem particularly apposite for ethics questions.

Also bear in mind the possibility of a criminal offence dimension to a particular exercise as well as a conduct/ethics dimension, as where conduct which is unethical, such as representing a false situation to the Home Office, might also bring liability in terms of seeking to obtain leave to remain via deception.

The question of how non Solicitor Regulation Authority regulated LSC examinees are tested on ethics is an unresolved one. Practice so far has been to make ethical issues non-specific to the Solicitor Regulation Authority Code of Conduct. Nevertheless, the code provides extremely useful general ethical guidance and the principles therein are certainly examinable.

Chapter 17: Practical skills

Asylum applications

Taking instructions

It is recommended that you are familiar with the ILPA Making an Asylum Application as to the best practice to follow throughout asylum applications, although we summarise most of the important points in this section – for example making sure you take instructions on other basis than asylum on which an application for leave to remain could be made (and indeed whether an article 8 human rights claim is a realistic option to going abroad and applying under the immigration rules), immigration history, the status of other family members, and ensuring you are aware of all relevant documents held by the client (e.g. documents going to the basis of stay of relatives and witnesses in the United Kingdom be it ILR on the basis of refugee status, or lesser forms of leave to remain, and accompanying statements).

Top tip

HJT strongly recommends reading the following ILPA best practice guides, which are essentially skills guides. They are written by skilled, experienced practitioners who have distilled their learning into readable and accessible form. Aspiring practitioners would be mugs to pass by the opportunity to learn from them! They are available to download from the ILPA website.

Best practice guide to asylum and human rights appeals, Mark Henderson (2003). An updated version (2009) is available electronically to subscribers of the Electronic Immigration Network. A new edition is due to be published by Legal Action.

Making an asylum application: a best practice guide, Jane Coker, Garry Kelly, Martin Soorjoo (2002)

Challenging immigration detention: a best practice guide, Emily Burnham (2003)

Working with children and young people subject to immigration control: guidelines for best practice, ILPA/Heaven Crawley (2nd edition, March 2012)

> Representation at immigration appeals: a best practice guide, Jane
> Coker, Jim Gillespie, Sue Shutter, Alison Stanley (2005)
>
> The detained fast track process: a best practice guide, Matthew
> Davies (2008)
>
> Working With Refugee Children: Current Issues in Best Practice
> (second edition, February 2012), Syd Bolton, Kalvir Kaur, Shu Shin
> Luh, Jackie Peirce and Colin Yeo for ILPA May 2011 (first edition)
>
> Resources Guide for Practitioners Working with Refugee Children
> (Second Edition) ILPA November 2011

Ensure you investigate whether there have been any other encounters with the authorities such as visa applications or other applications to remain in the United Kingdom.

Applications for asylum must be made in person, by appointment, and are often followed directly by the screening interview. It is useful to send clients along with written materials confirming that the firm is on the record. Give your client's name, firm's reference number for client, date of birth, and nationality, confirm you are instructed. After a claim has been lodged, confirm that the Home Office have recorded these details, confirm the temporary admission address (and that it is the correct and permitted address). Make sure you have a copy of the c=screening interview record and discuss it with your client. Make representations immediately where there are errors. See the asylum process and practice chapter for further details.

Where a non-compliance refusal is issued which is inaccurate (i.e. there has been compliance, overlooked or lost by the Home Office), an appeal should still be lodged, although it is possible the Home Office will recognise their oversight and issue a substantive decision in due course. Remember that on appeal, an Immigration judge may take into account the reasons for the non-compliance, but their overriding duty is to determine whether the immigration decision being carried out would breach the Refugee Convention, which requires they determine whether your client is a refugee or not, something as to which the non-compliance issue may be neutral (Haddad (starred) (00/HX/00926) 13 March 2000).

Substance of instructions

Ensure you deal with issues such as:

> ➢ Internal relocation and State protection issues
>
> ➢ Delay in leaving country of origin
>
> ➢ Time in third countries
>
> ➢ Family members left behind

- ➤ Delay in claiming asylum

- ➤ Possession of a national passport

Substance of initial advice

Ensure you deal with issues such as

- ➤ Possessing a nationality (or kind of case) liable to fast tracking, be that non-suspensive appeals with detention at Campsfield or elsewhere or accelerated appeals with detention at Harmondsworth or Yarl's Wood, or third countrying

- ➤ Liability to treatment as illegal entrant

- ➤ Being ready for the interview and the general non-readback policy, and the absence of clerks

- ➤ Entitlement to ARCs and asylum support

Re: witnesses, ensure that you know their:

- ➤ Immigration status (and have advised them of any possible adverse consequences of giving evidence, for example, whilst it is no doubt very unlikely indeed, there is a power to revoke leave available to the SSHD)

- ➤ If they are refugees or otherwise made applications to the SSHD, that you have details of those applications and any appeals (it can be a disaster if a statement or SEF turns up on the SSHD's file at court showing claims inconsistent with those already available).

Dealing with interpreters

Ensure that:

- ➤ The interpreter is competent to interpret both in the client's language to English and back again

- ➤ Interpreters do not interpolate information into questions or answers, nor summarise them, nor render "comprehensible" answers that if not so decoded would indicate mental health issues.

- ➤ Interpretation is in the first person

- ➤ The interpreter is conversant with the client's dialect as well as language, and does not intimidate them

The Best Practice Guide (BPG) advises of the possibility of errors resulting from the use of an under-qualified interpreter, or one who is inappropriate because he speaks a different dialect or because his cultural or ethnic background or gender inhibit communication

Practitioners should not proceed to use an interpreter who is inadequate. It will be preferable to make alternative arrangements even if this risks antagonising the client: it is better to explain the need for professional interpretation than to follow a client's wishes to proceed speedily by using a well-meaning friend. Using an inadequate interpreter runs a risk of acting incompatibly with the fundamentals of Solicitor Regulation Authority rules on acting in the best interests of the client and working on the case with due diligence.

Minors

Regarding claimants who are under 18:

> Make sure advisers working with children are accredited to IAAS Level 2, suitably experienced, and have had enhanced criminal record checks undertaken

> If unaccompanied they should be referred to the Refugee Council's Children's Panel of Advisors.

> Counselling

> Psychiatric report

> More attention should be afforded objective indications of risk. Just because the child is too young to understand their situation does not mean they do not have a well-founded fear in the sense of an objective risk of persecution that a third party would be able to determine whatever the child's own apprehension of future events (see the immigration rules).

It used to be unusual for a child to be interviewed, but under current practice;

352. Any child over the age of 12 who has claimed asylum in his own right shall be interviewed about the substance of his claim unless the child is unfit or unable to be interviewed. When an interview takes place it shall be conducted in the presence of a parent, guardian, representative or another adult independent of the Secretary of State who has responsibility for the child. The interviewer shall have specialist training in the interviewing of children and have particular regard to the possibility that a child will feel inhibited or alarmed. The child shall be allowed to express himself in his own way and at his own speed. If he appears tired or distressed, the interview will be suspended. The interviewer should then consider whether it would be appropriate for the interview to be resumed the same day or on another day.

Best practice requires a decision to be made quickly, within a month if there is no good reason to delay it. See: Processing an asylum application from a child (APG: Special cases).

Remember in making appointments for children to ensure they attend with an appropriate adult who is responsible for the child's welfare (e.g. panel adviser, foster parent or social worker). Try to avoid appointments that will disrupt school. Have breaks as often as required. Ensure you use appropriate language and pace of delivery. Information should be sought from other sources where possible: from parents, adults, or objective material regarding the country.

Section 55 of the Borders, Citizenship and Immigration Act 2009 introduced an obligation on the Secretary of State to make arrangements to ensure that specified functions are discharged having regard to the need to safeguard and promote the welfare of children who are in the United Kingdom. In so doing it aligns the duty imposed with that imposed on public authorities under the Children Act 2004, s.11(2).

The duty applies to the Home Office and also to those performing immigration functions, broadly defined. It only applies to children present in the UK, although the guidance (see below) encourages officials abroad to act compatibly.

By section 55(3), a person exercising any of the specified functions must, in so exercising them, have regard to any guidance given to the person by the Secretary of State for the purpose specified in BCIA 2009, s 55(1). The statutory guidance Every Child Matters: Change for Children was issued in November 2009.

Unaccompanied Asylum Seeking Children

The Secretary of State makes particular provision for unaccompanied asylum seeking children (UASCs):

An unaccompanied asylum seeking child is a person who, at the time of making the asylum application:

> ➢ is, or (if there is no proof) appears to be, under eighteen;

> ➢ is applying for asylum in his or her own right;

> ➢ and has no adult relative or guardian to turn to in this country (guardian is here used in a technical sense).

The policy of the Secretary of State is not to remove UASCs unless there are adequate reception facilities in the country of origin. If they are refused protection, they will be granted leave until they are 17½ under r.352ZC.

Disputed minors

These are extracts from the GOV.UK website regarding disputed minors:

6.1 Where an applicant claims to be a child but his/her appearance strongly suggests that he/she is over 18, UKBA's policy is to treat the applicant as an adult and offer NASS support (if appropriate) until there is credible documentary or medical evidence to demonstrate the age claimed. These applications are flagged as 'disputed minors' and they are treated as adult cases throughout the asylum process, or until we accept evidence to the contrary. In borderline cases UKBA gives the applicant the benefit of the doubt and treats the applicant as a minor.

Although it is rare, where social services disagree with the Home Office's assessment of age, it is Home Office's policy to accept the social services department professional assessment.

For guidance in dealing with age dispute issues it is a good idea to acquaint yourself with recent case law on the subject. Age assessment judicial reviews are heard by the Upper Tribunal (IAC) and reported (see e.g. http://www.bailii.org/uk/cases/UKUT/IAC/2013 (and search for AAJR cases)).

Women

The Home Office have now incorporated elements of the best practices contained in the old IAA Gender Guidelines and elsewhere in their APIs.

Thus they recognise that various sorts of ill-treatment that may particularly affect women may be persecution. They name marriage-related harm; violence within the family or community; domestic slavery; forced abortion; forced sterilisation; trafficking; female genital mutilation; sexual violence and abuse; and rape.

They also recognize that women may be subjected to discriminatory treatment that is enforced through law or through the imposition of social or religious norms that restrict their opportunities and rights. This can include, but is not limited to: Family and personal laws; Dress codes; Employment or education restrictions; Restrictions on women's freedom of movement and/or activities; and Political disenfranchisement.

The Convention reasons apply to women as men, although there are general considerations to be borne in mind in assessing the former's cases. There are cases where women are persecuted solely because of their family or kinship relationships, for example, a woman may be persecuted as a means of demoralising or punishing members of her family or community, or in order to pressurise her into revealing information. Whilst many women will be involved in such conventional political activities and raise similar claims this does not always correspond to the reality of the experiences of women in some societies. The gender roles in many countries mean that women will more often be involved in low level political activities for instance hiding people, passing messages or providing community services, food, clothing or medical care. "Low-level" political activity does not necessarily make it low-risk. The response of the state to such activity may be disproportionately persecutory because of the involvement of a section of society, namely women, who because of their gender it is considered inappropriate for them to be involved at all.

In terms of establishing the facts of their cases, it should be remembered that women who have been sexually assaulted may suffer trauma. The symptoms of this include persistent fear, a loss of self-confidence and self-esteem, difficulty in concentration, an attitude of self-blame, a pervasive loss of control and memory loss or distortion. Beware of inhibitors to taking instructions – the presence of family members, for example.

Vulnerable clients

Ensure that you create a suitable atmosphere for the interview. Seek a rapport, using body language, eye contact and tone of voice (though it will be appreciated that these devices may not survive cultural divides).

Make sure the client understands they can have another interpreter or even representative so long as that choice is made on grounds that are not themselves discriminatory.

Be aware of body language as a clue to distress.

Be aware of the possibility that the interview will be the first opportunity the individual has to relate the events to another person: this may lead to a release of pent-up emotion.

Be alive to the possible need to refer to a health care professional in extreme cases where there is a concern that the interview is threatening the health of the client. It would not be impossible for the account to be provided via a statement or summary produced by such a professional absent any other alternative.

Determine whether the client wishes to commit self-harm, and seek professional help for them if you judge there to be a real risk of this eventuating.

Advise them on the possibility of support and counselling from specialists.

Bear in mind the difficulties occasioned by recent arrival: disorientation, and fatigue.

Watch out for language that may imply sexual ill treatment (e.g. "I found myself naked in the street"). Late disclosure of this is to be expected; but it still needs to be dealt with (watch out for relying on explanations such as gender of interviewer or interpreter only to discover that the sought-for combination was available earlier in the process). Do not probe unnecessarily for details, but nor should you fail to obtain clear instructions unless the client's well-being is threatened by this.

Be alive to behaviour that suggests PTSD, such as extreme symptoms of, or a combination of: recurrent recollections (including nightmares) of past trauma; fear of figures of authority or other cues to past trauma; irritability; memory failure and poor concentration; fatigue.

Do not underestimate the impact on yourself of a traumatic interview.

Checklist regarding vulnerable clients

    (i) Where the client is an adult with a history of torture consider:

> ➢ Counselling
> ➢ Psychiatric Report
> ➢ Physical injuries report

(ii) Where the client is disabled consider:
> ➢ Their current health (e.g. are they well enough to attend an interview with us)
> ➢ Whether they will require assistance to attend our offices or any appeal
> ➢ Whether they will expect third parties to attend the interview
> ➢ Whether they will have special access requirements (e.g. parking close to the building, use of lifts, wheelchair access)

Professional Conduct Regarding Asylum Claims

Advise your client of the need for prompt disclosure, this will be in their interests, however upsetting they find it. If they cannot disclose details of their case for reasons of mental health, medical evidence should be sought to explain this on an objective basis.

Ensure that all relevant asylum claims are brought forwards – women or other dependants may have independent claims which are prejudiced by a failure to explore them sufficiently early on.

Bear in mind issues that might ensue from a conflict of interests – this may lead you to have to stop acting from one or more of your clients (the latter situation might arise where you are privy to information that could assist one or other to succeed in their case, where you have come into possession of the information due to the confidential lawyer/client relationship). There is a duty to keep your client's case confidential, however you receive information in relation to it – and this continues after you stop acting.

As to confidentiality more generally, an Appellant client might wish to give evidence in private (what used to be called in camera), Immigration and Asylum Appeals (Procedure) Rules 2005, r 54. Requests for anonymity need to be made in writing to the Tribunal (see: http://www.justice.gov.uk/forms/hmcts/immigration-and-asylum). Nevertheless, once an appeal has been made, the determination is in the public domain, although where anonymity has been requested all methods of identifying the appellant should be removed from the determination. The Secretary of State expressly tells asylum seekers that there are some foreign and domestic agencies to which he may reveal details of their asylum claim – however, in so doing, he may create additional risks which can be taken into account in any appeal - Bouamama (18630; 28 September 1998).

Expert evidence practice direction

It is important to be familiar with the practice direction on expert evidence in the tribunal. In particular, note the parts of the direction referring to the instructions to the expert and the contents and structure of the expert report.

10 Expert evidence

10.1 A party who instructs an expert must provide clear and precise instructions to the expert, together with all relevant information concerning the nature of the appellant's case, including the appellant's immigration history, the reasons why the appellant's claim or application has been refused by the respondent and copies of any relevant previous reports prepared in respect of the appellant.

10.2 It is the duty of an expert to help the Tribunal on matters within the expert's own expertise. This duty is paramount and overrides any obligation to the person from whom the expert has received instructions or by whom the expert is paid.

10.3 Expert evidence should be the independent product of the expert uninfluenced by the pressures of litigation.

10.4 An expert should assist the Tribunal by providing objective, unbiased opinion on matters within his or her expertise, and should not assume the role of an advocate.

10.5 An expert should consider all material facts, including those which might detract from his or her opinion.

10.6 An expert should make it clear:-
(a) when a question or issue falls outside his or her expertise; and
(b) when the expert is not able to reach a definite opinion, for example because of insufficient information.

10.7 If, after producing a report, an expert changes his or her view on any material matter, that change of view should be communicated to the parties without delay, and when appropriate to the Tribunal.

10.8 An expert's report should be addressed to the Tribunal and not to the party from whom the expert has received instructions.

10.9 An expert's report must:-
(a) give details of the expert's qualifications;
(b) give details of any literature or other material which the expert has relied on in making the report;
(c) contain a statement setting out the substance of all facts and instructions given to the expert which are material to the opinions expressed in the report or upon which those opinions are based;
(d) make clear which of the facts stated in the report are within the expert's own knowledge;
(e) say who carried out any examination, measurement or other procedure which the expert has used for the report, give the qualifications of that person, and say whether or not the procedure has been carried out under the expert's supervision;
(f) where there is a range of opinion on the matters dealt with in the report –
   (i) summarise the range of opinion, so far as reasonably practicable, and
   (ii) give reasons for the expert's own opinion;
(g) contain a summary of the conclusions reached;
(h) if the expert is not able to give an opinion without qualification, state the qualification; and
(j) contain a statement that the expert understands his or her duty to the Tribunal, and has complied and will continue to comply with that duty.

10.10 An expert's report must be verified by a Statement of Truth as well as containing the statements required in paragraph 10.9(h) and (j).

10.11 The form of the Statement of Truth is as follows:
"I confirm that insofar as the facts stated in my report are within my own knowledge I have made clear which they are and I believe them to be true, and that the opinions I have expressed represent my true and complete professional opinion".

10.12 The instructions referred to in paragraph 10.9(c) are not protected by privilege but cross-examination of the expert on the contents of the instructions will not be allowed unless the Tribunal permits it (or unless the party who gave the instructions consents to it). Before it gives permission the Tribunal must be satisfied that there are reasonable grounds to consider that the statement in the report or the substance of the instructions is inaccurate or incomplete. If the Tribunal is so satisfied, it will allow the cross-examination where it appears to be in the interests of justice to do so.

10.13 In this Practice Direction:-
"appellant" means the party who is or was the appellant before the First-tier Tribunal; and
"respondent" means the party who is or was the respondent before the First-tier Tribunal.'

Commissioning medical evidence

Identifying the issues

The legal professional, when setting out on the medical aspect of the case, must first evaluate what the Medical Expert can do for the case's presentation.

Medical evidence can be of use in a number of scenarios.

(i) In establishing the facts of the case independently of the client's oral evidence, e.g. by showing that there is scarring present, and perhaps also that it does not have any obvious explanation than that offered by the Appellant (e.g. bullet wounds, blade wounds to the back);

(ii) In showing physical evidence of past problems that might exacerbate risk on return to the country of origin, or in showing that present health questions may attract discrimination (e.g. HIV in some countries);

(iii) In establishing why the client cannot themselves give a coherent account, e.g. because they have mental health problems following serious ill treatment, or because it would be unusual for a victim of trauma to be able to give details of certain episodes in their life;

(iv) In establishing that the client has health problems counting against their return to their country of origin, where this would amount to a breach of ECHR Article 3 or Article 8 – this will be particularly relevant where they cannot access health care at all.

Before setting out to write your letter of instructions, you should determine which of these functions you hope that the evidence will serve.

Corroboration

Whilst there is no absolute requirement for corroboration, bear in mind that a lack of medical evidence that is in principle capable of being obtained is sure to raise doubts in the mind of a decision maker.

The tribunal will often say that the existence of an injury is not probative of its alleged causation. But the more particular the injury, the greater the argument for saying that it could not have an alternative history (contrast cigarette burns on the back with scarring on the knee).

In cases where the account of torture is, or is likely to be, the subject of challenge, Chapter Five of the United Nations Document, known as the Istanbul Protocol, submitted to the United Nations High Commissioner for Human Rights on 9 August 1999 (Manual on the Effective Investigation and Documentation of Torture and Other Cruel, Inhuman or Degrading Treatment or Punishment) is particularly instructive.

At paras 186-7, under the heading "D. Examination and Evaluation following specific forms of Torture" it states:

> 186... For each lesion and for the overall pattern of lesions, the physician should indicate the degree of consistency between it and the attribution
> (a) Not consistent: the lesion could not have been caused by the trauma described;
> (b) Consistent with: the lesion could have been caused by the trauma described, but it is non-specific and there are many other possible causes;
> (c) Highly consistent: the lesion could have been caused by the trauma described, and there are few other possible causes;
> (d) Typical of: this is an appearance that is usually found with this type of trauma, but there are other possible causes;
> (e) Diagnostic of: this appearance could not have been caused in anyway other than that described.
>
> 187. Ultimately, it is the overall evaluation of all lesions and not the consistency of each lesion with a particular form of torture that is important in assessing the torture story (see Chapter IV.G for a list of torture methods).

This is known as the Istanbul Protocol and medical reports documenting torture and scars should follow the language of the protocol. Its use was approved by the Court of Appeal in the case of SA (Somalia) v SSHD [2006] EWCA Civ 1302.

Credibility

Beware the expert commenting on credibility without good reason. However expert the expert may be immigration judges remain jealous of their independence on assessing truthfulness. If the expert has good reason to make a judgment on credibility, they should provide clear justification.

A decision in the Scottish courts reaffirms the judicial view that a Doctor's role is not to assess credibility, which remains the exclusive role of the decision maker at the tribunal; see M.E. v SSHD [2009] CSIH 86.

However, a medical report cannot simply be dismissed due to the poor credibility of the asylum seeker and the fact that the medical expert has accepted the asylum seekers account. The Court of Appeal has recently reviewed the meaning of 'independent evidence of torture' and the correct approach to the analysis of medical reports in R (on the application of AM) v Secretary of State for the Home Department [2012] EWCA Civ 521.

Giving the leading judgment of the Court of Appeal, Rix LJ disagreed that the nurse was merely taking everything AM said at face value:

> [Her] reports constituted independent evidence of torture. [She] was an independent expert. ... expressing her own independent views. ... it is evident from her assessment that she believed that AM had suffered torture and rape and that those misfortunes had rendered her the "grossly traumatized" woman that she found her to be, with "feelings of deep and intense shame and self disgust", "feelings of shame and stigmatization", and a "fragile mental state". Those findings are ... interpretation of what she found, they are not the mere assertions of AM.
>
> ...[Her] belief was her own independent belief, even if it was in part based on AM's account. ... the judge was mistaken to suggest that such belief was merely as a result of 'taking everything she said at face value' ... where the independent expert is applying the internationally recognised Istanbul Protocol... A requirement of "evidence" is not the same as a requirement of proof, conclusive or otherwise. Whether evidence amounts to proof, on any particular standard ... is a matter of weight and assessment.

Reviewing the medical report

The work is not finished with the arrival of the newly commissioned report. It is also necessary to determine whether the report requires further work. Always ask yourself: Why did I commission this report? And then review the report to determine whether your objectives have been met.

Sometimes the doctor gives an account that the asylum seekers have themselves given to them. Remember to check the account that the doctor receives is consistent with that which appears in the statements – there are lots of reasons why they may differ (the doctor may have less time than the solicitor to go into the story, and may have less experience of the pitfalls of working through interpreters, or does not attach quite the same weight to accuracy).

Bear in mind the chance that the witness will be found to lack credibility by the immigration judge who hears oral evidence. In such a case, the value of the report may be significantly diminished. Consider if it is possible to preserve some aspects of its value, e.g. comments on the impact of return on a traumatised individual may retain relevance even if the reasons for the trauma are rejected.

Checklist for medical evidence

The very best doctors, unless they have a great deal of experience of medico-legal report writing, are likely to be unaware of the strictures by which the Tribunal recommends medical evidence is to be assessed. Whilst it may be tempting to dismiss much of the Tribunal's guidance as neurotic or anti-expert, it remains the case that they are the ultimate arbiter of the weight to be given reports, and in order for your report to be taken seriously, it is advisable that it takes into account their approach.

(i) Has the doctor commented on credibility? If so, have they given reasons for their conclusions? For example, is there a careful analysis of the patient's manner of telling their story as well as the doctor's own expertise of assessing the truthfulness of patients?

(ii) Is the doctor, by their use of language, liable to be criticized by an immigration judge for seeming to become an advocate for the patient, or in commenting on matters that go beyond their actual medical expertise (e.g. making generalized comments on the availability of medical treatment in a country without having expertise on that issue), or beyond their own area of medical expertise (e.g. a physician making statements regarding PTSD)?

(iii) Has the doctor made judgments based on the truthfulness of the appellant's account? If so, does this mean the value of the report will be wholly lost if an adverse credibility finding is made based on the evidence "in the round", and is there anything that can be done about this (e.g. is it possible to isolate some elements of the report from the acceptance of the story)?

(iv) Has the doctor commented on the possible causes of the client's physical and mental presentation, if it is realistic to do so, and have they given the basis for their expertise in determining causation?

(v) Is there any reason to make the doctor available for cross examination, so as to be able to answer specific questions from an immigration judge?

(vi) Has the doctor provided their methodology including any relevant diagnostic criteria?

(vii) Has the doctor explained the reasons for their diagnosis and prognosis and any other conclusions, and is it clear how their conclusions are reached based on the presentation of the patient to them?

(viii) Is the doctor liable to criticism from an immigration judge for not having spent sufficient time with the patient to justify their conclusions?

Submitting the medical report to the court

It is advisable to submit your letter of instructions together with the report, because then the immigration judge can be certain of what the expert was asked; and it avoids any chance that the report will be given diminished weight on account of a lack of clarity over precisely what instructions were given to the expert.

As with any evidence that is specific to the case in hand, it is better to submit it in good time before the hearing, serving it on the Home Office as well as the court. Then any failure to grapple with its contents will be something that the Home Office representative has to address without being able to fend off the report's implications with a suggestion that the Secretary of State has had no effective opportunity to consider its contents. The Best Practice Guide to Asylum and Human Rights Appeals recommends that a direction be sought (at the First Hearing stage) that the Home Office expresses any challenge to the report in advance of the full hearing.

Make sure that the doctor has provided details of their qualifications, emphasizing weighty aspects of their curriculum vitae such as official appointments, and any experience that is particularly relevant to the case in hand.

Sometimes it may be desirable to submit photographic evidence of the scarring or other injuries of the appellant. It may be distressing, and inappropriate, for the appellant to be expected to display their scarring at court, which after all is a public hearing. Medical photography is available from the Photography & Illustration Department, University College London, tel: 020 7380 9079.

Referral onwards

Remember that, even if, or once, the medical "evidence" aspect of the health professional's work is done, there may remain an issue of desirable referral onwards for therapeutic reasons. Do not neglect this. Experts will not necessarily perceive their role as bringing with it a need to arrange treatment (the Medical Foundation is an exception to this).

Practicalities

Always check when instructing –

> ➤ Fees (clarify with the expert)

> ➤ Timing of report (almost inevitably there is a degree of urgency, and in any event you should agree a timetable)

> ➤ Availability for giving oral evidence

➢ And ensure that you

- Enclose all relevant documentation (a schedule is advisable for clarity)

- Explain the purpose of the report, succinctly and without legalese.

- Have asked all relevant questions, psychiatric and physical (including the impact of each on the other), dealing with future prognosis, present diagnosis, present and future treatment.

Commissioning country expert evidence

When to commission country expert evidence

To show that events are credible in the sense of being plausible

If there is a dearth of general material about an unfamiliar country; or if, re a more familiar country, the issues in question are not dealt with by the existing publicly available materials.

Examples of the assistance that expert evidence can give

There is an excellent section in the ILPA/RLG Best Practice Guide on Asylum Appeals which itemises various forms of assistance that might be derived from expert evidence.

A guide for experts, the Best Practice Guide for Country Evidence Experts in UK Immigration and Asylum Appeals, is available on the EIN website.

However, in short, expert evidence will potentially be available to prove any aspect of the case.

➢ The likely reaction of the authorities or other agencies to any aspect of your client's circumstances (including whether your client is "Low-level" and whether this matters) including whatever activities they have undertaken, and whether her sexuality or ethnicity will place her at risk;

➢ whether the criminal offence for which she is wanted may put her at risk of ill-treatment during interrogation, detention conditions that will be inhuman or degrading, or an unfair trial;

➢ the consequences of future actions that the client proposes on a return;

➢ whether she will be at risk of ill-treatment as an expelled asylum seeker;

➢ whether dissident activities abroad are monitored, and whether your client's activities in the UK may place her at risk.

➢ Any aspect of the case as to which evidence that you have to hand is lacking – e.g. parties or groups unmentioned in the country evidence.

➢ Questions of protection - whether the Government's statements on human rights are contradicted by its deeds and how effective are its investigations into human rights abuses by its security forces.

➢ You may be assisted in determining whether the relevant tests for the availability of internal location are met: (a) accessibility of safe haven; (b) safety in reaching the safe haven, or living there; (c) undue harshness in reaching the safe area, or living there; (d) discriminatory breaches of socio-economic rights.

➢ Where such matters are in dispute, it can be advisable to seek expert evidence on whether language and accent/dialect, behaviour, knowledge of local areas, are consistent with the client's account of their own background.

Human Rights Cases

➢ The likelihood of destitution (availability of social services, family networks, discrimination in access to human rights) may benefit from expert input. So too can expert input on medical treatment: remember, there is little reason to suppose that most doctors have knowledge of the state of medical care abroad, as opposed the consequences of removal on health.

➢ The level of stigma nationally and in local communities is relevant, e.g. regarding rape or HIV victims.

➢ You might wish for expert evidence as to the situation if family members were to relocate – medical treatment, discrimination or dangers aimed against Westerners, health and educational facilities for children.

Finding an expert witness

The ILPA Directory of Expert Witnesses, now available on the EIN, is one source. The School of Oriental and African Studies (SOAS) is also a useful resource, and the searchable Refugee Legal Group website can be very helpful (contact rlg@asylumaid.org.uk for details).

Testing the expert witness

Ensure that they are not partisan so as to give the appearance of a lack of objectiveness. Bear in mind the possibility that they give evidence in camera. Obtain a CV, bearing in mind the following indicia of expertise:

➢ Publications, especially recent and relevant ones.

> ➢ Journalism, particularly for media with a reputation for impartiality.

> ➢ Advising national or international bodies, and reputable NGOs. Obviously if an expert has at any stage advised the Foreign Office, or if the Home Office has relied upon their work, that will be of particular interest. The Canadian independent documentation centre, DIRB, is among foreign organisations perceived by the tribunal as reliable.

> ➢ Academic discipline, postings and research, and work with research organisations and think tanks.

> ➢ Relevant work with reputable NGOs, particularly human rights monitoring but also in the aid and development fields.

> ➢ Time spent in the country (but see the next paragraph)."

Determine whether the expert has given evidence in legal proceedings previously – and specifically whether they have done so in the immigration courts. Also always check:

> ➢ Fees

> ➢ Timing of Report

> ➢ Availability for giving oral evidence

Bear in mind the words of the BPG:

> Consult your client about choice of expert if she is to be interviewed by him, but distinguish between legitimate concession to her vulnerability and illegitimate discrimination.

Duties of expert witnesses

The impact of expert evidence can be seriously damaged by failing to take account any of the following common faults, taken again from the BPG:

> ➢ Expert evidence presented to the court should be and should be seen to be the independent product of an expert uninfluenced as to the form or content by the exigencies of litigation.

> ➢ An expert witness should provide independent assistance to the court by way of objective unbiased opinion in relation to matters within his expertise.

> ➢ An expert witness in the High Court should never assume the role of advocate (i.e. they should not argue the case for the asylum seeker).

> ➢ An expert witness should state the facts or assumptions on which his

544

opinion is based. He should not omit to consider material facts which detract from the concluded opinion.

> An expert witness should make it clear when a particular question or issue falls outside his expertise.

> If an expert's opinion is not properly researched because it considers that insufficient data is available then this must be stated with an indication that the opinion is no more than a provisional one.

> If after exchange of reports, an expert witness changes his view on a material matter, such change of view should be communicated to the other side without delay and when appropriate to the court.

> Where expert evidence refers to photographs, plans, calculations, survey reports or other similar documents, they must be provided to the opposite party at the same time as the exchange of reports.

The Civil Procedure Rules (Pt 35) provide further guidance on expert evidence in civil litigation which in light of their citation by the old Immigration Appeal Tribunal in the Starred determination of Slimani should be followed (and is reflected in the guidance given below).

The expert should address his report to the Court rather than taking the form of a letter addressed to the person commissioning it.

Doctrine of ultimate issue

It is advisable to avoid the expert stepping on the toes of the judicial decision maker by expressing conclusions on "ultimate issues" – i.e. by stating a fear of persecution is "well founded"; by saying that a particular form of harm is "persecution" or "inhuman or degrading treatment or punishment"; or by stating that protection is not satisfactory to the standard required by international law. It is preferable for the expert to give their opinion in their own words without using legal terms of art.

Experts should steer clear of stating that a claim is credible, although it is not inappropriate for them to comment on its consistency with country conditions, i.e. its plausibility.

Letter of instructions

This should ensure the expert understands the issues above, and that they are clear as to the ambit of their instructions (e.g. as to whether or not to comment on the plausibility of certain events):

Whilst your letter to the expert is privileged, beware asking loaded questions which will diminish the report's value:

> You should obviously ensure, regardless of the risk of disclosure, that your questions to the expert are fair and cannot be characterised as slanted or misleading: pose the question in a manner that you would not be embarrassed to have disclosed to the adjudicator.

Consider whether you wish to seek opinions in the alternative, e.g. on the basis of the account being found credible by an immigration judge, and upon the basis that the appellant is only considered to be a failed asylum seeker.

An expert can advise you as well as act as an expert, but beware crossing boundaries between those roles:

> 23.14 An expert can advise you on your preparation and conduct of the case as well as providing a report for disclosure. You might, for example, seek his comments on a document which your client has obtained from the country of origin and which you are unsure whether to submit (see further chapter 16). Traditionally, communications with an expert are privileged to the extent that he is acting in an advisory capacity rather than an expert witness. The CPR require an expert to state only the 'substance of all material instructions... on the basis of which the report was written' [emphasis added]. If the expert who produces a report could not also advise privately on other issues, that would encourage the practice of solicitors instructing a second 'shadow expert' to avoid the risk of his advice being disclosed. However, the matter is not free from doubt. Any issue on which you ask your expert to act in an advisory capacity should be clearly differentiated from those issues that he will address as an expert witness.

The expert should receive all documentation relevant to the matters in hand.

The expert may wish to meet the client. This will be of doubtful utility in cases other than nationality disputes, where face-to-face meetings can be vital.

The report

This is the BPG's summary of the key components of an expert report:

> ➤ An account of the expert's qualifications, training and experience, such as are relevant to his ability to assist the court reliably on the issues raised by his instructions.

> ➤ A statement setting out the substance of his material instructions (whether written or oral). The statement should summarise those facts and instructions provided to the expert which are material to the opinions expressed in the report or upon which those opinions are based (see by analogy CPR rule 35.10(3)).

> ➤ What documentation he has considered.

> ➤ His conclusions upon each question posed in his instructions, separating facts, inferences drawn from facts, and opinion.

> ➤ An explanation of how the expert arrived at each answer, including

particular aspects of his qualifications, training, experience or research which led him to the answer, and the sources upon which he has relied (see below).

➢ The declaration that the expert has complied with his duty to the Court and a 'statement of truth')."

➢ Always check the report for consistency against the versions of the appellant's account that you have, to ensure that the expert has not overplayed discrepancies, or given the appearance of a discrepancy when none truly exists.

➢ Watch out for emotive language.

Reusing expert reports

Here is the BPG guidance on this topic:

➢ The IAT expressed consistent concern about 'recycling' of expert reports and preferred to receive a report specifically directed to the appellant, and this has not changed under the AIT or the unified tribunal system.

➢ It will not consider a 'recycled' report at all unless the expert has given permission for it to be reused.

➢ Always obtain an individual report where possible.

➢ If that is impractical, strive to obtain the expert's consent to the use of a previous (relevant) report and ensure that it is anonymised.

➢ Consider obtaining a report that is expressly issue-based rather than client-based to deal with issues that arise repeatedly in the same form."

Also see the BPG on professional conduct and experts:

Although you can and should ask your expert to make necessary changes to his report, you must be careful not to overstep the mark into writing it for him. Expert reports must not be 'settled' by the lawyers.

List of Cases

(R on the application of TR (Sri Lanka)) v Secretary of State for the Home Department [2008] EWCA Civ 1549 288

'Limbuela' [2005] UKHL 66) 272

A v London Borough of Croydon & SSHD (Interested Party), WK v SSHD and Kent County Council [2009] EWHC 939 (Admin).......... 274

A, H and AH [2006] EWHC 526 (Admin) 81, 334

AA (Afghanistan) v SSHD [2007] EWCA Civ 12.......... 334

AA (Nigeria) v SSHD [2010] EWCA Civ 773 65

AA (Risk for involuntary returnees) Zimbabwe CG Rev 1 [2006] UKAIT 00061 229

AA (Somalia) v SSHD [2007] EWCA Civ 1040.......... 473

AA (Uganda) v SSHD [2008] EWCA Civ 579 250

AA and LK v SSHD [2006] EWCA Civ 401.......... 230

AB (Jamaica) v SSHD [2007] EWCA Civ 1302 327

AB (Protection - criminal gangs - internal relocation) Jamaica CG [2007] UKAIT 00018.......... 248

AB (Third-party provision of accommodation) [2008] UKAIT 00018 57

Abdi v SSHD [1996] Imm AR 148 .... 81, 334

Advic v United Kingdom 00025525/94 (6 September 1995).......... 323

AG and others (Policies; executive discretions; Tribunal's powers) Kosovo [2007] UKAIT 00082 .... 81, 334

AH Sudan in the Court of Appeal ([2007] EWCA Civ 297 249

Ahmad v SSHD [2014] EWCA Civ 988 352

Ahmed (Amos; Zambrano; reg 15A(3)(c) 2006 EEA Regs) [2013] UKUT 00089 (IAC) 369

Ahmed (benefits: proof of receipt; evidence) [2013] UKUT 84(IAC).......... 55

Ahmed and Another (PBS: admissible evidence) [2014] UKUT 365 (IAC).......... 210

Ahmut v. Netherlands (1997) 24 EHRR 62 322

Akhalu (health claim: ECHR Article 8) [2013] UKUT 00400 (IAC).......... 315

Alan v Switzerland (UNCAT) [1997] INLR 29 220

Aldogan (R on the application of) v Secretary of State for the Home Department [2007] EWHC 2586 (Admin) 385

Al-Mehdawi v Home Secretary [1990] 1AC 876 481

Al-Sirri v SSHD & Anor [2009] EWCA Civ 222 .... 255, 256

Alvi [2012] UKSC 33 .... 35, 159

AM (Ethiopia) & Ors v Entry Clearance Officer [2008] EWCA Civ 1082.......... 57

Amegnigan v The Netherlands.......... 313

AMM and others (conflict; humanitarian crisis; returnees; FGM) Somalia CG [2011] UKUT 445.......... 262

Amos v SSHD [2011] EWCA Civ 552 366

Amrollahi v Denmark (Appl no 56811/00; 11 October 2002).......... 326, 334

Anderson FE (AP), Re Judicial Review [2013] ScotCS CSOH_52) 83

AP and FP (Citizens Directive Article 3(2); discretion; dependence) India [2007] UKAIT 00048 (13 June 2007) 344, 355

Arman Ali.......... 300

Aydin v Turkey (1998) 25 EHRR 251 308

Azimi-Moayed and others (decisions affecting children; onward appeals) 101

B (DR Congo) [2003] UKIAT 00012 (12 June 2003) 222, 224

BA (Pakistan) v Secretary of State for the Home Department [2009] EWCA Civ 1072.......... 235

Bagdanavicius [2005] UKHL 38 312

Basnet (validity of application - respondent) Nepal [2012] UKUT 113 (IAC) (04 April 2012) 163

Batayav v SSHD [2003] EWCA Civ 1489 and again at [2005] EWCA Civ 366) 228, 261, 309

Baumbast [2002] EUECJ C-413/99 (17 September 2002) 364

BE (Iran) v SSHD [2008] EWCA Civ 540 240

Beldjoudi v France (1992) 14 EHRR 801 .... 300, 334

Bensaid v UK (2001) 33 EHRR 205 .... 312, 325, 329

Beoku-Betts v Secretary of State for the Home Department [2008] UKHL 39 (25 June 2008) 294, 335

Berrehab v. Netherlands (1989) 11 EHRR 322 .... 322, 334

Berthiaume v. Dastous [1930] AC 79 119

Bouamama (18630; 28 September 1998). 531

Boughanemi v. France (1996) 22 EHRR 228 322

Brown (Case 197/86, 1988 3 CMLR 403)). 220, 327

BT (Former Solicitors' alleged misconduct) Nepal [2004] UKIAT 00311 291

CA v Secretary of State for the Home Department [2004] EWCA Civ 1165.... 314, 482

Carcabuk & Bla (00/TH/01426; 18 May 2000)... 466

CB (Validity of marriage: proxy marriage) Brazil [2008] UKAIT 00080 119

Chahal v UK (1996) 23 EHRR 413... 305, 307, 311

Chikwamba v SSHD [2008] UKHL 40 328

Chiver (10758; 24 March 1994).. 224

CM (EM country guidance; disclosure) Zimbabwe CG [2013] UKUT 00059(IAC) 227

CO (EEA Regulations: family permit) Nigeria [2007] UKAIT 00070 361

D v SSHD [2012] EWCA Civ 39 445

D v UK (1997) 24 EHHR 423 .... 312, 315

DA (Unsigned interview notes) Turkey [2004] UKIAT 00104 (14 May 2004).... 222

Danian v SSHD [2000] Imm AR 96 230

Dauhoo (EEA Regulations - regulation 8(2)) Mauritius [2012] UKUT 79 (IAC). 359

Deliallisi (British citizen: deprivation appeal: Scope) Albania [2013] UKUT 439 (IAC) 407

Demirkaya v Secretary of State for the Home Department [1999] Imm AR 49. 227

Devaseelan 305, 473

Diatta v Land Berlin 1986 2 CMLR 164.. 366

Durrani (Entrepreneurs: bank letters; evidential flexibility) (Rev 1) [2014] UKUT 295 (IAC) 170

E v SSHD [2004] EWCA Civ 49 .... 474, 481

East African Asians v UK (1981) 3 EHRR 76 311

EB (Kosovo) v SSHD [2008] UKHL 41 .... 326, 332, 333

Edgehill & Anor v SSHD [2014] EWCA Civ 402 99

EK (Ankara Agreement - 1972 Rules-construction) Turkey [2010] UKUT 425 (IAC) 385

EK (Article 4 ECHR: Anti-Trafficking Convention) Tanzania [2013] UKUT 00313 266

Elgafaji (Justice and Home Affairs) [2009] EUECJ C-465/07 (17 February 2009) 261

EM (Lebanon) v SSHD [2008] UKHL 64. .... 305, 325, 326, 335

EN (Serbia) v SSHD [2009] EWCA Civ 630 258
Etame v Secretary of State for the Home Department & Anor [2008] EWHC 1140
    (Admin) (23 May 2008) 385
ex p. Onibiyo [1996] Imm AR 370 288
FA (Iraq) v Secretary of State for the Home Department [2010] EWCA Civ 696
    (18 June 2010) 260, 453
Fetle (Partners: two year requirement) [2014] UKUT 00267). 117
Fiaz (cancellation of leave to remain-fairness) [2012] UKUT 00057(IAC) 69
Fouzia Baig v SSHD [2005] EWCA Civ 1246.. 81
FP (Iran) v SSHD [2007] EWCA Civ 13.. 290, 472
FV (Italy) [2012] EWCA Civ 1199 .... 375, 376
Gashi [1997] INLR 97.. 236
Glowacka 421
Goudey (subsisting marriage – evidence) Sudan [2012] UKUT 00041(IAC).... 120
GS (Existence of internal armed conflict) Afghanistan CG [2009] UKAIT 00010
    .... 261, 262
GS and EO (Article 3 - health cases) India [2012] UKUT 397 (IAC)................ 314
Gul v. Switzerland (1996) 22 EHRR 93... 322
Gurung [2002] UKIAT 04870.. 254, 255
Guteirrez Gomez (00/TH/02257; 20 November 2000.................................... 245
GW (EEA reg 21: "fundamental interests") Netherlands [2009] UKAIT 00050 . 376
Haddad (starred) (00/HX/00926) 13 March 2000 525
Haddadi (00/TH/02141)... 247
Hardward v SSHD (00/TH/01522) 12 July 2000.. 149
Hariri v SSHD [2003] EWCA Civ 807 .... 228, 305
HH (Iran) v Secretary of State for the Home Department [2008] EWCA Civ 50320
HJ (Iran) and HT (Cameroon) v Secretary of State for the Home Department
    [2010] UKSC 31... 231, 232, 285
HK v SSHD [2006] EWCA Civ 1037.. 223
HLR v France (1998) 26 EHRR 29 312
Horvath [1999] INLR 7.. 222, 245, 246, 312
Huang.. 330
Ibrahim [2010] EUECJ C-310/08 367
ID and Others v The Home Office [2005] EWCA Civ 38 426
Iftikar Ahmed [2000] INLR 1... 231, 243, 245
IK (Returnees - Records – IFA) Turkey CG [2004] UKIAT 00312 229
in re Wasfi Suleman Mahmod [1995] Imm AR 311 409
Ireland v United Kingdom (1978) 2 EHRR 25..................................... 308, 309
IS (marriages of convenience) Serbia [2008] UKAIT 00031.......................... 356
Ishtiaq v SSHD [2007] EWCA Civ 386 135
Islam & Anor [2012] EUECJ C-83/11 358
J v SSHD [2005] EWCA Civ 629.. 316
JA (Ivory Coast) v SSHD [2009] EWCA Civ 1353 315
Jain v Secretary of State for the Home Department [2000] Imm AR 76 239
Jakitay (12658; 15 November 1995) 220
Janjanin v Secretary of State for the Home Department [2004] EWCA Civ 448
    324
Januzi v SSHD [2006] UKHL 5... 248, 249
JD (Congo) v SSHD [2012] EWCA Civ 327 484
JH (Zimbabwe) v SSHD [2009] EWCA Civ 78 41

K (DR Congo) [2003] UKIAT 00014 (23 June 2003) 224

Kagema [1997] IAR 137 238

Kalashnikov v Russia (2002) 36 EHRR 587 309

Karanakaran [2000] Imm AR 271 .... 216, 217

Kasolo (13190; 1 April 1996) 223, 224

Katrinak v SSHD [2001] EWCA Civ 832 237

Kaur (01/TH/02438; 26 September 2001) 514

Kaziu & Ors v Secretary of State for the Home Department [2014] EWHC 832 (Admin) 407

KB (Failed asylum seekers and forced returnees) Syria CG [2012] UKUT 426 (IAC) 215

Kempf v Staatsecretaris van justitie 1987 1 C.M.L.R 764 ECJ) 348

KH (Afghanistan) v SSHD [2009] **EWCA Civ 1354** 313

KH (Article 15(c) Qualification Directive) Iraq CG [2008] 260

Khaliq (entry clearance; para 321) Pakistan [2011] UKUT 350 (IAC) 69

Khatel and others (s85A; effect of continuing application) [2013] UKUT 44 (IAC) 52

KJ ("Own or occupy exclusively") Jamaica [2008] UKAIT 00006 58

KJ (Sri Lanka) v SSHD [2009] EWCA Civ 292 .... 254, 256

Klusova v London Borough of Hounslow [2007] EWCA Civ 1127 39

Krotov v SSHD [2004] EWCA Civ 69 240

KS (Burma) & Anor v Secretary of State for the Home Department [2013] EWCA Civ 67 231

Ladd v. Marshall [1954] 1 WLR 1489 .... 290, 291, 481

LB (Medical treatment of "finite" duration) Bangladesh [2005] UKAIT 00175 91

LC (China) v Secretary of State for the Home Department [2014] EWCA Civ 1310 443

LD (Article 8 best interests of child) Zimbabwe [2010] UKUT 278 (IAC) 332

LG (Italy) v Secretary of State for the Home Department [2008] EWCA Civ 190 (18 March 2008) 376

LS (Gambia) [2005] UKAIT 00085 463

Lumba v SSHD [2011] UKSC 12 .... 414, 415

LW (Cancellation refugee status: UNHCR Note) Ethiopia [2005] UKIAT 00042 252

M (Yugoslavia) [2003] UKIAT 00004 (29 May 2003) 224

M.E. v SSHD [2009] CSIH 86 535

M.S.S. v Greece and Belgium (Application no. 30696/09) [2011] ECHR 281

MA & Ors v SSHD [2013] EUECJ C-648/11 281

MA (Ethiopia) v Secretary of State for the Home Department [2009] EWCA Civ 289 (02 April 2009) 235

MA (Fresh evidence) Sri Lanka [2004] UKIAT 00161 (21 June 2004) 481

MA (rule 51(4) - not oral evidence) Somalia [2007] UKAIT 00079 463

Maaroui v France 319

Mahad [2009] UKSC 16 .... 55, 57, 301

Marckx v Belgium (1979) 2 EHRR 330 321

Mateta & Ors, [2013] EWCA Crim 1372 493

McCarthy v United Kingdom (Case C-434/09) 371

MG and VG Ireland [2006] UKAIT 00053 376

MJ and others (Art.12 Reg.1612/68, self sufficiency?) [2008] UKAIT 00034 366

MK (Somalia) v Entry Clearance Officer [2007] EWCA Civ 1521 54

MM & Ors v Secretary of State for the Home Department [2013] EWHC 1900 (Admin) 126

MM & Ors, R (On the Application Of) v SSHD (Rev 1) [2014] EWCA Civ 985 . 320

MNM (00/TH/02423; 1 November 2000) 319

MR and Others (EEA extended family members) Bangladesh [2010] UKUT 449 (IAC) 358

MS (Somalia) v SSHD [2010] EWCA Civ 1236 296

Mubilanzila Mayeka and Kaniki Mitunga v. Belgium, no. 13178/03, ECHR 314

Mundeba (s.55 and para 297(i)(f)) Democratic Republic of Congo [2013] UKUT 88 (IAC) 149

Munir & Anor, R (on the application of) v SSHD [2012] UKSC 32 79

Mwanza v SSHD (C/2000/0616; 3rd November 2000) 463

N v UK (Application no. 26565/05) [2008] ECHR 453 Strasbourg 312, 313, 314

NA v UK App. no. 25904/07 471

Nadarajah v Secretary of State for the Home Department [2003] EWCA Civ 1768 318

Naz (subsisting marriage – standard of proof) Pakistan [2012] UKUT 00040(IAC) 120

New London College Ltd) v SSHD [2013] UKSC 51 155

Niemietz v Germany (1992) 16 EHRR 97 323

Nmaju v ECO [2000] EWCA Civ 505 (C/2000/6263) 31 July 2000 148

NR (Jamaica) v SSHD [2009] EWCA Civ 856 467

NS (European Union law) [2011] EUECJ C-411/10 281

O v The Netherlands (Case C-456/12) 352, 353

OA (Alleged forgery; section 108 procedure) Nigeria [2007] UKIAT 00096 ..... 468, 470

OB (EEA Regulations 2006 - Article 9(2) - Surinder Singh spouse) Morocco [2010] UKUT 420 (IAC) 354

Ocalan v Turkey (2003) 37 EHRR 10 311

Odelola v SSHD [2009] 3 All ER 1061 80

Okonkwo (legacy/Hakemi; health claim) Nigeria [2013] UKUT 401 (IAC) .. 73, 333

OS (ten years' lawful residence) Hong Kong [2006] UKAIT 00031 82

Pankina [2010] EWCA Civ 719 159

Papajorgji (EEA spouse - marriage of convenience) Greece [2012] UKUT 38 (IAC) 356

Patel (revocation of sponsor licence – fairness) India [2011] UKUT 00211 (IAC) 158

Payir and Ozturk v Secretary of State for the Home Department (Case C-294/06; 24 January 2008) 380

PO (Nigeria) v SSHD [2011] EWCA Civ 132) 263

PR (Sri Lanka) & Ors v SSHD [2011] EWCA Civ 988 484

Pretty v United Kingdom (2002) 35 EHRR 1 .... 309, 324

PS (prison conditions; military service) Ukraine CG [2006] UKAIT 00016 310

QD Iraq v Secretary of State for the Home Department [2009] EWCA Civ 620 .... 261, 262

Quila & Anor, R (on the application of) v Secretary of State for the Home Department [2011] UKSC 45 120

R (Alconbury Developments Ltd) v Secretary of State for the Environment [2001] 2 WLR 1389 300

R (Dirshe) v SSHD [2005] EWCA Civ 421 270

R (Gungar) v Secretary of State [2004] EWHC 2117 (Admin) 7 September 2004 291

R (Iran) & Ors v SSHD [2005] EWCA Civ 982 474

R (Mahmood) v SSHD [2001] 1 WLR 840.. 326

R (on the app of I) v SSHD [2003] INLR 196.. 414

R (on the app. of Rahimi) v SSHD [2005] EWHC 2838 (Admin) 292

R (on the application of A) v London Borough of Croydon [2009] UKSC 8 275

R (on the application of A) v SSHD [2007] EWCA Civ 804 .... 275, 409

R (on the application of AA) (FC) v SSHD [2013] UKSC 49............................. 416

R (on the application of AM (Cameroon)) v Asylum and Immigration Tribunal [2007] EWCA Civ 131.. 467

R (on the application of AO) v Secretary of State for the Home Department [2011] EWHC 3088 (Admin) 339

R (on the application of B) v London Borough of Merton Council [2003] EWHC 1689 (Admin), ... 274

R (on the application of Bapio Action Ltd) v SSHD [2008] UKHL 27 80

R (on the application of D) v SSHD & Ors [2006] EWHC 980 (Admin)............. 416

R (on the application of English UK) v SSHD [2010] EWHC 1726 (Admin)...... 159

R (on the application of HSMP Forum Ltd) v SSHD [2008] EWHC 664 (Admin) 80

R (on the application of I & O) v SSHD [2005] EWHC 1025 (Admin)............... 416

R (on the application of JS (Sri Lanka)) v SSHD [2010] UKSC 15 255

R (on the application of K) v Secretary of State for the Home Department [2010] EWHC 3102 (Admin) 74

R (on the application of Kobir) v Secretary of State for the Home Department [2011] EWHC 2515 (Admin), ... 163

R (on the application of MK (Iran)) v Secretary of State for the Home Department [2010] EWCA Civ 115.. 260

R (on the application of S) v SSHD [2007] EWCA Civ 546 73

R (on the application of Shou Lin Xu) v SSHD (Legacy cases - "conclusion" issue) IJR [2014] UKUT 375(IAC).. 73

R (on the application of T) v London Borough of Enfield [2004] EWHC 2297 (Admin 274

R (on the application of YH) v Secretary of State for the Home Department [2010] EWCA Civ 116... 287, 288

R (on the application of) Nagre v SSHD [2013] EWHC 720 (Admin) 320

R (Veli Tum) v Secretary of State the Secretary of State [2004] EWCA Civ 788 384

R v Secretary of State for the Home Department & Immigration Appeal Tribunal ex parte Robinson [1997] Imm AR 568.. 249

R v Afsaw [2008] UKHL 31... 493

R v Governor of Durham Prison ex parte Hardial Singh [1984] 1 WLR 704 409

R v Kingston-upon-Thames Magistrates ex parte Martin [1994] Imm AR 172 .... 214, 464, 524

R v Secretary of State for the Home Department ex parte Adan [1998] Imm AR 338.. 241

R v Secretary of State for the Home Department ex parte Konan [2004] EWHC 22 Admin 425

R v Secretary of State for the Home Department ex parte Saadi & Ors [2001] EWCA Civ 1512... 318

R v Secretary of State for the Home Department, ex p Q [2003] EWHC 195 (Admin) 228

R v SSHD (ex parte Boafo) [2002] 1 WLR 1919 463

R v SSHD ex parte Thangarasa; Yogathas [2002] UKHL 36 283

R v SSHD, ex parte Husan [2005] EWHC 189 (Admin) 282

R v Tabnak [2007] EWCA Crim 380 499

R v Uxbridge Magistrates Court ex parte Adimi, & Ors [1999] Imm AR 560 .... 219, 220, 492

Raju & Ors [2013] EWCA Civ 754 52

Rashid [2005] EWCA Civ 744 .... 81, 334

Ravichandran [1996] Imm AR 97 216

Razgar [2004] UKHL 27 .... passim

RB (Algeria) v SSHD [2009] UKHL 10 319

RM (Kwok On Tong: HC395 para 320) India [2006] UKAIT 00039 467

RP (Proof of Forgery) Nigeria [2006] UKAIT 00086 .... 468, 470

RS (immigration and family court proceedings) India [2012] UKUT 00218(IAC) 78

RS (Zimbabwe) v SSHD [2008] EWCA Civ 839 314

RT (Zimbabwe) v SSHD [2012] UKSC 38 233

Rudralingam (00/TH/02264; 24 November 2000). 241

Ruiz Zambrano [2011] EUECJ C-34/09 367

S and Others [2002] EWCA Civ 539 486

S&K [2002] UKIAT 05613 (3 December 2002) 311

SA (Somalia) v SSHD [2006] EWCA Civ 1302 534

Saadi v UK 13229/03 [2008] ECHR 318, 411, 415

Said (Article 1D : meaning) Palestinian Territories [2012] UKUT 413 (IAC) 253

Sanade and others (British children - Zambrano - Dereci) India [2012] UKUT 48 (IAC) 370

Savas 383, 384

Sawmynaden (Family visitors – considerations) [2012] UKUT 00161(IAC) 87

SB (PSG, Protection Regulations, Reg 6) Moldova CG [2008] UKAIT 00002 .. 244

Selmouni v France (1999) 308

Sen v Netherlands (2003) 36 EHRR 81 322

Sepet and Bulbul v SSHD [2001] EWCA Civ 681 .... 238, 239, 485

SH (Afghanistan) v Secretary of State for the Home Department [2011] EWCA Civ 1284 277

Shabani v SSHD (EEA - jobseekers; nursery education) [2013] UKUT 315 369

Shah and Islam 243, 244

Shahzad (Art 8: legitimate aim) Pakistan [2014] UKUT 85 (IAC) 330

Shepherd Masimba Kambadzi v SSHD [2011] 415, 416

Singh v ECO New Delhi [2004] EWCA (Civ) 1075 322

Singh v Entry Clearance Officer New Delhi [2004] EWCA Civ 1075 150

Sivakumaran [1988] 1 AC 958 224

Slimani 541

SM (India) v Entry Clearance Officer [2009] EWCA Civ 1426 355

SM (Section 8: Judge's process) Iran [2005] UKAIT 00116 219

Soering v UK (1989) 11 EHRR 439 .... 305, 306, 307, 309

Somalia (AMM and others (conflict; humanitarian crisis; returnees; FGM) Somalia CG 2011] UKUT 445 (IAC)) 262

SS & Ors (Ankara Agreement, no in-country right of appeal) Turkey [2006] UKAIT 00074 (29 September 2006) 385

SSHD v K; Fornah v SSHD [2006] UKHL 46...244
ST (Libya) v Secretary of State for the Home Department [2007] EWCA Civ 24
    (12 January 2007) 219
Sufi and Elmi v United Kingdom (Application no 8319/07 and 11449/07) [2011]
    ECHR 1045 226
Suleyman (16242; 11 February 1998)...222
Surinder Singh (C-370/90, [1992] ECR I-4265)..352
Svazas v Secretary of State for the Home Department [2002] EWCA Civ 74..247
T, R (on the application of) v SSHD [2014] EWHC 2453 (Admin)...................132
T' (T v Secretary of State for the Home Department [1996] Imm AR 443).......254
TA and Others (Kareem explained) Ghana [2014] UKUT 316 (IAC)................119
Tanveer Ahmed [2002] UKIAT 00439 ....468, 470
TD (Paragraph 297(i)(e): "sole responsibility") Yemen [2006] UKAIT 00049 ...148
Thet v Director of Public Prosecutions [2006] EWHC 2701 (Admin)................498
TI v United Kingdom [2000] INLR 211..281
Tientchu v Immigration Appeal Tribunal (C/2000/6288; 18 October 2000).......239
TK (Tamils – LP updated) Sri Lanka CG [2009] UKAIT 00049........................471
TK (Tamils, LP updated) Sri Lanka (Rev 1) CG [2009] UKAIT 00049..............227
TM (Zimbabwe) v Secretary of State for the Home Department [2010] EWCA Civ
    916...232
TR (reg 8(3) EEA Regs 2006) [2008] UKAIT 00004.....................................358
TS (Political opponents – risk) Burma CG [2013] UKUT 00281 (IAC).............231
Tum and Dari v Secretary of State for the Home Department (C16-05; 20
    September 2007)...384
Tyrer v United Kingdom (1978) EHRR 1 310
Üner V. The Netherlands (Application No. 46410/99) 444
Ullah [2004] UKHL 26 ....236, 305, 325
Van der Elst...349
VW (Uganda) v SSHD [2009] EWCA Civ 5..326
WM (DRC) v SSHD [2006] EWCA Civ 1495 288
Y v SSHD [2006] EWCA Civ 1223 223
Yarce (adequate maintenance: benefits) [2012] UKUT 00425(IAC)..................55
YB (Eritrea) v SSHD [2008] EWCA Civ 360..230
YS (Egypt) v SSHD & Anor [2009] EWCA Civ 222 255
Z v Secretary of State for the Home Department [2002] Imm AR 560 325
Zambrano v Belgium (Case C-34/0)..369
ZB (Pakistan) v SSHD [2009] EWCA Civ 834 323
ZH (Bangladesh) v SSHD [2009] EWCA Civ 8..97
ZH (Tanzania) v SSHD [2011] UKSC 4...327, 332
Zhang, R (on the application of) v SSHD [2013] EWHC 891 (Admin).............328
ZL and VL v Secretary of State for the Home Department and Lord Chancellors
    Department [2003] EWCA Civ 25 277
ZT (Kosovo) v SSHD [2009]...283, 287